THE OBSERVER
FRENCH
COOKERY
SCHOOL

THE OBSERVER FRENCH COOKERY SCHOOL

BY ANNE WILLAN
OF LA VARENNE · PARIS

with
An Anthology of French Cooking
and Kitchen Terms
compiled by Jane Grigson

MACDONALD
MACDONALD FUTURA PUBLISHERS
LONDON

Kitchen equipment from Divertimenti,
Marylebone Lane, London W1

First published in *The Observer*
newspaper, in 16 parts, in 1980
Copyright in the text © Anne Willan
and Jane Grigson

First published in book form in 1980 by
Macdonald, London
Macdonald Futura Publishers Limited,
Paulton House, 8 Shepherdess Walk,
London N1

0 356 09782 X

New material copyright © Anne Willan
and Jane Grigson
Photographs and illustrations copyright
© *The Observer,* 1980
Photograph on page 217 copyright
© BPC Publishing Ltd
Chart on page 261 by kind permission
of The Eggs Authority

Printed and bound in Great Britain by
Purnell and Sons Ltd.,
Paulton (Bristol) and London

For my colleagues, family and friends
whose advice I have freely borrowed and whose
tastes I have so candidly exposed
to the public view. My warmest
regards and thanks.
Anne Willan

The anthology of French food which
follows I offer as a tribute to all those –
including Anne Willan – who are not upset
or made jealous by the thought of the
excellence of French food.
Jane Grigson

Acknowledgements

At La Varenne:
Research and recipe drafting
by Faye Levy
Editing by Judith Hill

At *The Observer:*
Series design by Graeme Murdoch
Photography by Victor Watts
Illustrations by Pamela Dowson
Editing by Joy Langridge

At Macdonald Futura:
Design by Sue Carter

Photograph on page 217
by Roger Phillips

CONTENTS

INTRODUCTION
Jane Grigson

Anne Willan opened her Paris cookery school, La Varenne, in 1975 in a street off the Place des Invalides on the Left Bank. She had read economics at Cambridge, studied and taught at London's Cordon Bleu school, and studied at the Ecole du Cordon Bleu in Paris, where she won the Grand Diplôme, the school's highest award. She had also worked for *Gourmet*, the top American food magazine, and as food editor for *The Washington Star*. With a library of 1,200 books, she has an equal interest in the history of food and in cooking.

Even with these qualifications, it seems daring, perhaps outrageous, for someone who was born in Newcastle and brought up in Yorkshire, to open a school of cookery in Paris. But Anne Willan felt she had something to contribute.

In France, cookery is a matter of mother and *métier*. Professional chefs and cooked food purveyors usually have the benefit of both, attending trade schools in long apprentice courses. Non-professionals make do with mother. You will not find French girls of 18 or thereabouts in the famous Parisian cookery schools such as the Cordon Bleu; their pupils are mainly foreigners, who come from all over the world to study at the source.

Unfortunately, they are often disappointed by the rigidities of the French style of education. Lessons are delivered from a spiritual, if not an actual, dais. Pupils struggle as best they may, take it or leave it. Questions are not encouraged. Anne Willan felt she could coax and persuade her staff of professional French chefs to adopt a different attitude, with the aid of a sympathetic translator and go-between.

Why 'La Varenne'? The name was chosen in honour of the writer of the first proper modern French cookery book. In 1651, the Sieur de la Varenne, master cook to Monsieur le Marquis d'Uxelles, published *Le Cuisinier François*. It opened, as French cookery books still do, with a recipe for basic stock. It contained a few traces of the medieval past, but showed how the French style – so much influenced by Italian cookery in the previous 150 years – had settled down to being itself. Recipes for meat, fish, eggs and vegetables are often for dishes that we still recognise as French. Others have passed into our own tradition so that they seem as English as boiled suet pudding (in fact, an English translation of the book appeared promptly in 1653, and had a strong influence in this country).

Anne Willan feels that it is the combination of skill and simplifying intelligence that has made French cookery for three centuries the liveliest in the world. It has never ossified. Yet it has never made the opposite error of dashing towards every new thing as it comes along. It is this confident discretion that she hopes to pass on to readers of this book.

THE STYLE OF LA VARENNE
Anne Willan

This book describes French cooking as we teach it at Ecole de Cuisine La Varenne in Paris. It will give you a glimpse of the way French chefs think about cooking – the importance they place on freshness of ingredients, their love of colour and presentation. It will show not only dishes and recipes, but also the principles that lie behind them.

The lessons – there are 30 in all – are not progressive in the sense that Lesson 1 is the easiest and Lesson 30 the hardest. Instead they are grouped by subject, with something in each for beginners and experienced cooks alike. The challenge comes in combining more and more basic techniques, using them as building blocks. A simple recipe like Escalopes de veau à la crème only requires a knowledge of how to sauté meat and reduce a sauce, whereas a pastry such as ponts neufs uses four subsidiary preparations: pâte brisée, choux pastry, pastry cream and apricot jam glaze.

At the school we follow exactly the same plan. Students start by learning a few techniques, combining them slowly, then faster and faster in more complicated dishes as their expertise increases. Classes are small and students cluster around the chef, working hard, asking questions, doing as they are told but contributing something of their own as well. At lunch and dinner their work is tasted, criticised, praised, so that soon they lose their inhibitions in talking about food at length, seriously, as do the French themselves.

Since opening the school in 1975, we've welcomed students from 23 different countries; Chef Fernand Chambrette, the school director, has brought back 6,000 kilos of butter and 300 crates of carrots from Rungis; Pâtissier Albert Jorant has taught puff pastry to more than 3,000 students; and Chef Claude Vauguet has demonstrated Bouillabaisse in London and Crème de crevettes aux petites quenelles in San Francisco, all in a day's work. Our curriculum is based on classical cuisine, but we've also tackled regional cooking and nouvelle cuisine, charcuterie and pastry work, not to mention some recipes from the original La Varenne.

When Jane Grigson, food writer of *The Observer*, came to visit La Varenne a couple of years ago, the two of us fell at once into culinary discussion. Is a copper pan really necessary to making good hollandaise? Should a soufflé be cooked in a moderate or a very hot oven? What are the merits of steamed as against boiled vegetables? A continuation seemed only natural and thus this two-part book was born, with Jane providing a glossary in her inimitable style to amplify and complement La Varenne's lessons.

Both Jane Grigson and I agree that without the right equipment and the right ingredients it is impossible to cook well. But this book will show that 'right' is a flexible term. The average French kitchen contains remarkably little equipment and what it has is solid, functional and built to last. One of the first things La Varenne students learn is how to improvise with what they have – where corners can be cut (and where they can't). Our recipes describe both hand and mechanised methods, since at the school we use both; time and labour is cut, but not standards. The same is true of ingredients. French chefs are past masters at making the most of what they have to hand, substituting one fish for another and using vegetables that are in season. The difference between British and French ingredients – mainly in the flour, cream and cuts of meat – need not stand in your way as in this book any necessary adjustments have been made.

Most important of all, we want to give you confidence. We want you to understand methods and techniques and why they work in a particular way. We want you to develop the basic skills, so that you come to regard recipes not just as blueprints to be followed to the letter, but as free-form sketches from which you can go on to create your own personal style.

1

BOILING, POACHING AND STEAMING
Getting into hot water

Two methods of cooking can claim to be prehistoric: grilling and boiling in water. Long before the invention of fireproof cooking pots, man learnt to boil water by dropping heated stones into a gourd or wooden container. But it was not until the development of cauldrons which could be placed directly over the fire that the art of cooking in water truly began.

For art it is, despite its apparent simplicity. The liquid may be plain water, salted water, court bouillon flavoured with onion, carrots and herbs, or stock made beforehand with the appropriate bones and vegetables. For sweet dishes the water may be flavoured with sugar and possibly with vanilla, lemon, wine or spices.

The flavour of the final dish also depends on the temperature at which its cooking began. For instance, if you begin with meat and simple salted water, yet want a rich broth either to serve with the poached meat or from which to make an accompanying sauce, then meat and water should start cooking together at room temperature so the meat juices are drawn out as the liquid heats. On the other hand, if the flavour of the meat alone is the overriding concern, it should be plunged into boiling water, thereby sealing in its juices and ensuring the best flavour. In this case the broth is usually too thin to be served as part of the meal.

Each approach has its devotees. Chef Chambrette at La Varenne is a broth man. When he embarks on one of his bouts of dieting, he cooks himself a huge 'marmite' of boiled beef. At lunch he sits down to a great bowl of beef and vegetables liberally soused with broth – excellent eating, though the slimming properties are more dubious. Some cooks solve the broth-versus-meat dilemma by cooking the meat so that it is as flavourful as possible, but doing so in stock rather than water so the resultant broth is also tasty.

The speed of cooking in liquid is all-important too. Green vegetables should be plunged into large quantities of boiling, salted water and boiled as fast as possible so as to keep their colour and flavour, but they

PECHES POCHES

Peaches poached in a sugar syrup – one of the several types of fruit that are suitable for this treatment

POIRES AU VIN ROUGE POIVREES

These pears are poached in a syrup flavoured with red wine, cinnamon and black peppercorns – a dessert from nouvelle cuisine

are something of an exception. Few foods should actually be cooked with the liquid at a full, rolling boil, as this tends to disintegrate the skin before the food is cooked in the centre. Boiled potatoes, for example, should be simmered, that is, cooked in liquid that is placidly bubbling, as should ham. Mixtures like stews and ragoûts cook thoroughly and evenly at a simmer, root vegetables become tender without breaking up, and pasta stays separate without the water boiling over.

At the lowest temperature, that for poaching, we enter the domain of grande cuisine. Here the liquid should not actually bubble, but cook at 90-95C (194-203F), a temperature signalled by a shivering of the liquid in one area of the pan. Poaching is indicated for delicate foods that break up easily like quenelles (meat or fish dumplings), sausages, fruits, and for foods that lose flavour quickly like fish. Dishes such as pot au feu that require several hours' cooking are also often poached rather than simmered as their excellence depends on drawing out flavours during the slowest possible cooking.

To maintain the right speed for poaching requires vigilance, and for some really tricky foods such as foie gras or a galantine, even the chefs like to use a thermometer. I have my own early warning system – my ear. Boiling involves a turbulent churning that instantly flashes danger, if only of an overflowing pan. Simmering is peaceful, a companionable murmur that means all is well. And poaching should make no noise at all.

An alternative to poaching that has recently become popular is steaming. Although it is traditionally English – it is no accident that steamer fittings for saucepans do not exist in France – avant-garde chefs have nonetheless adopted steam because of its delicate effects on fish, vegetables and small cuts of meat. Not for them plain water: they steam over aromatic infusions of vegetables, with the food laid on beds of herbs, sorrel, or even seaweed (a conceit initiated by Michel Guérard and copied by half a dozen famous names).

Blanching, the last direct use of water, usually prepares food for further cooking. As a general rule, the food is put in cold, unsalted water, brought slowly to a boil, skimmed, then simmered a few minutes. Green vegetables, however, are blanched in water which is already boiling. The term 'to blanch' is misleading, for as well as whitening, it removes salt and other strong flavours, notably from bacon; it firms meats like sweetbreads and brains; it sets the brilliant colour of green vegetables and herbs, which often do not need further cooking; it loosens the skin of nuts and fruits like almonds and tomatoes, and it rids rice and potatoes of excess starch.

Trust the French to have identified so many nuances in cooking with water. And trust them too, tongue in cheek, to characterise plain boiling and steaming as 'à l'anglaise'. A sly thrust that comes home to me, for seven long school years of steamed suet puddings and pallid root vegetables boiled to extinction remain all too heavily imprinted on my mind, or should I say palate? It has taken 15 years of French cuisine to eradicate a prejudice against anything to do with water, but now at last I *am* convinced of the merits of a pot au feu, simmered to just the right stage of spoon-soft tenderness, and am prepared to admit that a poached chicken (with the appropriate cream sauce) can be compared with one that is roasted. Perhaps one day I will also learn to appreciate the subtleties of fish steamed with seaweed and ham on a bed of hay, in the style of the new cuisine.

THE WAY TO SUCCESS

Meat and poultry

1 Trim off all excess fat.
2 Truss poultry and tie meat in a neat shape to ensure even cooking.
3 For a clearer cooking liquid, meat can be blanched before being poached: place meat in a pan with cold water to cover, bring just to the boil, drain and refresh under cold, running water.
4 Skim frequently during poaching so broth remains clear.
5 For poultry, be particularly careful not to allow the water to boil as the skin may burst or a stuffing leak.

Fish and shellfish

1 Always clean small fish through the gills, keeping the slit in the stomach as small as possible so the flesh cannot shrink and split during cooking. Large fish such as salmon, which do not have sharp gills, are also best cleaned in this way.
2 Make sure court bouillon or fish stock is cool before adding fish; hot liquid will contract the surface of the fish, spoiling its appearance and preventing even cooking. Shellfish, however, can be added to hot liquid as they are protected by their shells.
3 Fish and shellfish overcook rapidly; fish becomes soft and tasteless and shellfish rubbery; always undercook rather than overcook them.

Fruit

1 To keep fruit firm, the poaching syrup should have a higher sugar concentration than the fruit itself.
2 Do not bruise the fruit when peeling.
3 Soak dried fruits in cold water or another liquid before poaching.

Getting ahead

Preparing ahead really depends on the food used and how it is to be served, but here are a few general guidelines:

1 Blanching can always be done ahead. The blanched foods should be kept in the refrigerator.

2 Foods for steaming are normally chosen because they cook quickly, so they tend to overcook when reheated. The same is true for small cuts of meat and all fish that are poached.

3 Large cuts of beef and whole poultry can be poached ahead and reheated in the poaching liquid. However, they should be undercooked to allow for reheating. Fish to be served cold can also be poached ahead, allowed to cool to tepid, skinned, and kept in the poaching liquid.

4 Vegetables can be boiled or simmered ahead, drained, then reheated in butter; their taste is not as fresh as when boiled just before serving.

POULE AU POT HENRI IV

(Chicken in the pot Henry IV)

Poule au pot is practically the French national dish, known long before the jovial King Henri IV had his name permanently attached to it by declaring: 'Each Sunday, I want a chicken in every pot in my kingdom.' So popular has it continued to be that Curnonsky, the prince of gastronomes, was led to comment that he thought the spices in the stuffing of poule au pot must be aphrodisiac. Originally an old fowl was added to the soup pot with vegetables, to give more flavour to the soup. Now this richer version is often prepared both at home and in restaurants.

SERVES 6-8

1½ kg (3lb) rolled rump roast
1½ kg (3lb) short ribs of beef
1kg (2lb) veal bones
6 litres (10½ pts) water
12 peppercorns
large bouquet garni
tablespoon salt, or to taste
onion, stuck with a clove
chicken or boiling fowl of 1½-2kg (3 to 4lb)
1kg (2lb) beef marrow bones
6 carrots, halved and cut in 7.5cm (3in) lengths
6 onions, halved
3 medium turnips, cut in quarters
6 leeks, halved and cut in 7.5cm (3in) lengths
cabbage, quartered (optional)
6 stalks celery, cut in 7.5cm (3in) lengths
250g (8oz) piece liver (optional)
125g (4oz) vermicelli or very fine noodles or a small French loaf (for serving with broth)
coarse salt, pickles, gherkin pickles, horseradish and mustard (for serving with meat)

for the stuffing

onion, chopped
30g (1oz) butter
250g (8oz) minced pork
250g (8oz) raw smoked ham, minced
1 clove garlic, crushed
tablespoon chopped parsley
60g (2oz) fresh breadcrumbs
liver from the chicken, chopped
½ teaspoon ground allspice
salt and pepper

Put the beef with the veal bones (not the marrow bones) in a large saucepan with the water, peppercorns, bouquet garni and salt. Cut the onion in half and bake it on an electric burner or by holding it in a gas flame on a fork until charred, then add it to the pan; this gives colour to the broth. Bring the pot slowly to the boil, allowing at least 20 minutes, skimming often. Simmer and continue skimming for 10-15 minutes until all the thick, brown scum has risen. Cover the pot, leaving a small gap for evaporation and simmer for 2 hours, skimming occasionally.

To make the stuffing: cook the onion in the butter until soft but not brown. Add the pork and cook until browned. Stir in the ham, garlic, parsley, breadcrumbs, chicken liver, allspice and plenty of salt and pepper.

Put the stuffing into the bird and truss. Add the bird to the pot after 2 hours' cooking. Continue simmering for 1¼ to 1½ hours or until the bird and meat are tender.

Wrap the marrow bones in cheesecloth so the marrow does not fall out during cooking. If you like, also tie the vegetables in a large piece of cheesecloth so they are easy to lift out. Add marrow bones, liver, if included, and vegetables to the

pot and continue simmering for ¾ to 1 hour, or until the meat is very tender. Poule au pot can be prepared up to 48 hours ahead and kept in the refrigerator, but undercook it slightly to allow for reheating.

If serving broth with noodles: 10 minutes before the end of cooking, spoon 1-2 litres (2-3½ pints) broth into a separate pan and simmer the noodles in it for 5 minutes, or until tender. If serving with bread, cut the bread in 1cm (½in) diagonal slices and toast in a moderate oven, 180C (350F) gas 4, for 10-15 minutes until golden brown.

To serve: lift out the beef and vegetables. Carve the rump roast in 3mm (⅛in) slices and arrange overlapping down the centre of a large serving dish. Cut the ribs in pieces and pile at each end. Carve the chicken, and add it to the dish and arrange the vegetables in piles with the chicken stuffing around the meat and chicken pieces. Cover the dish with foil and keep hot. Strain the broth, skim off as much fat as possible, first with a metal spoon, then with strips of paper towel, and taste for seasoning. Either unwrap the marrow bones, spread marrow on the browned bread and put in soup bowls before pouring over the broth, or add the bones to the dish of meat and give guests spoons for scooping out the marrow.

The liver, which helps to clear the broth and give flavour, is discarded before the soup is served.

Croûtes for Poule au pot

To make the traditional croûtes for poule au pot: cut a thin loaf of French bread in half horizontally. Pull the soft bread away leaving a shell of crust. Cut crusts crosswise into 5cm (2in) pieces and dry them in a slow oven 140C (275F) gas 1, or sprinkle with fat skimmed from the poule au pot and brown in a moderate oven 190C (375F) gas 5. Use in place of the vermicelli or toast.

POISSON POCHE
(Poached fish)

A whole poached fish is usually served with the head on. Allow 375-500g ($\frac{3}{4}$-1lb) fish, depending on the size of the head, per person.

SERVES 4-5

about 2kg (4lb) whole fish, fish steaks or fillets (eg, salmon, halibut, cod, hake, trout)
3 litres (5pts) court bouillon, or to cover
hollandaise, beurre blanc or other butter sauce (page 194) if serving hot
mayonnaise (page 179) if serving cold
chopped parsley and lemon decorations (to garnish)

Make the court bouillon and allow it to cool.

Wash the fish, cut off the fins and trim the tail to a 'V'. To clean the stomach through the gills: cut a very small slit in the stomach near the tail. Pull out as much of the stomach contents as possible through the gills, carefully cutting out the gills also but leaving in the tiny bit attached to the head. Take out any remaining contents through the stomach slit, then hold the fish under the tap and run cold water in the mouth and out through the stomach until very clean.

Cleaned in this way the fish will look neat after cooking, but if the gills are hard and sharp, make a larger slit in the stomach and clean out the fish entirely through this. If the fish has large scales, scrape with the back of a knife to remove them, working from tail to head. However, if the fish has small scales – such as a trout or salmon – leave them on to protect the fish during cooking.

If poaching a large fish, set it stomach-down in a pan; if using a fish poacher, lay the fish on the rack. If the fish to be poached are small, lay them sideways on the rack or in the pan. Pour the court bouillon over the fish; it should cover it and if it doesn't, add more water. Cover the pan and bring the liquid slowly to the boil. If using a fish poacher, all cooking should be done on two burners or rings on top of the stove; if poaching small fish or fish fillets in a pan, once the court bouillon is hot, the cooking can be completed in a moderate oven, 180C (350F) gas 4.

For a large whole fish allow 8 minutes per $\frac{1}{2}$kg (1lb) for those under 2kg (4-5lb) and 6 minutes

per $\frac{1}{2}$kg (1lb) for larger fish. This includes the time needed for the liquid to come to a simmer. For pieces of fish and whole fish under 1kg (2lb), allow 8-20 minutes cooking time. For example, thin fillets of sole or flounder take 8-10 minutes and small, whole fish take 15-20 minutes depending on their size. Fish is cooked when the flesh is no longer transparent.

If serving fish hot, allow it to cool for a few minutes in the liquid, then lift out on the rack to drain, or drain on paper towels. Skin large fish, leaving head and tail, and remove the small bones running along the top of the backbone. Small fish may be skinned or left with the skin on as you prefer; steaks should have as much skin and bone removed as possible. Cover the fish loosely with foil and reheat for a few minutes in a hot oven, 200C (400F) gas 6, just before serving, or it can be kept warm in a low oven 130C (250F) gas $\frac{1}{2}$, for up to 30 minutes. Set the fish on a white napkin on a serving dish. Garnish the fish with parsley and lemon decorations just before

serving and serve the hollandaise or other butter sauce separately.

If the fish is to be served cold, leave it to cool in the poaching liquid until tepid, then drain and skin it. It can be kept, covered in the refrigerator, for up to 24 hours before serving. Serve it plain, with mayonnaise, or decorate it according to the individual recipe.

COURT BOUILLON

Court bouillon is used for poaching fish and sometimes offal or innards.
Makes 1 litre ($1\frac{3}{4}$ pints)

1 litre ($1\frac{3}{4}$pts) water
carrot, sliced
small onion, sliced
bouquet garni
6 peppercorns
teaspoon salt
300ml ($\frac{1}{2}$pt) dry white wine or 4 tablespoons vinegar or lemon juice

Combine all the ingredients in a large pan (not aluminium), cover and bring to a boil. Simmer uncovered for 15-20 minutes and strain.

LEMON GARNISHES

Lemons make a charming and functional decoration, particularly for fish. Other citrus fruits can be prepared in the same way to serve with any citrus-flavoured dishes, including desserts.

Fluted slices
1 Use a cannelle knife (canneleur) to cut grooves lengthwise down the lemon. Try to space the grooves evenly.
2 Cut the lemon in thin slices.
3 For fluted half-slices, halve the grooved lemon lengthwise, then lay it flat side down and cut in crosswise slices.

Wolf's teeth
1 Cut a thin slice from the top and bottom of the lemon so the two halves will stand up later.
2 With a small sharp knife cut a zig-zag line all around the lemon, slicing through to the centre.
3 Pull the two lemon halves apart.
4 If you like, place a small sprig of parsley in the centre, or sprinkle with chopped parsley.

Lemon baskets
1 Cut a thin slice from the bottom

of the lemon so the basket will stand up.
2 Cutting down from the top with a small sharp knife, remove nearly a whole quarter section from the top half.
3 Remove the other quarter section from the top half of the fruit leaving a strip in the centre wide enough to form the handle of the basket.
4 Cut away the flesh under the handle.
5 Either leave the bottom half of the lemon for squeezing or remove all the flesh, making a basket of peel to fill with sauce or cut vegetables or fruit.

Lemon knots
1 Cut a thin slice from the top and bottom of the lemon so the two halves will stand up later.
2 Halve the lemon crosswise.
3 Pare a narrow strip of rind from the cut edge, cutting nearly all the way around so the strip hangs free but remains attached to the lemon.
4 Make a simple knot in the rind so it stands out on the edge of the lemon half.

MELI MELO DE POISSONS A LA VAPEUR AU BEURRE ROUGE
(Steamed fish with red wine butter sauce)

For an attractive presentation, this dish should include fish of three skin colours: bass (blue), brill (white) and red mullet.

SERVES 6-8

4 red mullet
1½ kg (3lb) bass
1kg (2lb) brill or other flat white fish
court bouillon made with 1 litre (1¾pts) water, carrot, onion, bouquet garni, 6 peppercorns, teaspoon salt and pinch of cloves
salt and pepper
for the red wine butter sauce
7-8 shallots, very finely chopped
salt and pepper
1 litre (1¾pts) red wine
450g (1lb) butter

For the red wine butter sauce: boil the shallots with tiny pinches of salt and pepper in the red wine until reduced nearly to a glaze. The sauce can be prepared 2-3 hours ahead up to this point and kept in the refrigerator.

Scale, trim and carefully fillet all the fish, but leave the skin on. Leave the red mullet fillets whole. Wipe them clean but do not wash them or they will lose their colour. Cut each bass fillet in 5 diagonal pieces. Cut the brill fillets into diagonal pieces of similar shape and size to the bass. Wash the pieces of bass and brill.

Simmer the court bouillon ingredients for 15-20 minutes.

About 15 minutes before serving, bring the court bouillon to the boil, season the pieces of bass with salt and pepper and steam them on a rack or drum sieve or in a steamer above the boiling court bouillon for 5-6 minutes or until barely tender. Remove to a serving dish and keep warm. Season the brill fillets, steam for 4-5 minutes or until barely tender and arrange them on the serving dish with the bass. Then season the red mullet and steam for 3-4 minutes or until barely tender. (If there is room in the steamer for all the fish put the bass in first; 1-2 minutes later add the brill, and a minute after, add the mullet.) Keep warm on the serving dish.

To finish the red wine butter sauce: reheat the red wine glaze to boiling point. Beat in the butter gradually in small pieces without letting it melt. Work sometimes over very low heat and sometimes off the heat so that the butter softens and thickens the sauce without melting. Season to taste with salt and pepper. The sauce can be kept warm on a rack over warm, but not boiling, water.

To serve: arrange the fish attractively on the serving dish alternating the colours. Serve the red wine butter sauce separately.

SALADE DE HARICOTS VERTS ET DE TOMATES
(Green bean and tomato salad)

Test the green beans every few minutes while they are boiling to catch them at the perfect point of crunchiness between raw and overcooked.

SERVES 4

350g (¾lb) green beans, cut in 5cm (2in) lengths
4-5 medium tomatoes
salt
tablespoon chopped parsley (for sprinkling)
for the dressing
tablespoon wine vinegar
½ teaspoon Worcestershire sauce, or to taste
salt and pepper
75ml (3oz) olive or walnut oil

Cook the green beans in boiling salted water for 10-15 minutes or until just tender. Drain, refresh with cold water and drain again thoroughly. Scald the tomatoes for 5 seconds in boiling water. NOTE: this facilitates peeling. Peel them, halve them across the centre and squeeze to remove the seeds. Slice them, sprinkle with salt and leave to drain for 10-15 minutes. Toss in a colander to remove all the liquid. *For the dressing:* whisk the vinegar with the Worcestershire sauce and a little salt until the salt is dissolved. Gradually whisk in the oil so the dressing emulsifies. Taste for seasoning and adjust if necessary. Add the beans and tomatoes, mix carefully and taste again. The salad should be made at least 1 hour and up to 3 hours ahead; keep it covered in the refrigerator.

Sprinkle with chopped parsley just before serving.

To steam fish for meli melo de poissons: this can be done in an improvised steamer made from either a grill rack or, as shown here, a drum sieve placed over a pan of boiling court bouillon

QUENELLES DE VOLAILLE AUX POIREAUX

(Chicken quenelles with leeks)

Quenelles are essentially dumplings made of forcemeat finely minced or pounded to a paste. Pike quenelles are most common. Quenelles can be made of virtually any meat, game, poultry, fish or shellfish; here, chicken is used.

Makes 12 quenelles to serve 6 as a first course or 4 as a main course.

for the quenelles
1½kg (3lb) chicken
2 egg yolks
125g (4oz) butter, softened
salt and pepper
pinch of grated nutmeg
1 egg white
200ml (⅓pt) double cream
for the garnish and sauce
3 leeks
1 litre (1¾pts) chicken stock
salt and pepper
400-600ml (¾-1pt) double cream
60g (2oz) butter (to finish)

Bone the chicken completely, separating the flesh from the skin and bones. Using the knife with a scraping motion, remove as much flesh from the bones as possible, then use the bones to make chicken stock.

For the quenelles: weigh the chicken flesh – there should be 500g (1lb). Mince the chicken flesh in a blender or food processor together with the egg yolks and soft butter until the mixture turns into a very fine paste. Push the mixture through a drum sieve. NOTE: the flesh goes through the sieve much more easily when puréed with the yolks and butter. Place in a metal bowl. Set the bowl inside a larger bowl of ice and beat the mixture well so that it chills evenly. Add salt, pepper and nutmeg. Gradually beat in the egg white, then the cream, 2 tablespoons at a time, beating well between each addition. Chill the mixture thoroughly before shaping the quenelles.

Clean the leeks thoroughly, halve them lengthwise and flatten. Cut them into 4cm (1½in) lengths and then cut each lengthwise into thin julienne strips. Bring a medium-size saucepan of water to the boil

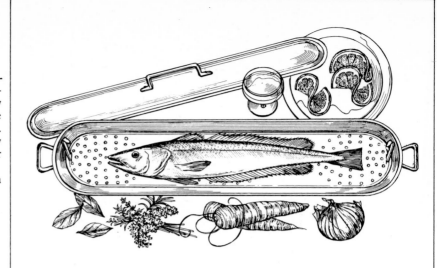

FISH POACHER

(Fish kettle)

A fish poacher is a satisfying piece of equipment; long and narrow, as deep as it is wide, it is shaped so the minimum of liquid is needed to cover the fish. A two-handled rack fits into the base so the fish can be removed easily. The finest material for a fish poacher is copper – and also the most expensive; a large poacher can run into hundreds of pounds. Tin-clad aluminium is the workaday alternative. Fish poachers are also available in stainless steel, at a price between copper and aluminium. The most important principle is to buy a large one which will accommodate all comers, large and small.

Plenty of substitutes for a fish poacher are available. An oval casserole will give an attractive curve to a large fish and a roasting pan will suffice, at a pinch. Fish steaks, fillets and little fish should, in any case, be poached in a shallow baking dish rather than a poacher, but never use unclad aluminium as the vinegar or white wine often used in the court bouillon in which the fish is cooked will attack the metal.

The most original makeshift device was the invention of gastronome Brillat-Savarin. Faced with an outsize turbot and no 'turbotière' (a diamond-shaped poacher), he ordered the copper laundry boiler to be cleaned – and poured in a court bouillon mixture. On a wicker tray suspended above it, he placed herbs and the fish. The resulting steamed turbot was the best he'd ever cooked.

and add salt and the leeks. Boil 2-3 minutes or until they are just tender, refresh in cold water and drain well.

To poach the quenelles: bring the chicken stock to a boil in a large sauté pan or shallow saucepan and add salt. Meanwhile, use 2 tablespoons to shape the quenelle mixture into ovals, dropping each one onto a dampened tray. With a rubber spatula, transfer the quenelles to the boiling stock. When the pan is fairly full, lower the heat and poach the quenelles for 10-15 minutes or until just firm. Lift them out with a draining spoon and dry them carefully on cloth or paper towels while poaching the remainder.

For the sauce: strain the stock and boil rapidly in 2 shallow pans until it is reduced to a syrupy consistency. Combine in one pan and add 400ml (¾pt) cream. Continue to reduce, whisking often, until the sauce is thick enough to coat a spoon lightly. Taste for seasoning and adjust if necessary; if the flavour of the sauce is too strong, add a little more cream. Stir in the leeks.

To finish: if necessary, reheat the quenelles covered with foil, in a moderate oven, 180C (350F) gas 4. Remove the sauce from the heat and gradually whisk in the butter. Spoon the sauce and leeks over the quenelles and serve.

OEUFS POCHES PATTI

(Poached eggs Patti)

The simple poached egg is here lifted to the heights of grande cuisine.

SERVES 8

pâte brisée (page 141) made with 250g (8oz) flour, 125g (4oz) butter, 2 egg yolks, level teaspoon salt and 3½-4 tablespoons cold water
sauce suprême (page 191) made with 300 ml (½pt) chicken stock, 20g (1½ level tablespoons) butter, 15g (½oz) flour, 30g (1oz) chopped mushroom stalks, 4 tablespoons double cream, salt, freshly ground pepper and 15g (½oz) butter
8 eggs
2 hard-boiled egg yolks (to finish)
150ml (¼pt) double cream
for the artichoke purée
lemon, halved
8 artichokes
2 tablespoons flour (for 'blanc')
30g (1oz) butter
salt and pepper

8 deep tartlet tins, 10cm (4in) in diameter

Make the pâte brisée and chill. Roll it out to just under 5mm (¼in) thick. Butter the tartlet tins, line them and chill until the butter is firm. Set the oven at hot, 200C (400F) gas 6. Fill the shells with beans, bake and cool according to the directions on page 142. The shells can be made up to 48 hours ahead and kept in an airtight container.

Make the sauce suprême. Rub the surface of the warm sauce with a piece of butter to prevent a skin from forming. The sauce can be made up to 24 hours ahead and kept covered in the refrigerator.

For the artichoke purée: prepare and cook the artichoke bottoms in a 'blanc' as for Salade Bramafan (page 184). Drain thoroughly and scoop out the choke with a teaspoon. Work the artichoke bases through a vegetable mill or purée them in an electric processor. The purée can be prepared 3-4 hours ahead and kept covered at room temperature.

Poach the eggs and keep them in a bowl of cold water. They can be prepared up to 4 hours ahead.

To finish: heat the tartlet shells in a low oven. Place the eggs in a bowl of warm water to heat them. Melt the 30g (1oz) butter in a saucepan, add the artichoke purée with salt and pepper and cook, stirring, until very hot.

Spoon some artichoke purée into each tartlet shell. Drain the eggs carefully on paper towels, arrange one on the artichoke purée in each tartlet shell and keep warm. Bring the sauce suprême just to the boil and spoon enough over each egg to coat it. Sieve a little hard-boiled egg yolk over each and serve immediately.

COMPOTE DE FRUITS

(Poached fruit)

Any of the given fruits, or a mixture of them, are suitable for poaching. They should be juicy but firm and not too ripe.

SERVES 4

500g (1lb) fruit (see right)
100g (3½oz) sugar, or to taste
600ml (1pt) water
vanilla pod
pared rind and juice of one lemon

Prepare the fruit.

Heat the sugar in a pan with the water, vanilla pod, lemon rind and juice until all the sugar is dissolved. Bring to the boil and add the prepared fruit. To keep fruit firm, plunge it in simmering syrup, then lower the heat to poaching heat. NOTE: the fruit should be completely covered by syrup, and large halves or whole fruits, such as pears or peaches, may need cooking in 2 batches or in a double quantity of syrup.

Poach gently until the fruit is semi-transparent and just tender when pierced with the point of a small knife. Cooking time depends on the ripeness and variety of the fruit.

Let the fruit cool to tepid in the syrup and use a draining spoon to transfer the fruit carefully to a glass serving bowl. Boil the syrup until fairly thick and reduced to 300ml (½pt). Allow to cool slightly, taste, add more sugar if needed and strain over the fruit. Serve cool or chilled.

FRUIT FOR POACHING

Apples: dessert apples such as Golden Delicious are excellent for poaching, or tart cooking apples may be used. NOTE: peel apples only just before cooking them and rub them immediately with a cut lemon as they quickly discolour. Scoop out the stalk and flower ends. If serving whole, core the apples and poach them, a few at a time, for 15-20 minutes, making sure that they are immersed in the syrup. For cut-up apples: halve them, scoop out the core and cut in quarters. Poach them a few at a time for 8-12 minutes.

Apricots: cut around the apricots through the indentation, twist them in half and discard the stones. Poach for 5-8 minutes.

Cherries: either sweet, dark Morello cherries or tart, red cherries can be used. Poached tart cherries are often served with meat, poultry or game but they need more sugar if they are to be served as dessert. Wash the cherries, discard the stems and, if you like, remove the stones with a cherry stoner or the point of a vegetable peeler. Poach the cherries for 8-12 minutes.

Cranberries: pick over the cranberries and wash thoroughly. Make the sugar syrup with 300g (10oz) sugar and 600ml (1pt) water. Add the berries and poach for 4-5 minutes. They overcook easily. As cranberries tend to be sour, they may need more sugar if you are serving them for dessert.

Peaches: cut around the peaches through the indentation, twist them in half and discard the stones. If desired, crack a few of the stones and use the kernels to give an almond flavour to the syrup. Poach the peaches, a few at a time, for 7-10 minutes. Allow them to cool to tepid, then peel them. Small peaches can also be poached whole – for 15-20 minutes. Allow them to cool to tepid and peel them. Poached white peaches are particularly good with brandy added.

Pears: firm pears such as Anjou or Bosc should be used for poaching.

NOTE: pears discolour very rapidly and must be rubbed with a cut lemon and immersed in syrup as soon as they are peeled. If serving whole: scoop out the flower end with the point of a knife and, if you like, insert a small sharp coffee spoon, grapefruit spoon or the tip of a vegetable peeler into the pear to scoop out the core; peel the pear, leaving the stalk. Poach the pears, a few at a time, for 20-25 minutes, making sure that they are immersed in syrup. For cut-up pears: peel them, discarding the flower end, halve them, cut out the core and stem, and quarter or slice them. Poach for 5-10 minutes.

Plums: make the sugar syrup with 450ml ($\frac{3}{4}$pt) water. Cut around the plums through the indentation and twist them in half, discarding the stones, or leave them whole. Poach them for 8-12 minutes. Poached plums are particularly good served with a sprinkling of cinnamon.

Rhubarb: make the sugar syrup with 300ml ($\frac{1}{2}$pt) water. Wash the rhubarb and cut in 5cm (2in) lengths. Poach for 5-10 minutes and then test the fruit; it overcooks very easily.

POIRES AU VIN ROUGE POIVREES

(Peppered pears in red wine)

The peppercorns add a surprising note to the flavour of this dish.

SERVES 4

8 firm pears
100g ($3\frac{1}{2}$oz) sugar
600ml (1pt) red wine
strip of lemon peel
5cm (2in) piece cinnamon
teaspoon black peppercorns
Chantilly cream made with 150ml ($\frac{1}{4}$pt) double cream, 2 teaspoons sugar and $\frac{1}{2}$ teaspoon vanilla essence (optional – for serving)

Choose a saucepan that just holds the standing pears. In it put the sugar, red wine, lemon peel, cinnamon and peppercorns and heat until the sugar is dissolved. Boil for 5 minutes and allow to cool slightly. Peel the pears, core them carefully from the base but leave the stalk. Cut a thin slice off the bottom of each so the pears stand up. Immerse the pears in the syrup, adding more wine if necessary to cover them. Cover with the lid and poach them

To transfer poached fruit to a serving bowl: once it has cooled, the fruit is carefully removed from the poaching liquid with a draining spoon. The syrup is then reduced until it is fairly thick

for 20-45 minutes or until tender. NOTE: cooking time depends on the variety and ripeness of the pears, but 20 minutes is a minimum to prevent discoloration around the cores.

Allow the pears to cool to tepid in the syrup, then drain them and arrange in a shallow dish. Strain the syrup and reduce until thick (do not allow it to caramelise); taste and add sugar or lemon juice if necessary. Allow to cool slightly and spoon it over the pears. Chill them thoroughly. The pears can be cooked 24 hours ahead and kept tightly covered in the refrigerator. Serve Chantilly cream separately.

2
BONING
The one-piece treat

'Bone the meat' is an instruction which makes all too many cooks turn hastily to the next page of recipes. Admittedly, boning is a skill which is rare nowadays – not because it is difficult, but because it takes time. Chefs and suppliers cannot afford to go in for boning unless the results can command a high price, as does a galantine of chicken decked in aspic or a boned shoulder of meat stuffed and tied for roasting. In our local shopping street in Paris there are three butchers, one of whom displays splendid boned roasts of veal stuffed with pork and pistachios, not to mention larded beef roasts and paupiettes of half a dozen different flavours. I pass by on the other side so as not to be tempted by such expensive luxuries.

Because of rising prices, it is increasingly useful to know how to bone at home. The best way to start is to look up instructions in a book or two, preferably one with illustrations. Study the anatomy of the meat or poultry or fish in front of you and don't hesitate to poke it with your fingers to locate the bones while you work. The aim is to keep the meat in one piece, as neat and intact as possible. While boning, you should cut away gristle, sinews and excess fat so that in the end you are left with a piece of meat that is totally edible. If the meat is simply being boned for chopping, of course, you can work faster as there is no need to keep it in one piece.

The French are great boners of meat, perhaps because boned cuts offer so many possibilities for cooking. Meat is rolled and tied in a neat cylinder so that it roasts or braises evenly. Often it is stuffed before rolling, or at the very least it is sprinkled with salt, pepper, herbs and perhaps a bit of garlic. A recipe can be transformed simply by adding a different stuffing, like the onion and mushroom mixture that is used for lamb in the Touraine, or the bread stuffing with garlic, shallots and parsley, backed up by a garnish of blanched and roasted sweet peppers, that the Basques prefer for lamb. The idea for a rice stuffing flavoured with raisins and pine nuts quite probably came from Provence, even though it is often called à la grecque. For some cuts, particularly shoulder of lamb or pork, the 'melon' approach is possible: the meat is stuffed, sewn up, rolled into a ball and tied, making segments with the string like those of a Charentais melon.

Poultry can also be shaped in the same way, but more often the meat and skin are sewn around the stuffing, then trussed so that the bird regains its original shape; the leg and wing bones may be left to improve appearances. Often the stuffed bird is poached in stock, or it can be baked in an oval terrine. A favourite exercise at La Varenne is the lesson on removing chicken breasts to make suprêmes, then boning the leftover legs to be stuffed and sauced. Two luxury dishes from one relatively inexpensive bird, plus the bones for stock – nothing could appeal more to the economical instincts of the chefs.

As for fish, even its most dedicated fans prefer it without the bones. It can be left whole with a stuffing taking the place of the backbone, in which case it is usually baked in the oven with a moistening of wine and melted butter. Or it can be taken completely off the bone in fillets – the best procedure when serving the fish in a sauce. During cooking, fillets tend to curl if they are left flat, so they are usually folded in half or three, or curled like a rollmop herring. Fish bones, like chicken bones, are a bonus for making stock. Meat bones (except those from veal) are not so useful, as they contain less of the gelatine that makes good stock, but never throw them away. Resting on the bottom of the braising or roasting pan, they will always add flavour to the gravy.

Most famous of the French boned dishes are ballotines and galantines. A galantine is made from boned poultry or meat that is stuffed, formed into a symmetrical shape, then poached in stock. The stock from cooking is almost always clarified for aspic – with which the galantine is then coated, making it one of the favourites for grand buffets. Ballotines are similar but are shaped like a bundle (ballot) and may be braised and served hot rather than poached and decorated with aspic.

Many elaborate boned dishes have an ancient history, dating from the days when kitchen help was cheap and chefs had time on their hands. A boned, stuffed peacock in full plumage was the crowning touch at medieval feasts, carried in procession around the hall by a lady of outstanding beauty and rank. Even more recherché was the 'rôti sans pareil' (roast without equal), consisting of a stoned olive wrapped in a boned garden warbler, wrapped in a boned ortolan, and so on through 15 different birds to end with a bustard. The result must have looked rather like a giant haggis.

Such an orgy of birds may be out of place today, but a knowledge of how to fillet and skin fish, how to bone poultry and one or two cuts of meat is certainly not. Boning not only gives a neatly shaped piece of meat

that cooks evenly, but also one that cooks more quickly and is less apt to dry out. And with the bones removed before cooking, serving is simple. The work is done beforehand in the kitchen rather than when carving at the dining table.

THE WAY TO SUCCESS

1 Before boning, try to picture the final product: are you trying to make a place for stuffing, to prepare a rolled roast, or simply to take meat from the bone?
2 Use a very sharp pointed knife, varying the size with the size of the bones.
3 Keep the knife blade against the bone to avoid cutting into flesh or skin.
4 Use the point of the knife to help locate the bones.
5 Scrape rather than cut the meat from the bones wherever you find them.
6 To help you see what you are doing, pull the flesh away from the bones with your fingers as you work.
7 Work with short sawing or stroking movements of the knife; avoid using force.

How to bone meat

Boning many cuts of meat forms a natural pocket. Sometimes this is enlarged to provide more room for stuffing; sometimes a pocket is cut deliberately. When this is done, an equal thickness of meat should be left all around the opening so the meat will cook evenly. After stuffing, the meat is closed using a trussing needle and string; it should not be sewn too tightly or the meat will burst during cooking.
Here a shoulder is used to exemplify the process of boning as it has an especially complicated bone structure.
1 A shoulder has three bones: the flat blade bone and two round bones. The blade bone forms a line with the first round (centre) bone, which fits into the second (arm) bone at approximately a right angle. As with any piece of meat, there are left- and right-handed shoulders.
2 Pull any skin from the shoulder, using a cloth to hold it and cutting it away with a knife where necessary.

3 Trim off most of the fat, leaving only just enough to keep the meat moist.
4 With the smooth side of the shoulder on the board, make a slit in the meat on the far side of the shoulder from the arm bone. You should be able to find a flat triangular bone with the point of your knife.
5 Uncover this blade bone with the point of your knife until it is completely visible.
6 Cut through the joint connecting it to the arm bone.
7 Strip out the blade bone by grasping the joint end and pulling it sharply towards you.
8 Take the protruding arm bone in your left hand and scrape downwards with short strokes to free the bone from the meat.
9 With the point of the knife, find the joint connecting this bone to the centre bone. Cut around the bone at the joint to release it.
10 The centre bone is now left and it is removed in 'tunnel' style: cut all the tendons around each end of the bone. Carefully scrape the meat from the bone, from the ends towards the centre.
11 When the bone is free, pull it out. The shoulder is now completely boned.

Tying the meat

The boned shoulder can be tied in different ways:
1 It can be rolled up lengthwise into a sausage shape and tied neatly in a cylinder. A stuffing can be added before it is rolled.
2 It can be stuffed and formed into a 'melon' shape (see Epaule d'agneau en melon): bring the edges of the meat into the centre to enclose the filling; then sew them. Encircle the meat twice with string at right angles like a parcel, and tie. Then, with a very long string, roll the meat round and round so that the string marks segments like those of a melon.

EPAULE D'AGNEAU EN MELON

Boned shoulder of lamb stuffed with a rice mixture which includes pine nuts and raisins. The melon shape results from the way in which the meat was tied before cooking. Tomatoes filled with extra stuffing and tomatoes provençale both garnish the serving dish

HOW TO BONE SHOULDER OF LAMB

When the flat blade bone has been scraped free of meat and the joint connecting it to the arm bone severed, grasp the joint end; remove the bone by pulling it sharply towards you

When only the centre bone remains, cut the tendons around each end, then free the meat from the bone in 'tunnel' fashion, scraping from the extremities to the middle of the joint

EPAULE D'AGNEAU EN MELON

(Melon-shaped stuffed shoulder of lamb)

To bone the shoulder, follow the instructions above and overleaf. If bought ready boned, it should weigh 1¼-1¾kg (about 2½-3½lb). You may prepare just one type of tomato garnish, if you prefer. If you're not preparing stuffed tomatoes, any left-over rice stuffing can be reheated to serve separately.

SERVES 4-6

shoulder of lamb weighing 2-2½kg (4-5lb) boned (bones reserved)
salt and freshly ground black pepper
2 tablespoons oil
onion, quartered
carrot, quartered
1-2 cloves garlic, peeled
teaspoon dried rosemary
150ml (¼pt) brown stock (optional)
½-¾ recipe for tomatoes provençale (page 29)
for the stuffing and garnish
30g (1oz) butter
medium onion, finely chopped
200g (7oz) rice
600ml (1pt) water
60g (2oz) raisins
salt and freshly ground black pepper
75g (2½oz) pine nuts or 100g (3½oz) whole blanched almonds
2 tablespoons chopped parsley
2 eggs
2-3 tomatoes, halved and seeded
2-3 tablespoons oil
for the gravy
150ml (¼pt) white wine
300-450ml (½-¾pt) brown stock
trussing needle and string

To make the stuffing: melt the butter in a flameproof casserole and slowly cook the onion until soft but not brown. Add the rice and cook, stirring, until the grains are transparent. Add the water with the raisins, salt and pepper, then cover and bring to the boil. Simmer on top of the stove or cook in a hot oven, 200C (400F) gas 6, for exactly 20 minutes. Leave for 10 minutes to cool before removing the lid. Stir to separate the grains and allow to cool to tepid. If using almonds, bake them in a hot oven, 200C (400F) gas 6, for 4-6 minutes until golden brown. Stir the pine nuts or almonds, the parsley and the eggs into the rice and taste – it should be highly seasoned.

Trim the skin and all but a thin layer of fat from the lamb. If necessary, enlarge the pocket formed when the lamb was boned. Season inside the pocket and fill with the cooled stuffing, reserving a little for the tomato garnish. Bring the sides to the centre to enclose the filling and tie with string to form a melon shape (see instructions). The lamb can be stuffed up to 6 hours before cooking but, if so, the stuffing must

be cold before it is put inside the meat. Keep in the refrigerator.

To make the stuffed tomato garnish: remove a little of the pulp from each tomato half to make room for the stuffing. Season the tomato with salt and pepper and add the remaining rice stuffing, mounding it slightly.

About 1½-2 hours before serving, set the oven at very hot, 230C (450F) gas 8. Pour the 2 tablespoons oil into the roasting tin, add the lamb bones, onion and carrot and place the lamb on top. Cut the garlic into slivers. Make several incisions in the meat with the point of a knife and insert the pieces of garlic. Sprinkle the meat with rosemary, salt and pepper and sear it for 10-15 minutes or until it browns. Lower the oven heat to hot, 200C (400F) gas 6, and continue roasting, basting often, for 1¼-1½ hours or until a meat thermometer inserted in the meat (not the stuffing) registers 66-68C (150-155F) for medium-done meat. If the pan juices brown too much, add 150 ml (¼ pint) of stock.

A few minutes before the lamb is done, cook the stuffed tomato garnish. The tomatoes provençale can also be cooked at the same time. Heat half the oil in a roasting tin and add the tomatoes, skin side down. Sprinkle both types of tomato with oil. Cover the stuffed tomatoes with foil to prevent them from drying out. Place in the hot oven, 200C (400F) gas 6. Bake for 10-12 minutes or until the tomatoes are tender and the stuffing is hot.

Transfer the lamb to a serving dish, remove strings and keep the meat warm. Leave it to rest for 15 minutes before carving. Pour out and discard the excess fat, but leave in the bones, onion and carrot.

While the meat is resting, make the gravy. Add the wine to the roasting tin and bring to the boil, stirring to dissolve the pan juices. Add the stock and simmer for 5-10 minutes until well reduced and strain the gravy into a small saucepan. Skim off the excess fat, bring back to the boil and taste for seasoning. Keep hot until ready to serve.

To serve: just before serving, sprinkle the stuffed tomatoes with a little oil. Brown them lightly under the grill. Surround the lamb with tomatoes provençale and tomatoes stuffed with rice. Carve the meat in wedges like a melon and serve the gravy separately.

HOW TO BONE A LEG OF LAMB TO MAKE ESCALOPES

1 Remove the skin and most of the fat from the lamb.
2 Place the leg on the board, skin side down. With the point of the knife, find the tail bone – the long, thin bone which runs across the wide end of the leg. The next bone which meets the tail bone is the hip, or aitchbone, and this is a very irregular shape. It also runs across the wide end of the leg at a slightly different angle from the tail bone. Cut the tendons that hold it in place and very carefully scrape it free of meat. Be especially careful here because of the irregular shape of the bone.
3 The hip bone meets the next bone, the leg bone (hip to knee), in a ball joint located near the centre of the hip bone. Free the hip bone at the joint and remove the bone.
4 Grasp the shank bone (knee to angle) located at the small end of the leg. Cut all the tendons at the base of the bone. Push and scrape the meat away from the shank bone, cutting on the side of the bone which contains little meat. Try to keep the meat on the other side of the bone in one piece.
5 When the bone has been scraped clean, find the knee joint, where the shank bone is connected to the leg bone at approximately a right angle. Cut the tendons at the joint to release the shank bone.
6 Now the leg bone is left in the centre of the meat. Carefully release each end of the bone from the meat; it is round at the lower end and is formed of two small parts at the upper end. When completely free of meat, twist the bone and pull it out. NOTE: proceed very carefully in order to obtain neat slices. Place it, skin side down, on your work surface and, using a very sharp knife, cut the meat into 2cm ($\frac{3}{4}$in) slices. Pound them a little to flatten them.

ESCALOPES DE GIGOT DE MOUTON AUX CONCOMBRES
(Escalopes of leg of lamb with cucumbers)

Although Frenchmen consider lamb and mint to be an English combination, the two are occasionally paired in French cuisine as in this delicious garnish of cucumbers, ham and mint for lamb escalopes.

Serves 6-8, depending on the size of the leg of lamb.

2-2$\frac{1}{2}$g (4-5lb) leg of lamb
1$\frac{1}{2}$ tablespoons butter
1$\frac{1}{2}$ tablespoons oil
salt and freshly ground black pepper
100ml (4fl oz) red or white wine
200ml ($\frac{1}{3}$pt) veal or beef stock
for garnish:
4 cucumbers
60g (2oz) butter, plus a little extra (optional)
4 shallots, finely chopped
250g ($\frac{1}{2}$lb) cooked lean ham, cut in julienne strips
white pepper
1$\frac{1}{2}$ tablespoons chopped fresh mint
60ml (2oz) double cream

For the garnish: peel the cucumbers, halve them lengthwise and scoop out the seeds. Cut them crosswise in 1cm ($\frac{3}{8}$in) crescents and blanch them in boiling salted water for 2 minutes. Drain, refresh the cucumber with cold water and drain again. Melt the butter in a saucepan and sauté the shallots until soft but not brown. Add the cucumber, ham and white pepper. NOTE: taste for salt, too, but the ham may have made the garnish salty enough. The garnish can be prepared 5-6 hours ahead.

Bone the leg of lamb, first freeing the tail and hip bones from the meat and then carefully scraping the meat from the shank and leg bones (follow the instructions above). Using a very sharp knife, cut the meat into 2cm ($\frac{3}{4}$in) slices.

Sauté the lamb slices in the butter and oil for 3-4 minutes on each side, adding more butter and oil if necessary. The escalopes should be rare. As each is cooked, season it and transfer to a serving dish, overlapping the slices. Keep them warm. Discard the fat from the pan and deglaze with the wine and stock, boiling to reduce well. Meanwhile in a separate pan, sauté the cucumber garnish with a little extra butter if necessary, until very hot. Add the mint and cream, taste for seasoning and arrange at each end or down one side of the lamb slices. Strain the gravy, taste for seasoning and serve at once.
NOTE: another recipe for using escalopes of lamb can be found in the chapter on grilling on page 112.

TOMATES PROVENÇALE
(Provençal tomatoes)

When tomatoes are at their best, these make an ideal accompaniment to lamb, beef or chicken dishes.

SERVES 4

4 tomatoes
salt and freshly ground black pepper
2 cloves garlic, crushed
2 tablespoons chopped parsley
3 tablespoons fresh breadcrumbs
4 tablespoons olive or vegetable oil

Cut the tomatoes in half, discarding the cores. Sprinkle them with salt and pepper. Chop together the garlic and the parsley, then mix with the breadcrumbs.

About 20-30 minutes before serving, heat the oven to hot, 200C (400F) gas 6. Heat 2 tablespoons of the oil in a roasting tin or baking dish. Put in the tomatoes, skin side down. Sprinkle them with 1 tablespoon of oil. Place in the hot oven and bake for 10 minutes. Sprinkle with the garlic mixture, then with another tablespoon of oil and bake for another 2-3 minutes. If you like, brown the tomatoes under the grill just before serving.

Scrape meat from the bones while easing the flesh from the carcass

When flesh is freed from both sides, cut along the breastbone

To bone completely: scrape flesh from wing, thigh and drumstick bones

HOW TO BONE A BIRD

All birds are boned in the same way. Sometimes they are partially boned, leaving the leg and wing bones to add shape when stuffing is added – this is usual for small birds and for chaudfroids for which appearance is very important. For galantines or ballotines, the bird is boned completely. For boning, choose a bird with the skin intact, so it can be kept whole to use for wrapping.

To bone the bird partially

1 Cut off the wing tip and middle section leaving the largest wing bone.
2 With the breast of the bird down, slit the skin in a line down the backbone from neck to tail, exposing the backbone.
3 Cut and scrape the flesh and skin away from the carcass, working evenly with short sharp strokes of the knife. After each stroke, carefully ease the flesh and skin away from the carcass with the fingers of your left hand.
4 Outline with the knife and cut the flesh from the sabre-shaped bone near the wing. As you reach the ball and socket joints connecting the wing and thigh bones to the carcass, sever them; the wing and thigh are thus separated from the carcass but are still attached to the skin.
5 Using longer strokes of the knife, continue cutting the breast meat away from the bone until the ridge of the breastbone, where skin and bones meet, is reached; take great care not to sever the skin here as it is very thin.
6 Turn the bird around and repeat on the other side.

When the skin and meat have been freed from the carcass on both sides of the bird, they will remain attached to the carcass only along the breastbone.
7 Lift up the carcass of the bird in one hand so that the skin and meat hang loose on each side of the breastbone. Cut against the ridge of the breastbone to free the skin and pull to remove the breastbone and the carcass from the flesh. Be careful – the skin here is easily pierced.
8 Spread the skin on the board, flesh side up. The bird is partially boned at this point; the wing and leg bones are still in place.

To bone the bird completely

9 For the wing bone: holding the end of the wing bone in one hand, cut through the tendons and scrape the meat from the bone, drawing the skin away inside out. Pull out the bone, using the knife to free it.
10 For the leg bone: holding the free end of the thigh bone firmly in the left hand, cut through the tendons attaching the flesh to the bone. Use the knife to scrape the meat from the thigh bone, pushing the meat away from the end of the bone as if sharpening a pencil. When you reach the joint between the thigh and drumstick bones, cut off the thigh bone. Scrape the flesh from the drumstick bone until completely clean, drawing the skin off inside out. Cut the drumstick bone free from the skin.
11 Repeat on the other side.
12 Push the skin from the legs and wings right side out. The completely boned bird will now be flat, with most of the skin lined with meat.

BALLOTINE DE DINDE
(Ballotine of turkey)

Serves 10-12 as a main course

4-5kg (8-10lb) turkey
for mousseline stuffing
1½kg (3lb) minced lean veal
6 egg whites
750ml (1¼pt) double cream
½ level teaspoon ground allspice
¼ level teaspoon ground nutmeg
salt and white pepper
for braising
30g (1oz) butter
2 onions, diced
2 carrots, diced
2 sticks celery, diced
2 shallots, finely chopped
clove garlic, crushed
level teaspoon tomato purée
250ml (8fl oz) white wine
750ml (1¼pt) veal stock
bouquet garni
salt and pepper
for the sauce
1 litre (1¾pt) espagnole sauce or fond de veau lié (page 191)
2 tablespoons brandy
3 tablespoons Madeira or sherry
trussing needle and string

For the stuffing: work the veal twice through the fine blade of a mincer. Pound the mixture in a mortar with a pestle until smooth, then gradually work in the egg whites; or, work the veal with the egg whites a little at a time in a blender or electric food processor. Place the mixture in a metal bowl over a bowl of ice and gradually work in the cream. NOTE: do not season the mousseline until all the egg whites and cream have been added, then add allspice, nutmeg, salt and pepper to taste.

Bone the turkey completely and spread it, skin side down, on a board, reserving the bones. Pile the stuffing in the centre, sew up the skin and tie the bird into a neat roll.

For braising: set the oven at moderate, 180C (350F) gas 4. Melt the butter in a heavy-based casserole and brown the turkey on all sides. Take it out, add the onions, carrots and celery, cover and cook over a low heat for 5-7 minutes or until the butter is absorbed and the vegetables are soft. Place the turkey on top and add the shallots, garlic, tomato purée, wine, stock, bouquet garni, turkey bones and salt and pepper. The ballotine should be half covered by the liquid. Cover, bring to the boil and braise in the heated oven for 1½-2 hours or until a skewer inserted in the centre of the ballotine for ½ minute is hot to the touch when withdrawn.

Meanwhile, make the espagnole sauce or fond de veau lié.

To finish: reheat the ballotine, if necessary, on top of the stove or in a moderate oven, 180C (350F) gas 4. When the ballotine is hot, take it out, remove the strings and keep the turkey warm. Strain the cooking liquid, pressing it well through the strainer to extract all the juices from the vegetables, then skim off any fat. Boil until reduced to 200ml (⅓pt). Add the cooking liquid to the espagnole sauce or fond de veau lié and, if necessary, reduce again.

Carve part of the ballotine in 1cm (½in) slices and arrange them overlapping down a serving dish with the remaining ballotine at one end. Add the brandy and sherry or Madeira to the sauce, bring just back to a boil and taste for seasoning. Coat the meat with some of the sauce and serve the rest separately.

CUISSES DE POULET FARCIES, SAUCE SUPREME
(Stuffed chicken legs suprême)

SERVES 8
8 chicken drumsticks
onion, sliced
carrot, sliced
750ml (1¼pt) chicken stock
bouquet garni
salt and pepper
for the stuffing
30g (1oz) chopped cooked ham
60g (2oz) minced veal or ½ chicken breast, chopped
100g (3oz) lean pork, chopped
100g (3oz) pork fat, chopped
egg, beaten to mix
pinch of grated nutmeg
tablespoon brandy
salt and pepper
canned truffle, with its liquid (optional)
for the garnish
250g (½lb) button mushrooms, stalks trimmed level with the caps
15g (½oz) butter
squeeze of lemon juice
for the sauce suprême
45g (1½oz) butter
30g (1oz) flour
the poaching liquid from the chicken legs and the mushrooms
250g (½lb) chopped mushroom stalks
125ml (4½oz) double cream

With a small pointed knife, bone the chicken legs, scraping the bones clean without slitting the meat.

For the stuffing: work the ham, veal or chicken, lean pork and pork fat twice through the fine blade of a mincer and mix in the egg, nutmeg, brandy and plenty of salt and pepper – the mixture should be highly seasoned. Drain the truffle, if included, and cut into 8 thick slices. Reserve these and chop any trimmings. Add the trimmings with the liquid to the stuffing. Fill the cavities in the chicken with stuffing, then roll and tie them into neat parcels to enclose the stuffing.

To cook the chicken: spread the onion and carrot slices in a saucepan, set the chicken legs on top, pour in the stock and add the bouquet garni and a little salt and pepper. Cover and poach for 35-45 minutes or until the chicken is tender. Allow to cool slightly, drain the chicken and remove the strings. Strain the cooking liquid. It can be cooked up to 48 hours ahead.

For the garnish: place the mushrooms in a saucepan with the 15g (½oz) butter, sprinkle with lemon juice, add 1cm (½in) of water and salt and pepper. Cover and cook them for 5-8 minutes or until tender.

For the sauce: melt the butter in a saucepan, stir in the flour and cook until foaming. Allow to cool slightly and then pour in the cooking liquid from the chicken and the mushrooms. Add the chopped mushroom stems and bring the sauce to the boil, whisking constantly. Simmer, stirring occasionally, for about an hour or until reduced to a coating consistency. Strain, add the cream and reduce again to a coating consistency. Taste and adjust the seasoning.

To finish: add the chicken rolls and mushrooms to the sauce and heat through gently. Spoon the sauce over the chicken to coat it, top each piece with a slice of truffle, if used, and arrange the mushrooms around the side. Serve the remaining sauce separately.

Hold the tail of the sole firmly with one hand, and pull the skin away with the other

Remove a fillet from a flat fish with a sweeping motion keeping the knife flat against the bone

After cutting one fillet from a round fish, cut under the bone to release the other one

HOW TO BONE FISH

There are two main types of fish: flat and round. Flat fish, such as sole, turbot and plaice, are easier to bone because the bones lie flat, with the rib bones fanning out horizontally from the central spine. They usually have four fillets, two lying above the backbone and two underneath (some fish such as bream and John Dory have only two fillets). In round fish, such as salmon, trout, whiting or hake, the backbone lies vertically rather than horizontally, and there is one fillet on each side.

A fish cannot be completely boned without being divided into its component fillets, though the backbone can be removed, leaving the head and tail. Boning therefore almost always includes filleting as well. If possible, always use a special fish-filleting knife, which has a very thin, flexible blade. Start by cutting off the fins, but do not bother to gut the fish; nor is there any need to scale the fish as the skin will be removed after filleting. Wash the fillets under cold running water before cooking.

To skin a Dover sole

Dover sole is the only fish that can be skinned before being filleted.
1 Make a small cut in the skin at the tail end. Scrape the skin off towards the head, until enough is free so you can get a good grip on it.
2 With your fingers, firmly grasp the skin and pull it towards the head of the fish, holding the tail with your other hand. If the fish or skin are slippery, hold them with a cloth or dip your fingers in salt.
3 Turn the fish over; remove skin from the other side in the same way.

To fillet a flat fish

If using Dover sole, skin it first (see above).
1 Cut to the bone just behind the head, outlining it.
2 Find the spine; in a skinned sole it is clearly visible and in other flat fish there is a central line in the skin that runs from head to tail.

3 Slit from head to tail along the spine, through to the bone, thus outlining the length of the fillets.
4 Keeping the knife almost flat, slip it between the fish flesh and the rib bones. Cut away the fillet, using a stroking motion and keeping the knife in contact with the bones.
5 When the fillet is detached, you will come to a line of small bones on the border of the fish. Free the fillet by cutting along this line of bones.
6 Turn the fish round and slip the knife under the flesh of the second fillet and remove it in the same way. Turn the fish over and remove the other two fillets in the same way.

To fillet a round fish

1 Cut down to the backbone just behind the fish head.
2 Holding the knife horizontally, slit the skin from head to tail.
3 Holding the knife flat on the backbone, cut flesh from above the bone, using stroking motion and keeping the knife in contact with the bone.
4 When the fillet is detached, cut carefully along the abdominal cavity of the fish to free it completely.
5 Cut under the bone with the same smooth motion to release the second fillet.
6 Turn the fish over and cut behind the head, freeing the fillet entirely.
7 If the fillets contain small bones near the centre, remove them with tweezers.

To remove the skin from fish fillets

1 Place the fillet, skin side down, tail end towards you.
2 Using a filleting knife, make a small cut to separate the skin end from the flesh at the tail.
3 Grasp the skin with the fingers of one hand, using a cloth or dipping your fingers in salt – if they slip.
4 Holding the knife almost parallel to the board, work away from you in a sawing motion, at the same time pulling the skin towards you with your other hand. Work carefully, so as not to damage the flesh.

TRUITES FARCIES AU CITRON
(Lemon-stuffed trout)

This boning technique provides servings that look like whole trout but are infinitely easier to eat.

SERVES 4

| 4 trout, each weighing about 250g (½lb) |
| 200ml (7fl oz) white wine |
| 60g (2 oz) butter |
| salt and pepper |
| ½ teaspoon dried thyme |
| *for the stuffing* |
| 60g (2 oz) fresh white breadcrumbs |
| grated rind of 2 lemons |
| 3 shallots or 1 onion, finely chopped |
| 90g (3oz) butter |
| salt and pepper |
| 6 tablespoons finely chopped parsley |
| juice of 1 lemon, or to taste |
| 1 egg, beaten |
| *for serving* |
| tablespoon chopped parsley |
| 4 lemon slices |

For the stuffing: mix the breadcrumbs with the lemon rind. Cook the shallots or onion in the butter until softened and add them to the breadcrumbs with plenty of salt and pepper, the chopped parsley and the lemon juice. Add the beaten egg to bind the mixture. Heat the oven to moderate, 180C (350F) gas 4.

To prepare the trout: snip off the fins and cut the tails into a neat 'V'; leave the heads intact. Slit the stomach, clean the fish and wash thoroughly. Cut along the backbone from just behind the head to the tail and slip the knife between the bones and the flesh to release the fillets. The two fillets should still be attached at the head and tail. Snip the backbone at each end with scissors and pull it out along with the fine bones attached. Sandwich the fillets with the stuffing.

Put the trout in an ovenproof baking dish and pour the white wine over them. Dot with the butter and sprinkle with salt, pepper and thyme. Bake in the heated oven for 15-20 minutes or just until the fish turns opaque; baste often during cooking.

Sprinkle them with chopped parsley, garnish each fish with a lemon slice and serve.

TURBOT A LA BOURGUIGNONNE

Steamed potatoes are the classic accompaniment to this dish. Sole, hake or any other well-flavoured fish can be substituted for the turbot.

SERVES 4

| 1½kg (3lb) turbot |
| fish glaze (page 219) made with the bones from the fish, slice of onion, 10g (⅓oz) butter, water to cover, 5 peppercorns and a bouquet garni |
| 3 shallots, chopped |
| 400ml (¾pt) red wine (preferably Burgundy) |
| kneaded butter made with 45g (1½oz) butter and 15g (½ oz) flour |
| tablespoon brandy |
| salt and pepper |
| 45g (1½oz) butter |
| tablespoon chopped parsley (for sprinkling) |

Fillet the turbot and use the bones to make a fish glaze. Butter a shallow ovenproof baking dish, spread the shallots in the bottom and lay the fish fillets on top. Pour over the wine and cover with a piece of buttered foil. Leave to marinate for 1 hour. Set the oven at moderate, 180C (350F) gas 4.

Poach the fish in the heated oven for 12-15 minutes or until the fillets just become opaque. Drain them on paper towels, arrange them on a serving dish and keep them warm. Strain the cooking liquid into a saucepan, bring to the boil and whisk in the kneaded butter a little at a time so that the sauce thickens to a coating consistency. Add ½ teaspoon of the glaze and the brandy, take from the heat and taste for seasoning. Whisk in the remaining butter a little at a time. NOTE: do not reheat the sauce or it will separate. Spoon the sauce over the fish, sprinkle with the parsley and serve at once.

3
BRAISING AND STEWING
Cultural clash with the casserole

In his admirable 'Food of France' (1958), Waverly Root points out that the French approach meat cookery quite differently from the British. To the French, a braise or a ragoût (stew), slowly simmered in a rich, balanced sauce, are both equal, if not superior, to any roast or grill. Ragoûts date back to the Renaissance and were, says Alexandre Dumas, the glory of ancienne cuisine. The gluttonous Catherine de Medici is said to have nearly died from over-indulgence in a ragoût of cockscombs, kidneys and artichoke hearts.

Braises and stews call for mature, tough meats whose flavour is devloped by long cooking. French animals are deliberately bred, fed and butchered to provide lean, close-textured meat with none of the streaks of fat that give tenderness to Scottish or Texan beef. The two aims are incompatible, so the British find French roasts inferior and the French think English stews lack body. In France, cooks go for muscular cuts from the shoulder and leg that contain plenty of gristle. Gristle may be something of an acquired taste, but given the right low-temperature treatment, it dissolves during cooking to give a flavour and syrupy texture which is highly prized. Calves' and pigs' feet and pork rind may be added for similar effect.

Stewing is a wide term, covering any dish in which the meat (or poultry) is cut in pieces, either browned or not, and cooked slowly in a good deal of liquid. From the French viewpoint, the word loses something in translation, for ragoût has none of the low budget, school-meal connotation of the English 'stew'. Braising is more narrowly defined: it refers to meat, usually a single, larger piece, that has been browned or at least lightly sautéed and then cooked slowly with a liquid, and a braise always uses a mirepoix or mixture of diced vegetables – carrots, onion, celery – for flavour. In the old days, the braising pot was buried in the ashes of the fire – hence the hollow lid, designed to hold the hot coals of the traditional braisière.

Like sauces and sautés, braises and ragoûts divide into brown and white, each with its appropriate ingredients. The 'brown' approach involving the use of red wine and brown stock is by far the more common, ideal for dark meats such as beef, mutton, game, goose and duck. Veal, pork, chicken and innards can be cooked either by the brown method or the white, which uses white wine and light stock. In the actual cooking, the difference between the brown and white appears to be slight: in one the meat is well browned, in the other it is not. But the characteristics of brown and white stews or braises are totally different, even when the same meat is used.

Beef is the favourite meat for ragoûts as stewing suits only the tougher meats. Long cooking is redundant for tender lamb, so with the exception of navarin printanière (in which spring lamb is combined in a stew with the first baby vegetables of the season) and creamy lamb blanquette, mutton is usually used. To balance its pervasive taste, strong-flavoured root vegetables are added, or dried beans may be used – as in Cassoulet or haricot of mutton, a dish featured in 18th-century English cookbooks. Pork and veal can be stewed, but the resulting sauce is less aromatic than that of a beef stew.

Although veal, lamb and innards can be braised to good effect, beef is the top choice for this method. So popular is braised beef that every region has its own version. Provençal daube, cooked with olives, tomatoes and a strip of orange peel until the meat is tender enough to cut with a spoon, has spread nationwide. Estouffade, derived from 'étouffer' meaning to smother, emphasises the slow cooking involved in dishes like the Gascon étouffat de Noël, in which beef is braised with Armagnac, wine and shallots for as long as twenty-four hours. La Varenne's Chef Chambrette regularly cooked braised beef overnight in his restaurant. He would bring the pot to the boil before closing time and put it in a very low oven. By the next morning, the meat was so tender that he had to lift it out carefully by hand; if he had used a fork, it would have fallen apart.

For poultry braises and ragoûts, tough old birds that have served their time in the farmyard are needed. This way go the elderly turkeys and chickens (geese and ducks are more often preserved in their own fat). Nothing, say the experts with a knowing wink, com-

BOEUF CHASSEUR

A hearty beef stew with mushrooms, shallots, herbs, wine and garlic. It tastes even better when it is reheated

EPAULE DE VEAU A LA BOURGEOISE

A boned shoulder of veal, stuffed with finely minced pork and herbs. It is braised in wine and veal stock and garnished here with 'turned' vegetables

pares with Coq au vin made with an old cock; battery chickens or young free-range chickens simply will not do. Mature birds are best, too, for cooking 'en cocotte'; a method by which meat or poultry is cooked in a covered casserole with fat and vegetables, but with no liquid except its own juices.

Perhaps the fullest flavoured ragoûts of all are made with game – the ragoûts of venison or wild boar using meats that are marinated for days before cooking. There is an anti-marinade movement in the nouvelle cuisine, but for game and some ragoûts such as beef bourguignon, a day or two of marinating transforms both flavour and texture. The marinade is invariably used in the sauce and sometimes, as in civet of hare, the sauce is thickened with blood. Braising and stewing are the age-old ways to deal with tough pheasant or grouse that are more than a year or two old. Equally traditional are ragoûts of innards such as kidneys, sweetbreads and tongue, though one recent revival from the 18th century by a three-star chef seems destined for instant oblivion. It consists of a ragoût of cockscombs, wild mushrooms and truffles served in a cornucopia made from a breadcrumbed and deep-fried sow's ear.

Braises and ragoûts, always favourites in brasseries and bistros as well as at home, are now enjoying a comeback in top restaurants too. Each method has its own appeal to the nouvelle cuisine chefs. In their rôle as self-appointed saviours of regional cooking, they enthuse the traditional braises – the daubes and éstouffades – essential to country cooking. Ragoûts are adored even more because, while smacking of a righteous return to simple, good cooking, they are less stereotyped. More or less anything can be added to a ragoût, and you can call it what you please. Already we have ragoûts of seafood and ragoûts of vegetables, and I'm still waiting for a ragoût of beef, crayfish and passion fruit juice. . . .

THE WAY TO SUCCESS

1 150g (5oz) boneless meat is the usual allowance per person.
2 Meat *must* be dry before frying, or it will steam rather than brown. If it is damp from marinating, dry it well on paper towels. Marinated meat can be browned in a frying pan rather than in a casserole; in a deep pan, steam tends to condense on the meat and prevent it browning.
3 Pieces of meat should be browned a few at a time; if the pan is too crowded, the temperature of the fat will be lowered and the meat will steam in its own juices.
4 Do not use stock that contains much salt. During cooking it will reduce, becoming saltier and saltier.
5 For extra richness, add pork rind – or calves' or pigs' feet to the pan.
6 A stew or a braise can be simmered on top of the stove instead of in the oven. Make sure the lid fits tightly and stir the sauce from time to time.
7 Braising and stewing is done at a slow, regular simmer; 180C (350F) gas 4 is the temperature usually recommended. If the liquid boils, the meat will dry and shrink.

When braising
8 Do not add too much liquid; the sauce should be flavoured with the concentrated essence of meat and vegetables, not just with wine and stock.
9 Towards the end of cooking when the sauce has reduced, turn and baste the meat often so that it does not dry out.

When stewing
10 At the beginning of cooking, the liquid should just cover the meat. At the end, the liquid should have reduced but still cover $\frac{1}{2}$ - $\frac{2}{3}$ of the meat. Add extra liquid during cooking if it evaporates too quickly. If the sauce is thin at the end of the cooking time, reduce it by boiling until concentrated.

Getting ahead
1 Almost all braises and stews are better when reheated because the sauce mellows on keeping. Keep covered in the refrigerator for up to 3 days.
2 When reheating, be careful not to overcook any of the vegetables in the garnish; deliberately undercook them when making the dish ahead.
3 Braised and stewed meats free well, particularly when covered in their sauce. Braised meat is also good served cold.

EPAULE DE VEAU A LA BOURGEOISE

(Shoulder of veal bourgeoise)

'Bourgeois' refers to a garnish of simple ingredients which accompanies braised meats, especially beef, veal or mutton. For greater elegance, chefs sometimes trim the carrots and potatoes of this dish to 3.5cm (1½in) long olive shapes before being cooked.

SERVES 6-8

2-2½kg (4-5lb) boned shoulder of veal
salt and freshly ground pepper
tablespoon oil
2 tablespoons butter
onion, diced
carrot, diced
2 stalks celery, diced
300ml (½pt) white wine
600-750ml (1-1¼pts) veal stock
2 teaspoons tomato purée
clove garlic, crushed
bouquet garni
60g (2oz) butter
30g (1oz) flour
2 tablespoons chopped parsley (optional)
for the stuffing
onion, chopped
2 tablespoons butter
75g (2½oz) fresh white breadcrumbs
4 tablespoons white wine
500g (1lb) finely minced pork, fat and lean mixed
2 cloves garlic, crushed
tablespoon chopped parsley
2 teaspoons chopped mixed herbs – thyme, rosemary, oregano
egg, beaten to mix
for garnish
750g (1½lb) baby carrots, or large carrots, quartered
750g (1½lb) baby onions, blanched and peeled
1kg (2lb) small new potatoes, peeled

For the stuffing: cook the onion in the butter until soft but not brown and allow to cool. Moisten the breadcrumbs with the wine. Mix the pork with the onion, breadcrumbs, garlic, parsley, herbs and plenty of salt and pepper; stir in the beaten egg.

Lay the meat, cut side up, on a board and sprinkle with salt and

FOR THE EPAULE DE VEAU

Spread the pork stuffing evenly over the boned veal shoulder and roll it into a compact cylinder before tying it

pepper. Spread it with the stuffing, roll up neatly and tie.

Heat the oil and butter in a large flameproof casserole and brown the meat on all sides. Take it out, add the onion, carrot and celery, cover and cook over low heat for 5-7 minutes until the fat is absorbed and the vegetables are slightly soft. Replace the veal, add the wine, 300ml (½pt) of the stock, the tomato purée, garlic, bouquet garni, and season with salt and pepper. Cover and bring to the boil. Braise the veal in a moderate oven, 180C (350F) gas 4, for 1½ hours or until almost tender. Take out the meat and strain the gravy. Replace the meat, put the baby carrots around it, pour over the gravy and add more stock if necessary to cover the carrots. Cover and continue cooking for 20 minutes. Add the onions, potatoes and enough stock to cover and continue cooking for 20-25 minutes or until both vegetables and meat are tender. Veal bourgeoise can be cooked 2-3 days ahead, but the vegetables should be slightly underdone to allow for reheating.

To finish: if necessary, reheat the meat in a moderate oven, 180C (350F) gas 4. Lift out the meat and vegetables and keep warm. Skim any fat from the gravy, taste it for seasoning and reduce if necessary until well flavoured. Mash the butter with the flour until smooth. Whisk enough of this kneaded butter bit by bit into the sauce to thicken it slightly. Strain it into a saucepan and keep hot. Discard the strings from the meat, cut it in 1cm (⅜in) slices and arrange them overlapping down the centre of a serving dish. Spoon the vegetables around and coat both meat and vegetables with a little sauce.

Sprinkle the vegetables with chopped parsley and serve the remaining sauce separately.

BOEUF CHASSEUR

(Beef chasseur)

Venison is also delicious cooked in this way. The flavour of the dish is even better when reheated.

SERVES 4

tablespoon oil
tablespoon butter
750g (1½lb) lean chuck or round steak, cut in 3.5cm (1½in) cubes
onion, chopped
level tablespoon flour
300-375ml (½-⅝pt) beef stock
150ml (¼pt) white wine
clove garlic, crushed
2 shallots, finely chopped
2 teaspoons tomato purée
bouquet garni
salt and freshly ground pepper
250g (½lb) mushrooms
tablespoon chopped parsley (for sprinkling)

Heat the oil and butter in a heavy-based flameproof casserole until foaming and brown the pieces of beef on all sides, a few at a time. Take them out, add the onion and sauté over moderate heat until lightly browned. Stir in the flour and cook, stirring, until richly browned – do not allow it to burn. Allow it to cool slightly and add 300ml (½pt) of the stock, the wine, garlic, shallots, tomato purée, bouquet garni and salt and pepper. Replace the beef and bring the mixture to the boil. Cover and simmer on top of the stove or cook in a moderate oven, 180C (350F) gas·4, for 1½-2 hours, or until the beef is very tender. Stir from time to time and add more stock if it looks dry.

Trim the mushroom stems level with the caps and quarter them if large. Fifteen minutes before the end of cooking, add the mushrooms to the stew, stir, and continue cooking. When the beef and mushrooms are tender, discard the bouquet garni and taste for seasoning. Transfer to a serving dish or serve from the casserole, and sprinkle with chopped parsley. The stew can be made a day or two ahead. Keep it covered in the refrigerator. It will freeze for up to 3 months.

FILET DE PORC NORMANDE

(Loin of pork Normande)

Here appears what one French gastronome has called 'the holy trinity' of apples, Calvados and cream – the classic ingredients of any dish named 'Normande'.

SERVES 4

tablespoon oil

tablespoon butter

boned fore loin of pork weighing about 750g or $1\frac{1}{2}$lb

2 medium onions, sliced

2 tart apples, peeled, cored and sliced

3 tablespoons Calvados

level tablespoon flour

375ml ($\frac{5}{8}$pt) veal or chicken stock

salt and pepper

100ml ($\frac{1}{6}$pt) double cream

for the garnish

2 tablespoons butter

2 firm dessert apples, unpeeled and sliced in 1cm ($\frac{3}{8}$in) slices

30g (1oz) sugar

bunch of watercress

Heat the oil and butter in a sauté pan or shallow flameproof casserole and brown the loin of pork on all sides. Remove it, add the onions and cook until soft but not brown. Add the apples and continue cooking over fairly high heat until the apples and onions are golden brown. Replace the loin, pour over the Calvados and flame (page 57). Stir the flour into the juices, add the stock, salt and pepper and bring to the boil. Cover and simmer, stirring occasionally, in a moderate oven, 180C (350F) gas 4, for $1\frac{1}{2}$-2 hours, or until the meat is tender. The pork can be prepared up to 48 hours ahead and kept covered in the refrigerator, or it can be frozen for up to 3 months.

For the garnish: heat the butter in a frying pan. Dip one side of each apple slice in the sugar. Cook the apple slices, sugared side down, in the hot butter over high heat for 4-5 minutes, or until the sugar caramelises. Sprinkle the rest of the sugar on the apples, turn over and cook for 4-5 minutes longer.

To finish: if necessary, reheat the pork on top of the stove. Lift out the loin, carve it in 6mm ($\frac{1}{4}$in) diagonal slices, arrange them on a serving dish and keep warm. Strain the sauce, pressing the apples and onions through the strainer, bring to the boil and reduce if necessary until thick enough to coat a spoon. Add the cream, bring just back to the boil and taste for seasoning. Spoon the sauce over the pork and garnish the dish with the caramelised apple slices and the watercress before serving with a rice pilaf.

Cuts of meat for braising and stewing

Beef	Veal	Lamb	Pork
Neck	Shoulder	Scrag	Neck
Top ribs	Breast	Shoulder	Shoulder
Aitchbone	Leg	Breast	Fore loin
Topside	Shin	Leg	Leg
Shin; cow heel		Middle neck	Hand and spring
Thick flank			
Thin flank			
Chuck steak			
Sticking piece			
Clod			
Brisket			

JAMBON BRAISE A LA PIEMONTAISE DE CAREME

(Carême's braised ham, Piedmont-style)

SERVES 12-16

6-8kg (12-16lb) uncooked country ham

2 bunches watercress

150g (5oz) grated Parmesan cheese

for simmering

4 carrots, quartered

4 onions, quartered and each stuck with 2 whole cloves

large bouquet garni

10 peppercorns

2 level tablespoons fresh basil leaves or 2 teaspoons dried basil

for braising

45g ($1\frac{1}{2}$oz) butter

3 carrots, diced

3 onions, diced

2 sticks of celery, diced

450ml ($\frac{3}{4}$pt) dry white wine

150ml ($\frac{1}{4}$pt) brandy

1 litre ($1\frac{3}{4}$pts) brown veal stock

2-3 level teaspoons arrowroot mixed to a paste with 2-3 tablespoons Madeira

for the rice piémontaise

375g ($\frac{3}{4}$lb) butter

800g ($1\frac{3}{4}$lb) long grain rice

$1\frac{3}{4}$ litres (3pts) white veal stock

salt and freshly ground black pepper

125g (4oz) grated Parmesan cheese

Scrub the ham, trim off some of the fat and, if the ham is salty, soak it for 12-24 hours in cold water, changing the water 2 or 3 times. Drain the ham, wrap it tightly in cheesecloth or muslin and put it into a very large saucepan with the ingredients for simmering. Add water to cover, bring to the boil and skim. Cover and simmer, allowing 12 minutes per 500g (1lb) and 12 minutes more. Allow the ham to cool to tepid and then peel off and discard the skin. Trim away all but a thin layer of fat. Set the oven at moderate, 180C (350F) gas 4.

To braise the ham: melt the butter in a large flameproof casserole and gently cook the diced carrots, onions and celery for 5-7 minutes or until soft but not browned. Add the wine and reduce for 5 minutes. Add the brandy with 2 cups of the veal stock, set the ham on top, cover and braise for 1 hour. The ham can be cooked 2-3 days ahead.

To make the rice: melt 250g (8oz) of the butter in a large, heavy-based pan and add the rice, stock and seasoning. Cover and bring to the boil. Simmer on top of the stove or cook in a moderate oven at 180C (350F) gas 4, for 18-20 minutes.

To finish: reheat the ham, if necessary, in the casserole then transfer it to a roasting tin and turn up the oven to very hot, 230C (450F) gas 8. Strain the cooking liquid and skim off the fat. Spoon a little of the liquid over the ham and roast, basting often, for 10-15 minutes to glaze it.

Heat the rice, if cooked ahead, in the oven or on top of the stove. When hot, leave it to stand in a warm place for 10 minutes, then remove the lid. Dot the top with the remaining butter and sprinkle with grated cheese. Leave for 1-2 minutes.

RIS DE VEAU BRAISES DEMIDOFF

The pair of sweetbreads on the plate are ready for blanching. Once blanched (see recipe), the excess skin is peeled off and they are pressed between two plates under a weight

At the very last moment before serving Ris de veau braisés Demidoff, the garnish is added to the sauce, gently reheated and spooned over the neatly sliced sweetbread 'escalopes'

Meanwhile finish the sauce: add the remaining stock to the braising liquid, bring to the boil and reduce, if necessary, until well flavoured. Whisk enough of the arrowroot and Madeira mixture into the boiling sauce to thicken it slightly. Taste for seasoning.

Spread the rice on a large serving dish, set the ham on top and garnish the dish with watercress. Serve the sauce and a bowl of grated Parmesan cheese separately.

RIS DE VEAU BRAISES DEMIDOFF
(Braised sweetbreads Demidoff)

This rich dish, which in classic cuisine also contains truffles cut into crescents, was named after the Russian prince Anatole Demidoff.

SERVES 4

1-2 pairs (750g or 1½lb) calves' sweetbreads
slice of lemon
salt and pepper
30g (1oz) butter
2 carrots, diced
2 onions, diced
50g (1⅔oz) flour
2 shallots, finely chopped
clove garlic, crushed (optional)
teaspoon tomato purée
300ml (½pt) veal or chicken stock
150ml (¼pt) white wine
bouquet garni
tablespoon chopped parsley (for sprinkling)

for the garnish

125g (¼lb) mushrooms, stems removed
4 stalks celery, peeled
2 carrots, peeled
turnip, peeled
medium onion
30g (1oz) butter

Soak the sweetbreads for 2-3 hours in cold water, changing the water once or twice. Drain, rinse and put them in a pan with cold water to cover, a slice of lemon and a little salt. Bring slowly to the boil, skimming occasionally, and simmer for 5 minutes. Drain, rinse the sweetbreads, peel them and remove the ducts. Reserve the trimmings. Press the sweetbreads between two large plates with a 1kg (2lb) weight on top and chill.

For the garnish: cut the mushrooms and celery in thin slices. Halve the carrots lengthwise, remove the centres and cut the carrots in thin, crescent-shaped slices. Prepare the turnip like the carrots, but a wide turnip must first be quartered. Quarter and slice the onion. The vegetables should all be crescent-shaped. Save all the vegetable trimmings, except those from the turnip.

Melt the butter in a sauté pan or shallow flameproof casserole. Add the diced carrot and onion and cook until golden brown. Dip the sweetbreads in 30g (1oz) of the flour, pat off the excess, and brown well on both sides in the butter. Add the shallots, garlic, tomato purée, stock, wine, bouquet garni, salt, pepper, and the trimmings from the sweetbreads and vegetables. Bring to the boil, cover and braise in a moderate oven, 180C (350F) gas 4, for 35-45

minutes, or until the sweetbreads are very tender.

To cook the garnish: spread a heavy-based pan with the rest of the butter, add the celery, carrots and onion with salt and pepper, press a piece of buttered foil on top and cover with the lid. Cook in a moderate oven, 180C (350F) gas 4, for 10 minutes, stirring occasionally, until nearly tender. Add the mushrooms and turnip and continue cooking, stirring occasionally, for 10-15 more minutes, or until all the vegetables are tender.

For the sauce: lift out the sweetbreads and allow to cool slightly. Strain the cooking liquid into a pan, pressing the vegetables well to extract all the juices. Boil it until glossy and well flavoured. Mash together the butter with the remaining flour until smooth. Over low heat, whisk in enough of this mixture, bit by bit, to thicken the sauce slightly.

Cut the sweetbreads in 'escalopes' – diagonal slices about 1cm (½in) thick. The sweetbreads can be prepared 24 hours ahead up to this point. Keep them in the sauce in the refrigerator, with the garnish separate. The sweetbreads, but not the garnish, can also be frozen.

To finish: if necessary, reheat the sweetbreads in the sauce on top of the stove. Lift out and arrange overlapping on a serving dish and keep warm. Add the garnish to the sauce, reheat gently and taste for seasoning. Spoon the garnish and sauce over the sweetbreads and sprinkle with chopped parsley. Serve any remaining sauce separately.

CIVET DE LIEVRE
(Hare civet)

A civet is a ragoût of furred game, usually hare, made with red wine, onions, lardons (bacon strips) and mushrooms and thickened with blood. There is no substitute for the blood of the hare except pigs' blood; without this thickener the civet becomes simply a ragoût.

SERVES 6

freshly killed hare of 2-2½ kg (4-5lb), blood reserved
for the marinade
2 tablespoons olive oil
4 tablespoons brandy
onion, cut in rounds
3 shallots, sliced
bouquet garni
for the sauce
tablespoon oil
250g (½lb) piece lean bacon, cut in lardons (strips)
2 onions, cut in quarters
3 level tablespoons flour
bottle red wine
300ml (½pt) brown veal stock
clove garlic, crushed
bouquet garni
salt and pepper
½ level teaspoon ground allspice
for the garnish
24 baby onions, peeled
3 tablespoons butter
½ level teaspoon sugar
250g (½lb) mushrooms, cut in quarters
for the croûtons
4 tablespoons oil and butter, mixed (optional – for frying)
6 slices bread, crusts removed, cut in triangles
tablespoon chopped parsley (for sprinkling)

Detach the thighs from the back and divide each thigh into three. Detach the forelegs and cut each in two. The head can be cut in two, the eyes removed and cooked in the civet to add flavour. *It is not served.* Slice off the neck and cut in two or three pieces. Divide the rib section in two along the backbone and cut each half in 4-6 pieces, depending on the size of the hare.

For the marinade: combine all the ingredients in a deep bowl. Add the pieces of hare and turn them so they are thoroughly coated with marinade. Cover and leave overnight at room temperature or in the refrigerator for up to 3 days; turn the hare pieces from time to time in the marinade.

For the sauce: heat the oil in a sauté pan and fry the bacon lardons until the fat runs. Add the onion quarters and cook until they begin to brown. Take out the bacon and onion and drain off all but 2 tablespoons of the fat. Meanwhile drain the pieces of hare, reserving the marinade, and pat them dry on paper towels. Sauté in the fat until lightly browned on all sides. Sprinkle in the flour and brown it also. Add the wine, boil it for 2-3 minutes to reduce it, then add the stock, garlic, bouquet garni, salt, pepper and allspice, and replace the bacon and onion.

Cover the pan and bring the liquid to the boil. Add the reserved marinade and flavourings and simmer very gently in a moderately low oven, 160C (325F) gas 3, for 1 hour or until the hare is very tender.

The hare can be cooked up to 48 hours ahead and kept covered in the refrigerator, or the dish can be frozen.

For the garnish: fry the onions in the butter for 10 minutes or until almost tender. Sprinkle with the sugar, season with salt and pepper and cook, shaking the pan, until caramelised. Take them out, add the mushrooms and sauté until tender.

For the croûtons: heat the oil and butter in a frying pan, add the triangles of bread and fry until golden brown on both sides. Drain thoroughly on paper towels. Alternatively the bread may be toasted, the crusts trimmed off and the bread cut into triangles.

To finish: if necessary, reheat the hare on top of the stove. Transfer the pieces of hare with the lardons of bacon to a serving dish and keep warm. Strain the sauce into a saucepan, add the garnish and heat gently. Skim off any fat that rises to the surface. Stir a little of the hot sauce into the hare blood. Pour this mixture back into the pan, off the heat, shaking so it is incorporated. If necessary, heat the sauce slightly so it thickens. NOTE: do not boil or the sauce will separate. Taste the sauce for seasoning and spoon it over the hare.

Sprinkle the dish with parsley and arrange the croûtons around the edge before serving.

POIVRADE DE PORC
(Pork poivrade)

The term 'poivrade' usually suggests game, and venison could be substituted in this recipe, but pork takes to the treatment admirably. Brussels sprout purée (page 231) makes a good accompaniment.

SERVES 8

2kg (4lb) boneless pork shoulder
3 tablespoons peppercorns
2 carrots, peeled
large onion, sliced
10 juniper berries
750ml (1¼pt) red wine
200ml (½pt) red wine vinegar
stock or water as required
30g (1oz) butter
60g (2oz) flour
3 tablespoons red currant jelly
3 tablespoons chopped chives

Trim the pork of all fat and sinew and cut it into large chunks. Put the meat, 1 tablespoon of peppercorns, the whole carrots, sliced onion, juniper berries, wine and vinegar into a heavy-based pan. Bring it to the boil and then simmer, uncovered for 1 hour. Add more stock or water as required so that the meat is always covered by liquid.

Remove the meat and strain the cooking liquid. Crush the remaining peppercorns. Melt the butter in a large saucepan and add the crushed peppercorns and the flour. Cook slowly until the flour browns. Whisk in the strained cooking liquid and bring to the boil. Stir in the red currant jelly and then add the pork. Simmer for 40 minutes. Taste for seasoning, add salt if necessary and serve sprinkled with the chives.

CASSEROLES FOR BRAISING

The traditional casserole for braising is called a braisière and is usually made of metal – cast iron, enamelled cast iron or, nowadays, stainless steel. The sides must be thick-walled and the base must be flameproof so ingredients can be browned directly over the heat. The lid must fit tightly so evaporation of the sauce can be controlled. The casserole should just hold all the ingredients – for poultry an oval pot is ideal. If the pot is too big, too much liquid is needed.

OIGNONS BRAISES AU VIN
(Onions braised in wine)

Because the recipe can be varied by using red or white wine and stock from any meat, poultry or game, these braised onions complement many main dishes.

SERVES 8

8 medium onions, peeled
tablespoon oil
150ml ($\frac{1}{4}$pt) red or white wine
300ml ($\frac{1}{2}$pt) stock or water
salt and pepper

Set the oven at moderately low, 170C (325F) gas 3. Heat the oil in a shallow flameproof casserole and put in the onions, root end down. They should be tightly packed. Heat until the oil sizzles, then add the wine, bring to the boil and boil for 1 minute. Add enough stock or water to come halfway up the onions and season well.

Bake, uncovered, in the heated oven for 1$\frac{1}{4}$-1$\frac{1}{2}$ hours or until the onions are tender. The cooking liquid should be well-reduced; if not, remove the onions and boil the liquid on top of the stove until syrupy. The onions can be cooked up to 3 days ahead and reheated, or they can be frozen.

MARRONS BRAISES
(Braised chestnuts)

Braised chestnuts are a favourite French accompaniment for goose and turkey.

SERVES 4

750g (1$\frac{1}{2}$lb) chestnuts
tablespoon oil
onion, chopped
stalk celery
450-600ml ($\frac{3}{4}$-1pt) white veal stock
salt and pepper
$\frac{1}{4}$ level teaspoon allspice

To peel the chestnuts: prick the shell of each nut with a sharp knife. Put the chestnuts in a pan of cold water, bring to the boil, then take the pan from the heat and quickly peel them with a small knife, a few at a time, while still hot, taking off both outer and inner skin.

Heat the oil in a casserole and fry the onion until soft but not brown. Add the chestnuts and celery, pour over 450ml ($\frac{3}{4}$pt) stock and add salt, pepper and allspice. Cover and simmer in a moderate oven, 180C (350F) gas 4, for 45 minutes or until the chestnuts are tender. Remove the celery. If too much stock evaporates during cooking, add more. If liquid is left at the end of cooking, remove the lid and boil rapidly to reduce until the chestnuts are coated with a shiny glaze.

CHOU ROUGE BRAISE
(Braised red cabbage)

Red cabbage is cooked with acid ingredients – vinegar, lemon juice, apples – to preserve its colour.

SERVES 4

30g (1oz) butter
medium onion, chopped
medium head of red cabbage, cored and shredded
3 tablespoons wine vinegar
tablespoon lemon juice
salt and pepper
2 tart apples, peeled, cored and diced

Set the oven at moderate, 180C (350F) gas 4. Melt the butter in a large pan and sauté the onion until soft but not brown. Add the cabbage and stir over heat until well coated with butter. Pour over the vinegar and lemon juice and stir well. Add salt, pepper and the apples; cover the pan and braise in the oven, stirring occasionally, for 30 minutes, or until the cabbage is tender but still slightly crisp.

4

CHOUX PASTRY
The magic of choux

To me, choux pastry always smacks of a conjuring trick. I can't get over my mistrust of the power of plain eggs to transform gluey butter, flour and water paste into crisp balloons of pastry with hollow centres, so neatly designed to hold rich fillings. As with soufflés, I find a certain challenge in baking choux and suffer a sneaking fear that, despite my best efforts, the dough may not rise. In fact, this feeling is quite unfounded, for choux is perhaps the easiest of all doughs to make.

Choux pastry is unlike any other, for it is cooked twice – its original name was pâte à chaud, or 'heated pastry'. In the first cooking, butter is melted in water and brought to the boil; then flour is beaten in off the heat. The heat of the butter and water mixture cooks the flour to a solid dough (a panade), which is usually dried slightly over the heat for half a minute. Then the eggs are beaten, one by one, into the dough, which should be warm enough to slightly cook the eggs.

Adding the eggs is the only tricky part in making choux pastry. Beating is quite hard work and each egg must be thoroughly incorporated before the next is added. At first the dough thickens, then it starts to thin and look glossy. At this point, the last egg is lightly beaten with a fork and added – little by little – until the dough just falls easily from the spoon. Eggs make the pastry light, so it's desirable to use as many as possible, but the dough mustn't be so soft that it doesn't hold its shape. For this reason, no recipe states exactly how many eggs to use when making choux. Quantities can vary depending on the size of the eggs, the dryness of the flour, the amount of water that evaporated as it was brought to a boil, and how much the panade was dried. I had a nasty moment giving a demonstration in the American northwest when my four-to-five egg quantity of choux dough absorbed seven eggs. The flour of the region is notoriously dry, but nonetheless, I was relieved when the pastry rose in the oven on schedule.

Choux pastry is traditionally shaped into mounds of various sizes – tiny for petits fours, 2.5 cm (1 in) for profiteroles, 5 cm (2 in) mounds for cream puffs. All will double in size as they're baked. The dough is best shaped with a piping bag and tube, though a couple of spoons will do an adequate job. Ovals of choux pastry are called salambos and strips of choux, éclairs. Choux can be piped in a large ring to make Gâteau Paris-Brest, which is filled with praline-flavoured pastry cream and there is a grand gâteau called a Réligieuse, which recreates a nun's robes, with upended chocolate and coffee éclairs for her skirt, a

plump ring for her bosom and a choux puff for her head.

The choux dough puffs both from the action of the eggs and from that of the steam created by the oven heat within the dough due to its high water content. (Choux pastry shapes must always be piped well apart on a baking sheet to allow for expansion.) The dough must dry as well as puff while cooking, and in an electric oven which has no ventilation, the door should be propped open half-way through the cooking with a small wooden spoon to allow steam to escape.

Do not, by the way, despise the spoon as an oven control. A generous chink in the door is much the quickest way to cool an overheated oven, though the draughts when it is fully open will endanger cakes and soufflés. When I was training in Paris, we had ovens that heated red-hot top and bottom, all or nothing, and the only way to control them was by adjusting the gap in the door.

Choux pastry invariably looks done before it is ready as it must continue to dry for 5 to 10 minutes after it has browned. One clue is given by the sides, which brown last. Any cracks that form should also be brown, not pale. When done, choux must be transferred at once to a rack and should be poked with a knife, or split, so that steam can escape from inside.

Baked choux pastry quickly loses its crispness, so it should be stored in an airtight container and filled not more than an hour or two before serving. It is edible, of course, for much longer – frankly, a truly fresh, crisp choux pastry with a melting filling is rare outside a home kitchen. That may explain the most expensive tea I ever had, at a grand hotel in Paris. Tea for two, with a couple of éclairs, admittedly spanking fresh, cost almost £10 without the tip.

Before baking, most choux are brushed with egg glaze to help them colour, and sweet choux may also

PROFITEROLES AU CHOCOLAT
Chocolate-topped puffs filled with a mixture of crème pâtissière and crème Chantilly

GATEAU PARIS-BREST
Choux pastry filled with praline butter cream. A praline crème St Honoré can be used instead

43

be sprinkled with flaked almonds, which then toast to a rich brown. After cooking, most are given an additional topping: simply, a dusting of icing sugar – especially if the choux are almond topped – or more elaborately, a coating of fondant icing. Alternatives are a light caramel (caramel-topped éclairs are called bâtons de Jacob), melted chocolate or glacé icing.

Like all pastry, baked choux is used primarily as a container for other ingredients. For choux gâteaux, the most common filling is pastry cream, partly because it keeps better than whipped cream, partly because it has less tendency to soak into the pastry. Flavours lean heavily towards the traditional vanilla, chocolate and coffee, but orange or lemon pastry cream make a pleasant change, or pastry cream flavoured with a spirit like rum or Kirsch. One excellent variation, choux normande, calls for pastry cream mixed with one third its weight in apple purée flavoured with Calvados, while in choux Montmorency the cream is flavoured with chopped cherries and cherry brandy.

A croquembouche, the standard 'pièce montée' – the table centre – for French weddings and anniversaries, is the most famous of all choux gâteaux. To make it, small choux puffs are glued together with light caramel to form a towering cone as much as a metre (three feet) high, which is then embellished with nougat shapes and sugared almonds. Because keeping the structure straight is not easy, some chefs use a special metal cone. Most have developed their own variant of croquembouche, and Chef Jorant of La Varenne recalls that, whenever he was commissioned to make a croquembouche at his pastry shop, he would make it an hour or two ahead to display in his window – the best possible advertisement of his skill.

But choux pastry is much more than just the basis of rich gâteaux. Savoury choux puffs can be served hot, filled with a béchamel sauce flavoured with mushrooms, ham or cheese or alternatively with fish mousse, while cold puffs are often stuffed with chicken and vegetables bound with mayonnaise. Baby choux, plain or cheese flavoured, are a good accompaniment to soup. Choux dough can also be deep fried, flavoured with mushroom or cheese for savoury fritters, or with sugar for sweet ones. Leftover dough, mixed with double the quantity of mashed potato then deep fried, makes one of my favourites – pommes dauphine. Choux pastry is also the binding agent in many types of quenelles and hot pâtés of fish. For gnocchi Parisienne, it is piped into little cork shapes, poached and then baked in a cream sauce.

Best of all, perhaps, is the Burgundian gougère: cheese-flavoured choux that is piped in a ring. As one wine connoisseur put it, 'Gougère is not a cheese, though it has that savour, not a pastry, though it has that appearance. It is the ideal bridge between main course and dessert, allowing the last glass of wine to be enjoyed with delight.'

THE WAY TO SUCCESS

1 Use a heavy-based pan so the dough does not scorch.
2 When heating the butter and water, cut the butter in pieces and let it melt before the water boils. Take from the heat *at once* so dough proportions are not altered by water evaporation.
3 Add flour to the butter/water mixture all at once and beat vigorously; if the flour is added little by little it will cook into lumps.
4 Do not dry the panade for more than $\frac{1}{2}$-1 minute, or water may evaporate and the butter start to separate from the dough.
5 Beware of a panade that looks grainy. This means it contains too much butter, either because of incorrect measurement, or because too much water evaporated during cooking. Try beating in a little water to make the panade smooth. If it is still grainy, do not waste eggs; make another panade.
6 If too little egg is added to the dough, it will not rise well. If too much egg is added, the dough cannot be shaped.
7 Baking sheets for choux dough should be very lightly buttered; if they're too dry, the dough will stick, but if too greasy, the choux will slide and become misshapen.

8 When brushing with glaze, do not allow any to drip and cause the dough to stick to the baking sheet.
9 Mark dough with the prongs of a fork so it will rise evenly. Choux cracks as it puffs and will rise best if the cracks are in regular patterns.
10 If the oven is not hot enough, choux will not puff well but will dry out and become brittle. If the oven is too hot, the dough will rise quickly, but often flattens again during baking.
11 The oven should be hotter for baking small shapes than for large ones.

Getting ahead

1 Though it doesn't puff quite so well as when used fresh, choux pastry can be made up to 8 hours before being baked. To prevent a crust from forming, the surface of the dough should be rubbed, while still warm, with butter. When the dough is cool, cover it tightly and keep in the refrigerator.
2 Baked choux pastry is best eaten the day it is made, but it can be stored in an airtight container, or in a plastic bag in the refrigerator for 1-2 days.
3 Choux puffs filled with pastry cream can be kept for only a few hours before becoming soggy.

PATE A CHOUX
(Choux pastry)

flour	75g (2½oz)
water	125ml (scant ¼pt)
salt	2g (⅓ level teaspoon)
butter	50g (1½oz)
eggs	2 large (sizes 2,3)

flour	110g (3½oz)
water	185ml (scant ⅓pt)
salt	3g (½ level teaspoon)
butter	75g (2½oz)
eggs	3-4 large

flour	150g (5oz)
water	250ml (scant ½pt)
salt	4g (¾ level teaspoon)
butter	100g (3½oz)
eggs	4-5 large

Sift the flour onto a piece of greaseproof paper. Heat the water, salt and butter in a saucepan until the butter is melted, then bring to the boil and take from the heat. NOTE: prolonged boiling evaporates the water and changes the proportions of the dough. As soon as the pan is taken from the heat add all the flour at once and beat vigorously with a wooden spatula for a few seconds until the mixture is smooth and pulls away from the pan to form a ball. Beat for ½-1 minute over low heat to dry the mixture.

Set aside one egg, break it and beat it in a bowl. With a wooden spatula, beat the remaining eggs into the dough, one by one, beating thoroughly after each addition. Beat enough of the reserved egg into the dough to make a mixture that is very shiny and just falls from the spoon. NOTE: all of the reserved egg may not be needed; if too much is added, the dough cannot be shaped.

Although the dough puffs better if used immediately, choux pastry can be stored for up to 8 hours before baking. Rub the surface with butter while the dough is still warm. When cool, cover tightly and store in the refrigerator.

Beat the panade of flour, water and butter vigorously for a few seconds until the mixture is smooth and shiny and pulls away from the sides of the pan. Continue beating over low heat to dry the mixture before adding eggs

Perfect choux dough should be like this: once the eggs have been beaten into the mixture, it should be smooth and shiny and just fall from the spoon. Do not add too much egg or it will be difficult to pipe the finished dough

CREME PATISSIERE
(Pastry cream)

6 egg yolks
125g (4oz) sugar
50g (1½oz) flour
450ml (¾pt) milk
pinch of salt
vanilla pod

Beat the egg yolks with the sugar until thick and light. Stir in the flour. Scald the milk by bringing it just to the boil with the salt. Add the vanilla pod to the hot milk, cover the pan and leave to infuse for 10-15 minutes. Remove the vanilla pod and reheat the milk to boiling point. Whisk the boiling milk into the egg mixture, return to the pan and whisk over gentle heat until boiling. NOTE: be sure the pastry cream is smooth before letting it boil. If lumps form as it thickens, take the pan from the heat and beat until smooth. Cook the cream gently, whisking constantly, for 2 minutes or until the cream thins slightly, showing the flour is completely cooked. Take it from the heat, transfer to a bowl, rub a piece of butter over the surface to prevent the formation of a skin and let it cool. Use as directed in the recipes.

THE WAY TO SUCCESS: Crème pâtissière

Pastry cream is the most common filling for sweet choux pastries. Here are a few ground rules:
1 Be sure to cook pastry cream thoroughly. Lightly cooked, it has an unpleasant taste of raw flour.
2 If the finished cream is too thick, simply thin it with a little milk.
3 Special care must be taken in keeping pastry cream since quickly cooked egg yolks spoil fairly rapidly. Refrigerate as soon as it is cool and keep for not longer than a day or two.
4 Thick pastry cream can be frozen, but thin cream made with a minimum of flour will separate on freezing.
5 Pastry cream is also commonly spread in tart shells (Chapter 17) and topped with fruit, or spread between layers of sponge cake.

PETITS CHOUX AU FROMAGE

(Little cheese choux puffs)

These puffs are a perfect accompaniment for cream soups but they can also be served as hors d'oeuvre. In more than one top Paris restaurant, a plateful arrives with the apéritifs. This quantity of choux pastry is the smallest it is possible to measure accurately.

Makes enough to serve 10-12

choux pastry made with 75g (2½oz) flour, 125ml (scant ¼pt) water, 2g (⅓ level teaspoon) salt, 50g (1½oz) butter and 2 large eggs

30g (1oz) grated Parmesan cheese

pastry bag and 3mm (⅛in) plain tube

Make the choux pastry, following the basic method. After adding the eggs, beat in the grated cheese. Put the mixture in a pastry bag with a 3mm (⅛in) plain tube and pipe thimble-sized mounds on a lightly buttered baking sheet. Bake the choux in a hot oven, 200C (400F) gas 6, for 12-15 minutes or until brown and crisp and allow to cool on a rack. (You should not need to pierce such small choux.)

They can be made 1-2 days ahead and kept in an airtight container. They can also be frozen.

GOUGERE

SERVES 6

choux pastry made with 110g (3½oz) flour, 185ml (scant ⅓pt) water, 4g (½ level teaspoon) salt, 75g (2½oz) butter, 3-4 eggs and freshly ground pepper

60g (2oz) diced Gruyère cheese

for the filling (optional)

thick béchamel sauce (page 192) made with 600ml (1pt) milk, slice of onion, small bay leaf, 6 peppercorns, 30g (1oz) butter, 30g (1oz) flour, salt and white pepper and a pinch of grated nutmeg

150g (5oz) diced cooked ham; or 150g (5oz) diced cooked chicken; or 150g (5oz) mushrooms, quartered and sautéed in 15g (½oz) butter; or 60g (2oz) grated Gruyère cheese and 2 tablespoons double cream

20-23cm (8-9in) diameter ovenproof baking dish or pie dish

Set the oven at hot, 200C (400F) gas 6. Make the choux pastry dough following the basic method and,

after adding the eggs, stir in the diced cheese. Season the dough to taste.

Butter the pie dish or baking dish and shape the dough in puffs with 2 tablespoons and arrange these round the sides of the dish, leaving a hollow in the centre. Score the dough lightly with the prongs of a fork. Bake the gougère in the heated oven for 30-40 minutes, or until the dough is puffed and brown.

If making a filling, first prepare a thick béchamel sauce, then add one of the four listed flavourings to the béchamel sauce and rub the surface with butter to prevent the formation of a skin.

When the gougère is baked, spoon the filling into the centre of the pastry ring. Return it to the oven for 3-5 minutes to reheat and serve within 5 minutes.

PROFITEROLES D'OEUFS A LA PUREE DE HARICOTS VERTS

(Choux puffs with poached eggs and green bean purée)

A light yet satisfying starter from nouvelle cuisine.

SERVES 8

8 eggs

choux pastry made with 75g (2½oz) flour, 125ml (scant ¼pt) water, 2g (⅓ level teaspoon) salt, 50g (1½oz) butter and 2 large eggs

1 egg beaten to mix with ½ teaspoon salt (for glaze)

for the green bean purée

250g (8oz) green beans

salt and pepper

15g (½oz) butter

for the tomato sauce

6 tomatoes, peeled, seeded and chopped

salt

sprig of thyme

15g (½oz) butter (to finish)

pastry bag and 2cm (¾in) plain tube

Set the oven at hot, 200C (400F) gas 6. Make the choux pastry dough.

Put the dough into the pastry bag fitted with a 2cm (¾in) plain tube and pipe 6.5cm (2½in) puffs of dough well apart onto a lightly buttered baking sheet, mounding the dough as much as possible. Brush

the puffs with egg glaze and score each puff with the prongs of a fork. Bake in the heated oven for 25-30 minutes or until the puffs are firm and brown. Transfer them to a rack to cool. While still warm, cut the top third from each puff to release the steam. Unfilled puffs can be kept overnight in an airtight container, but they are at their best eaten within a few hours of baking.

Poach the eggs for about 3 minutes and transfer them to a bowl of cold water.

For the green bean purée: cook the green beans in a large pan of boiling salted water for 7-10 minutes or until just tender. Drain thoroughly and work them through a drum sieve, or purée them in an electric food processor and strain to remove any strings.

For the tomato sauce: put the tomatoes, salt and thyme in a small saucepan and simmer for about 20 minutes or until tender. Purée the sauce in a food mill and return to the saucepan.

To finish: about 20 minutes before serving, reheat the choux puffs in a moderate oven, 180C (350F) gas 4. Transfer the eggs to a bowl of warm water to heat them. Heat one 15g (½oz) butter until nut brown, add the green bean purée, salt and pepper and cook, stirring, for 3-5 minutes or until nearly all the moisture has evaporated. Reheat the tomato sauce, remove it from the heat and whisk in the other 15g (½oz) butter. Taste for seasoning and adjust if necessary.

To serve: drain the eggs. Spoon some green bean purée into each choux puff, top with a poached egg and pour over some of the tomato sauce. Top each with its choux 'hat' and serve any remaining sauce separately. NOTE: assemble and serve the eggs at the last minute as the choux puffs very quickly become soggy.

WILD BARFIELD   BARLOW WHITNEY

Imperial Way Watford, Hertfordshire WD2 4QQ,

PROFITEROLES AU CHOCOLAT
(Chocolate profiteroles)

Chantilly cream is folded into the pastry cream filling of these profiteroles to lighten it, but Chantilly cream or pastry cream can be used alone. The puffs are also good filled with vanilla ice-cream and served with hot chocolate sauce.

SERVES 6-8

choux pastry made with 110g (3½ oz) flour, 185ml (scant ⅓ pt) water, 4g (½ level teaspoon) salt, 75g (2½ oz) butter and 3-4 eggs
1 egg, beaten with ½ teaspoon salt (for glaze)
Chantilly cream made with 150ml (¼ pt) double cream whipped with 2 level tablespoons icing sugar
pastry cream made with 6 egg yolks, 125g (4oz) sugar, 50g (1½ oz) flour, 450ml (¾ pt) milk, pinch of salt and a vanilla pod
for the chocolate sauce
100g (3½ oz) dark dessert chocolate
30g (1oz) butter
5 tablespoons water
tablespoon rum, brandy or Grand Marnier
pastry bag and 1cm (⅜ in) plain tube

Set the oven at hot, 200C (400F) gas 6. Prepare the choux pastry following the basic method.

Put the dough into a pastry bag fitted with a 1cm (⅜ in) plain tube and pipe 3.5cm (1½ in) mounds of dough well apart on a lightly buttered baking sheet. Score lightly with a fork and brush with egg glaze. Bake in the heated oven for 20-25 minutes, or until the puffs are firm and brown. Transfer the puffs to a rack to cool.

While they are still warm, split them to release the steam.

Make the pastry cream (page 45). *For the filling:* make the Chantilly cream and fold it into the cooled pastry cream. The filling can be made up to 4 hours ahead and kept in the refrigerator.

For the chocolate sauce: melt the chocolate and the butter in the water over low heat, stirring occasionally. Do not allow to boil. Stir in the rum, brandy or Grand Marnier. The sauce can be made up to 24 hours ahead and kept in the refrigerator.

Not more than 2 hours before serving: either use a teaspoon to fill the puffs or pipe in the filling.

To serve: pile the puffs in bowls and coat with the chocolate sauce.

CHOUX AU CAFE
(Coffee cream puffs)

These are best assembled at the last minute to ensure a fresh flavour and a pleasant contrast between the crisp pastry and the creamy filling.

Makes about twenty 7.5cm (3in) puffs.

choux pastry made with 150g (5oz) flour, 250ml (scant ½ pt) water, 4g (¾ level teaspoon) salt, 100g (3½ oz) butter and 4-5 large eggs
1 egg, beaten with ½ teaspoon salt (for glaze)
for the filling
pastry cream made with 6 egg yolks, 125g (4oz) sugar, 50g (1½ oz) flour, 450ml (¾ pt) milk and a pinch of salt
tablespoon dry instant coffee
for coffee glacé icing
about 200g (7oz) icing sugar
2 tablespoons water
teaspoon dry instant coffee dissolved in a tablespoon warm water
pastry bag and 1.25cm (½ in) and 5mm (¼ in) plain tubes

Set the oven at hot, 200C (400F) gas 6. Make the choux pastry dough and put it into a pastry bag fitted with a 1.25cm (½ in) plain tube. Pipe 3cm (1¼ in) mounds of dough well apart onto two lightly buttered baking sheets. Brush the puffs with egg glaze and score each puff with the prongs of a fork dipped in water. Bake in the heated oven for 20-25 minutes or until the puffs are firm and brown. NOTE: if using an unventilated electric oven, keep the door propped slightly open while baking the puffs. Transfer them to a rack to cool. While still warm, make a hole in the bottom of each to release the steam. Unfilled puffs can be kept overnight in an airtight container, but they are at their best eaten within a few hours of baking. *For the filling:* make the pastry cream, dissolving the coffee in the hot milk. Rub the surface of the finished cream with a little butter to prevent a skin from forming and leave to cool.

For the icing: sift the icing sugar and mix until smooth with enough water to make a paste that spreads easily; add the coffee and mix well. Warm the icing to tepid in a water bath – it should coat the back of a spoon, but if it is too thick, add more liquid. If it is too thin, beat in more sifted icing sugar. Dip the top of each choux puff in icing and leave to set. The pastry cream can be made and the puffs can be coated 4-5 hours before serving. Keep them in a dry place.

Not more than 2 hours before serving, put the pastry cream into a pastry bag fitted with a 5mm (¼ in) plain tube and pipe the cream into the puffs.

CHOUX PRALINES

Made with classic butter cream, these are meltingly rich petits fours.

MAKES 36

choux pastry made with 150g (5oz) flour, 250ml (scant ½ pt) water, 4g (¾ level teaspoon) salt, 100g (3½ oz) butter and 4-5 eggs
1 egg, beaten with ½ teaspoon salt (for glaze)
90g (3oz) chopped, browned almonds
icing sugar (for sprinkling)
for the filling
butter cream (page 100) made with 3 egg yolks, 90g (3oz) sugar, 65ml (2½ oz) water and 200g (6½ oz) butter
praline (page 129) made with 60g (2oz) unblanched almonds and 60g (2oz) sugar
pastry bag and 1cm (⅜ in) plain tube

Set the oven at hot, 200C (400F) gas 6. Make the choux pastry dough, fill a pastry bag fitted with a 1cm (⅜ in) plain tube and pipe 2cm (¾ in) mounds of dough well apart onto lightly buttered baking sheets. Brush with egg glaze, score lightly with the prongs of a fork and sprinkle with chopped almonds. Bake in the heated oven for 25 minutes or until the puffs are firm and brown. Transfer them to a rack to cool. While they are still warm, split them to release the steam. They can be kept overnight in an airtight container, but they are at their best eaten within a few hours of baking. Make the butter cream and beat in the praline.

To finish: fill the puffs with the praline butter cream and sprinkle with icing sugar. Serve these petits fours within 3-4 hours of making them.

GATEAU PARIS-BREST

Gâteau Paris-Brest can be made with several different fillings, but they are all flavoured with plenty of praline. Besides the delicate St Honoré cream and the Chantilly cream variation here, praline butter cream can be used. Chef Jorant at La Varenne says the ideal filling is a mixture of butter cream, pastry cream and meringue – easy enough in a pastry shop, but quite a task to prepare at home.

Makes 2 gâteaux to serve 8-10

choux pastry made with 150g (5oz) flour, 250ml (scant ½pt) water, 4g (¾ level teaspoon) salt, 100g (3½oz) butter and 4-5 eggs
1 egg, beaten to mix with ½ teaspoon salt (for glaze)
4 tablespoons sliced almonds
icing sugar (for sprinkling)
for the praline
100g (3½oz) whole unblanched almonds
100g (3½oz) sugar
for the St Honoré cream
375ml (⅝pt) milk
vanilla pod
pinch of salt
5 egg yolks
90g (3oz) sugar
40g (1⅓oz) flour
5 egg whites
4g (⅐oz) gelatine (optional)
pastry bag and 2cm (¾in) plain tube; large star tube

Set the oven at hot, 200C (400F) gas 6. Make the choux pastry dough.

Put the dough into a pastry bag fitted with a 2cm (¾in) plain tube and pipe a 20cm (8in) ring on a lightly buttered baking sheet. Pipe a second ring of dough just inside the first. Pipe another ring of dough on top, on the crack between the first two rings. Shape another gâteau in the same way. Brush them with egg glaze, score with the back of a fork and sprinkle with sliced almonds. Bake in the heated oven for 30-35 minutes or until the cakes are firm, brown and thoroughly baked. Transfer to a rack to cool and while the cakes are still warm, split them in half horizontally with a sharp knife so the steam can escape.

For the praline: put the almonds and sugar in a heavy-based pan and heat gently, stirring occasionally, until the sugar melts and caramelises. The almonds should pop, showing they are thoroughly toasted. Pour the praline onto an oiled marble surface or baking sheet and leave until cold and crisp. Grind it to a powder in an electric food mill or with a rotary cheese grater; then work through a coarse sieve. NOTE: any lumps will block up the star tube when piping.

Make the St Honoré cream as close to serving as possible. Make a pastry cream using the milk, vanilla pod, salt, egg yolks, 60g (2oz) of the sugar and the flour (see Chocolate profiteroles). At the same time, whip the egg whites until stiff and beat in the remaining sugar. Stir the praline powder into the pastry cream. If you have to make the St Honoré cream ahead, add the gelatine by softening it in 2 tablespoons of cold water, then stirring it into the hot cream. NOTE: if gelatine is added, the cream will not have so fine a texture.

While the cream is still very hot, quickly stir in a third of the stiffly whipped egg whites; then fold the cream into the remaining egg whites as lightly and as quickly as possible. The hot cream must cook the egg whites in order to be of a good piping consistency. NOTE: if the cream is folded too much, it will be too soft to pipe properly. The cream and the pastry rings can be made 5-6 hours ahead and kept at room temperature. Keep the pastry in an airtight container.

Not more than 2 hours before serving, complete the gâteaux: put the St Honoré cream into a pastry bag with a large star tube and pipe the filling onto the lower halves of the rings. Top with the upper sections – the cream should show round the sides. Sprinkle with icing sugar before serving.

Note: instead of the St Honoré cream, make Chantilly cream using 600ml (1pt) double cream and 30g (1oz) sugar. Fold in the praline. When filling the gâteau, reserve a little of the cream for decorating. Using the star tube, pipe rosettes on top of the gâteau and decorate each with a crystallised violet.

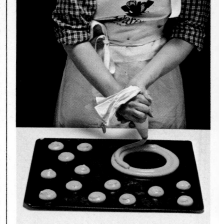

To make choux puffs: pipe them onto a lightly buttered baking sheet. They should be evenly spaced and of equal size. For a gâteau Paris-Brest, pipe two base circles, then a third to sit on top

To grind praline: use an electric food mill or a rotary cheese grater. Praline must be fine and free from lumps

BUTTER CREAM

The butter cream used to fill and decorate the gâteau Paris-Brest in the photograph on page 43 is a rich mixture of egg yolks, cooked sugar, butter and praline flavouring. The recipe is given on page 100, where it is used with génoise pastry.

To decorate the gâteau Paris-Brest: using a pastry bag with a large star tube, pipe the praline-flavoured cream on each lower half and top with the upper half. Sprinkle with icing sugar or decorate with rosettes of cream before serving

SALAMBOS

These orange-filled, caramel-topped petits fours are a delicious variation on the little oval salambos, which are usually filled with kirsch-flavoured pastry cream and finished with icing.

MAKES 36

choux pastry made with 150g (5oz) flour, 250ml (scant ½pt) water, 4g (¾ level teaspoon) salt, 100g (3½oz) butter and 4-5 eggs

1 egg, beaten with ¼ teaspoon salt (for glaze)

180g (6oz) sugar

125ml (scant ¼pt) water

for the filling

pastry cream (page 45) made with 5 egg yolks, 90g (3oz) sugar, 40g (1½oz) flour, 400ml (⅔pt) milk and a pinch of salt

grated rind of 1 orange

1-2 tablespoons Grand Marnier or other orange-flavoured liqueur

pastry bag and 1cm and 5mm (⅜ and ¼in) plain tubes

Set the oven at hot, 200C (400F) gas 6. Make the choux pastry dough. Put it into a pastry bag fitted with a 1cm (⅜in) plain tube and pipe lengths about 1cm (⅜in) wide and 3cm (1¼in) long onto lightly buttered baking sheets. Brush the choux lengths with egg glaze, score them lightly with the prongs of a fork, and bake them in the heated oven for 25 minutes or until they are firm and brown. Transfer the oval puffs to a rack to cool. While they are still warm, poke a hole in the bottom of each with the 5mm (¼in) tube. The pastries can be kept overnight in an airtight container, but they are at their best eaten within a few hours of baking.

For the filling: make the pastry cream and stir in the orange rind and Grand Marnier or orange liqueur. Rub the top with a little butter to prevent a skin from forming and allow to cool. The cream can be stored in the refrigerator, tightly covered, for 1-2 days.

To finish: put the orange pastry cream into the pastry bag fitted with the 5mm (¼in) tube and fill each salambo through the hole in the bottom. Dissolve the 180g (6oz) of sugar in 125ml (scant ¼pt) water in a heavy-based saucepan. Boil to a light golden caramel, then dip the base of the pan in water to stop the cooking. Dip the top of each salambo in the caramel, twisting it quickly so it is evenly coated. NOTE: if the caramel sets before all the petits fours are coated, heat it gently but do not allow it to cook further. Serve within 3-4 hours.

5
CONSOMME
Clarifying matters

Consommé is the simplest yet perhaps the most sophisticated, of the dishes made from stock. To make consommé, veal, beef, chicken or, more rarely, game or fish stock is reduced, then clarified to give a limpid, sparkling liquid. Its transparency is deceptive since good consommé has punch – a heady aroma and an equally powerful flavour that is neither bland nor salty, thin nor heavy. The balance is not easy to achieve, and consommé is one of the traditional tests of an accomplished chef.

The heyday of consommé was the 'belle époque', when after caviar, oysters or smoked salmon, soup was the standard second course in every 10- or 12-course dinner. Escoffier, Montagné and all the great names vied to produce the finest Consommé madrilène, garnished with tomatoes; Consommé brunoise, with its garnish of tiny diced vegetables; or the tricky Consommé royale, decked with minute shapes of pale golden egg custard.

Regardless of whether the finished dish includes a simple or elaborate garnish – or no garnish at all – the preparation of the consommé itself is always the same. Well-flavoured, fat-free stock is brought slowly to a boil while whisking with egg white – 3 whites to 1 litre (1¾ pints) stock is the standard proportion. As the egg white cooks, it traps the tiny particles that cloud the stock; and as soon as the mixture looks milky, whisking should be stopped so that the whites can rise gradually to the top of the stock in a grubby grey froth that coagulates to form a filter. Then the consommé is left to simmer quietly for half an hour or more, percolating constantly through the filter, until it is clean and sparkling.

The problem with egg whites is that while they clarify the liquid they also steal flavour. Reinforcements are therefore added along with them: vegetables such as carrots, leeks, celery (not too much) and skinned tomato, all finely cut so they yield their flavour in a short cooking time. Meat is also used: beef for beef consommé, chicken for chicken, and fish for fish – hence the term 'consommé double', for meat or fish is used twice in the preparation, both for making the stock and at the clarifying stage. All meat *must be*

CONSOMME BRUNOISE, MADRILENE AND JULIENNE

Consommé brunoise (left) is garnished with a tiny dice of vegetables; Consommé madrilène (front) has a tomato garnish; Consommé julienne (right) is garnished with matchstick-thin strips of vegetables

free of fat (for beef, the preferred cut is the tough, scrawny shin), and it is shredded or minced so that it cooks quickly. As well as adding flavour, red meats help to clear consommé as blood is a clarifying agent.

The basic clarifying mixture, then, is a combination of egg whites, vegetables and meat. Other possible flavourings are legion: herbs, celery leaves, sliced mushrooms and even (says Escoffier) caviar. Salt and pepper, too, should be added before rather than after the stock is clarified. No matter what they are, these extra ingredients are strained out at the end of simmering.

Opinions are mixed about the use of alcohol. A dash of sherry or Madeira added just before serving is generally acceptable; some chefs add white wine, sherry or Madeira and even a touch of brandy during the clarification. Either way, alcohol should be an embellishment, not a prop. Made from good stock and properly clarified, a consommé stands on its own, and no amount of alcohol will redeem an indifferent result.

Besides clarity and flavour, colour is important. A clear tint, light but not pale, is most attractive; consommé of beef or game should be slightly darker than that of chicken or of fish. Pinkness can be added during clarification by including plenty of tomatoes, but the only way of darkening a pallid stock is to use food colouring, and this should be avoided if possible. The key to the colour of consommé lies in colouring the original stock well.

It is the gelatine content of consommé which gives it a suave texture when hot and sets it, when chilled, to just the right shivering jelly. Ideally, the original stock should have been made with enough veal bones to make it set without additional gelatine. However, this can be asking too much, and sometimes gelatine is added (about 7g ($\frac{1}{4}$oz) per litre) while clarifying, to ensure that the consommé, hot or cold, comes out just right. On the other hand, too much added gelatine gives a heavy, cloying soup, so extra should be added only if really necessary.

Although 'consommé double' is perfection in itself, garnishing is another matter to consider. Escoffier rang the changes on 136 variations, from consommé aux ailerons (chicken consommé with stuffed chicken wings and rice) to consommé Zorilla (tomato-flavoured consommé with chickpeas and rice). If you use a garnish that is to be added to the consommé before serving, it is always cooked separately and put in at the last moment so that it cannot cloud the soup. A tablespoon of garnish per serving is sufficient as it must not detract from the clarity of the consommé. Some possibilities are tiny quenelles (meat or fish dumplings), crêpes cut in strips, small pasta shapes or chopped fresh herbs. Other garnishes may be served separately and placed in the soup at table, such as tiny choux puffs flavoured with cheese. Sautéed croûtons are frowned on as they form an oil slick over the beautiful, clear soup.

Consommé no longer occupies the important position on menus that it once did. Young chefs look for more instant appeal, finding the return too low on the care needed for the preparation of a good consommé. The truth is that making consommé tests many aspects of a cook's skill: a delicate touch with the seasoning, a sensitive eye for colour, careful judgment of texture, a gentle hand when straining, and skill in preparing the garnish.

THE WAY TO SUCCESS

1 Stock for consommé should be concentrated and well flavoured. If its flavour is weak, boil to reduce it before clarifying.

2 The stock must be *completely skimmed of all grease* as fat prevents clarification. To do this, chill the stock until set and skim the fat from the surface. Then gently heat the stock and remove any remaining fat by quickly drawing strips of absorbent kitchen paper across the surface. All the equipment used should also be free of grease.

3 Use a pan of stainless steel, tin-lined copper or enamel. The action of a whisk in an aluminium pan may give an unpleasant flavour and colour.

4 The number of egg whites needed depends on the stock. If the stock is very cloudy, add another egg white to the suggested amount.

5 Do not pour hot stock directly on the egg whites or they will coagulate too quickly. It is the slow coagulation of the egg whites that produces a clear consommé.

6 So that the globules of egg white will attract all the particles that cloud the stock, they must be thoroughly mixed with it.

7 Once the crust, or filter, begins to form, stop whisking. With a ladle or the handle of a wooden spoon, make a small hole through which the stock can bubble. Otherwise the movement of the liquid will break the filter.

8 When straining, use a ladle to take the liquid carefully from the hole in the filter and ladle it into a towel-lined strainer. Let the liquid drain through slowly and don't press the solids.

9 If, in spite of all precautions, the liquid running through the strainer is not sparkling clear, pour the liquid through again. If it *still* isn't clear, repeat the clarification process using an additional egg white; simmer for only 5-10 minutes before straining.

10 Egg whites, vegetables and meat left over after clarification can be added to another batch of simmering stock. They will add flavour and help to make it clearer.

Getting ahead

1 Consommé can be made ahead and kept several days in the refrigerator. It will not lose flavour, but it may become slightly cloudy.

2 Consommé can be frozen but, again, it will become less clear.

3 Most garnishes can be prepared in advance. Reheat them gently in a small amount of the consommé, then drain and add to the hot consommé just before serving.

CONSOMME OU GELEE

(Consommé or aspic)

1.5 litres (2¾pts) well flavoured beef stock
salt and freshly ground pepper
350g (¾lb) boneless shin of beef, chopped
2 carrots, chopped
green tops of 2 leeks, chopped
2 stalks of celery, chopped
2 tomatoes, quartered
3 egg whites
15-30g (½-1oz) gelatine (optional)
4 tablespoons Madeira or sherry (optional)

Skim all the fat from the stock, melt it in a large pan (not aluminium) and remove any remaining fat with strips of absorbent kitchen paper. Taste the stock for seasoning. In a bowl, thoroughly mix the beef, carrots, leeks, celery, tomatoes and egg whites. Pour on the warm stock, whisking with a balloon whisk, and return the mixture to the pan. Set the pan over moderate heat and bring slowly to the boil, whisking constantly – this should take about 10 minutes.

As soon as the mixture looks milky, stop whisking. NOTE: continuing to whisk prevents the formation of the filter. Let the filter of egg white rise slowly to the top of the pan, then turn down the heat. With a ladle or the handle of a wooden spoon, make a small hole in the egg white filter so the consommé bubbles through the filter only in that place. Let the consommé simmer gently for 30 minutes to an hour to extract all flavour from the beef and vegetables. If using gelatine, soften it in a little consommé and add it through the hole in the filter, then simmer for 2-3 minutes to be sure it's dissolved. Taste for seasoning and add Madeira or sherry, if desired.

Place a scalded dish towel or jelly bag in a strainer over a clean bowl and ladle the consommé into it, sliding out the filter intact. Do not press on the mixture in the towel and, if the consommé running through is not sparkling clear, strain it again through the cloth and filter.

If serving the consommé hot, bring it almost to a boil and add any flavourings and garnish just before serving. Do not cook the garnish in the consommé as it will cloud it.

If the consommé is served chilled, it should be lightly jellied. Just before serving, stir it with a fork to break it up, spoon into chilled bowls and top with any garnish.

CONSOMME BRUNOISE

Brunoise is one of the most classic garnishes for consommé. The tinier the vegetables are diced, the prettier the garnish. This is also a delicious dish for dieters.

SERVES 4

1 litre (1¾pts) beef consommé
for the brunoise garnish
small carrot
stalk celery (optional)
small, white turnip
small leek
150ml (¼pt) of the above consommé

Prepare the consommé.

Peel and cut the carrot, celery, turnip and leek into very thin strips, then into tiny dice.

Simmer the diced vegetables in 150ml (¼pt) consommé for 5-8 minutes or until tender, and drain. Add the garnish to the rest of the hot consommé just before serving.

CONSOMME NIÇOISE

SERVES 4

1 litre (1¾pts) beef consommé
for the garnish
small potato
4 fresh green beans
2 tomatoes

Prepare the consommé.

Cut the potato and the beans into 3mm (⅛in) dice and cook them in 150ml (¼pt) of the beef consommé for 8-10 minutes, or until tender. Drain well.

Peel and seed the tomatoes and cut the flesh into small dice. Add the cooked garnish to the rest of the hot consommé and put in the tomato dice just before serving.

MANDOLINE GRATER

A mandoline grater cuts perfectly even strips from firm-textured vegetables and is therefore an asset for making garnishes such as the one required for Consommé julienne. The strips can also be cut into fine dice and used to garnish such soups as Consommé brunoise.

The device is good, too, for cutting longer strips, slices of varying thicknesses and even latticed slices. The exact size and type of cut – and the resulting thickness of the strip or slice – can be regulated with levers.

If you decide to invest in a mandoline grater – and they are not cheap – it would be best to buy a sturdy metal one (as above). This should last a lifetime. The less expensive wooden models have a tendency to warp.

When clarifying stock to make consommé, whisk until the mixture looks milky. A filter will form and rise

When the filter has risen in the pan, gently make a hole in it with a ladle so the stock bubbles up through the filter

Carefully ladle the hot liquid through the hole into a towel-lined strainer set on a bowl, then lift out the filter intact

CONSOMME JULIENNE

SERVES 4

1 litre (1¾pts) beef consommé

for the garnish

small carrot

stalk celery (optional)

small, white turnip

white part of 1 small leek

Prepare the consommé.

Cut the vegetables into very thin julienne strips. Simmer them in 150ml (¼pt) of the beef consommé until tender and drain. Add this garnish to the basic consommé and serve.

CONSOMME OLGA

SERVES 4

1 litre (1¾pts) beef consommé

150ml (¼pt) port

for the garnish

¼ of a small celeriac

white part of a small leek

small carrot

5 small gherkins

Prepare the consommé.

Cut the vegetables into very thin strips and simmer them in 150ml (¼pt) of the consommé for 5-8

minutes, or until tender. Drain well.

Cut the gherkins into very thin strips. Just before serving, add the port, the vegetable garnish and the gherkins to the consommé.

CONSOMME MADRILENE

This consommé is named madrilène, which means 'from Madrid', because the French often associate tomatoes with Spanish cooking. It can be served hot or cold.

SERVES 4

1 litre (1¾pts) chicken consommé

2 tomatoes

for the garnish

3 tomatoes, peeled, seeded and cut in thin strips

Prepare the consommé, adding the extra 2 tomatoes, in addition to the tomatoes in the basic recipe.

Add the garnish to the consommé just before serving.

CONSOMME ROYALE

SERVES 4

1 litre (1¾pts) beef consommé

2 tablespoons sherry or Madeira

for the garnish

1 egg

3 egg yolks

salt and freshly ground pepper

Whisk the egg with the egg yolks and a generous 150ml (¼pt) of the beef consommé until thoroughly mixed. Season to taste and pour the mixture into a buttered dariole mould or ramekin dish set in a water bath (see Chapter 29). Bake in a moderate oven, 180C (350F) gas 4, for 20 minutes, until the custard is set. NOTE: do not overcook it or it will curdle.

Chill, then turn out the custard and cut it into tiny shapes – diamonds, crescents etc – using a knife and cutting round the larger end of a piping tube to make the crescents. Add the shapes to 1 litre (1¾pts) hot beef consommé, with the sherry or Madeira, just before serving.

6
CREPES
Suzette's not the only one...

There seems to be something provocative about a crêpe that tempts the most phlegmatic of adults to indulge in childish games. If you toss a crêpe on New Year's Day, one saying goes, a coin in your hand will multiply each day of the year. At Candlemas, count the stars in the sky as you toss your crêpes, and you'll find the same number of eggs in the hen-house next morning. And it's a dull chef indeed who does not occasionally forget his training and toss a crêpe blithely in the air instead of turning it prudently with a palette knife.

But crêpes offer far more than fun and games to a cook. They can be made at a moment's notice from three basic ingredients – flour, eggs and milk. They can equally well be prepared ahead against the arrival of an unexpected guest. They adapt to sweet or savoury fillings; they can be dressed up by flaming or dressed down with just a dusting of sugar or a spoonful of jam.

Eggs are the most important ingredient in crêpes. Flour provides the base and milk the liquid, but it is the eggs that give richness and flavour and bind the crêpes together in the pan. Usually white flour is used, but in Brittany crêpes are often made with buckwheat flour and then are called galettes; the buckwheat flour has a low gluten content, so these crêpes are very light. Cooks in Alsace sometimes replace the milk with beer, which also has a lightening effect. Salt is an indispensable seasoning in crêpe batter, and sugar can be added for sweetness.

CREPES SOUFFLES AU CITRON

These are thin French pancakes, filled with a lemon soufflé mixture which puffs up in the oven and raises the crêpes around the filling. They are served with raspberry purée flavoured with Kirsch

The vanilla, rum or liqueur called for in some recipes is gilding the lily, I think, since their flavour is inevitably lost during cooking. Much more important is the final ingredient, melted butter – almost the more the better. The more melted butter in the batter, the less often the pan needs to be greased, and the easier the frying.

Before you start frying, it is best to be organised. Assemble a jug of melted butter or cooking oil, a plate and a palette knife. Put a small ladle in the batter – it should scoop just enough batter to cover the bottom of the crêpe pan. Heat the pan, coat it with melted butter or oil and pour the excess back into the jug. Heat the pan again and test with a few drops of batter – if they splutter, the pan is ready. Add a ladle of batter, turning the pan with a sweep of the wrist and shaking at the same time so the bottom is coated. This movement is the key to thin, even crêpes, and it takes a bit of practice.

Put the pan back on the heat, brown one side of the crêpe, turn it carefully with a palette knife and brown the other, then turn the crêpe onto the plate. A good crêpe is easy to recognise: it is flexible and paper thin with a pretty marbled surface where it has browned in the pan. (The second side of a crêpe is never so handsome as the first, speckled for serving.) If the crêpe is heavy, the batter was too thick or the pan was not hot enough when the batter was added. If the crêpe split when it was turned, the batter was too thin.

Continue frying, piling the crêpes on a plate to keep them warm and moist. Grease the pan only when the crêpes start to stick; if the pan has been thoroughly proved and the batter contains a generous measure of butter, you should be able to fry at least 6 crêpes and probably more without greasing the pan again. With a bit of experience, you will soon get into a rhythm and will be able to keep two pans going at once; I can manage three and the chefs juggle with four, though the pace gets a little hectic and I've learned a colourful oath or two as a result.

With crêpes in hand, the sky is the limit. As versatile a wrapping as pastry, crêpes lend themselves to any filling from the simplest grated cheese and scrambled egg to the luxury of lobster, or sweetbreads moistened with a sauce. Dessert ideas range from a sprinkling of sugar and liqueur to fruit mixtures or pastry cream or, grandest of all, a soufflé mixture that puffs within the crêpes. The crêpes may simply be rolled around the filling like a cigar, or if the mixture tends to overflow, the ends of the crêpe can be turned in to make a parcel. Sometimes these little packages are dipped in coating batter and deep fried. Flamed dessert crêpes are often folded in four – this is traditional for Crêpes Suzette – and when enclosing a soufflé mixture, they must be very loosely wrapped so that the mixture inside has room to puff.

Leftover crêpes pose no problem: they can be eaten cold with butter and jam for breakfast; they can be shredded and scrambled with eggs, or added as a garnish to soup. They're fine reheated but can be a bit dry, so unless there is a very moist filling some kind of topping is important. Savoury crêpes can be sprinkled with melted butter, breadcrumbs and grated cheese; sweet crêpes can be sprinkled with butter and sugar which will caramelise in the oven. The last, mis-shapen crêpe of a batch, called a galichon, is given to the dog.

The infinite variety of crêpes has inspired chefs from Escoffier downwards – even his classic Crêpes Suzette can be done in several ways. There are crêpes belle Angevine filled with pears from the Loire valley and flamed in Curaçao, and crêpes Normande stuffed with caramelised apples and cream and flamed in Calvados. And there is the unadorned Brittany galette, considered by many the best crêpe of France. For these it is said you need a Breton fire, a Breton pan, wheat grown in Brittany and a Breton cook with a Breton soul.

THE WAY TO SUCCESS

1 The basic batter – flour, milk and egg – must be smooth. To avoid lumps, add only *part* of the milk to the flour at the beginning of mixing, then gradually stir in the rest. If the batter is lumpy, strain it.
2 Let batter stand for at least half an hour to allow the grains of starch in the flour to swell and lighten. It will thicken on standing.
3 If the batter is too thick, add more liquid. However, do this with care as a batter that is too thin is hard to rectify.
4 Use medium heat for cooking. Crêpes should be cooked briskly, but a high heat sets the batter too fast so the crêpe will be thick. Also the crêpe may scorch.
5 Before making each crêpe, stir the batter a little with the ladle to be sure the mixture has not separated slightly.
6 Grease the pan as little as possible: crêpes fried in too much butter are heavy and greasy. You can give an extra light coating of butter with a pastry brush.
7 The first crêpe is always a tryout, and crêpes cooked just after regreasing the pan are often heavy. Don't hesitate to discard any failures.
8 Crêpes with simple fillings such as grated cheese, scrambled eggs or jam are best eaten at once.

BASIC CREPES

	Makes:	Makes:
	18 crêpes	28 crêpes
flour	125g (4oz)	200g (7oz)
salt	2g ($\frac{1}{2}$ level teaspoon)	4g ($\frac{3}{4}$ level teaspoon)
milk	250ml ($\frac{3}{8}$pt)	375ml ($\frac{5}{8}$pt)
eggs	3	4 large
melted butter or oil	2 tablespoons	3 tablespoons
clarified butter or oil (for frying)	100g (3oz)	125g (4oz)

This neutral batter can be used for savoury or sweet crêpes. If you prefer a rich batter that calls for greasing the pan rarely – if at all – add 100g (3oz) melted butter to the batter for each 125g (4oz) of flour.

Sift the flour into a bowl, make a well in the centre and add the salt and half the milk. Gradually whisk in the flour to make a smooth batter. Whisk in the eggs. NOTE: do not beat the batter too much or it will become elastic and the finished crêpes will be tough. Stir in the melted butter or oil with half the remaining milk, cover and let the batter stand for 1-2 hours. It will thicken slightly as the grains of starch in the flour expand. The batter can be kept up to 24 hours in the refrigerator.

Just before using: stir in enough of the remaining milk to make a batter the consistency of thin cream. Brush or rub the inside of the crêpe pan with butter or oil and heat until very hot (a drop of batter will sizzle at once). Add 2-3 tablespoons of batter to the hot pan, turning it quickly so the bottom is evenly coated. Cook over fairly high heat until browned, then toss the crêpe, or turn it with a spatula. Cook for 10 seconds to brown the other side and turn out onto a plate. Continue cooking the remaining crêpes in the same way, greasing the pan only when the crêpes start to stick.

As the crêpes are cooked, pile them one on top of the other to keep the bottom ones moist and warm. Crêpes can be made ahead, layered with greaseproof paper and stored in a plastic bag. They can be kept in the refrigerator for up to 3 days, or for 2-3 months in the freezer.

Flaming food

Foods are flamed for two reasons: one is to add flavour, and sometimes colour; the other, frowned on by chefs but applauded by head waiters in slightly flashy restaurants, is that flaming makes a good show.

To flame food successfully, a high alcohol content is needed; this is found in brandy or rum, in fortified wines like sherry and Madeira, and in liqueurs like Cointreau and Grand Marnier. Plain wine will not do. The alcohol must be hot before it will light, and so must the food to be flamed – don't forget to use a flame-proof dish. When all the alcohol has burned off, the flame dies away naturally, leaving only the essence.

One method is to warm the alcohol slightly first, pour it over the food and then heat both together on top of the stove or a table burner. The alcohol is lit either with a match or by tipping the dish over a gas flame until the fumes ignite. However, this method occasionally fails if the alcohol has been absorbed by the food before it can be lit. More reliable, I think, is the first method. Heat the alcohol separately in a small pan, flame it, then pour it – flaming – over the hot food. This way the flames are also easier to control.

Baste the food with the flaming juices until the flames die; then serve at once.

Vital precautions:

1 *Stand back* when flaming.

2 *Never pour alcohol straight from the bottle* onto very hot food as the alcohol in the bottle can catch fire.

Getting ahead

1 Crêpe batter can be made up to 24 hours ahead and kept, covered, in the refrigerator. Melted butter should be added just before cooking or it will solidify into granules.

2 Unfilled crêpes can be made up to 3 days ahead, layered with greaseproof paper and stored in a plastic bag in the refrigerator. They can also be wrapped and frozen, but they tend to be brittle if kept for more than a month.

3 Filled crêpes, especially when coated with a sauce, can be kept in the refrigerator; keeping time depends on the filling. Crêpes in a sauce can be frozen for 2-3 months.

GALETTES DE SARRASIN

(Buckwheat galettes)

Galettes are traditionally made on large griddles. However, crêpe pans or large frying pans can also be used.

SERVES 4

125g (4oz) buckwheat flour
2g (⅓ level teaspoon) salt
300ml (½pt) milk
3 eggs
2 tablespoons melted butter or oil
100g (3oz) clarified butter or oil (for frying)

Make the crêpe batter, following the method given for Basic crêpes.

NOTE: do not beat the batter too much or it will become elastic and the finished galettes will be tough. Cover and let the batter stand for 1-2 hours, or it can be kept for up to 24 hours in the refrigerator.

Just before using: stir enough of the remaining milk to make a batter the consistency of thin cream. Brush or rub the frying pan or a large griddle with butter or oil and heat until very hot (a drop of batter will sizzle at once). Add 2-3 tablespoons of batter to the hot pan, turning it quickly so the bottom is evenly coated. Cook over fairly high heat until browned, then toss the galette or turn with a spatula. Cook for 10 seconds to brown the other side and turn out onto a plate.

Continue cooking the remaining batter in the same way, greasing the pan only when the galettes start to stick.

As the galettes are cooked, pile them one on top of the other to keep the bottom ones moist and warm. They can be made ahead, layered with greaseproof paper and stored as for crêpes (see Getting ahead).

For serving: the galettes are best served at once. Large ones are folded in four; small ones are folded in half.

For a savoury filling: sprinkle each galette with melted butter, grated cheese and top with a thin slice of ham. Dust with pepper, fold and sprinkle with a little more melted butter.

For a sweet filling: sprinkle each galette with melted butter, and top with a spoonful of jam, liqueur, or sugar. Fold and sprinkle again with butter.

CREPES DE FRUITS DE MER

(Seafood crêpes)

Any combination of fish and shellfish can be used. The dish is typical of Brittany, famous for crêpes and for excellent seafood.

Serves 4 as a main course; 8 as a starter

crêpe batter made with 125g (4oz) flour, 2g (⅓ level teaspoon) salt, 250ml (⅜pt) milk, 3 eggs and 2 tablespoons melted butter or oil
100g (3oz) clarified butter or oil (for frying)
fish stock (page 218) made with 1 onion, tablespoon butter, 500g (1lb) fish bones, 600ml (1pt) water, 10 peppercorns, bouquet garni and 300ml (½pt) dry white wine
250g (8oz) sole fillets, cut in strips
salt and pepper
125g (4oz) scallops
125g (4oz) mushrooms, quartered
juice of ½ lemon
125g (4oz) cooked lobster or crab meat
125g (4oz) cooked peeled shrimps, halved lengthwise
velouté sauce (page 190) made with 90g (3oz) butter, 75g (2½oz) flour, cooking liquid from the fish and mushrooms, pinch of nutmeg and salt and pepper
150ml (¼pt) double cream
2 egg yolks (optional)

Make the crêpe batter, following the method given for Basic crêpes, and fry them. They can be layered with greaseproof paper and kept in a plastic bag in the refrigerator for up to 3 days, or they can be frozen. *For the filling:* bring the fish stock to a boil, add the sole strips, salt and pepper and poach for 1-2 minutes or until just tender. Lift out with a draining spoon, add the scallops and poach these for 1-2 minutes until just tender. Drain them reserving the cooking liquid. Pu

MAKING CREPES

Ladle 2-3 tablespoons of the batter from the bowl into the hot, lightly greased crêpe pan, turning and shaking it at the same time to make sure the bottom is evenly coated. Stack the crêpes as each one is done to keep them moist and warm

the mushrooms in a saucepan with the lemon juice, season with salt and pepper and add a 6mm (¼in) layer of water. Cover and cook over high heat for 2-3 minutes until the liquid boils to the top of the pan and the mushrooms are tender.

Make the velouté sauce and mix half the sauce into the sole, scallops, lobster or crab meat, shrimps and mushrooms.

Put a spoonful of filling on each crêpe, roll up like cigars and arrange them diagonally in a shallow buttered baking dish. Stir the cream into the egg yolks, if using, add a little of the remaining sauce and stir this mixture back into the saucepan. Heat gently, stirring, until the sauce thickens slightly. If using only cream, bring the sauce just to the boil. Taste again and spoon the sauce over the crêpes. They can be prepared up to 3 days ahead and kept covered in the refrigerator, or they can be frozen, but if they are to be reheated, *do not add egg yolks to the sauce.*

To serve: reheat the crêpes if necessary, in a moderate oven, 180C (305F) gas 4 for 20-30 minutes, or until very hot and browned. If they are just cooked and already warm, brown them under the grill.

CREPES NIÇOISE

If you would like to try this with fresh tuna, allow a 750g (1½lb) piece and cook it with the tomato and onion mixture.

MAKES 18

crêpe batter made with 125g (4oz) flour, 2g (⅓ level teaspoon) salt, 250ml (⅜pt) milk, 3 eggs, 2 tablespoons melted butter or oil
100g (3fl oz) oil (for frying)
2 tablespoons olive oil
20-24 pickling onions
1 kg (2lb) fresh tomatoes, peeled, seeded and chopped; or 1kg (2lb) canned Italian-style plum tomatoes, drained and chopped
2 cloves garlic, crushed
2 teaspoons thyme
salt and pepper
600ml (1pt) white wine
360-420g (12-14oz) canned tuna fish, drained and flaked
60g (2oz) grated Parmesan cheese

for the sauce
45g (1½oz) butter
40g (1½oz) flour
250ml (scant ½pt) tomato juice
15-18cm (6-7in) crêpe pan

Make the crêpe batter.

Heat the olive oil in a sauté pan and brown the onions. Add the chopped tomatoes, garlic, thyme, salt and pepper and wine. Simmer the mixture for 20 minutes, then strain it, reserving the liquid. Stir the tuna fish into the onion and tomato mixture, taste for seasoning and adjust if necessary.

Fry the crepes and, as they are cooked, pile one on top of another to keep the first ones moist and warm. Fill the crêpes with the tuna fish mixture, rolling them like cigars, and arrange them diagonally in a shallow, buttered, ovenproof baking dish.

For the sauce: melt the butter in a saucepan, stir in the flour and cook until foaming. Allow to cool slightly, then stir in the reserved cooking liquid and the tomato juice. Bring to the boil; the sauce should coat the back of a spoon. Reduce it by further boiling if necessary. Taste the sauce for seasoning and adjust if necessary, then spoon it over the crêpes and sprinkle them with the grated cheese. They can be prepared up to 2 days ahead and kept, covered with plastic wrap, in the refrigerator, or they can be frozen.

To finish: bake the crêpes in a moderate oven, 180C (350F) gas 4, for 20-25 minutes or until hot and the cheese is browned.

CREPES SOUFFLES AU JAMBON ET AU FROMAGE

(Ham and cheese soufflé crêpes)

The ham in this filling should be cut into the finest possible dice so that the soufflé will rise well, but it should not be minced.

MAKES 18

crêpe batter made with 125g (4oz) flour, 2g (⅓ level teaspoon) salt, 250ml (⅜pt) milk, 3 eggs and 2 tablespoons melted butter or oil
100g (3½oz) clarified butter or oil (for frying)

for the soufflé mixture
béchamel sauce (page 192) made with 45g (1½oz) butter, 30g (1oz) flour, 250ml (⅜pt) milk, salt, pepper and a pinch of grated nutmeg
teaspoon prepared mustard
4 egg yolks
75g (2½oz) Gruyère cheese, grated
125g (4oz) ham, finely diced
6 egg whites

Make the batter and cook the crêpes in the clarified butter or oil. They can be made ahead and kept for up to 3 days in the refrigerator. The crêpes can also be frozen.

For the soufflé mixture: make the béchamel sauce. Remove from the heat and beat in the mustard and egg yolks. Return to low heat and cook, whisking constantly, for about ½ minute or until the mixture thickens slightly. Remove from the heat, allow to cool slightly and stir in the grated cheese and ham. Taste for seasoning and adjust if necessary. The mixture can be prepared 3-4 hours ahead up to this point. Rub the surface of the warm mixture with butter to prevent a skin from forming.

To finish: set the oven at very hot, 220C (425F) gas 7. Butter a heat-proof serving dish. Beat the egg whites until stiff, if possible using a copper bowl. Heat the cheese mixture, stirring constantly, until it is hot to the touch. NOTE: be careful not to heat it too much or the cheese will cook into strings. Add about a quarter of the egg whites and stir until well mixed. Add this to the remaining egg whites and fold together as lightly as possible.

Put about 2 tablespoons of the soufflé mixture on each crêpe, fold it in half and set it on the buttered serving dish. If the egg whites were beaten until *very* stiff, the filled crêpes can be kept in the refrigerator for 1 hour before baking; however, it is best to bake them as soon as possible. Bake in the heated oven for 5-6 minutes or until the crêpes are puffed. Serve them immediately.

CREPES SUZETTE

Opinions differ on whether this dish was created by Escoffier or the personal cook of the future Edward VII. But all agree that the inspiration for the dish originally came from a *petite amie* of the then Prince of Wales.

SERVES 4

crêpe batter made with 125g (4oz) flour, 2g (½ level teaspoon) salt, 250ml (⅜pt) milk, 3 eggs and 2 tablespoons melted butter or oil
100g (3oz) clarified butter or oil (for frying)
for orange butter
60g (2oz) butter
60g (2oz) sugar
grated rind of 1 orange
tablespoon orange Curaçao, Grand Marnier or other orange liqueur
for flaming
30-45g (1-1½oz) butter
2-3 tablespoons brandy, or to taste
2-3 tablespoons Curaçao, Grand Marnier or other orange liqueur
chafing dish and table burner – optional

Make the crêpe batter following the method given for Basic crêpes and fry them. There should be 16-18.

They can be layered with greaseproof paper and kept in a plastic bag in the refrigerator for up to 3 days, or they can be frozen and stored in the freezer for up to a month.

Not more than 3-4 hours before serving, make the orange butter. Cream the butter and beat in the sugar and orange rind until soft and light. Beat in the orange liqueur and spread the underside (the speckled side cooked first) of each crêpe with butter; stack them one on top of another. Keep them covered at room temperature. For flaming, have ready a chafing dish and table burner, butter, brandy, orange liqueur, a metal palette knife, fork, tablespoon and small pan.

To flame the crêpes: heat 1-2 tablespoons butter in a chafing dish or frying pan, add a crêpe, orange butter side down, and cook briskly for about 30 seconds until very hot. Fold in half and half again (this triangular shape is traditional) and leave at the side of the pan.

Similarly cook another crêpe,

To finish Crêpes Suzette: have the brandy and orange liqueur in a small pan ready to heat and flame. Heat each butter-coated crêpe, fold it in half and half again into the traditional triangular shape, then move it to the edge of the pan for flaming just before serving

fold and continue until the pan is full; by this time the orange butter should have caramelised on the bottom of the pan, adding a superb flavour. Heat the brandy and orange liqueur in a small pan, set it alight and pour it over the crêpes. Serve them at once.

If all the crêpes were not used for the first serving, repeat the heating and flaming process with the remainder.

CREPES SOUFFLES AU CITRON
(Lemon soufflé crêpes)

Soufflé crêpes are crêpes filled with a soufflé mixture, folded or rolled lightly and baked briefly in a hot oven so the soufflé mixture puffs.

SERVES 8

crêpe batter made with 125g (4oz) flour, 2g (⅓ level teaspoon) salt, 250ml (⅜pt) milk, 3 eggs, level tablespoon sugar and 2 tablespoons melted butter
100g (3oz) clarified butter or oil (for frying)
for the lemon marmelade
juice and finely chopped rind of 4 lemons
150g (5oz) sugar
for the soufflé mixture
pastry cream (page 45) made with 3 egg yolks, 60g (2oz) sugar, 25g (2 level tablespoons) flour and 250ml (⅜pt) milk
3 egg whites
for the raspberry purée
250g (8oz) fresh raspberries or 1 packet of frozen raspberries, thawed
icing sugar (to taste)
tablespoon Kirsch

Make the crêpe batter following the method given for Basic crêpes and fry them. They can be made ahead and kept, layered with greaseproof paper, for up to 3 days in the refrigerator, or they can be frozen. *For the lemon marmelade:* heat the lemon rind and juice with the sugar until dissolved; then cook, stirring, for 20-25 minutes until thickened so the mixture still falls easily from the spoon. NOTE: be careful not to let the mixture turn dark brown, or it will be bitter.

For the soufflé mixture: make the pastry cream and beat in the lemon marmelade. This lemon soufflé mixture can be made up to 12 hours ahead. Keep it in the refrigerator, with a piece of greaseproof paper pressed on top.

For the raspberry purée: work fresh or thawed raspberries through a strainer, or purée them in a blender and strain. Stir in icing sugar to taste (frozen raspberries may be already sweetened) and the Kirsch. This purée can be kept for up to a week in the refrigerator, or it can be frozen.

To finish: about half an hour before serving, set the oven at moderately hot, 190C (375F) gas 5. Beat the egg whites until very stiff. Meanwhile, heat the lemon soufflé mixture until hot to the touch. Stir in about a quarter of the egg whites, add this mixture to the remaining egg whites and fold together as lightly as possible.

Put 2 tablespoons of the soufflé mixture on each crêpe, fold in half and set on a flat buttered ovenproof dish. Continue until all the mixture has been used and the dish is full. Cook at once in the heated oven for 10-12 minutes until the crêpes are puffed. Spoon a ribbon of cold raspberry purée around the edge of the dish and serve the rest of the purée separately.

CREPES FOURREES A LA PRALINE

(Stuffed crêpes with praline)

Each element of this recipe can be made ahead; the crêpes can be filled a day before serving and simply heated and flamed at the last moment.

SERVES 4

crêpe batter made with
125g (4oz) flour
2g (⅓ level teaspoon) salt
250ml (⅜pt) milk, 3 eggs and
2 tablespoons melted butter or oil
100g (3oz) clarified butter or oil (for frying)
3-4 tablespoons rum (for flaming)
for the pastry cream filling
praline (page 129) made with 100g (3½oz) sugar and 100g (3½oz) whole unblanched almonds
pastry cream made with 6 egg yolks, 125g (4oz) sugar, 50g (1½oz) flour, 450ml (¾pt) milk, pinch of salt, and a vanilla pod
tablespoon rum

Make the crêpe batter following the method given for Basic crêpes and fry them. There should be 16-18. They can be kept refrigerated for 3 days, or frozen.

For the filling: make the praline and pour onto an oiled baking sheet or marble slab and leave until cold and crisp. Grind it to a powder in a blender, or with a rotary cheese grater.

Make the pastry cream and while still hot beat in the praline and rum. Transfer to a bowl, rub a piece of butter over the surface to prevent the formation of a skin and let cool. It can be kept, refrigerated, for 1 or 2 days.

Spread the filling over the pancakes, roll them and arrange diagonally in a buttered baking dish.

To finish: bake the crêpes in a moderately hot oven, 190C (375F) gas 5, for 10-15 minutes or until very hot. Heat the rum in a small pan, flame it, pour it over the crêpes and serve them while still flaming.

CREPE PANS

Crêpe pans once had handles as much as 1½ metres (about 1½ yards) long for cooking over an open fire, but now the handles have shrunk to a standard 17-20cm (7-8in). The pans themselves are made of cast iron with shallow sides to make turning easier, and most are 23cm (9in) across the rim. Larger sizes *are* available, but big crêpes need an expert touch. Other frying pans can be used, particularly those with a non-stick surface, but usually these cannot be strongly heated and the crêpes tend to cook too slowly.

Whatever pan you use, it must be heavy enough to distribute the heat evenly, but light enough to handle easily.

Like omelette pans, crêpe pans should never be washed. They should be thoroughly proved when new, and proved again each time they stick or have to be washed (page 75). While they are still hot after use, wipe them thoroughly with a cloth or paper towel.

CREPES AUX NECTARINES

(Nectarine crêpes)

Use this basic recipe for other fruits in season, and vary the liqueur as well if you like. Peaches, apples and pears would all be good substitutions for the nectarines, or combine fruits such as peaches and bananas.

SERVES 4

crêpe batter made with 125g (4oz) flour, 2g (⅓ level teaspoon) salt, 250ml (⅜pt) milk, 3 eggs, 30g (1oz) melted butter or oil, tablespoon Cointreau (optional)
100g (3oz) butter or oil (for frying)
4 tablespoons Cointreau (for flaming)
for nectarine filling
90g (3oz) butter
1kg (2lb) nectarines, peeled and sliced
120g (4oz) sugar, or to taste
4 tablespoons Cointreau

Make the crêpe batter, flavouring it with the tablespoon of Cointreau. Meanwhile, make the nectarine filling: heat the butter in a shallow pan, add the nectarines and cook over low heat, stirring often, for 20 minutes or until very soft and thick. Add the sugar and continue to cook very gently, stirring constantly, for 5 more minutes or until the mixture begins to stick to the pan. Remove from the heat and add the 4 tablespoons of Cointreau. Keep the filling warm.

Set the oven at very hot, 230C (450F) gas 8. Fill the crêpes with the warm nectarine mixture, roll them like cigars or fold them in half and arrange in one layer in a buttered baking dish. Bake 4-5 minutes until very hot.

To flame the crêpes: heat 4 tablespoons Cointreau in a small pan. Light the Cointreau, pour it flaming over the crêpes and serve at once.

7
DEEP FRYING
The element of surprise

In France, 'friture' has three meanings: the cooking method of deep frying, the deep fat itself and the food fried in it. The 'friteuse' is the pan for deep frying, and in grand kitchens there is even a 'friturier', a chef solely in charge of deep frying. I would love to claim that with all this attention the French are better at deep frying than anyone else, but alas the reek of deep fat, so evocative of roadside pull-ins and all-night cafés, is as typical of France as anywhere else. No method of cooking is quite so abused as deep frying, and the reasons are not hard to find. Like so much quick cookery, deep frying is not cheap. Good fat or oil is expensive, and there is a strong temptation to continue using it long after it has become scorched and dark. And because it is done at a high temperature, deep frying leaves no margin for error.

The aim of deep frying is to seal food in a crisp coating so all the flavour is captured within. Brillat-Savarin said it should be 'surprised'. The trouble is that foods are 'surprised' at different temperatures and some more easily than others. If food is fried too slowly, it is not sealed and absorbs fat. If the fat is too hot, the food is scorched. The correct temperature for the fat can vary from 180-200C (355-390F) and the larger the pieces of food, the lower the heat should be so that the outside does not burn before the inside is cooked. Raw foods also should be fried for a longer time at a lower temperature than cooked ones, which only need to warm through to the centre. Very high heat is needed for small pieces, like julienne (matchstick) potatoes, and for reheating deep-fried foods. A few foods, notably potato chips (see instructions), are fried twice, once at a lower temperature to cook them through, then at a high temperature to crisp the outside.

If you do much deep frying, it is well worth investing in a deep fryer with thermostatically-controlled heat. When using a simple stove-top deep fryer, guesswork can be reduced by the use of a deep fat thermometer, which should be dipped in hot water, dried, then clipped to the side of the pan so that the bulb of the thermometer does not touch the bottom. But at La Varenne, the chefs still trust mainly to intuition. They look to see when a haze is rising from the fat – at about 190C (375F). (Blue smoke shows the fat is burning and the heat must be lowered *at once*.) Then dip in a piece of bread or raw potato and watch the bubbles rise – at 180C (355F) the bread simmers and at 190C (375F) the bubbles are brisk. Another time-honoured test is to throw in a drop of water

which should rebound at once – the army canteen custom of spitting in deep fat is convenient but less commendable.

By no means can all types of fat be used for deep frying as it must be resistant to high temperatures. Butter burns long before it reaches the temperature required for deep frying. Olive oil is generally considered too strongly flavoured. Most popular today are peanut and corn oil as they are bland and do not burn easily; almost any vegetable or seed oil will do, but these are expensive. The traditional cheaper alternative is beef fat, preferably rendered from the kidney. One advantage is that beef fat can be heated to very high temperatures without burning, so it lasts a long time. It can also be mixed with lard. However, these animal fats give a heaviness to anything fried in them, so they are no longer popular.

Most deep fat can be used 3-6 times, depending on what has been fried in it. In a restaurant, fresh fat is reserved for fried potatoes and delicate fritters. After a few fryings, it is made to do duty with meats or breaded croquettes, then finally demoted to fish, which gives fat an ineradicable flavour. Between each frying, the fat should be strained through butter muslin or a fine sieve to remove any debris. This is particularly necessary when a breadcrumb coating has been used because the crumbs detach, then burn in and darken the fat. In a busy restaurant, constant straining may be impossible so it is easy to see why the fat is so often burnt.

Given the searing temperature of deep fat, it is not surprising that most foods need to be coated before frying. Flour, egg and breadcrumbs give the greatest protection, and they are used for soft mixtures like croquettes and pastry cream or for foods that are cooked for a long time like a whole fish. Fritter batter, based on flour and often lightened with beaten egg whites, is good for fruit, vegetables and some meats, while small pieces of food such as strips of fish or onion rings may be coated simply in flour. One delicious coating is pastry, usually pâte brisée or puff pastry, which is wrapped around food as a turnover (technically known as a rissole). Significantly, all

SOLE COLBERT

Pictured on the Normandy coast not far from where they were caught are these whole, boned sole. They are first coated in flour, egg and breadcrumbs and then deep fried and filled with maître d'hôtel butter

these coatings contain starch, and the only foods which can be fried without coating at all, such as potatoes and a few other root vegetables, also have a high carbohydrate content.

Given the right coating, an amazing variety of ingredients can be deep fried. If they have a soft melting texture to contrast with the crisp outside – sweetbreads, brains, courgettes, aubergines or fish for example – so much the better. Almost every French province has its own favourite, from the deep fried mussels of Provence to the baby eels of Bordeaux and the rissoles de Saint Flour of Auvergne (turnovers of pâte brisée filled with a mixture of fresh and Cantal cheeses, chives and chervil, bound with egg yolks).

Rissoles can be filled with leftover terrine, and croquettes are the classic repository for bits of cooked ham, chicken and fish. But they have acquired a bad name because some cooks vainly believe that they can disguise stale food by deep frying. 'Don't use the "friteuse" as a dust bin,' warns Favre, author of a ponderous 19th-century dictionary of cooking. No less apposite is the Provençal proverb reminding us that, 'A fish is born in water, but it should die in oil.'

As a method of cooking, deep frying is unusual in providing almost as many desserts as first courses and main dishes. All too many of these fried foods are in eclipse, outmoded by current fashions in diet. 'Atteraux', brochettes of mixed meats and vegetables that were breaded and deep fried, and the first course mixture of deep fried meats and vegetables called 'friture à l'italienne' are probably no loss. But what about fruit beignets, deep-fried fish and the delicious cheese or mushroom fritters that have almost disappeared from modern menus? Even choux pastry beignets are hard to find. Together with pommes Dauphine (potato purée mixed with choux pastry and deep fried), they are almost the only survival of a more hearty past.

Personally, I can hardly wait for a fried food renaissance.

THE WAY TO SUCCESS

1 In deep frying raw foods, the aim is to cook the interior in the same time as it takes to brown the outside. If foods are already cooked, they should only reheat while browning. Therefore, raw foods take slightly longer to cook and should be fried at a lower temperature.
2 Cut food in even-sized pieces so that it all cooks at the same speed.
3 The smaller the pieces, the higher the temperature for cooking the food.
4 Do not try to deep fry anything too large as the outside will brown before the interior is hot. Single fish of up to 350g (¾lb) is the largest raw food that can be used. Five minutes is the maximum frying time.
5 Coat food thoroughly so that foods brown evenly and soft mixtures do not burst through their coating.
6 Do not use a basket for batter-coated foods as they stick to the mesh.
7 Food, especially if it has been chilled, lowers the temperature of fat, and the heat should be adjusted.
8 Because of the cooling effect, never fry too much food at once. Deep frying is usually done in several batches.
9 If too much food has been added it is simmering rather than frying, remove at once and reheat the fat to the right temperature.
10 While frying, do not touch or stir the food as this can damage a crust that is not yet firm. Often chefs shake the pan to redistribute the food and prevent sticking, but this must be done gently to avoid spilling.
11 Reheat fat to the right temperature before adding another batch.

Getting ahead
Most food and coatings can be prepared ahead:
1 Food can be coated in egg and breadcrumbs up to 6 hours ahead and kept uncovered in the refrigerator. This dries the coating so it is crisper when fried. Many breadcrumbed foods such as croquettes and chicken Kiev can be coated and frozen.
2 Batter can be made ahead and kept overnight in the refrigerator. Food must be dipped in batter just before frying.
3 Food can be tossed in a flour coating 1-2 hours ahead. Often it is coated again just before frying for extra crispness.
4 Once cooked, deep-fried dishes should be served at once. When frying several batches, keep cooked food hot in a warm oven with the door ajar.

Safety and deep fat
The deep fryer is the most dangerous piece of equipment in the kitchen. In contact with hot deep fat, water vapourises so quickly that it explodes – hence the spluttering when any damp food is lowered into a pan of hot fat. When using a deep fryer, keep the handles of the pan pushed to the inside of the stove so it cannot be knocked over. Thoroughly dry ingredients for frying and, when adding anything damp to fat, use a basket so the food can be lifted quickly if the fat threatens to overflow. Stay by the stove while frying. Never fill the pan more than one-third full of fat. This will minimise the risk of it bubbling over or of spilling when the pan is moved.

If you do have a fire, turn out the source of heat. Cover the pan of fat with a lid or baking sheet, or smother the fire with a dry cloth or blanket. Never try to move the pan or to extinguish the fire with water.

Check the instructions on the packaging of the fat you buy – not all types of fat are suitable for deep frying.

THE PERFECT CHIP

Deep fat and potatoes form a natural union. The potatoes can be cut in half a dozen shapes:
Straw: the finest possible strips, about 8cm (3in) long.
Matchstick: julienne strips with a little more body than straw potatoes.
Pont Neuf: 1cm (½in) sticks about 6cm (2½in) long; so-called because they were sold on the Pont Neuf in Paris.
Gaufrette: lattice rounds cut with a mandoline grater (page 53).
Crisps: wafer-thin rounds (these are called 'chips' in France).
Mignonnettes: 5mm (¼in) sticks the same length as straw and matchstick potatoes.

Straw, matchstick, gaufrette potatoes and crisps are fried only once at 195C (385F). For best results, soak them for an hour or two in cold water to remove starch, then dry thoroughly before frying. Gaufrette potatoes and crisps can be kept for an hour or two in a warm place, or they can be reheated in the oven.

Pommes mignonnettes and Pont Neuf potatoes are fried twice, once at 160C (320F) to cook them until soft and just beginning to brown – time varies from 6-12 minutes depending on the size of the potatoes. Then they are drained. This frying can be done several hours ahead. Just before serving, they are fried at a high heat – around 190C (375F) – for 1-2 minutes until crisp and golden brown, drained well, salted and served at once.

CROQUETTES

Croquettes can be made of anything from artichokes to lobster, from rice to whiting. The food is cooked, chopped, then bound with a rich brown or white sauce and rolled into cork shapes before being breaded and deep fried. Meat or fish croquettes are usually served as a first course, while vegetable croquettes such as potato, chestnut or lentil are a good accompaniment to game and beef. Instructions for

NOTE: temperature equivalents, Centigrade to Fahrenheit, are calculated here more precisely for deep frying than for oven temperatures.

perhaps the richest croquette of all were given by Prosper Montagné at the turn of the century: 'Sandwich rather thick truffle slices with foie gras purée. Dip in fritter batter and deep fry.'

1 Follow the recipe proportions carefully, especially those concerning the quantity of flour used in the sauce and the amount of sauce relative to other ingredients. If the sauce is too thin, or if there is too much of it, the croquettes are impossible to shape; if the sauce is too thick, the croquettes are heavy; and if there is too little sauce, they will fall apart.
2 Cool the croquette mixture thoroughly before shaping, preferably overnight. Alternatively, it can be cooled quickly in ice-cube trays in the freezer.
3 Divide the croquette mixture into even pieces and shape the croquettes on a floured board so that they are as smooth as possible, to avoid cracking during frying.
4 Be generous with the egg and crumbs for coating. During frying this coating acts as a container for the soft filling, and it may burst through any thin patches.
5 Be sure that fat is hot enough, or the filling will melt before the coating is properly sealed.
6 If a croquette is cooked too long, the filling will boil and burst through the coating.

POMMES DAUPHINE

(Potatoes Dauphine)

In a restaurant, potatoes Dauphine are made with leftover mashed potatoes and choux pastry, allowing approximately double volume of mashed potatoes to choux pastry.

SERVES 8
deep fat (for frying)
choux pastry (page 45) made with 75g (2½oz) flour, 125ml (scant ¼pt) water, ¼ teaspoon salt, 50g (1¾oz) butter and 2 large eggs
for the mashed potatoes
750g (1½lb) potatoes, peeled and cut in 2-3 pieces
45g (1½oz) butter
salt and white pepper
pinch of grated nutmeg
about 100ml (⅙pt) hot milk

Make the choux pastry. If making ahead, rub the surface of the dough with butter while still warm. When cool, cover tightly and store in the refrigerator for up to 8 hours.

For the mashed potatoes: put the potatoes in cold salted water, bring to the boil and simmer for 15-20 minutes or until tender when pierced with a knife or skewer – they should be quite soft. Drain the potatoes and work them through a potato ricer or a sieve back into the pan. Add the butter, salt, white pepper, nutmeg and hot milk. Beat the potatoes with a wooden spoon over low heat until they are light and fluffy. Allow to cool and beat into the choux pastry. Taste for seasoning. The mixture can be made 4-5 hours ahead and kept tightly covered at room temperature.

To finish: heat the deep fat to 180C (355F) on a fat thermometer. Drop in half a dozen walnut-sized balls of potato mixture, shaping them with two teaspoons. NOTE: leave room for the potatoes to swell. Fry until golden brown, turning them so they brown evenly. Drain on paper towels and keep hot in a moderate oven, 180C (350F) gas 4, with the door ajar while frying the remaining potato mixture.

Potatoes Dauphine can be kept hot for 15-20 minutes as long as they are spread out so they do not touch each other.

VARIATIONS

Pommes Bussy: to the mixture for potatoes Dauphine, add 2 tablespoons chopped truffles and a tablespoon of chopped parsley. Use a

To finish potatoes Dauphine, use two teaspoons to form walnut size balls of the dough. Drop them into hot fat allowing room for them to swell up

pastry bag to pipe short lengths of the mixture into hot fat, cutting the mixture from the piping tube with a knife.

Pommes Chamonix: flavour the potato mixture with grated Gruyère cheese.

Pommes Lorette: divide the pommes Chamonix mixture into small pieces of about 60g (2oz) each. Flatten them into triangular shapes and then roll them up, starting at the base of the triangle. Before deep frying, bend the ends round to form crescents. They should look like miniature croissants.

BEIGNETS AU FROMAGE
(Cheese beignets)

Serves 6 as a starter, or makes an excellent cocktail hors d'oeuvre.

choux pastry (page 45) made with 110g (13½oz) flour, 185ml (scant ⅓pt) water, 4g (½ level teaspoon) salt, 75g (2½oz) butter and 3-4 eggs
100g (3½oz) Gruyère cheese, finely diced
pinch dry mustard
pepper
deep fat (for frying)

Make the choux pastry dough and beat in the diced cheese with the dry mustard and pepper to taste – it should be quite highly seasoned. The dough can be prepared up to 6 hours ahead and kept in the refrigerator, covered with a damp cloth.

A short time before serving, heat the deep fat to moderately hot, 180C (355F). Using two teaspoons dipped in the fat, drop 2.5cm (1in) balls of dough into the hot fat. Do not fry too many beignets at a time as they swell. At once increase the heat so that the temperature of the fat rises steadily to hot, 190C (385F), and the beignets gradually puff. NOTE: if the fat is too hot, the outsides of the beignets are sealed too quickly and they cannot swell properly; if it is too cool, they will be soggy.

Cook the beignets for 4-5 minutes until puffed and golden brown. Drain them on paper towels and keep them warm in a moderate oven, 180C (350F) gas 4, with the door ajar while frying the remaining dough. Serve at once.

BEIGNETS DE CHAMPIGNONS
(Mushroom beignets)

For the cheese in the above recipe substitute 350g (12oz) finely chopped mushrooms cooked with the juice of ½ lemon, 15g (½oz) butter and 1cm (½in) water. Use the cooking liquid instead of water to make the choux pastry. Season with nutmeg, not mustard, and salt and pepper.

CROQUETTES DE CAMEMBERT
(Camembert fritters)

These croquettes can be shaped in rounds as described in this recipe, or in the traditional cork shape: roll the mixture into a rope on a floured surface, cut it in 2.5cm (about 1in) lengths, then dip in egg and breadcrumbs. If there is no time to chill the mixture overnight, this method of shaping is often easier.

These fritters serve four as a starter, or they make delicious cocktail hors d'oeuvre when cut in small 2.5cm (1in) rounds.

béchamel sauce (page 192) made with 375ml (⅝pt) milk, slice of onion, small bay leaf, 6 peppercorns, 60g (2oz) butter and 60g (2oz) flour
250g (8oz) Camembert cheese
3 egg yolks
teaspoon Dijon mustard
salt and white pepper
pinch of grated nutmeg
deep fat (for frying)
bunch of parsley (optional – for garnish)

for coating:
30g (1oz) flour seasoned with ¼ teaspoon each of salt and pepper
1 egg, beaten to mix with 1 tablespoon water and 1 tablespoon oil
100g (3½oz) dry white breadcrumbs
3.75cm (1½in) plain round cutter

Make the béchamel sauce.

Discard the rind and chop the cheese. Add the cheese and egg yolks to the warm béchamel sauce and simmer, stirring constantly, for 2 minutes – or until smooth and almost as thick as choux pastry. Take from the heat and add the mustard, salt, pepper and nutmeg to taste. Pour into a buttered baking tray – or swiss roll tin or cake tin – to make a 1cm (½in) layer and chill overnight.

Warm the baking tray or tin over the heat to melt the butter and cut out 3.75cm (1½in) rounds of cheese mixture. Coat them with seasoned flour, then brush them with beaten egg and coat with breadcrumbs. The fritters can be prepared 24 hours ahead and kept uncovered in the refrigerator, or they can be frozen.

To finish: heat the deep fat to 180C (355F) on a frying thermometer. Fry the fritters a few at a time until golden brown and drain thoroughly on paper towels. Keep warm in a moderate oven, 180C (350F) gas 4, while frying the rest.

If garnishing with fried parsley, be sure it is dry; let the fat cool slightly, then toss in the parsley, standing back as it will sputter. After 30 seconds, or when the sputtering stops, lift out the parsley and drain it on paper towels. Arrange the fritters overlapping on a serving dish, sprinkle with fried parsley sprigs and serve at once.

TO COAT FOOD FOR DEEP FRYING

1 Have ready three trays or large plates.
2 On the first, put white flour generously seasoned with salt and pepper. On the second, break two or more eggs and beat with a large pinch of salt and a tablespoon of oil (this mixture is called an anglaise). Spread dry white breadcrumbs on the third plate.
3 Dip the food in flour; then transfer it to the beaten egg.
4 Brush the food with beaten egg until very thoroughly coated.
5 Transfer to the crumbs and turn until evenly coated, pressing firmly to make the crumbs adhere. Transfer to a clean plate to await frying.
6 If a coating falls off during frying, the fat was not hot enough.

CROQUETTES DE POISSON
(Fish croquettes)

These can be served as a starter or a main course or even, made smaller, as an hors d'oeuvre.

MAKES 10-12

thick béchamel sauce (page 192) made with 300ml ($\frac{1}{2}$pt) milk, slice of onion, bay leaf, a pinch of grated nutmeg, 6 peppercorns, 60g (2oz) butter, 60g (2oz) flour, salt and pepper

300g (10oz) flaked, cooked fish

salt and pepper

pinch Cayenne pepper

75g (2$\frac{1}{2}$oz) flour seasoned with $\frac{1}{2}$ level teaspoon salt and a pinch of pepper

2 eggs, beaten to mix with tablespoon oil and tablespoon water

125g (4oz) dry white breadcrumbs

to finish

béarnaise sauce (page 194) made with 180g (6oz) butter; 3 tablespoons vinegar; 3 tablespoons white wine; 10 peppercorns, crushed; 3 shallots, finely chopped; tablespoon chopped fresh tarragon stems or leaves or tarragon preserved in vinegar; 3 egg yolks; salt and white or Cayenne pepper; and, to finish, 1-2 tablespoons fresh tarragon leaves or tarragon in vinegar, finely chopped; and tablespoon chervil or parsley, finely chopped

deep fat (for frying)

bunch of parsley

Make the béchamel sauce, stir in the flaked fish and season well with salt, pepper and Cayenne. The mixture should be just soft enough to fall from the spoon. Dot with butter to prevent the formation of a skin. Spread the mixture in an ice cube tray and chill until very firm.

Sprinkle the seasoned flour on a board, turn out the croquette mixture and cut it in 2.5cm (1in) bars. Roll the bars into cylinders about 7.5cm (3in) long and 2.5cm (1in) in diameter. Brush the croquettes with the beaten egg mixture and roll them in breadcrumbs. NOTE: be sure the ends are well coated. Transfer to a plate or baking sheet and chill for no less than 30 minutes or up to 6 hours, uncovered.

To finish: make the béarnaise sauce and keep it warm in a water bath (lesson 16). Heat the deep fat to hot, 180C (355F), and fry the croquettes, a few at a time, for 2-3 minutes until golden brown. NOTE:

do not overcook, or they will burst. Keep them hot in a moderate oven, 180C (350F) gas 4, with the door ajar while frying the rest.
For the fried parsley: let the fat cool slightly. Toss in the parsley, standing back as it will sputter. After 30 seconds, or when the sputtering stops, lift out and drain well. Sprinkle the parsley over the croquettes and serve at once. Serve the béarnaise sauce separately.

RISSOLES

Serve these as a hearty starter; tiny ones are sometimes used to garnish meat dishes.

MAKES 12

pâte brisée (page 141) made with 300g (10oz) flour, 150g (5oz) butter, 2 egg yolks, teaspoon salt and 4-4$\frac{1}{2}$ tablespoons cold water

egg, beaten to mix with $\frac{1}{2}$ teaspoon salt (for glaze)

deep fat (for frying)

tomato sauce (page 230)

for the filling

15g ($\frac{1}{2}$oz) butter

shallot, finely chopped

150g (5oz) mushrooms, finely chopped

tablespoon chopped parsley

salt and pepper

100g (3$\frac{1}{2}$oz) pork fat, minced

300g (10oz) lean pork, minced

9-10cm (3$\frac{1}{2}$-4in) fluted cutter

Make the pâte brisée, wrap and chill it.
For the filling: first make the duxelles. Melt the butter in a frying pan and sauté the shallot until soft but not brown. Add the mushrooms and cook over high heat, stirring occasionally, until all the moisture has evaporated. Take from the heat, add parsley and seasoning and leave to cool. Mix the duxelles with the pork fat and lean pork, sauté a small piece and taste for seasoning.

Roll out the dough to about $\frac{1}{2}$cm ($\frac{1}{4}$in) thick and cut in rounds with the fluted cutter. Place a teaspoonful of filling on each round, keeping the edge free of filling. Brush egg glaze round the edges of each one, fold the pastry in half and seal the edges. NOTE: make sure the filling is tightly enclosed. Set aside to rest for $\frac{1}{2}$ hour or refrigerate for up to 24 hours.

Heat the deep fat to moderately hot, 180C (355F). Fry the rissoles for about 7-8 minutes. Remove from the fat and drain well on paper towels.

Serve hot with tomato sauce.

SOLE COLBERT

Several rich French dishes are named after Colbert, a powerful minister at the court of Louis XIV.

SERVES 4

4 whole sole each weighing 350-500g ($\frac{3}{4}$-1lb), with the heads on

deep fat (for frying)

bunch parsley (for garnish – optional)

for coating

seasoned flour made with 75g (2$\frac{1}{2}$oz) flour, $\frac{1}{2}$ teaspoon salt and $\frac{1}{4}$ teaspoon pepper

2 eggs, beaten with 1 tablespoon water and 1 tablespoon oil

60-90g (2-3oz) dry white breadcrumbs

for the maître d'hôtel butter

100g (3$\frac{1}{2}$oz) butter

1$\frac{1}{2}$ teaspoons lemon juice

tablespoon chopped parsley

salt and pepper

Slit the stomach of each fish and clean. Cut off the fins with scissors and cut the tail into a 'V'. Grasp the dark top skin of the fish firmly at the tail and rip it off up to the head. Dip your fingers in salt if the skin is very slippery. Scale the white, bottom skin but do not remove it. NOTE: the white skin is left on so that the fish

---

DEEP FRYING PANS

A deep fryer, whether it is heated on top of the stove or has an independent heat source, should have two characteristics: *it must be deep* so that the food is completely covered with fat without touching the bottom of the pan; *it should be stable* so that it does not tip.

Keep the pan clean both inside (because bits of food left will darken the fat) and outside (because spilt fat may catch fire). Usually a good wipe is sufficient, but if the pan is washed, dry it thoroughly before replacing the oil so no water is left to make the fat splutter. Never fill it more than one-third full of fat.

To coat fish for sole Colbert: first dip in seasoned flour, then brush with beaten egg and finally coat the fish with breadcrumbs, pressing them in well

POULET A LA KIEV
(Chicken Kiev)

The key to chicken Kiev is to fry just long enough so the chicken is cooked but the butter is not so hot that it bursts through the bread-crumb coating. Correctly, chicken suprêmes – that is, the whole of the white breast meat including the wing bone – should be used for this dish, but boned chicken breasts can be substituted.

SERVES 4

suprêmes cut from two 1.5-2kg (3-4lb) roasting chickens (see below)
deep fat (for frying)
for the herb butter
100g (3½oz) butter
grated rind and juice of 1 lemon
tablespoon chopped parsley
teaspoon tarragon
teaspoon chives
salt and freshly ground black pepper
for coating
30g (1oz) flour seasoned with ¼ teaspoon salt and pinch of pepper
1 egg, beaten to mix with ½ tablespoon oil and ½ tablespoon water
100g (3½oz) dry white breadcrumbs
4 paper cutlet frills

First detach the suprêmes from the chicken: cut down from the top of the breastbone with a sharp knife, taking care to keep the knife close to the rib cage so that all the white meat is detached in one piece. Cut through the wing joint so that the bone is attached to the breast. Cut through the next joint to detach the two small wing bones and discard them.

For the herb butter: cream the butter and beat in the lemon rind and juice, herbs and plenty of season-ing. Form it into a 6cm (2½in) square cake on a sheet of grease-proof paper. Cover and chill until very firm.

Cut the chilled butter into 4 sticks. There are two ways to insert it into the chicken breasts:

1 Lay the chicken suprêmes be-tween two sheets of greaseproof paper and beat them with a cutlet bat or rolling pin until thin. Set a stick of butter on each suprême, fold over the edge furthest from the wing bone and roll up so that the wing bone protrudes at one end.

2 Cut a horizontal slit in each su-prême and insert the butter. NOTE:

will hold together.

Working on the dark skin side, make a slit down the centre and cut the fillets from the bone with smooth strokes, using a flexible fish filleting knife, but leave them attached at the edges. Fold the fillets outwards to expose the bone and snip the backbone across in 2-3 places with scissors. NOTE: this makes the bone easy to remove after cooking. Coat the fish with season-ed flour, brush with egg and coat with breadcrumbs, pressing them in well. The fish can be prepared 2-3 hours ahead up to this point and kept, uncovered, in the refrigerator.

For the maître d'hôtel butter: cream the butter and beat in the lemon juice, parsley and plenty of season-ing. Keep it in the refrigerator.

To finish: remove the maître d'hôtel butter from the refrigerator so that it will be of spreading con-sistency. Heat the deep fat to 180C (355F) on a frying thermometer. Fry the fish, one by one, for 6-7 minutes until golden brown. NOTE: be sure the fish are flat and the fillets are folded outwards during frying. Drain them, pull out the backbone and keep hot while frying the remainder. Arrange the fish on a serving dish, spoon or pipe the maître d'hôtel butter into the cavity

where the backbone was, and serve.

If garnishing with fried parsley, let the fat cool slightly, then toss in the parsley. Stand back because it will sputter. After 30 seconds or when sputtering stops, lift out the parsley and drain it well. Decorate the serving dish and serve at once.

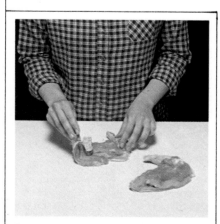

For chicken Kiev, either fold the breast around the butter and roll it up, or slip butter into a horizontal slit in the suprême, which is left flat (at front)

with both methods, it is important that the butter be completely enclosed.

Roll in seasoned flour, brush with beaten egg and coat with dry breadcrumbs, pressing them in well. Chill, uncovered, for at least 3-4 hours, or overnight. The prepared suprêmes can also be wrapped and frozen; let them thaw in the refrigerator for 6-7 hours before frying.

To finish: heat the deep fat to 180C (355F) on a frying thermometer. Fry the suprêmes two at a time, in the hot fat until golden brown – they should cook through in 5 minutes. Drain the suprêmes on paper towels. The suprêmes can be kept hot in an oven with the door ajar for 5-10 minutes.

BEIGNETS AUX FRUITS
(Fruit fritters)

Beer can be substituted for the milk in this recipe; it makes a light and well-flavoured batter. Beignets can also be made with other fruit such as apricots, figs, cherries, peaches, pears and plums. The fruit should be peeled and cut into halves or pieces of even size that are not too large.

SERVES 6-8

4 tart apples, peeled, cored and cut in 1cm ($\frac{1}{2}$in) rings; or 1 pineapple, peeled, cored and cut into 1cm ($\frac{1}{2}$in) rings; or 6-8 bananas, cut diagonally into 5cm (2in) lengths

deep fat (for frying)

sugar (for sprinkling)

apricot or raspberry jam, heated (optional)

for fritter batter

125g (4oz) flour

pinch of salt

tablespoon sugar

2 eggs, separated

about 200ml ($\frac{1}{3}$pt) milk

tablespoon melted butter or oil

For the batter: sift the flour with the salt into a bowl, add the sugar and make a well in the centre. Add the egg yolks and half the milk and stir, gradually drawing in the flour to make a smooth paste. Stir in more milk to make a batter that drops easily from the spoon, though not in a continuous ribbon. Beat it for 5 minutes, then cover and leave for 30 minutes. The grains in the starch will expand, and the batter will thicken.

It can be kept, covered, in the refrigerator overnight.

To finish: heat the deep fat to 195C (385F). Beat the egg whites until stiff and fold into the batter with the melted butter or oil. Using a fork, dip a piece of fruit into the batter, lift out, let the excess batter drip off for 2-3 seconds and lower the fritter gently into the hot fat. Fry the pieces of fruit a few at a time until golden brown, turning them once, and drain on paper towels. Keep warm in a moderate oven, 180C (350F) gas 4, with the door ajar while frying the remaining fruit.

Sprinkle with sugar and serve the fruit fritters at once, with a little warmed apricot or raspberry jam if you like.

8
EGGS
The versatility of eggs

'Larousse Gastronomique', which lists more than 400 recipes for cooking eggs, does not cover all the possibilities. What with scrambling, soft-boiling, hard-boiling, poaching, cooking them 'en cocotte', 'sur le plat' and in omelettes, not to mention dishes in which white and yolk are separated, the permutations are almost endless, especially since eggs blend accommodatingly with most other flavours – with spinach and mornay sauce in Oeufs florentine, with onions, peppers and tomatoes in Omelette basquaise, with everything from lobster – in eggs à l'américaine – to Brussels sprouts in oeufs à la bruxelloise.

An egg not only takes well to such theatrical makeup, but requires it if it is to look attractive for serving. For instance, a coating of sauce gives a cosmetic touch to the pallid surface of poached, mollet or hard-boiled eggs. Eggs lend themselves to all sauces – white, cheese, velouté, butter and even brown.

One of the most popular dishes of the moment is oeufs en meurette, a traditional Burgundian recipe of poached eggs coated with a red wine-flavoured brown sauce and garnished with bacon, mushrooms and often button onions. Omelettes can be topped with a spoonful of whatever flavouring is inside, plus a ribbon of sauce around the dish if you like, and scrambled eggs can be garnished in the same way. But a good thing should not be carried too far and the La Varenne chefs constantly admonish, 'It should be

OEUFS EN COCOTTE
(top left) Eggs in individual ramekins, each set on a bed of diced ham, bacon, chicken livers or vegetables

OEUFS POCHES SKABELEFF
(top right) Individual pâte brisée tartlet shells holding poached eggs coated with a tomato-flavoured mayonnaise and garnished with strips of smoked salmon

OMELETTE FINES HERBES
(bottom left) One of the classic ways of flavouring a plain omelette with chopped fresh chives, tarragon and chervil

OMELETTE ESPAGNOLE
(bottom right) Well-seasoned 'omelette plate' cooked with onion, tomatoes, green peppers and garlic that makes a meal in itself

scrambled eggs with peas, not peas with scrambled eggs!' Cold eggs can be coated or moulded in aspic, or topped with mayonnaise.

The serving dish itself forms the decoration for eggs en cocotte and eggs au plat, and I am constantly tempted to buy the pretty French flowered ramekins and entrée dishes designed for egg cookery. Scrambled eggs benefit from some kind of container – preferably edible – besides the plate, as do poached eggs and oeufs mollet. A pastry tartlet shell or a fried or toasted croûte of bread is good as the crisp texture contrasts with the soft egg. Lighter alternatives are a bed of vegetables such as spinach, mushroom purée (dux-elles) or sliced tomatoes, and artichoke bottoms are perhaps the most luxurious container of all. Never serve an omelette or scrambled eggs on a hot plate, say the experts, for once they reach their climax in the pan any further heat will destroy the perfection. This is not a *faux pas* likely to be committed in our house, where there seems to be a constant battle to have enough hot plates.

The number of eggs usually served per person varies very much depending on the way they are cooked. One egg is the usual portion if the egg is poached or mollet and a substantial garnish is added, such as the hollandaise, croûte and slice of ham called for in eggs Bénédict, or the generous coating of jelly in eggs in aspic. The helping may, of course, be doubled if the eggs are served as a main course rather than an entrée. For eggs en cocotte or boiled eggs, you can offer one or two, but anything less than two eggs au plat looks a bit mean.

For an omelette, two eggs per head is a minimum, and an extra egg 'for the pan' is often added. I personally regard six eggs as a maximum for a good omelette, though you can make them with eight or even 10 eggs if serving three or four. But with too many eggs, the omelette cooks slowly, setting evenly all through instead of browning on the outside and remaining *baveuse,* or runny, in the centre. Scrambled eggs never seem to go far, perhaps because they should be creamy with a few firm pieces to add texture, but never cooked enough to hold their shape. One scrambled egg on a plate looks like just a little blob of sauce and three eggs per person is the usual allowance, even when served as an entrée to be followed by a meat course. Perhaps not many people would eat more than three eggs at once, but when I'm trying to lose weight, I eat a huge six-egg omelette with a mound of spinach and a generous glass of white wine. I'm sure it's dreadfully unhealthy as a diet, but it works – I lose 3 or 4 pounds in a week.

In addition to being admirable eating in themselves, eggs are often an important ingredient within a dish. Whole, they act as binders in stuffings and terrines. Considered separately, the white and yolk have different properties. Whites lighten and bind quenelles, for example, and especially when beaten, make other ingredients rise – as in cakes. Egg yolks have quite a different effect, both enriching and thickening such preparations as custards and sauces. The traditional egg yolk liaison for soups and sauces is out of fashion because yolks curdle easily, and hurried chefs do not like to take the risk. I hope this is only a passing trend, for the smooth, rich texture and flavour of a sauce completed with a yolk liaison are hard to match. Often several of the properties of an egg are used, as in quiches, in which the whites puff the filling as it cooks and the yolks enrich and thicken the mixture.

In the old days, the freshness of eggs caused a lot of concern. Nineteenth-century cookbooks list elaborate ways to 'candle' eggs, illuminating the air pocket (the larger the pocket, the longer the egg has been evaporating through its porous shell into the open air). Or an egg was immersed in a 12 per cent solution of salt water to see if it would sink in proof of its freshness. Nowadays there is little need to fuss. Eggs are all of more or less the same age by the time they reach the kitchen: not fresh from the chicken, but not very stale either. They can be stored in nitrogen for months without changing state, and whatever one may think of this practice, it does ensure a supply of eggs at a relatively stable price throughout the year.

There are, of course, 'farm eggs' whose freshness is guaranteed – at a premium. Personally I think that for most egg recipes it is not worth the extra cost and good cooking is by far the most important part of the exercise. For two kinds of dishes, however, fresh eggs are essential: for soft-boiled eggs, in which the full flavour of the egg can be appreciated, and for poached eggs. In a very fresh egg, the white clings closely to the yolk so that when it is poached, the egg is a neat round shape. The older the egg, the more liquid the white so that in the poaching water it floats away from the yolk in strings. If the egg is really stale, the yolk can be left almost bald.

A bad egg is all too unmistakable and is nearly always due to a crack in the shell (sometimes almost invisible). Prudent cooks examine egg shells and then break eggs individually into a cup before adding them to anything else. But practice and precept are not always the same. I remember when I was training 20 years ago, my teacher, a starch-bosomed martinet if ever there was one, ignored her own rules and broke 20 eggs directly into a bowl. The 19th was bad; it was a lesson I have never forgotten.

For short-term storage, a refrigerator is not the ideal place for eggs because they dehydrate rapidly through the shell. However, the egg deteriorates more slowly at a lower temperature, so if you *must* keep eggs a long time (a week or more) the refrigerator is the best place. Egg yolks that are left over form a crust in the open air within 2-3 hours and even when tightly covered they tend to dry overnight. So if I have spare yolks, I moisten them by adding a whole egg or a spoon or two of water, then cover them tightly. Luckily, most kitchens have a surfeit of whites rather than yolks; they keep very well for up to three weeks in the refrigerator, or they can be frozen. Egg whites are one of the few foods that La Varenne chefs advocate freezing – they say they whip up better afterwards.

Eggs are graded by size (see the Anthology), and the price varies accordingly. Most recipes, including those from La Varenne, use large eggs – size 3 or 4. For something like an omelette, egg size doesn't matter much, but in cakes and soufflés it can make a good deal of difference, and the number of eggs you use should be adjusted. Here in France, brown eggs are more prevalent than white. It always amuses me that in America white eggs are more popular, presumably because they appear more pure. In point of fact, the colour of the shell has no bearing on the taste of the egg inside.

Eggs are good both in star and in supporting rôles, but I doubt if many cooks would go as far as Ali Bab, whose cookbook dating from the 1930s suggests this Symphony of Eggs: 'Chop two hard-boiled eggs. Poach six eggs and keep warm. Make an omelette from four eggs. Before folding it, sprinkle it with the chopped hard-boiled eggs and set the poached eggs on top. Fold the omelette and serve with tomato or cream sauce.' Egg-centric to say the least.

THE WAY TO SUCCESS

1 Eggs start cooking at the relatively low temperature of 70C (158F), and they cook quickly – an omelette takes 1-2 minutes and a poached egg 3-4 minutes. Twenty seconds can make the difference between eggs being done and being overcooked.

2 Eggs scorch easily, and fierce heat toughens them. In many dishes, the egg is cooked in its shell or in a container which protects it from direct heat. When eggs are in contact with the heat, as when they are fried, scrambled or cooked in an omelette, the heat must be very carefully watched.

3 Eggs to be served cold should be cooked until slightly firmer than those to be reheated, particularly if the eggs are to be in a sauce.

4 Eggs are often seasoned with white pepper as the appearance of specks of black pepper are considered unattractive.

Getting ahead

1 Eggs can be poached several days ahead and kept in a bowl of cold water in the refrigerator. To reheat, immerse them in hot water, around 65C (150F), for 3-4 minutes, then drain and pat dry on paper towels.

2 Eggs can also be cooked 'mollet' or boiled and kept at room temperature for up to 24 hours. If chilled, they become tough. Peeled eggs can be kept in a bowl of cold water at room temperature for up to 24 hours, but it is best to peel them when needed.

3 Scrambled eggs can be made a few minutes in advance if cooked just until very soft; keep them warm above a water bath.

4 Omelettes, eggs en cocotte and shirred eggs cannot be made ahead as they toughen if kept hot, but most garnish ingredients can be prepared in advance and kept in the refrigerator.

For perfect poached eggs, bring the water to a rolling boil, break an egg into a patch of bubbling water. The bubbles will spin the egg, setting the white round the yolk

Using a draining spoon, lift an egg out of the water to test. It is done when the white is firm, but the yolk is still soft. Transfer the egg to a bowl of cold water to stop cooking

OEUFS POCHES
(Poached eggs)

Poaching actually involves two cooking temperatures: a rolling boil when the eggs are added to the water, then just below a simmer to complete cooking.

Fill a sauté pan or shallow saucepan (preferably not aluminium) two-thirds full of water, add 3-4 tablespoons vinegar per litre (1¾pts) of water and bring to a rolling boil.

Holding an egg close to the water, break it into a bubbling patch; the bubbles spin the egg so the white sets around the yolk. (This can be easier if you break each egg into a cup before adding it to the water.) Repeat with more eggs, adding up to 8-10 to the pan, one by one. Turn down the heat so the water almost simmers and poach the eggs for 3-4 minutes.

Test each egg by lifting it out with a draining spoon and touching it – the white should be just firm and the yolk soft.

When done, transfer the eggs at once to a bowl of cold water to stop them cooking. To give the eggs a neat shape, trim any strings of cooked egg white, taking care not to break the yolk. Drain thoroughly on paper towels before using.

OEUFS POCHES FLORENTINE
(Poached eggs Florentine)

'Florentine' often refers to a garnish or bed of spinach, in tribute to the Florentine chefs who came with Catherine de Medici when she married King Henri II, and who introduced this vegetable to France.

SERVES 4

8 fresh eggs

30g (1oz) grated Parmesan or Gruyère cheese (for sprinkling)

1 tablespoon melted butter

for the spinach

1.25kg (2½lb) fresh spinach or equivalent of frozen leaf spinach

30g (1oz) butter

salt and freshly ground pepper

pinch of nutmeg

mornay sauce (page 192) made with 600ml (1pt) milk, 30g (2 level tablespoons) butter, 20g (2 level tablespoons) flour, salt, pepper, nutmeg, 2 egg yolks, 60g (2oz) grated Parmesan or Gruyère cheese and 1 teaspoon Dijon mustard

Poach the eggs (see previous recipe) for about 3 minutes, cooking them lightly so they are still soft. NOTE: they will cook further when the finished dish is browned. Transfer them to a bowl of cold water.

To cook the spinach: wash fresh spinach thoroughly, discard the stems and cook in plenty of boiling salted water for 5 minutes or until the leaves are wilted, stirring occasionally. Drain the spinach, refresh with cold water and drain it thoroughly. Cook frozen spinach according to the instructions on the packet. Squeeze it by handfuls to extract all the water.

Make the mornay sauce.

Transfer the eggs to a bowl of fresh warm water to heat them through. Melt 30g (1oz) butter in a pan, add the spinach and toss until very hot, seasoning it with pepper and a little nutmeg. Arrange the spinach down the centre of a buttered baking dish or heatproof serving dish. Drain the eggs on paper towels and arrange them on the bed of spinach.

Spoon the sauce over the eggs and spinach to coat them, sprinkle with the rest of the grated cheese and dribble on the melted butter. Brown the dish under the grill and serve.

The finished eggs Florentine can be kept hot in the oven for 10-15 minutes in a water bath, but the eggs easily overcook.

OEUFS POCHES SKABELEFF
(Poached eggs Skabeleff)

The names of French recipes often refer to an important ingredient in the garnish, as in this dish – the Russian name of which hints at the smoked salmon used for decoration.

SERVES 4

pâté brisée (page 141) made with 125g (4oz) flour, 60g (2oz) butter, 1 egg yolk, 2g (⅓ level teaspoon) salt and 1½-2 level teaspoons cold water

150g (5oz) shrimps, cooked, peeled and coarsely chopped

4 eggs

1 thin slice (about 60g or 2oz) smoked salmon (for decoration)

tomato and anchovy mayonnaise (page 179) made with 1 egg yolk, salt and white pepper, 1 tablespoon white wine vinegar, or to taste, a little dry mustard or Dijon mustard (optional), 300ml (½pt) oil, 1 teaspoon anchovy paste and 2 teaspoons tomato purée

4 deep tartlet tins, 10cm (4in) diameter

Make the pie pastry and chill. Roll it out to just under 5mm (¼in) thick. Butter the tartlet tins, arrange them side by side and place the rolled-out dough on top. Line the tins with rounds of dough, pressing it well down into the bases with a ball of dough dipped in flour. Press together the dough trimmings, roll out and line the remaining tins and chill until firm. Set the oven at hot, 200C (400F) gas 6.

Line the tartlet shells with rounds of paper and dried beans, or place a smaller tartlet tin inside each, put them on a baking sheet and bake in the heated oven for 8-10 minutes or until the pastry is set and lightly browned. Remove the paper and beans or small tins and return the shells to the oven for 5-7

EGGS AND SALT

Salt has an important effect on eggs: it breaks down the whites so they become liquid. This is useful when egg whites and yolks should blend, as in egg glaze – for which a whole egg is beaten with a good pinch of salt until the glaze is smooth. More often, however, the liquefying effect should be avoided so salt should be added to eggs at the last moment. An omelette or scrambled eggs will be watery if the eggs are mixed with salt more than a minute or two before cooking, and salt sprinkled on eggs au plat or eggs en cocotte before cooking gives a spotted effect when the egg is cooked. Even more disastrous is the effect of adding salt to water for poached eggs – the salt breaks down the egg white, which detaches itself in strings from the yolk. The correct addition to the poaching water is vinegar, which has the effect of sealing the egg white. When whipping egg whites, add a pinch of salt towards the end of beating.

minutes, or until crisp and brown. Allow to cool slightly, then remove the pastry shells from the tins and cool completely on a rack. They can be made up to 48 hours ahead and kept in an airtight container.

Make the mayonnaise and mix 6 tablespoons with the anchovy paste. Stir in the chopped shrimps and taste for seasoning. To the rest of the mayonnaise, add enough tomato purée to colour and flavour it. Poach the eggs (see Oeufs pochés) and keep them in a bowl of cold water. The eggs and mayonnaise can be prepared up to 6 hours ahead; keep both covered at room temperature.

Not more than 2 hours before serving, assemble the dish. Divide the shrimp mixture among the tartlet shells. Drain the eggs, dry and place each in a tartlet shell. Coat with the tomato mayonnaise. Cut the smoked salmon into thin strips and use to decorate the eggs.

OEUFS MOLLETS, A LA COQUE ET OEUFS DURS
(Mollet, soft and hard-boiled eggs)

To help prevent cracking, let the eggs come to room temperature before plunging into boiling water.

In a saucepan (not aluminium) bring enough water to the boil to cover the eggs generously. Using a very large spoon or small strainer, lower all the eggs together into the water. Bring back to the boil and begin counting the cooking time. For soft-boiled eggs, allow 4-4$\frac{1}{2}$ minutes; for mollet, allow 5-6 minutes; and for hard-boiled, allow 10-12 minutes.

To peel mollet or hard-boiled eggs, tap them gently all over to crack the shell and peel it away with the skin. *Be especially careful* with mollet eggs because the yolk is soft. If the egg is difficult to peel, put it under cold running water. However, some eggs will still be stubbornly hard to peel; this is due to the type of feed given to the hens.

OEUFS DURS BOULANGERE
(Hard-boiled eggs boulangère)

The name boulangère, or baker's wife, refers to the rolls used as containers for eggs and sauce.

SERVES 6

30g (1oz) butter

2 medium onions, thinly sliced

salt and white pepper

8 hard-boiled eggs

béchamel sauce (page 192) made with 600ml (1pt) milk, 1 slice onion, 1 bay leaf, 6 peppercorns, 45g (1$\frac{1}{2}$oz) butter, 40g (1$\frac{1}{2}$oz) flour, salt, pepper and a pinch of grated nutmeg

6 long crusty rolls

30g (1oz) grated Gruyère cheese (for sprinkling)

2 tablespoons finely chopped parsley (for sprinkling)

Melt the butter in a heavy-based pan, add the onions, salt and pepper and press a piece of buttered foil, non-stick vegetable parchment or greaseproof paper on top. Add the lid and cook very gently for 10-12 minutes until tender. NOTE: do not allow onions to brown.

Peel the eggs, cut two of them in half lengthwise, scoop out the yolks and reserve. Coarsely chop the halved egg whites with the rest of the eggs. Make the béchamel sauce and mix it with the chopped eggs and the onions. Rub the surface with butter to prevent a skin from forming.

The dish can be prepared up to this point 24 hours ahead and kept covered in the refrigerator.

About 30 minutes before serving, split the rolls in half lengthwise and remove most of the soft crumb, leaving a shell. Fill the shells with the egg and sauce mixture and sprinkle them with the grated cheese.

To finish: set the rolls on a baking tray and bake the filled rolls in a hot oven, 200C (400F) gas 6, for 15-20 minutes or until hot and appetisingly browned. Sieve the reserved yolks over the top.

Sprinkle the chopped parsley lengthwise down the centre of each roll and serve immediately.

OEUFS EN COCOTTE
(Eggs 'en cocotte')

Diced bacon, sliced ham, sliced cooked sausages, chicken livers and sliced or diced cooked vegetables are only a few of the possibilities for garnishing eggs en cocotte. Just place a little in the buttered ramekin and break the egg on top.

If using the oven set it at moderately hot, 190C (375F) gas 5. Arrange individual heatproof ramekins in a large shallow water bath (a roasting pan is ideal) – and add enough warm water to come two-thirds of the way up the sides of the ramekins. Allow 2 small or 1 large ramekin per person. In each ramekin put $\frac{1}{2}$ tablespoon butter, and a little salt and freshly ground black pepper. (The black pepper is hidden by the egg on top.) If the ramekins are large enough for two eggs, double these quantities. Heat the ramekins gently in the water bath on top of the stove until the butter has melted, then break one or two eggs into each. If you like, top with a tablespoon of cream.

Bake the eggs in the water bath in the heated oven for 5-6 minutes or until the whites are almost set – the eggs will continue cooking in the heat of the moulds, and when served the whites should be just set and the yolks soft.

OMELETTE PANS

One of the keys to success in making omelettes is a good pan. It can be made of aluminium or iron. The base must be thick to distribute the heat evenly and the sides fairly high, curved and gently sloping so the omelette can be folded easily. The handle is also angled to help folding.

The size of the pan can vary from about 17cm (7in) diameter for making a 2-3 egg omelette for one, to 25-28cm (10-11in) for an 8-egg omelette for 3 or 4. A 23cm (9in) diameter pan is right for a 4-5 egg omelette for two.

Omelette pans should be 'proved' before use: wash the pan well (without abrasives), dry and pour in a 1cm ($\frac{1}{2}$in) layer of oil and coarse salt. Leave for 12 hours, then heat gently until the oil is very hot and almost smoking (this can be done easily in the oven). Pour off oil and salt and wipe dry.

Stir briskly with a fork for 8-10 seconds until the beaten eggs start to thicken

Holding the pan handle in one hand, tip the pan and give the handle a sharp tap

Slide the omelette on to a plate, rolling it so it lands neatly folded into three

OEUFS AU PLAT
(Eggs 'au plat')

These eggs are sometimes called Oeufs miroir, a name derived from the shiny film that forms on the surface. The same garnishes can be used as for eggs en cocotte. Traditionally, Oeufs au plat are cooked and served in shallow, white heatproof dishes with two little handles, but they can be made in any shallow baking dish. If it is flameproof, the eggs can be cooked on top of the stove.

If using the oven, set it at moderately hot, 190C (375F) gas 5. Butter shallow individual baking dishes or one large baking dish and spread the chosen garnish in the bottom. If using a garnish, make a hollow for the eggs and break them into the dish, allowing two per dish if using individual dishes. Cover the dishes with a lid or foil and cook gently on top of the stove, or bake in the heated oven for 8-10 minutes, until the whites are set and the yolks are still soft. The eggs will continue cooking in the heat of the dish, particularly if it is metal, so stop cooking before the whites are quite set. Serve them at once.

OEUFS BROUILLES MAGDA
(Scrambled eggs Magda)

The slower scrambled eggs are cooked, the better; old cookbooks say 8 eggs should take 30 minutes!

SERVES 4

8 eggs
salt and pepper
200g (7oz) butter
4 thick slices bread, cut in triangles
30g (1oz) grated Gruyère cheese
2 teaspoons chopped mixed herbs (tarragon, chervil and chives)
2 level teaspoons Dijon mustard

Beat the eggs with salt and pepper until thoroughly mixed and frothy.

Melt half the butter in a frying pan and fry the slices of bread until golden brown on both sides. Drain well on paper towels and keep warm.

Melt the remaining butter in a heavy-based saucepan, add the eggs and stir constantly over low heat with a wooden spoon until the mixture begins to thicken. Continue cooking over very low heat, scraping the cooked egg from the bottom and sides of the pan so the dish becomes creamy and doesn't get lumpy. NOTE: If the eggs start thickening too quickly, take them from the heat and let them cool a little before continuing to cook. Scrambled eggs should be slightly undercooked as they will continue to cook in the heat of the pan.

Add the cheese and continue stirring until it melts into the eggs. Remove from the heat and stir in the chopped herbs and the mustard.

Pile into a shallow serving bowl or dish and surround with the bread triangles. Serve at once.

OMELETTE
(Plain omelette)

In France, in order to be considered an expert, a chef must make omelettes every day for 3 years! Allow 2-3 eggs per person for an omelette.

SERVES 2

4-5 eggs
salt and freshly ground black pepper
2 tablespoons butter
23cm (9in) diameter omelette pan

Beat the eggs with salt and pepper in a bowl with a fork until thoroughly mixed. Have ready a warm serving dish.

Melt the butter in the omelette pan over medium heat. When it foams, pour the eggs into the pan. Stir them briskly with the flat of the fork for 8-10 seconds until they start to thicken. Then quickly but carefully pull the egg that is cooking at the sides of the pan towards the centre, tipping the pan to pour uncooked egg to the sides. Continue until most of the egg is set, or some is still runny, depending on your taste, then leave the omelette to cook for 10-15 seconds to brown the bottom and set it slightly.

To fold the omelette: hold the pan handle in one hand, with the pan facing towards you. Tip the pan away from you and either give the handle a sharp tap with the other hand so the edge of the omelette flips or, with the help of the fork, fold over the edge of the omelette near the handle. Half roll, half slide the omelette into the serving dish so it lands folded into three. Neaten the omelette with a fork, and serve.

Cheese omelette
Just before folding the omelette,

add 2-3 tablespoons grated or finely diced Gruyère cheese.

Chicken liver omelette

Sauté 2-3 chicken livers with 1 finely chopped shallot (optional) in 2 teaspoons butter until browned but still pink in the centre. Slice the livers, return them to the pan and stir in 1 level teaspoon flour. Add 3-4 tablespoons stock and cook the mixture, stirring, for 2-3 minutes. Taste for seasoning and keep warm.

Spoon in just before folding.

Omelette fines herbes

When beating the eggs, add 2 teaspoons each of chopped fresh chives, chervil and tarragon.

Ham omelette

Stir 90g (3oz) cooked ham, diced or cut in julienne strips, into the beaten eggs.

Mushroom omelette

Sauté 125g (4oz) sliced mushrooms in 30g (1oz) butter until tender. Stir in 2 level teaspoons flour and add 3-4 tablespoons double cream, a squeeze of lemon juice, and salt and pepper to taste.

Morel omelette

If using fresh morels, wash them carefully, brushing to remove all the sand; cut them in two lengthwise. If using dried morels, cover them with boiling water and leave for an hour to swell. Melt 30g (1oz) butter in a saucepan, add 120g (4oz) fresh morels or 30g (1oz) soaked dried morels, 100ml (4oz) chicken stock, a squeeze of lemon juice, salt and pepper and cook over medium heat, stirring occasionally, for 10 minutes or until the morels are tender and all the liquid has evaporated. Taste them for seasoning and reserve a few morels for garnish. Make the omelettes as usual and spoon in morels just before folding.

Tomato omelette

Melt 30g (1oz) butter in a frying pan and slowly cook 2 tomatoes, peeled, seeded and coarsely chopped, with 1 finely chopped shallot, until soft but not browned. Add 1 clove garlic, crushed (optional); 1 teaspoon chopped mixed herbs (thyme, basil, parsley); salt and freshly ground black pepper; simmer until pulpy.

Keep the mixture hot. Just before folding the omelettes, spoon in the tomato mixture.

Omelette basquaise

Slowly cook 1 small onion, sliced, in 30g (1oz) butter until soft. Add ½ small green pepper, cored, seeded and coarsely chopped and season with salt and freshly ground black pepper. Cook, stirring, until the vegetables are soft. Stir in 2 tablespoons chopped parsley and keep the mixture warm. Add the basquaise mixture when the omelette is half cooked.

OMELETTES PLATES

('Flat' omelettes)

SERVES 2
4-5 eggs
salt and freshly ground black pepper
chosen flavouring (see below)
2 tablespoons butter
23cm (9in) diameter omelette pan

Beat the eggs with salt and pepper in a bowl with a fork until thoroughly mixed. Add the chosen flavouring. Melt the butter in the omelette pan over medium heat and, when foaming, add the eggs. Stir them briskly with the flat of the fork and when they start to thicken continue stirring until the mixture is almost as thick as scrambled eggs. Leave the omelette to cook for 15-20 seconds or until well browned on the bottom and almost firm on top. Take from the heat, set a heatproof plate over the top of the pan and invert the pan to turn out the omelette. Slide it back into the pan and brown the other side. Serve hot or cold.

OMELETTE ESPAGNOLE

(Spanish omelette)

Slowly cook 1 slice of onion in 2 tablespoons oil or butter until soft. Add ½ green pepper, cored, seeded and cut in strips; 2 tomatoes, peeled, seeded and coarsely chopped; 1 clove garlic, crushed (optional); salt and freshly ground black pepper. Cook, stirring, until the vegetables are soft. Add this mixture to the beaten eggs and make the omelette as above. Diced cooked ham and chorizo sausage can also be added.

OMELETTE PAYSANNE

(Peasant omelette)

Dice a 75g (2½oz) piece lean bacon and fry until the fat runs. Add 150g (5oz) potatoes cut in 1cm (½in) dice and cook over medium heat, stirring, until brown and tender. Stir in 2 tablespoons chopped parsley and freshly ground black pepper to taste. Add this mixture to the beaten eggs and make the omelette as above.

OMELETTE SAVOYARDE

SERVES 4
8 eggs
150g (5 oz) raw ham
100g (3½oz) grated Beaufort or Gruyère cheese
salt and pepper
30g (1oz) butter
2-3 tablespoons double cream

Butter an ovenproof serving dish and set aside. Beat the eggs, adding the ham and half the cheese. Season to taste. NOTE: the ham will make the eggs quite salty. Preheat the grill.

Heat the butter in an omelette pan, over high heat. Pour in the egg mixture and shake the pan until the omelette begins to set. When the omelette is fairly firm on the bottom, carefully slide it out onto the buttered dish. Spoon over the cream, sprinkle the remaining cheese on top and finish cooking for 1-2 minutes under the grill or until the omelette is golden on top. The omelette should still be creamy in the centre.

9
FROZEN DESSERTS
The Turks had a word for it

The first frozen dessert I ever ate was a dingy pink block of rock-hard ice in which were imprisoned a few parched strawberries, thirsting for release. It was a children's party in the early 1940s for which a kind great-aunt had done her best to re-create a peacetime treat during an ice-cream-less war. I'm afraid the effect was the opposite from what she had intended: we dispiritedly spooned the puddles of melting ice onto our plates. My aunt had, unwittingly, picked one of the most difficult of all frozen desserts – a fruit-based sorbet.

Sorbets were the first frozen desserts – the name comes from the Turkish word for a refreshing wine or fruit drink, no doubt originally chilled with snow. The Turks were by no means the first to appreciate the pleasure of chilled drinks in summer – Xenophon remarked on the Greek soldiers' taste for cold desserts made of honey and fruit juice, and Nero apparently regaled himself with snow flavoured with rose water, honey and raisins. But it was not until the Renaissance that ice-creams really came into their own, when Italian cooks discovered how to deal with the great enemy – water. During freezing, the water in an ice-cream mixture forms crystals or, in extreme cases like that of my great-aunt, a solid block of ice. To break up crystals and give a smooth texture, the mixture must be frozen as quickly as possible and stirred constantly while it is freezing. In the 16th century, a Sicilian found he could chill a mixture more quickly by adding saltpetre to ice, thus lowering its melting point, an effect modern cooks accomplish by adding salt. The idea was slow to spread north, but by 1782 the Café Procope in Paris was serving 80 different flavours, including orange, strawberry, raspberry, apricot, pineapple, rose, chocolate, coffee, walnut and chestnut (the Café Procope still exists, but its menu is now regrettably pedestrian).

The invention of the churn freezer further simplified the making of frozen desserts. The principle is simple: a central container, equipped with a paddle, is surrounded by ice and salt packed into a bucket. A crank handle turns the paddle so that the mixture in the container is churned constantly while being cooled by the salted ice.

Making ice-cream this way can be tedious, messy work – a good outdoor occupation for children on a hot day, but there are now several modern improvements. The churn can have an electric motor, and some new ice-cream makers are designed to operate inside a freezer so that no ice and salt are needed. The electric

MANDARINES GIVREES
Refreshingly tangy tangerine sorbet packed into the reserved, chilled shells of the fruit

ANANAS EN SURPRISE
A pineapple shell filled with a layer of the flesh cut in chunks and flavoured with Kirsch, heaped with scoops of pineapple sorbet and covered with meringue

SOUFFLES GLACES AUX FRAISES
Individual iced soufflés made of meringue and whipped cream and flavoured with strawberries

cord passes easily through the rubber seal on the freezer door to a plug outside. Most cooks I talk to are enthusiastic about these little machines, but I must confess I have had no luck with them, finding that the heat of the motor prevents the ice-cream or sorbet mixture from freezing to the right consistency. In any case, a three-star freezer is needed, not just the freezing compartment of a refrigerator, and rich mixtures can take a very long time to freeze.

Given constant churning at a low temperature, it is possible to freeze a wide range of mixtures. They fall into two main categories: sorbets made of fruit juice or purée, wine or liqueur, plus sugar and various flavourings, and richer mixtures based on eggs, milk and/or cream. Of the latter, by far the most common are custard ice-creams made of milk thickened with from 5 to 12 egg yolks per litre – three-to-six yolks per 600ml (1pt). Sometimes whipped or unwhipped cream is added too, the aim being a smooth texture to enhance the most important aspect – the flavour.

One of the best ices I have ever tasted was based on prunes soaked in Armagnac – unusual enough, particularly in France, where tastes have hardly changed since the heyday of Procope. Not for the French the rum-raisin and tutti-frutti concoctions of the USA. They prefer their vanilla to be plain vanilla, infused with vanilla beans split to release the full flavour (hence the specks of vanilla seed to be seen in the best ice-cream).

Chocolate is flavoured with melted chocolate and coffee with coffee extract – though I find that powdered instant coffee dissolved in a tablespoon of hot water is just as good. Pistachio is popular, as is the classic praline of caramel and toasted almonds – both made only with fresh nuts, ça va sans dire. The French rarely use fruit to flavour ice-cream – fruit flavours come through more clearly in a sorbet, without eggs or cream.

Richest of all are the iced desserts that reached their zenith in the 19th century. There are the parfaits, made with 32 egg yolks and a litre (1¾pts) whipped cream to every litre of concentrated syrup, and bombes frozen in layers in a spherical mould (hence their name) so they form rainbow stripes when cut into wedges for serving. During the 'belle époque', a chef was scarcely worthy of the name if he did not invent a new coupe of ice-cream or sorbet with some combination of fruit, sweet sauce, nuts, Chantilly cream or cystallised fruits – creations such as the famous poires Belle Hélène and pêches Melba of Escoffier. Still popular are iced soufflés, frozen in a soufflé mould heightened by a paper collar so that the 'soufflé' stands high above the rim when the collar is removed.

The relative popularities of the various frozen desserts are as changeable as is fashion. Now we are back at the beginning with sorbets: fruit sorbets, spiced sorbets, wine sorbets, even vegetable sorbets are a mandatory part of an up-to-date menu. One reason is that they epitomise the current fashion for lightness, colour, and clarity of flavour, but the recent develop-ment of small commercial ice-cream machines certainly has helped.

Sorbets offer a good deal of scope for experiment, but finding just the right balance of flavour and sweetness is not easy. Professional glaciers measure the density of sorbet mixtures (which varies according to the proportion of sugar) with a hydrometer and debate the relative merits of stirring sugar directly into a mixture as compared with making a sugar syrup. All agree that, in practice, there is no substitute for tasting, then adjusting ingredients until the combination is just right. Flavour at room temperature must be intense, for freezing attenuates the taste.

As with all cooking, good frozen desserts require the finest ingredients. Cheating is easy, and the manufacturing of commercial ice-cream is surrounded by regulations about the use of animal fat instead of cream, of additives such as cornflour, agar-agar and gelatine. Also, the bulk of an ice-cream can be increased enormously by whipping in air – compare the weight of 600ml (1pt) homemade ice-cream with commercial ice-cream, and you will see. In France, most commercially prepared fruit sorbets may contain as little as 15 per cent fruit (10 per cent for acid fruits like red currants or lemon). Since the rest is mainly sugar and water, no wonder they don't taste the same as homemade!

Given a good mixture and an ice-cream churn, whether electric or hand-operated, making ice-cream or sorbet is simple. Fill the container not more than two-thirds full (all mixtures expand when frozen), pack with ice and salt or put in the freezer, as appropriate, and churn until the mixture is set. This can take anything from ten minutes to half an hour, depending on the amount and type of the mixture.

If you don't have an ice-cream churn, there are still plenty of possibilities. The richest mixtures, such as iced soufflés, don't require churning at all (the recipes specify whether or not churning is necessary). Other mixtures can be frozen directly in the freezer, but they must be removed several times during freezing and thoroughly beaten to break up ice crystals; gelatine can be added to discourage crystallisation, too. However, with sorbets and plain ice-creams with a high water content, results are never very satisfactory.

A very little egg white or meringue may be added to a sorbet halfway through freezing to lighten the mixture and make it smoother. Egg white can give a slightly pasty texture, though, and detract from the flavour. At La Varenne we find that we're using it less and less.

In the old days, ice-creams were moulded and turned out onto a white napkin (to absorb the drips) or scooped into stemmed glasses for serving; sorbets were invariably served in glasses. But now the only limit on possible serving containers is your imagination. One of the prettiest presentations I have seen was an arrangement of five tiny scoops of different-coloured sorbets, five fruits to match and a vine leaf – a far cry from my first rock-hard strawberry ice.

THE WAY TO SUCCESS

1 When making the custard base for ice-cream, never leave the yolks in contact with the sugar without mixing, or the sugar will break down the yolks – the French call the reaction 'burning'.

2 If the custard overcooks slightly and begins to curdle, remove it from the heat immediately and whisk vigorously to make it smooth. If it is very overcooked, there is nothing to do but start again.

3 Mixtures should be highly flavoured as freezing diminishes taste.

4 Sugar and alcohol lower the freezing point of a mixture; if too much of either is added, it may not freeze at all. On the other hand, a sorbet with too little sugar will be hard and tasteless when frozen.

5 The mixture for fruit sorbets should be slightly sweeter than for one flavoured with wine or eau de vie. Lemon juice is added to most fruit sorbets to bring out their flavour.

6 To add flavour to citrus sorbets, rub lump sugar on the rind of the fruit to extract the oils from the zest, then use to sweeten the juice.

7 Prepare a churn with salt and ice 10-15 minutes ahead, so that the mixture is chilled as soon as it is put in. Proportions of ice to salt should be about 3 to 1. If too much salt is used, the mixture will freeze too quickly and will not be smooth. Take great care not to drop any salt into the container. If a mixture takes more than 30 minutes to freeze, add more salt.

8 All freshly frozen mixtures thaw very quickly (sorbet melts even more quickly than ice-cream), so handle as speedily as possible and always chill any spoon or other equipment that touches them.

9 When filling fruit shells such as oranges or pineapple with ice-cream or sorbet, be sure the shells are frozen before being filled.

Getting ahead

1 Fruit juice and purée can be prepared and frozen for sorbets later.

2 To store ice-cream, pack it into chilled metal moulds, cover tightly with foil or freezer wrap and keep in the freezer; use simple shapes since complicated ones do not turn out well. Alternatively, pack the ice or sorbets into dishes or individual cold-resistant glasses, ready for serving.

3 A freezer should not be set at its lowest temperature for storing ice-cream or sorbet; the lower the temperature, the quicker they crystallise.

4 Rich ice-creams can be stored for 2-3 months in the freezer, but mixtures such as sorbet that contain a high proportion of water tend to crystallise on standing and should be used within 2-4 weeks.

5 Ice-cream or sorbet that has been in the freezer for more than 12 hours should be left in the refrigerator for 1-2 hours to soften before serving.

CREME ANGLAISE
(Custard sauce)

This basic sauce is usually flavoured with vanilla but can be made with any number of other ingredients, such as lemon or orange rind or mint. It is used in many recipes including ice-cream, though in that case the proportion of sugar is much higher than usual because unsweetened cream is added during the freezing.

500ml (1pt) milk
vanilla pod or other alternative flavouring
6 egg yolks
60g (2oz) sugar

Bring the milk almost to the boil with the vanilla pod. Beat the egg yolks with the sugar until thick and light. Whisk in half the hot milk and then whisk the mixture back into the remaining milk. Cook over very low heat, stirring constantly with a wooden spoon, until the custard thickens slightly. Your

To test the crème anglaise base for ice-cream: lift the spoon and draw your finger across it. If a clear trail is left, the crème is thick enough to be used

finger should leave a clear trail when drawn across the back of the spoon.

Remove from the heat at once and strain. Cool, cover tightly and chill. The custard can be kept up to 2 days in the refrigerator.

GLACE AU CHOCOLAT
(Chocolate ice-cream)

Once, Chef Claude made super-rich ice-cream by doubling these quantities of chocolate and cream. Whichever version you choose, stir the chocolate thoroughly into the custard so there are no lumps.

Makes 1 litre (1¾pts)

200g (7oz) dark dessert chocolate, chopped
custard sauce made with 450ml (¾pt) milk, 5 egg yolks and 125g (4oz) sugar
225ml (⅜pt) double cream, lightly whipped

Melt the chocolate in a bowl over hot water. Make the custard sauce.

Take the custard from the heat, stir in the chocolate and strain the custard into a bowl. Allow to cool and pour it into a churn freezer. When the ice-cream is partly set, add the whipped cream to the mixture and churn until set.

GLACE AU GINGEMBRE

(Ginger ice-cream)

The strong flavour of ginger mellowed by the rich ice-cream is delicious, and the crystallised ginger adds textural interest.

Makes 1 litre (1¾pts)

---

custard sauce made with 450ml (¾pt) milk, 5 egg yolks and 150g (5oz) sugar

---

teaspoon ground ginger

---

2 level tablespoons chopped, crystallised ginger

150ml (¼pt) double cream, lightly whipped

Make the custard sauce. NOTE: do not overcook or boil it or it will curdle.

Take the custard at once from the heat, add the ground ginger and strain the custard into a bowl. Stir in the chopped crystallised ginger, allow to cool and pour into a churn freezer. After about 5 minutes, or when the ice-cream is partly set, add the lightly whipped cream to the mixture and churn until set.

GLACE AUX PISTACHES

(Pistachio ice-cream)

This ice-cream is good on its own, or it can be used as the outside layer of Bombe Véronique.

Makes 1 litre (1¾pts)

150g (5oz) shelled pistachios

---

custard sauce made with 450ml (¾pt) milk, 5 egg yolks and 125g (4oz) sugar

---

few drops green edible food colouring (optional)

225ml (⅜pt) double cream, lightly whipped

Blanch the pistachios in boiling water for 1 minute, drain and peel them. Pound them in a mortar with a pestle or work them in a food processor with 2 tablespoons of the cream to make a smooth paste. Heat the milk with the pistachio paste, cover and leave to infuse for 10-15 minutes.

Bring the flavoured milk almost to the boil and make the custard sauce. Remove the custard from the heat at once and strain it. Colour it lightly with a few drops of green food colouring. Cool and pour into a churn freezer. When the ice-cream is partly set, add the whipped cream to the mixture and continue churning until set.

BOMBE VERONIQUE

'Bombes' are called this because of their shape. They are made in moulds that are almost spherical, with a flat bottom. This shape made it easy to bury them in snow. Now, however, bombes are usually put in a freezer, and any shape of mould can be used – a charlotte mould, a stainless steel bowl or even a cake tin.

SERVES 8-12

750ml (1¼pt) pistachio ice-cream

25ml (1fl oz) brandy

50g (1½oz) candied orange peel, chopped

90g (3oz) dark dessert chocolate, chopped

60g (2oz) sugar

100ml (4fl oz) water

---

3 egg yolks

225ml (8fl oz) double cream, lightly whipped

---

bombe mould, 1½ litre (2½pt) capacity

Using a metal spatula, line the mould with the ice-cream and put in the freezer to set firmly. Pour the brandy over the candied orange peel and leave to macerate. Melt the chocolate in a water bath.

Heat the sugar with the water until dissolved, bring to a boil and cook to the thread stage (97C or 232F on a sugar thermometer). Beat the egg yolks until lightly thickened. Allow the bubbles in the hot syrup to subside, then add the syrup to the egg yolks, beating constantly. Continue beating the mixture until it is cool and thick. Set it in a bowl of ice and beat until chilled. Stir in the macerated orange peel, brandy and chocolate and finally fold in the whipped cream.

Spoon the bombe mixture into the mould, cover with the lid or with foil and freeze for at least 3 hours. The bombe can be kept for up to 3 months.

To serve: dip the mould into a bowl of cold water for 5 seconds. Uncover the bombe and set a serving dish on top. Reverse the mould, give a sharp shake to release it and lift it off.

CLEANING THE DASHER OF AN ICE-CREAM CHURN

With the electric motor and lid removed, lift out the dasher from the container inside and scrape the remaining ice-cream into a chilled bowl

POUDING NESSELRODE GLACE

(Iced Nesselrode pudding)

This dessert was created for the Comte de Nesselrode.

Makes about 1¼ litre (2¼pts)

500g (1lb) fresh, unpeeled chestnuts; or a 375g (¾lb) can sweetened chestnut purée

custard sauce made with 600ml (1pt) milk, 6 egg yolks and 60g (2oz) sugar

50g (2oz) dried currants

50g (2oz) raisins

65ml (3fl oz) rum

250ml (9oz) double cream, lightly whipped

Chantilly cream made with 200ml (7oz) double cream, 1-2 teaspoons sugar and a tablespoon rum (for decoration)

for cooking fresh chestnuts

60g (2oz) sugar, plus extra to taste

400ml (¾pt) water

vanilla pod

bombe mould or deep metal bowl, 1.25 litre (2¼pt) capacity; pastry bag and medium star tube

To peel the chestnuts: place the nuts a few at a time in boiling water and bring back to the boil. Take from the heat, lift out the nuts and use a peeling knife to remove both outer and the inner peel. NOTE: if the nuts become hard to peel, reheat them, but do not allow them to cook.

To cook fresh chestnuts: put the peeled chestnuts in a pan with the sugar, water and vanilla pod, cover and simmer for 40-50 minutes or until very tender and all the water has been absorbed. Add more water during cooking if the pan gets dry. Take out the vanilla pod to use for the custard sauce and purée the chestnuts a few at a time in an electric food processor or work them through a food mill or a sieve. Beat in extra sugar to taste – the purée should be quite sweet.

Make the custard sauce, bringing the milk almost to the boil with the vanilla pod. Remove the custard from the heat, take out the vanilla pod and beat the custard gradually into the chestnut purée. Mix in the dried fruit and rum. Freeze the mixture in a churn freezer. When firm, pack it into the mould, cover and freeze for at least 4 hours. This dessert keeps well in a freezer for 3-6 months.

To serve: dip the mould for a few seconds in tepid water, run a knife around the edge and turn out onto a serving dish. Pipe a puff of Chantilly cream around the edge of the frozen pudding with a pastry bag and medium star tube.

SORBET AU THE AU CITRON VERT

(Tea and lime sorbet)

Nouvelle cuisine has launched the two-flavoured sorbet – you can choose the balance in favour of tea or lime – whichever you prefer.

Makes 1 litre (1¾pts)

3 limes

300ml (½pt) water

10 high-quality tea bags

for the syrup

1 litre (1¾pts) water

250g (8oz) sugar

For the syrup: heat the sugar with 1 litre (1¾pts) water over low heat until dissolved; then boil for 2-3 minutes or until the syrup is clear.

Pare the zest from the limes and chop into the smallest possible pieces. Blanch by putting them in cold water and bringing to the boil. Refresh under cold running water and drain thoroughly. Simmer the blanched zest in 150ml (¼pt) of the syrup, stirring frequently, for about 15 minutes or until tender. NOTE: be careful that the syrup does not burn.

Bring 300ml (½pt) water to the boil, add the tea bags, remove from the heat and leave to infuse for 5 minutes. Remove the tea bags. NOTE: do not leave to infuse too long or the liquid will become bitter.

Squeeze and strain the juice from the limes. Mix together the syrup, the infused tea liquid, the cooked zest with any remaining syrup and the lime juice. Taste the mixture, adding sugar or lime juice if necessary. Pour into a churn freezer and freeze until firm.

SORBET DE GENIEVRE

(Juniper sorbet)

Not perhaps to everyone's taste, sorbet flavoured with juniper berries is a refreshing creation of the nouvelle cuisine.

Makes about 600ml (1pt)

600ml (1pt) water

200g (7oz) sugar

2 sticks cinnamon

4 tablespoons juniper berries

100ml (3½oz) juniper liqueur (Genièvre) or gin

egg white

Heat the water and sugar gently in a heavy-based pan without stirring until the sugar has dissolved. Bring to the boil and boil for 1 minute. Add the cinnamon and juniper berries, cover the pan and infuse over low heat for 15-20 minutes. Strain and allow to cool. Add the juniper liqueur or gin.

Freeze the mixture in a churn freezer until slushy. Beat the egg white until frothy, add 1-2 tablespoons of the beaten white to the mixture and continue freezing in the churn freezer until firm. Pack the ice into a container and keep in the freezer for at least 4 hours to mellow the flavour. If the sorbet is frozen for more than 12 hours, leave it in the refrigerator to soften for ½-1 hour before serving.

MANDARINES GIVREES

(Sorbet-filled tangerines)

Hollowed-out oranges, lemons or grapefruit or melon halves also make very attractive containers for sorbet.

Makes about 1 litre (1¾pts) sorbet, fills 8-10 tangerines

20 tangerines

juice of ½ lemon

100ml (⅙pt) water

a little icing sugar (optional)

for the syrup

250g (8oz) sugar

150ml (¼pt) water

juice of ¼ lemon

For the syrup: heat the sugar with the measured water and the lemon juice over low heat until dissolved; then boil just until the syrup is clear, about 2-3 minutes. Leave to cool.

Grate the zest from 10 of the tangerines and squeeze the juice from the fruit. Cut the remaining tangerines so each has a base and a lid, making a jagged edge if you like. Squeeze these, too, but be careful not to damage the skins, which should be saved. You need 750ml (1¼pts) juice. Add the grated zest, juice, lemon juice and the 100ml (⅙pt) water to the cooled syrup. Taste and add a little icing sugar or extra lemon juice if necessary. Freeze in a churn freezer until firm.

Meanwhile, carefully remove all the flesh and skin from the tangerine shells and chill them in the freezer. Pack the sorbet in the bases and cover with the lids to serve.

ANANAS EN SURPRISE

(Pineapple en surprise)

Pineapple en surprise is a variation of baked Alaska. Meringue is spread over fruit and sorbet and the whole is quickly baked in the oven.

SERVES 6

large ripe pineapple
2 tablespoons Kirsch
sugar to taste
for the pineapple sorbet
large, ripe pineapple
syrup made with 300g (10oz) sugar, 200ml (⅓pt) water and juice of ⅓ lemon (see Sorbet-filled tangerines)
250ml (⅓pt) water
½ lemon
2 tablespoons Kirsch
for the meringue
3 egg whites
180g (6oz) sugar
teaspoon vanilla essence
pastry bag and medium star tube (optional)

Cut the pineapple in half lengthwise, leaving the plume. With a curved grapefruit knife, cut out the flesh, leaving the shells in the form of a boat. Discard the centre core and cut the flesh into chunks. Sprinkle the chunks with Kirsch and sugar to taste. Cover and chill both pineapple flesh and shells for up to 8 hours.

For the pineapple sorbet: cut the plume and base from the pineapple, peel and core it. Pull the flesh into shreds with 2 forks or purée it in a food processor. Add the sugar syrup, water, lemon juice and Kirsch. Taste and add sugar or more lemon juice if necessary. Freeze in a churn freezer until firm. Spread the pineapple chunks in the shells, pack the sorbet over them and freeze until firm.

For the meringue: whip the egg whites until stiff, using a copper bowl if possible. Add 2 tablespoons of the sugar and continue whisking for 1 minute or until the mixture forms long peaks when the whisk is lifted. Fold in the remaining sugar with the vanilla. The meringue can be prepared up to 1 hour before serving; keep it covered with a damp cloth.

A short time before serving, heat the oven to very hot, 220C (425F) gas 8. Cover the sorbet with a layer of meringue, sealing the edges carefully so no heat can penetrate to the sorbet. If you like, put the remaining meringue into a pastry bag fitted with a medium star tube and decorate the meringue coating with rosettes, or cover the sorbet with all the meringue – making peaks with a spatula. Sprinkle it with sugar and bake in the heated oven for 8-10 minutes or until the meringue is browned. Set the pineapple halves on a napkin-covered serving dish and serve at once.

Variation: If preferred, another flavour of sorbet, such as orange or raspberry, can be used to fill the pineapple shell. If using raspberry sorbet, make it with 500g (1lb) raspberries, syrup made with 250g (8oz) sugar, 150ml (¼pt) water and the juice of ¼ lemon. Flavour with Kirsch and pack into the pineapple shells.

SOUFFLE GLACE

(Iced soufflé)

This basic iced soufflé, a combination of meringue and whipped cream, does not need to be churned during freezing. It can be made with most of the flavourings used for ice-cream or sorbet. Do not add too much alcohol or other liquid, however, or the mixture will separate.

SERVES 4

100g (3½oz) sugar
75ml (⅛pt) water
2 egg whites
chosen flavouring (see below)
250ml (scant ½pt) double cream, whipped until it holds a soft peak
for optional decoration
150ml (¼pt) double cream, whipped until stiff
4 walnut halves, toasted almonds, or crystallised violets
4 parfait glasses or heavy-stemmed glasses, or 4 small ramekins; pastry bag and medium star tube (for optional decoration)

If using ramekins, wrap a collar of foil or waxed paper around each one to extend 3·75-5cm (1½-2in) above the edge of the dish and tie with string. Place in the freezer until ready to use.

Heat the sugar with the water in a heavy-based saucepan until dissolved and bring to the boil. Boil to the soft ball stage (115C or 239F on a sugar thermometer, or see below).

Beat the egg whites until stiff and gradually pour on the hot sugar mixture, beating constantly. Continue beating until completely cool and very stiff. Fold in the chosen flavouring and the whipped cream.

Spoon the mixture into glasses or prepared ramekins, smoothing the top. Freeze for at least 2-3 hours or until firm. It can be kept in the freezer, tightly covered, for 2-3 months.

To finish: if desired, use a pastry bag and medium star tube to top each soufflé with a rosette of stiffly whipped cream. Top each rosette with a nut or crystallised violet. Discard the paper collars.

If the soufflés have been frozen for more than 24 hours, let them soften for 1-2 hours in the refrigerator before serving.

FLAVOURINGS

Iced coffee soufflés: dissolve 1 tablespoon instant coffee in 3 tablespoons warm water. Fold into the egg white and sugar mixture with the whipped cream.

Iced strawberry soufflés: purée 250g (8oz) strawberries in a blender or work them through a nylon strainer. Flavour the purée with 1 tablespoon Kirsch or lemon juice.

Fold into the egg white and sugar mixture with the whipped cream.

Iced raspberry soufflés: purée 250g (8oz) fresh or frozen raspberries in a blender and strain to remove the seeds, or work the raspberries through a nylon strainer. Flavour the purée with 1 tablespoon Kirsch or lemon juice. Fold into the egg white and sugar mixture with the whipped cream.

Paper collars that are wrapped round the ramekins holding soufflés glacés make a frozen dessert that has the traditional 'raised' appearance of a hot soufflé

85

10
GELATINE
Setting without strings

Gelatine is not a fashionable ingredient. The statuesque jellies and creams, the towering 'pièces montées' held together with gelatine that were so admired in the 19th century, are the antithesis of the new cooking in which simplicity, albeit a deceptive simplicity, is the *leitmotif*. But, whether or not they follow fashion, modern cooks cannot do without gelatine; with it would disappear far too many moulded desserts and, perish the thought for the dedicated caterer, there would be no aspic.

Aspic, the original airtight container, is used to coat poultry but can make a dressy ham or glistening fish as well. It is the savoury jelly that is used to coat meats and fish; it is also an essential of moulded dishes built in layers such as Boeuf à la mode en gelée and may be included in savoury mousses in preference to plain gelatine. Sweet jellies are simply gelatine, sugar and flavouring such as fruit juice or liqueur. Bavarian creams (Bavarois) – along with the many charlottes based on them – would fall flat without gelatine.

As far as the cook is concerned, there are two kinds of gelatine: natural gelatine, which is extracted from bones and skin during cooking, and commerical gelatine. The more natural gelatine that can be used in a dish, the better – it is commercial gelatine that is frowned on as 'artificial'. However, few savoury aspics can be relied upon to stay set in the heat of the average dining-room without the addition of some commercial gelatine, and without it many moulded desserts could not exist.

Natural gelatine is found chiefly in the knuckle bones of young calves. Pigs' feet also yield a good deal of gelatine, as do fish and chicken carcasses, but the content in beef and lamb bones is relatively low, so they are of little use. To extract natural gelatine, long, slow cooking is needed – up to 8 hours for veal bones – and this is usually done as part of the process of making stock. After straining, the stock is boiled down to reduce the gelatine to the right concentration for aspic. Aspic has, of course, the flavour of the bones from which it was extracted. Veal, with a neutral flavour, can be used with most meats and poultry; chicken aspic is usually reserved for chicken and fish for fish.

Commercial gelatine comes as a powder or, less commonly now, in sheets. Powdered gelatine should be sprinkled over a small quantity of liquid and left for a few minutes without stirring until it swells to a spongy consistency. This can then be melted and added to a warmish mixture, or it can be added directly to a mixture hot enough to melt it.

Leaf gelatine, generally used in France, should be soaked in cold water for two or three minutes until soft, then drained, squeezed of all water and melted or added to a warm mixture in the same manner as powdered gelatine. There is really nothing to choose between the two kinds: both are tasteless (almost) and equally easy to use. With either, be sure to stir so the gelatine is thoroughly incorporated and does not form strings or granules. There was a nasty occasion at La Varenne when an inexperienced student, trying to cut corners, added gelatine to a mixture that was too cool. All appeared to be well until lunchtime, when the chef extracted, one by one, the strings from his portion of mousse.

The trickiest part about aspics and moulded desserts is knowing how much commercial gelatine to add, for this can vary according to the heat of the day, the quantity of natural gelatine already present and how long the dish will be left to stand before serving (gelatine tends to stiffen in the refrigerator). We've all chewed on rubbery jellies, sweet or savoury, that would bounce if dropped and it is a great temptation to cut gelatine to a minimum. But even more disastrous are jellies that will not set. The legendary Chef Carême, writing during the First Empire, recorded his chagrin when a skimpy amount of gelatine failed to maintain the stability of his charlottes and they collapsed in ignominious heaps.

Better, then, to be safe rather than sorry. If after trying a recipe you think it has too much gelatine, reduce the quantity only a little next time. As a general rule, 30g (1oz) gelatine will set 1 litre (1¾pts) of liquid to a good consistency, but less gelatine will be needed for light mousse mixtures. To test a savoury aspic that

CHARLOTTE AUX FRAMBOISES

A shell of sponge finger biscuits filled with raspberry mousse; when turned out, the dessert is decorated with whipped cream and raspberries

BOEUF A LA MODE EN GELEE

Well-flavoured aspic jelly holds carefully arranged slices of succulent braised beef, together with rows of green beans, button onions, carrots and 'turned' turnips

already contains natural gelatine, put a little on a plate in the refrigerator. When set, you can judge how much more, if any, gelatine should be added.

Gelatine sets quite suddenly. When working with aspic, put it in a metal bowl set over ice and stir frequently until it appears oily. This shows it is about to set and is ready for use. Spoon it over food or into a mould, working quickly as it will set within one or two minutes. Leftover aspic that has set is melted to use again – most dishes need at least two coatings and moulds are usually filled in stages, layer by layer.

With desserts, too, the gelatine mixture should be stirred fairly constantly over ice as that part of the mixture in direct contact with the chilled bowl will set quickly. As soon as the mixture starts to thicken, fold in any whipped ingredients such as cream or egg whites (they lose volume if added too soon) and spoon the mixture into the mould at once. If a gelatine dessert separates in the mould, the chances are that the cream or egg whites were added too soon, before the mixture had begun to set.

Though always called 'cold', gelatine dishes are best served at room temperature, not chilled. They should be kept in the refrigerator, but be careful of cold air currents; when too cold, aspic and jelly will crystallise and your work will be entirely destroyed. For this reason it is risky to use a freezer for quick chilling when working with gelatine. If a dish does completely crystallise, the only way to save it is to melt it and start again.

Gelatine dishes have an enormous advantage when it comes to serving: all the work is done ahead. Moulds must be assembled at least 3-4 hours in advance so that the gelatine will set firmly before turning out, and 24 hours is perfectly acceptable. Meats coated in aspic are sealed from the air and are, in effect, preserved so their keeping time is greatly extended – one reason aspic dishes are so popular with professional chefs. Nor is much last-minute decoration needed. Desserts demand at most a few rosettes of whipped cream topped with whole strawberries or chocolate rounds, and for savoury dishes a bunch of watercress is more than ample. With their spectacular shapes and multi-coloured layers, gelatine dishes make their own show.

THE WAY TO SUCCESS

Using gelatine

1 For aspics or gelatine desserts which are served from the dish and not turned out, use less gelatine so the texture is less firm.
2 To melt gelatine after softening, put it in a water bath and leave until dissolved, shaking it from time to time. Do not put it over direct heat because gelatine can stick to the sides of the pan and burn.
3 To speed up setting, put the gelatine mixture in a metal bowl set over ice; it must be stirred until it is on the point of setting.
4 When on the point of setting, aspic or fruit jellies have the consistency of oil and creamy mixtures start to thicken. Use them at once.
5 If a mixture sets too soon, melt it for a few seconds in a water bath. However, do not heat desserts for very long. If they contain egg they will curdle, and whipped cream will melt.
6 Gelatine dishes look best served on plain dishes – silver, stainless steel or glass. Patterns detract from the decoration of the mould itself.

Making aspic

1 When making the original stock, be sure it only simmers; boiling will make it cloudy. The stock must be completely free of all fat, otherwise the aspic will not be clear.
2 To test whether more gelatine is needed for making aspic, check the consistency of stock as follows: pour a spoonful of stock on a small plate or saucer. Place the plate over ice or in the refrigerator. After a few minutes, see how well it has set. If still very liquid, add 30g (1oz) gelatine per litre (1¾pts) stock. If very set, do

not add any. If in-between, add 15-20g (½-⅔oz). If not sure, add less gelatine than you think you need, and test again.
3 Seasoning becomes less pronounced as food cools, so when tasting warm aspic, overseason it slightly.
4 Fortified wines and liqueurs, if used, should be added when the aspic is cool but still liquid. They lose their aroma if added to a hot mixture.
5 For moulding or coating, aspic should be at the setting point.

To mould and turn out aspics and sweet jellies

Choosing the mould: the taller the mould, the more spectacular the jelly will look, but the more likely it is to collapse. The more complicated the design of the mould, the more likely the mixture is to stick. Aspics and plain sweet jellies hold up well, but soft, creamy mixtures are best set in simple moulds that are relatively shallow, such as a moule à manqué. In a charlotte, sponge fingers (biscuits à la cuiller) help to retain the filling. Unclarified aspics such as beef à la mode look good set in a deep bowl; a loaf tin gives neat slices and a round mould lends itself to flowerlike designs of meat and vegetables.

Moulding: rinse out the mould with water, leaving it damp. (For aspics, the mould can be lightly oiled.) Chill the mould thoroughly, add a 1cm (⅜in) layer of aspic or jelly and chill until set. Arrange a layer of meat, vegetables, fruit or other recipe ingredients in the mould, add aspic or jelly to almost cover – the ingredients must not float – and chill again until set. Repeat until all the ingredients are used and the mould is full. NOTE: if the aspic or jelly does not set completely between adding each layer, the ingredients will float; however, if the jelly is left too long between each addition, it will set so firmly that the layers will tend to detach from each other when turned out.

Cover the mould with plastic wrap or greaseproof paper and keep in the refrigerator at least 3-4 hours until firmly set. Most moulds can be kept for up to 48 hours before turning out, but their consistency will be firmer, so use less gelatine in a mould that is to be kept for some time.

Turning out: lower the mould into a pan of hand-hot water so the water almost reaches the top. Leave it for 2-3 seconds and lift it out; metal moulds conduct heat better than other materials and should be dipped for a shorter time.

Tip the mould sideways and gently pull the mixture away from the edge with your fingers, repeating all round the mould; this breaks the airlock and helps prevent sticking. Rinse the serving plate with water so that if the jelly does not land in the middle of the plate, you can gently push it into place. Dry the mould with a cloth, set the plate upside down on top and quickly turn over both together. Give a sharp shake sideways and down and the jelly will fall onto the plate.

If the jelly sticks, give several sharp shakes. If it still sticks, put a hot wet cloth on top of the mould for 10-20 seconds – this works best with a metal mould. If the mixture continues to stick, dip the mould in warm water again.

If the jelly does not turn out neatly, don't despair. A little chopped parsley or small pieces of neatly 'turned' freshly cooked vegetables can cover faults in moulded aspics, and whipped cream does wonders for desserts.

Getting ahead

Of necessity, gelatine dishes must be made ahead because the gelatine must have time to set.

1 Meat or poultry aspic can be made up to 3 days ahead and kept covered in the refrigerator. Fish aspic should be used within 12 hours. To prepare the aspic for use, melt it over very low heat. NOTE: if it is heated above 40-45C (105-115F) it will quickly turn sour.

2 Dishes coated or set in aspic and gelatine desserts can be kept in the refrigerator for up to 24 hours. Gelatine tends to stiffen on standing, so slightly reduce the quantities when making up the recipe. Do not allow aspic dishes to become so cold that they crystallise.

3 Aspic dishes and gelatine-moulded desserts cannot be frozen.

SAUMON EN GELEE
(Salmon in aspic)

A large salmon coated with aspic makes a beautiful dish, but you can certainly use the basic idea on a smaller one than called for here or even on a different fish.

SERVES 8-10

3-4kg (6-8lb) whole salmon, cleaned

fish stock (page 218) made with 1½kg (3lb) fish bones, 2 onions, 15 peppercorns, small bunch of parsley, 600ml (1pt) dry white wine, 900ml (1½pt) water and salt

aspic (page 53) made with 1 litre (1¾pts) stock from cooking the fish, 15g (½oz) gelatine (optional), 100ml (4oz) dry sherry, 2 carrots, tops of 2 leeks, 2 stalks celery, 2 tomatoes and 2 egg whites

for serving

green mayonnaise (see Pâté de poisson la marée, page 152) made with 300ml (½pt) mayonnaise, 6-8 spinach leaves, 10g (⅓oz) watercress leaves, 10g (⅓oz) parsley sprigs, 2 tablespoons tarragon or chervil leaves, salt and pepper

for the garnish

2 cucumbers

salt and pepper

10-12 even-sized tomatoes

750g (1½lb) large, cooked and peeled prawns

fish poacher (kettle)

One to two days ahead, poach the salmon: make the fish stock and allow it to cool. Trim the tail of the fish to a 'V' and set it on the rack of a fish kettle. Tie it in place with string, put the rack in the kettle and pour over the cooled stock. Cover and bring slowly to the boil, allowing about 20 minutes. Simmer for 15-25 minutes, depending on the size of the fish. Allow it to cool to tepid in the stock. Take it out, peel off the skin and remove the fins, leaving the head attached. Scoop out the small bones along the spine and transfer the fish to a large serving dish or tray. Cover and chill thoroughly, preferably overnight. Boil the fish stock until reduced to about 1 litre (1¾pts) and chill. The next day, make the aspic.

For the garnish: peel a cucumber lengthwise, leaving strips of peel so it is striped. Cut the cucumber into very thin slices, sprinkle with salt and leave them to drain. Peel, seed and dice the remaining cucumber, sprinkle it also with salt and leave to drain. To make tomato baskets: cut almost a quarter of a tomato away, turn the tomato stem end down and, cutting down, remove nearly a whole quarter section. Remove another quarter section, leaving a strip in the middle wide enough to form the handle of a tomato basket. Cut away the flesh from under the handle and scoop the seeds from the bottom half, leaving a basket shape. Repeat with the rest of the tomatoes to make 10-12 tomato baskets. Fill them with the diced cucumber.

Put some of the aspic in a metal bowl and cool it in a bowl of ice until it is on the point of setting. Spoon it over the salmon at once and chill until set. Arrange the cucumber slices overlapping like scales on the salmon. Arrange the shrimps overlapping on one side of the serving dish and set the tomato baskets down the other; chill again. Cool more aspic until on the point of setting and coat the salmon and the garnish. Chill, repeat the coating if necessary and chill thoroughly.

Pour the remaining aspic into a dampened tray to form a 1cm (⅜in) layer and chill until set. Run a knife around the edge of the aspic and turn it out on a damp sheet of greaseproof paper. Cut out triangles or crescents and arrange them on the edge of the dish. The salmon can be prepared up to 24 hours ahead and kept in the refrigerator. NOTE: do not allow it to freeze or the aspic will crystallise.

Serve with Green mayonnaise.

TRUITES AU VIN BLANC EN GELEE

(Poached trout in white wine aspic)

This dish comes from Alsace, where the Riesling used for poaching the trout gives the aspic a special flavour. A touch of colour can be added by garnishing the dish with cooked prawns or crayfish.

SERVES 4

4 trout each weighing 350-450g ($\frac{3}{4}$-1lb), heads left on

fish stock (page 218) made with 700g (1$\frac{1}{2}$lb) fish bones, medium onion, sliced, 10 peppercorns, several sprigs of parsley, 600ml (1pt) Riesling and 600ml (1pt) water

about 1-1$\frac{1}{2}$ envelopes (the equivalent of 15-20g or $\frac{1}{2}$-$\frac{2}{3}$oz) gelatine (optional – see method)

3-4 tablespoons chopped parsley (optional)

salt and pepper

a few drops lemon juice

for garnish

3 lemons

Make the fish stock. NOTE: the stock must be simmered very gently so it is clear, not cloudy. Set the oven at moderate, 180C (350F) gas 4.

Wash the trout and, if possible, clean them through the gills so there are no slits in the stomachs. Leave the heads and trim the tail to a 'V' shape. Lay them in a baking dish, pour over the stock, cover and poach in the heated oven for 20-25 minutes, or until the flesh is firm and no longer transparent. Allow to cool to tepid in the cooking liquid, then drain the fish on paper towels and skin them, discarding the fins and small bones along the back, but leaving on the head and tail.

Arrange the trout close together in a deep dish and cut one lemon into thin slices. Overlap 2-3 slices of lemon along the back of each fish. Strain a spoonful or two of the cooking liquid onto a saucer and put it into the refrigerator. If it sets well, there is no need to add gelatine. If it does not set enough, add the gelatine: first sprinkle the gelatine over 150ml ($\frac{1}{4}$pt) of cool stock in a small bowl and leave for 5 minutes or until spongy. Reheat the rest of the stock and add the gelatine, mixing well to melt it. If using parsley, reheat the liquid to hot, then add the parsley. NOTE: this

makes it bright green. Add salt, pepper and lemon juice to taste – the liquid should be highly seasoned – and pour it over the trout. They should be completely covered. Cover the dish and leave for at least 2 hours or until set.

The trout can be prepared 24 hours ahead and kept covered in the refrigerator.

To finish: halve the 2 whole lemons and cut a slice from the base of each half so that they sit firmly. Or make knotted lemons by peeling a thin strip from around the top of each half and, before it is completely detached, knotting the strip so that the knot sits on the side of the lemon. Arrange these around the trout before serving.

MOUSSE D'AVOCATS

(Avocado mousse)

For an even richer starter or a light main course, serve a seafood salad in the centre of the dish.

SERVES 6

$\frac{1}{2}$ envelope gelatine (the equivalent of 7g or $\frac{1}{2}$oz)

4 ripe avocados

juice of $\frac{1}{2}$ lemon

mayonnaise (page 179) made with 1 egg yolk, salt and white pepper, mustard, about 150ml ($\frac{1}{4}$pt) oil and 2 teaspoons white wine vinegar

$\frac{1}{2}$ clove garlic, finely chopped

salt and pepper

pinch of Cayenne pepper

3 tablespoons double cream, lightly whipped

bunch of watercress (for garnish)

1.25 litre (2pt) capacity ring mould

Lightly oil the ring mould. Sprinkle the gelatine over 4 tablespoons cold water and allow to stand for 5 minutes or until spongy. Halve the avocados, discarding the stones, peel them and crush the flesh with a silver fork. (Aluminium discolours the pulp.) At once stir in the lemon juice to prevent them discolouring.

Melt the gelatine mixture over low heat and stir into the avocado pulp, followed by the mayonnaise, garlic, salt, pepper and Cayenne pepper. When the avocado mixture is cool, fold in the lightly whipped cream and taste for seasoning – it should be highly seasoned to counteract the avocados' blandness. Pour the mixture into the prepared mould, cover it tightly with plastic wrap and chill for at least 2 hours or

until set. NOTE: if the mould is not tightly sealed, the mousse will discolour. It can be made 12 hours ahead and kept in the refrigerator.

For an alternative way of serving, save the halved avocado skins and pipe the partly set mousse into them, using a piping bag and medium star tube.

Not more than 30 minutes before serving, run a knife around the edge of the mousse and turn it out onto a round serving dish, or arrange the avocado halves on a dish, if serving them the alternative way.

OEUFS EN GELEE

(Eggs in aspic)

The eggs can be poached or soft-boiled; they must be small so they fit into the moulds easily.

SERVES 6

aspic (page 53) made with 1 litre (1$\frac{3}{4}$pt) well-flavoured veal or beef stock, salt and pepper, 15-30g ($\frac{1}{2}$-1oz) gelatine, 2 carrots, green tops of 2 leeks, 2 sticks celery, 2 tomatoes, 50ml (2fl oz) Madeira or sherry, 2 egg whites and 200g (7oz) lean, chopped beef

6 small eggs

3 slices cooked ham

small can truffles; or 3 black olives; or few leaves of fresh tarragon or chervil (for decoration)

bunch of watercress (for garnish)

6 small oval moulds or ramekins

Chill the moulds in the refrigerator. Make the aspic (if using canned truffles, add the truffle liquid to the stock before clarifying). Poach or soft-boil the eggs and keep them in cold water. Cut 6 ovals of ham to fit the bases of the moulds.

For decoration: cut 6 slices of truffle or stone the olives and halve them lengthwise. If using tarragon or chervil, pick a dozen good leaves or sprigs, pour boiling water over them, leave them for 1 minute, then drain them on paper towels.

Pour enough aspic into each mould to make a 5mm ($\frac{1}{4}$in) layer. Stand the moulds in a roasting pan containing ice and water or place them in the refrigerator and leave until the aspic is set. Put a slice of truffle or a piece of olive cut side up, or two leaves of tarragon or chervil in the centre of each mould. Carefully spoon in just enough aspic to cover the decoration and chill to set.

Drain the eggs. If using soft-boiled eggs, peel them and dry them gently on paper towels. Set a piece of ham in the base of each mould and put an egg on top. Fill them two-thirds full of aspic and chill to set. Finally, fill the moulds to the brim with aspic, transfer them to the refrigerator and chill for 1-2 hours or until firmly set. The eggs can be prepared up to 24 hours ahead and kept, tightly covered, in the refrigerator.

Not more than 2 hours before serving, turn out the eggs: have ready a bowl of hand-hot water and the serving dish. Grasp a mould firmly by the top with the palm of your hand and immerse it in the hot water for 1-2 seconds. Still holding the mould, turn it over so your palm is underneath. Knock the mould sharply with the fingers of the other hand until the contents drop onto your palm. Leave the mould on the egg, slide the egg onto the serving dish and lift off the mould. Turn out the remaining eggs in the same way. Arrange them in a circle and set a bunch of watercress in the centre. The eggs can also be served on individual plates and each garnished with a sprig of watercress.

BOEUF A LA MODE EN GELEE
(Beef à la mode in aspic)

Many restaurants serve beef à la mode hot one day, then layer the beef and vegetables in a terrine to be turned out and served cold the next day. Either way, it is one of the mainstays of French bourgeois cooking.

SERVES 6-8

2kg (about 4lb) round roast of beef, larded and barded
calf's or pig's foot, split
250g (½lb) piece lean bacon, diced
600ml (1pt) white veal stock
salt and pepper
½ envelope (the equivalent of 7g or ¼oz) gelatine
4 tablespoons sherry or Madeira (optional)
for the marinade
3 medium onions, quartered
3 medium carrots, quartered
2 stalks celery, cut in 5cm (2in) sticks
clove garlic, peeled; large bouquet garni; 6 peppercorns and 3 cloves, tied together in cheesecloth or muslin
600ml (1pt) red wine
tablespoon oil

for garnish
1kg (2lb) small or medium carrots
1kg (2lb) button onions
a little sugar (for sprinkling)
1kg (2lb) turnips
700g (1½lb) green beans, trimmed and cut in 5cm (2in) lengths

2 litre (3½pt) capacity rectangular terrine mould or large oval casserole

Marinate the beef 3-4 days ahead. Put the piece of beef in a small deep bowl (not aluminium), add the onions, carrots, celery, the seasonings in cheesecloth or muslin and pour on the wine. Pour the oil on top. Cover and leave in the refrigerator for 12-24 hours, turning the meat from time to time.

Braise the beef 2-3 days ahead: first blanch the calf's or pig's foot by putting it in cold water, bringing to the boil, simmering for 5 minutes and draining. Blanch the bacon in the same way. Set the oven at moderately low, 170C (325F) gas 3. Drain the beef and pat dry with paper towels. Strain the marinade; reserve it and the vegetables and flavourings.

Fry the bacon in a casserole until browned, adding a little oil if necessary. Lift out with a draining spoon, add the beef and brown it on all sides. Remove the beef, add the onions, carrots and celery from the marinade and cook gently until beginning to brown. Replace the beef and bacon, add the reserved marinade, seasonings in cheesecloth or muslin, the stock and a little salt. Tuck the bones and calf's or pig's foot down beside the meat, cover the pan and bring to the boil. Braise in the heated oven, regulat-

For Boeuf à la mode en gelée: assemble the dish by arranging beef slices with some of the vegetables on a thin layer of set aspic jelly, then add most of the rest of the vegetables and enough of the cool aspic to fill the mould

ing the heat so that the liquid barely simmers, for 2½-3 hours or until the meat is very tender when pierced with a skewer. Let it cool to tepid, then drain it and chill for 5-6 hours or overnight. Strain the cooking liquid, pressing the vegetables well to extract the flavours, and chill.

To make the aspic: skim all fat from the stock; it should be firmly set but, if not, sprinkle the gelatine over 4 tablespoons water, allow to stand until spongy then melt it over a pan of hot water. Melt the stock, measure it and reduce it if necessary to 1 litre (1¾pts). Some of the liquid may be reserved for cooking the vegetables. Skim off any remaining fat with paper towels and add the soaked gelatine. Add sherry or Madeira if desired, then taste – it should be very well seasoned. If you like, add the gelatine and meat from the calf's or pig's foot, finely chopped, to the stock and allow it to cool. The aspic should be a rich golden brown. The beef and aspic can be prepared up to 48 hours ahead and kept covered in the refrigerator.

The garnish can be cooked up to 24 hours before serving: peel the carrots and 'turn' to shape them in 5cm (2in) ovals. Cook them in boiling salted water for 15-20 minutes or until tender and drain them. Blanch the onions in boiling water for 1 minute, drain and peel them. Cook the onions in boiling salted water for 12-15 minutes or until tender, drain and sprinkle with a little sugar. Peel the turnips and 'turn' to shape them into ovals, the same size as the carrots. Cook the turnips in boiling salted water for 3-5 minutes or until tender, drain and refresh with cold water. Cook the beans in boiling salted water for 8-10 minutes or until just tender, drain, rinse with cold water, and drain again. NOTE: be sure the vegetables are well cooked because if they are undercooked they will be hard when cool. If preferred, all the vegetables except the green beans can be cooked in some strained cooking liquid from the beef. Chill all the vegetables.

To assemble the dish: discard the outer fat and string from the meat and carve it in 1.25cm (½in) slices. Put the slices on a wire rack and chill.

Spoon a thin layer of aspic in the terrine or large oval casserole and chill until set. Arrange the slices of meat, overlapping on top of the aspic, down the centre of the terrine. On each side of the beef slices arrange lengthwise rows of green beans, baby onions, carrots and turnips, using half the vegetables. Spoon over enough aspic to cover the vegetables and to nearly cover the meat. Arrange another layer of vegetable rows on each side of the meat. Reserve the remaining vegetables. Spoon on enough aspic to cover the meat and vegetables and fill the terrine, and chill.

The mould can be assembled up to 24 hours ahead and kept tightly covered with plastic wrap, in the refrigerator. NOTE: do not allow the aspic to freeze, or it will crystallise.

Just before serving: turn out the beef onto a serving dish and surround with 'bouquets' of the remaining chilled vegetables.

MOUSSE DE JAMBON
(Ham mousse)

It is important to use a well-flavoured country-cured ham.

SERVES 8

| 1 litre (1¾pts) jellied beef stock |
| 15g (½oz) gelatine (optional) |
| 100ml (⅙pt) Madeira or sherry |
| 400g (14oz) cooked, lean smoked ham |
| velouté sauce (page 190) made with 30g (1oz) butter, 30g (1oz) flour, 350ml (⅗pt) veal or chicken stock, salt, pepper and squeeze of lemon juice |
| salt and freshly ground black pepper |
| 350ml (⅗pt) double cream, lightly whipped |
| *for decoration* |
| small can truffles with their liquid, or 2 hard-boiled eggs, or ½ cucumber |
| hot toast (for serving) |
| *1½ litre (2½pt) capacity soufflé dish* |

Tie a collar of greaseproof paper or foil around the soufflé dish to extend 5-7cm (2-3in) above the rim.

If the beef stock is not firmly jellied, soften the gelatine in 100ml (⅙pt) water and then melt it over a pan of hot water. Melt the stock and add the gelatine and half the Madeira or sherry with the truffle liquid, if using truffles. Allow it to cool. Cut even slices from the truffles or hard-boiled eggs and chop the rest. If using cucumber, peel it lengthwise, leaving strips of

peel so that it is striped. Cut it into thin slices.

Work the ham twice through the fine blade of a mincer and then pound in a mortar with a pestle, gradually working in the velouté sauce. Finally, work the mixture through a drum sieve. Alternatively, work the ham and sauce in a blender or electric food mill. Stir in half the aspic with the remaining Madeira or sherry, chopped truffle or egg, and salt and pepper to taste. NOTE: the ham is salty, so that extra salt may not be necessary.

Place the mousse in a bowl over a pan of iced water, stirring it occasionally until it starts to thicken. Fold in the whipped cream and pour it into the soufflé dish. Chill the mousse for 1-2 hours, or until it is firmly set.

To decorate: spoon over a layer of cool but still liquid aspic and chill. Pour a little aspic over the truffle or cucumber slices and arrange them overlapping round the edge of the mousse. The aspic should make them stick.

If using hard-boiled eggs for decoration, arrange the slices on top without first soaking them in aspic. Chill the mousse until the decoration is firm, spoon a thin layer of aspic over the top and chill again until set. Pour over the remaining aspic and chill for 2-3 hours, or until firm. The mousse can be made 24 hours ahead and kept in the refrigerator.

To finish: peel 'the paper collar from the mousse, detaching it carefully with the blade of a knife dipped in boiling water. Serve the mousse with hot toast.

Chicken mousse
To use the recipe to make a chicken mousse, substitute 250g (8oz) cooked chicken breasts for the ham and use chicken rather than beef stock for the aspic.

GALANTINE DE POULET
(Chicken galantine)

Strips of cooked ham and tongue and pieces of chicken liver form a pattern in the centre of each slice of galantine. Together with aspic made from the cooking liquid, they form the decoration for the dish. It should be cooked at least one day ahead.

SERVES 8-10

| 2-2½kg (4-5lb) chicken |
| 75ml (3fl oz) sherry or Madeira |
| salt and freshly ground black pepper |
| 5mm (¼in) slice cooked ham, weighing about 150g or 5oz, cut in strips |
| 5mm (¼in) slice cooked tongue, weighing about 150g or 5oz, cut in strips |
| 150g (5oz) chicken livers, including the liver from the bird |
| calf's or pig's foot, split |
| 1 litre (1¾pts) veal or chicken stock |
| aspic (page 53) made with the above litre (1¾pts) stock in which the chicken is cooked, 15-30g (½-1oz) gelatine (optional), 2 carrots, tops of 2 leeks, 2 sticks celery, 2 tomatoes, 50ml (2fl oz) Madeira or sherry, 2 egg whites and 250g (8oz) chopped lean beef |
| *for the stuffing* |
| 250g (8oz) minced pork |
| 250g (8oz) minced veal |
| 60g (2oz) pistachios (optional) |
| onion, chopped |
| 30g (1oz) butter |
| level teaspoon ground allspice |
| clove garlic, crushed |
| 150ml (¼pt) white wine |
| egg, beaten to mix |
| salt and freshly ground black pepper |
| *trussing needle and string* |

Bone the chicken completely and save the bones. Carefully remove the flesh from the skin, keeping the skin in one piece. Cut the breast meat into strips. Moisten them with 25ml (1oz) of the sherry or Madeira, sprinkle with salt and pepper, mix well and leave to marinate.

To make the stuffing: work the remaining chicken meat, the pork and the veal through the fine blade of a mincer. If using pistachios, blanch them in boiling water for 1 minute, then drain and peel them. Cook the onion in the butter until soft but not brown and add to the meat mixture with the pistachios if included, allspice, garlic, white wine, egg and the sherry or Madeira drained from the chicken pieces. Add plenty of salt and pepper – the mixture should be highly seasoned – and mix with the hand until the stuffing holds together.

Weigh the stuffing and then weigh the strips of chicken, ham and tongue, adding or subtracting strips until their weight equals that of the stuffing.

Spread the chicken skin, cut side up, on a board and fold the leg and the wing skin to close the openings. Spread a third of the stuffing mixture in a rectangle about 8cm (3in) wide, leaving a border of 4cm (1½in) of skin at each end and 8-10cm (3-4in) on each side. Arrange half of the strips of ham, tongue and chicken breast lengthwise down the stuffing and set the chicken livers on top. Build up more stuffing around the livers and then top them with the remaining strips of meat so that they are surrounded. Top with the remaining stuffing, shaping it to form a neat cylinder, and wrap the chicken skin around it. Sew the skin with a trussing needle and string and wrap it tightly in a scalded dish cloth. Tie both ends with string to keep the ballotine in shape and fasten the centre with a large safety pin. NOTE: any creases in the cloth will make wrinkles on the galantine.

To cook the galantine: blanch the calf's or pig's foot by putting it in cold water, bringing the water to the boil, simmering for 5 minutes and draining. Put the galantine in a large saucepan with the chicken bones, calf's or pig's foot, the remaining 50ml (2oz) sherry or Madeira, and enough stock to cover. Cover and bring slowly to the boil. Simmer for 1½-2 hours or until a skewer inserted in the centre of the galantine for ½ minute is hot to the touch when withdrawn. Leave it to cool to tepid in the liquid, then drain it. Rewrap it in the cloth as tightly as possible, put it on a deep serving dish, top with a board and a 1kg (2lb) weight and chill for 5-6 hours or overnight. Strain the cooking stock and chill it also.

Make the aspic by clarifying the chilled stock and adding gelatine if necessary.

To finish the galantine: unwrap it, carefully remove the trussing string and cut half to three quarters of the roll in 1cm (⅜in) slices. Put the slices on a wire rack and chill them along with the remaining roll. Spoon a layer of aspic on a serving dish and chill it until set. Cool some aspic in a bowl and coat the galantine slices, rolling them round 2-3 times; chill them thoroughly. Pour most of the remaining aspic into a tray to form a 1cm (⅜in) layer and chill until set.

To assemble the dish: put the uncut galantine at one end of the serving dish of set aspic and arrange the slices overlapping down the centre. Coat once more with aspic and chill thoroughly. Turn out the tray of aspic onto a sheet of wet greaseproof paper, cut out triangles or crescents and arrange them around the edge of the dish. Chop the remaining aspic and pile it around the sliced galantine.

The galantine can be prepared and decorated up to 24 hours ahead and kept in the refrigerator. NOTE: do not allow the aspic to freeze or it will crystallise.

POIRES ISABELLA
(Pears Isabella)

This recipe comes from the original 'Household Management' published by Isabella Beeton in 1861.

SERVES 6

| 4 large or 6 small firm pears, peeled, cored and halved |
| 1 litre (1¾pts) water |
| 200g (6½oz) sugar, or to taste |
| 8 cloves |
| 5cm (2in) cinnamon stick |
| 2 envelopes – 30g (1oz) gelatine |
| strip of lemon peel |
| juice of ½ lemon |
| 150ml (¼pt) Port |

2 litre or 3½pt capacity moule à manqué, springform mould or large sandwich tin

Set the oven at low, 150C (300F) gas 2. Put the pears with the water, sugar (the exact amount depends on the sweetness of the fruit), cloves and cinnamon into a casserole or heatproof dish and cover tightly. Bake in the heated oven for 1-1¼ hours or until the pears are very tender but not mushy. The length of the cooking time depends very much on their ripeness. Allow them to cool, then drain and measure 1 litre (1¾pts) juice, adding more water if necessary.

Wet the mould and arrange the halves of pear, rounded side down, in the bottom. Chill 150ml (¼pt) of the reserved pear juice in a bowl, sprinkle over the gelatine and allow to stand for 5 minutes until spongy. Put the remaining juice into a pan, add the lemon peel, lemon juice and Port and simmer for 5 minutes. Strain the hot liquid into the gelatine and stir until dissolved. Allow to cool to tepid and spoon some of the mixture over the pears to form a layer that almost covers

them. Chill until set, spoon over the remaining liquid and chill for 2 hours or until firmly set. The mould can be made 24 hours ahead and kept tightly covered in the refrigerator. Allow to stand at room temperature for 1-2 hours before turning out and serving.

BISCUITS A LA CUILLER
(Sponge fingers)

Besides being used to line charlotte moulds, fresh sponge finger biscuits are good served with coffee or with ice-cream.

Makes about 30

| 100g (3½oz) flour |
| tiny pinch of salt |
| 4 eggs, separated |
| 100g (3½oz) sugar |
| ½ teaspoon vanilla essence |
| icing sugar (for sprinkling) |

pastry bag; large plain tube

Set the oven at low, 150C (300F) gas 2. Cover a baking sheet with greaseproof paper, or grease it and coat it lightly with flour.

Sift the flour and salt together twice. Beat the egg yolks with half the sugar and the vanilla until light and thick enough to leave a ribbon trail. Whip the egg whites until stiff, preferably in a copper bowl, add the remaining sugar and beat for a further 20 seconds or until glossy. Place the sifted flour over the yolks. Add about a quarter of the egg whites to the egg yolk mixture and fold together with the flour as lightly as possible. Gently fold in the remaining egg whites in two batches. NOTE: the mixture must be folded as quickly as possible – but with great care – as it must remain stiff enough to pipe.

Spoon the mixture gently into a pastry bag fitted with a large plain tube and pipe fingers about 9cm (3½in) long and 2.5cm (1in) apart on the prepared baking sheet. Immediately sprinkle the tops with icing sugar, gently shake or blow off any excess sugar and bake in the heated oven, with the door held slightly open with a spoon, for 15-18 minutes. These sponge finger biscuits should scarcely be browned, but should be firm on the outside and still soft in the centre. Allow them to cool slightly; then transfer them to a wire rack to cool completely.

To pipe biscuits à la cuiller: hold the pastry bag in one hand, support it with the other and pipe 9cm (3½in) strips on the baking sheet, keeping them apart

To line a charlotte mould: after lining the sides of the mould with the biscuits à la cuiller, cover the base with triangular pieces cut off from the rest

CHARLOTTE AUX FRAISES OU AUX FRAMBOISES

(Strawberry or raspberry charlotte)

Charlottes are thought to be named after Queen Charlotte, the wife of George III. They can be filled with Bavarian cream, fruit purée, or even ice-cream, as well as a mousse mixture like this one. If you do not have time to make your own sponge fingers (see the recipe left), try to find ready-prepared ones that are not too dry.

SERVES 6-8

20-22 sponge fingers
250g (8oz) fresh strawberries, hulled, or raspberries
½ envelope (the equivalent of 7g or ¼oz) gelatine
juice of ½ lemon
3 eggs
2 egg yolks
180g (6oz) sugar
300ml (½pt) double cream, lightly whipped
tablespoon Kirsch
for decoration
Chantilly cream made with 150ml (¼pt) double cream, tablespoon sugar and teaspoon vanilla essence
few whole strawberries or raspberries
2 litre or 3½pt capacity charlotte mould; pastry bag and medium star tube

Line the sides and bottom of the mould with sponge fingers, trimming the sides so they fit tightly. Work the fruit through a sieve, or purée in a blender and then work through a sieve. Sprinkle the gelatine over the lemon juice in a small pan and allow to stand for 5 minutes or until spongy.

Put the eggs, egg yolks and sugar in a bowl, a copper bowl if possible, and beat until mixed. Set the bowl over a pan of hot but not boiling water and beat until the mixture is thick and light and leaves a ribbon trail when the beater is lifted. Take from the heat.

Melt the softened gelatine over low heat, beat into the hot egg mixture and continue beating until cool. Stir in the fruit purée, set the bowl over ice and chill, stirring occasionally, until the mixture starts to set. At once fold in the lightly whipped cream with the Kirsch and pour into the charlotte mould. NOTE: if the mixture is not on the point of setting, it will soak into the sponge fingers. Cover and chill for at least 2 hours or until firm.

The charlotte can be made up to 48 hours ahead and kept in the refrigerator. However, gelatine tends to stiffen on chilling, and the charlotte should stand at room temperature for an hour or two before serving.

One or two hours before serving, turn out the charlotte: trim the sponge fingers level with the top of the mould, set a plate on top and carefully turn both upside down so the charlotte falls out onto the plate. Decorate the base and sides of the charlotte with Chantilly cream, using a pastry bag and medium star tube, and top it with a border of rosettes. Set fresh whole strawberries or raspberries on the rosettes. Keep in a cool place, or the refrigerator, until serving.

BAVAROIS RUBANE

(Ribboned Bavarian cream)

The secret of making this spectacular dessert is to be organised: once the three custard flavours, the whipped cream, bowl of iced water and mould are ready, assembling it is easy.

SERVES 8-10

1¾ envelopes (about 25g or ⅝oz) gelatine
60g (2oz) dark dessert chocolate, chopped
level tablespoon dry instant coffee dissolved in 2 tablespoons warm water
375ml (⅝pt) double cream, whipped until it holds its shape
vanilla custard sauce (page 81) made with 1.5 litres (2½pts) milk, vanilla pod, 12 egg yolks and 200g (6½oz) sugar
for decoration
Chantilly cream (optional) made with 150ml (¼pt) double cream
tablespoon sugar and ½ teaspoon vanilla essence
coffee dragées or chocolate caraque (optional)
2.5 litre (4pt) capacity tall mould; pastry bag and medium star tube

Rinse the mould with cold water. Sprinkle the gelatine over 150ml (¼pt) water in a small bowl and leave 5 minutes or until spongy. Set the chocolate on a plate over a pan of hot water and leave until melted. Set aside until cool but still soft. Make the vanilla custard sauce. NOTE: do not overcook or allow it to boil or it will curdle. Take the custard from the heat at once and strain it into a bowl. Melt the gelatine in the bowl over a pan of hot water, add the melted gelatine to the hot custard and stir well. Divide the custard into thirds and put each third in a separate bowl.

Stir the dissolved coffee into one bowl of custard and the melted, cooled chocolate into another; leave the remaining bowl of custard simply flavoured with vanilla. Leave the custards until cool, then set the coffee custard in a bowl of iced water and stir until it starts to thicken. Fold in one third of the lightly whipped cream and pour the custard into the prepared mould. Put it in the refrigerator until firm.

Stir the vanilla custard also until on the point of setting, fold in half the remaining whipped cream and pour gently into the mould. NOTE: the coffee custard must be quite firmly set or it will mix with the vanilla when it is added; if it is very hard, however, the layer of vanilla will slide off when the dessert is turned out. Put in the refrigerator again until firm.

Lastly, set the bowl containing the chocolate custard over ice and stir. When on the point of setting, fold in the remaining cream and pour into the mould. Cover tightly and chill for at least 2 hours or until it is firmly set. The cream can be made up to 24 hours ahead, but it tends to stiffen and must be removed from the refrigerator 15-20 minutes before serving to soften.

Not more than 2 hours before serving, turn out the dessert: run a knife around the edge, pull the Bavarian cream away from the mould with a finger to release the airlock, set a serving dish upside down on the top and turn over mould and serving dish together.

If you like, decorate the base of the dessert with rosettes of Chantilly cream, using a pastry bag and star tube, and decorate the rosettes with coffee dragées or chocolate caraque.

CHARLOTTE AUX FRUITS
(Fruit charlotte)

If no fresh mint leaves are available, use dried mint to flavour the Bavarian cream.

SERVES 8
génoise (page 100) made with 125g (4oz) flour, pinch salt, 60g (2oz) butter, 4 eggs and 125g (4oz) sugar
peach
pear
4 Chinese gooseberries, peeled and sliced
a little icing sugar (for sprinkling)
125g (4oz) strawberries, hulled and halved lengthwise
250g (8oz) raspberries
icing sugar (see method)
for the sugar syrup
100g (3½oz) sugar
600ml (1pt) water
for the Bavarian cream
12g (½oz) gelatine
custard sauce (page 81) made with 600ml (1pt) milk, 3 mint leaves, 8 egg yolks and 150g (5oz) sugar
375ml (scant ¾pt) double cream, lightly whipped
23cm (9in) diameter cake tin; 8 individual soufflé dishes

Make the génoise and pour the mixture into the prepared tin. Bake in a moderate oven, 180C (350F) gas 4, for 25-30 minutes or until the cake shrinks slightly from the sides of the tin and the top springs back when lightly pressed with a fingertip. Run a knife around the edge of the cake and turn it out onto a rack to cool.

Make the sugar syrup by heating the sugar and water together until the sugar is dissolved, then bringing the mixture to the boil. Peel, halve and core the peach and pear and poach them in the syrup until tender. Remove the fruit, chop it into 1cm (⅜in) cubes and drain on paper towels. Reduce the syrup to 250ml (scant ½pt) and set aside to cool.

Cut the cake in half horizontally and then cut 8 rounds to exactly fit the soufflé dishes. Brush each round of cake with the reduced syrup. Butter the dishes, sprinkle them with icing sugar and arrange a few slices of Chinese gooseberry in the bottom of each one.

To make the Bavarian cream: sprinkle the gelatine over 75ml (⅛pt) water to soften it. Make the custard sauce. NOTE: do not overcook or boil or it will curdle. Take the custard from the heat and strain it into a bowl. Melt the gelatine in a small pan or bowl set in a water bath. Add the melted gelatine to the hot custard and stir well. Put the bowl into a larger bowl filled with ice and cool, stirring constantly, until the mixture just begins to thicken. Remove from the ice and fold in the lightly whipped cream.

Just cover the slices of fruit in the bottom of each dish with the Bavarian cream. Top with the peach and pear cubes, then divide the remaining Bavarian cream among the dishes. Slide the strawberry halves in around the edges, flat sides outward, and finish each dessert with a circle of cake, syrup side down. Refrigerate for at least 2 – and up to 24 – hours.

To finish: purée the raspberries by pushing them through a drum sieve or by working them in an electric food processor, then sieving to remove the seeds. Sweeten the purée with icing sugar if necessary. Turn out each charlotte by running a knife around the edge, dipping the bottom briefly in warm water and turning it out onto an individual serving plate. Encircle each charlotte with a ring of raspberry purée.

11

GENOISE AND 'BISCUIT'
Sponge with a light touch

Génoise bears the same relation to pastry as brown
sauce to savoury dishes – it is the cornerstone of
innumerable classic recipes. Hundreds of gâteaux are
built up from a foundation of génoise sponge (or its
cousin, 'biscuit') elaborated with butter cream, pastry
cream, whipped cream, fondant icing, Italian meringue and various flavourings. There are time-honoured
combinations such as gâteau moka, made of génoise
that is sandwiched and coated with coffee butter cream
and bordered with browned almonds, or gâteau fraisier
filled with whole strawberries and Kirsch-flavoured
butter cream and topped with pink marzipan. At La
Varenne, when the chefs want to keep the students
quiet, they assign them gâteau opéra, a stunning
confection of almond génoise cake, coffee syrup,
coffee butter cream and chocolate cream filling, all
coated with a thick layer of chocolate and decorated
with royal icing. It takes at least three hours' work
from start to finish. Happily no-one, not even a master
pâtissier, is expected to have every possible gâteau at
his fingertips and most chefs keep to a dozen or so
popular favourites.

There is little to choose between génoise and
'biscuit'. Both are made with the same ingredients of
eggs, sugar, flour and butter, in the same proportions.
The only difference is in the method of mixing:
génoise uses whole eggs, whereas for 'biscuit', the
eggs are separated. When baked, 'biscuit' is slightly

GATEAU A LA MOUSSE AU CHOCOLAT
*A cake made of chocolate génoise filled and masked with
chocolate mousse, decorated with chocolate shapes and whipped
cream*

SUISSES
(back)
*Rounds of génoise sponge topped with mounds of butter cream
and glacé cherries, covered with fondant icing*

PRINTANIERS
(centre)
*Thin layers of génoise sponge sandwiched with vanilla butter
cream and decorated with strips of pistachio, vanilla and
strawberry-flavoured butter cream*

NOISETTES
(front)
*Squares of génoise filled with coffee butter cream, each topped
with coffee-flavoured fondant icing*

drier and lighter because of the beaten egg whites, so gâteaux made with it are often soaked with liqueur or served with poached fruit or a sweet sauce. Perhaps the most common form of 'biscuit' is sponge finger biscuits ('biscuits à la cuiller') whose main rôle is to line the mould and provide a plain background for creamy charlotte fillings.

Génoise and 'biscuit' once mixed will not wait, so advance preparation is at least as important as the mixing itself. The oven must be preheated. The shelf should be set two-thirds down in the oven, and a cake tin of the right size prepared. Equipment must be assembled: paper and strainer to sift the flour, bowl and whisk for the eggs, wooden spatula or metal spoon for folding, rubber spatula for scraping the bowl. After the ingredients are measured, the butter is melted slightly to make it easier to mix. Some chefs like it to be pourable but still creamy, others melt it and still others flavour it by cooking it to a nut brown. Whatever the stage of cooking, the butter must be left to cool before adding to the mixture.

At last comes the action, designed to give the maximum of air to the cake. Two points are crucial: whisking the eggs and sugar to the right consistency and folding in the flour and butter as lightly as possible. The egg and sugar mousse for génoise is ready, say the chefs at La Varenne, when you can write your name with the ribbon trail from the whisk, but I think they exaggerate, particularly when the mousse has been whisked over heat and will thicken as it cools. I whisk only until the trail shows for a few seconds, then disappears.

As for folding, génoise and 'biscuit' rival a soufflé for capriciousness: the classic cutting and scooping motion that turns over the ingredients with a minimum of disturbance works well when adding the flour, but the whisked mixture visibly loses volume once the butter is added. One way to mix it quickly is to add a couple of spoonfuls of whisked mixture to the melted butter, fold both together and then fold this mixture into the rest.

For 'biscuit', the same general principles apply. The egg yolks and sugar are whisked until thick and light, some of the sugar being kept to make a meringue with the whipped egg whites. Then the meringue is folded into the yolk mixture alternately with the flour.

Baking time depends on the size of the cake: when it starts to shrink from the sides of the pan it is nearly ready, and when the centre springs back after being pressed with a fingertip, the cake is done. Tip the cake upside down on a rack lined with paper so the cake cannot stick. If a cake sticks, ease it away from the sides of the tin with a knife. A tin that habitually sticks is a nuisance, and Chef Jorant jokes that he used to sell pastry still attached to such bugbears. A sponge that is to be rolled should be covered with a cloth so that its own steam keeps it moist and pliable.

The filling and decoration are where the fun begins. To keep sponge cake moist, pastry chefs often brush (but not soak) the layers with liqueur-flavoured syrup; for simplicity and a more alcoholic kick, I often just sprinkle the cake with liqueur. For filling, there are many possibilities. Butter cream is the clear favourite as its richness complements the plainness of a sponge and it lends itself to almost any flavour. Pastry cream is lighter, especially when mixed with whipped cream, but it does not keep well. Plain whipped cream separates within a few hours so it is rarely used, and then only when mixed with Italian meringue or some other stabiliser. Recently, young chefs have been filling cakes with mousse mixtures, often made with fruit. The most popular of these new cakes is sandwiched and coated with chocolate mousse and decorated with chocolate curls – hardly bearing out nouvelle cuisine's reputation for lightness.

Butter cream has the added advantage of doubling as filling and coating. The other two usual professional coatings for cakes, fondant icing and marzipan are best obtained commercially from pastry supply houses; both require some practice to use. Italian meringue is a frosting that is easy and impressive: it is spread on the top and sides of a cake, piped in rosettes, then browned in the oven to give an American-style finish that is, in fact, entirely French. Glacé icing is another easy one, and simplest of all is a coating of apricot glaze into which chopped browned almonds are pressed – a favourite for rolled 'biscuit'.

Decorations for génoise and 'biscuit', could fill a whole book, and the more obvious include rosettes of filling, marzipan flowers and the mundane glacé cherry. The chefs whip up little paper piping cones and trace delicate patterns of melted chocolate or royal icing. Less artistically gifted, I'm a great devotee of wafer-thin rounds or ovals of chocolate (see the recipe for Chocolate mousse gâteau) and all the ready-made little nothings like chocolate-coated coffee dragées that cost a small fortune but go a long way. Dark coffee or chocolate butter cream can be highlighted by a sprinkling of icing sugar, particularly in a pattern. For stripes, lay parallel bands of paper across the cake, dust with a thick coating of icing sugar, then carefully remove the paper. For a spider's web, set one of those round wire cake racks on top of the cake and sprinkle with sugar. On light butter cream, the same decoration can be done with powdered chocolate.

Possibilities for génoise and 'biscuit' even within the classic repertoire seem almost endless – and indeed they are. I once demonstrated a different French gâteau every afternoon for three months, and I still had scarcely scratched the surface. The best pictorial record I know of these cakes is in 'Recettes d'un Compagnon du Tour de France' by Yves Thuries. (M. Thuries is referring to the gastronomic society, not the bicycle race.) The great strength of génoise gâteaux is that they include something for everyone, from the challenges of an opéra or a bûche de Noël, to a simple rolled 'biscuit' filled with raspberry jam.

THE WAY TO SUCCESS

1 Be sure to measure ingredients accurately.

2 All eggs used should be of sizes 3 or 4.

3 When the eggs and sugar for génoise are beaten by hand, the bowl is put over low heat. Do not overheat the mixture or the eggs will coagulate and prevent the cake from rising properly.

4 It is better to slightly overbeat the mousse for génoise than to underbeat it. When it reaches the ribbon stage, the mixture will be completely smooth; if it still has bubbles, it has not been beaten enough.

5 After pouring batter into the tin, hollow the centre slightly as the centre of the cake tends to rise more than the edges. The tin should be about two-thirds full.

6 Before baking, bang the tin briskly once on the table to knock out any large air bubbles.

7 Be sure the oven has reached the right temperature before baking.

8 While a cake bakes, check the oven occasionally to be sure it is not browning too fast. If it is, cover the cake loosely with foil and, if the cake is firm enough to be moved, lower the oven shelf.

9 If the baked cake does not come out of the tin easily, leave it upside down for a minute to allow its own steam to loosen it. You can also run a knife between the cake and sides of the pan, but be careful not to cut into the crust.

10 Let a cake cool thoroughly before cutting into layers. It will tend to fall apart if cut while still warm.

11 To split a cake easily, set it flat on a table, steady it with one hand on top and cut horizontally with a long serrated knife.

12 To make handling while decorating easier, cut a circle of cardboard to fit the base of the cake and stick the two together with a dab of filling.

13 Do not moisten all the layers with syrup at once before assembling a gâteau because they will soften and be hard to move. Instead, brush syrup on each layer as it is used.

14 Refrigerate a gâteau as soon as it is assembled so the butter cream can harden before the cake is decorated, especially if fondant is used – as it must be spread while slightly warm and it tends to melt the butter cream. Refrigerate the gâteau again before slicing.

Butter cream

1 Always use unsalted butter. Thoroughly cool the yolk mixture before adding butter or the butter will melt.

2 If butter cream separates, which can happen if it is stored in a cold place, warm it gently in a water bath, whisking until it is soft and smooth again.

3 If butter cream is too stiff to smooth evenly over a cake, use a metal spatula heated for a moment or two in hot water or over a gas burner.

4 Be sure a cake is cool before spreading with butter cream, or the butter cream will melt.

Getting ahead

1 The whisked mixture for génoise and 'biscuit' should be baked as soon as it is mixed.

2 Once baked, however, cakes made from génoise or 'biscuit' can be stored for several days in an airtight container, or wrapped and put in the refrigerator. They can also be frozen.

3 The syrup for moistening the layers can be kept, covered, for up to one month in the refrigerator.

4 If a cake is to be kept, sprinkle each layer generously with sugar syrup before filling. This helps prevent it from drying.

5 Butter cream keeps well because the yolks in it are thoroughly cooked by the boiling sugar syrup. Unless it contains fruit purée, it will last in the refrigerator for up to a week. It can also be frozen. Allow it to come to room temperature before using.

6 Butter cream can be made in large quantities without flavouring, then flavouring added as needed.

7 Once filled and decorated, gâteaux can be kept as long as their fillings and icings will last. With butter cream filling, gâteaux keep well in the refrigerator for a few days and can also be frozen. Italian meringue coating holds up for about 24 hours, fondant lasts 2-3 days but can dry and crack, and almond paste keeps for a week or more; none of these toppings can be frozen. Pastry cream can be kept for 36 hours, not more, and any cake with whipped cream should be eaten within 6 hours.

To prepare cake tins

1 The diameter of a cake tin is measured across the upper edge. Tins vary in shape from shallow (usually used in twos or threes for layer cakes), to deep (often with springform sides), to the French cake tins with sloping sides called 'moules à manqué'. These are designed so that the icing flows easily down the sloping sides.

2 To butter the pan, brush it with an even layer of very soft or melted butter, using a pastry brush. Hold the tin up to the light to check for any missed spots. Turn the tin upside down and leave the butter to set.

3 To flour it, add a handful of flour to the buttered tin and turn it, tapping at the same time so the flour sticks. Discard excess flour and tap the tin upside down on the table to leave a thin, even coating of flour.

4 This coating of butter and flour should be sufficient. However, if the tin is new or inclined to stick, line the base with a circle of greaseproof paper. Cut a circle of paper the diameter of the tin. Butter the tin, press in the paper, butter it also and then flour as above.

5 Handle a prepared tin by the base so as not to disturb the coating.

6 Never wash a cake tin. Wipe it while still warm with a damp cloth. Any fat left will help prevent it from rusting. If a cake pan sticks badly and must be washed, rub it with butter after washing and wipe it clean.

GENOISE
(Basic recipe)

If you use a big electric mixer to beat génoise, the mixture need not be heated. However, this step cannot be eliminated when using a small or hand-held electric beater.

125g (4oz) flour
pinch of salt
60g (2oz) butter (optional)
4 eggs
125g (4oz) sugar
for flavouring
one of the following:
½ teaspoon vanilla essence; or grated rind of 1 lemon; or grated rind of 1 orange; or teaspoon orange flower water
23cm (9in) diameter round cake tin

Brush the inside of the cake tin with melted butter. If you like, line the base with a circle of greaseproof paper that exactly fits and butter it also. Leave for a few minutes and then sprinkle the tin with flour, discarding the excess. Set the oven at moderate, 180C (350F) gas 4. Sift the flour with the salt 2-3 times.

Clarify the butter by melting it over low heat and skimming off the froth; pour into a bowl, leaving the milky sediment behind.

Put the eggs in a large bowl, preferably of copper, and gradually beat in the sugar. Set the bowl over a pan of hot but not boiling water, or over very low heat, and beat for 8-10 minutes or until the mixture is light and thick enough to leave a ribbon trail when the whisk is lifted. Take the bowl from the heat, add the chosen flavouring and continue beating until cool.

Sift the flour over the mixture in three batches, folding in each batch as lightly as possible with a wooden spatula or metal spoon. Just after the last batch, add the butter and fold in both together. NOTE: the whisked mixture quickly loses volume after the butter is added.

Pour the mixture into the prepared tin and bake in the heated oven, allowing 35-40 minutes, or until the cake shrinks slightly from the sides of the tin and the top springs back when lightly pressed. Turn it out on a rack to cool.

Chill thoroughly before cutting into petits fours or before coating and decorating.

To 'ribbon trail': make the egg mousse for génoise sponge by beating eggs and sugar until the lifted whisk leaves a ribbon trail – as shown here

CREME AU BEURRE
(Butter cream)

Since butter is the main ingredient in this cream, which doubles as filling and icing, use the best you can find. Butter cream is also often spread between large or small rounds of nut meringue to make spectacular gâteaux.

Makes about 500ml (scant 1pt)

4 egg yolks
125g (4oz) sugar
100ml (⅙pt) water
250g (8oz) butter
chosen flavouring (see below)

Beat the egg yolks lightly in a bowl until mixed. Heat the sugar with the water until dissolved, bring to the boil and boil until the syrup reaches the soft ball stage, 115C (239F) on a sugar thermometer.

Gradually pour the hot sugar syrup onto the egg yolks, beating constantly, and continue beating until the mixture is cool and thick. Cream the butter and gradually beat it into the egg mixture. Beat in the chosen flavouring.

FLAVOURINGS

Chocolate: to every 250g (8oz) butter cream add 100g (3½oz) dark dessert chocolate, chopped, melted over hot water and left until cool.
Coffee: to every 250g (8oz) butter cream add 2-3 level teaspoons instant coffee powder dissolved in a tablespoon of hot water.
Lemon or orange: into every 250g (8oz) butter cream beat the finely grated zest of 2 lemons or 1 orange. To orange butter cream add 1 tablespoon of an orange liqueur such as Grand Marnier.
Praline: heat equal weights of blanched or unblanched almonds and granulated sugar in a small pan, allowing 40g (1⅓oz) almonds and 40g (1⅓oz) sugar for every 250g (8oz) butter cream. Heat the mixture, stirring, until the sugar melts and cooks to a dark brown caramel. Pour onto a greased marble slab or baking sheet and leave until cold and crisp. Pound the praline or grind it in a rotary cheese grater and beat it into the butter cream.
Raspberry: purée fresh raspberries or frozen raspberries, thawed and thoroughly drained, by working them through a sieve or puréeing them in a blender and straining to remove seeds. Gradually beat in the purée, allowing 150ml (¼pt) purée to every 250g (8oz) butter cream. Add ½-1 tablespoon Kirsch.
Strawberry: purée fresh strawberries in a blender or work them through a sieve. Gradually beat the purée into butter cream, allowing 150ml (¼pt) purée to every 250g (8oz) butter cream and add ½-1 tablespoon Kirsch.
Vanilla: into every 250g (8oz) of butter cream beat a teaspoon of vanilla essence.

GLACAGE SIMPLE
(Glacé icing)

Glacé icing makes an easy substitute for fondant, if necessary.

Makes about 250ml (scant ½pt)

about 200g (7oz) icing sugar
1-4 tablespoons water
edible food colouring (optional)
for flavouring
one of the following: (see individual recipes)
½ teaspoon vanilla essence; or 1 level teaspoon instant coffee dissolved in 1 tablespoon warm water; or 30g (1oz) dark dessert chocolate; or 2-3 tablespoons lemon or orange juice; or 1-2 tablespoons Kirsch, rum or liqueur

Sift the icing sugar into a bowl. If using chocolate, chop it, melt it on a heatproof plate over a pan of hot water and allow to cool. Add chocolate or other chosen flavouring to the icing sugar with 1-2 tablespoons of the water. Mix to a smooth, stiff paste. Set the bowl in a pan of hot water and heat to lukewarm; icing should be thick enough to coat the back of a spoon. If too thick, add more water; if too thin, beat in more icing sugar. Add colouring, if required. Icing should be delicately, not brightly coloured. Use at once while still warm.

FONDANT

Fondant can also be turned slowly in an electric mixer with a dough hook, a great saving on the muscles. The basic fondant is generally not flavoured. Because it keeps so well, it is practical to make it in quantity and flavour just what is needed for a given recipe.

Makes 600ml (1pt)

500g (1lb) sugar

250ml (9fl oz) water

50g (1⅔oz) corn syrup or glucose; or pinch of cream of tartar dissolved in 1 teaspoon of water; or ½ teaspoon lemon juice or vinegar

Heat the sugar and water in a heavy-based pan until the sugar dissolves. Add the corn syrup or glucose or cream of tartar or lemon juice or vinegar. Bring the sugar to the boil and boil steadily without stirring to the soft ball stage (115C or 239F). If crystals form on the sides of the pan during boiling, wash them down with a brush dipped in water. Take the pan at once from the heat, let the bubbles subside and pour the mixture slowly, from a height, onto a dampened tray. Sprinkle with a little water to prevent the formation of a crust.

When cool, put the mixture on a cool surface. Run a sugar scraper or a metal spatula up one side of the mixture. When you get to the far corner, lift the fondant, folding it over on itself and returning the scraper to the end nearest you. Turn the scraper over to keep the side facing the working surface clean, run it up the other side and pull the fondant back as before. Repeat, working the fondant vigorously until it becomes white and creamy – it will do this suddenly and become too stiff to work. If fondant gets very hard and seems impossible to work, put a bowl over it for a few minutes; the humidity will soften it.

Work a small piece of fondant at a time with the hands until smooth. Pack it into an airtight container and allow it to stand for at least an hour and preferably 2-3 days to mellow. Fondant can be kept in an airtight container for up to a year.

NOISETTES

Fondant icing is not easy to make; if you do not find it easily obtainable from trade suppliers, use glacé icing (see left).

Makes about 20

basic génoise

butter cream made with 2 egg yolks, 60g sugar, 3 tablespoons water and 125g (4oz) butter

3-4 teaspoons dry instant coffee dissolved in warm water (see below)

50g (1½oz) hazelnuts

500g (1lb) fondant icing; or glacé icing made with about 200g (7oz) icing sugar and 1-4 tablespoons water

Bake the génoise as described. Make the butter cream following the basic recipe and flavour it with 2-3 teaspoons of the instant coffee dissolved in the tablespoon warm water. Brown the hazelnuts in a moderate oven, 180C (350F) gas 4, and rub them with a cloth to remove the skins. Finely chop half of them and add to the butter cream.

Trim the génoise, cut it in half horizontally and sandwich with the flavoured butter cream. If using fondant, soften it with a little warm water, set the bowl in a water bath and heat until just warm to the touch. Make the glacé icing if using this instead. Flavour the fondant or glacé icing with 1 teaspoon instant coffee dissolved in 1 tablespoon warm water and ice the top of the cake. Carefully cut the cake into 4cm (1½in) squares with a sharp knife and top each with a toasted hazelnut.

SUISSES

Makes about 18

basic génoise

butter cream made with 4 egg yolks, 125g (4oz) sugar, 100ml (⅙pt) water and 250g (8oz) butter

200ml (⅓pt) strawberry purée

2 tablespoons Kirsch

red food colouring

18 glacé cherries

500g (1lb) fondant icing; or glacé icing made with about 200g (7oz) icing sugar and 1-4 tablespoons water

3cm (1¼in) round cutter, pastry bag and 1·25cm (½in) plain tube

Bake the génoise as described. Make the butter cream following the basic recipe and flavour it with the strawberry purée and 1 tablespoon Kirsch. Colour the butter cream pink with red food colouring. Cut 4cm (1½in) rounds from the cake. Pipe a mound of butter cream on each one, top each with a glacé cherry and chill thoroughly.

If using fondant, soften it with a little warm water, set the bowl in a water bath (Chapter 29) and heat until just warm to the touch. Make the glacé icing if using this instead. Flavour the fondant or glacé icing with 1 tablespoon of Kirsch. Coat the cakes with the icing – it should be thin enough for the cherries to show through.

PRINTANIERS

Makes 40

basic génoise

butter cream made with 4 egg yolks, 125g (4oz) sugar, 100ml (⅙pt) water and 250g (8oz) butter

2 tablespoons strawberry purée

red and green edible food colouring

2 tablespoons blanched finely ground pistachios

teaspoon vanilla essence

pastry bag and small star tube

Bake the génoise as above. Make the butter cream as in the basic recipe. Flavour ⅙ of the butter cream with strawberry purée and colour it pink; flavour another ⅙ with the ground pistachios and colour it green; flavour the rest with vanilla essence and leave white.

Split the cake in half horizontally and fill with about ⅔ of the vanilla butter cream. Using a pastry bag and small star tube, pipe strips of white butter cream across the cake, leaving room for a coloured strip between every two white ones. Pipe pink butter cream into half the open spaces. Lastly, pipe green butter cream into the remaining spaces. Chill thoroughly, then heat a sharp knife by dipping it into boiling water and wiping dry. Cut into 2·5cm by 5cm (1in by 2in) pieces.

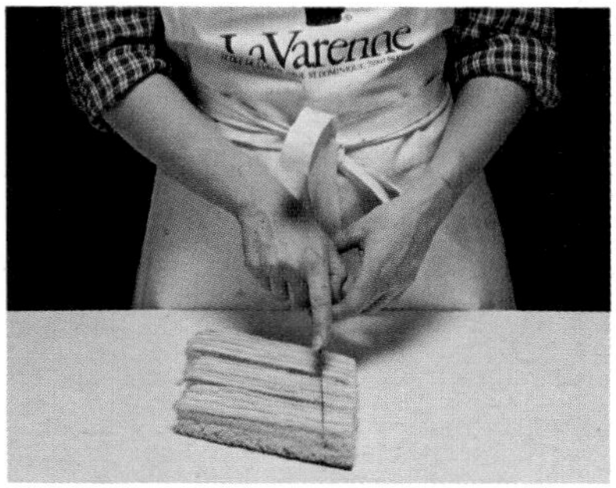

TO CUT PRINTANIERS

After heating a knife so that it will slip easily and cleanly through the butter cream, cut the whole decorated cake into neat and even-sized petits fours

GATEAU GRAND MARNIER

If the cake has been refrigerated, bring it to room temperature before serving so that the butter cream will soften.

SERVES 6

génoise made with 90g (3oz) flour, tiny pinch of salt, 45g (1½oz) butter, 3 eggs, 90g (3oz) sugar and the grated rind of 1 orange
100g (3½oz) candied fruit, finely chopped
tablespoon Grand Marnier
for the syrup
100g (3½oz) sugar
100ml (4fl oz) water
tablespoon Grand Marnier
butter cream (page 100) made with 3 egg yolks, 90g (3oz) sugar, 3 tablespoons water and 180g (6oz) unsalted butter
2-3 tablespoons Grand Marnier, or to taste
for the decoration
125g (4oz) chopped almonds
4-5 glacé cherries, halved; or wide strips of candied orange peel cut into 8-10 round pieces
23cm (9in) diameter cake tin; pastry bag and medium star tube (optional)

Set the oven at moderate, 180C (350F) gas 4, and prepare the cake tin. Make the génoise mixture and bake in the heated oven for 25-30 minutes or until the cake shrinks slightly from the sides of the pan and the top springs back when lightly pressed with a fingertip. Run a knife around the edge of the cake and turn it out onto a rack to cool. Mix the chopped candied fruit with the Grand Marnier and leave to macerate.

Spread the chopped almonds on a baking sheet and toast in the heated oven for 8-12 minutes or until golden brown. The browned nuts can be kept for 1-2 weeks in an airtight container.

For the syrup: bring the sugar and water to the boil in a saucepan and boil for 1-2 minutes or until the syrup is clear. Remove from the heat, cool, and add the Grand Marnier. The syrup can be kept for 3-4 weeks in the refrigerator.

Make the butter cream and flavour to taste with Grand Marnier. It can be kept for up to a week in the refrigerator.

To assemble the cake: holding a knife diagonally, bevel the top edge of the cake all round to give the génoise a slightly domed look. Split the cake into 3 layers and brush each with syrup. Sandwich the layers with about half of the butter cream and all of the chopped candied fruit. Coat the top and sides of the gâteau with most of the remaining butter cream.

For decoration: press the browned almonds on the sides of the cake with a metal spatula. Decorate the top with the halved glacé cherries or pieces of candied orange peel. If you like, pipe rosettes of the remaining butter cream onto the cake, using a pastry bag and medium star tube.

The cake can be kept, refrigerated, for up to a week depending on the freshness of the butter cream.

GATEAU A LA MOUSSE AU CHOCOLAT

(Chocolate mousse gâteau)

Mousse is becoming more and more popular as a filling for gâteaux in France because it is rich yet lighter than butter cream.

SERVES 6-8

for the génoise
100g (3½oz) flour
30g (1oz) cocoa powder
½ level teaspoon baking powder
pinch of salt
60g (2oz) butter
4 eggs
150g (5oz) sugar
½ teaspoon vanilla essence
for the chocolate mousse
150g (5oz) dark dessert chocolate, chopped
3 eggs, separated
90g (3oz) butter
½ teaspoon vanilla essence or tablespoon Grand Marnier liqueur
120g (4oz) dark dessert chocolate (for chocolate curls and decorations)
Chantilly cream made with 300ml (½pt) double cream, tablespoon sugar and ½ teaspoon vanilla essence
23-25cm (9-10in) diameter round cake tin or moule à manqué; 7·5cm (3in) diameter plain round cutter; pastry bag and medium star tube

Set the oven at moderate, 180C (350F) gas 4, and prepare the cake tin (see basic instructions). Sift the flour with the cocoa, baking powder and salt and make the génoise mixture following the basic recipe. Add the vanilla essence. Pour the mixture into the prepared tin and bake in the heated oven for 35-40 minutes or until the mixture springs back when lightly pressed with a fingertip. Run a knife around the edge of the cake and turn it out onto a rack to cool. The cake can be baked ahead and kept in an airtight container for 2-3 days, or it can be frozen.

For the chocolate mousse: melt the chocolate in a pan over hot water and stir until smooth. Take from the heat and beat the egg yolks one by one into the hot mixture so it thickens slightly. Beat in the butter and vanilla or liqueur. Allow to cool slightly. Whip the egg whites until

TO DECORATE GATEAU A LA MOUSSE AU CHOCOLAT

Using a vegetable peeler, scrape curls from a bar of chocolate straight onto the top of the cake. This is easiest to do with a fairly large piece of chocolate

To make shapes, first stamp out rounds from the thin layer of set chocolate, then cut out three leaf shapes from each, still using the circular cutter

stiff, add the tepid chocolate mixture to them and fold the two together as lightly as possible; the warm mixture will lightly cook and stiffen the whites. Leave to cool at room temperature but do not refrigerate otherwise the mousse will harden and become difficult to spread.

For the chocolate decorations: melt 90g (3oz) of the chocolate in a pan over hot water and stir until smooth. Pour the chocolate onto a piece of greaseproof paper and allow to cool until set. Use the 7·5cm (3in) cutter to make rounds of chocolate, then cut 3 almond shapes from each round.

To assemble the gâteau: split the génoise into 3 layers. On the bottom layer spread two-thirds of the chocolate mousse. Place the second layer of génoise on top and spread it with two-thirds of the Chantilly cream, reserving the remaining cream for decoration. Top with the third layer and spread the remaining mousse on the top and sides of the cake. Decorate the top with chocolate curls made by scraping curls off a bar of dessert chocolate with a vegetable peeler. It is easier to make the curls from a large piece of chocolate, but actually only about 30g (1oz) of chocolate will be used in the curls. Chill until the gâteau is firm.

To finish: place the chocolate shapes around the edge, sticking them in at an angle. Using the pastry bag and medium star tube, pipe vertical ruffs of Chantilly cream between them.

GENOISE AUX FRUITS
(Génoise with fruit)

This is the perfect cake to make when fresh fruit is in season. It doesn't keep well but is usually eaten too quickly for that to be a problem.

SERVES 4

génoise made with 90g (3oz) flour, pinch salt, 45g (1½oz) butter, 3 eggs, 90g (3oz) sugar and ½ teaspoon vanilla essence

icing sugar (for sprinkling)

for the filling

250g (8oz) fresh raspberries or strawberries or 2-3 peaches

Chantilly cream made with 250ml (8oz) double cream, 1-2 tablespoons sugar and teaspoon vanilla essence or tablespoon brandy

23cm (9in) diameter cake tin; pastry bag and medium star tube (optional)

Make the génoise and pour the mixture into the prepared cake tin. Bake in a moderate oven, 180C (350F) gas 4, for 25-30 minutes or until the cake shrinks slightly from the sides of the tin and the top springs back when lightly pressed with a fingertip. Run a knife around the sides of the cake to loosen it and turn it out onto a rack to cool.

To finish: not more than 3-4 hours before serving, prepare the fruit. Pick over the raspberries, or hull and halve the strawberries or scald, peel and slice the peaches. Reserve 6-8 whole raspberries or strawberries for decoration. Split the cake horizontally, spread with about half of the cream and top with the fruit. Add most of the remaining cream, top with the second round of cake and press lightly. Sprinkle the top with icing sugar and, if you like, decorate the top with 6-8 rosettes of the remaining Chantilly cream, using a pastry bag and medium star tube. Top each rosette with a whole raspberry or strawberry. Refrigerate the cake until serving.

GATEAU MIMOSA

So named because it resembles mimosa in bloom.

SERVES 8

génoise made with 180g (6oz) flour, ½ teaspoon salt, 90g (3oz) butter, 6 eggs, 180g (6oz) sugar and ½ teaspoon vanilla essence

vanilla or Kirsch-flavoured pastry cream (page 45) made with 5 egg yolks, 90g (3oz) sugar, 40g (1½oz) flour, 375ml (scant ¾pt) milk, pinch of salt and vanilla pod or 1 tablespoon Kirsch

Chantilly cream made with 200ml (⅓pt) double cream, 2-3 teaspoons sugar and ½ teaspoon vanilla essence

two 20-23cm (8-9in) diameter cake tins

Make the génoise and pour the mixture into prepared cake tins. Bake in a moderate oven, 180C (350F) gas 4, for 25-30 minutes or until the cakes shrink slightly from the sides of the tins and the tops spring back when lightly pressed with a fingertip. Run a knife around the edge of the cakes and turn out onto a rack to cool. Make the pastry cream, coat with a little butter to prevent a skin from forming and leave to cool. Make the Chantilly cream.

To assemble the gâteau: split one cake horizontally into three layers. Cut the other cake into 1cm (⅜in) dice. Fold the pastry cream and Chantilly cream together as lightly as possible. Sandwich the split cake with about half the cream, mounding it to a slight peak in the centre of each slice so that the cake is domed when it is assembled. Spread the top and sides of the cake with the remaining cream. Press the cake dice into the cream until it is completely covered.

Refrigerate until serving. The cake is best eaten the day it is made.

BISCUIT
(Sponge cake)

125g (4oz) flour

pinch of salt

4 eggs, separated

180g (6oz) sugar

½ teaspoon vanilla essence; or grated rind of 1 lemon or 1 orange; or teaspoon orange flower water; or 2-3 drops 'anise' oil (for flavouring)

23-25cm (9-10in) diameter cake tin

Brush the cake tin with melted butter. If you like, line the base with a circle of greaseproof paper and butter it also. Sprinkle the inside of the tin with flour, shake to coat and discard the excess. Set the oven at moderate, 180C (350F) gas 4. Sift the flour with the salt 2-3 times.

Beat the egg yolks with half the sugar and the flavouring until thick and light and the mixture leaves a thick ribbon trail when the whisk is lifted. Beat the egg whites until stiff. Add the remaining sugar and beat for a further 20-30 seconds or until it is glossy. Fold the flour and egg whites into the egg mixture in 2-3 batches.

Pour the mixture into the prepared tin and bake in the heated oven for 30-35 minutes or until the cake shrinks slightly from the sides of the pan and the top springs back when lightly pressed with a fingertip. Run a knife around the edge of the cake to loosen it and turn it out onto a rack to cool.

The cake is best served fresh, but it can be kept for a day or two in an airtight container. It freezes well.

BISCUIT ROULE
(Sponge roll)

Do not overbake this cake or it will crack when rolled.

SERVES 6-8

100g (3½oz) flour
pinch of salt
4 eggs, separated
180g (6oz) sugar
½ teaspoon vanilla essence
coffee or chocolate butter cream made with 3 egg yolks, 90g (3oz) sugar, 4 tablespoons water, 180g (6oz) unsalted butter and 2 teaspoons dry instant coffee dissolved in 1 tablespoon water; or 30g (1oz) dark dessert chocolate, melted; or 180g (6oz) raspberry or strawberry jam
icing sugar (for sprinkling)

Set the oven at hot, 200C (400F) gas 6. Butter a baking sheet, line it with greaseproof paper and butter it also. Sprinkle the paper with flour.

For the sponge roll: sift the flour with the salt. Beat the egg yolks with two-thirds of the sugar until thick and light; beat in the vanilla essence. Whip the egg whites until stiff in a copper bowl if possible, and beat in the remaining sugar until the mixture is glossy. Carefully fold one-third of the flour, then one-third of the egg whites into the egg yolk mixture. Repeat with another third of flour, followed by egg whites, then fold in the remainder. Spread the sponge mixture on the prepared baking sheet to a 30×40cm (12×16in) rectangle. Bake in the heated oven for 8-10 minutes or until browned around the edges. Cover with a cloth and a wire rack, turn upside down, lift off the baking sheet and leave to cool. NOTE: the cloth and paper prevent the cake from drying.

Meanwhile make the coffee or chocolate butter cream, or melt the jam and allow to cool. When the cake is cool, peel away the paper. Trim the short edges and spread the cake with butter cream or melted jam. Roll it up beginning with a short side and trim the ends. The sponge roll keeps for 2-3 days, but is best eaten on the day of baking.

Just before serving, sprinkle it with icing sugar and transfer to a serving dish.

GATEAU AUX AMANDES AU CARAMEL
(Almond and caramel gâteau)

Making your own caramel for flavouring is not difficult, but do be careful to avoid getting the hot caramel, which can stick and burn, on your hands.

SERVES 6-8

250g (8oz) sliced almonds (for decoration)
for the almond 'biscuit'
110g (3½oz) blanched almonds
110g (3½oz) sugar
30g (1oz) clarified butter
3 eggs
3 egg whites
30g (1oz) flour
for the caramel
100g (3½oz) sugar
60ml (2½oz) cold water
30ml (1oz) warm water
for the syrup
100g (3½oz) sugar
100ml (4fl oz) water
tablespoon caramel (see above)
butter cream (page 100) made with 4 egg yolks, 60g (2oz) sugar, 60ml (2oz) water, 250g (8oz) butter and 4 tablespoons caramel, or to taste (see method)

20-23cm (8-9in) diameter cake tin; pastry bag and medium star tube

Set the oven at moderate, 180C (350F) gas 4.

For the almond 'biscuit': grind the 110g (3½oz) blanched almonds in a rotary cheese grater or an electric food processor. Reserve 1 tablespoon of the sugar for beating into the egg whites. Spread the sliced almonds for decoration on a baking sheet and toast in the heated oven for 8-12 minutes or until golden

Starting with a short side, roll the cake into as compact a cylinder as possible, using the cloth to guide it into shape

brown.

Mix the ground almonds and remaining sugar in a bowl, add one egg and beat until the mixture is very light and thick. Add the other 2 eggs one at a time, beating well after each addition.

Beat the egg whites until stiff, if possible in a copper bowl. Add the reserved tablespoon of sugar and beat for a further 20-30 seconds or until glossy. Sift the flour over the almond mixture and, using a wooden spatula or metal spoon, fold it in as lightly as possible. Fold in the egg whites in 2-3 batches and lastly, fold in the clarified butter.

Pour the mixture into the prepared cake tin and bake in the heated oven for 40-45 minutes or until the cake shrinks slightly from the sides of the pan and the top springs back when lightly pressed with a finger-tip. Run a knife around the sides of the cake and turn it out onto a rack to cool.

For the caramel: heat the sugar gently with the cold water in a heavy-based saucepan until the sugar has dissolved. Bring to the boil and cook steadily to a rich brown caramel. The caramel must be well browned or it will be unpleasantly sweet, but do not let it burn or it will turn bitter. Take from the heat and at once add the warm water, standing well back because the caramel will sputter. Heat gently until the caramel has melted and let it cool.

For the syrup: bring the sugar and water to a boil in a saucepan and boil for 1-2 minutes or until the syrup is clear. Remove from the heat and stir in 1 tablespoon of the caramel.

Make the butter cream and beat in the remaining cooled caramel. NOTE: the butter cream is made with less sugar than usual to allow for the sweetness of the caramel.

To finish the cake: split the 'biscuit' into 2 or 3 layers, brush each layer with syrup and sandwich with butter cream. Coat the top and sides with the remaining butter cream, reserving a little for decoration. With a metal spatula or with your hands, press the browned almonds over the top and sides of the cake, covering it completely. Put the remaining butter cream in a pastry bag with a star tube and decorate the top of the cake with 6-8 rosettes. The gâteau keeps well, refrigerated, for 2-3 days.

GATEAU OPERA

A beautiful cake popular in classic and nouvelle cuisine restaurants alike. It is often cut into small squares and served as petits fours.

SERVES 8

for the almond 'biscuit'
110g (3½oz) blanched almonds
110g (3½oz) sugar
3 eggs
3 egg whites
30g (1oz) flour
30g (1oz) clarified butter
for the syrup
100g (3½oz) sugar
100ml (4oz) water
teaspoon instant coffee
butter cream (page 100) made with 3 egg yolks, 90g (3oz) sugar, 60ml (2½oz) water and 200g (7oz) butter and 4 teaspoons instant coffee dissolved in 1 tablespoon hot water
for the ganache mousse
250g (8oz) dark dessert chocolate, chopped
125ml (4½oz) milk
250ml (9oz) double cream, lightly whipped
to finish
150g (5oz) dark dessert chocolate, chopped

Set the oven at hot, 200C (400F) gas 6. Butter a baking sheet, cover it with a sheet of greaseproof paper and butter that also. Grind the blanched almonds in a rotary cheese grater or an electric food processor. Reserve 1 tablespoon of the sugar to beat into the egg whites.

Mix the ground almonds and remaining sugar in a mixing bowl, add one egg and beat until the mixture is very light and thick. Add the other eggs, one at a time, beating well after each addition.

Beat the egg whites until stiff, if possible in a copper bowl. Add the reserved tablespoon of sugar and beat 20-30 seconds longer or until glossy. Sift the flour over the almond mixture and, using a wooden spatula or metal spoon, fold it in as lightly as possible. Fold in the egg whites in 2-3 batches and last fold in the clarified butter.

Spread the mixture in a smooth layer about 5mm (¼in) thick on the prepared baking sheet. Bake in the heated oven for 12-15 minutes or until just firm but still moist. Remove the cake with its paper to a rack to cool. When cool, carefully peel off the paper and cut the cake into 3 equal pieces.

For the syrup: bring the sugar and water to a boil in a saucepan and boil for 1-2 minutes or until the syrup is clear. Add the instant coffee and stir until dissolved.

Make the butter cream and beat in the dissolved coffee.

For the ganache mousse: melt the chocolate in a water bath and stir until smooth. Bring the milk to the boil in a small saucepan, pour the boiling milk over the melted chocolate and stir well. Leave to cool at room temperature. When cool but still liquid, fold in the lightly whipped cream.

To assemble the cake: place one layer of cake on a serving dish and brush it generously with syrup. Spread it with the butter cream. Place the second layer on top, brush it with syrup and spread it with over half of the chocolate mousse. Top with the third layer and brush with syrup. Spread with a thin layer of chocolate mousse and smoothe it with a metal spatula to make the surface as flat as possible. Chill thoroughly.

To finish the cake: melt the chocolate as gently as possible in a water bath. Spread on top of the cake and leave to set. The cake keeps for 4-5 days in the refrigerator.

12
GRILLING AND BARBECUEING
Ancient and modern

Grilling is the most ancient and the most modern cooking technique. If man once knew no way to cook his meat other than holding it over a fire, he has now come full circle and would give his right arm – or charred forefinger – for a charcoal grill. Simple as it looks, grilling often proves difficult. It can display the best and worst in food, making the most of tender meat and full-flavoured fish but leaving inferior ingredients all too naked and ashamed.

To grill properly, a fierce heat is essential. The rate of cooking, which should always be relatively fast, is controlled by altering the position of the grill rack, not by lowering the heat. The more robust the meat, the more quickly it should be cooked so that the juices are sealed; the whole point of grilling is to concentrate flavours inside the food rather than draw them out into a sauce. Beef, game and lamb must be seared quickly on both sides, at 10-12.5cm (4-5in) distance from the grill flame, or about 7cm (3in) in the case of an electric grill, the heat from which is less strong.

If more cooking is needed, the rack is then moved away from the heat to finish cooking. Pork, veal and chicken are cooked more slowly, further away from the heat, but they still need to brown well for flavour. Fish and shellfish are trickiest of all. To prevent them sticking to the rack, brush them with oil or clarified butter and turn them with a fish slice.

Meat for grilling should be cut in pieces not more than 5cm (2in) thick, and only the most tender cuts, liberally marbled with fat, are suitable. Beef steak is the obvious candidate – together with lamb chops and cutlets. Lamb steaks cut from a boned leg are an unusual alternative, but they need regular basting, as do pork chops (despite its reputation as a 'fat' meat, little fat enriches the lean of pork). Poultry suffers from the same problem, and I find the famous American barbecued chicken much overrated – unless it has been well moistened with butter or oil. Equally, I don't think veal, fish or shellfish do well under a grill unless

IN A PARTY MOOD
An appetising way of serving food out of doors.
On the barbecue: Côtes de pork grillées (front left);
plain grilled pork chops for serving with
sauce Robert; Brochettes de coquilles St Jacques et
crevettes (front right); seafood marinated in wine,
then skewered and grilled for serving with
béarnaise sauce and Poulets à la crapaudine
(centre and left). And you can make your own
French sausages (Boudins blancs) – Chapter 24

they have been marinated beforehand, then basted with the marinade during cooking.

Fillets of almost any fish can be grilled, but best of all are small fish on the bone like trout, herring, small mackerel and bream. Significantly that old favourite, grilled Dover sole, is left on the bone to keep it moist; even then it is often served drenched in melted butter. Much more reliable are grilled innards, for a touch of charring balances what can be a slightly sickly richness. Liver is good grilled, with a couple of slices of bacon on top to baste it. Brochettes of veal or lamb kidneys, pink in the centre and slightly charred on the outside, make a dish that is fit for a king – or a three-star chef.

Careful seasoning adds that extra dimension to grilled meats. They may be marinated beforehand to add flavour and make them tender, the type of marinade and length of time depending on the food. Unless they have already been marinated, all meats benefit from being brushed with clarified butter or oil before grilling, and you can satisfy a creative urge by adding lemon juice, herbs, wine or garlic.

To salt – or not to salt – before grilling is a controversial question. Many cookbooks say that salt should never be sprinkled on the surface of raw meat – particularly beef – as it draws out the juices, with the result that the meat stews rather than grills. However, when salt is added *after* cooking it is never absorbed in quite the same way. No harm is done by adding salt before cooking, say the La Varenne chefs, provided it is done at the last minute and in practice I have found that they are right. Pepper and other dry seasonings pose no such problems. If grilling indoors, have good ventilation as grilling can make a lot of smoke. Many domestic cookers have the grill inside the oven, but unless the door is left open the food tends to roast rather than grill. The English cookers with eye-level grills are excellent, but then grilling is an English speciality, and the 'mixed grill' an English invention. To America, I suppose, must go credit for the popularity of the barbecue, in its contemporary form, replete with all its gadgetry. The same foods are suitable for barbecueing out of doors as for indoor grilling, and the same principles for seasoning and cooking apply. The characteristic barbecue flavour is given, not by the coals, but by melted fat which falls into the coals and flares, singeing the meat. Too much flame is disastrous, and to avoid a raging inferno when the food is put on the grill, the fire must be given time to burn down to a dull grey. In the US, professionals keep two bowls beside the fire, one of sauce for basting and the other of water to extinguish any flames. Actually, I've found a water pistol the best flame douser, in keeping with the carnival spirit of most barbecues.

Europeans have never taken to barbecuing in quite the same way, their enthusiasm dampened, literally, by the weather. Instead, they are partisan to another offshoot of grilling – pan-grilling or dry frying. Pan-grilling means cooking quickly over high heat in a heavy frying pan with little or no fat so that the food is seared in much the same way as in grilling. The French use a special pan with a ridged base so that the food can be marked with a diamond pattern, but any heavy pan will do. It should be more or less the same size as the food to be cooked so that the food is not crowded, nor is the pan base so bare that the food will scorch.

To pan-grill, heat a very small quantity of clarified butter or oil until just smoking, add the food and sear it, exactly as in grilling. If using a ridged pan, shift the food 80 or 90 degrees after a few moments' cooking to mark a lattice, then turn and cook it in the same way on the other side.

All meats that can be grilled can also be pan-grilled; it is a particularly good method for veal and pork, which otherwise tend to dry out. Pan-grilling has a very French advantage: the juices that congeal in the pan during cooking make an excellent 'small' sauce. At the end of cooking, drain the pan of fat (there should not be much in any case) and add wine, stock, or even water. Boil until well reduced and the coagulated juices are dissolved; then season according to your taste with salt, pepper, chopped herbs, green peppercorns, perhaps a dash of Madeira or a touch of cream. Strain the sauce over the meat and serve.

There is something indecent about a piece of grilled meat or fish without an accompaniment. A bunch of watercress is the least of garnishes, with wedges or baskets of lemon for fish. A cohort of colourful vegetables is acceptable with almost anything, though few vegetables except mushrooms and tomatoes lend themselves to grilling with the meat and most must be cooked separately. Grilled food may be topped with a generous pat of butter seasoned with herbs or perhaps with anchovy essence. Or, most interesting of all, it may have a sauce.

Classic meat/sauce combinations are: for beef and lamb – truffle, madère or béarnaise sauces; for pork – diable or Robert (both piquant); for fish – hollandaise or sauce beurre blanc. But there are endless unorthodox possibilities. Tartare sauce goes well with grilled chicken, béarnaise is delicious with salmon, and I've had pistachio sauce with chicken and Roquefort sauce with veal.

Grilling will always have a place in the cooking repertoire as one of the quickest and simplest ways of producing a hot meal. As a method of cooking, it has attracted attention recently not only because of its speed but because it lowers calories by dissolving the maximum amount of fat. Unfortunately that's only when the meat is not accompanied, as I like it, by a rich sauce!

THE WAY TO SUCCESS

1 For most meats and fish, allow 150-200g (5-7oz) per person and up to double that for a cut of meat containing a large amount of bone, for unboned fish and also for unboned fowl.

2 Leave meat at room temperature for 1-1½ hours before grilling so that its temperature is uniform, thus allowing it to cook evenly.

3 Before putting any food on the rack, heat a gas or electric grill for at least 5 minutes so it is very hot. For oven grills, leave the rack and pan inside to heat also. If using a charcoal grill, light the fire about an hour in advance; the coals should be grey and scarcely glowing when the cooking begins. If the grill is not hot enough, the meat won't sear and the juices will run into the fire.

4 Do not trim all fat from meat because it adds flavour. If there is a border of fat around steak, slash it with a knife to prevent it curling.

5 A hot grill rack prevents food from sticking. To help further, grease the grill so the food does not tear when turned or removed.

6 Sear the outside of food as quickly as possible and do not move it until ready to turn, as it may stick until a crust has formed.

7 Meats are best handled with an implement like tongs that will not prick them and let juices escape.

8 Grilling needs constant attention to avoid overcooking and burning.

9 Grilled foods should be served sizzling hot; they cannot wait.

10 Serve grilled food with the side that was first cooked upwards.

Getting ahead

Grilled, barbecued and pan-grilled foods must be cooked at the last minute; they cook so fast that cooking ahead would achieve little.

1 Meat can be trimmed, skewered and otherwise prepared for grilling a few hours ahead and kept in the refrigerator.

2 If marinating the meat, this should of course be done ahead.

3 Accompanying sauces and flavoured butters can be made ahead. Most can be made at least one day in advance, except emulsified sauces such as hollandaise which should not be kept waiting too long.

How to tell when grills are done

The cooking of grills depends enormously on the temperature of the grill and on individual taste so it is impossible to give *exact* cooking times.

Very rare (bleu): The meat is cooked just long enough to seize all the surfaces and offers no resistance when touched. When cut, it is rare-to-blue inside. For steak and some game.

Rare (saignant): Turn the meat when the blood has just come to the surface and brown the other side. The meat offers little resistance when touched and feels spongy. When cut, it is deep pink inside. For steak, game, kidneys and sometimes lamb.

Medium (à point): Before the meat is turned, drops of juice are clearly visible on the surface showing that the centre of the meat is warm. When pressed with a finger, the meat resists because it is sufficiently cooked to have contracted. When cut, the colour is rose pink inside. For steak, lamb, kidneys, liver, veal and duck. Some nouvelle cuisine chefs cook fish so that it is still pink next to the bone. Chicken should be medium to well done.

Well done (bien cuit): The meat is very firm to the touch because the heat has entirely reached the centre. When cut, there is no trace of pink inside. For pork, chicken, fish and shellfish. Some people insist that red meats – steak or kidneys – should be well done, but this is anathema to any chef.

MARINADES

A marinade is a highly flavoured liquid in which food is soaked before cooking to give it flavour, to prevent it drying out and to tenderise it slightly.

There are two types of marinade: raw and cooked. Raw marinades such as those for fish or chicken, in which the ingredients are simply mixed together and poured over the food, are used when the food is to be marinated for a short time. Cooked marinades in which the ingredients are simmered until tender, then completely cooled before pouring over the food, are intended to give stronger flavours. They are used with beef and game and generally contain red wine, herbs and spices such as juniper and peppercorns as well as onion, carrot, garlic and shallots. For lighter meats, the marinade ingredients are lighter too – white wine is used and fewer spices – and for uncooked marinades the ingredients are minimal – white wine or lemon juice, herbs, pepper and a slice or two of onion.

Lamb is good with oriental spiced marinades; pork takes to sweet-sour combinations or Indonesian saté seasonings laced with peanut oil. All marinades for grilling must contain a good proportion of oil, especially if used for basting.

The longer food is left in a marinade, the more it absorbs its flavour. In traditional cooking, 2-3 hours in the refrigerator is usual for fish fillets, 6-8 hours for veal and chicken and about 24 hours for lamb. Game and beef can be left for up to 3 days, by which time the flavour is quite strong, and nouvelle cuisine chefs have cut these times severely. The food should be turned from time to time in the marinade; it will mature twice as fast if left at room temperature rather than in the refrigerator. Before grilling, drain the food and thoroughly dry it on kitchen paper, otherwise it will not brown but simply stew in the excess moisture.

SAVOURY BUTTERS

Savoury butters of various flavours are a favourite accompaniment to grilled meats and fish – and to boiled or steamed vegetables. The butter can be shaped into a 2·5-cm (1-in) diameter or a rectangle about 1cm (⅜in) thick, wrapped in grease-proof paper and chilled until hard. Slice it into rounds or cut it in squares and set on the hot food just before serving. Alternatively, cream the butter and serve a spoonful of this softened butter on grilled food. For dry-fried meats, add a little savoury butter to the deglazed pan juices to enrich the sauce.

Anchovy butter

Soak 4 anchovy fillets in a little milk for about 20-30 minutes to remove excess salt, and drain. Crush in a mortar and pestle and work in 60g (2oz) creamed butter with freshly ground black pepper to taste. For fish.

Garlic butter

Blanch 4 peeled cloves of garlic in boiling water for 5 minutes, and drain. Crush them and beat into 60g (2oz) creamed butter with salt and pepper. For red meats and scampi.

Lemon butter

Beat the grated rind of a lemon and a teaspoon of lemon juice into 60g (2oz) creamed butter. For fish and vegetables.

Maître d'hôtel butter

Beat 2 teaspoons chopped parsley and a teaspoon of lemon juice with salt and pepper to taste into 60g (2oz) creamed butter. Serve with meat, chicken, fish and vegetables.

Maltaise butter

Beat the grated rind of half an orange, a teaspoon of orange juice and a teaspoon of tomato purée into 60g (2oz) creamed butter. For lamb chops, steaks and fish.

Mustard butter

Beat 2-3 teaspoons Dijon mustard into 60g (2oz) creamed butter. For steaks, fish and vegetables.

Paprika butter

Beat 2 teaspoons paprika pepper and a teaspoon of tomato purée into 60g (2oz) creamed butter. For veal, chicken and vegetables.

Shellfish butter

Pound 250g (8oz) crushed shellfish shells and trimmings (crayfish, shrimp, lobster, etc) in a mortar and pestle with 6 tablespoons creamed butter until smooth, or work the mixture in a blender. Rub through a very fine sieve or squeeze in cheesecloth or muslin to extract the butter, then season with salt and freshly ground pepper. For fish.

Tomato butter

Beat a tablespoon of tomato purée and a crushed clove of garlic (optional) into 60g (2oz) creamed butter. For steak or, without garlic, for fish and vegetables.

Ravigote butter

Chop together 2 shallots, 1 teaspoon fresh tarragon, 1 teaspoon fresh chervil, 1 teaspoon fresh parsley and 6-8 spinach leaves. Blanch for 5 minutes in boiling water, then plunge into cold water, drain and dry on a towel. Pound in a mortar or bowl or work in a food processor. Gradually add 60g (2oz) butter. For fish.

BROCHETTES DE COQUILLES ST JACQUES ET CREVETTES
(Scallop and shrimp brochettes)

Mussels, scampi tails, pieces of fish fillets and mushrooms are other possibilities for seafood brochettes. Choron sauce or sauce beurre blanc (page 194) can also be served. The brochettes can be served on a bed of boiled rice or rice pilaf. If possible, use only fresh herbs in the marinade.

SERVES 4

450g (1lb) scallops
450g (1lb) raw peeled shrimps
melted butter (for basting)
90g (3oz) freshly ground black pepper
½ teaspoon paprika
for the marinade
300ml (½ pint) white wine
2 tablespoons oil
tablespoon chopped tarragon
2 teaspoons chopped fresh mixed herbs – thyme, oregano, basil, parsley
for the béarnaise sauce (optional)
180g (6oz) butter
3 tablespoons vinegar
3 tablespoons white wine
10 peppercorns, crushed
3 shallots, finely chopped
tablespoon chopped fresh tarragon stems, or tarragon leaves preserved in vinegar
3 egg yolks
salt and white or cayenne pepper
1-2 tablespoons finely chopped fresh tarragon or tarragon leaves preserved in vinegar
tablespoon chopped chervil or parsley
lemon wedges (optional) for garnish
8 kebab skewers

Discard the small membrane adhering to the side of each scallop and put them in a bowl (not aluminium). Make the marinade: combine the wine, oil and herbs and pour this over the scallops and shrimps. Mix well, cover and leave to marinate in the refrigerator for at least 2 and, if possible, up to 8 hours.

For the béarnaise sauce: melt the butter, skim any froth from the surface and allow it to cool until just tepid. Boil the vinegar and wine in a small saucepan with the peppercorns, chopped shallots and 1 tablespoon of the tarragon stems or leaves until reduced to 2 tablespoons. Allow to cool, then add the egg yolks, a little salt and pepper and whisk for 30 seconds until light. Set the pan over low heat or in a water bath (bain marie) and whisk constantly until the mixture is very thick. Take from the heat and whisk in the tepid butter, a few drops at a time. When the sauce has thickened, the butter can be added faster. Do not add the milky sediment from the bottom of the pan. When all the butter has been added, strain the sauce, pressing it well through the sieve. Add the rest of the chopped tarragon, the chervil or parsley and taste for seasoning.

To finish: heat the grill or barbecue. Drain the scallops and shrimps and thread them on kebab skewers. NOTE: scallops are threaded through their diameter. Brush them generously with melted butter, sprinkle with black pepper and paprika and grill them with the rack about 7·5cm (3in) from the heat for 4-5 minutes, or until they are browned and tender. Turn them once during cooking and baste often with melted butter.

Serve the brochettes on a dish garnished with lemon wedges, or serve béarnaise sauce separately.

POULET A LA CRAPAUDINE
(Spatchcock chicken)

Another version of devil sauce (sauce diable) can be found on page 191. Instead of devil sauce, grilled chicken may be topped with maître d'hôtel butter.

SERVES 2

small chicken weighing about 750g-1kg (1½-2lb)
salt and freshly ground black pepper
2 tablespoons oil or melted butter
bunch of watercress (for serving)
for the devil sauce
150ml (¼pt) white wine
75ml (⅛pt) white wine vinegar
4 shallots, finely sliced
freshly ground black pepper
450ml (¾pt) veal or chicken stock
tablespoon meat glaze (page 219)
teaspoon chopped fresh or ½ teaspoon dried tarragon
tablespoon fresh tarragon leaves (optional – to finish)
30g (1oz) butter (to finish)
salt
2 skewers

Place the chicken on a board, breast side down. Cut along one side of the backbone with poultry shears or a heavy knife so the chicken can be pulled open. Remove the backbone by cutting along its other side. Snip the wishbone in half. Turn the chicken breast side up. With a sharp movement of the heel of the hand, press the chicken flat, breaking the breastbone. Skewer the chicken crosswise in order to hold it flat. Preheat the grill.

Meanwhile, make the sauce: in a small saucepan (not aluminium), boil the white wine, vinegar, shallots and pepper until reduced by one third. Add the stock and simmer for 10 minutes. Add the meat glaze and chopped or dried tarragon and continue cooking for 10 minutes more. This sauce can be prepared up to 3 days ahead and kept in the refrigerator, or it can be frozen.

Sprinkle the chicken with salt and pepper and brush with oil or melted butter. Place on the grill rack, skin side towards the heat and grill until well browned. Turn and continue grilling until tender, basting often. The total grilling time should be about 12-16 minutes, depending on the size of the chicken and the heat of the grill.

Just before the chicken is ready, finish the sauce. Bring it back to the boil. Blanch fresh tarragon leaves, if using, in boiling water for 1 minute, then drain, refresh with cold water and drain again thoroughly. Take the sauce from the heat, add the butter in small pieces, shaking the pan so it is incorporated. Add the tarragon leaves, taste for seasoning and serve with the chicken.

POULET A LA CRAPAUDINE
(Spatchcock chicken)

To prepare Poulet à la crapaudine for grilling: split the chicken, cut away the backbone, turn the bird breast side up and press down hard with the heel of the hand to break the breast bone and flatten out the chicken. Thread it on a pair of skewers to hold it flat, then preheat the grill and make the sauce

LEGUMES GRILLES
(Grilled vegetables)

For grilling it is best to choose fairly large mushrooms and to buy tomatoes that are ripe but not soft. The preferred type of onion to cook by this method is the large, mild Spanish onion.

SERVES 4

200g (8oz) mushrooms
3 tablespoons butter
salt and pepper
2 tomatoes
¼ teaspoon finely chopped garlic
4 teaspoons dry breadcrumbs
2 Spanish onions
teaspoon sugar

Remove stems from the mushrooms and fill the cavities with butter, reserving 2 teaspoonsful for the tomatoes. Season with salt and pepper.

Halve the tomatoes crosswise and cut out the core but do not peel. Sprinkle with garlic, salt, pepper and breadcrumbs and dot each with half a teaspoon of butter.

Peel the onions and cut crosswise into thick slices. Sprinkle one side with sugar, salt and pepper.

Arrange the vegetables, seasoned side up, on a baking sheet and grill without turning for 5 minutes, or until lightly browned.

ESCALOPES DE GIGOT DE MOUTON AU COULIS D'AIL ET D'ECHALOTTES

(Escalopes of leg of lamb with garlic and shallot purées)

Lamb is often flavoured with garlic, but serving garlic purée with lamb escalopes is an exciting new way of combining them. Purée of shallot, which like garlic belongs to the onion family, adds another note.

SERVES 6-8

leg of lamb weighing about 2-2.5kg (4-5lb), boned but kept whole (see page 29 for the boning method)
pinch each of pepper and thyme
tablespoon oil
crushed bay leaf
4 egg whites (to finish)
salt
for the garlic purée
10 heads of garlic, cloves separated and peeled
45g (1½oz) butter
salt and freshly ground pepper
for the shallot purée
40 shallots, peeled
45g (1½oz) butter
salt and freshly ground pepper

Remove the skin and most of the fat from the lamb and place it skin side down on your work surface. Using a very sharp knife, cut the meat into 2 cm (¾in) slices. Pound them to flatten them a little.

Place the escalopes in a shallow dish and sprinkle with pepper, thyme, oil and crushed bay leaf. Leave them for about an hour to absorb the seasonings.

For the garlic purée: place the garlic in cold water, bring to the boil and boil for 5 minutes. Drain thoroughly. Heat the butter in a pan, add the garlic and cook *very slowly*, stirring frequently, for 20-30 minutes, or until nearly all the moisture has evaporated. NOTE: garlic burns easily. Work the garlic purée through a drum sieve and season to taste with salt and pepper.

For the shallot purée: proceed to cook the shallot purée exactly as for the garlic purée.

About 15 minutes before serving, whip the 4 egg whites until stiff. Bring the garlic and shallot purées to the boil in separate pans and remove from the heat. Add half the beaten egg whites to each purée, whisking vigorously, and return to the boil. Remove from the heat and taste each for seasoning.

Keep the purées warm over a pan of hot water while grilling the drained meat.

To finish: grill the lamb for about 3-4 minutes on each side or until still very rare in the centre. Sprinkle with salt and serve with purées.

BROCHETTES DE ROGNONS

(Kidney brochettes)

SERVES 4

6-8 lambs' kidneys or 4 veal kidneys
60g (2oz) clarified or melted butter
salt and freshly ground black pepper
bunch of watercress (for garnish)
for the mustard sauce
180g (6oz) butter
3 tablespoons water
3 egg yolks
salt and Cayenne pepper
juice of ½ lemon, or to taste
1-2 teaspoons Dijon mustard
6-8 kebab skewers

To prepare the kidneys: peel off any skin and cut away as much of the core as possible with scissors or a small knife. Cut lambs' kidneys almost in half, leaving them joined on the curved side, and flatten them to form a butterfly shape. Cut veal kidneys almost in half also, spread them flat and secure in position with skewers.

For the mustard sauce: melt the butter, skim the froth from the surface and allow to cool until tepid. Lightly whisk the water and egg yolks with a little salt and Cayenne pepper in a small saucepan, then continue whisking over low heat until the mixture is thick enough for the whisk to leave a trail on the base of the pan. Take from the heat and whisk in the tepid melted butter, a few drops at a time.

When the sauce has started to thicken, add the butter a little faster. *Do not add the milky sediment* from the bottom of the pan. Stir in the lemon juice and mustard and taste for seasoning.

Keep the sauce warm in a water bath or bain marie.

Heat the grill. Brush the kidneys, cut side up, with butter and sprinkle with salt and pepper. Grill them 10-12.5cm (4-5in) from the flame, allowing 2-3 minutes on each side and brushing often with butter – they should remain pink in the centre. Remove the skewers, arrange the kidneys on a platter and garnish with watercress. Serve at once, with mustard sauce handed separately.

Matchstick-thin julienne or soufflé potatoes are the classic accompaniment to grilled kidneys.

COTES DE PORC GRILLEES SAUCE ROBERT

(Grilled pork chops, sauce Robert)

Hearty accompaniments are needed for pork: mashed or sautéed potatoes are the most popular. Devil sauce (page 191) can be served instead of sauce Robert.

SERVES 4

4 pork chops
3 tablespoons oil
salt and freshly ground pepper
bunch of watercress (for garnish)
for the sauce Robert
½ onion, chopped
tablespoon butter
75ml (⅛pt) white wine
2 tablespoons white wine vinegar
300ml (½pt) Basic brown sauce (page 191)
1-2 teaspoons Dijon mustard

For the sauce Robert: slowly cook the onion in the butter until soft but not brown. Add the wine and vinegar and reduce until about 2 tablespoons of liquid remain. Add the Basic brown sauce (fond de veau lié) and bring back to the boil. Rub the surface of the warm sauce with butter to prevent a skin forming. The sauce can be made a day ahead and then kept covered in the refrigerator.

Trim off the fat from the chops. Heat the grill. When hot, brush the chops with oil, season, and grill about 12.5cm (5in) from the heat source. When browned on one side, turn over, brush again with oil and season. Continue grilling until the chops are well done, about 10-14 minutes – the juices escaping from the meat should be clear.

To finish: just before the meat is done, bring the sauce to the boil. Remove from the heat, stir in the mustard and taste for seasoning. Do not allow the sauce to boil again. Arrange the pork chops on a platter, garnish with a bunch of watercress and serve the sauce separately.

TOURNEDOS EN SANGLIER

(Tournedos as mock wild boar)

As the name of this dish suggests, when beef steak is marinated it develops a flavour remarkably like that of wild boar.

SERVES 4

4 tournedos steaks, cut 3-5cm (1½-2in) thick
tablespoon oil
15g (½oz) butter
salt and freshly ground black pepper
75ml (3fl oz) veal stock
3 tablespoons cream
bunch of watercress (optional – for decoration)
for the cooked marinade
2 tablespoons oil
onion, sliced
carrot, sliced
2 shallots, sliced
stick of celery, sliced (optional)
600ml (1pt) red wine, plus a little extra (see method)
6-8 peppercorns
4-5 juniper berries
pinch of rosemary
pinch of thyme
2 bay leaves
tablespoon vinegar
for the vinegar mirepoix
½ onion, sliced
½ carrot, sliced
150ml (¼pt) vinegar
pinch of salt
2 peppercorns
4 juniper berries
for the sauce
2 tablespoons oil
30g (1oz) butter
½ onion, sliced
½ carrot, sliced
30g (1oz) flour
300ml (½pt) marinade (from the beef)
300ml (½pt) veal stock
tablespoon red currant jelly
salt and freshly ground black pepper
30g (1oz) butter (to finish)
for the croûtons
4 slices white bread
3 tablespoons oil
45g (1½oz) butter

For the marinade: heat half the oil in a saucepan (not aluminium), add the onion, carrot, shallots and celery and cook slowly until soft but not brown. Add the wine, peppercorns, juniper berries, rosemary, thyme and bay leaves, bring back to the boil and simmer for about 30 minutes or until the vegetables are tender. Leave until cold and add the vinegar.

Place the steaks in a small deep dish and pour the cold marinade over them to cover them completely. Sprinkle with the rest of the oil. Leave 2-3 days in the refrigerator. The longer the meat is marinated, the stronger the gamey flavour.

Drain the meat and pat dry with paper towels. Strain the marinade, reserving the vegetables and spices. Measure the liquid and, if necessary, add enough red wine to make it up to 300ml (½pt).

For the vinegar mirepoix: place the sliced onion and carrot in a small saucepan with the vinegar, salt, peppercorns and juniper berries. Bring slowly to the boil and boil until nearly all the liquid has evaporated.

For the sauce: heat the 2 tablespoons oil and add the 30g (1oz) butter. Add the sliced onion and carrot and sauté until lightly browned. Add the flour and cook slowly, stirring constantly until golden brown. Add the marinade, the reserved vegetables and spices, the veal stock and a little salt. Bring to the boil, stirring often. Cover and simmer over low heat or in a very hot oven, 220C (425F) gas 7, for 1 hour, stirring occasionally. Add the vinegar mirepoix and the red currant jelly and simmer for a further 20 minutes.

For the croûtons: cut rounds from the bread the same size as the tournedos and sauté them in the oil and butter until browned on both sides. Drain them on paper towels and keep at room temperature.

To finish: heat the oil and the butter in a sauté pan. Season the steaks with salt and pepper and sauté for 4-5 minutes on each side for rare steak. Transfer them to a serving dish and keep them warm. Discard the fat. Pour the 75ml (3fl oz) stock into the pan to deglaze it, add the cream and bring to the boil. Strain the sauce into the pan and bring to the boil again. Taste for seasoning and add plenty of freshly ground black pepper. Cut the 30g (1oz) butter into small pieces and add, shaking the pan, or stirring with a whisk to incorporate them. NOTE: pepperiness is characteristic of the sauce, but if pepper is cooked for too long it becomes bitter. Set the tournedos on the croûtons on a serving dish and spoon a little sauce over them. Garnish the dish with watercress and serve the remaining sauce separately.

13
MAIN COURSE SOUPS
Tour de France

The French are past masters at the proverbial one pot meal, and indeed the word supper comes from 'soupe'. No other nation seems to have quite the same flair for packing their 'marmites' with fish, meat, fowl and vegetables in permutations that vary from region to region. Cotriade, with its white fish in a cream sauce, glistening black mussels, and seaweed green sorrel, evokes the rocky Atlantic coast of Brittany as clearly as bouillabaisse depicts the colours of the Mediterranean – saffron orange, tomato red and multi-hued fish and shellfish. The flavour of cotriade is subdued and serious, whereas bouillabaisse is heady with herbs and piquant with spice. Even the cooking methods contrast: bouillabaisse must be recklessly boiled to emulsify the liquid, with the attendant risk of overcooking the fish, while cotriade is cooked at a steady simmer.

Inland, the possibilities are even more varied. Potée, a soup of pork and cabbage that dates back to the Gauls, can be flavoured with garlic sausage (in Auvergne), with ham (in the Morvan) or even with lamb or duck (in Brittany). It is a kind of pot au feu of pork and reflects the lack of standard recipes – the cook simply adds what happens to be at hand that day. The only difference between such soups and a stew is that they have enough liquid to form an excellent broth that can either be served separately as a first course, or in a bowl together with the meat and vegetables.

Unlike the English 'soup' the French term does not cover the refined bisques, and consommés of classical cooking. 'Soupes' are simple peasant affairs, often based on vegetables. Bacon and sausages may be pressed into service to give flavour to kitchen garden products like cabbage, leeks and the full range of roots. Typical of main course soupes is Garbure, made with bacon or a bit of confit of goose, plus leeks, carrots, onions, potatoes and any other available vegetables. Garbure can be served as a purée, or the vegetables can be left in thin slices in the broth. Croûtons are an essential accompaniment, sometimes toasted, sometimes spread with a spoonful of the puréed vegetables from the soup. In the old days, soupes always included bread, and even now most are served with fried or baked croûtons that add body to the liquid.

Garbure is a full meal, despite the lack of meat, and the same can be said of many other regional vegetable soups: Provençal chick pea soup flavoured with onion, leeks and tomatoes; the leek and potato soup of Flanders; and Normandy potato soup, flavoured with sorrel and enriched with egg yolks and cream. Touraine, famous for its fine vegetables, has a soup of leeks, turnips, cabbage and green peas flavoured with pork, and in Gascony goose giblets and barley are added to the local vegetables. Auvergne is famous not only for its potée, but for innumerable cabbage soups, for chestnut soup, and for a local garlic soup which is made simply of sliced bread rubbed with garlic, sprinkled with olive oil and moistened with boiling water.

This is an example of soupe at its most basic, and alas, what abuses are perpetrated in that name. 'Mange ta soupe, chérie,' still echoes in my ears from the year I lived with a family whose six small children were served a watery vegetable purée five nights out of seven (meat in the evening being considered bad for infant digestions). Such travesties are mercifully rare on adult tables, but the simplicity of soupes should be maintained. Any tendency to dress them up – to refine the cooking or add unnecessary garnishes – is a mistake. As Chef Chambrette impresses on over-eager students at La Varenne, knowing when to leave well alone is as important as the cooking itself.

Bread and soup

Most regional soups require bread, which is sometimes toasted in the oven. It can be added directly to the bowl; usually slices are layered alternately with the soup. This is an excellent use for stale bread.

Often the bread is made into croûtes: French bread is sliced and either baked in the oven or fried. For croûtons cut in cubes or other shapes, white sandwich bread is used. Frying in oil results in crisper croûtons, but butter gives better flavour, so a mixture of the two is the usual compromise. For garlic-flavoured soups, croûtes are often rubbed with a cut clove of garlic after frying; the crust of a whole French loaf can be rubbed with garlic, then the loaf sliced.

COTRIADE BRETONNE

Many versions of Cotriade exist in Brittany and this is one of the richest. It is made from a mixture of firm-fleshed white and oily fish to which onions, leeks, sorrel and mussels are added and the soup is then thickened with cream. The heart-shaped croûtes of fried bread are flavoured with garlic

THE WAY TO SUCCESS

1 When there is a choice of ingredients, particularly vegetables, try to contrast textures and colours.
2 Do not use large quantities of strong flavours like celery and leek.
3 Cut the vegetables and other ingredients into the sizes indicated in the recipe. Any change in shape or size can have a great effect on cooking time.
4 Acid ingredients such as onions and many green vegetables will curdle milk or cream unless they are thoroughly cooked beforehand.
5 Ingredients should be added to soups in an order determined by their cooking times; green vegetables, for instance, generally go in last.
6 Season soups lightly at first; add more salt during cooking if needed.

Getting ahead

1 Nearly all robust soups can be made at least one day ahead and kept covered in the refrigerator.
2 Vegetables that tend to fall apart, such as potatoes, should be slightly undercooked to allow for reheating. Noodles and delicate vegetables like spinach are best added when the soup is reheated.
3 Most soups can be frozen, but they will lose aroma and any crunchy texture. Soups containing cream tend to curdle, so cream should be added on reheating rather than earlier.

COTRIADE BRETONNE

SERVES 6

1.5kg (3lb) fish – a mixture of any of the following: lotte or monkfish, whiting, sole, turbot, mackerel, conger eel, hake
1 litre (¾pts) fish stock (page 218)
4 potatoes
2 onions, chopped
2 leeks, chopped
2 cloves garlic, chopped
30-60g (1-2oz) butter
bouquet garni
500g (1lb) raw or 250ml (⅜pt) cooked sorrel
750ml (1¼pts) mussels, cleaned
250ml (⅜pt) double cream
for the croûtons
6-8 slices white bread, cut in heart shapes, crusts discarded
6 tablespoons oil (for frying)
clove garlic, cut

Cut the fish into chunks and use the heads and tails of all except the mackerel to make the fish stock.
For the croûtons: fry the heart-shaped pieces of bread in the oil until golden brown on both sides. Drain on paper towels. Rub each croûton with the cut clove of garlic.

Quarter the potatoes and cut each quarter in thin slices. Chop the onions, leeks and garlic together and cook them slowly in 2 tablespoons of the butter. Add the fish stock, bouquet garni and potatoes and simmer for about 5 minutes, or until the potatoes are partly cooked. Add the monkfish and conger eel, if using, and simmer for about 3-4 minutes, then add the softer fish. Simmer for 5 more minutes.

If using raw sorrel, remove the stems, wash and cook in 2 tablespoons of butter for 15 minutes, stirring often, until very soft. When the fish are nearly tender, add the cooked sorrel, the mussels in their shells and the cream. Cook just until the mussels open. Serve the croûtons separately.

When preparing fish for any fish soup, cut the fish into equal-sized portions. This improves the appearance of the dish and the fish cooks through evenly

---

BOUILLABAISSE

True bouillabaisse uses Mediterranean fish, but an excellent imitation can be made with other sea fish. The greater the variety used, the better the bouillabaisse will be, and some white, some rich-fleshed fish and some shellfish should always be included.

Because many different kinds of fish are included, it is hard to cut down quantities in this recipe.

SERVES 8-10

1.5kg (3lb) white fish such as lotte or monkfish, John Dory, red mullet, whiting, bass, hake, perch, haddock and plaice
1kg (2lb) rich fish such as conger eel, Moray eel, gurnard, eel
2 litres (3½pts) fish stock (page 218)
large spiny lobster or 8-10 small lobster tails
2 large crabs or 8-10 small crabs
200ml (⅓pt) olive oil
2 medium onions, sliced
white part of 2 leeks, sliced
2 stalks celery, sliced
3 tomatoes, peeled, seeded and chopped
3-4 cloves garlic, crushed
bouquet garni
strip of orange rind, without pith
2 sprigs of fresh fennel or 1 teaspoon dried fennel
¼ teaspoon saffron
salt and pepper
tablespoon tomato purée
tablespoon anise liquor (Pernod or Pastis)
4 tablespoons chopped parsley (for sprinkling)

for the marinade
3 tablespoons olive oil
2 cloves garlic, finely chopped
pinch of saffron
for the croûtes
long loaf of French bread, cut into about 20 diagonal slices
150ml ($\frac{1}{4}$pt) olive oil
clove garlic
for the sauce rouille (optional)
1 chili pepper
1 slice bread, crust removed
3-4 cloves garlic, crushed
1 egg yolk (optional)
salt
150ml ($\frac{1}{4}$pt) olive oil

Cut the fish in chunks, discarding skin and fins. Use the fish heads and tails to make fish stock. Meanwhile, marinate the fish in a bowl with the olive oil, garlic and saffron. Leave all shellfish in their shells. With a cleaver, chop the large crabs and spiny lobster into pieces and discard the stomach and 'dead men's fingers'.

In a very large, wide pan or flameproof casserole heat the 200 ml ($\frac{1}{3}$ pt) oil, add the onions, leeks and celery and sauté lightly until soft but not brown. Add the tomatoes, garlic, bouquet garni, orange rind and fennel. Add the fish stock. Sprinkle in the saffron and add salt and pepper. Bring to a boil and simmer for 30-45 minutes. The bouillabaisse can be prepared 2 hours ahead up to this point; keep it in the refrigerator.

For the croûtes: lightly brown the sliced bread on both sides in the olive oil in a heavy frying pan. Halve the clove of garlic and rub each croûte with it.

For the optional sauce rouille: chop the chili pepper. Soak the bread in water and squeeze dry. Work the chili, garlic, bread, egg yolk and salt together with a little of the oil. Gradually whisk in the remaining oil. Season to taste.

Twenty minutes before serving: bring the liquid to a boil, uncovered, add the rich fish and shellfish and boil as hard as possible for 7 minutes. Do not stir, but shake the pan from time to time to prevent the mixture from sticking. Put the white fish on top and boil for 5-8 minutes longer or until the fish just flake easily, adding more water, if necessary, to cover all the pieces of fish. NOTE: it is important to keep the liquid boiling rapidly so that the oil emulsifies with the broth and does not float on the surface.

Bouillabaisse is served in two dishes, one for the pieces of fish, the other (a bowl or soup tureen) for the broth. Take the bouillabaisse from the heat and transfer the fish to a hot deep serving dish.

Whisk the tomato purée and anise into the hot broth and taste for seasoning. Pour the broth into the tureen. Sprinkle broth and fish with chopped parsley and serve at once along with the croûtes and the sauce rouille. Though the liquid and fish are served in separate dishes, they are brought to the table at the same time. Guests spread the croûtes with the sauce rouille and drop them into the broth. For an even stronger flavour, more sauce can be stirred directly into the soup.

MATELOTE

Matelote is found all over France in different versions. Eel is a favourite ingredient, but other freshwater fish such as perch, carp, pike or trout are appropriate.

SERVES 4

$\frac{3}{4}$-1kg ($1\frac{1}{2}$-2lb) eel, cut in 5cm (2in) pieces
salt and pepper
3 tablespoons brandy
450ml ($\frac{3}{4}$pt) dry red wine
onion, sliced
carrot, sliced
clove of garlic, sliced
2 shallots, sliced
2-3 sprigs parsley
bay leaf
sprig of fresh thyme or $\frac{1}{2}$ teaspoon dried thyme
kneaded butter made with 2 level tablespoons butter and 2 level tablespoons flour
30g (1oz) butter, to finish
for garnish
16 pickling onions, peeled
250g (8oz) mushrooms, stems trimmed level with the caps
15g ($\frac{1}{2}$oz) butter
juice of $\frac{1}{2}$ lemon
for the croûtons
8 slices of white bread
3 tablespoons oil
45g ($1\frac{1}{2}$oz) butter

Sprinkle the fish with salt and pepper, pour over the brandy and mix well. Cover and leave to marinate in the refrigerator for 1-2 hours. Put the wine, onion, carrot, garlic, shallots, parsley, bay leaf and thyme in a saucepan (not aluminium) and simmer for 30 minutes, covered.

For the garnish: simmer the onions in boiling salted water for 12-15 minutes or until tender, then drain. Put the mushrooms in a pan with the butter, lemon juice and 1cm ($\frac{1}{2}$in) water. Cover and simmer for 5 minutes, or until the mushrooms are tender.

For the croûtons: cut heart shapes from the bread slices and fry them in oil and butter until golden brown on both sides. Drain on paper towels and keep warm.

Arrange the eel in a shallow pan, and strain over the hot wine – it should cover the fish. Cover the pan, bring to a boil and simmer for 15 minutes or until the fish flakes easily. Transfer the fish to a deep serving dish or tureen and keep warm.

Bring the cooking liquid to the boil and whisk in the kneaded butter a piece at a time, so that the soup thickens to the consistency of thin cream.

Add the onions and the mushrooms with their liquid, heat thoroughly and taste for seasoning. Take the soup from the heat and stir in the 30g (1oz) butter in small pieces. NOTE: do not reheat the soup after adding the butter. Spoon the liquid over the fish, arrange the heart-shaped croûtons around the edge and serve.

It is possible to prepare the matelote 6-8 hours ahead and reheat it, but do so with care, so that the fish does not overcook. Wait until just before serving to add the butter enrichment.

POCHOUSE

For this variation on matelote, lardons of smoked bacon are added to the soup with the garnish of tiny onions and heart-shaped croûtons. Allow 125g (4oz) of derinded bacon cut into strips, and blanch the lardons first by putting them in cold water and bringing it to the boil. Drain well, then sauté them in 15g ($\frac{1}{2}$oz) butter. Add to the soup with the onions and the mushrooms.

MARMITE DIEPPOISE

In this soup, the fish of the Normandy coast are lightly flavoured with the exotic spices that the French sailors brought back to the port of Dieppe.

SERVES 8

| 4 sole or plaice weighing 350-500g ($\frac{3}{4}$-1lb) each, filleted and with the bones removed |
| 2kg (4lb) turbot or halibut, cut into 8 steaks |
| 1 litre (1$\frac{3}{4}$pts) mussels |
| 300ml ($\frac{1}{2}$pt) dry white wine |
| 500g (1lb) cooked, peeled shrimps (optional) |
| 90g (3oz) butter |
| 2 leeks, chopped |
| 2 stalks of celery, chopped (optional) |
| 2 large onions, chopped |
| 3 dried fennel twigs tied with string, or teaspoon fennel seeds |
| 2 tomatoes, peeled, seeded and chopped |
| salt and pepper |
| 8 prawns or scampi (optional) |
| 8 scallops (optional) |
| 60g (2oz) flour |
| 300ml ($\frac{1}{2}$pt) double cream |
| pinch of Cayenne pepper |
| $\frac{1}{2}$ teaspoon curry powder |
| *to finish* |
| pinch of paprika |
| tablespoon chopped parsley |

Cut each sole or plaice fillet in half crosswise and each turbot or halibut steak into 4 pieces, removing the bone. Use the bones of the sole and the turbot to make a simple fish stock: wash them, just cover with water, bring to the boil and simmer for 20 minutes. Strain and add enough water to make 1$\frac{1}{4}$ litres (2$\frac{1}{4}$pts).

Scrub the mussels thoroughly under running water and remove any weed. Discard broken shells and any open ones that do not close immediately when tapped. Put them into a saucepan with the wine, cover and cook over high heat, tossing occasionally for 5-7 minutes, or until the mussels open. Drain, reserving the liquid and discard any mussels that remain closed. Discard the top shells, leaving the mussels in the bottom shells. Put them into a bowl with the shrimps and keep warm.

Heat 30g (1oz) of the butter in a large saucepan, add the chopped leeks, celery, onions and fennel and cook over low heat, stirring, until soft but not brown. Add the tomatoes and simmer, stirring, for 10 minutes. Stir in the fish stock and a little salt and pepper. Add the turbot, bring to a simmer for 2 more minutes. Add the scampi and scallops, if included, and the sole, and simmer for 5 more minutes, or until all are just tender.

Transfer the fish to a serving bowl or tureen and keep warm, reserving the liquid.

Heat the remaining butter in a saucepan, add the flour and cook over low heat, whisking, until foaming but not brown. Whisk in the fish liquid and then carefully add the reserved mussel liquid, leaving any sand and grit behind. Bring to the boil, whisking, and simmer for 2 minutes. The soup should be lightly thickened. Stir in the cream, Cayenne and curry powder and taste for seasoning. Pour the liquid over the fish in the serving bowl and sprinkle with paprika and chopped parsley. Top with the mussels and prawns or scampi and serve.

POTEE AUVERGNATE

This 'soupe' is an ideal winter dish. Stuffed cabbage rolls accompany the cooking broth; then the meat and vegetables come as a main course.

SERVES 6

| 1kg (2lb) rolled pork shoulder |
| 500g (1lb) piece bacon |
| 1kg (2lb) veal bones |
| 4 litres (7pts) water |
| 6 peppercorns |
| bouquet garni |
| 1$\frac{1}{2}$ teaspoons salt, or to taste |
| onion, stuck with a clove |
| 3 carrots, halved and cut in 7 · 5cm (3in) lengths |
| 3 stalks celery, cut in 7 · 5cm (3in) lengths |
| 3 onions, halved |
| 2 medium turnips, cut in quarters |
| 3 leeks, halved and cut in 7 · 5cm (3in) lengths |
| 3-4 long crusty rolls, cut in 1 · 25cm ($\frac{1}{2}$in) slices (for croûtes) |

for cabbage rolls

| outer leaves of a Savoy cabbage |
| 250g ($\frac{1}{2}$lb) minced pork |
| clove garlic, crushed |
| 75g (2$\frac{1}{2}$oz) fresh white breadcrumbs |
| $\frac{1}{4}$ teaspoon grated nutmeg |
| salt and freshly ground black pepper |
| 1 egg, beaten to mix |

Put the pork, bacon and bones in a large pan with the water, peppercorns, bouquet garni tied in cheesecloth, and the salt. Cut the onion in half across the rings and bake it on an electric hot plate or held on a fork over a gas flame until charred, then add it to the pan. NOTE: this gives colour to the broth.

Bring the water slowly to the boil, allowing at least 20 minutes and skimming often. Simmer and continue skimming for 10-15 minutes until all the thick brown scum has risen and been discarded. Cover the pot, leaving a small gap for evaporation, and simmer for 2$\frac{1}{2}$ hours, skimming occasionally. Tie the vegetables in a large piece of cheesecloth so they will be easy to lift out of the cooking pot.

For the cabbage rolls: remove any wilted leaves and blanch the cabbage in a large pan of boiling water for 5 minutes. Drain it and remove 12-14 outside leaves. The remaining cabbage can be used in another dish. Mix together the minced pork, garlic, breadcrumbs, nutmeg and plenty of salt and pepper and stir in the egg to bind the mixture. Put a spoonful of stuffing on each cabbage leaf and roll it up, turning in the sides to enclose the stuffing. Pack the cabbage leaves tightly in a shallow pan so they do not unroll and spoon over enough broth from the pork to cover them. Cover and simmer for $\frac{3}{4}$-1 hour or until the stuffing is firm.

Add the bag of vegetables to the large pan and continue simmering for $\frac{3}{4}$-1 hour, or until the meat is very tender and the vegetables are cooked. The potée and cabbage rolls can be prepared up to 48 hours ahead and kept in the refrigerator, but undercook the vegetables slightly to allow for reheating. Bake the bread slices in a low oven until crisp to make them into croûtes.

To serve: lift out the meat, carve the pork in 1cm ($\frac{3}{8}$in) slices and arrange overlapping down the centre of a large serving dish. Slice the bacon and pile at each end.

Arrange the vegetables around the meat, cover the dish with foil and keep hot.

Strain the broth and add the liquid from the cabbage rolls. Reheat the broth, taste for seasoning and skim off as much fat as possible. Put 2-3 cabbage rolls in each soup bowl with a few croûtes, pour over the broth and serve, passing the platter of meats and vegetables as a second course.

GARBURE

These vegetables are a base to which others such as peas and green beans are added in season. In some richer versions of garbure, bacon or confit of goose is also used.

SERVES 6

45g (1½oz) butter
medium white turnip, thinly sliced
2 large carrots, thinly sliced
¼ medium head of cabbage, shredded
white part of 3 leeks, thinly sliced
2-3 stalks celery, thinly sliced
2 medium potatoes, thinly sliced
2 litres (3½pts) veal or chicken stock or water
salt and pepper
for the dried beans
60g (2oz) dried white haricot beans, soaked overnight and drained
½ onion, stuck with 2 cloves
small carrot
bouquet garni
salt and pepper
for the croûtes
2 crusty rolls or 1 long thin loaf of bread, crust removed and bread cut in 1·25cm (½in) slices
3 tablespoons oil and 3 tablespoons butter (for frying)
60g (2oz) grated Gruyère or Parmesan cheese (for sprinkling)
tablespoon melted butter
to finish
30-45g (1-1½oz) butter
2 tablespoons chopped parsley

For the dried beans: put the beans, onion with cloves, carrot and bouquet garni in a pan with water to cover. Simmer for 2-3 hours or until the beans are tender, adding more water if necessary. Add salt and pepper halfway through the cooking time. Drain the beans and discard the onion, carrot and bouquet garni.

To make the garnish for garbure: spread the fried bread croûtes with some of the vegetables from the soup made into a purée. Sprinkle with grated cheese before putting them in the oven to brown well. They are handed separately

In a large heavy-based flameproof casserole or pan melt 30g (1oz) of the butter, add the turnip, carrot, cabbage, leek, celery and potato and press a piece of buttered foil on top. Cover and cook very gently, stirring occasionally, for 15-20 minutes or until the vegetables are fairly tender. NOTE: do not let them brown. Add the beans, 1·5 litres (2½pts) stock or water, season with salt and pepper and cover and simmer for 20-30 minutes, or until the vegetables are very tender.

For the croûtes: fry the sliced bread in the oil and butter until golden brown on both sides and drain on paper towels.

Set the oven at moderately hot, 190C (375F) gas 5. Lift out about a quarter of the vegetables from the soup with a slotted spoon and purée them in a blender or work them through a food mill. Melt the remaining butter in a small pan, add the purée and cook, stirring constantly, until it thickens to the consistency of mashed potatoes. Spread the purée on the croûtes, doming it well, sprinkle with grated cheese and dribble on the melted butter. Bake the croûtes in the heated oven for 10-12 minutes or until well browned.

Meanwhile purée the remaining soup in a blender or work it through a food mill. Reheat it and add enough of the remaining stock or water to thin it to the consistency of

cream. Taste it for seasoning. The soup and croûtes can be made 48 hours ahead; keep them covered in the refrigerator.

To finish: bring the soup to a boil and warm the croûtes in the oven. Take the soup from the heat, stir in the butter in small pieces, spoon into bowls and sprinkle with chopped parsley. Serve the croûtes separately.

VARIATION

Follow the recipe for garbure, but purée all the vegetables together. Just before serving, add the butter and parsley to the soup and pour it into heatproof serving bowls. Cover the surface of each bowl with thin overlapping slices of crusty bread and sprinkle each bowl with 2-3 tablespoons grated Gruyère or Parmesan cheese. Dribble on a little melted butter. Bake in a very hot oven, 240C (475F) gas 9, until browned, or brown under the grill.

14

MERINGUES
Secrets of Carême's Castle

Meringues are essentially frivolous. No one could take seriously a confection that bursts into a cloud of white at the touch of a fork, then melts to nothing in the mouth, leaving a tantalising honey-sweetness. Child's play to eat, and seemingly child's play to make as well, meringues need only two ingredients – egg whites and sugar. Methods of mixing are surprisingly diverse, resulting in three different kinds – Swiss meringue, Italian meringue and cooked meringue, or 'meringue cuite'.

Simplest of all is Swiss meringue, where the sugar – a whopping 60g (2oz) for each egg white as for all meringues – is folded into the whipped egg white. Despite the minimal ingredients, though, there is a catch: if the sugar is over-mixed, the meringue dissolves to make a syrup that glues the mixture to the baking sheet and forms a sticky centre in the finished meringue. It may still be delicious, but it is incorrect.

Not only is Swiss meringue tricky to make (it happens to be one of my personal bêtes noires), but it separates if kept for more than an hour or so before it is baked. So I prefer to follow the lead of most professional chefs and make Italian meringue, where the egg whites are beaten with scalding sugar syrup and cooked to an indestructible snow-white mousse that can be kept for hours, or even days, in the refrigerator before baking. Making Italian meringue, particularly with an electric mixer, is foolproof *provided* the sugar syrup is cooked to the right temperature. Because of its heat the egg whites expand, with the result that Italian meringue has almost double the volume of the same quantity of Swiss meringue.

Cooked meringue – or 'meringue cuite' – I leave, frankly, to the professional chefs. It is prepared by beating egg whites with icing sugar over steam or very low heat and the muscle power needed to thicken and lighten the mixture correctly is prodigious. Even the chefs look wary when cooked meringue is mentioned and tend to reserve it for boisterous students who regard cooking as an active sport.

Once prepared, any meringue is invaluable (and remarkably inexpensive). With no addition save a few drops of vanilla for flavour, Swiss meringue can be baked to sandwich with cream to make meringues Chantilly, piped into individual baskets to fill with fruit, or spread on fruit pie as a topping. Swiss meringue makes delicious cakes when mixed with ground almonds or hazelnuts and filled with various flavours of butter cream. Classics include japonais (made with ground almonds, filled with Kirsch-flavoured buttercream and coated with white praline), progrès (with ground almonds and hazelnuts, praline-flavoured buttercream and icing sugar) and succès (made with ground almonds, filled with praline butter-cream and with a coating of browned almonds) as well as the Dacquoise given here. No cake tins are needed for meringue and, though it is often shaped with a pastry bag and piped into the appropriate rounds or ovals, it can be simply spread on baking trays with a knife.

More durable than Swiss meringue, Italian meringue is even more versatile. It can be substituted for Swiss meringue in any recipe, though the texture is somewhat finer and softer when baked. Italian meringue is the basis for a multitude of petits fours such as Rochers de neige – snow 'rocks' flavoured with almonds – and Noix au café – hemispheres of coffee-flavoured meringue sandwiched with the same meringue, uncooked. Equal parts of Italian meringue, whipped cream and fruit purée make the perfect iced soufflé and pâtissiers keep a jar of Italian meringue on hand to sweeten pastry cream and whipped cream (the results are lighter and smoother than if sugar is used).

Above all, Italian meringue is the mortar for a Vacherin – that dazzling operetta castle turreted with whipped cream and emblazoned with fresh fruit. The bricks of these castles are normally made of Swiss meringue, with a solid circle of meringue as base. When baked, the 'bricks' are mounted on the circle and mortared with Italian meringue, piped with rosettes, then recooked until crisp, and filled with cream and fruit.

Such fanciful confections hark back to another age. Marie Antoinette, most lighthearted of queens, whipped up meringues for her friends in the Trianon, and it was the greatest pâtissier of all time, Carême, chef to Tsar Nicholas I, to the Prince Regent and to Talleyrand, who remarked, 'Of the five fine arts, the fifth is architecture, whose main branch is confectionery'. Today's trend towards simplicity belies his words, but the Vacherin has survived in triumph to attest to his claim.

VACHERIN

A Vacherin is a fairytale concoction of Swiss meringue, held together and decorated with Italian meringue. This one is filled with Chantilly cream and topped with strawberries.

MONTS BLANCS

These individual Monts Blancs have a meringue base supporting a nest of chestnut purée filled with Chantilly cream.

THE WAY TO SUCCESS

1 When making Swiss meringue, do not overfold the sugar: when the egg whites are stiff enough to hold peaks, add 2 teaspoons sugar per egg white and beat vigorously for a few seconds to 'cook' the whites, giving them body and gloss. Fold the remaining sugar carefully into the mixture. The meringue should be stiff enough to retain peaks so it can be piped.

2 When making Italian meringue, boil the sugar to the right temperature. When testing, a sugar thermometer should register 120C (248F). When hand-testing the syrup should form a firm ball when rolled between fingers and thumb. Lift out syrup in a spoon, plunge into cold water and, still in the water, roll into a ball.

3 To prevent meringues sticking during cooking: thoroughly butter baking sheets, allow the butter to set, then sprinkle evenly with flour. Do not add flour while the butter is still soft. Alternatively, use silicone non-stick vegetable parchment to line baking sheets. (The paper can be used several times.) Pipe or spoon the meringue evenly onto the baking sheet. Even if meringues do stick, all is not lost. With ice-cream, or whipped cream and fruit, a meringue-based dessert is always delicious.

4 Set the oven at very low – the lower the better, as meringues should dry out rather than bake. Professional pastry books recommend cooking them for 3 hours or more, depending on size, at 80-100C (176-212F) gas low. Note that domestic oven thermostats are rarely accurate at such low levels, so watch meringues while baking.

Getting ahead

1 Although Swiss meringue must be baked as soon as it is made, Italian meringue can be kept for up to a week in a covered container in the refrigerator.

2 All baked meringues, whether Swiss or Italian, with or without nuts in the mixture, keep well for several weeks in an airtight container. They can be frozen for up to 3 months.

3 If for some reason a meringue loses its crispness (this can happen in damp weather), reheat in a very low oven for 25-30 minutes to dry it.

VACHERIN

SERVES 6

for the Swiss meringue

4 egg whites

240g (8oz) caster sugar

$\frac{1}{2}$ teaspoon vanilla essence

icing sugar (for sprinkling)

for the Italian meringue

240g (8oz) caster sugar

150ml ($\frac{1}{4}$pt) water

4 egg whites

8-10 candied cherries (optional)
or 18-20 hazelnuts (optional)

for the filling

Chantilly cream made with 300ml ($\frac{1}{2}$pt) double cream, tablespoon caster sugar and teaspoon vanilla essence

250-350g (8-12oz) fresh strawberries or raspberries or any suitable poached fruit

pastry bag; medium plain and star tubes

Set the oven at 120C (250F) gas low; thoroughly butter and flour two baking sheets and mark four 18-20cm (7-8in) rounds using a pan lid or flan ring as a guide.

For the Swiss meringue: using a copper bowl and whisk or an electric mixer, beat the egg whites until they hold stiff peaks. Add 2 tablespoons of the sugar and continue beating for 30 seconds, or until the mixture holds long peaks when the beater is lifted, and is slightly glossy. Fold in the remaining sugar, a few tablespoons at a time. Fold in the vanilla with the last spoonful of sugar. Put it into a pastry bag with a medium plain tube, and pipe 16-20 fingers 10cm (4in) long and one 18-20cm (7-8in) solid circle, starting from the centre and spiralling outwards. Sprinkle the meringues with icing sugar and bake in the heated oven for 1-1½ hours, or until crisp and very lightly browned. NOTE: if the meringues start to brown during cooking, turn down the heat.

For the Italian meringue: heat the sugar with the water over low heat until dissolved. Bring to the boil and boil without stirring until the syrup reaches the hard ball stage (120C, 248F, on a sugar thermometer). NOTE: while boiling, wash down any sugar crystals from the sides of the pan with a pastry brush dipped in water. Meanwhile, stiffly whip the egg whites. Gradually pour the very hot syrup onto them, whisking constantly at high speed, and continue whisking until the meringue is completely cool.

When the Swiss meringues are cooked, loosen them with a sharp knife and transfer to a rack to cool. Cut a small piece from each biscuit to make one end flat. Using a piping bag and a medium star tube, pipe a line of Italian meringue near the edge of the circle. Place 2 meringue fingers upright on the Italian meringue, flat end down and rounded side outwards. Pipe 2 lines of Italian meringue between the fingers, one outside, one inside. NOTE: this provides extra support. Continue in this way until the 'case' is complete.

Put the remaining Italian meringue into a pastry bag fitted with a star tube and decorate the top and sides of the vacherin with rosettes. If you like, you can decorate the rosettes with halved candied cherries or hazelnuts. Continue baking it for an hour, or until crisp. Let it cool on a rack. A vacherin can be baked 2-3 weeks ahead and kept in an airtight container, or frozen.

For the filling: to make the Chantilly cream, whip the cream in a cold bowl until it starts to thicken. Add the sugar and vanilla and continue beating until the cream holds a shape and sticks to the whisk.

To finish: not more than 3-4 hours before serving, fill the vacherin with Chantilly cream, using a pastry bag and star tube, if you like. Layer and top the cream with fruit.

Vacherin can also be made as individual gâteaux. It can also be made by piping rings of meringue the same diameter as the solid circle base. Mount these on the base circle, cement and cover the whole vacherin with Italian meringue.

THE HARD BALL STAGE

To cook sugar syrup to the hard ball stage for Italian meringue, boil without stirring until it reaches 120C (248F). To test by hand, lift a bit of syrup from the pan with a spoon, plunge it into cold water and roll into a ball

TO FILL A PIPING BAG

Twist the tube into the piping bag so the mixture won't drip out. Holding the bag in one hand, fold the top down with the other to form a collar. Scoop the mixture into the bag, pull up the top and twist to close it

TO PIPE A MERINGUE BASE

Mark a circle on a well-floured baking sheet as a guide and pipe meringue in a spiral, starting from the centre. Hold the bag firmly upright as you are piping and keep the top closed

TO MAKE A VACHERIN

Each flat 'biscuit' of Swiss meringue is attached to the meringue base and sandwiched with ribbons of Italian meringue, first inside, then outside. The whole case is baked again before being filled

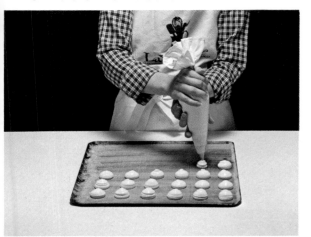

TO PIPE INDIVIDUAL MERINGUES

Holding and squeezing the bag in one hand and using the other for support, pipe walnut-sized meringues onto a well-floured baking sheet to make the little Noix au café

MONT BLANC

Mont Blanc should be piled high in the centre, mountain style. It can be made as one large gâteau or as 6 individual ones.

If fresh chestnuts are not available, an 880g (1lb 15oz) can of sweetened chestnut purée can be substituted. In this case do not make a syrup.

Unsweetened canned chestnut purée is best kept for savoury stuffings. Canned whole chestnuts may be used as they will save a good deal of work. Put them in the pan with the water and vanilla pod and cook until tender – this will only take a few minutes. Continue as directed.

SERVES 6

for the Swiss meringue
4 egg whites
240g (8oz) caster sugar
½ teaspoon vanilla essence
for the chestnut purée
1kg (2lb) chestnuts
1 vanilla pod
90g (3oz) sugar
150ml (¼pt) water
to finish
150ml (¼pt) double cream
½ teaspoon vanilla essence
1 egg white
1-2 tablespoons caster sugar
15g (½oz) dark dessert chocolate, grated
pastry bag; 1cm (½in) and 3mm (⅛in) plain tubes

Thoroughly butter a baking sheet and leave until the butter is set. Flour lightly and evenly and mark a 25cm (10in) circle on it with a flan ring or pan lid. Set the oven at 120C (250F) gas low.

For the Swiss meringue: using a copper bowl and whisk or an electric mixer, beat the egg whites until they hold stiff peaks. Add 2 tablespoons of the sugar and continue beating for 30 seconds, or until the mixture holds long peaks when the beater is lifted, and is slightly glossy. Fold in the remaining sugar, a few tablespoons at a time. Fold in the vanilla with the last spoonful of sugar.

NOTE: do not overmix the meringue or it will turn to liquid as the sugar dissolves.

Using the pastry bag and 1cm (½in) plain tube, pipe the meringue with a spiralling motion in a 25cm

(10in) solid circle on the prepared baking sheet, starting from the centre. Bake in the heated oven for 1-1½ hours or until the meringue is firm to the touch. If it starts to brown during cooking, turn the heat down or prop open the oven door with a wooden spoon. Transfer the meringue to a rack to cool. It can be stored in an airtight container for a few weeks.

To peel the chestnuts: pierce each nut with a sharp knife and bring to the boil a few at a time in a pan of water to cover. Remove the pan from the heat and lift out the nuts with a slotted spoon. Take off the outer and inner peel. If they become difficult to peel, reheat them in the water as it is easier to peel chestnuts while still hot.

For the chestnut purée: put the peeled nuts in a saucepan with the vanilla pod and water to cover and bring to the boil. Cover and simmer for 25-30 minutes, or until the nuts are very tender. Drain the nuts and work through a food mill to purée them. Wash the vanilla pod to use again. In a small saucepan, bring sugar and measured water to the boil to make a thin syrup. Allow this to cool. Beat the syrup into the chestnut purée to thin it, adding enough to make the purée thin enough to pipe but thick enough to hold a shape. Fill into the pastry bag fitted with the 3mm (⅛in) plain tube.

To finish: stiffly whip the double cream and add the vanilla. Stiffly whip the egg white, add the sugar and continue to beat until glossy. Fold into the cream until just mixed. Using the 3mm (⅛in) tube, pipe the chestnut purée in the shape of a nest around the edge of the meringue base and pile the whipped cream in the centre. Sprinkle grated chocolate over the whipped cream and chill well.

The Mont Blanc can be made 3-4 hours before it is required and stored in the refrigerator.

GATEAU SUCCES

This cake is better if made a day ahead so the meringue will soften.

SERVES 6

for the almond meringue layers
180g (6oz) blanched almonds
15g (½oz) corn or potato flour (fécule)
180g (6oz) sugar
6 egg whites

for the praline butter cream
butter cream (page 100) made with 4 egg yolks, 90g (3oz) sugar, 60ml (2oz) water and 250g (8oz) butter
praline (page 129) made with 110g (3½oz) whole unblanched almonds and 110g (3½oz) sugar
to finish
icing sugar
125g (4oz) chopped, toasted almonds
pastry bag and 1cm (⅜in) plain tube

In a blender, electric food processor or rotary cheese grater, grind the blanched almonds to a powder a few at a time. Butter and flour one or two baking sheets and mark three 23cm (9in) diameter circles with a flan ring or pan lid as a guide. Turn the oven to very low, 130C (250F) gas ½.

For the almond meringue layers: mix together the almonds, flour and all but 2 tablespoons of the sugar. Beat the egg whites until stiff, if possible in a copper bowl. Beat in the remaining 2 tablespoons of the sugar for 30 seconds until the egg whites are glossy. Fold in the almond mixture as quickly and lightly as possible. Using the pastry bag and plain tube, pipe the mixture in 23cm (9in) rounds on the prepared baking sheets and bake in the heated oven for about 40-50 minutes or until the layers are crisp, dry and just beginning to brown. Trim the rounds neatly with a sharp knife while they are still hot and then transfer them to a rack to cool. They can be kept up to 2 weeks in an airtight container.

For the praline butter cream: make the butter cream and praline and combine. The butter cream can be kept, refrigerated, for up to a week.

To assemble the gâteau: sandwich the meringue layers with about half of the butter cream. Spread the remaining butter cream over the top and sides. The cake can be kept refrigerated for up to a week depending on the freshness of the butter cream. Bring to room temperature before serving. Sift a layer of icing sugar over the top and press the chopped, toasted almonds around the side before serving.

DACQUOISE

SERVES 6

for the almond Swiss meringue

100g (3½oz) blanched almonds

level tablespoon cornflour

4 egg whites

150g (5oz) caster sugar

½ teaspoon vanilla essence

for the filling

Chantilly cream made with 300ml (½pt) double cream, tablespoon caster sugar, teaspoon vanilla essence

250g (8oz) strawberries, raspberries or pineapple

icing sugar (for sprinkling)

pastry bag and medium star tube

Set the oven at 150C (300F) gas low. Butter and flour a baking sheet and mark two 20cm (8in) circles with a pan lid or flan ring as a guide. *For the almond Swiss meringue:* in a nut mill, rotary grater or electric food processor grind the almonds to a powder, a few at a time. Mix them with the cornflour. Beat the egg whites until they hold stiff peaks. Beat in 2 tablespoons of the sugar and continue beating for 30 seconds or until the whites are glossy. Fold in the remaining sugar, a few tablespoons at a time. Sprinkle the ground almond mixture over the meringue in 2 or 3 portions and fold in each portion as lightly as possible. Lastly, fold in the vanilla. Spread the mixture in two rounds on the prepared baking sheet and bake in the heated oven for 40-50 minutes, or until crisp, dry and lightly browned. Trim the rounds, then transfer to a rack to cool.

For the filling: to make the Chantilly cream, whip the cream in a cold bowl until it starts to thicken. Add the sugar and vanilla and continue beating until the cream holds a shape and sticks to the whisk.

Hull the strawberries, rinse them if sandy and halve if large. Pick over raspberries, reserving a few whole berries of either fruit for decoration. Thinly slice the pineapple. Quarter a few of the slices to make crescents and reserve for decoration; dice the remaining pineapple.

To assemble: spread two-thirds of the Chantilly cream on one meringue layer and pile the fruit on top. Place the other meringue layer on top and sprinkle with icing sugar. Refrigerate the cake for at least 3 hours before serving so it softens and can be cut into neat slices without crumbling. It can be assembled up to 24 hours ahead.

Decorate the gâteau just before serving. Using the pastry bag and medium star tube, pipe rosettes of the remaining Chantilly cream around the top edge of the cake. Top each rosette with fruit.

NOIX AU CAFE

MAKES 12-16

240g (8oz) caster sugar

150ml (¼pt) water

4 egg whites

teaspoon coffee essence, or to taste

pastry bag; 6mm (¼in) plain tube

Thoroughly butter a baking sheet and leave until the butter is set. Flour lightly and evenly. Set the oven at 150C (300F) gas low.

Heat the sugar with the water over low heat until dissolved. Bring to a boil and boil without stirring until the syrup reaches the hard ball stage (120C, 248F, on a sugar thermometer). NOTE: while boiling, wash down any sugar crystals from the sides of the pan with a pastry brush dipped in water.

Meanwhile, stiffly whip the egg whites, beginning at low speed and gradually beating faster and faster. Gradually pour the very hot syrup onto the stiff egg whites, whisking constantly at high speed, and continue whisking until the meringue is completely cool – it will be stiff and glossy. Beat in the coffee essence to taste.

Reserve about a quarter of the mixture for filling. Place the remaining mixture in a pastry bag fitted with a 6mm (¼in) plain tube and pipe walnut-sized mounds on the prepared baking sheet. Bake in the heated oven 1-1½ hours, or until crisp. To test if they are done, remove one, let it cool and taste to see if it is crisp. Transfer the meringues to a rack to cool. The unfilled meringues can be kept for several weeks in an airtight container, or 3 months in the freezer.

When completely cool, sandwich them with the reserved coffee meringue mixture.

PETITS TURQUOIS

MAKES 12-14

for the almond meringue layers

180g (6oz) blanched almonds

15g (½oz) corn or potato flour (fécule)

180g (6oz) sugar

6 egg whites

for the chocolate mousse

250g (8oz) dark dessert chocolate, chopped

4 eggs, separated

100g (3½oz) butter

tablespoon Grand Marnier

30g (1oz) sugar

to finish

chocolate 'vermicelli'

plain chocolate bar (for making curls)

icing sugar (for sprinkling)

6.5cm (2½in) diameter plain biscuit cutter; pastry bag and 1cm (⅜in) plain tube

Set the oven at very low, 130C (250F) gas ½, and butter and flour two baking sheets. Mark 30 circles on the sheets with the biscuit cutter, spacing them well apart.

For the almond meringue layers: grind the almonds to a powder a few at a time. Mix the almonds, flour and all but 2 tablespoons of the sugar. Beat the egg whites until stiff. Beat in the remaining 2 tablespoons of the sugar for 30 seconds or until the egg whites are glossy. Fold in the almond mixture as quickly and lightly as possible. Put the mixture into the pastry bag fitted with a 1cm (⅜in) plain tube and pipe 6.5cm (2½in) rounds on the prepared baking sheets. Bake in the heated oven for 30-40 minutes or until the cakes are crisp, dry and just beginning to brown. Trim the cakes while still warm and soft and transfer them to a rack to cool.

For the chocolate mousse: melt the chocolate in a water bath. Take from the heat and beat the egg yolks one by one into the hot chocolate so it thickens slightly. Beat in the butter and Grand Marnier. Allow to cool slightly. Beat the egg whites until stiff and beat in the sugar until the egg whites are glossy. Fold the egg whites into the chocolate mixture as lightly as possible; the warm mixture will lightly cook and stiffen the whites. Leave to cool at room temperature but do not refrigerate.

To assemble: sandwich pairs of rounds with a 1cm (⅜in) layer of the chocolate mousse. Spread the tops and sides with mousse also. Press chocolate 'vermicelli' round the sides. Top with chocolate curls and sprinkle icing sugar on top. Chill thoroughly before serving. The cakes keep well in the refrigerator for 2-3 days.

15
NUTS
The subtlety of nuts

As a child I hated nuts. There was something about their crunchiness, their earthy taste, that set my teeth on edge, and I fancied I could detect the smallest particle of nut in any dish. I was in my teens before I realised what I was missing. Enlightenment began with macaroons and maids of honour, and from there I progressed rapidly to almond cakes, almond and hazelnut pastries, spiced cocktail nuts and – dare I breath the name – peanut butter. At last the chestnut stuffing in the Christmas turkey no longer elicited a 'moue' of distaste but tempted me to a second helping.

But the full impact of nuts in cooking did not burst upon me until I came to France. Who else would have thought of putting pistachios into a terrine or making a velouté-based soup garnished with chicken quenelles (dumplings) and hazelnuts? I became aware of the subtleties of white praline, made with ground blanched almonds and sugar syrup, and dark praline made with unblanched almonds and caramelised sugar – the difference between the two being rather like that between white and black pepper. White praline is used almost exclusively to decorate the chewy nut-based meringue gâteaux of which the French are so fond, but dark praline is a universal flavouring for the pastry and butter creams and for custards, nearly as useful as coffee and chocolate.

In the nut family, ground almonds surely rank first as far as the French cook is concerned. Almond meringue-based Dacquoise, almond petits fours, macaroons, gâteau Alcazar with its almond-flavoured filling, all are staples of the modern pâtissier's repertoire. And medieval cooks appreciated almonds even more. Their cultivation in Europe was encouraged by the Arabs, who loved marzipan, nougat and other nutty sweetmeats. In the 14th century, Taillevent, cook to King Charles VI of France, bound sauces with ground almonds and, of course, used them as the principal ingredient in blanc-manger, a symbol of purity. Blanc-manger could be made of any white mixture, not necessarily sweet; it was often based on chicken or veal and held together with ground almonds.

The French, with some inspiration from the Italians, also exploit chestnuts to the full. These nuts contain more starch and less oil than most and so can be cooked differently. They are the only nut that is treated like a vegetable and at La Varenne, Chef Chambrette has a special way of glazing chestnuts to a lustrous brown for serving with turkey, goose and especially game. Chestnuts are often simmered and sieved to a purée to accompany meat dishes, or to make

desserts like Mont blanc and Pavé aux marrons.

Of the other common nuts, pistachios are valued in cooking mainly for their colour. For a truly brilliant green, you should shell them then boil them in water a few moments before peeling off the inner skin. They are used for decorating pastries and provide a vivid note when mixed in terrines, stuffings for galantines and the new 'sausages' of shellfish. Hazelnuts are used ground in cakes and pastries and whole for decoration. Walnuts can double for hazelnuts in baking, but they are usually not browned because this can make them bitter. They are best, I think, in first course salads of greens and fish, to which the nuts add texture, and walnut oil can be used in the dressing. Such combinations are typical of the nouvelle cuisine.

This oil content of nuts is important in cooking. Nuts with a good deal of oil like almonds, peanuts, hazelnuts and walnuts must be ground carefully and handled lightly during mixing if the oil is not to separate and make the mixture heavy. Peanut oil, light and with a high scorching point, is excellent for deep frying and for neutral salad dressings. The use of walnut oil is a matter of taste – its flavour is pronounced and, delicious though it may be in dressings, a little goes a long way.

Because of their oil content, nuts easily turn rancid – and with a rancid mixture, nothing can be done. Nuts should therefore always be stored in an airtight container, preferably at a low temperature. They should be chopped or ground just before using as, once cut, they deteriorate rapidly. Nuts keep much better in their shells and freeze excellently.

Nut trees, and the recipes that go with them, are very much a matter of the local soil and climate. Almond trees withstand frost; chestnut trees can be found in most places, but plump chestnuts worth the peeling come mainly from central France, Italy and Spain. Although hazelnuts grow all over Europe, we have dozens of the bushes in our garden in Normandy that never seem to produce a nut, and walnut trees can be equally cantankerous. 'A woman, a dog and a walnut tree, the more you beat 'em, the better they be.'

GATEAU DE NOISETTES AUX FRUITS

The finished gâteau is a luscious concoction of hazelnut pastry, whipped cream and fruit, topped with a rosette of whipped cream. Other fruits can be used in season

Almonds, pistachios, walnuts and chestnuts are blanched before peeling. Hazelnuts are toasted in the oven. For almonds, pistachios and walnuts: bring water to the boil. At least double the volume of the nuts should be used. Add all the nuts and bring just back to the boil. Lift one out with a slotted spoon, and peel it. If it peels easily, drain the rest and rinse with cold water. If the nuts are hard to peel, continue boiling for a few moments but do not allow the nuts to cook.

To peel almonds and pistachios, take a nut between your thumb and index finger, press firmly and the nut should pop from the skin. Pistachio skins may be stubborn and require scraping with a knife. Scrape walnuts with a knife. They are somewhat troublesome and not often peeled. Dry thoroughly before using. For chestnuts: pierce the shell of each nut with a pointed knife before blanching in boiling water and cooking for 1-2 minutes. Leave the nuts in the hot water while peeling and reheat them if they become hard to peel as they cool. Use a small knife to cut away both shell and inner skins at the same time. For hazelnuts: grill the nuts as below until golden brown; the skins will crack and start to peel. Let the nuts cool slightly, then rub off the skins with a coarse cloth.

Grilling nuts

Spread nuts in one layer in an ungreased baking tin.

Bake in a moderate oven, 180C (350F) gas 4, for 8-15 minutes, depending on the size of the nuts, until golden brown. Nuts brown easily, so they should be carefully watched and stirred occasionally for an even result. Remove them from the baking tin, allow to cool and store them in an airtight container.

Grinding nuts

Nuts are best ground by hand with a rotary cheese grater as this method does not bring out their oil. However, they can be ground in small quantities in a blender or food processor provided they are not worked for too long; if flour or sugar are to be added to the ground nuts, add them to the unground nuts in the machine so as to keep them as dry as possible.

Getting ahead

1 Nuts can be peeled and kept in an airtight container for several weeks. *Be sure they are very dry* before storage.
2 Nuts can be toasted and kept tightly covered. This helps keep them from turning rancid.
3 Store ground nuts in an airtight container and keep them for as short a time as possible.
4 Because of the high oil content, mixtures containing nuts mellow on keeping. Nut cakes, biscuits and pastries should be stored in an airtight container. They all freeze well.
5 If nut pastry softens on standing, reheat it in a low oven to dry it; it will become crisp when it cools.

GATEAU DE NOISETTES AUX FRUITS

(Hazelnut and fruit torte)

Use any colourful fresh or poached fruit to make this torte. If you prefer, make individual tortes, using one 10cm (4in) round of hazelnut pastry for each.

SERVES 6-8

for the pastry
150g (5oz) flour
½ level teaspoon salt
250g (8oz) hazelnuts, toasted, peeled and ground
125g (4oz) sugar
125g (4oz) butter
1 egg yolk
for the fruit
one of the following: large pineapple, peeled, sliced, cored and poached; 4 peaches, scalded and peeled, either fresh or poached (page 23) or 500g (1lb) fresh strawberries, hulled

to finish
Chantilly cream made with 450ml (¾pt) double cream, teaspoon vanilla essence and tablespoon sugar
2 tablespoons apricot jam glaze – page 144 (optional)
pastry bag and medium star tube

For the pastry dough: sift the flour with the salt onto a board or marble slab and add the ground nuts and the sugar. With your fist or a rolling pin, pound the butter to soften it. Make a large well in the centre of the flour mixture, add the softened butter and egg yolk and work them to a paste with the fingertips. Gradually draw in the flour mixture, using the fingers and heel of the hand. When the dough is smooth, press it into a ball, wrap it in plastic wrap or a plastic bag and chill for ½-1 hour or until firm. Set the oven at moderately hot, 190C (375F) gas 5.

Divide the dough into three portions and, with the heel of the hand or with a tablespoon, press out each portion on a baking sheet to a 17-20cm (8in) round, using flan rings if possible to prevent the dough from spreading. Bake in the heated oven for 10-12 minutes, or until golden brown. If necessary, while the rounds are still warm, trim them neatly with a knife, using a plate or pan lid as a guide. Cut one round into 6-8 equal wedges. Transfer the pastry to a rack to cool; it can be kept for 4-5 days in an airtight container, or frozen for up to 3 months.

Reserve 2-3 pineapple slices, each cut into 3 wedges, 6-8 peach slices for decoration or 6-8 whole strawberries (the number depends on how many the cake is to serve). Slice the remaining peaches, halve the strawberries or cut each pineapple slice into 5 sections. Set one round of pastry on a serving dish, spread it with one-sixth of the Chantilly cream and top with half the sliced fruit. Cover with another sixth of the cream, set the second round of pastry on top and cover with another sixth of the cream. Using the remaining cream, pipe 6-8 decorative lines from the edge of

To peel hazelnuts: grill until the skins crack, cool slightly, then rub off the skins by working the nuts in a cloth

While the pastry rounds are still warm, cut one of them into 8 equal wedges. These are to be used for decoration

Sandwich the hazelnut pastry rounds with layers of whipped cream and your chosen fruit – La Varenne used fresh pineapple. Then pipe 'spokes' of crème Chantilly to support the slices of fruit and the hazelnut pastry wedges on top

the round to the centre thus dividing it into 6-8 equal sections. Top with the wedges of pastry and pieces of fruit, placing each wedge, supported by a line of Chantilly cream, at a 45° angle. Rosettes of cream can be piped under the wedges if additional support is needed. Leave enough cream to pipe a rosette in the centre of the cake for decoration. Chill until serving.

TO MAKE PRALINE

For a basic praline to flavour creams and ice-creams, put 100g (3½oz) whole unblanched almonds in a heavy-based pan with 100g (3½oz) sugar. Heat gently, stirring occasionally, until the sugar melts and caramelises. The almonds should pop, showing they are thoroughly toasted. Pour the praline onto an oiled marble surface or baking sheet and leave it until cold and crisp, like toffee. Grind it to a fine powder in an electric food mill or with a rotary cheese grater. Work through a fine sieve and store in a screwtopped jar. To make white praline for decorating cakes: cook sugar to the soft ball stage (115C (239F) on a sugar thermometer), add the same weight of ground blanched almonds as you have used of sugar and stir over the heat for about 1 minute. Cool on an oiled surface and work through a coarse sieve.

PAVE AUX MARRONS

(Chestnut paving stone)

The name of this dessert refers to its shape which echoes the wooden blocks that used to line the streets of Paris. If fresh chestnuts are not available, canned whole chestnuts or purée may be used; if the purée is sweetened, decrease the amount of sugar in the recipe.

SERVES 8

1kg (2lb) chestnuts, weighed unpeeled, or 250g (8oz) chestnut purée or canned whole chestnuts
1 vanilla pod
250g (8oz) dessert chocolate, chopped
150ml (¼pt) water
200g (7oz) unsalted butter
200g (7oz) sugar
2 tablespoons brandy
for decoration
Chantilly cream made with 150ml (¼pt) double cream, 1-2 tablespoons sugar and teaspoon vanilla essence
crystallised violets (optional)
medium loaf tin (20×10×6cm or 8×4×2¼in); pastry bag and medium star tube

Lightly oil the inside of the loaf tin, line the base with greaseproof paper or non-stick vegetable parchment and oil the paper. Peel the chestnuts. *To cook the chestnuts:* put the peeled nuts in a pan with the vanilla pod and enough water to cover. Cover the pan and simmer for 25-30 minutes or until the nuts are very tender. Remove the vanilla pod, drain the nuts a few at a time and work them through a vegetable mill or sieve. Drain and purée canned chestnuts, if using these.

Gently melt the chocolate in the measured water over low heat. Let it cool. Cream the butter, work in the sugar and beat until light and soft. Stir in the cooled chocolate, add the chestnut purée and flavour with brandy. Pack the mixture into the prepared tin, cover with greaseproof paper and chill overnight. The pavé can be kept up to a week in the refrigerator, or it can be frozen.

Not more than 3-4 hours before serving, unmould the pavé onto a serving dish and mark the top in a lattice pattern with the back of a knife. Decorate round the base of the pavé with rosettes of Chantilly cream, using a pastry bag and medium star tube.

Top the rosettes with crystallised violets and serve more cream separately if you like.

GATEAU ALCAZAR

Apricot is the classic glaze for this cake, but red currant glaze can be used as it is also attractive. Both are on page 144.

SERVES 6-8

pâte sucrée (lesson 4) made with 200g (6½oz) flour, ¼ teaspoon salt, 100g (3½oz) butter, 80g (2½oz) sugar and 3 egg yolks
100ml (⅙ pt) apricot jam glaze
for the almond filling
125g (4oz) whole blanched almonds, ground
160g (5oz) sugar
3 eggs
½ teaspoon vanilla
2 tablespoons Kirsch
60g (2oz) melted butter
for decoration
100g (3½oz) whole blanched almonds, ground
100g (3½oz) sugar
1 egg white, beaten until frothy
4 tablespoons apricot jam glaze
6-8 shelled pistachios, blanched and halved
20cm (8in) diameter cake tin; pastry bag and 6mm (¼in) plain tube

Make the pâte sucrée following the directions given on page 141 and chill for 30 minutes. Line the bottom of the cake tin with a round of paper and butter it generously. Roll out the dough and line the bottom and sides of the tin. Prick the bottom and spread with the 100ml apricot jam glaze. Set oven at moderately hot, 190C (375F) gas 5.

To make the almond filling: in a mortar with a pestle or in a bowl with the end of a rolling pin, pound the ground almonds with the sugar until almost paste-like. Add 1 egg, the vanilla and Kirsch and beat until thick and light-coloured. Alternatively, work the almonds, sugar, 1 egg, vanilla and Kirsch in a blender. Separate the remaining eggs and beat the yolks, one by one, into the mixture until it is thick. Whip egg whites until stiff. Fold the melted butter into the almond mixture and then fold in the egg whites as lightly as possible.

Pour the almond filling into the lined cake tin and bake in the heated oven for 35-45 minutes or until browned and a skewer inserted in the centre comes out clean. Turn it out and leave to cool on a wire rack. Turn the oven down to moderate, 180C (350F) gas 4.

For the almond decoration: pound the almonds with the sugar until paste-like and then beat in enough egg white to make a smooth paste that holds its shape. Alternatively, work the almonds and sugar with the egg white in a blender. Put the almond mixture into a pastry bag fitted with the plain tube and pipe the mixture in a diamond lattice on top of the cake. Bake the cake in the heated oven for a further 10 minutes or until the almond decoration is lightly browned.

Put the 4 tablespoons of apricot jam glaze in a pan and reduce until very thick. Brush it in each diamond of the lattice and set half a pistachio in the centre of each diamond.

GATEAU GRENOBLOIS AUX NOIX

(Grenoble nut cake)

This rich mixture, scarcely a cake at all, is baked in a water bath to ensure that it will cook slowly and evenly. Grenoble, near the French Alps, is famous for its walnuts.

SERVES 6

100g (3½oz) dark dessert chocolate
5 eggs, separated
120g (4oz) sugar
200g (7oz) walnuts, ground
100g (3½oz) hazelnuts, peeled and ground
Chantilly cream made with 150ml (¼pt) double cream, teaspoon sugar and ¼ teaspoon vanilla essence
angel cake tin with cover; water bath (see Chapter 29)

Set the oven at low, 150C (300F) gas 2. Thoroughly butter inside the cake tin.

Melt the chocolate over a pan of hot water. Beat the egg yolks with two thirds of the sugar until the mixture is light and creamy. Stir in the ground walnuts and hazelnuts and the melted chocolate. Mix well. Beat the egg whites until they form stiff peaks. Add the remaining sugar and beat for 20-30 seconds longer or until glossy. As lightly as possible, fold the egg whites into the chocolate nut mixture in 2-3 batches, using a wooden spatula or metal spoon.

Turn the mixture into the cake tin, cover, set in a hot water bath and bake in the centre of the heated oven for 1½ hours.

Allow the cake to cool thoroughly before turning it out of the tin. It can be made a few days ahead, wrapped and stored in the refrigerator, or it can be frozen. Just before serving, spread lightly sweetened Chantilly cream on top and slice into wedges.

BOULES A L'ORANGE

(Orange biscuits)

These almond biscuits are easier to make than macaroons. You can use candied lemon peel instead of the orange if you like.

MAKES 40-45

250g (8oz) almonds, blanched and peeled
250g (8oz) icing sugar
125g (4oz) candied orange peel, cut in small pieces
2-3 egg whites
to finish
1 egg white, lightly beaten
icing sugar

Lightly grease a heavy baking sheet and line it with non-stick vegetable parchment. Set the oven at hot, 200C (400F) gas 6.

Grind the almonds with the icing sugar and candied peel in a food processor until very fine. With the blades still turning, gradually add the egg whites until the mixture is moist enough to shape but not sticky.

Shape the mixture with your hands into balls the size of small walnuts. Roll each in the beaten egg white, then in icing sugar and place on the baking sheet. Bake in the hot oven for 10-12 minutes or until they crack on top but are still soft inside. Remove them from the paper and transfer to a wire rack to cool.

If it is difficult to remove the biscuits from the paper, lift one end of the paper slightly and pour a glass of water under the paper onto the baking sheet. The hot baking sheet will cause steam to form, making them easy to remove after a few minutes.

The biscuits can be stored for 1-2 weeks in an airtight container, but they tend to harden with time.

MACARONS
(Macaroons)

MAKES 12

125g (4oz) almonds, blanched, peeled and ground
1½-2 egg whites
160g (5⅓oz) sugar
½ teaspoon vanilla essence
2 tablespoons icing sugar, sifted (for sprinkling)

Line a heavy baking sheet with non-stick vegetable parchment and grease the parchment. Set the oven at hot, 200C (400F) gas 6.

Using a mortar and pestle, pound the ground almonds, adding ½ an egg white a little at a time. Keep pounding until you get a smooth and very fine paste. Add half the sugar and incorporate it into the mixture using the pestle. Next, add another ½ egg white and continue working the dough with the mortar and pestle. In the same way, incorporate the remaining sugar, then another ½ egg white. Beat in the vanilla. NOTE: the dough should be soft but not runny. If necessary add a little more egg white.

Shape the mixture with your hands into balls the size of walnuts. Arrange them on the prepared baking sheets and flatten them slightly. Brush each ball with a little water and sprinkle the surface of each with sifted icing sugar. Put the baking sheet in the top third of the heated oven and bake for 18-20 minutes, or until the tops are lightly browned.

Take the baking sheet from the

To loosen macaroons or boules à l'orange: as soon as they are taken from the oven, lift one corner of the paper and pour a glass of water onto the baking sheet. The steam will make it easy to remove the macaroons

oven and carefully lift one end of the paper slightly and immediately pour a glass of water under the paper. NOTE: the hot baking sheet will cause the water to form steam, thus making it easy to remove the macaroons. Leave for a few minutes, then remove the macaroons from the paper and transfer them to a wire rack to cool. They can be stored for 1-2 weeks in an airtight container, but as they tend to harden with time, it is better to eat them while still fresh.

NOISETTES SABLES
(Hazelnut sablé biscuits)

These unusual biscuits can be made 2 or 3 days ahead and kept in an airtight container.

MAKES 10-12

125g (4oz) shelled hazelnuts
60g (2oz) flour
pinch of salt
60g (2oz) butter
60g (2oz) sugar
to finish
about 4 tablespoons thick honey
125g (4oz) plain dark dessert chocolate, chopped

6cm (3½in) diameter plain round biscuit cutter

Set the oven at moderate, 180C (350F) gas 4. Cook the hazelnuts in the heated oven for 8-12 minutes or until browned. While still hot, rub them in a cloth to remove the skins and then leave the nuts to cool. Grind the nuts with a rotary cheese grater or nutmill onto a marble slab or a board and sift the flour over them. Make a well in the centre, add the butter and sugar and work them to a paste with the fingertips. Gradually draw in the flour and nuts, using the whole hand. When smooth, knead the dough with the heel of the hand until pliable and then chill the dough for 30 minutes or until firm.

Roll out the dough to a 7mm (¼in) thickness and cut into rounds with the biscuit cutter. Line a baking sheet with foil, set the biscuits on it and bake them in the heated oven for 7-10 minutes or until firm. NOTE: do not allow the biscuits to brown or they will taste bitter. Transfer them to a rack to cool.

Melt the chocolate on a heatproof plate over a pan of hot water. Allow it to cool to tepid, then work with a metal spatula until creamy. Spread half the biscuits with a smooth coating of chocolate. Put the remaining chocolate in a small strong plastic bag and snip off one corner with scissors so that the chocolate can be piped in a thin thread. Decorate each of the chocolate-coated biscuits with a diamond lattice pattern and leave to set. Spread the remaining biscuits with honey and set a chocolate-coated round on top of each one.

PRALINES
(Caramelised nuts)

Caramelised nuts, so often used ground as a flavouring, can also be formed into bite-size pieces and served as an accompaniment to ice-cream, or with coffee after dinner.

MAKES 12-15

100g (3½oz) shelled, unblanched almonds; or shelled and peeled hazelnuts
100g (3½oz) sugar
paper sweet cases

Oil a baking sheet. Put the nuts and sugar in a heavy-based pan and heat gently without stirring until the sugar starts to melt. Continue cooking, stirring occasionally until the sugar is a dark brown caramel and the nuts pop. Dip the base of the pan in a bowl of warm water to stop the cooking. Allow the caramel to cool for 1-2 minutes until it starts to thicken and then drop the mixture teaspoon by teaspoon onto the oiled baking sheet. Leave until cold and crisp, then transfer the nuts to an airtight container as they soften quickly. They can be kept, layered in greaseproof paper, for a week or more if the container is completely sealed. Set them in paper cases for serving.

16
PASTA
Rolling your own

Legend has it that Marco Polo brought pasta back from one of his trips to the Orient. Utter nonsense! The Roman Apicius, who lived at the time of Christ, gives a recipe for fried pasta strips with pepper and honey; and in 1279, a decade or more before Marco Polo's return from his travels, a chest of macaroni was listed as part of a Genoese inheritance. Through the centuries what is basically a flour and water dough has been transformed into an ever more fantastic number of patterns and shapes. Flamboyant sauces have been added, and the union of pasta and Parmesan cheese has been sanctified. However, it was not until the mid-19th century, with the invention of the extrusion machine for mass production, that pasta became an everyday staple food rather than a feast-day treat.

French cooks have never approached the Italian virtuosity with pasta; not surprisingly, many French pasta dishes bear Italian names – macaroni à l'Italienne (with Gruyère and Parmesan cheeses and butter), à la napolitaine (with beef stewed in red wine and tomatoes, grated cheese and butter) and à la sicilienne (with grated cheese, butter and puréed chicken livers). But the French have their own ways with pasta as well.

The Alsace region is famous for homemade noodles rich with egg yolks. These are often topped with toasted breadcrumbs and butter. Sometimes cream and a few drops of vinegar are added to the noodles, with a winter touch of wild mushrooms and, for the well-heeled, diced foie gras. In Languedoc, macaroni is prepared with aubergines, tomatoes, mushrooms and garlic, and it is no surprise to hear that ravioli and cannelloni have spread along the Riviera from Italy to Provence. (For cognoscenti, by the way, there's even a spaghetti museum near Imperia not far from Genoa.)

The Corsicans fill their ravioli with a mixture of fresh sheep's cheese, mint, fennel and lambs' lettuce. More orthodox ideas include pasta shells with onions, à la lyonnaise, and a delicious Provençal cannelloni filled with fresh sardines and spinach, coated with white sauce and sprinkled with cheese.

Pasta is at its best when freshly made, and in Italy fresh pasta is sold by every grocer. As well as serried trays of green, pink and cream-coloured noodles, bows, shells and several kinds of ravioli, many shops have a machine for making tortellini. The mesmeric regularity with which the hopper spits out a stream of plump cages filled with veal, cheese, chicken or Parma ham invariably draws a little crowd of onlookers.

However, the freshest of bought pasta rarely com-pares with that made at home. Ingredients for the dough are minimal: flour, salt, eggs (which for economy may be replaced by water) and a spoonful or two of oil to make the mixture easier to handle. The finished dough, made by the universal method of sifting the flour on a board then adding the liquid ingredients to a well in the centre, should be supple and moist. Don't be afraid of working pasta dough well – it should be a good deal more elastic than pâte brisée dough, and I like to pick it up and slap it on the table with a rhythm that works wonders on frayed nerves; if the dough tends to stick, work in a little flour, but never let it get dry or it will crack during rolling. The right consistency is aptly described in an old Alsatian recipe which calls for mixing one egg per person in a bowl, then beating in flour by spoonfuls until the dough is 'too stiff to beat'.

It is the rolling that takes time and skill. I have seen a little old Italian chef, who trained under Escoffier, make and roll dough by hand to wafer thinness in under 20 minutes, but he was a master. He used quantities of flour, shifted the dough and turned it from one side to another constantly and, by sheer muscle power and a heavy rolling pin, reduced the elastic ball of dough to a vast sheet the texture of velvet. Then, sprinkling with yet more flour, he loosely folded the sheet and cut it across in even strips to make perfect, even noodles.

For less intrepid cooks like me, it helps to leave the dough for an hour or so (covered with an overturned bowl to prevent drying) so that it loses some of its elasticity before rolling is attempted. A pasta machine, which works on the principle of a laundry mangle, simplifies the task still further. The dough is passed several times through the machine, each time with the rollers closer together, until the pasta emerges in a ribbon of the required thickness – as thin as possible.

Whether fresh or bought ready-made, and of what-ever form, all pasta is cooked in the same way. It should be immersed in large quantities of boiling liquid – at least 2 litres (3½pts) for 250g (8oz) pasta. Of course, almost all pasta is cooked in salted water –

NOUILLES AU BEURRE ET AU FROMAGE

Fresh noodles are cooked, drained and tossed in butter with salt and plenty of freshly ground black pepper. A generous sprinkling of Parmesan cheese adds the finishing touch. For a change, try making tomato-flavoured red noodles or spinach-flavoured green ones and serving them together with the plain ones

allow 8-10g salt (2 teaspoons) per litre (1¾ pts), but when you have it, stock will add flavour and richness. (This stock cannot be used afterwards because the paste will shed quite a lot of excess starch during cooking.)

Always simmer pasta, do not boil it, and stir it several times during cooking to separate the strands. Timing depends on type and size, and dried pasta takes much longer to cook than fresh. Homemade noodles, for instance, are done when brought back just to the boil; whereas commercial noodles can take 8-12 minutes. The only reliable test for cooking pasta is to taste it; it should still be resilient to the bite yet not taste of uncooked flour. The Italian phrase *al dente* perfectly sums up the correct texture – chewy to the teeth. When ready the pasta is drained, rinsed thoroughly with hot water to wash away excess starch and finished according to the recipe.

Much depends on this final stage as character is given to pasta by other ingredients. Pasta can be used in soup, from minestrone, with its elbow macaroni, to consommé with *semi di meloni* (melon seeds). When the pasta is to accompany a richly sauced dish, it is often tossed in butter, or better still in browned butter or beurre noisette. One of the most popular dishes at La Varenne is Sole Carlier – sautéed filets of sole served with a white wine and butter sauce on a bed of fresh, buttered noodles.

More elaborate sauces transform pasta from an accompaniment into a first course, varying from the classic macaroni Nantua, layered with a crayfish sauce, to the more peasant-style macaroni aux anchois, combined with anchovies cooked in a butter and tomato sauce.

Serving possibilities are so many, and the flavour of pasta itself is so unobtrusive that it is hard to imagine anyone disliking it. On the contrary, pasta is addictive. When he was Consul in Alexandria, Ferdinand de Lesseps would regale the plump son of the Egyptian Viceroy with secret feasts of macaroni. When the son became Viceroy in his turn, he permitted de Lesseps to try out his engineering talents on Egyptian soil. The Suez Canal, the eventual result, can therefore be said to be based on macaroni . . .

THE WAY TO SUCCESS

Flour for pasta
Strong white bread flour, made partly from hard (durum) wheat, has a high gluten content and makes very good pasta. Semolina flour or meal, produced from hard wheat, with its high gluten content, is sometimes recommended for pasta because it will hold up better and remain firm in cooking. Some people also find it tastier. Plain flour may also be used. Do not use self-raising flour.

Fresh pasta dough
1 Let the finished dough rest for about an hour before rolling, whether by hand or with a machine. Dough that is elastic will be tough when cooked.
2 Always roll the dough to a thin sheet; thick pasta is heavy when cooked.
3 When rolling by hand, be sure the sheet of dough is of even thickness so that it all cooks at the same speed.
4 A firm dough is needed for rolling pasta by machine so it does not stick. Flour the ball of dough thoroughly before passing it through the machine for the first time and sprinkle the machine rollers lightly with flour between each rolling.
5 When cutting noodles by hand, leave the sheet of dough to dry first for 30 minutes so it does not stick to itself when folded. If time is short, sprinkle the dough thoroughly with flour before folding.
6 All stuffings can be used for all types of pasta that are suitable for filling. Stuffings for pastas that are stuffed before cooking, such as ravioli and tortellini, should be drier than those used in cannelloni and other pastas that are cooked *before* being filled.

When cooking pasta
1 Allow 250g (8oz) pasta for four people, as a side dish or starter, or 500g (1lb) pasta for four as a main course. Proportionately less will be needed if the pasta is served with a rich sauce or stuffing.
2 Cook in at least 2 litres (3½pts) water per 250g (8oz).
3 A tablespoon of cooking oil added to simmering pasta helps prevent it sticking and keeps the water from boiling over.
4 An onion studded with cloves and a clove or two of peeled garlic will add flavour to the water for cooking.
5 Pasta that is to be baked or otherwise cooked further with other ingredients should be slightly undercooked when simmering. When cooking noodles and spaghetti, handle them with forks so that the strands remain separate.
6 Rinse very thoroughly in a colander under hot running water to wash away excess starch.
7 Serve very hot, with hot sauce, on heated plates.

Getting ahead
1 Fresh pasta dough can be made ahead and shaped into tagliatelle, spaghetti, cannelloni and other types of noodles. These can then be left to dry and stored in the refrigerator for up to one week. Pasta can also be frozen and kept for up to six months. However, the longer it is kept, the drier and more like bought pasta it will become.
2 Pasta should be cooked just before serving.
3 To keep it hot for up to 15 minutes, return the drained pasta to a saucepan and cover with 2·5-5cm (1-2in) or hot water; drain just before serving.

NOUILLES FRAICHES

(Basic recipe for fresh noodles)

Makes 250g (8oz) pasta; enough for 4 as a starter or side dish.

250g (8oz) strong white bread flour or semolina flour
teaspoon salt
tablespoon olive oil
2½ eggs (see below), beaten to mix
tablespoon water
to finish
salt and freshly ground black pepper
60g (2oz) butter

For ½ an egg, beat an egg and use half. Sift the flour onto a marble slab or board. Make a well in the centre and add the salt, oil, eggs and water. Work in the flour with the fingertips just as you would for pâte brisée (page 141), adding more liquid if necessary to make a smooth dough that is soft but not sticky. Knead the dough thoroughly for 5 minutes (if you don't have a pasta machine) until it is very smooth and elastic. Cover it with an inverted bowl and let it stand for 1 hour to lose some of its elasticity.

Working on a floured board, divide the dough in half and roll each into as thin a sheet as possible. Leave both to dry for ½-1 hour or until fairly stiff, then roll loosely and cut crosswise into 1·25-2 cm (½-¾in) slices. Spread the strips on a cloth or paper and leave to dry for a further 1-2 hours.

Alternatively, use a pasta cutting machine: divide the dough into 4 pieces and work them through the machine 3-4 times each on the first

The pasta dough needs to be of a firm consistency if a pasta machine is used. Flour the dough well, then roll it several times until it is thin enough, then pass it through the cutting blades

setting until very smooth, then once on each of the following settings which roll out the dough progressively thinner. Leave to dry and then cut the dough into noodles.

Dry the noodles for 2-3 hours before cooking. They can be made a week ahead if they are coiled loosely and left for 12-24 hours in the open air to dry very thoroughly. Wrap them in a plastic bag and store in the refrigerator. They can also be frozen once they are dried.

To cook the noodles: bring a large pan of salted water to the boil. Add the noodles, bring the water back to the boil and simmer for 1-2 minutes until almost tender – *al dente.* NOTE: they should have plenty of room to cook without touching. Fresh pasta cooks more quickly than bought or dried pasta. Drain the noodles, rinse with hot water to wash away the starch and toss in melted butter with salt and plenty of freshly ground black pepper and Parmesan cheese, or finish according to the individual recipe, with a sauce of your choice.

For a colourful, unusual dish, cook together equal quantities of red, green and plain noodles and serve with plenty of butter and grated Parmesan cheese.

NOUILLES ROUGES

(Red noodles)

Make the noodle dough following the instructions given for making fresh noodles (left), adding 2 tablespoons tomato purée to the well with the other ingredients. Use only 1-2 teaspoons of water.

NOUILLES VERTES

(Green noodles)

Remove the stems from 250g (8oz) spinach, wash thoroughly and cook for 2-3 minutes in a large saucepan of boiling salted water. Rinse under cold running water, drain well and squeeze out the excess liquid. Purée the spinach in a blender until very fine. Place in a small saucepan and dry out over low heat, stirring constantly, for 2-3 minutes.

Make the noodle dough following the instructions given for making fresh noodles, adding the spinach to the well with the other ingredients. Omit the water from the method.

FETTUCCINE ALFREDO

Serves 4 as a starter

250g (8oz) fresh noodles made from the basic recipe or
250g (8oz) dried noodles, bought ready made
180g (6oz) unsalted butter, softened
150ml (¼pt) double cream
100g (3½oz) freshly grated Parmesan cheese
freshly ground black pepper

Make fresh noodles following the instructions given in the basic recipe and dry them for 2-3 hours. Add fresh or dried noodles to plenty of boiling salted water and cook, allowing 2-3 minutes for fresh pasta and 8-10 minutes for dried pasta, or until it is almost tender – *al dente.* Drain and rinse well with hot water to wash away excess starch.

Heat the butter in a saucepan until creamy, add the noodles and toss, off the heat. Add the cream and toss over low heat. Remove from the heat, add the cheese and continue tossing until the mixture is very hot. Sprinkle with black pepper and serve at once.

NOUILLES FRAICHES, FROMAGE DE CHEVRE ET CIBOULETTE

(Red noodles with goat cheese and chives)

Serves 4 as a starter
250g (8oz) fresh red noodles
60g (2oz) unsalted butter, softened
175ml (6oz) double cream
125g (4oz) fresh goat's cheese, crumbled
2 tablespoons minced chives
1 egg yolk

Make the red noodles. While they're cooking, heat the butter and cream separately until warm. Drain the noodles well, return to the warm pan and toss them with the butter. Add cream and mix over low heat. Add the cheese and chives and allow to heat just until cheese melts. Remove from heat, add the egg yolk and toss well.

135

RAVIOLI

The name ravioli probably comes from *rabiole* meaning 'leftovers' in the Ligurian dialect.

Makes about 36 to serve 6 as a starter, 4 as a main course.

250g (8oz) pasta dough made from the basic recipe
chosen filling (see below)
1·5 litres (generous 2½pts) veal or chicken stock, or water (for cooking)
120g (4oz) grated Parmesan cheese (for serving)

Make the dough as for fresh noodles. Cover with an inverted bowl and leave for about an hour so the dough will lose its elasticity.

Cut the dough in half and roll out one half on a lightly floured board until paper thin; roll out the second piece the same way. Brush one piece of dough with water and set out teaspoonfuls of filling at 4cm (1½in) intervals. Cover with the remaining sheet of dough, lifting it on a rolling pin and, with a small ball of dough dipped in flour, press the top piece gently down to seal around each mound of filling, making sure all the air is removed.

Stamp out each square with a ravioli cutter, or cut in squares with a fluted pastry wheel. Transfer to floured greaseproof paper and leave for 2-3 hours to dry. Ravioli can be made 2-3 days ahead and kept covered with transparent plastic wrap in the refrigerator, or they can be frozen. In this case, thaw thoroughly before baking. If they are not being cooked the same day, let them dry for at least 6 hours and toss in flour before covering.

To finish: poach the ravioli in simmering water in a large saucepan or roasting pan of stock or salted water for 8-10 minutes, or until almost tender – *al dente* – and drain. Serve the grated Parmesan cheese separately.

Ham or chicken ravioli

Mix 250g (8oz) cooked, minced ham or chicken with 4 tablespoons béchamel sauce (page 192), tomato sauce or double cream, and a tablespoon of chopped parsley or fresh mixed herbs (basil, chives, oregano). Bind with a lightly beaten egg and season to taste.

Spinach ravioli

Wash 250g (½lb) fresh spinach, dis-

Before cutting pasta dough into required shapes by hand or by machine, spread out the thinly rolled dough and allow it to dry for ½-1 hour, or until it is fairly stiff

carding the stems, and cook in 1cm (½in) boiling, salted water until the leaves wilt, or cook 1 small packet of frozen spinach according to the directions on the packet. Drain the spinach thoroughly and squeeze it dry. Allow it to cool, then chop it and mix with 120g (4oz) Ricotta cheese, or creamed cottage cheese, ¼ teaspoon freshly grated nutmeg and salt and pepper to taste.

Cheese ravioli

Mix 60g (2oz) grated Parmesan cheese, 120g (4oz) Ricotta or creamed cottage cheese, 1 lightly beaten egg, tablespoon chopped fresh basil or parsley and salt and freshly ground black pepper to taste.

Meat ravioli

Heat 30g (1oz) butter in a heavy-based pan, add 150g (5oz) minced pork, 150g (5oz) minced veal and 150g (5oz) minced cooked ham and cook, stirring, until lightly browned. Add 4 tablespoons Marsala or sherry, salt and freshly ground pepper, then cover and cook for 20 minutes. Work through the fine blade of the mincer, taste and adjust the seasoning, if necessary, then add 1 lightly beaten egg to bind the mixture.

Ravioli in cream sauce

Make a béchamel sauce (page 192) with 750ml (1¼pts) milk, a slice of onion, blade of mace, bay leaf, 6 peppercorns, 60g (2oz) butter, 60g (2oz) flour and salt and pepper. Add 150ml (¼pt) double cream, taste for seasoning and keep warm. Cook the ravioli in plenty of salted water, drain and layer in a shallow buttered baking dish with the sauce, coating the last layer with sauce. Sprinkle with 60g (2oz) grated Parmesan cheese.

The ravioli can be kept for 2-3 days in the refrigerator, or they can be frozen.

To finish: bake in a moderately hot oven, 190C (375F) gas 5, for 20-25 minutes until the top is bubbling and browned. If the dish has been frozen, lengthen the cooking time to 40-45 minutes – make sure it is thoroughly heated before serving.

Ravioli in tomato sauce

Make a tomato sauce with 45g (1½oz) butter; 2 chopped onions; 30g (1oz) flour; 600ml (1pt) stock, or stock and juice from canned tomatoes; 6 fresh tomatoes, peeled, chopped and seeded or 700g (1½lb) canned tomatoes, drained and chopped; 2 crushed cloves garlic; bouquet garni; teaspoon sugar; salt and pepper. Cook the ravioli in plenty of salted water, drain and layer them in a shallow, buttered baking dish with the tomato sauce, ending with a layer of sauce. Sprinkle with 60g (2oz) grated Parmesan cheese. The ravioli can be kept for 2-3 days in the refrigerator, or frozen.

To finish: bake them in a moderately hot oven, 190C (375F) gas 5, for 20-25 minutes until bubbling and browned. They will need longer if they have been frozen.

CANNELLONI A LA CREME

Makes about 16 to serve 8, as a starter or 4 as a main course.

250g (8oz) pasta dough made from the basic recipe
for the sauce
90g (3oz) butter
90g (3oz) flour
900ml (1½pts) milk
salt and freshly ground pepper
600ml (1pt) double cream
pinch of nutmeg
30g (1oz) grated Parmesan cheese
for the filling
350g (¾lb) raw veal, minced
350g (¾lb) raw pork, minced
3 egg yolks
pinch of ground mace or nutmeg
salt and freshly ground pepper
to finish
60g (2oz) grated Parmesan cheese (for sprinkling)
30g (1oz) melted butter

Make the dough as for fresh noodles. Roll it out as thinly as possible with a rolling pin, or use a pasta machine. Cut it into 10cm (4in) squares, spread it on greaseproof paper or paper towels and leave for 2-3 hours to dry. If making ahead, pack the squares between sheets of greaseproof paper – or non-stick vegetable parchment and store in a plastic bag in the refrigerator for up to 4 days.
For the sauce: melt the butter, whisk in the flour and, when foaming, pour in the milk. Bring to the boil, whisking, season with salt and pepper and cook for 2 minutes. Add enough cream to make a fairly thick sauce and take from the heat. Add nutmeg to taste and adjust the seasoning, if necessary. Rub the surface of the sauce with butter to keep a skin from forming.
For the filling: stir 600ml (1pt) of the sauce into the minced meats, add the egg yolks and season well with mace or nutmeg, salt and pepper.

Cook the cannelloni squares, 6-8 at a time, in a large pan with plenty of simmering salted water for 6-8 minutes or until almost tender – *al dente*. Stir the pasta from time to time to prevent sticking. Transfer the cooked squares to a pan of cold water.

To assemble: drain the squares on paper towels and fill each one with 1-2 tablespoons of filling; roll them like cigars and place side by side in a buttered baking dish. Reheat the sauce and stir in the remaining cream. Take from the heat, stir in the 30g (1oz) grated cheese and taste for seasoning. Spoon the sauce over the cannelloni – it should cover them completely.

To finish: sprinkle the cannelloni with grated cheese, dribble on the melted butter, cover the dish and bake in a moderate oven, 180C (350F) gas 4, for 40-45 minutes. Ten minutes before the end of cooking, remove the lid so the cheese browns.

The cannelloni can be prepared ahead and reheated; keep them in the refrigerator. They can also be frozen and will keep for 3 months.
To make lasagne: the same filling and sauce can also be layered with cooked lasagne noodles in a baking dish, then sprinkled with grated cheese and gratinéed – placed under a hot grill for the top to brown before serving.

FILETS DE SOLE AUX PATES FRAICHES ET AUX CREVETTES

(Sole fillets with fresh noodles and crayfish)

The sheer luxury of this dish makes sole seem especially appropriate, yet many other fish could be used and another shellfish substituted for the scampi.

SERVES 6

green noodles (page 135) made with 375g (12oz) strong white bread flour, 1½ teaspoons salt, 1½ tablespoons oil, 4 eggs, 1½ tablespoons water and 375g (12oz) spinach
30g (1oz) butter
500g (1lb) unshelled scampi
½ carrot, thinly sliced
¼ onion, chopped
2 tablespoons Cognac
600ml (1pt) double cream
salt and pepper
1kg (2lb) sole fillets
hollandaise sauce (page 193) made with 120g (4oz) butter, 2 tablespoons water, 2 egg yolks, salt and Cayenne pepper and drops of lemon juice to taste

Make the noodles.

Melt the butter in a heavy-based pan, add the scampi and sauté them for about 5 minutes or until the shells begin to turn red. Add the carrot and onion and cook over low heat, stirring often, until soft but not brown. Add the Cognac and flame briefly. Stir in half the cream, season with salt and pepper and simmer for 10 minutes. Remove the scampi and shell them, reserving the shells. Pound the heads and shells in a mortar with a pestle or in a bowl with a bottle. Return them to the cooking liquid and simmer for a further 10 minutes. Strain through a fine sieve into a small saucepan and boil, if necessary, to reduce to a syrupy consistency. The scampi can be cooked up to 1 day ahead and kept in the refrigerator.

Fold the fish fillets in half crosswise and put them in a buttered ovenproof dish. Pour over the remaining cream. Heat the oven to hot, 200C (400F) gas 6.

Make the hollandaise sauce and keep warm in a water bath.

A short time before serving, cook the sole in the heated oven for 10 minutes or until the fillets just turn opaque. Meanwhile, cook the noodles in a large pan of boiling salted water and drain thoroughly. Drain the fish, reserving the liquid, and keep them warm. Add the scampi reduction to the cooking liquid and boil them together until slightly thickened and of a syrupy consistency. Whisk in the hollandaise sauce and stir in the scampi. Taste for seasoning, adjust if necessary and keep warm in a water bath.

To serve: arrange a bed of noodles on a large heated serving dish. Top with the fish fillets and spoon over the sauce and scampi.

17

PATE BRISEE AND PATE SUCREE
The quick and the cool

To think of French cooking without pastry is like imagining a house without beams – half the structure would fall apart. Where would be the mouthwatering open-faced fruit tarts that form the centrepiece of every pâtisserie window? Where would be the sweet custard flans and the savoury quiches crammed with onions, bacon, cheese, mushrooms or shellfish? What about the innumerable kinds of meat and poultry pâtés? (Technically speaking, a pâté should be wrapped in pâte, i.e. pastry.) The foundation of all these creations, cornerstone of home and professional kitchen alike, is pâte brisée.

Pâte brisée means 'broken dough' since the ingredients are worked and 'broken' until they are as pliable as putty. And here lies the main difference between pâte brisée and English shortcrust: the French regard their pâte brisée as a *container*. They want it to be thin yet robust, with none of the crumbly, melting texture that is the pride of English cooks. For these qualities, French cooks turn to their puff pastries. The similarity between shortcrust and pâte brisée is, in fact, deceptive since the French never add lard or shortening to their pâte brisée and they always finish the preparation by kneading the dough with the heel of the hand in a movement called 'fraiser', which thoroughly incorporates the butter and gives the dough its characteristic consistency.

Pâte brisée consists of four or five ingredients: flour, butter, salt, water and often, but not necessarily, egg yolks. The flour should be plain, not self-raising – wholemeal flour can be used, but it makes heavier pastry and absorbs more liquid during mixing. The butter can be salted or unsalted, and the amount of water needed will vary with such factors as the age and brand of the flour, the quality of the butter and even the humidity in the kitchen. Egg yolks add richness to the dough and make patching easy. For sweet tarts, 2-3 tablespoons of sugar may be added.

The preparation of pâte brisée is a good example of French economy in ingredients and utensils. No bowl, no pastry cutter; all that is needed is a metal or plastic scraper, a jug of cold water and a spoon for measuring for the fainthearted. Flour is sifted in a heap on the table and swept into a ring with a quick movement of the hand. Into this 'well' are put the remaining ingredients: butter, egg yolk, the minimum quantity of water indicated in the recipe, salt and, for sweet dough or pâte sucrée, a little sugar. These ingredients are worked with the fingertips, then the flour is incorporated with the aid of the scraper. More water is added if the dough is dry. Just before pressing the dough into a ball, the hands are dipped in the flour box, then rubbed to loosen every errant morsel of dough – no waste is countenanced. Then it is time to 'fraiser' before putting the dough in the refrigerator to chill.

Making pâte brisée is a quick process. From start to finish, the pastry chef at La Varenne takes about 2 minutes. My personal record is about 3 minutes, and even a novice takes no more than 10 minutes.

The quicker the better, not only to save time, but because the longer the dough is worked, the more elastic it becomes as the gluten in the flour is developed. Elastic dough is difficult to roll; it shrinks during cooking, and the texture is tough. To a certain extent, elasticity is lost when the dough is left to 'relax' in the refrigerator, but overworked dough will never completely regain the right texture.

Pâte brisée is most often used for lining a tart tin or

TARTE DE POMMES A LA NORMANDE

A pâte brisée shell is spread with almond cream and topped with apple slices. The slices of each apple half are kept together and arranged like the spokes of a wheel. During cooking, the almond cream rises to fill the spaces

TARTELETTES AUX FRUITS

Small pâte sucrée shells are simply filled with fresh fruit and glazed

139

flan ring, or for making tartlets or barquettes (little boats). No matter what shape is chosen, the method of lining the tin is always the same. Sometimes tops are put on tarts, or the surface may be criss-crossed with a lattice of pastry strips, or pâte brisée may be rolled in a sheet to wrap the ingredients for one large pâté or lots of little ones. Here the ingredients of the dough may be changed, transforming it into a pâte à pâté: lard is substituted for butter to give more flavour and a whole egg is added so the pastry sets firmly in the oven. Pâte à foncer (lining pastry), a plain version of pâte brisée, has a lower proportion of butter and no egg yolks, and is used for lining flan rings and tins.

By far the most popular – and delectable – variation of pâte brisée is pâte sucrée, sometimes called 'sandy' pastry or pâte sablée. Here, so much sugar is added that it totally changes the character of the dough, making it crumbly to handle and as crisp as a biscuit. The dough must be rolled thicker than for pâte brisée and its sweetness makes it a favourite for fruit tarts, particularly for little tartlets filled with strawberries

and raspberries, or poached fruit in season.

In Normandy, the excellent butter has made pâté sucrée biscuits or sablés a local speciality, and the little pastry shop near our house on the coast always displays a pile of sablés, topped by the reassuring sign 'guaranti pur beurre'.

Such refinements of basic pâte brisée date back to the Renaissance. In early days, pastry was literally a paste, a flour and water dough used to enclose and protect food while it was baking. Recipes for baking birds or ham (in pastry made of flour and oil) were given by Apicius, who lived in ancient Rome. Even as late as the 19th century, the straight-sided serving dishes called timbales were normally made of pastry, instead of the biscuit-coloured pottery that is often used today. But now, despite the current preoccupation with calories, any French-style restaurant invariably offers a savoury quiche on its menu. An open tart, filled with the fruits of the season, is the undisputed king of the dessert trolley. Pastry will never lose its appeal – or its convenience.

THE WAY TO SUCCESS

Pâte brisée

When making the dough
1 Marble is the ideal working surface because it is cold and smooth. However, Formica or wood are both perfectly adequate.
2 Keep the dough cool. Butter should be cold, though soft enough to knead. Use cold water, in summer ice cold water. Work the dough as rapidly as possible, using a scraper to minimise contact with your hands.
3 The standard proportion of salt for pâte brisée is 4-5 level teaspoons (20-25g, $\frac{2}{3}$-$\frac{5}{6}$oz) for 1kg (2$\frac{1}{4}$lb) of flour, when using unsalted butter. If the butter is salted, the salt in the dough should be reduced to 2$\frac{1}{2}$-3 level teaspoons per 1kg of flour.
4 Salt and sugar should be sprinkled over the water in the 'well', so that they dissolve completely.
5 At the beginning of mixing, add the minimum quantity of water indicated; halfway through mixing, the dough will start to form large crumbs. If these are dry, add more water so that the crumbs stick together. The finished dough should be soft but not sticky. If too moist, work in a little flour.
6 The dough is then kneaded, working down and away from you with the heel of the hand in the 'fraiser' motion. This distributes the fat throughout the dough and gives it the putty-like texture characteristic of all the pâte brisée family.
7 To avoid developing elasticity in the dough, work it as lightly as possible, using the fingertips, rather than the whole hand until the 'fraiser' stage. All dough is somewhat elastic and should be left to 'relax', covered

in the refrigerator, for at least 15 minutes before rolling. If necessary, leave it for 2-3 hours or even overnight. To test for elasticity, press with a fingertip – the dough should not spring back.

When shaping the dough
1 Use a heavy rolling pin – chefs favour the long, straight, cylindrical kind without handles. When rolling, start with the shape you want at the end – for a circle, start with a ball and for a square or rectangle, start with a square.
2 Roll out only as much dough as you need, to avoid trimmings. Dough is tougher when rolled a second time.
3 Chill the dough thoroughly in the refrigerator or freezer after shaping or lining it into a tin; it should be firm, showing that the fat has set. Chilling helps the dough to hold its shape during baking and reduces shrinkage.

When baking the dough
1 Preheat the oven. The baking of tarts, tartlets and pâtés is usually begun at 200C (400F) gas 6. This 'seizes' the dough so it does not melt out of shape. For pâtés and larger pastries, the heat is often reduced for the rest of the cooking time.
2 Use heavy baking sheets and grease them lightly if placing dough directly on the sheet. Lightly butter tins. For tarts, use a flan ring, or a flan tin with a removable base so the tart is easy to transfer to a plate.

3 To avoid a soggy crust, fillings that are already cooked – and soft fillings like the custard used in a quiche – are best put into a shell that is partly baked 'blind', or empty.
4 Once the filling is added, bake the dough at once.
5 Do not add hot filling to dough, whether baked or unbaked.

Getting ahead

1 Pâte brisée and pâte sucrée can be made ahead and stored, wrapped, in the refrigerator for up to 3 days. They can also be frozen for about a month if tightly sealed. If frozen too long, they tend to dry out. Thaw them thoroughly before rolling.
2 Better still, shape the dough into tart tins or tartlet shells, freeze, then remove the tins to use again. Store the unbaked shells, tightly wrapped, in the freezer.
3 Baked shells, unfilled, can also be frozen, though they are best reheated to crisp them before using.

4 Some baked, filled pastries can be frozen, but any filling with a high water content, such as a quiche, tends to separate slightly on thawing. The pastry itself can also be soggy when thawed.

Pâte sucrée

The points mentioned for pâte brisée apply to pâte sucrée. Also:
1 The high sugar content of pâte sucrée reduces its elasticity but also makes it crumbly and difficult to handle. Chill it well before rolling and, if necessary, press it into shape rather than rolling out. Any cracks or holes can easily be patched with a small piece of dough.
2 Pâte sucrée scorches easily because of the sugar in it. Once it starts to brown in the oven, watch it carefully.
3 Any leftover pâte sucrée makes delicious biscuits.

Pâte brisée

A 125g (4oz) quantity of dough will line a 20cm (8in) flan tin or 5 individual 10cm (4in) tartlet tins. A 200g (6½oz) quantity of dough will line a 26cm (10in) flan tin or 7 individual 10cm (4in) tartlet tins. A 250g (8oz) quantity of dough will line a 30cm (12in) flan tin or 8 individual 10cm (4in) tartlet tins.

flour	125g (4oz)	200g (6½oz)	250g (8oz)
butter	60g (2oz)	100g (3½oz)	125g (4oz)
egg yolk(s)	1	1	2
salt	2g (⅓tsp)	4g (¾ tsp)	5g (level tsp)
cold water	1½-2 tbsp	2½-3 tbsp	3½-4 tbsp

Sift the flour onto a marble slab or board and make a large well in the centre. Pound the butter to soften it slightly. Place the butter, egg yolk(s), salt and the smaller amount of water in the well and work together with the fingertips until partly mixed. Gradually work in the flour, using the fingertips to pull the dough into large crumbs. If the crumbs are dry, sprinkle over a tablespoon more water. Press the dough firmly together; it should be soft but not sticky.

To mix the dough thoroughly, work it in a few batches by pushing it across the working surface away from you with the heel of the hand and gathering it up with a dough scraper until smooth and pliable. Press the dough into a ball, roll lightly in flour to smooth it, and wrap in non-stick vegetable parchment, aluminium foil, plastic wrap or a plastic bag. Chill for at least 30 minutes or until firm. The dough can be stored, tightly wrapped, in the refrigerator for up to 3 days, or it can be frozen.

Pâte sucrée

A 125g (4oz) quantity of dough will line a 20cm (8in) flan tin or 5 individual 10cm (4in) tartlet tins. A 200g (6½oz) quantity of dough will line a 26cm (10in) flan tin or 7 individual 10cm (4in) tartlet tins. A 250g (8oz) quantity of dough will line a 30cm (12in) flan tin or 8 individual 10cm (4in) tartlet tins.

flour	125g (4oz)	200g (6½oz)	250g (8oz)
salt	pinch	pinch	large pinch
caster sugar	50g (1½oz)	80g (2½oz)	100g (3½oz)
egg yolks	2	3	4
vanilla essence	½ tsp	½ tsp	1 tsp
butter	60g (2oz)	100g (3½oz)	125g (4oz)

Sift the flour onto a marble slab or board and make a large well in the centre. Put the salt, sugar, egg yolks and vanilla in the well and mix them with your fingers until the sugar dissolves. Pound on the butter to soften it slightly, add it to the well and quickly work it with the other ingredients, using the fingertips, until partly mixed. Gradually work in the flour, using the fingertips to pull the dough into large crumbs. To mix the dough thoroughly, work it in a few batches by pushing it across the working surface away from you with the heel of the hand and gathering it up with the dough scraper until it is smooth and pliable. Press the dough into a ball, roll lightly in flour to smooth it, and wrap in non-stick vegetable parchment, aluminium foil, plastic wrap or a plastic bag. Chill for at least 30 minutes or until firm.

The dough can be stored, tightly wrapped, in the refrigerator for up to 3 days. It can also be frozen.

141

To line tartlet moulds quickly, group them together and cover them all at once with a sheet of dough rolled loosely around the rolling pin

Line a flan ring set on a baking sheet by pressing the dough well into the corners of the ring, then pushing the sides up slightly to extend above the top

For baking blind, when the pastry has set and begun to brown, lift out the lining paper and beans, and return to the oven to continue baking

TO LINE INDIVIDUAL TARTLET TINS

Chill the dough thoroughly before rolling out; butter inside the tins lightly to prevent sticking. The thickness needed depends on the size of the tins and the type of pastry. Large tins may need lining with dough of up to 6mm ($\frac{1}{4}$in) thickness, while dough for small tins may be rolled out as thin as 3mm ($\frac{1}{8}$in). Roll out brittle dough such as pâte sucrée fairly thick, but firm doughs such as pâte brisée can be rolled thinner. The trimmings can be pressed together to roll again, but all doughs become heavy if overworked.

Line large or deep tins with dough rounds stamped out with a cutter, the size depending on the depth of the tin; the rounds should be 2–3·5cm ($\frac{3}{4}$–1$\frac{1}{2}$in) larger than the diameter of the tins. Use fluted cutters for tartlets containing delicate mixtures and desserts; plain edges are suitable for more robust savoury mixtures. Set the rounds on the tins and, using a small ball of dough dipped in flour, press the dough well down into the base of the tin.

Small round and boat-shaped tins can be lined several at a time: roll out the dough slightly thicker than when stamping out rounds. Set half a dozen tins touching one another, fold the dough around the rolling pin and unroll it over the tins. With a ball of dough dipped in flour, press and pat the dough into the tins, easing it down gently. Roll the rolling pin across the top to cut off the dough.

With finger and thumb, press up the edge of dough vertically, so that it extends a little above the edge of the tin. Prick the bases and chill the tins well before baking.

TO LINE A FLAN TIN

An 18-20cm (7-8in) flan needs 125g (4oz) pastry; serves 3-4

A 24-26cm (9-10in) flan needs 200g (6$\frac{1}{2}$oz) pastry; serves 5-6

A 28-30cm (11-12in) flan needs 250g (8oz) pastry; serves 8

Place the chilled ball of dough on a lightly floured working surface. Pound it lightly with the rolling pin to flatten it, then roll it out, working from the centre of the ball to the edges and turning the dough after each stroke into an even round.

If using a flan ring, set it on a baking sheet; lightly butter the ring and baking sheet; do the same if using a flan tin with a removable base. Roll out the dough to a round about 6mm ($\frac{1}{4}$in) thick and 5cm (2in) larger than the flan ring or tart tin. Roll the dough around the rolling pin, lift it over the flan ring or tart tin and unroll it. Let the dough rest over the edge of the tin or ring, overlapping it slightly inside, and being careful not to stretch it. Gently lift the edges of the dough with one hand and press it well into the corners of the tin with the other, using a small ball of dough dipped in flour. Roll the rolling pin over the top to cut off any excess.

Using forefinger and thumb, press the dough evenly up the edge to increase the height. Neaten the edge with the finger and thumb and, for a sweet pie, flute it. Do not let the dough overlap the edge. Prick the base of the shell thoroughly and chill well before baking.

TO BAKE BLIND

Set the oven at hot, 200C (400F) gas 6.

For a flan or tart, cut a round of greaseproof or brown paper 5cm (2in) larger than the diameter of the tart. For individual tartlet moulds, cut small rounds or crumple small pieces of the paper. Line the flan, tart or tartet shell first with pastry, then with the paper, pressing it well into the corners. Fill the lined shells three-quarters full with uncooked beans or rice to hold the dough in shape. For individual tartlets, instead of using paper and beans, you can place a smaller mould, lightly buttered on the underside, in the lined mould.

Bake a large shell in the heated oven for 15 minutes and small tartlet shells for 6-10 minutes, or until the pastry is set and lightly browned. Lift out the paper and beans and continue baking a tart shell for a further 6-8 minutes and tartlet shells for about 5 minutes longer, or until golden brown. Let the shells cool slightly, then transfer to a rack to cool completely.

QUICHE AU ROQUEFORT ET AUX OIGNONS
(Roquefort and onion quiche)

This basic quiche recipe has many possible variations. For a shellfish quiche, omit the onions and replace the Roquefort with 450g (1lb) cooked peeled shrimps, or crab-meat, or pieces of lobster. For a vegetable quiche, halve the quantity of onions and replace the Roquefort with 350g (12oz) thinly sliced, sautéed mushrooms, sautéed julien-ned courgettes or chopped, cooked spinach. Be sure to season well, adding a little finely diced ham or Gruyère cheese if you like.

SERVES 6

pâte brisée made with 125g (4oz) flour, 60g (2 oz) butter, 1 egg yolk, $\frac{1}{2}$ level teaspoon salt and 1½-2 tablespoons cold water
for the Roquefort-onion mixture
30g (2 tablespoons) butter
3 large onions, thinly sliced
salt and pepper
pinch of powdered thyme
200g (7oz) Roquefort, crumbled
for the custard filling
1 egg
2 egg yolks
4 tablespoons milk
200ml ($\frac{1}{3}$pt) double cream
salt and pepper
pinch of grated nutmeg
shallow 22cm (9in) diameter tart or pie tin or flan ring

Make the pâte brisée as on page 20 and wrap and chill for 30 minutes.

Set the oven at 200C (400F) gas 6. Lightly butter the flan ring or tin. Roll out the dough, line the ring; chill until firm. Prick the bottom with a fork and bake for 12-15 minutes until the pastry is set and beginning to brown. Remove the paper and beans and bake the shell for 5-7 minutes more, or until the bottom is no longer soft. Remove from the oven and let the pie shell cool slightly. Lower the oven temp-erature to 190C (375F) gas 5.

Melt the butter in a heavy-based pan, add the onions with the salt, pepper and powdered thyme, press a piece of buttered foil on top and cover with a lid. Cook very gently, stirring occasionally, for 20-30 minutes until the onions are very soft. NOTE: do not allow them to brown. Add the Roquefort and stir in with a wooden spoon over low heat until dissolved and smooth. Let this mixture cool slightly, then spread it in the tart shell.

Beat the egg and egg yolks thoroughly with the milk and cream and add salt, pepper and nutmeg.

Add the custard filling to the pie shell, filling it three-quarters full, and bake in the heated oven for about 15 minutes. When the filling is partly set, add more custard filling to completely fill the shell. Bake all together for 25-30 minutes or until the custard is set and the top browned. NOTE: do not overcook or the egg custard will curdle. Serve hot or cool, but not chilled.

BARQUETTES AUX CREVETTES, SAUCE MORNAY
(Prawn boats mornay)

Follow this rich starter with a simple roast or grill.

MAKES 12-15

pâte brisée made with 200g (6$\frac{1}{2}$oz) flour, 100g (3$\frac{1}{2}$oz) butter, 1 egg yolk, 4g ($\frac{3}{4}$ level teaspoon) salt and 2$\frac{1}{2}$-3 tablespoons cold water
250g (8oz) cooked, peeled prawns, coarsely chopped
mornay sauce (page 192) made with 300ml ($\frac{1}{2}$pt) milk, slice of onion, small bay leaf, 6 peppercorns, 15g (level tablespoon) butter, 10g (level tablespoon) flour, salt, white pepper, grated nutmeg, egg yolk, 30g (1oz) grated Gruyère cheese and teaspoon Dijon mustard
30g (1oz) Gruyère cheese, grated (for sprinkling)
30g (1oz) melted butter (to finish)
8cm (3in) boat-shaped tins

Prepare the pâte brisée and chill it. Roll it out to just under 5mm ($\frac{1}{4}$in) thick and line the tins. Chill them until firm; set the oven at hot, 200C (400F) gas 6.

Prick the bases of the shells, line them with paper and fill with dried beans. Place them on a baking sheet and bake in the heated oven for 8-10 minutes or until the pastry is set and lightly browned. Remove the paper and beans and return the shells to the oven for a further 5-7 minutes or until they are crisp and brown. Allow to cool slightly, remove them from the tins and set on a rack to cool completely. The shells can be made up to 48 hours ahead and kept in an airtight container.

Make the mornay sauce. Mix the chopped prawns into the sauce. Place the boats on a baking sheet and set the oven at very hot, 220C (425F) gas 7.

Just before serving, spoon the prawn filling into the boats, sprinkle with the grated cheese and dribble on the melted butter. Bake in the hot oven until the tops are bubbling.

SABLES AU FROMAGE
(Cheese sablés)

A good hors d'oeuvre with cock-tails, these can also be made with aged Cheddar cheese.

MAKES ABOUT 30

about 100g (3$\frac{1}{2}$oz) flour
$\frac{1}{2}$ teaspoon salt
black pepper and Cayenne
90g (3oz) butter
90g (3oz) freshly grated Parmesan or Gruyère cheese
1 egg, beaten to mix with $\frac{1}{2}$ teaspoon salt (for glaze)
30g (1oz) coarsely chopped walnuts; or 60g (2oz) grated Parmesan or Gruyère (for sprinkling)

Sift the flour onto a flat surface with salt, pepper and a touch of Cayenne. Add the butter and rub it in with the fingertips until the mixture resem-bles fine crumbs. Add the cheese and press the dough together. It should be soft, but not sticky. If it is too moist, add 2-3 more tablespoons flour. Knead on a lightly floured surface, pushing it away with the heel of the hand and pulling it up with the fingers until it is as pliable as putty. Chill the dough for 30 minutes.

Set the oven at moderately hot, 190C (375F) gas 5. Roll out the dough to a rectangle 1cm ($\frac{3}{8}$in) thick. Cut the rectangle into 6.5cm (2$\frac{1}{2}$in) squares, cut each square into two triangles and brush the dough with egg glaze. Set the sablés a little apart on an ungreased baking sheet and sprinkle each one with chopped walnuts or grated cheese. Bake in the heated oven for 15-18 minutes or until golden brown. Transfer to a rack to cool. The sablés can be stored for up to a week in an airtight container, or they can be frozen for 1-2 months.

PETITS PATES CHAUDS

(Individual hot meat pâtés)

MAKES 6-8 SMALL PATES
60g (2oz) veal escalope, diced
60g (2oz) cooked ham, diced
60g (2oz) piece fat bacon, diced
for the marinade
2 tablespoons white wine
2 tablespoons brandy
2 tablespoons Madeira
pinch of thyme
bay leaf
$\frac{1}{2}$ onion, chopped
$\frac{1}{2}$ tablespoon oil
for the pastry
350g (11$\frac{1}{2}$oz) flour
180g (6oz) butter; or 60g (2oz) lard and 12g (4oz) butter
1 egg
tablespoon oil
7g (1$\frac{1}{2}$ teaspoons) salt
2-3 tablespoons cold water
1 egg, beaten to mix with $\frac{1}{2}$ teaspoon salt (for glaze)
for the filling
100g (3$\frac{1}{2}$oz) lean pork
100g (3$\frac{1}{2}$oz) fat pork
100g (3$\frac{1}{2}$oz) veal
90g (3oz) chicken livers
2 tablespoons white wine
tablespoon brandy
1 egg
teaspoon ground allspice
salt and freshly ground black pepper

Place the veal escalope, ham and bacon in a shallow dish. Add 2 tablespoons white wine, 2 table-spoons brandy, the Madeira, thyme, bay leaf, onion and oil, mix well and leave to marinate for about 30-45 minutes.

For the pastry: sift the flour on to a marble slab or board and make a large well in the centre. Pound the butter or butter-lard mixture to soften it. In the well, place the butter or butter-lard mixture, egg, oil, salt and water and work together with the fingertips until well mixed. Gradually work in the flour, pulling the dough into large crumbs, and adding more water if the crumbs are dry. Press the dough together and work it in two or three portions on the board until smooth and pliable. Press into a ball, wrap and chill 30 minutes.

PETITS PATES CHAUDS
These individual hot savoury pâtés are wrapped in dough, brushed with egg glaze and decorated with pastry trimmings

For the filling: work the lean and fat pork with the veal and chicken livers twice through the fine blade of the grinder. Mix with the white wine, brandy, egg, allspice and season with plenty of salt and pepper. Work with the hand until the mixture holds together. Drain the diced veal, ham and bacon, adding any marinade liquid to the minced meat mixture and discarding the bay leaf and onion. Mix the diced meats with the minced meat mixture.

Roll out the pastry dough on a floured marble slab or board to 6mm ($\frac{1}{4}$in) thickness and cut it into 15cm (6-in) squares. In the centre of each square, spread a layer of filling in a rectangle measuring 3.5cm × 10cm (1$\frac{1}{2}$in × 4in), mounding it well. Cut 2.5-cm (1-in) squares from each corner of the dough rectangles, brush the remaining dough with egg glaze and wrap up the pâtés like a parcel, sides over middle. Turn them over and set them, seam-side down, on a baking sheet. Brush with egg glaze.

Roll out the dough trimmings and decorate the top of the pâtés with strips or leaves or shells made by marking small fluted rounds of dough with the back of a knife in a rayed pattern – or with whatever design you like. Brush the decoration with egg glaze. Make a small hole in the top of each pâté with the point of a knife and insert a 'chimney' made of a strip of foil or wax paper rolled around a spoon handle.

(This allows steam to escape.) Chill the pâtés for at least 15 minutes. They can be prepared up to 8 hours ahead and kept covered in the refrigerator, or they can be frozen.

To finish: set the oven at hot, 200C (400F) gas 6. Bake the pâtés in the hot oven for 12-15 minutes or until beginning to brown. Lower the heat to moderate, 180C (350F) gas 4, and continue baking for 25-30 minutes or until a skewer inserted in the centre of the pâtés for $\frac{1}{2}$ minute is hot to the touch when withdrawn. If the pâtés brown too quickly, cover them loosely with foil during cooking. Discard the paper chimneys and serve.

NAPPAGE A L'ABRICOT

(Apricot jam glaze)

In a small pan (not aluminium) melt 350g (12oz) apricot jam with the juice of $\frac{1}{2}$ lemon and 2-3 tablespoons water or enough to make a glaze that can be poured. Work the hot jam through a strainer and store in an airtight jar. Reheat the glaze to melt it before using; the quantities given above make a generous 300ml ($\frac{1}{2}$ pint) of glaze.

GELEE DE GROSEILLE

(Red currant jelly glaze)

In a small pan (not aluminium) melt 350g (12oz) red currant jelly with 1 tablespoon water. Stir the jelly gently, but do not whisk or it will become cloudy. Be careful not to cook it for more than 1-2 minutes after melting or the jelly will darken. Store any leftover glaze in an airtight jar and reheat to melt it before using. The quantities given above make a generous 300ml ($\frac{1}{2}$ pint) of glaze.

TARTE DE POMMES A LA NORMANDE
(Normandy apple tart)

In France, fruit tarts and pies are everywhere, profiting from the finest products of the region. For holidays in Alsace, cooks traditionally make fruit galettes as big as bicycle wheels. In Provence, lemon pie is enriched with ground almonds; in the Vosges the fruit is baked in a custard mixture, like quiche; and in Normandy the variations of apple pie are as many as the cooks who make them.

SERVES 8-10

pâte brisée made with 200g (6½oz) flour, 100g (3½oz) butter, 1 egg yolk, ¾ level teaspoon salt and 2½-3 tablespoons cold water
3-4 ripe dessert apples
for the frangipane
100g (3½oz) butter
100g (3½oz) caster sugar
1 egg, beaten to mix
1 egg yolk
2 teaspoons Calvados or Kirsch
100g (3½oz) whole blanched almonds, ground
2 level tablespoons flour
to finish
caster sugar (for sprinkling)
150ml (¼pt) apricot jam glaze
25-27cm (10-11in) diameter tart or pie tin or flan ring

Make the pâte brisée and wrap and chill for at least 30 minutes.

Set the oven at hot, 200C (400F) gas 6, and place a baking sheet in the oven to heat. Roll out the dough, line the tart tin with it, prick lightly with a fork, flute the edges and chill again until firm.

To make the frangipane: cream the butter, gradually beat in the sugar and continue beating until the mixture is light and soft. Gradually add the egg and yolk, beating well after each addition. Add the Calvados or Kirsch, then stir in the ground almonds and the flour. Pour the frangipane into the chilled pastry, spreading it evenly.

Peel the apples, halve them and scoop out the cores. Cut them crosswise in very thin slices and arrange them on the frangipane to make the spokes of a wheel, keeping the slices of each half apple together. Press them down gently until they touch the pastry dough base.

Bake the pie on the hot baking sheet near the bottom of the heated oven for 10-15 minutes until the pastry dough is beginning to brown. Turn down the oven heat to moderate, 180C (350F) gas 4, and continue cooking for 15-20 minutes, or until the apples are tender and the frangipane is set.

Ten minutes before the end of cooking, sprinkle the tart with caster sugar and continue cooking until the sugar melts and caramelises slightly. Transfer to a rack to cool. A short time before serving, brush the tart with melted apricot jam glaze and serve at room temperature.

Normandy apple tart is best eaten the day it is baked, but it can also be frozen. Just before serving, reheat to lukewarm in a low oven.

TARTE A LA CREME D'AMANDES
(Almond cream pie)

Serve it as it is or decorate with a spiral of Chantilly cream and toasted flaked almonds.

SERVES 6

For the almond pastry
150g (5oz) flour
pinch of salt
150g (5oz) ground blanched almonds
125g (4oz) sugar
3 egg yolks
125g (4oz) butter
for the filling
250ml (8fl oz) milk
250ml (8fl oz) single cream
vanilla pod, split
pinch of salt
90g (3oz) sugar
2 eggs
2 egg yolks
1-2 tablespoons Kirsch or Maraschino
75g (2½oz) finely chopped mixed candied fruit

25cm (10in) diameter flan ring or pie tin with a removable base

For the almond pastry: sift the flour with the salt onto a working surface, add the ground almonds and make a large well in the centre. Add the sugar and egg yolks and work with the fingertips until they are mixed.

Pound the butter to soften it slightly and add it to the well. Work the butter, sugar and yolks with the fingertips until mixed and then gradually draw in the flour and almonds. When the dough is smooth, push it down and away from you with the heel of the hand in the 'fraiser' motion. Roll the dough into a ball, wrap it and chill for 30 minutes. Butter the pie tin or flan ring.

Roll out the dough on a floured surface, line the ring or tin and flute the edges. Chill it for 15 minutes. Set the oven at moderate, 180C (350F) gas 4. Line the dough with greaseproof paper, fill with beans and bake it in the heated oven for 12-15 minutes, or until set and just beginning to brown. Remove the paper and beans and allow the shell to cool.

For the filling: scald the milk and cream by bringing it just to the boil with the vanilla pod, salt and half the sugar. Cover and leave to infuse for 10-15 minutes. Add the remaining sugar and whisk until dissolved. Beat the eggs and egg yolks until mixed and stir in the hot milk mixture. Flavour the custard to taste with Kirsch or Maraschino.

Sprinkle the candied fruit in the pie shell and strain over the custard. Bake it in the heated oven 25 minutes or until browned and just set. NOTE: reduce the oven temperature to 170C (325F) gas 3 if the pie is browning too quickly. Do not overcook or it will curdle. Transfer the pie to a rack to cool.

It is best eaten the day it is baked.

BARQUETTES AUX MARRONS

(Chestnut boats)

In recipes requiring sweetened purée, canned chestnuts can be substituted for fresh with almost no loss of flavour.

MAKES 14

pâte sucrée made with 200g (6½oz) flour, pinch salt, 80g (2½oz) sugar, 3 egg yolks, ½ teaspoon vanilla essence and 100g (3½oz) butter

chestnut purée made with 750g (1½lb) chestnuts, vanilla pod, 180g (6oz) sugar and 125ml (scant ¼pt) water; or 500g (1lb) canned, sweetened chestnut purée

tablespoon rum

120g (4oz) dark dessert chocolate, chopped (to finish)

10cm (4in) boat-shaped tins

Make the pastry and chill it. Roll it out to about 5mm (¼in) thick and line the buttered tins. Chill them until the dough is firm. Set the oven at hot, 200C (400F) gas 6.

Prick the bases of the shells, line them with paper and fill with dried beans. Place them on a baking sheet and bake in the heated oven for 8-10 minutes or until the pastry is set and lightly browned. Remove the paper and beans and return the shells to the oven for a further 5-7 minutes or until they are crisp and brown. Allow them to cool slightly, then remove them from the tins and place on a rack to cool completely. The shells can be made up to 48 hours ahead and kept in an airtight container.

To peel fresh chestnuts: put the nuts a few at a time in boiling water and bring back to the boil. Take from the heat and lift out the nuts. Remove the outer and inner peel with a knife. If the nuts become difficult to peel, reheat them briefly in the water.

For the chestnut purée: put the peeled nuts in a saucepan with the vanilla pod and water to cover and bring to the boil. Cover and simmer for 40-50 minutes or until the nuts are very tender. Drain them and push through a sieve, work through a food mill or purée in an electric food processor. Wash the vanilla pod to use again. In a small saucepan bring the sugar and 125ml (scant ¼pt) water to the boil; leave it to cool. Stir in the rum and then add enough of the syrup to the chestnut purée so it just falls from a spoon.

If using canned purée, stir in the rum.

Mound the chestnut purée neatly in the boat shells, so that it comes to a peak in the centre. Chill thoroughly.

To finish: melt the chocolate in a water bath. Spread it evenly over the chestnut filling with a metal spatula. Chill until ready to serve.

TARTELETTES AUX FRUITS

Tartlets filled with fruit in contrasting colours make an attractive display. Red fruits should be coated with red currant jelly glaze and green and yellow fruits with apricot jam glaze.

MAKES 7-8

pâte sucrée made with 200g (6½oz) flour, tiny pinch of salt, 80g (2½oz) caster sugar, 3 egg yolks, ½ teaspoon vanilla essence (optional) and 100g (3½oz) butter

for the filling

350-450g (12-16oz) fresh fruit – strawberries, raspberries, grapes, cherries, apricots, tangerines

300ml (½pt) apricot jam or red currant jelly glaze, or 150ml (¼pt) of each

7-8 tartlet tins 8-10cm (3-4in) diameter; fluted biscuit cutter 10cm (4in) diameter

Make the pâte sucrée following the method given on page 20 and wrap and chill for 30 minutes.

Roll out the dough to 6mm (¼in) thickness, stamp out 10cm (4in) rounds with a fluted cutter and line them into tartlet tins. Alternatively, arrange the tartlet tins together and put the rolled sheet of dough over them all at once. Press the dough well into the base with a ball of dough dipped in flour. Press together the trimmings of dough, roll out and line the remaining moulds with it. Chill until firm. Set the oven at hot, 200C (400F) gas 6.

To bake the tartlet shells blind, line them with paper and dried beans and bake in the heated oven for 6-10 minutes or until the pastry is set and lightly browned. Lift out the paper and beans and continue cooking for 5 minutes, or until golden brown. NOTE: sweet pastry is unpleasantly bitter when too brown so make sure this does not happen.

Let the shells cool slightly, then transfer them to a rack to cool completely. They can be stored for 3-4 days in an airtight container.

To prepare the filling: hull strawberries, washing them only if they are sandy, and halve them if large; pick over raspberries; stone grapes if necessary; stone cherries; halve apricots, discarding the stones; peel tangerines and divide into segments, discarding pith and pips and any tough membrane or skin around each segment.

Not more than 3-4 hours before serving, brush tartlets with the appropriate melted glaze. NOTE: this helps prevent the fruit juice from making the pastry soft. Arrange a generous portion of fruit in each tartlet shell. It is possible to mix fruits in each shell, but tartlets filled with a single fruit is usually more attractive. Brush the fruits thoroughly with glaze, filling in all the cracks.

TARTELETTES AU CAFE ET AUX NOIX

(Coffee and walnut tartlets)

These little tartlets are so rich and delicious that they make all the work worthwhile.

MAKES ABOUT 30

pâte sucrée made with 250g (8oz) flour, large pinch salt, 100g (3½oz) sugar, 4 egg yolks, teaspoon vanilla essence and 125g (4oz) butter

for the almond cream

60g (2oz) butter, softened

60g (2oz) sugar

egg, beaten to mix

teaspoon rum

60g (2oz) blanched almonds, ground

10g (scant ½oz) flour

for the coffee walnut butter cream

butter cream (page 100) made with 4 egg yolks, 125g (4oz) sugar, 100ml (4oz) water and 250g (8oz) butter

tablespoon coffee essence, or to taste

75g (2½oz) finely chopped walnuts

to finish

glacé icing (page 100) made with 400g (14oz) icing sugar, 2-8 tablespoons water; or fondant (page 101) made with 500g (1lb) sugar, 250ml (9fl oz) water and 50g (1⅔oz) corn syrup or glucose, pinch of cream of tartar dissolved in 1 teaspoon of water; or ½ teaspoon lemon juice or vinegar

1 teaspoon instant coffee dissolved in 1 tablespoon water

30 walnut halves

thirty 5cm (2in) diameter tartlet tins

Make the pâte sucrée and chill it. Roll it out to just under 5mm ($\frac{1}{4}$in) thick and line half the tins. Chill the lined tins and set the oven at hot, 200C (400F) gas 6.

For the almond cream: cream the butter, gradually beat in the sugar and continue beating until the mixture is light and soft. Add the egg, beat well and then stir in the rum, ground almonds and the flour.

Coat the tartlet shells with the almond cream. Bake them in the heated oven for about 15 minutes or until the pastry is browned and crisp and the filling lightly browned. Allow the tartlets to cool slightly, then transfer them to a rack to cool completely.

Meanwhile, prepare the butter cream and flavour it with coffee essence. Stir in the chopped walnuts. When the tartlets are completely cool, spread them with the butter cream, giving them a smooth domed shape. Chill in the refrigerator until firm.

To finish: if using fondant, soften it with a little warm water, set the bowl in a water-bath (Chapter 29) and heat until just warm to the touch. Make the glacé icing if using this. Flavour the fondant or glacé icing with the dissolved coffee. Coat the tartlets as smoothly as possible with the glacé icing and top each with a walnut half.

PONTS NEUFS

Ponts Neufs can also be made as individual dessert tartlets rather than as petits fours.

Makes 25 very small tartlets

pâte brisée made with 250g (8oz) flour, 125g (4oz) unsalted butter, 2 egg yolks, 5g (teaspoon) salt and 3$\frac{1}{2}$-4 tablespoons cold water

egg, beaten with $\frac{1}{2}$ teaspoon salt (for glaze)

for the filling

choux pastry (page 45) made with 75g (2$\frac{1}{2}$oz) flour, 125g (scant $\frac{1}{4}$pt) water, 2g (1$\frac{1}{2}$ level teaspoon) salt, 50g (1$\frac{1}{2}$oz) butter and 2 large eggs

thin pastry cream (page 45) made with 5 egg yolks, 125g (4oz) sugar, 30g (1oz) flour, 400ml ($\frac{3}{4}$pt) milk, pinch of salt and vanilla pod

2 teaspoons orange flower water; or 25ml (1oz) rum

to finish

icing sugar (for sprinkling)

apricot jam glaze – made with 125g (4oz)

(4oz) apricot jam, lemon juice to taste and a tablespoon water

twenty-five 4cm (1$\frac{1}{2}$in) diameter tartlet tins

Make the pâte brisée and chill it. Roll it out to just under 5mm ($\frac{1}{4}$in) thick and line the tins. Reserve about $\frac{1}{8}$ of the dough for decoration. Chill the shells until firm. Set the oven at moderately hot, 190C (375F) gas 5.

For the filling: make the choux pastry and the pastry cream. NOTE: this pastry cream should be sweeter and thinner than usual. Beat the pastry cream into the choux pastry and flavour it with orange flower water or rum to taste. Fill the tartlets with the mixture, doming it in each shell. Place the tartlets on a baking sheet.

Roll out the reserved dough, cut it in very thin strips long enough to reach over the filling of each tartlet from edge to edge. Criss-cross two strips on top of each mound to divide each tartlet into 4 sections. Brush them with egg glaze and bake them in the oven for about 30 minutes or until they are puffed and brown. Transfer them to a rack to cool.

To finish: cut a round of cardboard slightly bigger than the tartlets and then cut away one quarter of the round. Holding the cardboard round above the tartlet so that all of the tartlet is covered except one section, shake icing sugar over that section. Next shake the sugar over the opposite section. Melt the apricot glaze in a small saucepan and brush it over the 2 remaining sections.

SABLES DE CAEN

Although these sablés originated in Caen, a town in Normandy, sablés with various flavourings can be found in most French pastry shops. The triangular design is traditional.

MAKES 12-14

330g (11oz) flour

$\frac{1}{4}$ level teaspoon salt

125g (4oz) icing sugar

250g (8oz) butter

3 hard boiled egg yolks, sieved

grated rind and juice of 1 orange

1 egg, beaten to mix with $\frac{1}{2}$ level teaspoon salt (for glaze)

9-10cm (3$\frac{1}{2}$-4in) biscuit cutter

Sift the flour on to a marble slab or board, make a large well in the centre and add the salt, sugar, butter, sieved egg yolks, grated orange rind and orange juice. Work these ingredients with the fingertips until mixed, then gradually draw in the flour, using the whole hand. Knead the dough with the heel of the hand until it is smooth and it peels easily from the board in one piece. Wrap and chill it for 30 minutes.

Set the oven at moderately hot, 190C (375F) gas 5, and butter 2 baking sheets. Roll out the dough to 6mm ($\frac{1}{4}$in) thickness, stamp out rounds with a 9-10cm (3$\frac{1}{2}$-4in) biscuit cutter and set them on a baking sheet. Press the pastry trimmings to a ball, roll and cut out more. Brush the sablés with beaten egg and, with the prongs of a fork, mark a triangle on each one. Chill for 10-15 minutes, then bake in the heated oven for 7-10 minutes or until lightly browned. NOTE: if overcooked, they will be bitter. Transfer them to a rack to cool.

18
PATES AND TERRINES
The rough and the smooth

Pâtés and terrines represent much of the best in French cooking: the combination of a large number of flavours to good effect; virtuosity in applying a simple cooking method to a wide variety of different ingredients; and an astonishing range of sophistication, from the sumptuous pâtés of fresh foie gras studded with truffles to rustic terrines de campagne that are no more than the Gallic version of a meat loaf. Pâtés and terrines cover almost the whole meal from fish through meat to vegetables, and we only need some wit of the nouvelle cuisine to invent a fruit terrine for the menu to be complete.

Pâtés and terrines are traditionally forcemeat, varying in texture from velvety smooth to coarsely chopped, which is seasoned and baked in the oven, usually until firm enough to turn out for serving. The forcemeat can be used alone or it can be layered with strips of meat such as veal, ham or game, often marinated in brandy; it can be dotted with liver for texture, or with pistachios, truffles or pieces of blanched green and red pepper for colour.

Pâtés are very local, reflecting the produce of the region. One of the best terrines I ever tasted was made with venison and studded with whole toasted hazelnuts, which gave a delicious crunch to the texture. I was in Orléanais, a hunting territory that is well known for its nuts.

Strictly speaking, a pâté is baked in pastry (pâte), and a terrine – the word comes from 'terre', earth – is cooked in a special earthenware mould (a terrine), but the definitions have become blurred over the years. In general, finer-textured, richer mixtures used to be

RILLETTES DE SAUMON *(left front)*
This starter is a good example of nouvelle cuisine. Slowly baked rillettes of pork, goose, duck and rabbit are traditional, but only recently have mixtures of similar consistency and richness been made of salmon and other fish. It's a new twist to an old idea in French cuisine, but salmon rillettes are very similar to potted salmon, in fact

PATE DE POISSON LA MAREE *(left back)*
Green and red peppers and black olives decorate the top of this delicate mousseline of fish layered with strips of salmon. It can be served either hot or cold

TERRINE DE CAMPAGNE *(right)*
Pistachio nuts and strips of ham add colour to a terrine of pork, veal and chicken livers. It is in the tradition of simple country terrines – gherkins are the usual accompaniment

baked in pastry, so these have become known as pâtés, though the pastry has often disappeared and been replaced by a terrine mould. To distinguish them, true pâtés are often called pâtés en croûte. The dough was originally made of flour and water and was not eaten, but nowadays most people tuck into the richer butter or lard-flavoured doughs that are used. Large pâtés en croûte are popular for dinner parties, and the little ones are a common snack, really no more than a glorified sausage roll. Pâtés en croûte can be served hot or cold – when eaten hot, the fat content of the forcemeat is usually reduced.

Pâtés and terrines probably began as a way of using up bits of the most common meat – pork. Pork is still the favourite ingredient – classic proportions for a forcemeat are one kilo (2lb) of veal, game or poultry meat, 500 grams (1lb) of lean pork (or pork and veal) and 750 grams (1½lb) of pork fat. This is half as much fat as lean – seemingly a high proportion, but the forcemeat tends to be dry without it. Often, for economy, some veal or pork is substituted for the game. Veal is used in forcemeats because its gelatine gives body.

The meat can be coarsely or finely minced in a mincer or, best of all, very finely chopped by hand. One day, a student at La Varenne was giving Chef Claude a hard time, so Claude put him to chopping the forcemeat for the duck terrine. Chopping does not bruise meat like a mincer and when, three days later, we compared the hand-chopped terrine with an identical one made with machine-cut meat, the result was a revelation. But the class did not forget the work involved. Equally demanding are the forcemeats used for fish and liver pâtés since, for the smoothest texture, they must be worked through a drum sieve. Mincing (or working in a food processor) does not extract fibres as a sieve does.

The seasoning of a forcemeat is even more important than the texture. Salt and freshly ground black pepper are indispensable – our chefs' proportions are 12 grams (2½ level teaspoons) of salt and 4 grams (scant level teaspoon) of pepper per kilo (2¼lb) of forcemeat, but this can vary depending on the meat used. Spices such as nutmeg, allspice, ginger and cloves lend flavour, as does a spoon or two of brandy or Madeira. Herbs, garlic, onion or shallot finely chopped and sautéed, and green peppercorns are all possible additions. Orange and lemon are great favourites with duck. The only way to test seasoning is by tasting: when all the ingredients are mixed, fry a little of the mixture or bake it in the oven and taste it. The seasonings should balance without one being predominant. Cold food requires more seasoning than hot and, if in doubt, I think too much is better than too little.

To keep forcemeat moist during cooking, it is always wrapped either in pastry (for pâté) or in barding fat (for a terrine). For poultry terrines, the skin of the bird may be used instead of barding fat. The lid of the terrine mould can also be sealed with a luting paste made of flour and water. Pâtés, however, are cooked simply on a baking sheet or in a topless pâté en croûte mould. Next comes baking, starting in a fairly high oven for a pâté so the dough sets, then lowering the heat to finish cooking the forcemeat inside. A terrine should be cooked in a water bath to ensure even heat – the mould is set in a tin of hot water, brought to the boil on top of the stove and cooked in a moderate oven.

Testing a terrine is vital, as an uncooked terrine will not keep and an overdone mixture will be dry. For pâtés, and for terrine moulds with a hole in the lid, use a primitive meat thermometer: insert a thin skewer or a piece of wire into the centre of the mixture, leave it for 30 seconds to absorb the heat, then at once touch it quickly to the back of your hand. If cold, the heat has not penetrated to the centre of the mixture and more cooking is needed; if hot, the mixture is done; if burning, it is overcooked. Terrines can also be tested by removing the lid: if the terrine is firm to the touch and the liquid bubbling at the sides is clear, showing the meat juices are cooked, the terrine is done. In case you should wonder why commercial terrines retain a pink tinge, this is not due to undercooking, but to the addition of saltpetre, which lengthens their shelf life.

At this stage, transfer pâtés to a rack to cool, and leave terrines undisturbed. When terrines are cool, but not cold, they should be pressed to make them compact for slicing: put a flat plate on the terrine and top with a 1½-1¾kg (3-4lb) weight – a copper saucepan or several tins are good. Leave overnight or until very cold. If you want to keep the terrine more than 3-4 days, make sure it is completely covered in fat, adding more if necessary. Then cover with the lid and keep in a cool place.

The classic pâtés and terrines are not the end of the story, though, for there are several other members of the terrine family. Rillettes resemble potted meat and are made by baking a fat meat, such as pork, goose or duck (cut in cubes and sealed in an earthenware pot or pottery jar with a very little water, salt and pepper) until the meat falls apart. When cool, the meat is pulled apart with forks and mixed with the rendered fat to give a characteristic rough texture. Lately fish rillettes have appeared; they have the same rough texture, but are made differently, being simply mixtures of cooked fish and butter. Salmon, eel and smoked fish are favourites for rillettes.

Fish rillettes are an invention of nouvelle cuisine, and young chefs are vying with each other in the creation of new pâtés and terrines as well, made of fish, not meat. Fish terrines have been thoroughly explored during the past 15 years – terrines of salmon, of sole, of scallops and other shellfish, often arranged in multi-coloured layers and seasoned with sorrel and green herbs. Now they are rivalled by an even trickier concoction – the terrine of vegetables. This is made by layering a variety of lightly cooked vegetables with a forcemeat of ham or veal to give a gaily striped slice dotted with carrots, peas, green beans, mushrooms, artichokes and so on. However, vegetables are not as accommodating as meat and fish: they lose flavour easily and render water during cooking. Making a terrine that holds together with vegetables of crisp texture and plenty of flavour is not easy.

Now – who's going to invent a new masterpiece – that fruit terrine?

THE WAY TO SUCCESS

1 If barding fat is not available to line a terrine mould, use caul fat. Alternatively cut pork back fat as thin as possible and pound it even thinner.

2 If game is being used, it should be fresh, not hung.

3 For most pâtés and terrines, especially delicate ones, the ingredients for forcemeat should be minced as fine as possible. The texture of country terrines, however, should be coarser.

4 For coarser terrines, the meat can be minced in a machine or by hand; for fine fish pâtés or liver pâtés, it should also be worked through a drum sieve after mincing. Mincing can be done in a food processor or an electric or hand mincer.

5 If adding ham or bacon to a pâté or terrine, season the forcemeat with less salt.

6 Add seasoning gradually, testing to get the right balance.

7 Pâtés and terrines shrink as they cook, so pack them down well and fill the mould completely.

8 To prevent forcemeat sticking to your hands, dampen them occasionally.

9 When layering the mixture, be sure to place meat strips lengthwise so they are cut through when slicing.

10 If raw strips of meat or poultry are used, they can shrink during cooking, leaving gaps in the terrine. To avoid this, sauté them lightly in butter to 'stiffen' and shrink them before using in the terrine.

11 Extra forcemeat can be used to stuff vegetables or can be baked in ramekins as individual servings.

12 So that cooking time can be measured accurately, always bring the water bath to a boil before putting a terrine mould in the oven; the oven should be hot enough to keep the water bubbling.

13 Do not cut a terrine until thoroughly chilled, or it will crumble.

Getting ahead

1 Pâtés, terrines and rillettes are intended to be made ahead. Although fish and vegetable terrines can be eaten warm directly from the oven, they can also be kept up to 3 days before serving. Meat mixtures mellow on keeping; they should be left at least 3 days and up to 10 days in the refrigerator or a cool place.

2 Once a meat pâté or terrine is cut open, it should be eaten within 48 hours (24 hours in the case of vegetables and fish mixtures). Cover the cut surface with plastic wrap to prevent discoloration.

3 If you want to keep a pâté or terrine even longer, when cold seal it with a generous layer of melted clarified butter or lard. This will double the time it will last.

4 The fat in meat rillettes helps to preserve them by sealing the meat from contact with the air. They can be kept for several weeks in a cool place. Fish rillettes should be covered with clarified butter for storage.

5 Terrines can be frozen, but they will be tougher and slightly damp when thawed. The texture of pâtés is spoiled by freezing, but rillettes, because of their high fat content, freeze very well.

PETITS PATES DE POISSON
(Little fish pâté)

These small fish pâtés were described in a book by Menon, a famous chef of the mid-eighteenth century. You could update them to nouvelle cuisine by serving them with white butter sauce.

SERVES 8

puff pastry (page 163) made with 100-125g (3½-4oz) butter, 125g (4oz) flour, 3g (½ level teaspoon) salt, ½ teaspoon lemon juice and 65-75ml (3fl oz) water
2 slices white bread, crusts removed
250g (½lb) salmon, whiting, pike, haddock or other well-flavoured fish
250ml (8oz) double cream
teaspoon salt
freshly ground black pepper
pinch grated nutmeg
2 shallots, finely chopped
2 tablespoons chopped parsley
egg yolk
15g (½oz) softened butter
egg, beaten to mix with ½ teaspoon salt (for glaze)
eight 8cm (3in) diameter tartlet tins; 9 and 10cm (3½ and 4in) diameter round biscuit cutters

Make the puff pastry dough and chill.

Bake the bread in a very low oven, 130C (250F) gas ½, until dry but not brown. Work it to crumbs in a food processor or rub it through a sieve. Remove all the skin and bones from the fish, and chop the flesh. Mix the fish with the breadcrumbs, cream, salt, pepper, nutmeg, shallots and parsley. Purée the mixture a little at a time in a food processor until smooth. Alternatively, pound the fish, breadcrumbs and seasonings in a mortar with a pestle and gradually work in the cream. Taste the mixture for seasoning and adjust if necessary; it should be highly seasoned. Beat in the egg yolk and butter. Set the oven at hot, 200C (400F) gas 6.

Roll out the pastry to a 5mm (¼in) thickness or thinner and stamp out eight 9cm (3½in) rounds, and eight 10cm (4in) rounds. Line the tins with the larger rounds, fill them with the fish mixture and moisten the inside edges with egg glaze. Cover with the smaller rounds and press the edges gently together. Brush the tops with glaze and chill for 15 minutes. Set the tins on a baking sheet and bake in the heated oven for 30 minutes or until a skewer inserted in the centre of one of the pastries for ½ minute is hot to the touch when withdrawn. Serve the pastries as soon as possible.

PATE DE POISSON LA MAREE
(Fish pâté la marée)

For fish pâtes, the forcemeat is usually a mousseline, a delicate mixture of ground raw fish, egg whites and cream. This mixture can also be packed in buttered dariole moulds or ramekins, cooked in a water bath until firm, turned out and served hot with sauce vin blanc. The recipe for sauce vin blanc is given on page 195 – it is served exclusively with fish dishes as it contains fish glaze. Green mayonnaise makes the perfect accompaniment if this pâté is served cold. The basic recipe for mayonnaise is given on page 179. If sliced truffles are used, they can either be placed on the bottom of the mould before cooking as directed, or on top after the pâté is turned out.

SERVES 4

for decoration

250g (½lb) sole or salmon, free of skin and bone (optional)
½ small green pepper, cored and seeded
½ small red pepper, cored and seeded
2 canned truffles with their liquid; or 2 black olives, stoned

for the fish mousseline

750g (1½lb) pike, halibut, whiting or salmon, free of skin and bone
3 egg whites, lightly beaten
salt and white pepper
pinch of grated nutmeg
300ml (½pt) double cream

for serving

white wine sauce (page 195) (if serving hot)
green mayonnaise (if serving cold)
bunch of watercress (optional)

1.5 litre (2½pt) capacity terrine mould or loaf tin

Set the oven at moderate, 180C (350F) gas 4. Butter the terrine or loaf tin, line the base with a strip of non-stick vegetable parchment and butter the paper.

If using a white fish for the fish mousseline, use salmon for decoration; if using salmon for the mousseline, use sole for decoration. Cut the 250g (½lb) of fish in thin strips and dry very well. Chop some of the peppers for adding to the mousseline and cut the rest in large pieces for the decoration. Blanch the peppers in boiling salted water for one minute, drain, refresh and

drain thoroughly. If using truffles drain them, reserving the liquid, chop one of them and slice the other.

For the fish mousseline: work the 750g (1½lb) fish twice through the fine blade of a mincer or work it in an electric food mill. Pound the mixture in a mortar with a pestle until very smooth or work it through a sieve. Transfer the mixture to a metal bowl and set it over a pan of iced water. Using a wooden spoon, gradually beat in the egg whites; then beat in the salt, white pepper and nutmeg. NOTE: the ice and the chemical action of the salt will make the mixture thicken slightly. Beat in the cream by spoonfuls, beating well between additions. The mixture should be very thick. Beat in the truffle liquid, if included, stir in the chopped peppers and chopped truffles and taste – the mixture should be quite highly seasoned.

Arrange large pepper pieces and olives (or truffle) in the base of the mould. Place half the mousseline in the mould and arrange the strips of fish lengthwise on the mixture. Put the rest of the mousseline mixture on top and cover with buttered greaseproof paper and with the terrine lid. If the tin or mould has no lid, cover with several layers of foil. The pâté can be prepared up to 8 hours ahead and kept in the refrigerator.

To cook the pâté: set the pan in a water bath and bring to the boil on top of the stove. Cook it in the heated oven for 30-35 minutes or until it is firm to the touch and hot when tested with a skewer. Meanwhile make the sauce vin blanc or green mayonnaise. Keep the sauce vin blanc warm in a water bath, or keep the mayonnaise covered at room temperature.

To finish: if serving it hot, the cooked pâté can be kept warm in a low oven, 150C (300F) gas 2, for 15-20 minutes. Just before serving, run a knife around the edge and turn the pâté out on a serving dish. If serving cold, let the pâté cool in the mould. It can be kept up to 24 hours in the refrigerator but must come to room temperature before serving. Garnish the serving dish with watercress.

MAYONNAISE VERTE
(Green mayonnaise)

Makes about 300ml (½pt)

6-8 fresh spinach leaves (stems removed)
10g (⅓oz) watercress leaves
10g (⅓oz) parsley sprigs
2 tablespoons tarragon or chervil leaves
600ml (1pt) boiling water
300ml (½pt) mayonnaise (page 179) made with 2 egg yolks, salt and white pepper, Dijon mustard, 2 tablespoons white wine vinegar or tablespoon lemon juice and generous 300ml (½pt) oil
salt and white or Cayenne pepper

Blanch the spinach, watercress, parsley and tarragon or chervil in the boiling water. Drain thoroughly, refresh with cold water and squeeze in a towel to obtain a green liquid. Stir 2 tablespoons of this liquid into the mayonnaise, or enough to colour the mayonnaise a pale green. Taste for seasoning and adjust if necessary.

Serve with the fish pâté or with any cold fish or vegetables, or with hard-boiled eggs.

RILLETTES DE SAUMON
(Salmon rillettes)

No wonder young chefs have seized on recipes like this one for fish rillettes. They are infinitely quicker and easier to make than terrines and can be kept, sealed under a top layer of clarified butter, for up to a week.

SERVES 6-8

500g (1lb) piece of fresh salmon, with the bone
375g (¾lb) smoked salmon
375g (¾lb) butter, softened
salt and pepper
pinch of grated nutmeg

for poaching the fresh salmon

75ml (3fl oz) white wine
fish stock (page 218) made with the salmon bone, onion, 15g (½oz) butter, 1 litre (1¾pts) water, 10 peppercorns and bouquet garni

for cooking the smoked salmon

30g (1oz) butter
tablespoon water

Remove the bone from the fresh salmon and use it to make the fish stock. Poach the salmon with the white wine and enough fish stock to cover for 5-7 minutes or until tender. NOTE: do not add salt because the smoked salmon will be salty. Leave to cool in the cooking liquid; then remove the salmon from the liquid and discard the skin. Cool thoroughly.

Melt the 30g (1oz) butter in a sauté pan; add the smoked salmon and 1 tablespoon water. Cover and cook for 3 minutes or until no longer transparent. Leave it to cool.

Shred the fresh and the smoked salmon with a fork and mix well. Cream the remaining butter and gradually mix it into the finely shredded salmon using a fork. Season to taste with salt, pepper and nutmeg. Pack the mixture in individual ramekins or in a pottery mould and chill thoroughly. Serve with fresh bread or toast.

For Terrine de campagne, a mould is lined with barding fat or strips of bacon and then packed with a forcemeat which is flavoured with onion, garlic, spices and brandy. The forcemeat is layered in the terrine with strips of ham

TERRINE DE CAMPAGNE
(Country terrine)

Nearly every charcuterie in France sells country terrine. The mixture should not be finely minced. Cream adds moistness but shortens the keeping time.

SERVES 8

250g (½lb) sliced barding fat or mild cure bacon
tablespoon butter
onion, chopped
500g (1lb) pork (half fat, half lean), minced
250g (½lb) veal, minced
250g (½lb) chicken livers, finely chopped
2 cloves garlic, finely chopped
¼ teaspoon ground allspice
pinch ground cloves
pinch ground nutmeg
2 small eggs, beaten
150ml (¼pt) double cream (optional)
2 tablespoons brandy
salt and pepper
75g (2½oz) shelled pistachios (optional)
slice of cooked ham (about 250g or ½lb), cut in strips
bay leaf
sprig of thyme
luting paste to seal mould (see the box on the right)

2 litre (3½pt) capacity terrine or casserole with tight-fitting lid

Line the terrine or casserole with barding fat or bacon, reserving a few slices for the top. Set the oven at moderate, 180C (350F) gas 4.

Melt the butter in a small pan and cook the onion slowly until soft but not brown. Mix the onion with the pork, veal, chicken livers, garlic, allspice, cloves, nutmeg, eggs, cream, brandy and plenty of salt and pepper. Beat with a wooden spoon to thoroughly distribute the seasoning. Sauté a small piece and taste for seasoning – it should taste quite spicy. Add the pistachios, if included, and beat the mixture until it holds together.

Spread a third of the mixture in the lined terrine, add a layer of half the ham strips and top with another third of the pork mixture. Add the remaining ham and cover with the last third of the pork. Lay the reserved barding fat or bacon slices on top, trimming the edges if necessary. Set the bay leaf and sprig of thyme on top of the barding fat or bacon and cover with the lid. Seal the gap with luting paste.

Set in a water bath (Chapter 29), bring the water to the boil on top of the stove and cook the terrine in the heated oven for 1¼-1½ hours or until a skewer inserted for ½ minute into the mixture is hot to the touch when withdrawn. NOTE: regulate the heat so the water keeps simmering; if much of it evaporates, add more. Cool until tepid, remove the luting paste and lid and press the terrine with a board, plate or the terrine lid turned upside down, and a 1kg (2lb) weight until cold.

Keep the terrine in the refrigerator for at least 3 days or up to a week to allow the flavour to mellow before serving. It can be frozen for up to 3 months.

To serve: unmould the terrine, cut part of it in thick slices and arrange them overlapping on a serving dish. Alternatively, serve the terrine in the mould.

LUTING PASTE
To make luting paste for sealing you will need:

200g (7oz) flour
225-300ml (8-10fl oz) water

Put the flour in a small bowl. Make a well in the centre, add 225ml (8oz) of the water and mix with your fingers, adding more water if needed, to obtain a soft paste just firm enough to shape. Do not beat the mixture or it will become elastic and may shrink and crack during cooking.

Turn onto a floured board and roll with your hands into a rope the length of the perimeter of your terrine mould. Put it around the rim and press on the lid. The paste hardens quickly and prevents all steam from escaping.

TERRINE DE FOIES DE VOLAILLE
(Chicken liver terrine)

The veal and pork in this terrine make it mellower than versions containing only chicken livers. Don't hesitate about including the high proportion of fat, which makes it smooth and rich, but not too greasy.

SERVES 12-16

500g (1lb) veal
500g (1lb) lean pork
1kg (2lb) pork fat
650g (1¼lb) chicken livers
2 eggs
3 tablespoons Cognac
salt and pepper
½ teaspoon dried thyme
pinch allspice
250g (½lb) barding fat
bay leaf
sprig of thyme
3 litre (5pt) capacity terrine mould

Mince together the veal, lean pork and pork fat and 500g (1lb) of the chicken livers. Combine the meats, eggs, Cognac, salt, pepper, thyme and allspice and work them together with your hands. Sauté a small piece of the mixture, taste, and adjust the seasoning if necessary. Line the terrine mould with barding fat and put in half the mixture. Arrange the remaining chicken livers down the centre and then fill the mould with the remaining mixture. Put the bay leaf and sprig of thyme on top and cover with the terrine lid. Set the oven at moderately hot, 190C (375F) gas 5.

Put the terrine in a water bath, bring the water to a boil on top of the stove and cook it in the heated oven for 2½-3 hours, or until a skewer inserted for ½ minute into the meat through the hole in the terrine lid is hot to the touch when withdrawn. NOTE: regulate the heat so the water keeps simmering; if much of it evaporates, add more.

Cool until tepid, remove the lid and press the terrine until cold with a board or plate topped by a 1kg (2lb) weight. Keep the terrine in the refrigerator for at least 3 days or up to a week before serving to allow the flavour to mellow. It can also be frozen for up to 3 months.

To serve, turn out the terrine, cut part of it in thick slices and arrange them overlapping on a serving dish.

TERRINE MOULDS

Terrine moulds are believed to have originated in Strasbourg, where a potter had the idea of cooking goose livers in earthenware containers.

Now terrine moulds come in materials varying from ovenproof porcelain through Pyrex to enamelled cast iron. Manufacturers have given full rein to the imaginations of their designers, and terrine moulds are ablaze with flowers, fruit and, more appropriately, vegetables. They come in many colours, the most successful, I think, being earth tones of orange, biscuit and brown. Some of the most expensive terrines are crowned in traditional style with pottery lids made to resemble birds and animals designating the contents. The cheapest, made of plain old-fashioned earthenware, probably remain the best.

Moulds vary from rectangular loaf shapes to ovals intended for terrines of boned, stuffed poultry. Long, narrow terrines are easy to slice. The shape of the terrine mould has considerable effect on the cooking time and so does the material in which it is made, as metal transmits heat much more quickly than pottery or porcelain. All terrines should have a tight-fitting lid with a hole in it. This serves the dual purpose of letting steam escape and allowing the insertion of a skewer into the terrine mixture to test for cooking. If you have no mould, you can improvise with a heavy baking dish and several layers of foil as a lid.

TERRINE DE CANARD AU POIVRE VERT
(Duck terrine with green peppercorns)

Green peppercorns are preserved in brine. They should be drained thoroughly before using.

SERVES 10

large duck, weighing about 2-2½kg (4-5lb)
tablespoon brandy
for the forcemeat
750g (1½lb) lean meat – combination of duck scraps, veal and pork
250g (½lb) fat pork
375g (¾lb) pig's liver (optional)
the duck liver
2 cloves garlic, crushed
2 tablespoons brandy
½ teaspoon ground allspice
¼ teaspoon ground cloves
¼ teaspoon ground nutmeg
3 tablespoons drained green peppercorns
2 eggs
salt and freshly ground black pepper
luting paste to seal mould
2-2.5 litre (3½-4½pt) capacity oval terrine mould; trussing needle and string

Set the oven at moderate, 180C (350F) gas 4. Completely bone the duck (page 30). Leave the meat attached to the skin, which should remain intact. Remove any untidy-looking bits of meat and save for the forcemeat. Sprinkle the duck skin with the tablespoon of brandy.

For the forcemeat: work the lean meat, fat pork, pork liver, duck liver and garlic twice through the fine blade of a mincer. Stir in the brandy, allspice, cloves, nutmeg, green peppercorns and the eggs and season well with salt and pepper. Sauté a small piece and taste for seasoning; it should taste quite spicy. Stir the mixture until it holds together.

Pack the stuffing into the duck skin and sew the seam together so the stuffing is completely enclosed. Set the duck seam side down in the terrine mould and top with the lid. Seal the gap between the terrine mould and lid with the luting paste.

Set the terrine in a water bath, bring it to the boil on top of the stove and cook it in the heated oven for 1¼-1½ hours or until a skewer, inserted for ½ minute into the mixture through the hole in the terrine lid, is hot to the touch when withdrawn. Cool until tepid, remove the luting paste and lid and press the terrine with a board, plate or the terrine lid turned upside down and a 1kg (2lb) weight until cold.

Keep the terrine in the refrigerator for at least 2 days or up to a week to allow the flavour to mellow before serving. To serve, turn out, discard the strings and cut in thick slices. It can also be served from the mould.

PATE CHAUD DE VEAU ET DE JAMBON EN CROÛTE

(Hot veal and ham pâté en croûte)

This pâté can be baked on a baking sheet or in a special hinged pâté en croûte mould.

SERVES 8-10

150g (5oz) veal escalope
very thick slice (about 150g or 5oz) cooked ham
125g (¼lb) piece fat bacon
for the marinade
2 tablespoons white wine
2 tablespoons brandy
2 tablespoons Madeira
pepper
for the pâté pastry dough
500g (1lb) flour
250g (8oz) butter or 100g (3oz) lard and 150g (5oz) butter
2 eggs
2 tablespoons oil
10g (2 level teaspoons) salt
2-3 tablespoons water
1 egg, beaten to mix with ½ level teaspoon salt (for glaze)
for the forcemeat
500g (1lb) lean minced veal
500g (1lb) lean minced pork
375g (¾lb) fat minced pork
100g (3oz) chicken livers, finely chopped
4 tablespoons white wine
2 tablespoons brandy
2 eggs, beaten to mix
small can chopped truffles, with their liquid (optional)
pinch of nutmeg
salt and freshly ground black pepper
(2-2·5cm) ¾-1in fluted biscuit cutter (optional) and a hinged pâté en croûte mould (optional)

Cut the veal escalope, ham and bacon into 5mm (¼in) strips, pour over the wine, brandy and Madeira, add pepper and mix well. Cover and leave to marinate for about 30-45 minutes.

For the pâté pastry dough: sift the flour onto a marble slab or board and make a large well in the centre. In the well place the butter or butter/lard mixture, eggs, oil, salt and water and work in the flour, pulling the dough into large crumbs and adding a little more water if the crumbs are dry. Press the dough firmly together and work it in two or three portions on the board until smooth and pliable. Press into a ball, wrap and chill for 30 minutes.

For the forcemeat: work the veal, lean and fat pork with the chicken livers twice through the fine blade of the mincer. Mix with wine, brandy, eggs, truffles and liquid, if included, the nutmeg and plenty of salt and pepper. Add any marinade from the meat. Cook a tiny piece of the mixture in a frying pan and taste – it should be highly seasoned.

Roll out the dough to a 35×50cm (14×20in) rectangle. Divide the forcemeat into 4 portions and spread one portion lengthwise on the dough in a 10×35cm (4×14in) strip. Top with a layer of strips of ham, veal and bacon, using half the veal and a third of the ham and bacon. Cover with another portion of forcemeat, add half the remaining strips of ham and bacon and cover them with forcemeat. Top with the remaining strips of veal, ham and bacon and cover with the last portion of filling. Mould the filling with your hands so that the rectangle is as tall and neat as possible.

Cut a square of excess dough from each corner and brush the edges of the rectangle with egg glaze. Lift one long edge of the dough on top of the filling and fold over the opposite edge to enclose it.

Press gently to seal the dough and fold over the ends to make a neat parcel. Roll the parcel over onto a baking sheet so that the seam is underneath. Brush the pâté with glaze.

Alternatively, line a hinged pâté en croûte mould with the dough. Arrange the filling and strips inside as described above and cover with another piece of dough. The pâté is then baked in the mould.

Roll out the dough trimmings, cut a long strip and set it around the edge of the pâté. Decorate the top with leaves and a pastry rose, or with shells made by stamping out 2.5cm (1in) rounds with a fluted cutter and marking them with the back of a knife. Brush the decoration with egg glaze. Make a hole near each end of the pâté and insert a roll of paper as a 'chimney' so that steam can escape. Cover and chill the pâté for 20-30 minutes or up to 3 hours.

To finish: set the oven at hot, 200C (400F) gas 6. Bake the pâté in the hot oven for 15 minutes or until the pastry is set and starts to brown. Turn down the heat to moderate 180C (350F) gas 4 and continue baking for 1 hour or until a skewer inserted in the centre of the pâté for ½ minute is hot to the touch when withdrawn. If the pastry browns too much during cooking, cover it loosely with foil. Serve warm or cool.

The pâté can be cooked up to 3 days ahead and reheated in a moderate oven, 180C (350F) gas 4 or it can be frozen, but the pastry will not be quite so crisp.

For cold Pâté en croûte

Increase the amount of fat pork in the forcemeat to 500g (1lb) to prevent dryness. Chill well and, if you like, pour cool aspic (lesson 29) through a funnel set in one of the holes used as chimneys.

Refrigerate to set.

19
PETITS FOURS
Small but perfectly formed

'Petits fours' are called, so goes the story, after the little ovens invented in the 17th century for baking them. It is a beguiling name for what I have to confess are one of my great weaknesses. I can resist the allure of an overladen dessert trolley with hardly a pang, but set a plate of innocent, freshly-baked petits fours in front of me and I am overcome. Should I choose one of the curved 'tuiles', or a crisply rolled 'cigarette', or a melting miniature fruit tartlet, a tiny génoise cake, or one of those fruits dipped in sugar that seem to explode in your mouth? On reflection, what better way to accompany a second cup of coffee than with one of each?

Tempting they certainly are, innocent they may look, but do not be deceived. Petits fours have been the undoing of many an ambitious chef. When properly made, each type should conform to exact standards: they should all be of the same size, baked to the same colour, shaped to the same characteristic form and decorated in precisely the same way. And they must be absolutely fresh.

There are literally hundreds of different petits fours, since most large pastries and cakes can be made in a small size, as well as the biscuits, glazed fruits and other 'bonnes bouches' that are specifically petits fours. Pâtissiers divide them into two categories: fresh and dry. Fresh petits fours cannot be kept for more than 24 hours; they may contain fruit, or butter, or pastry cream, or involve some kind of sugar coating that softens in humid air. Often they are based on choux pastry, or génoise sponge. Dry petits fours can include little meringues, miniature puff pastries, and the 'cigarettes', 'tuiles' (tiles) and other piped and shaped biscuits that are the subject of this chapter. Unfortunately, even dry petits fours cannot be kept for more than a week; most are best eaten within a day or two.

Cigarettes russes and Palets de dames are made of essentially the same rich mixture of flour, butter, egg whites and sugar that is piped onto the baking sheet. Flavourings can include vanilla, lemon or orange rind, chocolate, cinnamon, finely chopped candied fruit, dried fruits and finely sliced or ground almonds. For

PETITS FOURS

From top left: Palets de dames, thin flat biscuits topped with currants; Tuiles aux amandes, made in the curved shape of Provençal roof tiles; Cigarettes russes, thin round biscuits rolled into cigarette shapes and Petits fours aux amandes, made from a ground almond mixture piped into two classic shapes

tuiles the mixture is dropped, rather than piped, on the baking sheet, then spread to wafer thinness with a fork.

When baked, palets de dames remain as small, round biscuits, but 'cigarettes' and tuiles spread, so while they are still hot they can be curled to the shapes their names suggest. The mixture for 'cigarettes', which is slightly thicker than other mixtures, is particularly versatile: it can be twisted into a cone, or pressed over a tumbler or into a brioche mould to make 'tulipes', edible containers for serving ice-cream and sorbets. Chef Jorant, La Varenne's pâtissier, even has a confection called 'Paris paquets', for which génoise is soaked in liqueur, filled with pastry cream, then wrapped in sheets of warm cigarette 'biscuit' – a tour de force that requires – as do all these rolled biscuits – a mixture of just the right consistency, baked to just the right stage.

Because the consistency can vary with the dryness of the flour or the size of the egg whites used, it is best to bake a trial 'cigarette' or tuile to test the mixture. If it barely spreads and does not cook in the middle, it is too thick and a little more egg white should be added. If, on the other hand, the batter is too thin and spreads all over the baking sheet, stir in a little more flour. Bake only one sheet of petits fours at a time as they must be shaped quickly once they come out of the oven. Loosen them with a metal spatula and immediately shape them around a pencil or wooden spoon handle – for 'cigarettes' – or over a rolling pin – for tuiles. If they become too crisp to roll, warm them for a short while in the oven.

Almond petits fours pose no such technical problems. The basic mixture, made of ground almonds and sugar, is mixed with just enough egg white so that it can be piped. To avoid their sticking to the baking sheet, the petits fours are baked on a sheet lined with greaseproof paper or non-stick parchment. They are piped in varying shapes, such as figures of eight, rosettes, tear-drops, loops or rings and cooked until brown (but not dry), and while hot they must be brushed with a glaze of sugar and milk to make them moist and shiny.

Don't let yourself be distracted by the range of petits fours made by a professional pâtissier. He, poor man, must please his customers with a good spread and must sell all, fresh or stale, if he is to make a profit. You can rival him any day with two or three kinds of simple petits fours fresh from the oven. I well remember dinner in a nondescript restaurant in the main square of an equally nondescript town. Hors d'oeuvre and main course were without distinction. On the dessert menu was a single word – tuiles. When they came they were crisp, see-through thin, and the size of a real-life Provençal tile. For once was the word *unique* appropriate.

THE WAY TO SUCCESS

1 Ingredients must be of the finest quality. Petits fours are not cheap to make. Artificial flavourings, nuts that are not fresh or – perish the thought – margarine, are instantly detectable.
2 Delicate biscuits will pick up stray flavours and stick to the baking sheet if it is not thoroughly cleaned beforehand.
3 When adding egg whites to a butter and sugar mixture, whisk them in gradually so the mixture does not separate.
4 Petits fours must all be the same size, so spoon or pipe exactly equal amounts of batter onto the baking sheet.
5 Petits fours should not be too large – professionals count 12-15g ($\frac{1}{4}$-$\frac{1}{2}$oz) weight for each one.
6 Petits fours that spread during baking must be spaced well apart.
7 Baking time is critical; if underbaked, petits fours are soggy; if overbaked, they taste bitter and will be too dry to shape.
8 Oven heat may circulate poorly with the result that the petits fours do not all bake at the same speed. Some may need to be taken from the oven before others.

Getting ahead

1 The basic mixture for most dry petits fours can be made ahead and kept for 1-2 hours, covered, in the refrigerator.
2 The petits fours can be prepared and left on baking sheets ready for baking. They will keep without harm for 1-2 hours.
3 Petits fours are best eaten within a day or two of baking. However, if packed in an airtight tin as soon as they are cool, most biscuit fours can be kept for up to a week. If they become soft, heat in a low oven to crisp them.
4 Almond 'fours' must be kept, layered in greaseproof paper to prevent sticking, in an airtight tin. They should keep well for up to a week – they tend to dry rather than soften on standing. Dry petits fours freeze well.

CIGARETTES RUSSES

('Russian cigarettes')

Makes about 40

150g (5oz) butter

250g (8oz) icing sugar, sifted

6 egg whites

150g (5oz) flour

tablespoon double cream

teaspoon vanilla essence

pastry bag and 1cm (⅜in) plain tube

Grease two or three baking sheets and set the oven at very hot, 230C (450F) gas 8.

Cream the butter and the icing sugar and gradually beat in half the egg whites. Add 1 heaped teaspoon flour and mix well. Gradually beat in the remaining egg whites. Stir in the remaining flour, then add the double cream and vanilla and mix well. Put the mixture in a piping bag fitted with the 1cm (⅜in) plain tube and pipe mounds the size of a walnut, well apart, on the prepared baking sheet. Bang the baking sheet sharply on the table to flatten the mounds and bake in the heated oven for 4-5 minutes or until they brown around the edges.

Loosen the biscuits from the baking sheet with a pliable knife or metal spatula but leave them on the baking sheet. Place one upside down on a table and roll quickly around a knife-sharpening steel, the handle of a wooden spoon or a pencil. Remove the biscuit at once; leave on a rack to cool and roll up the remaining biscuits as quickly as possible. If they become too hard to roll, put them back in the oven for 1 minute to soften. NOTE: As a precaution, pipe and bake one test 'cigarette' first. If it is not crisp when rolled, add a tablespoon of melted butter. If it is too brittle, add 1-2 tablespoons more flour.

Shape cigarettes russes round the handle of a wooden spoon, tuiles over a rolling pin – while they're still warm

PETITS FOURS AUX AMANDES

(Almond petits fours)

Makes 12-14

200g (7oz) whole blanched almonds, ground

150g (5oz) sugar

teaspoon apricot jam glaze (optional)

2 egg whites, beaten to mix

½ teaspoon vanilla essence or ¼ teaspoon almond essence

for decoration

one or more of the following possibilities: blanched almonds, split in half; glacé cherries or candied orange peel, cut in pieces; small diamonds of angelica; raisins

for glaze

tablespoon icing sugar

2 tablespoons milk or water

greaseproof paper; pastry bag and large star tube

Line a baking sheet with greaseproof paper. Set the oven at moderate, 180C (350F) gas 4.

Mix the ground almonds and sugar, add apricot glaze and stir in enough egg white to make a mixture that is soft enough to pipe, but still holds its shape. Beat in vanilla or almond essence. Put the mixture in a pastry bag fitted with a large star tube and pipe the mixture in flowers, rosettes, zigzags or figure eights onto the prepared baking sheet. Decorate each one with your almonds, pieces of glacé cherry or candied orange peel, angelica or raisins and bake in the heated oven 15-20 minutes or until the petits fours are just beginning to brown. *For the glaze:* heat the sugar with the milk until dissolved and brush the glaze over the petits fours while they are still hot. Lift one end of the paper slightly and immediately pour a glass of water under the paper. NOTE: the hot baking sheet will cause the water to form steam, making it easy to remove the petits fours. Leave them for a few minutes, then remove them from the paper and transfer to a rack to cool. Store up to one week.

PALETS DE DAMES

Makes about 24

30g (1oz) currants or raisins

100g (3½oz) flour

pinch of salt

100g (3½oz) butter

100g (3½oz) sugar

2 egg whites, beaten to mix

½ teaspoon vanilla essence

pastry bag and 1cm (⅜in) plain tube

Set the oven at hot, 200C (400F) gas 6, and grease and flour 2 baking sheets. Pour boiling water over the currants or raisins, allow them to stand for 10 minutes or until plump, then drain and dry well on paper towels. Sift the flour with the salt.

Cream the butter, beat in the sugar and continue beating until the mixture is light and fluffy. Beat in the egg whites, a little at a time, beating well after each addition. Stir in the vanilla, then fold in the flour. Put the mixture in a pastry bag fitted with a 1cm (⅜in) plain tube and pipe 2.5cm (1in) mounds onto the prepared baking sheets, leaving plenty of room for the mixture to spread. Put one or two currants or raisins on each mound.

Bake the palets for 8-10 minutes or until the edges are golden, the centres still pale. Transfer to a rack to cool. They can be kept in an airtight container for up to a week.

TUILES AUX AMANDES

(Almond tile biscuits)

Makes about 20

90g (3oz) butter

90g (3oz) icing sugar, sifted

teaspoon rum

2 egg whites

75g (2½oz) flour

pinch of salt

100g (3½oz) slivered almonds

½ teaspoon vanilla essence

Set the oven at hot, 200C (400F) gas 6, and grease several baking sheets. Heat the butter very slowly until it is pourable but not melted. Mix together in a bowl the icing sugar, rum, egg whites, flour, salt, almonds and vanilla. Gently stir in the butter.

Drop the mixture by teaspoonfuls onto the prepared baking sheets, leaving plenty of room for each biscuit to spread. Flatten each with a fork dipped in cold water.

Bake for 6-8 minutes or until the edges are browned. Remove immediately from the baking sheet, shape around a rolling pin straight away or place them in a ring mould and leave until firm.

159

20
PUFF PASTRY
All done by hand

To the aspiring cook, puff pastry or pâte feuilletée, is the ultimate challenge. The word 'feuilleté' means multi-leaved – as good puff pastry should be, with its feather-light, flaky layers that seem to defy the weight of the butter that flavours them. Apprentices are trained for weeks before their puff pastry technique is acceptable and some fully-fledged chefs never achieve quite the right touch. For in making puff pastry, it is the 'tour de main' that counts, the feeling in the hands that tells you if the dough is too sticky or too dry, too hot or too cold. Recipes – and there are several variants – are secondary.

Puff pastry is raised by literally hundreds of layers of butter (729 to be precise) that are interspersed with flour-and-water dough. In the oven the butter melts, detaching the dough layers, while at the same time the water in the dough and in the butter turns to steam, raising the pastry to three or four times its original thickness. It is hard to believe that puff pastry is made with exactly the same basic ingredients as shortcrust, though admittedly the butter content is much higher, often equalling the weight of the flour. Exact quantities are hard to fix as the amount of water absorbed by the flour can depend on its type, dryness and even the humidity of the day. Some chefs prefer to weigh the dough after mixing, then add half its weight in butter.

Butter it must be, not margarine. The flavour of margarine in pastry is instantly recognisable and, to me, to spend time making puff pastry with it is wasted labour. In France, the best unsalted butter with a very low whey content is used. Lightly salted butter can be substituted, but less salt should then be added to the flour.

To make the flour and water dough – graphically called the 'détrempe', or 'soaking' – the flour is sifted onto a marble slab, and the water, salt and a little butter are added. (Puff pastry is disappointingly bland without a good dose of salt.) Some chefs like to add a spoon of lemon juice to the détrempe to discourage the development of gluten. Gluten gives elasticity, a quality vital to good bread, but a problem in puff pastry in which it makes dough 'fight back' so it is hard to roll, tends to make the butter 'break through', and toughens the finished pastry.

Once the dough has been mixed as gently as possible to a soft, slightly sticky mass (a few unmixed bits of flour do not matter – the essential thing is to avoid overworking it), the butter must be incorporated. A block of butter approximately half the weight of the détrempe is sprinkled with flour and pounded with a rolling pin. It is folded and shaped to a 12.5 or 15cm (5 or 6in) square that is as pliable as putty. The closer the consistency of the butter approaches that of the dough, the more easily the two can be rolled out together. The détrempe is rolled to a rough 25.5 or 30.5cm (10 or 12in) circle, just large enough to enclose the butter with the centre of the dough slightly thicker than the edges. The butter is wrapped in the dough ready for the real rolling.

It is this phase that gives puff pastry its many layers. Practice and a heavy rolling pin are required to roll the stolid square of dough to a rectangle almost three times as long as it is wide, working always away from you. The width and length of the rectangle vary from 15×45.5cm (6×18in) to 30.5×92cm (12×36in), depending on the quantity of dough. Half a pound (250g) of flour is a minimum, and I've seen our chefs, who are accustomed to heavy work in the kitchen, rolling 2kg (4lb) quantities, though this stretches even their biceps to the limit. Pastry shops dealing in bulk have mechanical rollers.

Then the rectangle of dough is folded in three to form a square again and turned through 90 degrees so three layers rather than a folded edge face the person rolling. This is called a 'turn' and ensures that the dough is rolled first in one direction, then in the other. The dough is rolled again to a strip, folded, sealed lightly at the edges with taps of the rolling pin so that the layers stay in place, and marked with two finger-prints to show it has received two 'turns'. (Turns are always given in twos.) Already it has nine layers, and each subsequent rolling multiplies them three times.

Up to this stage, the process of making puff pastry is non-stop. It should also be quick – not more than 8 to 10 minutes, so that the dough is worked as little as possible and stays cool. Do not be tempted to stop in the middle of a pair of turns as this will jolt the pastry's internal time clock, which many chefs insist is

FEUILLETEES DE FRUITS DE MER AUX EPINARDS
Diamonds of puff pastry are filled with mussels, sole, scallops, prawns and spinach – all in a white wine butter sauce. A nouvelle cuisine delight . . .

GATEAU PITHIVIERS
Two rounds of puff pastry are filled with a rich almond mixture, sealed together, glazed and finally scored in the traditional pattern before being baked

as real as a baby's. After the first two turns, a rest of 15 minutes (and not more than half an hour) is mandatory before the dough receives a further two turns, bringing the total to four. Then the pressure eases and the dough can be stored, well wrapped, in the refrigerator overnight, or it can be frozen. Finally, it must be given two last turns before it is used.

Throughout this process, low temperature is vital to puff pastry; if the butter warms enough to melt, it will break the dough, glueing layers together and ruining the skyscraper effect of stacked stories. A marble slab is ideal for making puff pastry, though in cool weather a smooth Formica or stainless steel surface can be used. In well-equipped pastry shops, the marble is refrigerated, and in summer in Paris we improvise by cooling the marble beforehand with a pan of ice, and by chilling the flour and the rolling pin. In a restaurant, puff pastry is always made first, before the kitchen heats up, and in the hotel in Venice where I taught for one season, the pastry chef rose (he said) at 5 a.m. to make puff pastry in the cool early morning.

By this stage, good puff pastry dough is easily recognised: it has a soft, matt surface, unmarked by pocks of flour or butter, and a texture which is pliable but not elastic. Do not worry if it has one or two air blisters, testifying to its airtight layers. For use, it is rolled to the appropriate thickness (thinner than one might think as too much dough weighs itself down) and cut to shape. This must be done with a sharp knife or cutter so the layers are not torn. Then the pieces of dough are pressed lightly in place on a dampened baking sheet. The water sticks the dough in place and helps reduce shrinkage.

Shrinkage is a bugbear of puff pastry, caused by elastic dough that has been overworked, or not left long enough to rest before baking. It leads to misshapen pastries, heavier pastry (because of reduced size) and can make bouchées topple over. So after the final two turns and shaping, puff pastry should be chilled for at least half an hour before baking, and I have heard chefs recommend covering it and leaving it overnight in the refrigerator.

The glazing and decorating of puff pastry are almost as important to the finished appearance as shaping. Glazing with egg must be done with particular care, so no glaze drips down the sides, glueing the pastry layers together. The lattices, chevrons and leaves cut into the surface are not just for show: they ensure that the dough breaks into a pretty pattern as it cooks, rather than cracking indiscriminately. The scalloped edges of vol-au-vents are there to straighten the sides and help them rise.

To this point, every step in making puff pastry is geared to producing a dough that is stacked in even layers. In the oven, the aim is to detach the layers one from the other so that they rise and cook. A quick boost of heat is the ideal way to begin, so as to melt the butter layers and at the same time convert the water to steam, raising the dough. Then, once the dough has risen and is brown on top, the heat can be lowered to cook it thoroughly inside. If the oven is too low, or the dough is not chilled before baking, the butter tends to melt and run from the pastry, which then cooks into a solid mass without rising.

With good puff pastry in hand, the sky is the limit. It makes the perfect airy container for shellfish, creamed chicken, ham and mushrooms, or the almost overwhelming vol-au-vent financière – a Renaissance dish of sweetbreads, which should include quenelles, mushrooms and olives as well as cockscombs, cocks' kidneys and Madeira sauce. Puff pastry is a luxurious wrapping for whole baked fish, for boeuf en croûte and for those delicious pâtés of ham and veal that are the ideal opening to a grand lunch.

Puff pastry is equally at home in nouvelle cuisine, where it forms the foundation of little feuilletées of crayfish and spinach in a butter sauce, asparagus with chervil butter, or green beans with hot foie gras. The only concession to the new spirit of lightness is in the shaping of the dough, which is baked in thinly rolled diamonds, then split and sandwiched with filling – rather than being cut in rounds for bouchées and vol-au-vents. The young chefs claim that these feuilletées use less dough, without so much as a mention of the other advantage of the new shape: it is much quicker to make.

Sweet puff pastries are legion – gâteau Pithiviers with its almond filling and distinctive circular shape; jalousie filled with jam and slashed on top so it looks like the shutters of a window; dartois – a jalousie without the slashes; cream horns, and the incomparable mille feuilles. (I cannot, however, subscribe to the current craze for mille feuilles filled with warm pastry cream – a horribly glutinous combination.)

Important, too, are the trimmings, which can amount to half the original dough. Leftovers should be piled side by side or one on another so the layers are maintained, never crushed in a ball. All sorts of ways to use them have been devised, and my favourite, I think, is palm leaves (palmiers) – curls of pastry rolled with sugar. 'Ox tongues' are made with puff pastry brushed with royal icing and baked to a crisp beige, and Sacristains look like cheese straws sprinkled with sugar and almonds. Savoury versions of all these pastries exist to serve with cocktails, usually made smaller so they are bite-size.

Puff pastry is also one of the few preparations tackled by both pastry and cuisine chefs. At La Varenne it is always a special moment when Chef Jorant (in the pâtisserie corner) and Chef Chambrette (in the cuisine corner) can be persuaded to fight it out in the ring. Like a true pastry chef, Jorant weighs each pat of butter and gram of salt; he rolls his corners with geometric precision and calculates his timing with the clock. Chef Chambrette relies on instinct for measurements and makes a dreadful mess when rolling out. He slashes his dough in a fury and bangs his baking sheet into the oven. Yet the result of the contest is always a draw – a victory for the diversity of approach in French cooking that enriches every meal in France.

THE WAY TO SUCCESS

1 If you are a newcomer to making puff pastry, let the dough rest for longer periods than specified in the recipes, so that it is thoroughly chilled and rolling is easier.

2 Ideally, the butter and détrempe should be of the same consistency; in summer when butter is very soft, a little more water should be used in the détrempe.

3 Before rolling dough for a set of turns, be sure that the work surface is cleaned of any leftover flour or scraps of dough.

4 Keep the dough moving when rolling, lifting it often and flouring the work surface. However, do not add more flour than is needed to prevent sticking as this changes the proportions of the dough.

5 When rolling dough into a rectangle for a turn, keep the sides straight and corners square, so that the layers can be aligned when it is folded.

6 When making turns, it is often easier to keep the dough in an even rectangle if the seam, or unfolded, side of the dough faces downwards.

7 Always roll dough to an even thickness, both for turns and before shaping.

8 During turns, roll dough only away from, or towards you, not sideways. However, when dough is rolled for the last time just before shaping, it can be rolled in any direction.

9 Puff pastry should be rolled to quite a thin sheet (6mm or $\frac{1}{4}$in) for small pastries and only a little thicker (about 1cm or $\frac{3}{8}$in) for large ones. If it is too thick, the dough weighs itself down and does not rise well.

10 A double coating of egg glaze gives a rich golden colour.

11 When cutting shapes from dough, brush each piece with glaze, rather than brushing the whole surface of dough with glaze. Glaze on leftover pastry trimmings prevents them from rising.

12 Use heavy baking sheets so that the pastry does not burn on the bottom. If the bottom does start to brown too much, put another cold baking sheet directly underneath for protection. If the top of the pastry browns too much, cover it with foil.

Getting ahead

1 The détrempe can be made ahead and kept overnight, tightly wrapped, in the refrigerator.

2 After 4 turns, puff pastry dough can be kept tightly wrapped for 4-5 days in the refrigerator, or it can be frozen for up to six months. It can also be kept after 6 turns, but will not rise quite so well. Be sure to wrap the dough tightly; if the surface dries the dough will crack when rolled out.

3 If chilled for a long time, let the dough come to room temperature before rolling, otherwise it will tear. Defrost frozen pastry thoroughly before use.

4 Puff pastry can be shaped a day ahead and kept in the refrigerator; it can also be shaped and then frozen. Small shapes can be baked from the frozen state, though large ones should be defrosted first.

5 Because puff pastry dough freezes so well, it is useful to make a double quantity, then shape and freeze what dough you do not need for immediate use.

6 Puff pastry is best eaten the day it is baked. However, it can be stored in an airtight container or frozen. Do not attempt to refrigerate baked puff pastry or it will turn soggy.

7 Baked puff pastry reheats well in a low oven. However, any creamy filling should be added at the last minute so that the pastry stays crisp.

PATE FEUILLETEE
(Puff pastry)

unsalted butter	200-250g (7-8oz)	unsalted butter	300-375g (10-12½oz)	unsalted butter	400-500g (14oz-1lb)
flour	250g (8oz)	flour	375g (12½oz)	flour	500g (1lb)
salt	5g (level teaspoon)	salt	7g (1½ level teaspoons)	salt	10g (2 level teaspoons)
lemon juice – (optional)	teaspoon	lemon juice – (optional)	1½ teaspoons	lemon juice – (optional)	2 teaspoons
cold water	130-150ml (scant ¼pt)	cold water	180-200ml (scant ⅓pt)	cold water	275-300ml (scant ½pt)

For puff pastry it is important to work on a cold surface. If your working surface is warm, chill it by putting ice trays on top before making the détrempe and before every 2 turns. Dry the working surface well after removing the ice.

Melt or soften one tenth of the butter. Keep the rest of the butter cold. Sift the flour onto a cold marble slab or board, make a well in the centre and add the salt, lemon juice, most of the water and the melted or softened butter. Work together with the fingertips until well mixed; then gradually work in the flour, pulling the dough into large crumbs with the fingertips of both hands. If the crumbs are dry, add more water – the amount of water needed depends very much on the type of flour used.

Cut the dough several times with a dough scraper to ensure that the ingredients are evenly blended but do not knead it. Press the dough to form a ball. It should be quite soft. This dough is called the détrempe. Wrap it in greaseproof paper, plastic wrap or a plastic bag and chill for 15 minutes.

The amount of butter used depends on how rich you want the dough to be and on your experience. The usual practice is to use half the weight of the détrempe in butter, but you may use up to the maximum indicated in the recipe. Lightly flour the butter and flatten it with the rolling pin. Fold it and continue pounding and folding until pliable but not sticky – the butter should be the same consistency as the détrempe. Shape it into a 15cm (6in) square and flour it lightly. Roll out the dough on a floured marble slab or board to a 30cm (12in) square, thicker in the centre than at the sides. Set the butter in the centre and fold the dough around it like an envelope.

Making sure your working surface is well floured, place the 'package' of dough on it seams down and bring the rolling pin down on the dough 3-4 times to flatten it slightly. Roll it out to a rectangle 18-20cm (7-8in) wide and 45-50cm (18-20in) long. Fold the rectangle of dough into three, one end inside, as if folding a business letter, with the layers as accurately aligned as possible. Seal the edges with the rolling pin and turn the dough a quarter turn (90°) to bring the closed seam to your left side so the dough 'opens' like a book. This is a turn. Roll out again and fold in three. This is the second turn. Keep a note of these turns by marking the dough lightly with the appropriate number of fingerprints. Wrap and chill for 15 minutes.

Repeat the rolling process, giving the dough 6 turns altogether with a 15-minute rest in the refrigerator between every two turns. Chill for at least 15 minutes before using.

Fold the dough around the square of soft butter as if forming an envelope

PATE FEUILLETEE

Fold the rolled dough in three as if it were a business letter, and seal edges

Turn the folded dough so that one open end faces you and roll out again

FEUILLETEES DE COCKTAIL
(Cocktail puff pastries)

Be sure to make these pastries as small and uniform as possible. The fillings and shapes can be varied. For example, you can make cheese fingers by sprinkling a glazed strip of dough with grated Parmesan cheese, then cutting it in fingers and baking. Adapt the ham crescents by substituting chopped cooked chicken or fish for the ham and binding with white sauce or a spoonful of cream.

puff pastry made with 200-250g (7-8oz) unsalted butter; 250g (8oz) flour; 5g (level teaspoon) salt; teaspoon lemon juice (optional) and 130-150ml (scant ¼pt) cold water; or the equivalent in puff pastry trimmings

1 egg, beaten to mix with ½ teaspoon salt (for glaze)

chosen fillings (see individual recipes)

Make the puff pastry dough and chill thoroughly. Roll it out slightly thinner than 5mm (¼in) thick, fill with chosen filling and shape according to the individual recipe. Set the pastries on a dampened baking sheet and chill for 15 minutes. Set the oven at very hot, 220C (425F) gas 7. Bake the pastries in the heated oven for 8-12 minutes or until puffed and brown; transfer them to a rack to cool.

The pastries are best eaten the day they are baked, but they can be kept for a day or two in an airtight container. They can also be frozen, baked or unbaked, for up to six months.

FEUILLETEES AUX ANCHOIS
(Anchovy fingers)

Makes about 30

Roll out the pastry dough to a strip 15cm (6in) wide. Cut in half lengthwise and trim the edges. Brush 1 rectangle with egg glaze and lay drained anchovy fillets crosswise on it at 3.5cm (1½in) intervals. Place the second rectangle on top and press down gently with a fingertip to outline the anchovies. Brush with egg glaze and cut between each fillet to form fingers. Decorate each finger in a lattice pattern with the back of a knife and bake as for the basic recipe.

FEUILLETEES AUX FOIES DE VOLAILLE
(Chicken liver fingers)

Makes about 40

Melt 30g (1oz) butter in a frying pan and fry 1 chopped onion until soft. Add 250g (8oz) chicken livers and sauté until brown on all sides but still pink in the centre. Add 2 tablespoons brandy, a pinch of Cayenne and plenty of seasoning and continue cooking for 1 minute. Allow to cool, then chop. Roll out the pastry dough to a strip 15cm (6in) wide and spoon the chicken liver mixture on one half of the pastry but not to the edge. Brush the edge of the pastry with egg glaze, fold over one side to meet the other, covering the chicken liver mixture, and press the edge to seal. Trim the edges, brush with egg glaze and cut into 2.5cm (1in) fingers. Bake as for the basic recipe.

For ham crescents, roll up each triangle of pastry, starting at the long edge

FEUILLETEES AU JAMBON
(Ham crescents)

Makes about 50

Roll the pastry dough to a strip 15cm (6in) wide and trim the edges. Cut in half lengthwise and then make crosswise cuts to form 7.5cm (3in) squares. Cut each square into 2 triangles and in the centre put a small teaspoon of finely chopped Parma ham or cooked ham mixed with a little Worcestershire sauce. Roll up the triangles starting at the long edge, then roll on the table with your hand to elongate the roll slightly and seal it. Shape it into a crescent on a dampened baking sheet, brush with egg glaze and bake as for the basic recipe.

FEUILLETEES DE FRUITS DE MER AUX EPINARDS
(Seafood feuilletées with spinach)

Serves 6 as a main course

puff pastry made with 300-375g (10-12½oz) unsalted butter, 375g (12½oz) flour, 7g (1½ level teaspoons) salt, 1½ teaspoons lemon juice (optional) and 180-200ml (scant ⅓pt) cold water

1 egg, beaten to mix with ½ teaspoon salt (for glaze)

for the filling

1kg (2lb) fresh spinach
15g (½oz) butter
salt and freshly ground pepper
pinch of grated nutmeg
1 litre (1¾pts) mussels
shallot, finely chopped
4 tablespoons dry white wine
3 small sole fillets (about 500g or 1lb)
250g (8oz) scallops
90g (3oz) scampi or prawns, cooked or uncooked

for the white wine sauce

fish stock (page 218) made with 750g (1½lb) fish bones; medium onion; bouquet garni and 750ml (1¼pts) water; or 1 teaspoon fish glaze (page 219)
2 shallots, finely chopped
250g (8oz) butter
100ml (⅙pt) dry white wine
tablespoon double cream
juice of ¼ lemon
salt and pepper

Make the pastry dough and chill. Set the oven at very hot, 220C (425F) gas 7. Roll out the dough into a large rectangle and cut it into 10cm (4in) diamonds (that is, each side should measure 10cm or 4in). Set them on a dampened baking sheet and brush with egg glaze. With a sharp knife, trace a line about 1.25cm (½in) from the edge of each diamond, without cutting all the way through the pastry; a small diamond is thus traced, which will form the 'hat' for the pastry case. Mark a design inside this diamond with the knife. Chill for 15 minutes and bake in the heated oven for 18-20 minutes or until puffed and brown. With a knife, outline and remove the 'hats' and scoop out any uncooked dough inside. Transfer the cases and hats to a rack to cool.

Make the fish stock and cook to reduce to a glaze, if necessary.

Pull out and discard the stems from the spinach and wash the leaves in several changes of water. Put them in a large pan of boiling, salted water and cook for 5 minutes, stirring once or twice. Drain the spinach thoroughly, refresh with cold water and thoroughly drain again. The spinach can be cooked up to 6 hours ahead and kept covered.

Scrub the mussels, removing all the weed and discarding any mussels that are open. Put the shallot and wine in a large pan, bring to the boil, add the mussels, cover tightly and cook over high heat for 5-7 minutes or until opened, stirring once. Shell them, remove the 'beards' and discard any shells that do not open. Strain the cooking liquid through muslin or cheesecloth and reserve it.

Steam the sole fillets (Chapter 1) above boiling water or fish stock for about 5 minutes or until just tender. Remove, then steam the scallops for 3-4 minutes or until they are just tender. Remove, and steam the scampi or prawns if uncooked.

For the white wine sauce: sauté the shallots in 15g (½oz) of the butter, stirring constantly. Add the wine and mussel juice and cook for about 5 minutes or until reduced almost to a glaze. Add the cream and reduce again. Cut the remaining butter in small pieces and whisk it in. Work sometimes over very low heat and sometimes off the heat so that the butter thickens the sauce without melting. Add the lemon juice, fish glaze, and salt and pepper to taste.

To finish: reheat the spinach in the butter and season it with salt, pepper and nutmeg. Spread some inside each pastry case. Cut the sole fillets in 3 or 4 diagonal pieces. Arrange with the other seafood on the spinach. Warm in a low oven 130C (250F) gas ½. Spoon a generous tablespoon of the sauce over each. Set each 'hat' on top. Serve the rest of the sauce separately.

CHAUSSONS AUX CHAMPIGNONS
(Mushroom turnovers)

Be certain to press the edges together firmly so the filling can't leak out.

MAKES 20-25

puff pastry made with 200-250g (7-8oz) unsalted butter, 250g (8oz) flour, 5g (1 level teaspoon) salt and 130-150ml (scant ¼pt) cold water; or an equivalent quantity of puff pastry trimmings

egg beaten with ½ teaspoon salt (for glaze)

for the filling

2 tablespoons oil

2 tablespoons butter

500g (1lb) mushrooms, thinly sliced

3 shallots, finely chopped (optional)

2 cloves garlic, finely chopped (optional)

400 ml (¾pt) double cream

salt and freshly ground pepper

2 egg yolks, beaten

6-7cm (2½-3in) plain biscuit cutter

Make the puff pastry dough and chill it.

For the filling: heat the oil in a frying pan and add the butter. Put in the mushrooms and sauté them over high heat until well browned, tossing often. When the mushrooms are nearly brown, add the shallots and garlic, if included, and toss together. Bring the cream to the boil in a heavy-based saucepan. Stir in the mushrooms, shallots and garlic and boil until the mushrooms have absorbed all the cream. Season to taste with salt and freshly ground pepper and allow to cool slightly. Beat in the egg yolks. Spread in a shallow tray or dish, leave to cool, then chill in the refrigerator.

Set the oven at very hot, 220C (425F) gas 7. Roll out the puff pastry to 5mm (¼in) thickness and stamp out 6-7cm (2½-3in) rounds with the biscuit cutter. Put a spoonful of cold filling in the centre of each, brush the border with egg glaze and fold the dough over to make a semi-circular turnover. Press the edges to seal them and put the pastries on a lightly buttered baking sheet. Brush the top of each turnover with egg glaze and make decorative slits in the tops with the point of a knife. Chill for 10-15 minutes.

Bake the turnovers in the heated oven for 20-25 minutes or until puffed and browned. Serve hot, or at room temperature. The turnovers are best eaten the day they are baked, but they can be frozen, either baked or unbaked.

TALMOUSES

Talmouses date back to the Middle Ages. The triangular shape specified in this recipe is traditional. This size is suitable for a starter; for hors d'oeuvre, they should be made with a 6cm (2½in) cutter.

MAKES 18

puff pastry made with 200-250g (7-8oz) butter, 250g (8oz) flour, 5g (1 level teaspoon) salt, teaspoon lemon juice (optional) and 130-150ml (scant ¼pt) cold water; or the equivalent in puff pastry trimmings

egg, beaten to mix with ½ teaspoon salt

for the filling

choux pastry (page 45) made with 75g (2½oz) flour, 125ml (scant ¼pt) water, 2g (⅓ teaspoon) salt, 50g (½oz) butter and 2 large eggs

125g (¼lb) Gruyère cheese, cut in small dice

salt and freshly ground black pepper

9-10cm (3½-4in) biscuit cutter; piping bag and large, plain tube (optional)

Make the puff pastry dough and chill it for 30 minutes.

For the filling: make the choux pastry dough, beat in the cheese, reserving 2-3 tablespoons for garnish, and season well.

Roll out the puff pastry dough to a sheet 3mm (⅛in) thick and cut out rounds with the biscuit cutter. Transfer the rounds to lightly buttered baking sheets and put a spoonful of the filling in the centre of each one, or pipe on a ball of filling using a piping bag and large, plain tube. Brush the edges with egg glaze. Fold over the sides in three places to form a triangle and press the edges together firmly, leaving a small open hole in the centre. Pile the dough trimmings together, roll them, cut out more rounds and fill them. Sprinkle the filling with the reserved diced cheese, brush the talmouses with egg glaze and chill them for 15-20 minutes. Set the oven at very hot, 220C (425F) gas 7.

Bake the talmouses in the heated oven for 12-15 minutes, or until puffed and brown; serve hot.

CORNETS A LA CREME
(Cream horns)

The pastry for these cornucopias must be rolled out to an exceptionally thin sheet.

MAKES 10-12

puff pastry made with 200-250g (7-8oz) butter, 250g (8oz) flour, 5g (level teaspoon) salt, teaspoon lemon juice (optional), and 130-150ml (4½-5oz) cold water; or the equivalent quantity of puff pastry trimmings

egg, beaten with ½ teaspoon salt (for glaze)

icing sugar (for sprinkling)

2-3 tablespoons raspberry or strawberry preserve

Chantilly cream made with 200ml (7oz) double cream, 1-2 tablespoons sugar and teaspoon vanilla essence or tablespoon brandy

1-2 tablespoons finely chopped pistachio nuts (to finish)

10-12 cream horn moulds; pastry bag and medium star tube

Make the puff pastry dough and chill. Lightly grease the moulds and a baking sheet. Roll out the dough to 3mm (⅛in) thickness, cut it into long strips 2.5cm (1in) wide and 23cm (9in) long and brush each strip with egg glaze.

To shape the cornets: pinch one end of a strip of dough onto the point of a mould and wind the strip, glazed side out, around the mould spiralling downwards and overlapping as you go. Trim the end. Form the rest of the horns in the same way and set them on the baking sheet. Brush again with glaze and chill for 15 minutes. Set the oven at very hot, 220C (425F) gas 7.

Bake the horns in the heated oven for 10-12 minutes or until crisp and brown. Sprinkle on some icing sugar and bake for 3 more minutes or until glazed. Transfer them to a rack, remove the moulds and leave to cool. The horns can be baked 1-2 days ahead and kept in an airtight container, but they are best eaten on the day they are baked.

To finish: not more than 3-4 hours before serving, stand the horns point end down in a brioche mould or a bowl so that they are easy to fill. Put a teaspoonful of jam in the bottom of each horn. Fill a piping bag with a star tube with the Chantilly cream and fill the horns. Sprinkle chopped pistachios on each one.

SACRISTAINS

Savoury sacristains can be made by replacing the sugar with grated Gruyère cheese.

Makes about 36

puff pastry made with 200-250g (7-8oz) unsalted butter, 250g (8oz) flour, 5g (level teaspoon) salt, teaspoon lemon juice (optional), and 130-150ml (4½-5oz) cold water; or the equivalent in puff pastry trimmings

1 egg, beaten to mix with ½ teaspoon salt (for glaze)

100g (3½oz) finely chopped or sliced almonds

200g (7oz) sugar

Make the puff pastry dough and chill thoroughly. Roll out to a rectangle slightly thinner than 5mm (¼in) thick and trim the edges. Brush the dough with egg glaze, sprinkle with half the almonds, then with half the sugar. Turn the dough over, brush the other side with egg glaze and sprinkle with the remaining almonds and sugar. Cut the dough into two 12cm (5in) strips, then crosswise into fingers 2cm (¾in) wide. Twist them several times and transfer to a baking sheet. Press the ends down firmly so that they do not unroll during baking. Chill for 15 minutes.

Set the oven at very hot, 220C (425F) gas 7. Bake the pastries in the heated oven for 8-12 minutes or until puffed and brown. NOTE: be very careful as these burn easily. Transfer to a rack to cool.

To shape sacristains, twist strips of the sugar-and-almond-sprinkled dough and press the ends firmly onto the baking sheet so that they stick firmly

For palmiers, fold the dough in towards the centre twice from each side so that the folds nearly meet

Cut folded dough into slices and place slightly open on a baking sheet, leaving room for them to puff up well

PALMIERS

Do not seal palmiers too tightly, or they will not puff to their characteristic heart shape. The palmiers' sweetness comes from rolling out the pastry on sugar instead of flour for the last 2 turns and for the final shaping.

Makes about 36

puff pastry made with 200-250g (7-8oz) unsalted butter; 250g (8oz) flour; 5g (level teaspoon) salt; teaspoon lemon juice (optional) and 130-150ml (scant ¼pt) cold water; or the equivalent in puff pastry trimmings

granulated sugar (for sprinkling)

If making new puff pastry, do only 4 turns and chill thoroughly. Sprinkle the working surface with granulated sugar and roll out the dough (whether new or trimmings) on the sugar to a 15×45cm (6×18in) rectangle. Sprinkle with sugar, fold in three, turn and roll again. Sprinkle again with sugar, fold and chill for 15 minutes.

Roll out the dough to a rectangle slightly less than 5mm (¼in) thick, still using sugar instead of flour, and trim the edges. Fold one long edge over twice to reach the centre of the dough. Repeat on the other side, press lightly to seal with a rolling pin and fold one rolled section of dough on top of the other. Cut into 1cm (⅜in) slices with a sharp knife. Lay these, cut side down, on a baking sheet, leaving room for them to spread. Chill for 15 minutes.

Set the oven at very hot, 220C (425F) gas 7. Bake the pastries in the heated oven for 8-12 minutes or until puffed and brown. If they don't brown enough on top, turn each one over and bake for a few more minutes.

NOTE: be very careful in baking these as they burn very easily. Also be careful when turning them, because the caramelised sugar is extremely hot.

Transfer palmiers to a wire rack to cool.

JALOUSIE

Jam is the easiest and most usual filling, but almost any sweet filling that is solid enough not to run out the slits could be used.

SERVES 4-5

puff pastry made with 200-250g (7-8oz) unsalted butter, 250g (8oz) flour, 5g (level teaspoon) salt, teaspoon lemon juice and 130-150ml (about ¼pt) iced water; or an equivalent quantity of puff pastry trimmings

5-6 tablespoons strawberry, apricot or raspberry jam

1 egg white, beaten until frothy

granulated sugar (for sprinkling)

Make the pastry dough and chill. Set the oven at hot, 220C (425F) gas 7.

Roll out the dough to a 20×30cm (8×12in) rectangle. Trim the edges neatly and cut it in half lengthwise. Fold over one piece lengthwise and, with a sharp knife, cut across the fold at ½cm (¼in) intervals to within 1cm (½in) of the outer edge. Spoon the jam or apple filling down the centre of the uncut piece of dough to within 2.5cm (1in) of the edge.

Brush the edges with cold water and set the cut rectangle on top with the fold in the centre. Open out the folded dough and press the edge down onto the lower piece. Trim the edges to neaten them and chill the jalousie for 10-15 minutes.

Bake the pastry in the heated oven for 25-30 minutes or until puffed and browned. About 5-10 minutes before the end of baking, brush the jalousie with the beaten egg white, sprinkle generously with sugar and continue baking. Serve the jalousie hot, or slide it onto a rack to cool and serve at room temperature. It is best eaten the day it is baked, or it can be frozen, baked or unbaked.

GATEAU PITHIVIERS

This gâteau is incredibly rich, with buttery almond filling enclosed in equally buttery pastry. On Sundays and holidays, rows of gâteaux Pithiviers of various sizes are displayed in the windows of most pâtisseries.

SERVES 6-8

puff pastry made with 300-375g (10-12½oz) butter; 375g (12½oz) flour; 7g (1½ level teaspoons) salt; 1½ teaspoons lemon juice and 180-200ml (about ⅓pt) cold water

1 egg beaten with ½ teaspoon salt

granulated or icing sugar; or 100g (3½oz) apricot jam glaze (page 144)

for the almond filling

125g (4oz) butter, softened

125g (4oz) sugar

1 egg

1 egg yolk

125g (4oz) whole blanched almonds, peeled and ground

15g (½oz) flour

2 tablespoons rum

Make the pastry dough and chill.
For the filling: cream the butter in a bowl, add the sugar and beat thoroughly. Beat in the egg and the yolk; then stir in the almonds, flour and rum.

Roll out half the puff pastry to a circle, about 27cm (11in) across. Using a pan lid as a guide, cut out a 25cm (10in) circle from this with a sharp knife, angling the knife slightly. Roll out the remaining dough slightly thicker than for the first round and cut out another 25cm (10in) circle. Set the thinner circle on a baking sheet, mound the filling in the centre, leaving a 2.5cm

To score gâteau Pithiviers, trace graceful curves on the top with a sharp knife. The slits should be shallow and not pierce right through to the filling

(1in) border, and brush the border with egg glaze. Set the second circle on top and press the edges together firmly. Scallop the edge of the gâteau by pulling it in at intervals with the back of a knife. Brush the gâteau with egg glaze and, working from the centre, score the top in curves like the petals of a flower. NOTE: do not cut through to the filling. Chill the gâteau for 15-20 minutes. Set the oven at very hot, 220C (425F) gas 7.

Bake the gâteau in the heated oven for 30-35 minutes or until it is firm, puffed and brown. Sprinkle the top with sugar and grill until shiny. Alternatively, brush the gâteau while still hot with melted apricot glaze. Transfer to a rack to cool.

FEUILLETEES DE POIRES AU CARAMEL
(Pear feuilletées with caramel)

Cold whipped cream in warm puff pastry with warm pear slices balanced on top and caramel over all – a typical nouvelle cuisine dessert.

SERVES 8

puff pastry made with 300-375g (10-12½oz) butter, 375g (12½oz) flour, 7g (1½ level teaspoons) salt, 1½ teaspoons lemon juice (optional) and 180-200ml (scant ⅓pt) cold water

egg, beaten to mix with ½ teaspoon salt (for glaze)

Chantilly cream made with 200ml (⅓pt) double cream, tablespoon sugar and ½ teaspoon vanilla essence

4 ripe pears

4-6 tablespoons caster sugar

for the caramel

150g (5oz) sugar

100ml (4oz) water

12cm (4½in) biscuit cutter; 9cm (3½in) biscuit cutter

Make the puff pastry dough and chill it for at least 30 minutes. Set the oven at very hot, 220C (425F) gas 7.

Roll out the dough to a sheet 3mm (⅛in) thick and stamp out eight rounds with the larger cutter. Put them on a buttered baking sheet and brush them with egg glaze. Stamp out an equal number of rings, using the larger cutter to cut out rounds and the smaller cutter to remove a round from the centre of each. Put a ring on top of each round. Decorate the rings by scoring them lightly with a small, sharp knife. Brush the rings with glaze and chill the feuilletés for 15 minutes.

Bake them in the heated oven for 20-25 minutes, or until they are puffed and brown. Transfer them to a rack and, while still warm, lift out the 'hat' and scoop out any uncooked dough with a teaspoon.

Make the Chantilly cream and refrigerate it until thoroughly chilled.
For the pears: butter a shallow ovenproof baking dish. Peel the pears, halve them and scoop out the cores and stem fibres. Cut them crosswise in very thin slices, keeping the slices of each half pear together. Put them in the baking dish and sprinkle them with sugar. NOTE: the amount of sugar depends on the sweetness of the pears. Caramelise the pears under the grill.
For the caramel: heat the sugar gently with the water until dissolved, then bring to the boil and cook steadily to a light brown caramel. NOTE: do not let it burn or it will turn bitter. Remove from the heat and dip the bottom of the pan in cold water to stop the cooking.

To finish: reheat the feuilletés and pears if necessary in a low oven, 130C (250F) gas ½. Spoon some cold whipped cream into each feuilleté and place the 'hat' on top of it, upside down. On each hat place the slices of one half pear. Reheat the caramel and pour a little over each half pear, taking care not to let too much drip down the sides as it will stick to the plate.

21
ROASTING
By guess and by God...

Roasting is one of the first and most basic skills to be learned by an apprentice cook. Nothing appears simpler than to roast a piece of meat, topped with fat and seasoning, either in an oven or on the traditional spit before the fire. But mistakes cannot be hidden and, like so many simple processes, roasting can be a false friend.

Of prime importance is the meat, which must be the best both in quality and cut. If in doubt, it is much wiser to pot roast or braise with liquid, than to expose an indifferent piece of meat to the dry, searing heat of true roasting. Should the meat be boned? Here the chefs at La Varenne and I diverge. I like the bones left inside, so that the meat juices are retained and there is less shrinkage. The French have a different aim: they like tidy pieces of meat that will cook evenly and slice well.

The British may be right to retain the bones, but in trussing and tying meat for roasting, French cooks are unrivalled. First they trim meat thoroughly, removing sinews and cartilage and cutting away all but a thin layer of outside fat. If the meat has no natural fat, it is often rolled in a sheet of 'barde' (thinly sliced pork fat). Sometimes herbs and other seasonings are added, and the meat may be larded (threaded with strips of fat). Pretentious butchers also go in for larding with truffles, pistachios and other conceits, but there I think they gild the lily – and the bill. Even a layer of barding fat is shunned by some cooks, who insist that it prevents the meat from being sealed by the heat.

Whether boned, tied and barded or 'au naturel', the meat or bird is impaled on a spit or set in a roasting tin. The tin must fit the meat – if it is too large, the meat juices will burn on the bottom of the pan during cooking; if too small or too deep, the meat tends to steam. To improve the flavour of the gravy, you can add a coarsely chopped carrot and onion to the tin, plus any bones removed from the meat. For both spit and oven roasting, the surface of the meat should be spread with butter (if you are French) or with dripping (if you follow English habits), then sprinkled with salt and pepper.

In a modern kitchen, roasting is almost invariably done in the oven. There are purists who insist that the term is inappropriate and that true roasting can only be done on a spit before an open fire. Certainly the effect of oven roasting is not quite the same, especially when a closed electric oven is used, as this traps moisture so the food tends to steam. But fun though it is, spit roasting often disappoints as heat control is such a

problem. So a spit has become a gimmick, as outmoded as the rôtisseur who once roamed city streets with his own spit (turned by a treadmill or sometimes by a dog), ready to cook any meat brought to him from the surrounding houses.

There are various theories about what temperature to use for roasting, but I don't think you can beat the French principle of starting at a high heat to sear the meat and seal in its juices, then lowering the temperature to finish cooking. An approximate cooking time can be calculated from the type of meat and its weight (see chart), but it is very rough as it varies with the shape of the meat. A chef tests, it always seems to me, by guess and by God. He scrutinises the meat, pokes it with a finger (the firmer it is, the more 'done') and pronounces judgment. But it is never easy to gauge the cooking of a roast, as was discovered by the Army cooks deputed to roast a whole ox in Windsor Great Park for the Queen's Jubilee. Optimistically, they kept the fire burning for 12 hours, only to find at the end of it all that the centre of the beast was still red raw.

They would have been wiser to use a meat thermometer – or rather a giant skewer, to take the inner temperature of the meat. This is how a French chef does it: he inserts a skewer into the centre of the meat, leaves it for thirty seconds and then withdraws it and touches the back of his hand with it. If the skewer is cold, the meat is not done, and if the skewer is warm, the meat is rare. If quite hot, it is pink, and if scalding, the meat is well done.

During cooking, delicate meat and poultry should be basted. Roasting juices must not be allowed to burn, though they should brown well to give colour to the gravy. If the juices do brown too much, add a little stock or water, but do this only if really necessary as it will produce steam and soften the seared crust of the meat.

Last but by no means least comes the gravy, and here I'm united with the French in preferring no thickening and a minimum of additions – the flavour of the meat itself should suffice. The colour of gravy should suit the meat – dark for beef and lamb and lighter for pork, veal and poultry. The gravy can be made while the meat is 'resting', for all roasts should wait for about 10 or 15 minutes before being carved so the juices, which retreat to the centre during roasting, will redistribute themselves again. One of the most effective demonstrations I've seen at La Varenne was performed by Chef Claude Vauguet. He roasted two pieces of beef to the rare stage, sliced one immediately

DINDE AUX MARRONS

The turkey is stuffed with a rich-tasting pork and chestnut 'farce' or stuffing and roasted to a golden brown

and left the other to sit before cutting. The first had an eye of deep pink, but the second was uniformly rosy with only a narrow rim of browned meat.

Accompaniments to roast meats are very much a matter of individual and national taste. In Paris the idea of serving mint sauce with lamb and cranberry jelly with turkey evokes a shudder, yet cherries, peaches or oranges are all considered ideal foils for duck. Most people would agree on the suitability of potatoes, but in France they would be boiled or fried in butter – no equivalent of the English roast potato exists. Where the French do excel is in vegetable garnishes – gleaming carrots, turnips and onions à la bourgeoise, or colourful mounds of spring vegetables flanking a roast 'à la printanière'.

It was the gastronome Brillat-Savarin who observed 'On devient cuisinier, mais on naît rôtisseur' – a cook can be made but a roasting chef is born. In these days of thermostats and meat thermometers, this may seem an exaggeration, but roasting still calls not only for experience and close attention, but also a touch of intuition.

THE WAY TO SUCCESS

1 Meat for roasting should be at room temperature so the heat will evenly penetrate the joint.

2 Preheat an oven or spit for at least 20 minutes. If cooking is started at too low a heat, the roast is not seared but tends to soften and stew.

3 To prevent stewing in the fat and the juices at the bottom of the tin, lift meat or poultry on a rack, or set it on the bones and vegetables which have been added to improve the gravy.

4 When basting, try to use only the fat in the bottom of the tin, not the meat juices. If the fat is hard to spoon, brush the meat instead with a little extra melted fat or butter.

5 In contrast to other meats, pork does not benefit from spit roasting, as it tends to dry.

6 Small roasts of red meat, notably fillet of beef and best end of neck of lamb, are cooked at a very high temperature for a short time, without lowering the heat to finish cooking.

7 A large roast needs relatively less time than a small one, because it continues cooking with retained heat for up to 10 minutes after being removed from the oven.

8 For roast duck, when the breast is served rare in French style, the thighs will be underdone. They are usually detached, cooked further under the grill and then passed as a second helping.

Making gravy

1 If pan juices have not browned enough during roasting, transfer the pan to the top of the stove and cook until the drippings colour.

2 Pour excess fat from the pan – some fat can be left for flavour, particularly with veal and poultry.

3 For a given amount of gravy, add twice the quantity of liquid to the pan. The liquid may be stock or water plus a little red or white wine, if you like.

4 Boil hard, shaking and stirring to dissolve the pan juices – this is called deglazing.

5 When reduced to half its volume, strain the gravy into a saucepan, removing bones and vegetables.

6 Skim off any unwanted fat, season the gravy and continue boiling if necessary to reduce until well flavoured.

7 About 100ml ($\frac{1}{6}$pt) of gravy should serve four people.

Getting ahead

1 Meat and poultry can be stuffed up to 6 hours ahead and kept in the refrigerator, providing that the stuffing was completely cold before adding. Meat stuffings taint a roast more quickly than stuffings made with rice or bread.

2 Except for the brief resting period of 10-15 minutes before carving, roast meats should not wait. Rare meats such as lamb and beef are particularly hard to keep hot as they overcook easily; however, pork, chicken and other meats that are eaten well done can be kept warm for a short time without harm.

3 Leftover roast meat can be stored covered in a cool place at a temperature below 60F (15C) for 2 days; it tends to lose flavour if refrigerated and it dries out if frozen.

4 Leftover roast meat or poultry is best served cold, perhaps with a piquant mayonnaise, or marinated in vinaigrette seasoned with shallots and capers.

5 Leftover white meat such as chicken, veal and pork can be reheated, particularly in a sauce. Roast red meats do not reheat so well; they must be warmed gently, not boiled, or they will toughen. One suggestion is to cut them in very thin slices, and then pour a very hot sauce over, perhaps sauce italienne or sauce diable. NOTE: Never reheat meats then keep them warm. Under these conditions, bacteria develop rapidly.

TRUSSING A TURKEY

Holding the legs of the bird so that they point straight up, stick the trussing needle into one leg, run it through the bird and bring it out through the other leg, leaving a length of string to tie

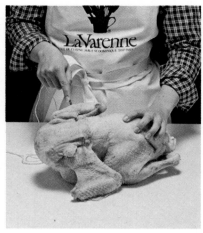

Turn the bird over onto its breast and catch the wing. Run the needle through the neck skin, attaching it to the body. Next, catch the other wing and tie the two ends of string together firmly

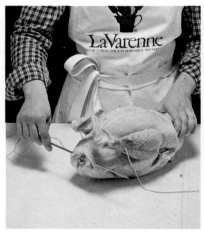

The most usual way of trussing in France uses two strings. The second one is pulled through both legs, then the tail end and tied securely. The legs of the bird are cut below the joint

DINDE AUX MARRONS

(Turkey with chestnuts)

SERVES 6-8

3-4kg (6-8lb) turkey
60g (2oz) butter
salt and freshly ground black pepper
450-600ml ($\frac{3}{4}$-1pt) chicken or turkey stock
150ml ($\frac{1}{4}$pt) white wine
for the stuffing
700g (1$\frac{1}{2}$lb) chestnuts
750ml (1$\frac{1}{4}$pts) chicken or veal stock
salt and freshly ground black pepper
2 onions, chopped
30g (1oz) butter
700g (1$\frac{1}{2}$lb) minced pork, fat with lean
4 tablespoons brandy
level teaspoon allspice
$\frac{1}{4}$ level teaspoon nutmeg
trussing needle and string

To skin and cook the chestnuts: pierce each one with a pointed knife. Cover the nuts with cold water in a saucepan, bring to a boil and take them from the heat. Drain and peel them a few at a time. If they become cool and difficult to peel, reheat them but do not cook them further or they will be impossible to peel. Put the peeled nuts in a pan with the 750ml (1$\frac{1}{4}$pts) stock, salt and pepper, then cover and simmer for 20-30 minutes or until tender. Allow to cool to tepid; then drain them.

For the stuffing: slowly cook the onions in the butter in a frying pan until soft but not brown. Add the pork and cook, stirring to break up the meat, until lightly browned. Add the brandy, allspice and nutmeg, and season with salt and pepper. Continue cooking for 2 minutes. Take the pan from the heat and stir in the chestnuts gently so that they do not break up. Taste and adjust the seasoning if necessary. Let the stuffing cool. Fill the turkey with the stuffing and truss (see the photographs). The turkey can be stuffed 3-4 hours ahead and kept in the refrigerator, but the stuffing must be completely cold before it is added.

To roast the turkey: set the oven at moderate, 190C (375F) gas 5. Spread the bird with butter, sprinkle it with salt and pepper and set it on one side in a roasting tin. Pour in 150ml ($\frac{1}{4}$pt) of the stock, cover the bird loosely with foil and roast in the heated oven, for 2$\frac{1}{2}$-3 hours or until the thigh is tender when pierced with a skewer. Turn the turkey from one side to another and then on to its back during cooking and baste it often. If the tin gets dry, add more stock. Remove the foil during the last half hour of cooking so the turkey browns and the skin crisps.

To serve: transfer the turkey to a carving board and keep warm. Add the remaining stock to the pan with the wine and deglaze the juices, boiling to reduce them well. Taste for seasoning and strain. Discard the trussing strings from the turkey and carve the bird in the kitchen, or at table. The serving dish can be garnished with watercress. A little gravy is spooned over the bird and the rest is served separately.

DINDE AUX TRUFFES
(Turkey with truffles)

Peel 2 fresh truffles and cut 8-10 thick slices from them. Chop the remaining pieces with the truffle peelings and add to the stuffing. Carefully insert the truffle slices in 2 rows between the breast and skin of the turkey, being careful not to let the skin tear. Stuff and truss the turkey and continue as for turkey with chestnuts.

ROASTING TIMES

	STARTING TEMPERATURE			AFTER 15 MIN TURN TO			COOKING TIME		TEMPERATURE ON MEAT THERMOMETER	
	C	F	GAS	C	F	GAS	(MIN PER KG)	(MIN PER LB)	C	F
BEEF & GAME	250	(475)	9	200	(400)	6	Rare: 12	6	60	140
							Med: 15	8	70	160
							Done: 18	9	75	170
LAMB	250	(475)	9	200	(400)	6	Med: 22	11	70	160
							Done: 25	12	80	175
VEAL	220	(425)	7	200	(400)	6	Pink: 30	15	75	165
							Well: 35	17	80	175
PORK	220	(425)	7	200	(400)	6	Done: 35	15	75	170
CHICKEN	200	(400)	6	180	(350)	4	Done: 30	15	80	175
DUCK	200	(400)	6	180	(350)	4	Done: 30	15	80	175
GOOSE	200	(400)	6	180	(350)	4	Done: 40-50	22-25	85	185
TURKEY	200	(400)	6	180	(350)	4	Done: 40-45	20-22	75	170
under 5kg (10lb)							36	18	85	185
5-6kg (10-12lb)							34	17	85	185
over 6kg (12lb)										

FILET DE BOEUF FARCI

To stuff the fillet of beef: first cut the cooled roast beef into slices, cutting almost to the base of the meat. Spread each slice thickly with the savoury filling and press the meat back into its original shape around the filling

FILET DE BOEUF FARCI
(Stuffed fillet of beef)

This is one of the few roast beef recipes which reheats well.

SERVES 8-10

1½-2kg beef fillet (3-4½lb), trimmed and tied with string

salt and freshly ground black pepper

6 tablespoons oil

2 tablespoons chopped parsley (for sprinkling)

for the stuffing

3 shallots

200g (6½oz) bacon

2 stalks celery, finely chopped

675g (1½lb) mushrooms, finely chopped

6 large tomatoes weighing about 1.25kg (2¾lb), seeded and chopped

salt and freshly ground black pepper

Madeira sauce (page 191) made with 6 tablespoons Madeira; 600ml (1pt) basic brown sauce, salt and pepper

Set the oven at very hot, 450F (230C) gas 8. Sprinkle the beef with salt and pepper. Heat the oil in a roasting tin until very hot and brown the meat well on all sides. Roast the meat in the very hot oven for 11 minutes. Remove the meat from the tin and leave to cool. Discard the fat from the tin.

For the stuffing: in a blender or electric food processor, chop the shallots and bacon together to a fine paste. In a frying pan or sauté pan, heat the shallot and bacon paste for 1-2 minutes. Add the chopped celery and mushrooms, mix well and add the tomatoes, salt and pepper. Cook over high heat, stirring often, for 15-18 minutes or until the moisture has evaporated. Taste for seasoning and leave to cool completely.

When the fillet of beef is cool, remove the strings. Slice it in 2cm (3-4in) slices, leaving each slice attached at the base. Spread 1-2 tablespoons of the filling on each slice and press the fillet back into its original shape. Wrap the beef in 2 layers of aluminium foil. The beef can be prepared ahead up to this point and kept wrapped in the refrigerator. Keep any remaining stuffing in a bowl and store, covered, in the refrigerator.

Make the Madeira sauce.

To finish: remove the beef from the refrigerator and allow it to come to room temperature. Set the oven at very hot, 220C (425F) gas 7. Put the beef, still wrapped in foil, in a roasting tin and reheat in the oven for 15 minutes or until the filling is hot. Leave the fillet wrapped in a warm place until ready to serve. Reheat the extra stuffing and spread a layer of it down the centre of an oval serving dish.

To serve: unwrap the beef, saving the juices that escape, and set it on the stuffing on the serving dish. Add the juices to the sauce, bring to the boil and spoon it over the beef. Sprinkle with chopped parsley before serving.

GIGOT D'AGNEAU A LA BRETONNE

(Breton roast leg of lamb)

'A la bretonne' means a garnish of dried white beans, tomatoes and onions. At the end of the 18th century, gastronome Grimod de la Reynière remarked: 'It is far easier to find a sensible woman than a tender leg of lamb'.

SERVES 6

a small leg of lamb weighing about 2½kg (5-6 lb)
2 tablespoons oil
onion, quartered
carrot, quartered
clove garlic, cut in 4-5 slivers (optional)
2 teaspoons rosemary (optional)
salt and freshly ground black pepper
bunch of watercress (for garnish)
for the beans
450g (1lb) dried white beans
onion, stuck with 4 cloves
carrot
bouquet garni, including a stalk of celery
salt and pepper
2-3 tablespoons chopped parsley (to finish)
for the tomatoes
2 tablespoons butter
2 onions, finely chopped
clove garlic, finely chopped
6 tomatoes, peeled, seeded and chopped; or 750ml (1¼pts) canned tomatoes, drained and chopped
75ml (⅛pt) white wine
bouquet garni
salt and pepper
for the gravy
300ml (½pt) brown veal stock or water
150ml (¼pt) white wine

For the beans: soak overnight in plenty of cold water and drain. Put them in a large pan with the onion stuck with cloves, carrot, bouquet garni and water to cover by at least 2.5cm (1in). Bring to the boil and simmer for 1-2 hours or until the beans are very tender, adding salt and pepper halfway through the cooking time. Add more water during cooking as it is absorbed; at the end of cooking the beans should be moist but not 'soupy'. Discard the onion, carrot and bouquet garni.

For the tomatoes: melt the butter in a sauté pan or shallow saucepan, add the chopped onions and garlic and cook slowly, stirring often, for 3-5 minutes or until soft but not browned. Add the tomatoes, white wine, bouquet garni, salt and pepper and cook over medium heat, stirring often, for 15-20 minutes or until nearly all the moisture has evaporated. Remove the bouquet garni, add the tomatoes to the beans and taste for seasoning. The beans can be cooked up to 2 days ahead and kept in the refrigerator.

One and a half to two hours before serving, set the oven at very hot, 250C (475F) gas 9. Trim the skin and all but a thin layer of fat from the lamb. Pour the oil into the roasting tin, add the quartered onion and carrot and place the lamb on top. If you like, make several incisions in the lamb with the point of a knife and insert the slivers of garlic – the flavour will permeate the meat. Sprinkle the meat with rosemary, salt and pepper and place in the hot oven. Sear the meat at a very high heat for 10-15 minutes or until it browns, lower the oven heat to hot, 200C (400F) gas 6 and continue roasting. For medium meat, allow 22 minutes per kg (11 minutes per lb) plus 11 minutes, or until a meat thermometer inserted into the meat registers 70C (160F). Baste the lamb often during cooking and, if the pan juices start to brown too much, add 125ml (¼pt) stock or water.

Reheat the beans if necessary in the oven or on top of the stove. Take from the heat and stir in 2 tablespoons chopped parsley.

Transfer the lamb to a serving dish and allow to stand in a warm place for 15-20 minutes before carving. Pour out and discard the excess fat but leave in the onion and carrot.

For the gravy: add the stock or water, and wine to the roasting tin and boil, stirring to dissolve the pan juices. Simmer for 5-10 minutes until well reduced and strain the gravy into a small saucepan. Skim off the excess fat, bring the gravy to a boil and taste for seasoning. Keep hot until ready to serve.

To serve: carve the lamb and replace it on the bone. Spoon the beans around the lamb and garnish the dish with watercress. Alternatively, place the uncarved leg of lamb on a serving dish garnished with the watercress; carve it at the table and serve the beans separately, sprinkled with more chopped parsley. In either case, spoon a little gravy over the meat to moisten it and serve the rest in a sauceboat.

NOTE: to shorten the time necessary for soaking the beans, bring them to the boil with enough water to cover them by 5cm (2in). Cover the pan and then remove them from the heat and allow them to stand and soften for about an hour. At the end of that time, you can pour out the water and proceed as if the beans had been soaked overnight.

CARRE DE PORC EN COURONNE
(Crown roast of pork)

A crown roast is always dramatic, and a choice loin of pork deserves this special treatment.

SERVES 8-10

rib sections of 2 pork loins, each weighing about 2kg or 4lb, made into a crown roast
3-4 tablespoons meat dripping or oil
250ml (scant ½pt) white wine
500ml (scant pint) beef or veal stock
for the stuffing
2 onions, finely chopped
30g (1oz) butter
375g (¾lb) minced pork
375g (¾lb) minced veal
250g (½lb) chopped cooked ham
125g (4oz) fresh white breadcrumbs
tablespoon chopped parsley
2 teaspoons mixed herbs – thyme, rosemary, oregano – ground or crushed
2 cloves garlic, finely chopped
salt and freshly ground black pepper
2 eggs, beaten to mix
16-20 paper frills

Set the oven at moderate, 180C (350F) gas 4.

For the stuffing: cook the onions in the butter until soft but not brown. Cool and combine with the pork, veal, ham, breadcrumbs, parsley, herbs and garlic. Add salt and plenty of pepper to taste. Stir in the beaten eggs. Cook a little piece of the stuffing in a frying pan and taste for seasoning.

Put the meat in a large round cake tin and set it in a roasting tin. Pile the stuffing in the centre and spoon the dripping or oil over the meat. Roast it in the heated oven, allowing 2½-3 hours or until a meat ther-

mometer registers 85C (185F); baste the meat and stuffing often during cooking.

To finish: remove the strings from the roast, transfer the meat to a serving dish and keep warm. Discard the fat from the pan, add the white wine and stock and deglaze the juices, boiling until the gravy is well reduced. Taste it for seasoning and strain into a sauceboat. Put a frill on each chop bone. The meat is carved down between the chop bones in wedges, so each chop includes a slice of the stuffing.

ROTI DE VEAU PRINTANIERE
(Roast veal printanière)

The garnish of spring vegetables, which gives this dish its name, is also good with roast lamb.

SERVES 6-8

1½-2kg (3-4lb) rolled veal roast
60g (2oz) softened butter
2 teaspoons mixed thyme, oregano and rosemary
salt and freshly ground black pepper
600-750ml (1-1½pt) stock
250ml (scant ½pt) white wine
for garnish
500g (1lb) spring or medium carrots
2 teaspoons sugar
75g (2½oz) butter
375-500g (¾-1lb) green beans, cut in 7.5cm (3in) lengths
24 button onions
750g (1½lb) tiny new potatoes
2 tablespoons chopped parsley

Set the oven at moderate, 180C (350F) gas 4. Put the meat in a roasting tin, spread it with the softened butter, sprinkle with herbs, salt and pepper and pour 125ml (4fl oz) stock and 125ml (4fl oz) white wine round the joint. Roast the veal in the heated oven, allowing about 30 minutes for each 500g (1lb) for slightly pink meat (70C or 160F on a meat thermometer) – the cooking time depends on the shape of the roast. Add more stock during cooking if the tin gets dry.

For the garnish: peel spring carrots or peel and quarter medium carrots lengthwise and trim them. Put them in a pan with water to cover, add 1 teaspoon sugar, ½ teaspoon salt and 15g (½oz) butter and boil, uncovered, until the liquid has evaporated to a glaze and the carrots are tender.

Cook the green beans in boiling salted water for 10-12 minutes or until just tender, drain, refresh with cold water and drain thoroughly. Blanch the onions in boiling water for 2 minutes and peel them. Melt 30g (1oz) butter in a heavy-based pan, add the onions, sprinkle with 1 teaspoon sugar, salt and pepper and cook gently, shaking the pan so that the onions cook evenly, for 15-20 minutes or until they are tender and brown with caramelised sugar.

Cook the potatoes in boiling salted water 15-20 minutes and drain. The vegetables can be cooked 2-3 hours ahead and reheated just before serving.

To finish: transfer the roast to a serving dish and allow to stand in a warm place for 15-20 minutes. Reheat the carrots and onions separately over low heat, shaking the pans from time to time. Melt 15g (½oz) butter in each of two more pans. Put the beans in one and the potatoes in the other and heat them gently, tossing them from time to time.

For the gravy: add the remaining stock and wine to the roasting tin and boil, stirring to deglaze it. Strain the gravy into a small pan, bring to a boil and taste, reducing it if necessary. Carve half or all the veal into 1cm (⅜in) slices and arrange them overlapping down the centre of a large serving dish. Add a tablespoon of chopped parsley to both the carrots and the potatoes and toss to mix. Arrange the vegetables in 'bouquets' around the veal, spoon a little gravy over the meat and serve the rest separately.

22
SALADS
The Anglo-French debate

In the old days, salads were not thought of as being typically French. In France 'raw' (cru) tends to be equated with 'crude' – the horror of any well-trained chef, and until a few years ago, salads suffered benign neglect. There were honourable exceptions, of course: dandelion salad in hot bacon dressing, made with tender leaves that had caught the first frost, lentils with a shallot and garlic vinaigrette, and mussels in herb mayonnaise. And, in the south of France, one could rely on a cornucopia of vegetable salads, both fresh and cooked. On the whole, however, 'salad' meant green salad tossed in vinaigrette dressing and served after the main course to brace the digestion for the onslaught of cheese and dessert.

Now all is changed, thanks to nouvelle cuisine. Young chefs give pride of place to their first course salads, with names – 'salade folle', 'salade fantaisie', 'salade volcan' – that are as fanciful as the mixture of ingredients. Among the three-star chefs, Michel Guérard combines smoked salmon and sturgeon with a julienne of vegetables, avocado and fresh ginger. Roger Vergé mixes wild mushrooms and quail with a vinaigrette of olive oil. The Troisgros brothers toss freshly sautéed foie gras and spinach leaves in a light version of mayonnaise. Perhaps the most imitated conceit is Jean Delaveyne's creation of foie gras, truffle, crayfish and artichoke bottoms in vinaigrette, now on offer in restaurants the length and breadth of France from Provence to Picardy.

These new salads have put all the old traditions in question. Root vegetables have escaped from the inevitable mayonnaise; meat and fish are no longer segregated; and fruit, which was once suspect in French salads, is now combined with everything – greens, fish or meat. Recently in a leading Paris restaurant, I had a salad of sweetbreads and oranges, which, despite my misgivings, proved to be delicious. Flavourings like ginger, green peppercorns and saffron are the rage. And the temperature – hot, cold or tepid, at which a salad may be served – is up to the chef; hot and cold ingredients are even mixed on the

SALADE DE CHOUX ROUGES AUX LARDONS ET AU ROQUEFORT
Shredded red cabbage, placed on a bed of lettuce leaves and dressed with a mustard vinaigrette. The salad is garnished with fried bread, crisply sautéed bacon and crumbled Roquefort cheese

same plate. But in trying these different ideas, chefs are very conscious that the old rules were not invented without reason. Colour, texture and flavour are still the three criteria by which a salad (or any dish) are ultimately judged.

Contrast of colour has always been an outstanding attribute of a good salad, as witness the two standbys of vegetable macédoine (multi-coloured dice of carrot, green peas, green beans and turnip) and rice salad, with its cheerful pot-pourri of tomato, carrot and green and red peppers, against a snowy background. Now, eye-catching salads often take an oriental turn with meticulous arrangements of ingredients sliced, diced or cut in julienne, and set off by sprigs of a carefully selected herb.

The French have tended to be rather less careful about the textures of their salads than their appearance. All too often vegetables were cooked to a uniform softness and dressed in a glutinous mayonnaise, but here again there has been an improvement. The current fashion for vegetables cooked briefly to retain their crispness has brought in salads based on green beans, for example, and has helped revive old favourites like vegetables à la grecque. More use is being made of croûtons, nuts and fried bacon to add contrasting texture, along with raw vegetables or fruit, such as celery and apple.

The remaining characteristic of a good salad, flavour, depends on two elements: the ingredients and the dressing that binds them. 'Bind' is perhaps the wrong word, for nowadays lighter and lighter dressings are favoured, and the old standby, mayonnaise, is sparingly used. Attention is thus focused on the type of oil or vinegar, and there is great play on nut oils, olive oil and on sherry and fruit vinegars. The dressings must be suited to the ingredients they marry: strong flavours like those of meats, root vegetables and peppery watercress can take a piquant sauce; whereas chicken, fish and the more delicate vegetables need lighter seasoning. Mayonnaise improves hard-boiled eggs, chicken or shellfish, but is less palatable with meats. Almost as important are the little touches that give a salad character – the herbs, gherkins, olives, chopped shallots, the spoon of caviar and the ever-present truffle, whose popularity never wanes despite its astronomic price.

The cardinal principles of colour, texture and flavour apply equally to the simplest salad of all – the green salad. With the exception of chicory (which should be simply wiped with a damp cloth), all salad greens are prepared in the same way: stems are trimmed, wilted leaves discarded and then inner leaves are separated for washing. All salad must be very well washed – nothing is worse than gritty greens. The leaves must also be well dried, or the dressing will not cling and the salad will taste watery.

The La Varenne chefs and I will never agree on the next step. While they leave greens at room temperature, I think an hour or two in the refrigerator crisps the texture without affecting the flavour. And, to my dismay, they insist on leaving even the largest lettuce leaves whole, for cramming into one's mouth only at the peril of makeup and clothes. For their part, they regard my habit of tearing leaves into handy-sized pieces as equally uncouth.

On the question of dressing, thank goodness, we are united. A good dressing for greens, as for any salad, is one that brings out the flavour of the ingredients it accompanies, without overwhelming them. It is unobtrusive without being bland and clings to salad leaves without being heavy. Certainly vinaigrette causes more discussion at La Varenne than almost anything else. Each day we use the same oil, vinegar and seasonings (mustard, salt, pepper, sometimes a little garlic), and one member of the lettuce family or another; yet each day the salad is different, the personal creation of the student who made it. Nothing shows more clearly the differences in individual taste.

The last step – mixing the salad greens with the dressing – must be done just before serving. At La Varenne the student responsible for the green salad jumps up from the table and (while everyone is finishing the main course) adds the vinaigrette to the leaves and tosses them well. Since the leaves wilt slightly as they absorb the dressing, the French call this reaction 'fatiguer' – 'to tire'. It is served at once since the leaves would become unpleasantly soggy within the hour. Exceptions to this rule are tough greens like endive or dandelion leaves, which are mixed with the dressing 1-2 hours ahead and thus become more tender.

Recently chefs have become more adventurous, dressing up their greens with cubes of Gruyère or Roquefort cheese; or flavouring them with sautéed chicken livers and cubes of crisply fried duck skin, as well as the more usual garlic croûtons and bacon. Recipes for these inspirations scarcely exist as they vary with the season, the weather, the contents of the refrigerator and the chef's whim. A hard-boiled egg or two may be chopped and added, as well as a pinch of spice or fresh herbs if they are to hand.

Perhaps the most satisfying salads are neither old nor new and abide by no rules at all. They are what I call household salads – the kind Chef Chambrette concocts for Saturday lunch at the cooking school when he wants to find a tidy refrigerator on Monday morning. There are certain recognised combinations like salade parisienne (beef vinaigrette, often with potatoes) and salade normande (potatoes with celery, ham and a cream dressing), but most have a handful of this, a pinch of that and, above all, a generous helping of imagination.

Mayonnaise

Mayonnaise is used in stuffed eggs and as a binder for salad ingredients; it is often used for coating food and makes an attractive piped decoration for cold fish, salads or canapés.

1 Have all ingredients at room temperature or even lukewarm.

2 Use a balloon whisk, not a spoon or spatula, for beating in the oil.

3 The bowl should have a small base so each stroke of the whisk reaches a large part of the mixture.

4 Do not add the oil too quickly, particularly at the beginning of mixing, or the mayonnaise may separate.

5 If too much oil is added, the mayonnaise will become very stiff and finally will separate. On the other hand, if not enough oil is added, the mayonnaise will be thin and have a taste of raw egg. The egg is primarily a binding agent and its flavour should not overpower that of the oil.

6 If it does separate, there are several ways to save it. In a warm bowl, whisk the curdled mixture drop by drop into any of the following:

a a few drops warm water

b a few drops of vinegar

c a little mustard

d another egg yolk

7 Mayonnaise can be varied in a number of ways. Flavour it with tomato purée for instance, or with blanched and puréed greens such as spinach and watercress, with garlic or curry powder, or mix it with half the quantity of whipped cream.

8 To prevent discoloration do not keep mayonnaise in an aluminium, copper or other metal bowl (except stainless steel) and do not leave a silver spoon in it.

9 Chefs do not advise chilling mayonnaise because the oil can congeal and separate from the sauce. However, if kept in the least cold spot of the refrigerator and allowed to return to room temperature before it is stirred, it usually survives.

Salads

1 Make sure all raw ingredients are thoroughly washed – nothing is worse than a gritty salad.

2 Cut ingredients to the size indicated – a change in size can radically change the effect of the finished arrangement.

3 Beware of strong flavourings like garlic, onion or green pepper. Chop very fine and, if you like, blanch them before using.

4 Taste constantly, particularly if changing the proportions of ingredients or using an unfamiliar oil or vinegar.

5 Whenever possible, toss a salad with the dressing; this coats the salad more evenly than simply spooning the dressing over it.

6 To keep the serving bowl clean, toss the salad separately in a large bowl.

Getting ahead

1 Vinaigrette can be made ahead in a screw-top jar. Shake the dressing well to re-emulsify it just before using.

2 All salads spoil more quickly when mixed with dressing. Prepare ingredients and dressing separately and mix them just before serving.

3 Salads dressed with vinaigrette can be kept for 12 hours or so if the ingredients are robust, such as cold meat. However, the more delicate the ingredients, the shorter the time they can be left to marinate.

4 Salads containing mayonnaise ferment particularly rapidly and should not be kept for more than a few hours after mixing.

5 Salads made ahead should be served at room temperature.

MAYONNAISE

La Varenne chefs usually add a teaspoon of French mustard to the egg yolks before beating in the oil as this helps to emulsify it. All the ingredients for mayonnaise must be at room temperature. On a cold day, warm the bowl and whisk in hot water before beginning.

Makes about 375ml (generous ½pt)

2 egg yolks
salt and white pepper
Dijon or dry mustard (optional)
2 tablespoons white wine vinegar or tablespoon lemon juice
375ml (⅝pt) oil

With a whisk or an electric beater, beat the egg yolks in a small bowl with a little salt, pepper, mustard, and 1 tablespoon of the vinegar (or ½ tablespoon lemon juice) until thick. Add the oil, drop by drop, whisking constantly. NOTE: if oil is added too quickly, the mayonnaise will curdle. When 2 tablespoons of oil have been added, the mixture should be very thick. The remaining oil can be added a little more quickly, either 1 tablespoon at a time or in a thin steady stream.

When all the oil has been added, stir in the remaining vinegar or lemon juice to taste, more mustard, salt and white pepper if necessary. The amount of seasoning depends very much on the type of oil and vinegar used and what the mayonnaise is to accompany. Thin the mayonnaise, if necessary, with a little warm water.

Mayonnaise is best stored in a covered container at room temperature, but if it is kept in the refrigerator, it should be brought to room temperature before stirring; otherwise it may curdle. It can be kept for 2-3 days.

If mayonnaise does curdle during making or on standing, beat in a tablespoon of boiling water. If it does not re-emulsify, start again beating a fresh egg yolk with salt and pepper, then whisking in the curdled mixture drop by drop. Alternatively, if the mayonnaise is to be flavoured with mustard, the curdled mixture can be gradually beaten into a teaspoonful of Dijon mustard.

179

VINAIGRETTE DRESSING

Four men, say the French, are needed for a good vinaigrette: a spendthrift for the oil, a miser for the vinegar, a wise man for the salt and a madman for the pepper.

The oil can be peanut (agreeably light), olive (rich and unmistakable in flavour), walnut (if you like walnuts), corn, sunflower, soybean (innocuous) or a novelty such as grape-pip oil.

The vinegar can be made from wine (red or white), sherry or Champagne (very fashionable), cider (low acidity), or fruits such as raspberry and cherry (for special effects); it can be flavoured with shallots or garlic (reserve this for strong-flavoured ingredients), or herbs; for a Mediterranean touch, use lemon juice instead of vinegar.

The standard proportion for vinaigrette dressing is 1 part vinegar to 3 parts oil, but this can vary enormously, depending on the kind of oil and type of vinegar used, the ingredients they are to dress, and the taste of the cook.

Salt and freshly ground black pepper are indispensable and chefs usually include a teaspoon of French mustard to help emulsify the mixture. Other favourite flavourings include herbs (they should be fresh), garlic (but in very small quantities), and very finely chopped shallot or onion.

Vinaigrette is made by whisking the vinegar with seasonings, including mustard, until smooth, then whisking in the oil, little by little, so that a thick emulsion is formed. The emulsion may separate on standing, but it will return with more whisking.

About 4 tablespoons of vinaigrette are enough for 500g (about 1lb) of salad greens, to serve 4.

SALADE AU PEAU DE CANARD

(Green salad with duck skin)

This salad, which is suitable for any tough-leaved greens, is served lukewarm after the meat course. The duck skin and croûtons add a pleasant crispness. The skin can be trimmed from the neck of a bird for roasting or, very commonly nowadays, it is cut from the breast, leaving the breast meat to form a kind of duck steak called a *magret*.

SERVES 4

skin from the breast of 1 fat duck
1 head of endive; or 700g (1½lb) dandelion leaves
salt and freshly ground black pepper
2 tablespoons wine vinegar
clove garlic, very finely chopped
for the croûtons
3-4 slices white bread, crusts removed, diced; or ½ loaf French bread, thinly sliced and cut in triangles
6 tablespoons oil (for frying)
clove garlic (optional)

For the croûtons: if using white bread, fry the diced bread in the oil until golden brown and pour into a strainer to drain. The croûtons can be made 2-3 hours ahead and kept at room temperature. If using French bread, rub the pieces with a cut clove of garlic; do not fry.

Cut the duck skin into small pieces.

Wash the greens, trim the stalks of dandelion leaves, and dry thoroughly. Place in a salad bowl and season with salt, pepper, vinegar and garlic.

Fry the duck skin until well browned and crisp, then pour the contents of the pan over the salad greens and toss until the greens wilt slightly. Add the croûtons, taste for seasoning and serve.

SALADE DE COURGETTES

(Courgette salad)

The inspiration for this salad comes from Maestro Martino, cook to the Renaissance Cardinal Ludovico Trevisan, known from his extravagance as the Lucullan cardinal. Martino was very keen on vegetable recipes – this was a clear break with the past, when vegetables were the food of the poor.

SERVES 4

450g (1lb) small courgettes
4 tablespoons olive oil
2 shallots, finely chopped
1½ teaspoons paprika
salt and freshly ground black pepper
½ teaspoon sugar
½ teaspoon dill seed or 1 teaspoon chopped fresh dill
2-3 tablespoons white wine vinegar

Wipe the courgettes and slice them thinly, discarding the ends. Heat the oil, add the shallots and courgettes and cook over low heat, stirring from time to time, for 5 minutes without allowing them to brown. Add the rest of the ingredients and continue cooking for 5 more minutes, or until the courgettes are just tender. Transfer to a salad bowl and serve at room temperature.

SALADE AUX FOIES DE VOLAILLE

(Green salad with chicken livers)

This salad, suitable for any tough-leaved greens, is served lukewarm as a first course.

SERVES 4

1 head of endive; or 700g (1½lb) dandelion leaves or young spinach
4 chicken livers, halved
vinaigrette dressing made with 2 tablespoons wine vinegar, salt, black pepper and 6 tablespoons oil
2 tablespoons oil (for frying)
salt and freshly ground black pepper
2 tablespoons wine vinegar

Wash the greens; trim the stalks of dandelion leaves and remove the stalks of spinach leaves. Dry thoroughly. Trim any green spots from the livers.

Shortly before serving, unless using fresh spinach, add the vinaigrette to the leaves to soften.

Just before serving, heat the oil in a frying pan until very hot. Season the livers with salt and pepper, and sauté in the hot oil over very high heat for 1-2 minutes on each side, or until well browned on the outside but still soft inside. Remove with a slotted spoon and place on the salad. Discard any fat remaining in the pan and immediately add the vinegar. Bring to a boil to deglaze the pan, pour over the leaves and mix well. Serve immediately.

Quarter and core the red cabbage before cutting it into the thinnest possible strips for using to make the Salade de choux rouges aux lardons et au Roquefort

Dry salad greens by swinging them in a traditional salad basket, rolling them gently in a kitchen towel, or whirling them in a plastic salad spinner

SALADE DE CHOUX ROUGES AUX LARDONS ET AU ROQUEFORT

(Red cabbage with bacon and Roquefort)

This colourful salad makes a refreshingly different first course.

SERVES 6

small head of red cabbage
4 tablespoons vinegar
250g (8oz) piece uncooked bacon, diced
tablespoon oil
16-20 lettuce leaves
90g (3oz) Roquefort cheese
for the croûtes
1 long French bread stick or 3-4 crusty white rolls, cut in 1cm (½in) slices
4-6 tablespoons oil (for frying)
for the vinaigrette dressing
tablespoon Dijon mustard
3 tablespoons vinegar
salt and freshly ground black pepper
200ml (⅓pt) oil

Quarter the cabbage, remove the core and shred the leaves finely lengthwise with a knife to obtain long strips. Place the cabbage strips in a bowl.

Bring the 4 tablespoons of vinegar to the boil, pour it over the shredded cabbage and mix well.

NOTE: the cabbage will turn bright red. It can be prepared an hour in advance and kept at room temperature.

Blanch the diced bacon by placing it in a pan of cold water, bringing to the boil, and draining. Refresh by rinsing under cold running water, and drain again thoroughly. Heat the oil in a frying pan, add the bacon and sauté until crisp. Place on paper towels to absorb the excess oil.

For the croûtes: heat the 4-6 tablespoons oil in the frying pan used for the bacon and fry the slices of bread until golden brown on both sides. Place them on paper towels to absorb the excess oil.

For the vinaigrette dressing: whisk the mustard with the vinegar, salt and pepper. Gradually whisk in the oil until the dressing emulsifies and taste for seasoning.

Just before serving, mix the cabbage with enough vinaigrette to moisten it well.

To serve: arrange beds of washed and well-dried lettuce leaves on 6 large plates. Pile the cabbage salad in a high dome in the centre of each plate. Place the croûtes on the lettuce leaves at equal intervals. Sprinkle the bacon on the cabbage. Lastly, scrape the Roquefort cheese over the cabbage with a fork, so that each portion has both white and green parts of the cheese. Serve immediately.

SALADE DE PISSENLITS

(Dandelion and bacon salad)

Dandelion salad is popular all over France in winter. The recipe can also be made with other tough-leaved greens such as lambs' lettuce and endive.

SERVES 4

450-700g (1-1½lb) dandelion leaves
5-6 rashers streaky bacon, diced
clove garlic, crushed
3 tablespoons wine vinegar
2 hard boiled eggs, chopped
freshly ground black pepper
a little salt, if necessary

Pull the dandelion leaves apart, trim the stalks, wash them thoroughly and dry on paper towels. Put the leaves in a salad bowl.

Fry the diced bacon until lightly browned, add the garlic and cook until brown and crisp. Pour the hot bacon and fat over the salad greens and toss until they wilt slightly. Add the vinegar to the pan, heat, stir to dissolve any pan juices and pour over the greens. Add the hard boiled eggs and plenty of pepper and toss. Taste for seasoning – if the bacon is salty, salt may not be necessary. Serve warm.

CRUDITES

This salad, served always as a starter, varies enormously from season to season. At least three of the following suggestions should be included, and they should be chosen so colours and textures contrast. The salad is arranged in neat piles on individual serving plates.

1 Celeriac cut in julienne strips and moistened with mustard-flavoured mayonnaise.

2 Sliced tomatoes dressed with a herb and shallot-flavoured vinaigrette.

3 Peeled and thinly sliced cucumbers mixed with vinaigrette and snipped chives.

4 Grated carrots in a simple vinaigrette dressing.

5 Cooked beetroot, skinned, diced and mixed with a vinaigrette.

6 Red, green or yellow peppers cut in strips, blanched and tossed with a garlic-flavoured vinaigrette.

7 Fennel bulbs thinly sliced, blanched and then combined with a vinaigrette dressing with lemon juice.

POIREAUX VINAIGRETTE

(Leeks vinaigrette)

Lightness, fresh flavour and low cost make this one of the most popular first courses in France, both at home and in restaurants.

SERVES 4

700g (1½ lb) leeks
salt
vinaigrette dressing made with 2 tablespoons white wine vinegar, salt, black pepper and 6 tablespoons oil
2 hard boiled eggs, chopped
2 medium shallots, finely chopped
tablespoon chopped parsley

Trim the leeks, discarding the green tops, split them twice lengthwise almost to the root and wash thoroughly. Tie in bundles and cook in a large pan of boiling salted water for 8-12 minutes, or until tender. Drain thoroughly. They can be cooked 6-8 hours ahead and kept covered at room temperature.

Make the vinaigrette and add the hard boiled eggs, shallots and parsley. Remove the strings from the leeks and cut in 3·5cm (1½in) lengths if you like. Arrange on a dish and spoon over the dressing. Serve at room temperature.

SALADE DE BETTERAVES AUX NOIX

(Beetroot salad with walnuts)

The greens for this salad can be varied according to season.

SERVES 4

2 plump heads of chicory, weighing about 250g (½ lb)
a few bunches lambs' lettuce, weighing about 125g (¼ lb)
2 large cooked beetroot
60g (2oz) walnuts, coarsely chopped
vinaigrette dressing made with tablespoon vinegar or lemon juice, teaspoon mustard, salt, freshly ground black pepper and 3 tablespoons walnut oil

Wipe the chicory, discard any wilted leaves and trim the stems. Cut them into diagonal slices. Wash the lambs' lettuce very thoroughly to remove all sand. Mix the chicory and the lambs' lettuce in a salad bowl. The greens can be prepared a few hours ahead and kept, covered, in the refrigerator.

Make the vinaigrette dressing.

Just before serving, cut the beetroot in medium-sized dice, add to the greens and toss with the vinaigrette. Taste for seasoning and sprinkle with the chopped walnuts.

LEFTOVER SALAD

Leftover salad cannot be served again, but it makes excellent soup: drain the greens of excess dressing, then cook them in a large saucepan until very limp. For each 500g (1lb) limp greens, stir in about 1 tablespoon flour, then 750ml (1¼pts) milk, chicken stock, or a mixture of the two. Cover and simmer very gently for 10-15 minutes. Purée in a blender or electric food processor, strain to remove fibres and taste for seasoning.

Reheat and, if you like, add a little lemon juice just before serving; the flavour of the soup should have a slight bite, left by the vinaigrette dressing.

SALADE MUGUETTE

Once rare, salads combining fruit and vegetables are now very much the rage in France.

SERVES 4

medium head of curly endive
celery heart
vinaigrette dressing made with 1 tablespoon vinegar, salt, freshly ground black pepper and 3 tablespoons walnut or peanut oil
2 tablespoons double cream
4 medium tomatoes
2 Golden Delicious or other crisp dessert apples
100g (3oz) walnut pieces
salt and freshly ground black pepper

Pull the endive leaves apart, discarding the tough green ones, wash and dry thoroughly. Chill for 1-2 hours to crisp them. Cut the celery heart in matchstick thin julienne strips and soak for 1-2 hours in ice cold water.

To finish the salad: make the vinaigrette dressing in a large bowl (see above) and whisk in the cream so the dressing thickens slightly. Peel the tomatoes, cutting the peel from one of them in a long strip and saving it for decoration. Remove the seeds from the tomatoes and cut the flesh in strips. Wipe the apples but do not peel; quarter, core and slice them into the dressing and toss at once so they are well coated with dressing and do not discolour.

Drain the celery, dry on paper towels and add to the apples with the tomatoes and walnut pieces. Mix carefully and taste for seasoning. Arrange the endive leaves around the edge of a salad bowl and pile the salad in the centre. Curl the strip of tomato peel round to resemble a rose and set in the middle of the salad.

Chill the salad and serve within 2 hours.

SALADE DE BOEUF A LA PARISIENNE

(Beef salad parisienne)

Traditionally, this salad is made with the leftovers of a pot au feu.

SERVES 4

750g (1½lb) potatoes
500-750g (1-1½lb) boiled beef, cut in 1cm (⅜in) slices
for the dressing
teaspoon Dijon mustard, or to taste
3 tablespoons wine vinegar
salt and freshly ground black pepper
9 tablespoons olive or salad oil
2 shallots, very finely chopped
2 tablespoons very finely chopped parsley
1½ tablespoons very finely chopped capers
1½ tablespoons very finely chopped pickled gherkins
clove garlic, crushed (optional)
for garnish
3-4 hard-boiled eggs, quartered
3-4 medium tomatoes, peeled and quartered

Put the potatoes, unpeeled, in cold salted water, cover and bring to the boil. Simmer for 15-20 minutes or until just tender and drain. Cut the beef in thin slices.

For the dressing: whisk the mustard with the vinegar, salt and pepper and gradually beat in the oil so the dressing emulsifies. Stir in the shallots, parsley, capers, gherkins and garlic, if included, and taste – it should be highly seasoned.

Peel the potatoes while still warm, cut them in 1cm (⅜in) slices and arrange them in a salad bowl in layers with the beef, spooning a little dressing over each layer and ending with a layer of potatoes. Cover and leave the salad in a cool place or the refrigerator for at least 2 hours, and up to 12 hours for the flavours to mingle.

A short time before serving, arrange the eggs and tomatoes around the edge.

SALADE DE TOMATES FARCIES GOUJONNETTES DE PLIE

(Stuffed tomato salad with goujonnettes of plaice)

This first course salad is typical of nouvelle cuisine: bright colours, careful garnishing and an offbeat combination of flavours.

SERVES 4

4 tomatoes
salt
12 large prawns, cooked and unpeeled
2 plaice fillets, cut in diagonal strips
16-20 lettuce leaves
teaspoon chopped chervil (for sprinkling)
teaspoon chopped tarragon (for sprinkling)
for the green bean salad
250g (½lb) green beans, trimmed
vinaigrette dressing (page 180) made with ½ tablespoon mustard, tablespoon vinegar, 3 tablespoons oil, salt and pepper
for the herb mayonnaise
mayonnaise (page 179) made with 1 egg yolk, salt, pepper, tablespoon vinegar, ½ tablespoon mustard, 100ml (⅙pt) vegetable oil and 100ml (⅙pt) olive oil
tablespoon lemon juice
2 tablespoons grapefruit juice
tablespoon tomato ketchup
teaspoon chopped chervil
teaspoon chopped tarragon

Cut a 'lid' off the top of each tomato at the flower end. With a teaspoon, or your finger, carefully remove the seeds. Sprinkle the inside of the tomato with salt, turn upside down and leave to drain. Peel the prawns but leave the heads on them.

For the green bean salad: cook the green beans in a large pan of boiling salted water for about 5-7 minutes or until barely tender. Drain, refresh under cold running water and drain thoroughly. Mix the green beans with enough vinaigrette to moisten.

For the herb mayonnaise: make the mayonnaise, using half vegetable oil and half olive oil. Mix it with the lemon juice, grapefruit juice, tomato ketchup, chopped chervil and tarragon. Taste and adjust the seasoning if necessary.

Poach the plaice fillets in salted water for 2-3 minutes, or until tender but still quite firm so that they do not break up when being mixed with the mayonnaise. Drain thoroughly and dry well. Cool and mix very carefully with the herb mayonnaise.

To assemble: put the strips of plaice standing up inside the tomatoes. Decorate with the prawns by also placing them inside the tomatoes, facing each other. Arrange a bed of lettuce leaves on each plate. Place a stuffed tomato in the centre of each.

Arrange a portion of the green bean salad in a wreath around each tomato and sprinkle chopped chervil and tarragon on each portion of the fish.

SALAD BOWLS AND SPOONS

Nearly as important as freshness is the way salads are mixed and presented. Wood is the ideal material for both bowl and serving spoons – a well-seasoned bowl of olive or some exotic wood is almost an heirloom. Neither wooden bowl nor servers should ever be washed, but wiped with paper towels after use. Glass or plastic are attractive alternatives to wood. Salad should never be served in metal bowls (except stainless steel) or with metal servers, as the acid in the dressing will react with the metal.

PILAF DE MOULES
(Mussel pilaf)

For a hot pilaf, substitute 6 table-spoons double cream for the vinaig-rette; stir it in just before serving. Serves 4 as a starter or 2-3 as a main course.

2 litres (3½pts) mussels
150ml (¼pt) white wine
clove garlic, crushed (optional)
30g (1oz) butter
onion, thinly sliced
300g (10oz) long grain rice
salt and pepper
vinaigrette dressing made with tablespoon white wine vinegar, salt, freshly ground black pepper and 3 tablespoons oil
2 tablespoons chopped parsley

Wash the mussels under running water, removing any weed. Discard broken shells or any which do not close when tapped. Put the mussels in a large pan, add the white wine and garlic, if included; cover and cook over high heat, stirring once, for 5-7 minutes or until opened. Remove from their shells, discard the beards and reserve the mussels. Strain the cooking liquid through muslin and add enough water to make it up to 600ml (1pt).

Set the oven at moderate, 180C (350F) gas 4. Melt the butter in a heavy-based pan and cook the onion slowly until soft but not brown. Add the rice and cook, stirring, until the grains are transparent and the butter is absorbed. Add the mussel liquid with pepper (if the mussels were salty, no extra salt will be needed). Cover the pan, bring to the boil and cook in the oven for 15 minutes.

Stir in the mussels, cover and

To shell mussels

Remove the mussels from their shells — an already emptied shell makes a convenient pair of pincers. Then pull the beard from each mussel. A mussel and beard are separately shown in front

continue cooking for a further 5 minutes. Allow the rice to stand for 5-10 minutes. The pilaf can be cooked up to 8 hours ahead and kept covered in the refrigerator.

One to two hours before serving, gently stir in the vinaigrette dressing and taste the salad for seasoning. Cover and leave in the refrigerator for the flavours to blend. Just before serving, stir in the chopped parsley.

SALADE ITALIENNE

To the French, a dish 'à l'italienne' always includes ham or pasta, and often olives.

SERVES 4

125g (4oz) dried pasta shells
125g (4oz) cooked ham, cut into strips
75g (2½oz) ripe olives, halved and stoned
mayonnaise (page 179) made with 1 egg yolk, salt and white pepper, tablespoon white wine vinegar and 150ml (¼pt) oil

Bring a large saucepan of salted water to the boil, add the pasta shells and simmer gently for about 8 minutes or until *al dente*. Drain, refresh with cold water and drain again. Mix the pasta with the ham, olives and mayonnaise in a bowl, taste for seasoning and arrange in a dish to serve. The salad can be prepared up to 6 hours ahead and kept covered at room temperature.

SALADE BRAMAFAN

SERVES 4

lemon, halved
4 large artichokes
250g (8oz) crayfish or scampi, cooked and peeled
125g (4oz) mushrooms, very thinly sliced
8 walnuts
tablespoon chopped chives or parsley
for cooking artichoke bottoms
1 litre (1¾pts) water
2 level tablespoons flour
salt
for the dressing
teaspoon lemon juice
tablespoon wine vinegar
salt and freshly ground pepper
4 tablespoons walnut oil
clove garlic, finely chopped

To prepare the artichoke bottoms: add the juice of ½ lemon to a bowl of cold water. Break the stem of each artichoke. Using a very sharp knife and holding it vertically against the side of the artichoke, cut off all the large bottom leaves, leaving a soft cone of immature leaves in the centre. Trim this cone level with the edge of the artichoke base. Rub the sides of the base well with half a cut lemon. NOTE: this prevents the artichoke from discolouring. Trim the base with a knife, removing the leaves underneath and giving the base an even round shape. Also trim the top to make a neat bevelled edge. At once rub it with the cut lemon and drop into the water.

To prepare a 'blanc' for cooking the artichokes: stir about 4 tablespoons of the water into the flour to make a smooth paste; bring the rest of the water to a boil and stir in the flour paste until well mixed. Add the salt.

To cook the artichoke bottoms: drain the artichokes and add to the pre-pared blanc along with the juice from the lemon half used to rub them. Simmer for 15-20 minutes or until they are tender. NOTE: cooking in a blanc prevents them from dis-colouring. Leave them to cool to tepid, then drain and scoop out the central choke with a teaspoon.

For the dressing: whisk the lemon juice and vinegar with salt and pep-per and gradually whisk in the oil. Add the garlic.

For the salad: reserve 4 crayfish or scampi and chop the rest. Pour the dressing over the mushrooms and chopped crayfish or scampi, mix well, cover tightly and leave to mari-nate for at least 2 hours.

Not more than an hour before serving, stir the walnuts into the salad and taste for seasoning. Arrange the artichoke bottoms on individual plates and pile the salad in the middle. Top each with a whole crayfish or scampi. Sprinkle with chopped chives or parsley.

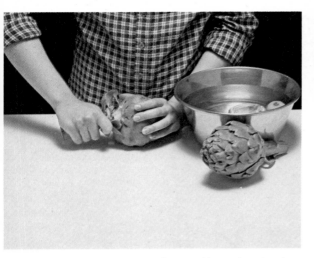

To prepare an artichoke: hold it firmly with one hand and snap off the stem sharply downwards with the other

Using a very sharp knife held firmly against the side, cut off all the bottom leaves to expose the pale flesh

Slice the remaining cone of smaller leaves from the top. This leaves you with the choicest part – the base

Trim the base flat and 'bevel' the top edge, then rub with half a cut lemon and drop the base into acidulated water

After cooking and allowing the bases to cool to lukewarm, scoop out the inedible hairy choke with a teaspoon

23
SAUCES
Well-turned complements

'Sauces are to cookery what grammar is to language and melody is to music.' Like so many catchy quotations, this lyrical outburst is attributed to at least three celebrities, in this case all of them chefs. It certainly sums up the Frenchman's almost reverential attitude to a sauce. To a chef sauces give structure – the grammar – to his repertoire, while defining the theme – the melody – of a particular dish. The analogy I would use is more mundane. I think of sauces as the mortar that holds dishes together, giving them coherence, so that cooks can build an almost infinite number of variations from a few basic ingredients.

God forbid, however, that a sauce should have the texture of cement. Even the thickest of sauces, designed to give body to foods like vegetables with a high water content, should not have a glutinous quality. Sauces for coating should coat lightly, so that the shape and colour of the food beneath are still discernable. And brown sauces to accompany roasts and grilled meats should be light, no more thick than oil. Often they contain no thickener at all.

For centuries the most common thickener has been a roux, a paste of melted butter (or oil) and flour that is cooked until frothy (for white sauces) or until a rich brown (for brown sauces). But flour-based sauces are comparatively modern. In medieval times sauces were thickened with eggs, with breadcrumbs, sometimes with vegetable purées, but never with flour.

The first French cook who seems to have used flour for thickening a sauce was La Varenne (*floreat* 1650), and it was not until the following century that the familiar range of white and brown sauces was developed. Some were named after contemporary personalities, such as the Marquis de Béchamel and the Duc de Mornay. Brown sauce (flavoured with ham) was called espagnole as the finest hams of the day came from Montanchez in the west of Spain. And so these classics have continued to the present, with more and more variations being added over the years.

All are based on four mother or 'mère' sauces, two white and two brown: there is béchamel, made of milk thickened with a white roux; velouté made of fish, chicken or veal stock; espagnole, made of brown stock with a brown roux in which oil replaces the butter; and fond de veau lié. This last sauce, the title of which is virtually untranslatable, is a basic brown sauce which has almost entirely replaced espagnole in everyday use. It consists of brown veal stock thickened, usually with arrowroot or potato flour, near the end of cooking.

On the foundation of these four sauces, innumerable others are constructed by adding such ingredients as wine, shallots, mushrooms, tomatoes, cheese, herbs or garlic. Bordelaise sauce for serving with steak, for example, is a reduction of red wine and shallots added to brown sauce; bretonne, for roast lamb, is composed of brown sauce with a reduction of white wine and onions, tomatoes and garlic; the famous sauce suprême is a chicken velouté flavoured with mushroom stems and enriched with cream.

The key to a good sauce is reduction: boiling to concentrate the flavour and produce just the right consistency. As a general rule, the longer a sauce is simmered, the more subtle and mellow it will be. Shortest cooking time is given to white sauces: 5-10 minutes suffice for béchamel, although there are chefs who like to give it half an hour to be sure that any flavour of uncooked flour has disappeared. Velouté, particularly when made with veal or chicken stock, should simmer for at least 15 minutes and preferably half an hour, while a good brown sauce needs an hour or more. A good deal of the reduction process can take place before the sauce is thickened, thus decreasing the danger of scorching. This is one reason for the popularity of fond de veau lié, which is thickened at the end of the cooking time.

Chefs who still make espagnole cook it for three or four hours; in its heyday, the sauce took two days. First the roux was slowly browned, rather like toasting coffee beans to develop the flavour. Then a rich brown stock was added, itself a day-long preparation, together with veal, ham, boiling fowl and sometimes game birds. The mixture was simmered, with frequent stirrings, skimmings and strainings to obtain a dark, rich, glossy sauce. Louis Diat, who presided over the

LA VELOUTE
One of the basic or 'mother' sauces, made from fish, chicken or veal stock thickened with a roux

SAUCE ITALIENNE
This sauce consists of thickened brown veal stock, flavoured with wine, mushrooms and ham

SAUCE BECHAMEL
One of the most important and familiar of the basic French 'mère' or 'mother' sauces. It is made of flavoured milk thickened with a white roux

187

kitchens of the old Ritz-Carlton Hotel in New York from 1910 to 1951, describes his training in France: 'The work with sauces was the most important part of a long and arduous apprenticeship. . . . I can see myself, a very young sous-chef, in front of a hot range, pushing and turning a sturdy wooden spatula as the sauces reduced in the big copper pans, and standing with bated breath while the chef des cuisines went through his daily routine of tasting the sauces for the day. The practised eye and sensitive tongue of this culinary expert could detect the slightest deviation from perfection, and his Gallic temper would soon let the kitchen know it. *Zut!* down the drain would go what we had thought a perfectly good sauce, and to the tune of a torrent of French fury.' No wonder young chefs, short of trained help, are adopting the traditional household solution of a fond de veau lié which entails no risk of scorching and takes 30 seconds to thicken at the last minute.

Emulsified sauces, those darlings of nouvelle cuisine, are currently ousting the traditional béchamels, veloutés and espagnoles. In search of lightness, more and more chefs are turning from traditional flour-based sauces to the delicate emulsions whose principle ingredient is butter. Chief among these, of course, are hollandaise and béarnaise, but this type of sauce has been with us a couple of centuries, and it is their cousin, beurre blanc, made without egg yolks, that is hitting the menu headlines.

Delicacy, both of flavour and texture, is the main characteristic of all emulsified sauces. A touch too much seasoning, a touch too much heat, and the sauce is ruined. Most of them are based on reductions: that is, liquid (often wine) boiled with chopped shallots, sometimes until most of the liquid had evaporated. Shallots must be thoroughly cooked and wine or vinegar well reduced if the sauce is to avoid acidity; lemon juice must be added with a light hand. In texture, butter sauces range from quite thick (béarnaise) to flowing (beurre blanc). Sometimes, as in eggs Bénédict, the butter sauce is spooned over the food it accompanies, but more often it is served apart, so that it doesn't separate upon coming into contact with very hot food.

When I trained in Paris 20 years ago, sauce beurre blanc, composed of shallots, Sancerre wine, vinegar and Nantais butter, was a little known regional curiosity from the Loire valley. Today the vast majority of restaurants with even a pretence to sophistication offer a beurre blanc or one of its sister sauces like beurre rouge (made with a red instead of white wine and no vinegar) or sauce vin blanc (a reduction of white wine, fish stock and shallots emulsified with butter). Chefs ring the changes with different kinds of vinegar, spices like green peppercorns, or a julienne of vegetables. Some like a touch of cream – one of La Varenne's 'secrets' is adding a spoonful of cream to the reduction for a beurre blanc – which discourages this most delicate of all sauces from separating.

Emulsified sauces are certainly prone to separation due to being mixed too quickly, subjected to high temperatures or allowed to stand for too long. When making them, adding the butter to the base is easy enough; the critical element is the base itself. At La Varenne for egg yolk sauces we prefer the mousse method, by which the yolks are whisked with a tablespoon or two of water (for béarnaise) until they are light yet thick enough to leave a ribbon trail. Cooking must be done slowly, whisking constantly, in a heavy-based pan, preferably of copper. Then clarified butter is added; but not for French cooks the agonising drop-by-drop suggested in some cookbooks. A half smile on his face, Chef Chambrette regularly draws gasps from his audience as, having briskly fluffed up his egg yolk mousse, he casually whisks in a panful of clarified butter in a steady steam. But there is method in this mad pouring and whisking, for he has saved himself endless time. And time is money for a professional cook. On the rare occasion that the sauce does separate, he equally swiftly re-emulsifies it.

Beurre blanc, however, is a different story. As sauces based on wine and stock separate even more easily than hollandaise and béarnaise, they should never be heated above tepid and should be made at the last possible minute. This is not difficult since the reduction of the wine and stock to syrupy glaze can be done ahead. The sauce is finished in a few moments by 'mounting' with butter – ie., adding butter in chunks over a very low heat, or off the heat altogether. The butter can be incorporated with a swirling motion of the pan, or by using a whisk or wooden spoon. Unlike that in hollandaise, the butter should not melt to oil, but soften to form a creamy sauce.

A sweet emulsified sauce also exists – sauce sabayon – which is the French version of Italian *zabaglione*. It is made rather like hollandaise by whisking egg yolks with liquid (usually white wine) and sugar to a light, fluffy mousse that is still thin enough to pour. Sauce sabayon is often served with poached fruit or génoise sponge cake. It, too, separates easily.

If emulsified sauces are so tricky, why are they so popular? Few other sauces are so quick to make; they require little equipment and a minimum of ingredients; and they complement a wide variety of dishes.

For a sauce does not exist in limbo – it is always destined to display other ingredients to their best advantage, to complement without overwhelming them. As with the selection of red or white wine, there is a recognised rule for sauces: the lighter the meat, the paler the sauce. Béchamel and hollandaise, as the lightest of the classic sauces, are reserved for vegetables, eggs, fish and sometimes for chicken; velouté sauces, invariably made from the stock in which veal, chicken or fish are cooked, are ideal to serve with them, while brown sauces are destined for dark meats, particularly beef and game. But jurisdictions overlap, especially for chicken and veal, so that a rich red wine sauce may be served with fish, or a light cream sauce with pheasant. A well-thickened piquant béarnaise is an excellent accompaniment not only to steak and lamb cutlets, but also to chicken, salmon and even poached eggs. The very origin of the name, from the Latin *salsa* meaning salty, emphasises the rôle a sauce always plays in highlighting the seasoning of a dish. This is why no sauce should taste good on its own – its flavour should be much too concentrated.

Flour-based sauces are in eclipse. Even the traditionally thick white sauces are getting thinner and thinner, relying on the gelatine from good stock and a generous swirl of butter to give body. One or two idealists have gone so far as to ban flour altogether from the cuisine section of the kitchen.

But flour-based sauces are a long way from disappearing altogether. Too many favourite dishes, old and new, depend on a full-bodied, roux-thickened sauce for their excellence. French cuisine would be unimaginable without its crisply browned gratins, based on a creamy béchamel, or without its regional ragoûts with their rich brown sauces – the carbonnades of Flanders and the daubes of Provence. Flour-thickened sauces form the base of many fillings, and without them the fabled French soufflé could scarcely exist. As an English expatriate living in France, I have to applaud the diversity and echo Voltaire's disapproval when he remarked, 'In England there are sixty different religions, but only one sauce.'

THE WAY TO SUCCESS

flour-based sauces

Although sauce-making demands a trained palate, anyone who likes to cook can easily learn it with practice.

1 Use a heavy-based pan. Tin or stainless-steel lined copper is ideal but stainless steel or aluminium are all right. A thin-based pan may scorch the sauce. For mixing, use a wire whisk but note that, in an aluminium pan, a wire whisk may discolour any sauce with acid ingredients such as wine.

2 The flavour of velouté and brown sauces depends very much on the quality of the stock; it should be well reduced and not cloudy.

3 The roux must be thoroughly cooked so that it does not impart an unpleasant taste of raw flour to the sauce. Even for béchamel, the roux should be cooked until frothing in little bubbles.

4 Stir a roux constantly to prevent uneven cooking and the possibility of scorching.

5 For béchamel and velouté sauces, the roux must not brown, although it can be slightly darker for velouté than for béchamel.

6 To save time whisking a sauce as it comes to the boil, add hot liquid. Before adding the liquid, let the roux cool slightly to avoid lumps.

7 Add the liquid in a steady stream to the roux, whisking constantly. There is no need to go slowly.

8 To avoid lumps and give the sauce a gloss, whisk constantly as it comes to the boil. If lumps form, do not cook them. Take the sauce from the heat and whisk it well. If the lumps persist, strain the sauce.

9 Remember to season a sauce during cooking. If all the salt and pepper are added at the end, they will not be well blended. If the sauce is to be reduced, season very lightly because the seasoning will become concentrated as the liquid reduces.

10 Condiments and seasonings must be used sparingly. They should bring out the natural flavours rather than impart new ones. Seasoning can always be added if necessary, but cannot be removed.

11 Spirits used to flavour a sauce are added directly to the sauce and brought just to the boil, but wine must first be well reduced in a separate pan to mellow the flavour.

12 Let the sauce simmer gently, stirring it frequently, so as to cook the flour thoroughly and prevent scorching. Béchamel burns particularly easily because the lactose (milk sugar) in the milk caramelises.

13 The right consistency for a sauce depends on its type and use. If it is too thin, simmer it to reduce until thick enough; if too thick, add liquid.

14 Brown sauces are strained in a chinois or conical mesh strainer. Press with a small ladle to extract all the juices from the vegetables. White sauces can also be strained to increase their glossy appearance.

15 Always taste a sauce for seasoning before serving.

Getting ahead

1 If a flour-based sauce is not to be used immediately, rub the surface of the warm sauce with a small piece of butter, or press a piece of greaseproof paper directly on the surface. This will prevent a skin forming.

2 Sauces based on béchamel or velouté can be stored, tightly covered, in the refrigerator for up to 3 days; brown sauces can be similarly kept for a week. Any butter, cream or egg yolks used for enriching the basic sauce should be added only when reheating.

3 Brown and velouté sauces freeze well, so it is worth making a large batch and packing them for use in small quantities. White sauces containing egg yolks separate when defrosted and all sauces containing cream tend to thin when thawed. If the consistency of a defrosted sauce is not smooth, it can be worked through a fine strainer or re-emulsified in a blender.

Thickening sauces without flour
Arrowroot or potato flour
Arrowroot or potato flour is added at the end of the cooking time because both will thin if simmered for more than 2-3 minutes. For every 600ml (1pt) liquid,

THREE STAGES IN SAUCE-MAKING

While adding liquid to a roux, it is important to stir constantly to avoid lumps. Adding hot liquid instead of cold will save time while whisking

Strain a sauce through a chinois, or conical strainer to strain out any solid ingredients and to give a greater gloss

If the sauce is not to be used immediately, rub the surface with butter to prevent a skin from forming. A fork makes a useful tool

mix 2-3 level teaspoons arrowroot or potato flour with 2-3 tablespoons cold water or cold liquid such as stock. Whisk enough of this liquid into the boiling sauce to thicken it to the desired consistency; it should be light and slightly syrupy.

When short of time just before serving, a roux-based sauce that is too thin can also be thickened this way, for example sauces that have thinned after de-frosting.

Arrowroot and potato flour are often used in brown sauces, and occasionally for velouté.

Cornflour

Cornflour is used in the same proporation as arrowroot. The result is slightly more sticky and the sauce does not thin when cooked further.

Cornflour is often used for thickening sweet sauces.

Eggs yolks and cream

Egg yolks with cream should be added just before serving, as the sauce will curdle if it gets too hot on standing. Mix the yolks with about an equal volume of cream, then stir in some of the hot sauce to partially cook the mixture. Whisk this mixture into the remaining sauce, off the heat. Then cook, whisking constantly, until the sauce thickens slightly. If the sauce contains no flour, do not boil or it will curdle. If it has a roux base, bring it just back to a boil after adding the egg yolks and cream.

Use for velouté sauces, occasionally for béchamel.

Kneaded butter

Kneaded butter or beurre manié is a roux of butter and flour added to thicken the mixture at the end, rather than at the beginning, of cooking. To make it, cream the butter and work in an equal weight of flour with a fork or wire whisk. Drop pieces of this kneaded butter into the boiling liquid, whisking hard. The butter will melt and distribute the flour evenly through the liquid. Keep adding pieces of kneaded butter until the sauce has thickened to the right consistency, then continue simmering for at least five minutes to thoroughly cook the flour.

Kneaded butter is little used nowadays but it is a useful way of thickening robust dishes such as boeuf bourguignon at the last minute.

LA VELOUTE

Velouté sauce is often made with the cooking liquid of veal, chicken or fish instead of stock. This basic sauce is usually enriched with egg yolks, cream and/or butter just before being served, and can accompany eggs, fish, poultry, white meats and vegetables.

Makes about 300ml (½pt)

300ml (½pt) well-flavoured veal, chicken or fish stock (page 218)
20g (1½ level tablespoons) butter
15g (1½ level tablespoons) flour
salt and pepper

Bring the stock to the boil. Meanwhile make the roux. Melt the butter in a heavy-based saucepan, whisk in the flour and cook for 1-2 minutes until foaming but not browned. Let the roux cool, then gradually whisk in the hot stock. Bring the sauce to the boil, whisking constantly, and add a little salt and pepper; the flavour of the sauce will be concentrated during later cooking. Simmer, skimming occasionally, for 15-30 minutes – or until it is the required consistency. Taste again for seasoning.

SAUCE SUPREME

This is usually served with chicken.

Makes about 300ml (½pt)

basic velouté made with 300ml (½pt) chicken stock, 20g (1½ level tablespoons) butter and 15g (1½ level tablespoons) flour

30g (1oz) mushroom stalks, chopped

4 tablespoons double cream

salt and freshly ground white pepper

15g (level tablespoon) butter

Make a basic velouté sauce (see previous recipe) using the chicken stock, butter and flour and add the chopped mushroom stems to the basic velouté with the stock. Simmer for 15-30 minutes. Strain the sauce, return to the pan and continue simmering, adding the cream a little at a time, for about 5-10 more minutes. Taste for seasoning. Take from the heat and add the butter just before serving.

SAUCE AURORE

This is served with eggs, fish, veal, pork and sweetbreads.

Makes 300ml (½pt)

basic velouté made with 300ml (½pt) chicken or fish stock, 20g (1½ level tablespoons) butter and 15g (1½ level tablespoons) flour

2 level tablespoons tomato purée

salt and freshly ground pepper

30g (2 tablespoons) butter

Make a basic velouté sauce with the stock butter and flour. Whisk in the tomato purée and season to taste. Remove the sauce from the heat and add the butter before serving.

FOND DE VEAU LIE
(Basic brown sauce)

Fond de veau lié has almost entirely replaced espagnole sauce in French restaurants as the basis of other brown sauces, and as a thickener for the cooking liquid of braised or stewed meats.

Makes 600ml (1pt)

generous 600ml (1pt) brown veal stock

2 level tablespoons arrowroot or potato flour

4 tablespoons Madeira or cold water

salt and freshly ground black pepper

Bring the stock to the boil and, if necessary, boil until the flavour is concentrated. Mix the arrowroot or potato flour to a paste with the Madeira or cold water. Gradually pour the mixture into the boiling stock, whisking constantly and adding just enough to thicken the sauce to the desired consistency. For most dishes, the sauce should be just thick enough to lightly coat the back of a spoon. Bring back to the boil, season to taste with salt and pepper and strain.

FOND DE VEAU LIE/2
(Variation on Basic brown sauce)

This is a richer version of the basic fond de veau lié, approaching the traditional espagnole sauce and is used with rich roast meat dishes – noisettes of lamb or tournedos of beef, for example.

Makes 600ml (1pt)

15g (tablespoon) butter

½ leek, diced

carrot, diced

onion, diced

stick celery, diced

750ml (1¼pt) white or brown veal stock

2 tomatoes, diced

bouquet garni

tablespoon tomato purée

2 level tablespoons arrowroot or potato flour

4 tablespoons Madeira or water

salt and freshly ground black pepper

Heat the butter in a heavy-based pan and add the diced leek, carrot, onion and celery. If using white stock, sauté the vegetables until well browned. If using brown stock, sauté them until lightly browned. Add the stock, tomatoes and bouquet garni, bring to the boil, and simmer for 30-45 minutes or until the vegetables are very tender. Add the tomato purée and return to the boil. Mix the arrowroot or potato flour to a paste with the Madeira or cold water. Gradually pour the mixture into the boiling sauce, whisking constantly, adding enough to thicken the sauce to the desired consistency. Bring back to the boil, taste for seasoning and strain.

SAUCE MADERE
(Madeira sauce)

This sauce is a classic accompaniment to fillet of beef, veal, ham and innards such as tongue and kidneys.

Makes about 600ml (1pt)

6 tablespoons Madeira, or to taste

600ml (1pt) basic brown sauce (fond de veau lié)

salt and freshly ground black pepper

Simmer 3 tablespoons of the Madeira with the basic brown sauce for 8-10 minutes, add 3 more tablespoons Madeira or to taste, and bring just back to the boil. Taste again for seasoning.

SAUCE ITALIENNE
(Italian sauce)

This rich sauce goes well with roast beef, steak, veal and pasta.

Makes about 750ml (1¼pts)

15g (level tablespoon) butter

½ onion, finely chopped

125g (4oz) mushrooms, finely chopped

300ml (½pt) dry white wine

600ml (1pt) basic brown sauce (fond de veau lié)

60g (2oz) cooked lean ham

salt and freshly ground black pepper

Heat the butter in a saucepan, add the onion and cook slowly for 5-7 minutes until soft but not brown. Add the mushrooms and cook them over high heat, stirring frequently, until soft. Add the wine, bring to the boil and boil until reduced to 150ml (¼pt).

Stir in the basic brown sauce and bring to the boil. Cut the ham in very small neat cubes or dice, add to the sauce and taste for seasoning.

SAUCE DIABLE
(Devil sauce)

This sharp-flavoured sauce livens roast or grilled meat or chicken.

Makes about 600ml (1pt)

150ml (¼pt) dry white wine

150ml (¼pt) white wine vinegar

2 shallots, finely chopped

2 teaspoons tomato purée

600ml (1pt) basic brown sauce (fond de veau lié)

pinch of Cayenne

salt and freshly ground black pepper

In a small saucepan (not aluminium) boil the wine, vinegar, shallots and tomato purée until reduced to about 100ml (⅛pt). Stir in the basic brown sauce and bring to the boil. Take from the heat, add just a touch of Cayenne and taste again for seasoning.

SAUCE BECHAMEL

The quantities below make a sauce of medium thickness, for serving with eggs, vegetables and pasta. For a thin sauce for making cream soups, use only 15g (level tablespoon) butter and 10g (level tablespoon) flour. For a thick sauce for binding soufflé mixtures, use 30g (2 level tablespoons) butter and 20g (2 level tablespoons) flour.

Makes 300ml ($\frac{1}{2}$pt)

300ml ($\frac{1}{2}$pt) milk
slice of onion, small bay leaf and 6 peppercorns (for infusing – optional)
20g ($1\frac{1}{2}$ level tablespoons) butter
15g ($1\frac{1}{2}$ level tablespoons) flour
salt and freshly ground white pepper
pinch of grated nutmeg

Scald the milk by bringing it just to the boil in a saucepan. If you like, add the onion, bay leaf and peppercorns and leave over very low heat for 5-10 minutes to add flavour.

Meanwhile make the roux: melt the butter in a heavy-based saucepan, whisk in the flour and cook for 1-2 minutes until foaming but not browned; let it cool. Strain in the hot milk, whisk well, then bring the sauce to the boil, whisking constantly, and add salt, pepper and nutmeg to taste. Simmer for 3-5 minutes. If not used at once, rub the surface of the sauce with butter or cover with greaseproof paper to prevent a skin forming.

Béchamel sauce can be kept covered for 2-3 days in the refrigerator, or it can be frozen.

SAUCE MORNAY

Mornay sauce is excellent served with eggs, fish, white meats, vegetables and pasta and is an important ingredient in most gratins. Well-aged Gruyère or Parmesan, or a mixture of both, are the best cheeses to use; you will find the flavour of Parmesan is somewhat sharper.

Makes about 300ml ($\frac{1}{2}$pt)

300ml ($\frac{1}{2}$pt) milk
slice of onion, small bay leaf and 6 peppercorns (for infusing – optional)
15g (level tablespoon) butter
10g (level tablespoon) flour
salt and freshly ground white pepper
pinch of grated nutmeg
1 egg yolk
30g (1oz) grated cheese
level teaspoon Dijon mustard (optional)

Make thin béchamel sauce (see previous recipe) with the milk, onion, bay leaf, peppercorns, butter, flour, salt, pepper and nutmeg. Take the pan from the heat, beat in the egg yolk, cheese and mustard and taste for seasoning. Serve at once.

Do not reheat the sauce or you will find that the cheese will cook into strings.

THE WAY TO SUCCESS

hot emulsified sauces

1 For richer sauce, increase the butter to about 300g (10oz). Do not use less than 180g (6oz) butter or the taste of egg will be too strong.
2 Clarify the butter, then cool slightly before adding to the egg yolks. Hot butter will curdle the sauce.
3 Thoroughly cook the egg yolk mousse that forms the base of the sauce: use low heat and whisk for several minutes so the mousse thickens lightly and evenly. Too sudden heat will make the eggs granular.
4 Remove the egg yolk mousse from the heat as soon as it is thick enough; overcooking will scramble it.
5 Add the butter in a slow but steady stream so it thickens the sauce without separating from it.
6 Never stop whisking while cooking the yolks or when adding the butter.
7 If the sauce is not perfectly smooth, strain it. Granules may form if the sauce is kept for some time and the yolks will scramble slightly.
8 If the sauce is too thick, add a tablespoon of tepid water. If the sauce is too thin, but not separated, continue cooking over low heat, whisking constantly until it thickens.
9 Add lemon juice to the sauce just before serving; if it is added too soon to a sauce that is kept warm for some time, it may cause fermentation.

10 Both sauces will discolour silver badly; do not use a silver sauceboat or a silver spoon.

To rescue curdled butter sauces
The sauce almost always curdles because it is too hot. If so:
1 Remove sauce at once from the heat and whisk in an ice cube.
a If this is not successful, gradually whisk the curdled mixture, drop by drop, into one tablespoon of cold water in a clean pan.
b If still unsuccessful, start the sauce again; whisk one egg yolk and one tablespoon water over low heat to a mousse; then gradually whisk in the curdled mixture, drop by drop.
c However, if the sauce is so badly curdled that the egg yolks have cooked into granules, the mixture must be discarded.
2 Very occasionally the sauce separates because it is too cool and has not been sufficiently cooked. Try bringing a tablespoon of water to the boil and then whisking in the turned sauce drop by drop over low heat.
3 Butter sauces without an egg yolk base cannot be rescued once curdled.

Getting ahead

1 In general, it is best to make emulsified sauces just before serving. However, egg yolk based emulsified sauces can be made up to 30 minutes ahead and kept warm in a pan over hot, but not boiling water. Check the sauce and whisk often to be sure it has not separated. If the sauce was made in a tin-lined copper pan, remove to another pan to keep warm. Never leave it in the copper pan.

2 Leftover hollandaise and béarnaise can be kept covered in the refrigerator for up to 2 days. They can be gently reheated, by whisking constantly in a water bath but the risk that the sauce might separate is high. high.

3 Cold hollandaise or beurre blanc are excellent for enriching white and velouté sauces and any cream soups to which lemon juice or vinegar can be added. Just before serving, remove the sauce or soup from the heat and whisk in the cold sauce a piece at a time.

CLARIFYING BUTTER

After melting the butter and skimming it of froth, pour it out carefully, leaving the milky residue behind in the pan

TO MAKE HOLLANDAISE OR BEARNAISE

Make the mousse base of the sauce by whisking the yolks constantly over low heat until they are thick and creamy

When a little of the clarified butter has been gradually whisked in the rest can be added in a slow but steady stream

SAUCE HOLLANDAISE

(Hollandaise sauce)

Makes about 300ml (½pt)
180g (6oz) butter
3 tablespoons water
3 egg yolks
salt and Cayenne pepper
juice of ½ lemon, or to taste

Melt the butter, skim the froth from the surface and allow the butter to cool to tepid. In a small saucepan, whisk the water and egg yolks with a little salt and Cayenne pepper for 30 seconds until light. Set the pan over low heat or in a water bath and whisk constantly until the mixture is creamy and thick enough for the whisk to leave a trail on the base of the pan. The base of the pan should never be more than hand-hot.

Take from the heat and whisk in the tepid butter, a few drops at a time. NOTE: do not add the butter too fast or the sauce may curdle. When the sauce has started to thicken, the butter can be added a little faster. Do not add the milky sediment from the bottom of the pan.

When all the butter has been added, stir in the lemon juice and taste for seasoning, adding salt, Cayenne pepper and lemon juice to taste. Hollandaise is served warm, not hot, and it should be kept warm in a water bath to avoid curdling.

SAUCE MALTAISE

(Maltese sauce)

To 300ml (½pt) hollandaise sauce, add the juice of ½ orange and the pared rind of ½ orange, cut in needle-like shreds, blanched in boiling water for 1-2 minutes and drained. Taste for seasoning and serve, particularly with asparagus.

SAUCE MIREILLE

To 300ml (½pt) hollandaise, add 1½ tablespoons tomato purée and ½ teaspoon finely chopped basil. Taste for seasoning. Serve with eggs, asparagus, artichoke bottoms or offal (innards).

SAUCE NOISETTE

Use noisette, rather than clarified butter. When clarifying the butter, cook it over medium heat until nut brown. NOTE: do not allow the butter to burn. Otherwise, proceed as usual. Serve this sauce with eggs or vegetables.

SAUCE MOUTARDE

To 300ml (½pt) hollandaise sauce, add 1-2 teaspoons Dijon mustard or to taste. Serve with eggs and fish.

SAUCE CHANTILLY, MOUSSELINE OU VIERGE

To 300ml (½pt) hollandaise sauce, add 4 tablespoons stiffly whipped double cream and taste for seasoning. Serve with asparagus, fish, chicken and sautéed sweetbreads.

BLENDER HOLLANDAISE SAUCE

Hollandaise sauce made in a blender or electric food processor has a fluffier, less creamy consistency than hand-made hollandaise, but it is very quick and easy to do.

Use the same ingredients and quantities as when making by hand. Heat the butter until hot but do not allow it to brown; discard any scum from the surface. Put the egg yolks with the water and a little salt and pepper in a blender and blend at medium speed, adding about a third of the butter in a very slow stream. When the mixture is quite thick, add the lemon juice and continue adding the butter slowly, increasing the blender speed as the mixture thickens. Do not add the milky liquid at the bottom of the butter.

When all the butter has been added, pour the sauce at once into a sauceboat or serving bowl, as it will quickly thicken too much to pour from the blender. Taste it for seasoning, adding salt, pepper and lemon juice to taste, and thin with a little warm water if necessary.

SAUCE BEARNAISE
(Béarnaise sauce)

Some writers argue that sauce béarnaise was originally made in Bearn, in southwest France, using oil, not butter. Others think the name Béarnaise honours Béarn-born King Henry IV, 'Le Grand Béarnais,' who loved spicy food. But most agree that the sauce became famous at the Pavillon Henri IV restaurant at Saint Germain-en-Laye, which was named after the king.

Makes about 300ml (½pt)

| 180g (6oz) butter |
| 3 tablespoons vinegar |
| 3 tablespoons white wine |
| 10 peppercorns, crushed |
| 3 shallots, finely chopped |
| tablespoon chopped fresh tarragon stems or leaves of tarragon preserved in vinegar |
| 3 egg yolks |
| salt and white or Cayenne pepper |

to finish

| 1-2 tablespoons finely chopped fresh tarragon leaves or tarragon leaves in vinegar |
| tablespoon chopped chervil or parsley |

Melt the butter, skim any scum from the surface and allow it to cool to tepid. Boil the vinegar and white wine in a small saucepan with the peppercorns, chopped shallots and tarragon stems or leaves until reduced to 2 tablespoons. Allow to cool, add the egg yolks, a little salt and pepper and whisk for 30 seconds or until light. Set the pan over low heat or in a water bath and whisk constantly until the mixture is creamy and quite a bit thicker than for hollandaise. The base of the pan should never be more than hand-hot.

Take the pan from the heat and whisk in the tepid butter, a few drops at a time. When the sauce has thickened, the butter can be added faster. Do not add the milky sediment from the bottom of the pan.

When all the butter has been added, strain the sauce, pressing well to extract all the mixture. Add the chopped tarragon and the chervil or parsley and taste again for seasoning. Béarnaise sauce should be quite piquant.

SAUCE CHORON
(Tomato béarnaise)

To 300ml (½pt) béarnaise sauce, add 1½ tablespoons tomato purée. Serve with steak, fish and eggs.

SAUCE FOYOT
(Béarnaise with meat glaze)

To 300ml (½pt) béarnaise sauce, add 1 teaspoon meat glaze (lesson 6). The sauce should be the colour of café au lait. Serve with steak.

SAUCE PALOISE
(Mint béarnaise)

Substitute chopped fresh mint for the tarragon. Serve this variation with steak, duck and fish.

BEARNAISE AU POIVRE VERT
(Green peppercorn béarnaise)

Omit the chopped tarragon and chervil leaves added to béarnaise sauce and add 1 level tablespoon drained and crushed green peppercorns to every 300ml (½pt) of sauce. (Green peppercorns preserved in vinegar are obtainable at delicatessens; once opened they can be kept in their liquid, tightly covered in the refrigerator, for 1-2 months.) Serve with steak and salmon.

SAUCE BEURRE BLANC
(White butter sauce)

White butter sauce comes from the Loire valley and traditionally is served with pike from the river, although it is delicious with any poached or steamed fish and also with vegetables.

Makes about 300ml (½pt)

| 3 tablespoons white wine vinegar |
| 3 tablespoons dry white wine |
| 2 shallots, very finely chopped |
| 250g (8oz) butter, very cold |
| salt and white pepper |

In a small saucepan (not aluminium), boil the wine vinegar, wine and shallots until reduced to 1 tablespoon. Set the pan over low heat and whisk in the butter gradually, in small pieces, to make a smooth, creamy sauce. Work sometimes over low heat and sometimes off the heat, so that the butter softens and thickens the sauce without melting. Season to taste with salt and white pepper and serve as soon as possible – if kept warm, it easily melts and becomes oily. If it must be kept warm for a few minutes, keep it in a pan over warm, but not boiling, water.

SAUCE BEURRE ROUGE
(Red butter sauce)

Substitute 90ml (3oz) red wine for the vinegar and white wine in sauce beurre blanc. Proceed as for sauce beurre blanc.

SAUCE VIN BLANC
(White wine sauce)

Because of the fish glaze which is always an ingredient of sauce vin blanc, it is served only with fish.

Makes about 225ml (8fl oz)

2 shallots, finely chopped
250g (8oz) butter, very cold
100ml ($\frac{1}{6}$pt) white wine
tablespoon double cream
juice of $\frac{1}{4}$ lemon
$\frac{1}{2}$ teaspoon fish glaze (page 219)
salt and pepper

In a small saucepan (not aluminium) soften the shallot in 15g ($\frac{1}{2}$oz) of the butter, stirring constantly. NOTE: do not allow the shallots to brown. Add the wine and cook for about 5 minutes or until reduced to 1-2 tablespoons. NOTE: The mixture will be very thick and syrupy. Add the cream and reduce again to 1-2 tablespoons. Set the pan over a low heat and gradually whisk in the rest of the butter in small pieces to make a smooth, creamy sauce. Work sometimes over low heat and sometimes off the heat so that the butter softens and thickens the sauce without melting. Whisk in the lemon juice and fish glaze and season to taste with salt and pepper.

The sauce can be kept for a few minutes over warm but not boiling water, but it is best to serve it immediately.

SABAYON SAUCE

The amount of sugar needed depends on the sweetness of the wine. Nearly any white or fortified wine can be used. Sabayon sauce can be served warm or cold.

SERVES 4

4 egg yolks
60g (2oz) sugar, or less
150ml ($\frac{1}{4}$pt) dry white wine
grated rind of 1 orange or 1 lemon (optional)

Put the egg yolks, sugar and wine in a copper bowl over a pan of hot water, or in the top of a double boiler, and whisk over hot but not boiling water until the sauce is frothy and almost thick enough to leave a ribbon trail. NOTE: do not heat the sauce too much or overcook it, or it will curdle. Add the grated orange or lemon rind.

If serving the sauce warm, serve it at once. If serving the sauce cold, whisk it until cool, then set the bowl in a pan of iced water and continue whisking it until the sauce is cold. It will hold up without separating for about an hour.

SABAYON AU MADERE

Use only 45g (1$\frac{1}{2}$oz) sugar and substitute 3 tablespoons Madeira for the white wine. Whisk the egg yolks, sugar and Madeira well, off the heat, then continue as above.

24
SAUSAGES
High class convenience food

A sausage is simply a filled 'casing' – a convenient way of packing meats and seasoning for cooking – so it's no surprise that there are so many different kinds. I know of no comprehensive list of sausages; every country has its own versions, and for France and Germany alone the lists run into the dozens – if not the hundreds. There are fresh sausages, cooked sausages, dried sausages and smoked sausages, plus various combinations of the four that give at least a dozen possibilities before you even start to consider the different types of meat and seasonings.

However, many sausages are not suitable for making at home. Minced meat quickly spoils so, in the damp English climate, and indeed anywhere in northern Europe, making dried sausages is risky. When we run the summer charcuterie course at La Varenne, Chef Chambrette always takes the salami-type sausages with him to Brittany to dry during his August vacation. So far he's always fallen on the couple of sunny weeks needed to dry the sausages properly, but he's been lucky. Smoked sausages, too, require the right conditions. If you have a smokehouse, all well and good; if not, hanging sausages at the back of the hearth in Tudor style is chancy – to say the least.

So that leaves fresh sausages and cooked sausages to make at home – and there's still plenty of choice. The simplest sausages of all consist of fresh minced pork including some – but not too much – fat, seasoned with salt and pepper and sometimes with spices. You'll find them almost everywhere. In England they are packed in skin or casings that are chipolata-size – and rusks are added as a filler. In France adding cereal fillers is frowned upon and is, in fact, illegal if the sausages are to be sold. They come in two usual thicknesses, 4cm (1½in) thick and the smaller chipolata. Seasonings vary from place to place and butcher to butcher and can include spices and herbs.

All sorts of variations are possible. Crépinettes – bundles of sausagemeat wrapped in lacy caul fat instead of packed in casings – are sold in all French charcuteries (pork butchers). Some butchers like to add beef to balance the richness of the pork, or a

BOUDIN BLANC, POMMES EN L'AIR

White 'boudin' are sausages made with cream and light meats, such as chicken breast and veal. For this recipe, they are cooked in butter, then served with caramelised apple slices

binding agent such as cornflour or dried milk. A small amount of liver transforms the sausage into a saucisse de Toulouse. Any sausage may have saltpetre added. Thus cures the mat so that it turns a pretty pink and keeps for much longer. Saltpetre can taste bitter, so it is always used in small quantities, with double its weight in sugar. You can buy it at the chemist – the technical name is potassium nitrate – and the usual allowance is 2g (about ½ teaspoon) saltpetre per kilo (2¼lb) meat.

Other additions to fresh sausages are up to you – if you find a type you like in the shops, try to reproduce the seasoning at home. Onion, celery or shallot are possible flavourings; good herbs to use include chives, crushed bay leaf, tarragon and chervil, and almost any spices are suitable – including juniper berries, caraway seeds and star aniseed. A dash of red or white wine never comes amiss and vinegar adds bite. The principle is to retain the earthy character of pork sausages; champagne, brandy and truffles are not appropriate here, although they can be used in another type of sausage – boudin blanc.

Boudins are akin to the black and white puddings still found in English country districts (indeed, the two words have a common root) and can be classed as cooked sausages since they are simmered by the butcher (or by you) and need only to be finished off by grilling or sautéing before being eaten. Boudin noir is a blood sausage, rich, powerful in flavour and typical bistro fare. In Normandy, boudin noir is made with diced fat, onions simmered to a pulp, salt, pepper, pigs' blood, and still made at home.

Boudin blanc is the queen of sausages. Plump and pearly, it is made with white meat – chicken or veal – held together with eggs and breadcrumbs (an exception among French sausages) and enriched with pork fat and cream. The seasoning of boudin blanc should be delicate – white pepper, a little onion, and perhaps some allspice. Some charcuteries put brandy, champagne or foie gras into their boudin blanc. This increases the price but does little, I think, for the flavour. Truffles, showing jet black against the white of the sausage, are the classic extra ingredient, but you need a number of them to make much impression. Personally I think an unadorned boudin blanc, freshly made with a minimum of seasonings, cannot be beaten.

The type of meat used in making sausages is important: leftover bits that are too tough to be used for anything else are instantly detectable. For pork, beef and veal, the shoulder and neck yield good lean meat that is not too expensive. Fresh leg of pork is excellent if you can afford it; any lean beef is good, and most cuts of veal are suitable as the meat is young and tender. The fat called for in sausages is almost always pork, and the best comes from the back. As each animal has large and small intestines, skins come in half a dozen sizes, each traditional for a different type of sausage. In France 'saucissons' are generally packed into large skins and 'saucisses' are smaller.

The size of the skin can change the character of a sausage – large ones retain their flavour better, but they must be cooked more slowly as they burst easily.

Sausages can be cooked for serving by grilling, baking in the oven, frying or poaching. Rich sausages, like fresh pork sausages or boudins noirs, are usually baked in the oven or grilled, perhaps on a barbecue. Frying in butter suits many types. Poaching is generally limited to delicate sausages that are likely to burst, to smoked sausages (cooking in water takes away too pronounced a flavour) and to pre-cooking various types before finishing by another method.

Accompaniments to sausages are time-honoured. Boudin, whether white or black, comes with potato purée or apples fried in butter. Saucisse de Toulouse go with white beans, as do many other types – Cassoulet would lack its essential punch if there were no sausages. Sauerkraut and braised cabbage are other favourite accompaniments; the widespread cabbage-based stew called 'potée' could hardly exist without saucissons.

Sausages can be compared to cheese, with similar regional associations and a close link to the soil. They evoke equally strong reactions. I am a devotee of sausages; my husband is not. In vain have I tried to tempt him with the pleasures of a freshly grilled boudin blanc or a plate of assorted 'saucissons secs'. At the smell of a poaching garlic sausage, perfume to my nostrils, he wrinkles his nose in distaste. We are united only over the merits of the fresh sausages from our local charcuterie – which resemble nothing so much as the good old English 'banger'.

THE WAY TO SUCCESS

Making sausagemeat

1 Try to get meat from an 'overweight' pig; the pork found in supermarkets is often too lean and may be tasteless.
2 Before mincing meat for sausages, remove all sinews and tendons.
3 Mince together the different meats used, for example the lean and fat pork, or pork plus other meats. This ensures that the meats will be perfectly mixed.

4 Add seasonings to the meats as you mince them. The seasonings will be distributed more evenly, and crushing will bring out their flavour.
5 Use a high percentage of fat in the mixture so it will remain moist.
6 To give the sausages a close, smooth texture, beat the filling with your hand or a wooden spoon until it comes away from the sides of the bowl.
7 The meat can be left to absorb seasonings and 'cure' for 12-24 hours in the refrigerator.

Sausage skins and how to stuff them

Sausage casings, made of animal intestines that have been thoroughly cleaned, are available from butchers who make their own sausages. The most common ones are those that are made from the large pork intestines – about 4cm (1½in) in diameter when stuffed – and the small intestines – about 2cm (¾in) in diameter when stuffed. You can sometimes buy fresh skins, but usually they are salted so that they can be stored in the refrigerator for a week or two. Both fresh or salted skins can be kept in the freezer for several months.

To stuff skins: soak them overnight in cold water to remove any salt and make them pliable. Drain them and dry lightly.

Tie one end closed and attach the open end to the base of the funnel or sausage-stuffer. Push the skin up the funnel until the closed end is reached. Work the sausage filling through the funnel into the skin, letting the skin fall as the stuffing fills it. If using a sausage-stuffer attached to a mincer, work the stuffing through the mincer into the skins. Do not pack the filling in too tightly, or they will burst during cooking.

When a length of skin has been stuffed, tie the end closed with string. Work the skins at intervals with your fingers to divide the filling into sausages of the desired length, then twist or tie with string. Cut before or after cooking, depending on the type of sausage.

Cooking sausages

1 Sausages burst easily. Prick the skins before cooking and cook them slowly.

2 Do not, however, prick boudins before poaching. When poaching, do not let the liquid boil.
3 Do not prick sausages when hot as they will lose juice and may burst. Handle them with care.
4 When cooking with highly seasoned sausages, do not overseason any accompaniment such as potatoes or a vegetable purée.

Getting ahead

Naturally, sausages can be made ahead of time and their storage time depends entirely on how they were made:

Fresh sausages can be kept in the refrigerator for up to 3 days, or a day or two longer if they are very highly seasoned.

Lightly smoked fresh sausages will stay fresh in the refrigerator for a week or so.

Precooked sausages, depending on how they were cured and seasoned, are all right if kept from one to two weeks in the refrigerator.

Cooked smoked sausages Most heavily smoked sausages, destined to be eaten as they are, can be kept for a month or more in a cool place. However, if they require further cooking, two weeks in the refrigerator is the longest recommended keeping time.

Dried sausages keep longest of all. Drying can last 6 months and, if you keep them at room temperature, the drying process simply continues. They will, however, eventually become unpleasantly strong and dry.

All sausages can be frozen and fresh sausages freeze very well indeed.

SAUSAGEMEAT

If the sausagemeat is to be used for stuffing vegetables such as tomatoes, cabbage or marrow, herbs make a pleasant addition. Allow 2 tablespoons of chopped fresh parsley, tarragon, chives, basil, thyme or sage, or a mixture of several.

Makes about 1kg (2¼lb)

650g (1lb 7oz) lean pork
100g (3½oz) lean beef
250g (8oz) fat pork
3 tablespoons water
16-20g (4-5 level teaspoons) salt
1.5g (⅓ level teaspoon) white pepper
1g (¼ level teaspoon) allspice

Mix together the lean and fat meat and mince them. Add water and seasoning. Continue to mix until completely bound and well blended.

CREPINETTES

(Flat sausages)

1kg (2lb) sausagemeat
caul fat

Soak the caul fat in cold water, rinse and drain.

Prepare the sausagemeat following the basic recipe and divide into portions of about 125g (4oz). Form each portion into a rectangle about 2cm (¾in) thick.

Spread out the caul fat and place the portions of sausagemeat on top, spacing to allow for wrapping. Cut the fat and wrap the portions, keeping their rectangular shape.

To serve: pan fry or, alternatively, brush with melted butter or beaten egg, roll in dry breadcrumbs and grill.

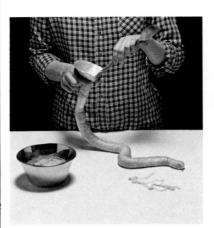

Tie one end of the casing or skin and push the sausagemeat through a stuffing funnel into the open end to fill it

After stuffing, the filled sausage skin is tied into the appropriate lengths – here they are approx. 15cm (6in) each

SAUCISSES DE TOULOUSE
(Toulouse sausages)

Makes 1¼kg (about 2½lb)

1kg (2¼lb) sausagemeat
(see basic recipe)

100g (3½oz) pork liver (optional)

1-1¼m (1-1½ yards) pork intestine

sausage stuffer or large funnel

Soak the intestines in cold water. Rinse and run water through them. Mince the pork liver with the sausagemeat. Fill the intestine without pressing too hard. Prick the sausages if necessary in order to prevent air pockets forming and twist into 15-18cm (6-7in) lengths. Serve – or keep – as for chipolatas.

SAUCISSES AU VIN BLANC SUR TOASTS
(Sausages with white wine on bread cases)

As an alternative, serve the sausages on a bed of boiled rice or pilaf.

SERVES 4

1kg (2¼lb) chipolata or Toulouse sausages

30g (1oz) butter

2 shallots, finely chopped

6 tablespoons white wine

6 tablespoons basic brown sauce (page 191)

salt and freshly ground black pepper

30g (1oz) butter (to finish)

2 tablespoons finely chopped parsley

for the bread cases

4 thick slices white bread, crusts removed

6 tablespoons oil (for frying)

To make the bread cases: cut 3 parallel indentations in each slice of bread with a small knife; each indentation will hold one sausage.

Heat the oil in a heavy based frying pan and add the bread cases, cut side down. Brown the cut side, turn over and brown the other. Drain. The cases can be made 2-3 hours ahead and kept at room temperature.

Melt 30g (1oz) butter in a sauté pan and sauté the sausages for 2-3 minutes or until brown. Remove them from the pan, add the shallots and wine and simmer for 3-5 minutes, or until the shallots are tender and the wine is reduced. Whisk in the basic brown sauce,

bring to the boil and season to taste. NOTE: the sauce should be slightly acid. Return the sausages to the sauce, cover; remove from the heat.

To finish: reheat the sausages in the sauce. Place one sausage in each indentation on the bread cases and arrange these on a plate. Remove the sauce from the heat and whisk in 30g (1oz) butter, in small pieces. Add the chopped parsley and spoon the sauce over the sausages.

CASSOULET

To ease preparation, the cassoulet can be made in steps, up to 3 days before serving.

SERVES 8-10

4-5 pieces, about 500g (1lb), confit of goose or duck; or 1 small fresh duck, weighing about 1¾-2kg (3½-4¼lb)

2 tablespoons goose or duck fat, or lard

500g (1lb) shoulder or breast of lamb, cut into 2.5cm (1in) pieces

500g (1lb) boneless pork loin or shoulder, cut into 2.5cm (1in) cubes

2 onions, chopped

4 cloves garlic, chopped

50ml (2fl oz) white wine

4 tomatoes, peeled, seeded and chopped; or 500g (1lb) canned tomatoes, drained and chopped

salt, pepper and a bouquet garni

375g (¾lb) piece lean salt pork, rind scored deeply, blanched

1 litre (1¾pt) stock or water

500g (1lb) Toulouse sausage

for the beans

1kg (2lb) dried haricot or white beans

carrot, quartered

onion, stuck with 4 cloves

bouquet garni

salt and pepper

to finish

100g (3½oz) breadcrumbs (optional)

2 tablespoons duck or goose fat

For the beans: soak them overnight in plenty of cold water and drain. Put them in a large pan with the carrot, onion stuck with cloves, bouquet garni and water to cover by at least 5cm (2in). Cover and simmer for 2½ hours or until the beans are almost tender. Add salt and pepper halfway through the cooking time. Drain the beans and discard the onion, carrot and bouquet garni; reserve the cooking liquid.

If using a fresh duck, cut it into

6 pieces and season them. In a flameproof casserole or frying pan, heat the goose fat or lard and brown the duck pieces on all sides, allowing 10-15 minutes so the duck's fat dissolves. Take out the duck, pour off and save all but 2 tablespoons of the fat, put in the lamb and brown it also on all sides. Take it out, put in the pork and brown it too. Remove the pork, replace with the chopped onions and brown them lightly. Add the garlic, sauté for a few seconds, then add the wine.

In a very large, deep baking dish or casserole, layer the confit or the browned fresh duck with the lamb, fresh pork, onion mixture, tomatoes and season with salt and pepper. Add a bouquet garni, set the salt pork on top and pour in enough of the stock or water to barely cover the meat. Cover and simmer very slowly on top of the stove or bake in a low oven, 150C (300F) gas 2, for 2-3 hours or until the meat is nearly tender, adding more liquid if the mixture becomes dry. Add the sausage and beans and continue cooking for another hour, moistening with the reserved bean liquid as needed.

Remove the salt pork and sausage, slice and replace them. Taste for seasoning, sprinkle breadcrumbs on top and dot with the fat.

The cassoulet can be prepared ahead up to this point and kept in the refrigerator, or it can be frozen.

To finish: cook the cassoulet in a moderately hot oven, 190C (375F) gas 5, for 1¼–1½ hours or until the top is browned. If the cassoulet was already warm, allow only ¾ hour for browning. Serve in the casserole.

SAUCISSES DE TOULOUSE AUX HARICOTS
(Toulouse sausages with white beans)

Sausages and beans seem to make natural partners and this is a particularly satisfying, simple dish.

SERVES 4

1kg (2¼lb) Toulouse sausages

30g (1oz) butter

for the beans

500g (1lb) dried white beans

onion, stuck with 4 cloves

carrot

bouquet garni

salt and pepper

For the beans: soak them overnight in plenty of cold water and drain. Place them in a large pan with the onion stuck with cloves, the carrot, bouquet garni and water to cover by at least 2.5cm (1in). Bring to a boil and simmer for $1\frac{1}{2}$ to 2 hours or until the beans are very tender, adding salt and pepper halfway through the cooking time. Add more water during cooking as it becomes absorbed; at the end of cooking the beans should be moist but not soupy. Discard the onion, carrot and bouquet garni. The beans can be cooked up to 2 days ahead and kept covered in the refrigerator.

Melt the butter in a sauté pan and sauté the sausages until well browned and cooked through. Add the beans and simmer together for 5 minutes so that the flavours blend, and serve.

BOUDIN BLANC
(White boudin)

Makes about 1kg ($2\frac{1}{4}$lb)

150ml ($\frac{1}{4}$pt) double cream

100g ($3\frac{1}{2}$oz) breadcrumbs

1-$1\frac{1}{4}$m (1-$1\frac{1}{2}$ yards) pork intestine

250g (8oz) lean veal

250g (8oz) fat pork

250g (8oz) boned chicken breast, or a
further 250g (8oz) lean veal
---
onion, chopped
---
3 eggs
---
level teaspoon ground allspice
---
salt and white pepper
---
for cooking

$1\frac{1}{2}$ litres ($2\frac{1}{2}$pts) water

750ml ($1\frac{1}{4}$pt) milk
---
sausage stuffer or large funnel

Scald the cream by bringing it just to the boil, pour it over the breadcrumbs and leave to cool. Soak the pork intestine in cold water.
For the filling: work the veal, fat pork, and chicken if used, twice through the fine blade of a mincer, adding the onion before the second mincing. Alternatively, work the meat and onion a little at a time in an electric food processor. Put the mixture in a bowl and stir in the soaked breadcrumbs, eggs, allspice and plenty of salt and pepper. Sauté a small ball of the mixture in a little oil and taste for seasoning – the mixture should be quite spicy. Beat with a wooden spoon or your hand until very smooth.

To fill the sausages: drain the pork intestine – it should be pliable. Tie one end, insert the sausage-stuffer or funnel in the other and spoon in the filling, shaking it down the skins. Do not fill them too tightly or they will burst during cooking. Tie into 15cm (6in) sausages.

Bring the water and milk to a boil in a large pan. Lower the sausages into the pan. Cover and poach for 18-20 minutes. Allow the sausages to cool to tepid in the liquid, then drain them and leave to cool completely. They can be cooked up to 24 hours ahead and kept covered in the refrigerator.

BOUDIN BLANC, POMMES EN L'AIR
(White boudin with apples)

The phrase 'pommes en l'air', apples in the air, happily evokes the way these fried apples should be tossed in the frying pan; faint-hearted cooks can turn them with a spatula.

SERVES 6

1kg ($2\frac{1}{4}$lb) white boudin

60g (2oz) butter
---
for garnish
---
4 firm apples, unpeeled

30g (1oz) butter

30g (1oz) sugar

For the boudin: melt the butter in a frying pan and gently fry the sausages for 4-5 minutes or until very hot and golden. Alternatively, brush with melted butter and grill them.
For the garnish: halve and core the apples and cut in thin slices. Melt the butter in a frying pan. Dip one side of each apple slice in the sugar. Cook the apple slices, sugared side down, in the hot butter over high heat for 4-5 minutes or until the sugar is caramelised. Sprinkle the rest of the sugar on the apples, toss, or turn them with a spatula and brown the other side. NOTE: do not overcook the apples, or they will turn to purée.

CHIPOLATAS

Makes 1kg ($2\frac{1}{4}$lb)

1kg ($2\frac{1}{4}$lb) sausagemeat
(see basic recipe above)

1-$1\frac{1}{4}$m (1-$1\frac{1}{2}$ yards) small intestines of
mutton
---
sausage stuffer or large funnel

Soak the intestines in cold water. Rinse and run water through them.

Prepare the sausagemeat. Fill the intestines without pressing too hard and prick if necessary in order to prevent air pockets. Twist to divide into 5-6cm (2-$2\frac{1}{2}$in) lengths. They can be kept in the refrigerator for up to 3 days. Brush with melted butter and grill, or poach for about 10 minutes in water to cover.

CHIPOLATAS AUX CHOUX NOUVEAUX
(Chipolata sausages with new cabbage)

This is a novel way of presenting the traditional combination of sausages and cabbage.

SERVES 4-6

20-24 chipolata sausages

60g (2oz) butter
---
about 30 cabbage leaves, preferably
from small new cabbages
---
salt and pepper

Melt half the butter in a frying pan and sauté the sausages for about 3 minutes or until brown but not yet cooked through.

Drop the cabbage leaves into a large pan of boiling salted water and boil, uncovered, until just tender, about 5 minutes for new cabbage and 10-15 minutes for older cabbage. Drain the leaves and dry them thoroughly. Season with salt and pepper. NOTE: a few more cabbage leaves than needed are cooked in case some of them tear.

Roll up each sausage in a cabbage leaf like a cigar and secure it with 2 cocktail sticks.

To finish: melt the remaining butter in a sauté pan and add the wrapped sausages. Cover with a buttered paper, top with a lid and heat gently for about 10 minutes or until the sausages are cooked through.

25
SAUTES
Don't drown in sauce

'Sauter' is one of those tantalising words that are untranslatable. When faced with the incongruities of 'leap the beef' or 'jumped potatoes', translators have given up looking for an equivalent and to sauté has entered the English cookery vocabulary intact. Appropriately so, for sautéing is a very French process, calling for just the right amount of oil or butter, a brisk but even heat in the pan, and the cook's total concentration. The resulting food, whether meat, fish, poultry or vegetables, should be golden brown and lightly crisp, and may – or may not – be cooked further. Sautéed food is never drained on paper towels but should be moist from the cooking fat. Confusion can arise because the French verb 'sauter' also means, simply, to fry.

The dish called a sauté is an extension of this method of cooking. A sauté is a kind of quick stew, where the meat (or poultry) is first sautéed in fat until partly done, then cooked rapidly with wine, stock, cream, tomatoes, water or a combination of them all, until the sauce reduces to the correct consistency. Sautés differ from stews in that only a small quantity of liquid is used, so that the food steams rather than simmers in the sauce. This calls for careful handling. Not until the invention (about 200 years ago) of the closed range with a flat, evenly heated top could the speed of cooking be controlled sufficiently to produce the essence of juices appropriate to a sauté, rather than the bath of liquid associated with a stew. 'Don't drown it in sauce!' is one of the perennial cries of the chefs at La Varenne, as impatient students tire of waiting for a sauce to reduce to the correct consistency. If the pan is covered, reduction will take longer.

Because of their fast cooking, sautés demand more luxurious ingredients than stews. Small chickens of $1\frac{1}{4}$-$1\frac{1}{2}$kg (or about $2\frac{1}{2}$-3lb) are ideal, as are duck, rabbit, pheasant and partridge (provided they are young and tender), firm fish like eel or monkfish and meats such as veal escalopes, chops and kidneys. With the exception of lamb cutlets and beef steak, most other cuts of lamb and beef take too long to cook to be suitable for a true sauté, and the so-called sautés of beef, such as boeuf chasseur, are really stews requiring a good deal of liquid.

Whatever the meat, it must be cut into medium, even-sized pieces that will cook together at the same speed. Chicken for a sauté is divided in a special way, a detail that makes poulet sauté Angevine one of the favourite examination dishes of the apprentices who take the official three-year training course for their Certificate d'aptitude professionelle, as it enables them to demonstrate their special skill. Then the meat or chicken is sautéed in clarified butter, or in butter with a dessertspoon or two of cooking oil added to raise the scorching point (butter alone burns at too low a temperature). For stronger-flavoured meats like pork or kidneys, you can, if you like, use dripping or lard.

Dark meats should be thoroughly browned, whereas chicken and the lighter meats should be golden or, when a white sauté is being made, simply 'stiffened' in the fat without browning. This distinction between brown and white is very French and evokes all kinds of comparisons with night and day, masculine and feminine, winter and summer. In cooking, red wine, brown stock and meat glaze count as 'brown' ingredients, while cream, white stock and white wine epitomise 'white' ones.

Once the meat for a sauté has been browned and is partly cooked (the exact timing depends on the individual recipe), liquid is added to deglaze the pan to a depth of about 6mm ($\frac{1}{4}$in). Then comes the garnish. A sauté is one of those splendid dishes in which anything goes. Sometimes the garnish is cooked together with the meat; more often it is sautéed separately and added towards the end of cooking so that the flavours have just time to blend. The choice is almost infinite. The chefs' eyes light up when there is a sauté on the menu because they can use up the leftover bits of this and that from the refrigerator: an onion or two, a few mushrooms, the odd tomato, a sliced courgette, some diced bacon – even shrimps may be added to the pan.

Of course, there are classic combinations like sauté of chicken chasseur, with mushrooms and shallots in a white wine tomato sauce, or veal chops paysanne with bacon, baby onions and diced potatoes. One of my own favourites is sauté of duck with Madeira, where the fat from the duck is thoroughly rendered before the bird is simmered in a rich wine and mushroom sauce. Then there is pheasant from the Auge valley in Normandy, famous for its Calvados and cream, and a sauté of rabbit with prunes. In La Varenne's rabbit recipe you will see that the sauce is thickened with a prune purée instead of flour, giving the lighter texture that is the hallmark of 'nouvelle

SAUTE DE POULET A L'INDIENNE
Chicken sauté, lightly flavoured with curry powder, ginger and saffron and served with boiled rice

cuisine'. More traditional methods of thickening sauces for sautés include sprinkling the meat with flour before browning, or adding kneaded butter (beurre manié) or arrowroot at the end of cooking. The aim is always the same – a light, highly concentrated sauce that scarcely coats the meat.

By varying the meat, cooking liquid or garnish, you can invent an almost infinite number of sauté dishes of your own. For example, rabbit sauté with prunes can be made with duck. If you replace the mushrooms in Escalopes de veau à la crème with lardons (strips) of bacon and flavour the sauce with mustard, you have a classic veal escalopes Dijonnaise. In fact the culinary Bible, Escoffier's 'Guide Culinaire', lists 65 variations on chicken sauté alone.

Perhaps the most famous chicken sauté of all is à la marengo, an implausible combination of chicken with tomatoes and mushrooms, garnished with croûtons and fried eggs and embellished with crayfish displayed in their shells 'en bellevue'. The dish was supposedly thought up by Napoleon's chef on the battlefield of Marengo, using ingredients on hand, but its studied virtuosity smacks to me of a Parisian kitchen. So indeed do all sautés. Quick, amusing, versatile, they give a touch of urban finesse to comfortable, country ingredients.

THE WAY TO SUCCESS

1 Choose a pan of the right size so that the meat fills the pan but each piece still touches the bottom.
2 Cook in very hot fat, so that the surface of the meat is 'seized', and forms a crust that retains the juices inside the meat.
3 Use just enough fat to circulate freely under the food; too much fat will give the effect of deep-frying.
4 *Discard all fat* (particularly with fatty meats like duck) before adding liquid to the pan.
5 For brown sautés, be sure the meat juices are thoroughly reduced and caramelised on the bottom of the pan before deglazing with liquid.
6 Traditionally, cooking is finished on top of the stove, but less attention is needed if a sauté is put in the steady heat of a moderate oven, 180C (350F) gas 4.

In this case, make sure the handle of your sauté pan will withstand the heat.
7 If a sauté starts to dry out before the meat is cooked, add a little more liquid and cover the pan. If, on the other hand, the meat is cooked before the sauce is properly reduced, transfer the meat to a dish to keep warm and boil the sauce down to the right consistency.

Getting ahead
1 Sautés can be made ahead and reheated, though some of their fresh flavour will be lost. Undercook both the meat and garnish slightly.
2 If freezing a sauté, increase the quantity of sauce so that the meat is covered when packed for freezing.

SAUTE DE POULET A L'INDIENNE

(Sauté of chicken in curry sauce)

SERVES 4
1½ tablespoons oil
1½ tablespoons butter
salt and freshly ground black pepper
1¼-1½kg (2½-3lb) roasting or spring chicken, cut in 6 pieces
1 onion, thinly sliced
clove garlic, crushed
level tablespoon flour
teaspoon curry powder, or to taste
¼ teaspoon ground ginger
pinch of Cayenne
300ml (½pt) chicken stock
pinch of saffron
250g (½lb) cooked peeled shrimps
for serving
boiled rice (see below)
chutney and grated fresh coconut (optional)

Heat the oil in a sauté pan and add the butter. Season the pieces of chicken and add to the hot fat, cut-side down, starting with the leg and thigh pieces because they take the longest time to cook. When they begin to brown, add the breast pieces. When all are brown, turn them over and brown on the other side for 2 minutes. Remove the chicken pieces from the pan.

Add the sliced onion and cook slowly until soft but not brown. Add the garlic, flour, curry powder, ginger and Cayenne and cook gently, stirring for 2 minutes. Return the chicken pieces to the pan. Add the stock, saffron and a little salt and cover and simmer for 20-25 minutes until the chicken is tender. Five minutes before the end of cooking, add the shrimps, stirring to mix them with the sauce.
For the boiled rice: bring 3 litres (5pts) of salted water to the boil in a large pan. A slice of lemon in the water will bleach the rice and add flavour. Add 250g (8oz) rice and boil for 10-12 minutes, stirring occasionally with a fork until the rice is tender but still resistant to the teeth. Do not overcook. When cooked, drain and rinse well with hot water.

Spoon the rice down one side of a serving dish and arrange the pieces of chicken down the other. Reduce the sauce if necessary to 5-6 tablespoons and taste it – it should be piquant but not overpowering. Spoon it over the chicken and serve.

The sauté can be prepared up to 3 days ahead and kept, covered, in the refrigerator, or it can be frozen.

In this case, reheat the thawed sauté on top of the stove. Reheat the rice on a buttered baking sheet in the oven and stir with a fork to fluff the grains. Finish as above.

Chutney and grated fresh coconut make good accompaniments.

TO CUT UP POULTRY IN EIGHT PIECES

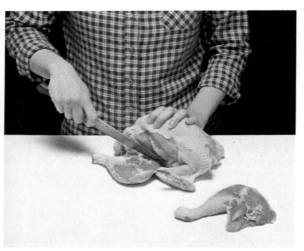

First, sever the skin between leg and breast. Cut, following the outline of the thigh, until a joint is visible

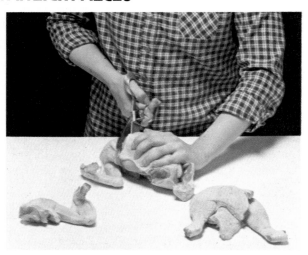

Cut the wings from the carcass with poultry shears or scissors. Be sure to include a piece of the breast with each

Cut away the backbone and ribs with poultry shears or scissors. Use in stock or to enhance flavour of the sauce

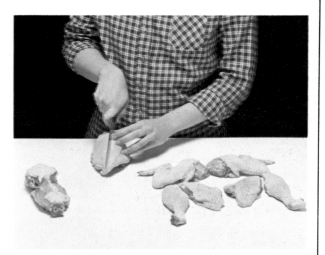

Cut the breast in two lengthwise. In the foreground are the backbone and ribs, the two wings and the divided legs

TO CUT UP POULTRY FOR A SAUTE

The bird for a sauté should be cut into 4, 6 or 8 pieces, according to its size.

1 Using a heavy knife, chop off the feet, leaving the drumstick knuckle attached to the leg bone.

2 With a sharp knife, sever the skin between leg and breast. Continue cutting through the skin, following the outline of the thigh, until the joint attaching the thigh to the carcass is visible. Use the knife to locate the oyster meat, which lies against the carcass, and cut around it in a half circle so that it remains attached to the thigh meat.

3 Holding the body with one hand, gently but firmly pull on the leg and thigh with the other, to break the joint. Pull the leg away from the body, cutting the meat, including the oyster, away from the carcass. Repeat with the other leg.

4 If cutting the bird into four, cut away the backbone and ribs with poultry shears or scissors. These can be used to make stock or sautéed with the other pieces to give the sauce more flavour. Divide the breast section in two by cutting lengthwise through the breastbone.

5 If cutting the bird into six or eight, cut off each wing together with a small portion of the breast meat. Cut away the backbone and ribs. Cut the breast section in two lengthwise.

6 If cutting in eight, cut the leg pieces in half, using the white line of fat on the underside as a guide to the position of the joint.

7 After cooking, trim the drumstick knuckles with poultry shears or scissors.

SAUTE DE CANARD AU MADERE
(Sauté of duck in Madeira)

This classic dish is especially useful if you want to serve duck without the last-minute fuss of carving.

SERVES 4

large duck of 2-2½kg (4-5lb)
tablespoon oil
1 onion, chopped
level tablespoon flour
150ml (¼pt) red wine
200ml (⅓pt) chicken or duck stock
bouquet garni
2 shallots, chopped
clove garlic, crushed
salt and freshly ground black pepper
125g (¼lb) mushrooms, thinly sliced
3 tablespoons Madeira
tablespoon chopped parsley (for garnish)
for croûtons
4 tablespoons oil and butter (for frying)
3 slices bread, crusts removed, cut in triangles

Cut the duck in quarters, discarding the backbone. Heat the oil in a sauté pan and sauté the pieces of duck, cut-size down, for 1-2 minutes to seal in the juices. Turn over and cook, skin-side down, for 15-20 minutes, or until well browned and all the fat has been extracted. NOTE: the duck must be sautéed thoroughly or the finished dish will be greasy.

Remove the duck and pour off all but 2 tablespoons of fat from the pan. Add the onion, cook slowly until lightly browned, then stir in the flour and cook, stirring, until browned. Add the wine, 150ml (¼pt) stock, bouquet garni, shallots, garlic, and salt and pepper. Return the duck to the pan, cover and simmer for 15-20 minutes, or until the duck is tender, adding more stock if the sauce gets too thick.

Remove the duck and trim the leg and knuckle bones with scissors. Strain the sauce into another pan, skim off any fat, add the mushrooms and Madeira and simmer for 2-3 minutes. Return the duck to the sauce and taste for seasoning. The duck can be cooked up to 48 hours ahead; keep it in the sauce, covered, in the refrigerator, or freeze it.
For the croûtons: heat the oil and butter in a frying pan, add the triangles of bread and fry until golden brown on both sides. Drain well on paper towels. The croûtons can be made 3-4 hours ahead and kept at room temperature.

To finish: reheat the duck in its sauce on top of the stove, if necessary. Arrange the pieces of duck on a platter, spoon the mushrooms and sauce over them and place the croûtons round the edge of the dish. Sprinkle with parsley and serve.

SAUTE DE FAISAN VALLEE D'AUGE
(Pheasant sauté Vallée d'Auge)

SERVES 4

young pheasant
tablespoon oil
tablespoon butter
2 medium onions, sliced
2 tart apples, pared, cored and sliced
2 tablespoons Calvados
450ml (¾pt) chicken or pheasant stock
bouquet garni
salt and freshly ground pepper
150ml (¼pt) double cream
for the garnish
2 tart apples
30g (1oz) butter
tablespoon sugar

Cut the pheasant into 4: 2 leg pieces and 2 breast pieces, reserving back, neck and wing pinions for stock.

Heat the oil and the butter in a sauté pan or shallow casserole and brown the pheasant pieces on all sides. Remove them and discard all but 1 tablespoon of fat. Put the onions in the pan and cook slowly until softened. Add the sliced apples and continue cooking over fairly high heat until the apples and onions are lightly browned. Return the pheasant to the pan, pour over the Calvados and flame. Add the stock, bouquet garni, salt and pepper and bring to the boil. Cover and simmer for about 30 minutes or until the pheasant is tender. The sauté can be prepared up to 3 days ahead and kept covered in the refrigerator, or it can be frozen.
For the garnish: peel and quarter the apples. Heat the butter in a frying pan, add the apples and sauté over high heat, tossing often, for 4-5 minutes or until lightly browned. Sprinkle with the sugar and continue to sauté for 4-5 minutes more or until the apples are tender and the sugar is lightly caramelised.

To finish: if necessary, reheat the pheasant in the sauce on top of the stove. Remove the pheasant pieces from the sauce, arrange them on a serving dish and keep warm. Strain the sauce into another pan, pressing hard to purée the apples and onions. Skim off as much fat from the sauce as possible, bring back to the boil and reduce if necessary to a coating consistency. Add the cream, bring just back to the boil and taste for seasoning. Spoon the sauce over the pheasant and garnish the dish with the caramelised apple quarters.

POUSSINS SAUTE SUR SON COULIS D'OIGNONS ET SCAROLE
(Sautéed baby chickens with onion and cos lettuce)

SERVES 4

4 baby chickens, each weighing 400g (13oz); or 1.5kg (3lb) chicken breasts
salt and pepper
⅛ teaspoon ground ginger
tablespoon oil
50g (1½oz) butter
4 onions, thinly sliced
4 heads cos lettuce

Remove the backbone by cutting along either side with kitchen scissors. Split each chicken in two at the breastbone and flatten the halves with a cleaver.

Season the chicken with salt, pepper and ginger. Heat the oil and butter in a sauté pan, add the chicken pieces and sauté them over high heat for 5-6 minutes or until browned. NOTE: use a second pan and more butter and oil if necessary. Remove the chicken pieces and put in the sliced onions and season with salt and pepper. Cook slowly, stirring occasionally, for 7-10 minutes or until they are soft but not brown.

Trim the stems of the lettuce; wash and drain well. Cut each in four. Add the pieces to the pan and cook with the onions for about 5 minutes or until softened. Return the chicken to the pan on top of the vegetables, and cook for about 15 minutes or until tender.

To serve: arrange the onions and greens on a serving dish and the chicken on top.

SAUTE DE LAPIN AUX PRUNEAUX

(Rabbit sauté with prunes)

Rabbit with prunes is a favourite country dish, from Picardy in the north to the Loire Valley.

SERVES 4

rabbit, skinned
250g (½lb) prunes
tablespoon oil
tablespoon butter
teaspoon vinegar
300ml (½pt) red wine
300ml (½pt) veal or chicken stock
clove garlic, crushed
bouquet garni
salt and freshly ground black pepper
tablespoon chopped parsley
for the marinade
150ml (¼pt) red wine
large bouquet garni
1 onion, coarsely chopped
1 carrot, coarsely chopped
6 peppercorns, slightly crushed
tablespoon oil

To cut up the rabbit: trim away any flaps of skin, excess bone and the tips of the forelegs. Using a heavy knife or cleaver, separate the legs from the body and cut off the upper section of the rabbit. Chop this in two to separate the forelegs. Cut across the back into two pieces.

To marinate the rabbit: put the six pieces in a bowl (not aluminium) and add the wine, bouquet garni, onion, carrot and peppercorns. Pour the oil on top. Cover and leave at room temperature, turning occasionally, for 4-12 hours. Alternatively, the rabbit can be marinated in the refrigerator for 1-2 days. Pour boiling water or tea over the prunes and leave to soak for 1-2 hours.

To cook the rabbit: drain the pieces and pat dry with paper towels. Strain the marinade and reserve the vegetables and liquid. Heat the oil and butter in a sauté pan or shallow casserole and brown the rabbit pieces on all sides. Remove from the pan, add the onion and carrot from the marinade and sauté lightly until they soften. Add the vinegar, the liquid from the marinade and the red wine and bring to a boil. Add the stock, garlic, bouquet garni and seasoning. Replace the rabbit pieces. Drain the prunes, add to the

pan, cover and simmer for 35-45 minutes, or until the rabbit is tender.

Remove the rabbit pieces and prunes and strain the sauce into another pan. Skim off as much fat from the sauce as possible. Stone and purée one-third of the prunes in a blender or food processor; alternatively, push them through a sieve. Reheat the sauce and whisk in the prune purée. If necessary, boil to reduce the sauce to a thin coating consistency. Taste for seasoning. The rabbit can be cooked up to 3 days ahead and kept covered in the refrigerator, or it can be frozen. In this case, reheat it on top of the stove in its sauce.

To serve: transfer the rabbit to a serving dish and spoon over the prunes. Spoon the sauce over the rabbit and sprinkle with parsley just before serving.

ESCALOPES DE VEAU A LA CREME

(Veal escalopes in cream sauce)

Veal chops can be prepared in the same way, but they should be cooked for 5 minutes on each side.

SERVES 4

700g (1½lb) veal escalopes
75g (2½oz) flour, seasoned with ½ teaspoon salt and ¼ teaspoon pepper
60-75g (2-2½oz) clarified butter
150ml (¼pt) white wine
150ml (¼pt) veal stock
250g (½lb) mushrooms, thinly sliced
150ml (¼pt) double cream
salt and freshly ground pepper
tablespoon chopped parsley

Flatten the escalopes to 6mm (¼in) thickness by beating them between sheets of greaseproof paper with a rolling pin.

Coat the escalopes with seasoned flour, patting them to remove the excess. Melt 50g (1½oz) of the butter in a sauté pan and sauté several escalopes over medium heat until browned, allowing 2-3 minutes on each side. Take out, arrange them, overlapping, on a serving dish and keep warm. Sauté the remaining escalopes in the same way, adding more butter if necessary, then arrange them with the others.

Deglaze the pan by adding the wine and stock and bringing to the

boil. Add the mushrooms and simmer until they are tender and the sauce is well reduced and slightly thickened. Add the cream, bring just to the boil, taste for seasoning and spoon the sauce over the escalopes. Sprinkle with parsley and serve.

The escalopes can be cooked up to 48 hours ahead and kept in the sauce in a refrigerator. They can also be frozen. In this case, reheat the thawed escalopes in the sauce over medium heat. Make sure that the escalopes are thoroughly heated through, but take care not to overcook them.

ROGNONS SAUTES AU MADERE

(Sautéed kidneys with Madeira)

Crisp fried potatoes are the perfect complement for these kidneys with Madeira.

SERVES 4

3-4 veal kidneys; or 4-6 lamb kidneys weighing about 750g (1½lb)
tablespoon oil
15g (½oz) butter
15g (½oz) flour
3 tablespoons Madeira or Port
200ml (⅓pt) veal stock
30g (1oz) butter (to finish)
tablespoon chopped parsley (for sprinkling)

Skin the kidneys if necessary and cut out the cores with kitchen scissors. Cut veal kidneys in thick slices or halve lamb kidneys.

Heat the oil and the 15g (½oz) butter in a sauté pan until foaming. Put in the kidneys and cook quickly for 2-3 minutes, turning them so that they brown on all sides. Drain off all but a tablespoon of fat, sprinkle in the flour and toss so that the kidneys are coated. Pour in the Madeira or Port and flame. Add the stock and bring to a boil, stirring.

Taste for seasoning and adjust if necessary. Simmer for 4-5 minutes or until the kidneys are cooked but still just pink in the centre. Take from the heat and add the remaining butter in small pieces, shaking the pan so the butter is incorporated. Taste the sauce again for seasoning, transfer the kidneys to a serving dish, sprinkle with parsley and serve.

26
SOUFFLES
Increasing the volume; exploding the myths

What is a soufflé? A great many things. Technically speaking, a soufflé is a highly flavoured sauce or purée mixed with stiffly whipped egg whites, which expand and puff in a hot oven. But any soufflé has charisma. It is just about my favourite dish to cook and to serve. The risk involved is amply rewarded by applause, making a soufflé the perfect opening or ending to an outstanding meal.

Tricky it may be, but there is no mystery to the making of a good soufflé. Three points are crucial: the consistency of the basic mixture, the process of beating the egg whites, and the technique for folding them in so as to retain maximum volume and lightness.

For savoury soufflés the base is usually a béchamel, cream or velouté sauce combined with whatever flavouring is chosen, although unthickened fish or vegetable purées can be used alone. Egg yolks are nearly always added for richness, but for extra-light diet soufflés they may be omitted. Most dessert soufflés are based on pastry cream (crème pâtissiere), which can be thought of as a sort of sweet béchamel sauce, again combined with any one of a variety of ingredients.

Best known of the soufflé bases are those flavoured with cheese, chocolate and Grand Marnier, but they are only the beginning of the repertoire. You'll find seafood soufflés in Brittany, chicken soufflés in the region of Bresse, Kirsch soufflé in Alsace and apple soufflé with Calvados in Normandy. Soufflés can also add a touch of elegance to mundane leftovers such as chopped ham or sweetbreads and are absolutely regal with yesterday's lobster or smoked salmon. You make scanty ingredients go further, add a 'surprise' of poached or soft-cooked eggs or, for a sweet soufflé, boudoir biscuits, or diced fruit macerated in liqueur.

Whatever its composition, the basic mixture should be soft enough so that it falls easily from a spoon; if it is too thin, the egg whites will be difficult to fold in, but if it is too thick the soufflé will be sodden. Of course, comparatively thick soufflés such as those including a vegetable purée never rise as much as light ones like cheese soufflés.

As with sauces, there is now a crusade for dispensing with flour in soufflé bases. But flourless soufflés are nothing new. Certain basic mixtures such as those for potato or chocolate soufflés do not need flour as a thickener. Some of the finest sweet soufflés are based on confiture russe – fresh fruit purées beaten for half an hour or more with sugar so that the mixture 'cooks'

slightly but retains its fresh flavour. My own favourite non-flour soufflé is one based on lemon curd (Soufflé chaud au citron). However, most attempts to bind heavy, moist ingredients like vegetables without using flour are doomed to disappoint.

Turning now to the egg whites, one-third to two-thirds more egg whites than yolks should be added to a soufflé to ensure lightness; the volume of beaten egg whites should be at least double that of the basic mixture. Egg whites are best beaten in a copper cowl with a balloon whisk. Aluminium or stainless steel bowls are passable alternatives to copper, but volume is lost in glass or pottery bowls as egg whites will not cling to these materials. Nor does an egg whisk or hand electric beater give as good a result as a bicep-building wire balloon whisk – a beater merely sits in the bottom of the bowl and less air is incorporated into the mixture.

When the egg whites have been whisked until stiff, it is vital for the success of a sweet soufflé to 'meringue' them: add a tablespoon of sugar to every three or four egg whites and continue beating for half a minute until the whites are glossy; this makes them much firmer and easier to fold.

For savoury soufflés, many cooks recommend adding a pinch of salt or cream of tartar just before the end of beating.

Given a good soufflé base, whether savoury or sweet, and stiffly whipped whites, the last essential ingredient for success is combining the two as lightly as possible. Heat the base mixture until hot but not scalding to the touch. Off the heat, add about a quarter of the whipped whites and stir lightly but thoroughly; the heat of the mixture will cook the whites so that they become firm. Tip this mixture into the whipped whites still in the mixing bowl, gently fold them in and turn the mixture into a buttered soufflé dish.

SOUFFLE AU GRAND MARNIER

*One of the most celebrated and delicious of
the classic French soufflés, flavoured
with the famous orange liqueur and decorated
with segments of orange*

SOUFFLES AU GINGEMBRE

*These individual soufflés make a change from the
traditional manner of serving and they
are just as simple to make. They are flavoured with
powdered ginger and candied ginger (left).
They can be sprinkled with icing sugar before serving*

The chefs at La Varenne never bother using a paper collar to support the rising soufflé, and after working with them for three years neither do I. When the dish has been thoroughly buttered and the soufflé mixture is appropriately stiff, it rises without any spills.

A hot soufflé, by the way, is not to be confused with the cold version, which is not a true soufflé at all but a fluffy mousse mixture that is set with gelatine and needs a high collar round the outside of the dish; when the collar is removed, the mixture looks as if it has puffed, like a true soufflé.

Besides the superfluity of a collar for a hot soufflé, another hint I have learnt is that a soufflé *can* wait before baking. At La Varenne it is standard practice to keep a soufflé for an hour or two in the refrigerator, then bake it at the last moment, and a wait of three or four hours is not uncommon. Although longer waits are not recommended, one memorable day a trainee left a flourless chocolate soufflé (one of the most delicate) in the refrigerator for 36 hours. Not wanting to waste it, she put it in the oven; it rose without a tremor.

The importance of a certain oven heat is another soufflé myth: a good mixture will rise at almost any temperature. The French like to cook soufflés fast, at 200C (400F) gas 6 or 220C (425F) gas 7, so they rise quickly and stay soft in the centre yet are crisp and brown on the outside. In an oven at 180C (350F) gas 4, a soufflé takes longer to cook (the exact time depends on the size and shape of the dish) and will be firm right through – a good method for heavier soufflés based on vegetable and fish purées. Nor will anything disastrous happen if you open the oven door during baking to turn the soufflé round so that it cooks evenly. But do avoid draughts.

When ready, a soufflé should be brown and should have increased by half or two-thirds in volume and risen above the rim of the dish. Shake it gently – if it quakes all over, it is not done; if it still wobbles in the middle, it is done to the French taste. However, if you prefer a firm soufflé, continue cooking for 2-3 minutes. Never overbake a soufflé. When left in the oven too long, a soufflé will deflate and turn into a tough, dry pancake.

Set the dish on a plate at once and rush it to the table with steady hand – at this point a soufflé waits for no one. It should be served with two spoons, breaking the crust and scooping into the centre so each person has some of the soft centre and a section of the firmer outside.

So those are the rules, to be followed the first time, then adapted according to experience. And if a soufflé doesn't rise as high as your hopes, don't despair. Even a failed soufflé is very edible – if savoury, call it a savoury mould; if sweet – call it, quite simply, a pudding.

THE WAY TO SUCCESS

Whisking egg whites

Egg whites whisked for soufflés or meringues in a copper bowl with a balloon whisk acquire a greater volume and denser texture than those whipped using any other equipment. Bowls of other metals and a balloon whisk or a heavy duty electric beater are the next best choices.

1 Clean the inside of a copper bowl by rubbing the surface with 1-2 tablespoons salt and 1-2 tablespoons vinegar, or use salt rubbed on with the cut surface of a lemon. Rinse and dry thoroughly. The copper will be shining and almost pink in colour. The bowl can be cleaned 1-2 hours ahead but not more, and *it must be cleaned every time it is used.*

2 Add the egg whites; they should be at room temperature.

3 To whip properly, the egg whites must be completely free of any trace of yolk, and the bowl and whisk must be equally free of water and grease.

4 With a large balloon whisk, start beating the egg whites slowly, working at first in the bottom of the bowl and then lifting the whisk high in a circle to beat in as much air as possible. As the whites break up and become frothy, increase the size of the circles until you are using the whole bowl area and whisking as fast as possible, still lifting the whisk high out of the bowl in a circle.

5 When the egg whites are quite stiff, change the motion by whisking in large circles as fast as possible with the whisk always down in the egg whites and in contact with the bowl. This stiffens and 'tightens' the whites rather than beating air into them. For sweet soufflés, reserve a little of the sugar to add when tightening the whites.

6 Continue beating 1-2 minutes until the egg whites form a shallow peak when the whisk is lifted. They should be smooth and so stiff that they would not fall out if the bowl were turned upside down.

7 If beating egg whites in a machine, start beating slowly and only gradually increase the speed. Do not overbeat them or they will 'grain' and separate into dry and lumpy particles.

Folding egg whites into other light mixtures

Folding two mixtures together lightly is a knack that is good to have, but takes practice to develop; it is an important technique in making cakes and desserts as well as soufflés.

1 Mixtures blend more easily if their consistency is similar.

2 With a spoon or rubber spatula, cut down into the centre, scoop under the mixture and turn bottom to top in a rolling motion. Proceed in this fashion, working clockwise. With the other hand, turn the bowl in the opposite direction, anti-clockwise.

3 Continue folding only until the mixture is blended; if it shows signs of going liquid (as with egg whites) or curdling (as with whipped cream), stop at once. Better a few patches of unmixed egg whites or cream than a heavy mixture.

Soufflés

1 Have everything prepared for baking and serving: arrange the oven shelf so there is plenty of room for the soufflé to rise without catching on the roof of the oven. Preheat the oven. Butter the soufflé dish; if using ramekins, place them on a baking sheet so they can be moved in and out of the oven easily. Have ready your serving tray and spoons.

2 For all soufflés, spread the dish, and especially the rim, generously with butter so that the mixture slips easily up the sides. You may coat inside the buttered dish with breadcrumbs for savoury soufflés or with sugar for sweet soufflés.

3 To be sure that the soufflé will rise well above the dish, the uncooked mixture should fill the dish to within 6mm (½in) of the rim.

4 If you want the soufflé to form a central 'top hat' as it bakes, trace a circle with a knife on the surface of the unbaked mixture near the edge.

5 Do not bake anything else in the oven at the same time as a soufflé.

6 You can open the oven during baking but avoid cold draughts. Never remove a soufflé from the oven during baking.

7 Remember that soufflés that are cooked for a relatively short time in a hot oven will sink more quickly when removed from the oven than those that are cooked more slowly at a lower temperature.

Getting ahead

'A soufflé can be awaited, but it must never wait.' Although this has long been considered the golden rule of the soufflé, I would amend the second half to, '. . . but once cooked it must never wait.' And with preparation done ahead, you needn't keep guests waiting either.

1 The base mixture for all soufflés can be prepared several hours or even a day ahead and kept in the refrigerator. Cover it tightly by pressing transparent plastic wrap on the surface.

2 Although it is preferable to beat the egg whites and fold them into the base mixture just before baking the soufflé, if they are very stiffly beaten they can be folded into the base mixture up to 2 hours ahead. Put the mixture in the soufflé dish and keep, covered, in the refrigerator until ready to bake.

3 A baked soufflé must be served at once. If a five-minute wait is unavoidable, open the oven door and leave the heat on. The outer side of the soufflé will shrivel, but the inner side will stay puffed. After a few minutes in the oven, turn the soufflé halfway round so that the fallen side faces the heat. This procedure is recommended only for a dire emergency.

MAKING A SOUFFLE

It is better to beat egg whites in a copper bowl with a wire whisk to achieve greater volume and lightness by incorporating as much air as possible. Use a circular motion and lift the whisk well out of the whites each time

When folding the beaten egg whites into a heavier mixture such as the basic sauce, cut down the centre. Scoop under the mixture, turning bottom to top with a rolling motion. Scoop one way, turning the bowl the other

When the egg whites are folded into the basic mixture, turn the uncooked soufflé into its dish and carefully smooth over the top with a metal spatula. Then trace a circle with a knife not far from the edge

SOUFFLE DE POISSON, SAUCE CURRY
(Fish soufflé with curry sauce)

This soufflé has a closer texture than the usual French soufflé and is cooked in a lower oven for a longer time so it is fairly firm in the centre. The curry sauce provides a spicy contrast in flavour.

SERVES 4

2 tablespoons browned breadcrumbs (for preparing the dish)
thick béchamel sauce (page 192) made with 150ml ($\frac{1}{4}$pt) milk, slice of onion, bay leaf, 6 peppercorns, 45g (1$\frac{1}{2}$oz) butter, 2 shallots, finely chopped and 30g (1oz) flour
350g ($\frac{3}{4}$lb) cooked, flaked fish (salmon, cod, smoked haddock)
4 tablespoons double cream
pinch of dry mustard
salt and pepper
4 egg yolks
6 egg whites
for the curry sauce
30g (1oz) butter
2 shallots, finely chopped
2-3 teaspoons curry powder
30g (1oz) flour
300ml ($\frac{1}{2}$pt) milk, infused with slice of onion, pinch of nutmeg, bay leaf and 5 peppercorns
salt and pepper
4 tablespoons double cream
1.5 litre (2$\frac{1}{2}$pt) capacity soufflé dish

Butter the inside of the soufflé dish well and sprinkle with browned breadcrumbs. Infuse the given quantities of milk for both the soufflé and sauce: scald the milk by bringing it just to the boil, add the onion, nutmeg, bay leaf and peppercorns, leave over very low heat for 5-10 minutes, then strain.

Make the béchamel sauce, sautéing the shallots in the butter before adding the flour. Stir in the fish and cream with dry mustard, salt and pepper to taste – the mixture should be highly seasoned. Take from the heat and beat the egg yolks into the hot mixture so it thickens. The soufflé can be prepared 3-4 hours ahead up to this point. Rub the surface of the fish mixture with butter or place a layer of greaseproof paper over it to prevent a skin forming.

For the curry sauce: melt the butter in a saucepan, add the shallots and curry powder and cook gently, stirring occasionally, for 3-4 minutes. Stir in the flour, cook until foaming, then add the infused milk. Bring to the boil, stirring, add salt and pepper and simmer for 2 minutes. Taste the sauce for seasoning and rub the surface with butter to prevent a skin forming. The sauce can also be prepared 3-4 hours ahead.

To finish the soufflé: set the oven at moderately hot 190C (375F) gas 5. Whip the egg whites until stiff, if possible using a copper bowl. Gently heat the fish mixture until hot to the touch. Add about a quarter of the egg whites and stir until well mixed. Add this to the remaining egg whites and fold together as lightly as possible. Pour this mixture into the prepared soufflé dish, smooth the surface and bake in the heated oven for 20-25 minutes or until the soufflé is puffed and brown. Meanwhile, heat through the curry sauce, stir in the cream and taste for seasoning.

Serve the soufflé at once, with the sauce in a separate dish.

SOUFFLE AU FROMAGE
(Cheese soufflé)

The best cheese for a soufflé is a mixture of Parmesan and Gruyère, but dry, sharp Cheddar can also be used. If you have too much mixture for your soufflé dish, bake the remainder in buttered ramekins for 6-8 minutes.

SERVES 4

2 tablespoons browned breadcrumbs (optional)
thick béchamel sauce (page 192) made with 45g (1$\frac{1}{2}$oz) butter, 30g (1oz) flour, 300ml ($\frac{1}{2}$pt) milk, slice of onion, salt and freshly ground pepper and a pinch of grated nutmeg
teaspoon prepared mustard or $\frac{1}{4}$ teaspoon dry mustard
4 egg yolks
75g (2$\frac{1}{2}$oz) grated cheese
6 egg whites
tablespoon grated cheese
1.25 litre (2$\frac{1}{4}$pt) capacity soufflé dish

Butter the soufflé dish well; sprinkle with the breadcrumbs.

Make the béchamel sauce. Take the pan from the heat, stir in the mustard and beat the egg yolks into the hot sauce so it thickens. Let it cool slightly, stir in the grated cheese and taste for seasoning. The mixture should be highly seasoned.

The soufflé can be prepared 3-4 hours ahead up to this point. Rub the surface of the cheese mixture with butter or cover with dampened greaseproof paper.

To finish the soufflé: set the oven at very hot, 220C (425F) gas 7. Whip the egg whites until stiff, if possible using a copper bowl. Heat the cheese mixture until it is hot to the touch. NOTE: do not heat it too much or the cheese will cook into strings. Add about a quarter of the egg whites and stir until well mixed. Add this mixture to the remaining egg whites and fold together as lightly as possible. Pour the mixture into the prepared soufflé dish and smooth the surface. Sprinkle with the tablespoon of cheese and bake in the heated oven for 12-15 minutes or until the soufflé is puffed and brown.

SOUFFLE AU FROMAGE EN SURPRISE
(Cheese soufflé surprise)

Follow the above recipe for cheese soufflé and, at the same time as preparing the basic cheese mixture, simmer 4 eggs in water for 6-7 minutes, drain, cover with cold water and leave to cool. Prepare a 1.5 litre (2$\frac{1}{2}$pt) soufflé dish or 4 individual dishes of 375ml ($\frac{5}{8}$pt).

To finish: carefully peel the eggs and immerse them in hot water. Whip the egg whites and finish the cheese soufflé mixture. Put a little in the dish, add the eggs (or put a single egg in each individual dish) and add the remaining mixture. Finish and bake as above – ramekins for 8-10 minutes.

SOUFFLE AUX EPINARDS
(Spinach soufflé)

SERVES 4

3 tablespoons browned breadcrumbs
350g (¾lb) fresh or equivalent of frozen leaf spinach
30g (1oz) butter
thick béchamel sauce (page 192) made with 30g (1oz) butter, 20g (2 level tablespoons) flour, 150ml (¼pt) milk, 150ml (¼pt) double cream, pinch of grated nutmeg and salt and freshly ground pepper
4 egg yolks
6 egg whites
4 level tablespoons grated Parmesan or Gruyère cheese
1.5 litre (2½pt) capacity soufflé dish

Butter the inside of the soufflé dish well and sprinkle it with 2 tablespoons of the breadcrumbs. Wash the spinach thoroughly, discarding the stems, and cook it in boiling salted water for 2-3 minutes, or until tender. Drain the spinach, refresh by rinsing with cold water, and drain thoroughly. Squeeze handfuls of the spinach to extract all the liquid, then finely chop or work it to a purée in an electric food mill. Thaw frozen spinach according to the directions on the packet. Melt the butter in the pan and cook the spinach, stirring until dry.

Make the béchamel sauce. Stir in the spinach and heat thoroughly. Take the pan from the heat and beat the egg yolks into the hot mixture so it thickens. Taste for seasoning – the mixture should be highly seasoned. The soufflé can be prepared up to this point 3-4 hours ahead. Cover the surface of the spinach mixture with dampened non-stick vegetable parchment, or dab with butter to prevent a skin from forming.

To finish the soufflé: set the oven at very hot, 220C (425F) gas 7. Whip the egg whites until stiff, if possible using a copper bowl. Heat the spinach mixture until it is hot to the touch. Remove from the heat, add about a quarter of the egg whites and stir in until well mixed. Add this and 3 tablespoons of the cheese to the remaining egg whites and fold them together as lightly as possible.

Pour the mixture into the pre-pared soufflé dish and sprinkle with a mixture of the remaining breadcrumbs and grated cheese. Bake in the heated oven 12-15 minutes, or until the soufflé is puffed and brown.

Serve at once.

SOUFFLE AUX AUBERGINES
(Aubergine soufflé)

Salt draws juices from the flesh of vegetables – a process called 'dégorger' in French. For aubergines this not only gets rid of excess moisture but of bitterness as well.

SERVES 4

2 medium aubergines each weighing about 375g (¾lb)
2 tablespoons butter
2 tablespoons oil
thick béchamel sauce (page 192) made with 250ml (⅜pt) milk, slice of onion, bay leaf, 6 peppercorns, 30g (1oz) butter, 30g (1oz) flour, salt, pepper and a pinch of nutmeg
4 egg yolks
30g (1oz) grated Parmesan cheese
salt and white pepper
6 egg whites
tablespoon grated Parmesan cheese mixed with 1 tablespoon toasted breadcrumbs (for sprinkling)
1 litre (1¾pt) capacity soufflé dish

Butter the soufflé dish and, if you like, sprinkle it inside with browned breadcrumbs.

Wipe the aubergines, trim their stems and cut them in half lengthwise. Run the point of a knife around the inside of the skin and score the flesh. Sprinkle them with salt and leave for 30 minutes to drain. Rinse the aubergines with cold water and dry them well on paper towels. Heat the butter and oil in a frying pan and fry the aubergines, cut side down, until brown. Transfer them to a moderately hot oven, 190C (375F) gas 5, and bake for 10-15 minutes or until they are tender. Allow them to cool slightly and then scoop out and chop the flesh.

Make the béchamel sauce and stir in the aubergine purée. Beat in the egg yolks one by one and cook the mixture over low heat, stirring, until it thickens slightly. Take from the heat, stir in the 30g (1oz) grated cheese and taste – the mixture should be highly seasoned. The soufflé can be prepared up to this point 3-4 hours ahead. Cover the surface of the aubergine mixture with wet greaseproof paper or rub it with butter to prevent a skin from forming.

To finish the soufflé: set the oven at very hot, 220C (425F) gas 7. Beat the egg whites until stiff, if possible using a copper bowl. Heat the aubergine mixture until it is hot to the touch. NOTE: be careful not to heat it too much or the cheese will cook into strings. Add about a quarter of the egg whites and stir until well mixed. Add this to the remaining egg whites and fold together as lightly as possible. Pour the mixture into the prepared soufflé dish, sprinkle with the cheese and breadcrumb mixture and bake in the heated oven for 15-18 minutes or until the soufflé is puffed and brown. Serve at once.

SOUFFLE DISHES

Originally, soufflés were cooked in pastry cases that had the same straight sides as today's dish; the pastry was not eaten. The classic soufflé dish is made of white, ovenproof porcelain with straight sides ribbed on the outside, but nowadays glass, earthenware and metal are also used. They come in several sizes, the smallest individual ones being called ramekins.

Soufflé dishes are available in many diameters, and it is the capacity or volume measure which is important. As a guide, a 1.25 litre (2pt) soufflé dish is just right for a 5-egg-white mixture. For individual soufflés, 150ml (¼pt) porcelain ramekins are a useful size. Both ramekins and soufflé dishes are useful for baking other mixtures such as Crème caramel (Chapter 29) and preparing cold and iced soufflés (Chapter 9).

If a soufflé dish is not available, a charlotte mould or any deep, heatproof dish can be used instead. The handles on a charlotte mould make it easy to transport from oven to table, but because the mould is deeper than a soufflé dish, there is greater risk of collapse.

SOUFFLE AU CRABE

(Crab soufflé)

A soufflé is an ideal way of stretching expensive crab meat. This same recipe could also be used with lobster.

SERVES 4

2 tablespoons toasted breadcrumbs

béchamel sauce (page 192) made with 250ml (8oz) milk, slice of onion, bay leaf, 6 peppercorns, 45g (1½oz) butter, 2 finely chopped shallots and 25g (1oz) flour

25ml (1oz) sherry or white wine

½ teaspoon paprika

75ml (2½oz) double cream

pinch of Cayenne

salt and pepper

4 egg yolks

250g (8oz) crab meat, flaked

6 egg whites

30g (1oz) grated Parmesan cheese (optional)

1.5 litre (2½pt) capacity soufflé dish

Butter the soufflé dish generously and sprinkle it with the breadcrumbs. Make the béchamel sauce, cooking the shallots in the butter before adding the flour. Stir in the sherry or wine, paprika and cream, season with Cayenne, salt and pepper and simmer for 2 minutes. Take from the heat and beat the egg yolks into the hot mixture so that it thickens. Add the crab meat and taste; it should be highly seasoned. The soufflé can be prepared 3-4 hours ahead up to this point. Cover the surface of the crab mixture with wet greaseproof paper to prevent a skin from forming.

To finish the soufflé: set the oven at very hot, 220C (425F) gas 7. Beat the egg whites until stiff, if possible in a copper bowl. Heat the crab mixture until it is hot to the touch. Add the cheese, if included, and about a quarter of the egg whites. Stir until well mixed. Add the mixture to the remaining egg whites and fold together as lightly as possible. Pour the mixture into the prepared soufflé dish and bake in the heated oven for 12-15 minutes or until the soufflé is puffed and brown. Serve at once.

SOUFFLE AU GRAND MARNIER

(Grand Marnier soufflé)

You can use any favourite liqueur or eau de vie to flavour this soufflé; the name of the soufflé and its taste will change accordingly, but the texture will always be light and airy.

SERVES 4

thick pastry cream (page 45) made with 300ml (½pt) milk, grated rind of 2 oranges, 3 egg yolks, 60g (2oz) sugar and 30g (1oz) flour

orange segments (see below)

3-4 tablespoons Grand Marnier

5 egg whites

icing sugar (for sprinkling)

1.25 litre (2¼pt) capacity soufflé dish

Butter the soufflé dish, being especially careful to butter the rim generously to prevent the soufflé from sticking. Sprinkle the dish with sugar, discarding the excess.

For the soufflé base: make a thick pastry cream. Scald the milk by bringing it just to the boil. Grate the rind of the 2 oranges. Beat the egg yolks with the orange rind and half the sugar until thick and light, and stir in the flour. Whisk the boiling milk into the yolk mixture, blend well and return to the pan. Whisk over gentle heat until boiling and smooth.

Simmer, constantly, for about 2 minutes or until thickened, then take the pan from the heat, let the mixture cool slightly and stir in the Grand Marnier.

To prevent a skin from forming, rub the surface of the mixture with butter. The soufflé can be prepared

SERVING A SOUFFLE

The best way of serving a soufflé is to break the crust with two spoons and scoop well down into the centre

3-4 hours ahead up to this point.

For the decoration: using a serrated edged or paring knife, cut all the pith from one of the oranges. Then cut down between the segments to separate them, folding back the membrane between them like the leaves of a book.

Twenty to 30 minutes before serving: set the oven at very hot 220C (425F), gas 7. Whip the egg whites until stiff, preferably using a copper bowl. Add the remaining sugar and beat for 20 seconds longer or until glossy. Heat the Grand Marnier mixture until hot to the touch, take it from the heat and stir in about a quarter of the egg whites. Add this mixture to the remaining egg whites and fold them together as lightly as possible.

Spoon the mixture into the prepared dish, smooth the surface and quickly place the orange sections on top in a star pattern. Bake at once in the heated oven for 12-15 minutes or until the soufflé is puffed and brown.

Sprinkle it with icing sugar and serve at once.

SOUFFLE AU GINGEMBRE

(Ginger soufflé)

SERVES 4

thick pastry cream (page 45) made with 225ml (⅜pt) milk, 3 egg yolks, 75g (2½oz) sugar, 30g (1oz) flour

½ teaspoon powdered ginger

2 tablespoons candied ginger, chopped

4 egg whites

icing sugar (for sprinkling)

1 litre (1¾pt) capacity soufflé dish or 4 ramekins

Butter the soufflé dish, being especially careful to butter the rim well.

For the soufflé base: make a thick pastry cream. Simmer, whisking constantly, for about 2 minutes, or until the pastry cream has thickened. Stir in the powdered ginger and the chopped candied ginger. To prevent a skin from forming, rub the surface of the mixture with butter. The soufflé can be prepared 3-4 hours ahead up to here.

Twenty to 30 minutes before serving, set the oven at very hot 220C (425F) gas 7. Whip the egg whites until stiff, preferably using a copper bowl. Add the remaining sugar and beat for 20 seconds longer or until glossy. Heat the ginger mixture until hot to the touch, take away from the heat and stir in about a quarter of the egg whites. Add this mixture to the remaining egg whites and fold them together as lightly as possible. Spoon the mixture into the prepared dish or dishes, smooth the top and bake at once in the heated oven for 10-12 minutes (5-7 minutes for ramekins), or until the soufflé is puffed and brown. Sprinkle with icing sugar and serve at once.

SOUFFLE AUX POIRES FRAICHES
(Fresh pear soufflé)

An exceptionally light soufflé made without flour, milk or egg yolks.
SERVES 4

vanilla custard sauce (optional) page 81, made with 375ml (14oz) milk, vanilla pod, 5 egg yolks and 50g (1½oz) sugar
2 large or 3 medium ripe dessert pears, weighing about 500g (1lb)
juice of ½ lemon
25ml (1oz) pear liqueur or Kirsch
100g (3½oz) sugar, or to taste
5 egg whites
sugar (optional – for sprinkling)
1.25 litre (2¼pt) capacity soufflé dish

Make the vanilla custard sauce if using, pour it into a sauceboat and chill. Butter the soufflé dish and sprinkle it inside with sugar. Turn it over to dislodge any excess.

Not more than 2 hours before serving, make the pear purée. Peel and core the pears and purée them in a food mill or electric food processor with the lemon juice, liqueur and half the sugar. Pour into a bowl and press a piece of plastic wrap over the top to exclude all the air. NOTE: the purée will discolour rapidly and must be made and covered as quickly as possible.

To finish: set the oven at moderately hot, 190C (375F) gas 5. Beat the egg whites until stiff, beat in the remaining sugar and continue beating for 30 seconds or until glossy. Fold about a quarter of the egg whites into the pear purée, mixing thoroughly. Add the mixture to the remaining egg whites. Fold them together as lightly as possible and pour into the prepared soufflé dish. Bake immediately in the heated oven for 15-20 minutes or until puffed and brown. If you like,

sprinkle with sugar and continue cooking for a further 1-2 minutes or until glazed. Serve at once, with the chilled vanilla custard sauce.

SOUFFLE AU CHOCOLAT
(Chocolate soufflé)

No flour is needed to thicken this soufflé as the chocolate itself is quite thick and rich enough to bind the mixture.
SERVES 4

125g (4oz) dark dessert chocolate, chopped
150ml (¼pt) double cream
3 egg yolks
1½ tablespoons brandy
½ teaspoon vanilla essence
5 egg whites
3 tablespoons caster sugar
icing sugar (for sprinkling)
1·25 litre (2pt) capacity soufflé dish or four 300ml (½pt) capacity soufflé dishes

Butter the soufflé dishes and sprinkle the insides with sugar, discarding any excess. Heat the chocolate with the cream in a heavy-based pan over low heat, stirring until melted. Take the pan from the heat and beat the egg yolks into the hot mixture so that they cook and thicken it. Stir in the brandy and vanilla essence. The soufflé can be prepared to this point 3-4 hours ahead. Keep the mixture, covered, at room temperature.

Twenty or 30 minutes before serving: set the oven at very hot 220C (425F) gas 7. Whip the 5 egg whites until stiff, preferably using a copper bowl. Add the caster sugar and beat for 20 seconds longer, or until the mixture looks glossy. Gently heat the chocolate mixture until just hot to the touch, take from the heat and stir in about a quarter of the egg whites. Add this mixture to the remaining egg whites and fold them together as lightly as possible.

Spoon the mixture into the prepared dish or dishes and bake at once in the heated oven, allowing 12-15 minutes for a large soufflé or 7-9 minutes for small ones, or until puffed. Sprinkle with icing sugar and serve at once.

SOUFFLE CHAUD AU CITRON
(Hot lemon soufflé)

The tangy lemon flavour really comes through in this flourless soufflé. Be sure to cook the lemon curd mixture until quite thick.
SERVES 4

60g (2oz) butter
125g (4oz) sugar
100ml (6 tablespoons) lemon juice (from about 3 lemons)
4 egg yolks
grated rind from 2 lemons
5 egg whites
icing sugar (for sprinkling)
1 litre (1¾pt) capacity soufflé dish

Butter the soufflé dish and sprinkle with sugar, discarding the excess. In a heavy-based pan (not aluminium) heat the measured butter with half the sugar and all the lemon juice until the butter and sugar are melted. Take from the heat and beat in the 4 egg yolks, one by one. Add the lemon rind. Heat very gently, whisking constantly, until the mixture thickens to the consistency of double cream. NOTE: do not let it get too hot or it will curdle. The soufflé can be prepared 3-4 hours ahead to this point. Keep the mixture, covered, at room temperature.

Twenty to 30 minutes before serving, set the oven at very hot, 220C (425F), gas 7. Whip the egg whites until stiff, preferably using a copper bowl. Add the remaining sugar and beat for 20 seconds longer or until glossy. Gently heat the lemon mixture until hot to the touch and stir in about a quarter of the egg whites. Add this mixture to the remaining egg whites and fold them together as lightly as possible.

Spoon the mixture into the prepared dish, smooth the surface and bake at once in the heated oven for 9-10 minutes, or until the soufflé is puffed and brown.

Sprinkle it with icing sugar and serve at once.

27
STOCKS
Stirrings, skimmings and strainings

French classical cooking can be thought of as the House that Jack Built – ingredients are added stage by stage to assemble the final dish. And one of the most vital parts of the house is stock. It is no accident that the French word for stock is *fond*, foundation. Without it there would be few French soups, even fewer sauces and hardly any braises or ragoûts at all.

Stock is not an end in itself; it is always used to make some other dish, or as a basis for classic white or brown sauces. The best stock is based on raw bones, with vegetables such as onion, carrot and celery added for flavour. Starchy vegetables such as potato or turnip would cloud the stock, and cauliflower and other members of the cabbage family are too strongly flavoured. Peppercorns are the invariable seasoning (ground or milled pepper turns bitter during long cooking), plus a bouquet garni of parsley, bay leaf and thyme. Salt, however, is taboo because even a small amount in the original liquid will become dangerously concentrated as the stock is boiled down. It is much wiser, say most chefs, to add salt when the stock is used in the final cooking. For veal stock, optional additions are garlic and a clove or two, and for a fish stock – white wine or lemon juice.

Both brown and white stock are made with the same veal bones, sometimes a few beef bones and vegetables, but for brown stock the bones and vegetables are *very thoroughly* browned before adding water. Brown stock should be rich, full-flavoured and concentrated and is used mainly with beef, game and lamb. White stock, intended for lighter meats, is more delicate – for the flavour of the stock should never overwhelm the other ingredients. Stocks for chicken and fish are similarly light-coloured and should be full-flavoured, but not strong.

In cooking stock the prime essential is patience. Classic cookbooks recommend cooking veal stock for 10-12 hours. Three hours will suffice for chicken stock, and fish stock is completed relatively quickly in half an hour. Once brought to a boil and skimmed, however, stock can be left untended to simmer at the back of the stove for the remaining time. It must not be allowed to boil hard (my recurring sin), as it will turn cloudy and acquire an unpleasant taste of bone.

During the cooking process, all the flavour should have been extracted from the bones and vegetables, leaving them tasteless. (This is what distinguishes stock from the broth in dishes such as pot au feu, which is much lighter because most of the flavour is left in the meat and vegetables.)

As well as flavour, good stock should acquire body from bone marrow and when chilled it will set to a jelly. Veal, being a young meat, is prized for making stock since it contains a good deal of gelatine, particularly in the knuckle bones. Beef knuckle bones are next best. Fish bones are also high in gelatine – in the 19th century, the gelatine which was used to set the elaborate moulded desserts so admired by Victorian matrons had the disconcerting name of 'fishglue'.

At the end of cooking, stock is strained and skimmed of excess fat. The modern trend is then to reduce the stock by boiling it down to half its volume or less. This is partly for convenience in storing, but mainly to make easy the 'small' sauces that are becoming more and more popular. Most of these are based on pan juices dissolved in stock, sometimes with other ingredients added, and the more concentrated the stock, the less reduction will be needed at the last minute. In fact, thorough reduction of stock is nothing new. Carried to the extreme, it results in meat (or fish) glaze, a syrupy liquid that, once cool, sets like India rubber. Just a teaspoon or two of meat glaze picks up the flavour of stews, and it is a standard ingredient in many classic sauces. Over 200 years ago, cookbooks suggested cutting meat glaze into dice for taking on journeys – the fore-runner of the bouillon cube.

Brown, white, chicken, fish – these are the classic stocks designed for classic dishes. There is also a simple version, household stock, at which chefs tend to turn up their noses, because they cannot rely on its effect in a sauce since it never tastes the same twice. But I am a devotee of household stock.

It is made with raw vegetable trimmings and left-over bones from raw or cooked meat and poultry. Everything is simmered together in happy abandon, bones and trimmings are thrown in as they accumulate and the stock is drawn off as needed and replenished with more water. At the end of ten days, my pot is usually so full that I have to strain the stock and start again, using this brew as a good starter for the next.

The stock should be boiled each day for 10 minutes so it does not go sour, and it is best kept in the refrigerator overnight, although I find this unnecessary in colder weather. When we go away, I simply put the whole pot in the freezer. I suppose one could go on thus for years, but my longest vintage lasted about three months before some oversight caused its demise.

Whether you choose classic recipes or my lazybone version, you will find stock a firm foundation for your own cuisine.

1 Stock pots are usually made of thick aluminium. It is best to use a deep pot, so evaporation won't be too rapid. Choose a pot that will be nearly filled by the stock mixture so it will be easy to skim.

2 As the stock is coming to the boil, it should be skimmed often, so that it will be clear.

3 Good stock should be clear, with a colour ranging from beige or straw (for veal and chicken stock) to medium brown (for beef).

4 Before using, it is best to chill stock so that any fat will solidify and can easily be skimmed from the surface. If you don't have enough time to chill it, skim off as much fat as you can with a spoon or ladle, then draw paper kitchen towels quickly across the surface to absorb and remove the last drops of fat.

5 If you need brown stock but have only white, a quick brown stock can be made by thoroughly browning chopped onions and carrots in a little fat and simmering them with white stock and a little tomato purée for about 30 minutes. Strain before using.

Getting ahead

1 Once stock has come to the boil and simmered for half an hour or more, the cooking can be interrupted for a day without harm. Keep the stock in the refrigerator until ready to continue cooking.

2 Meat can be kept for several weeks in the refrigerator if it is brought to a boil and boiled for 10 minutes every 3-4 days. Boil fish and chicken stock every 2 days.

3 Stock can be frozen almost indefinitely. To avoid using too much freezer space, reduce the stock until it is very concentrated and freeze it in ice-cube trays; a few cubes can then be diluted with water and heated as needed.

4 Stock that is to be kept should be completely cooled before covering or it may sour.

FOND BLANC DE VEAU
(White veal stock)

White stock is used for soups, velouté sauce (page 190), white sautés and stews. Because of its neutral flavour, it blends with almost any meat or poultry.

2·25kg (4-5lb) veal bones, cracked or cut in small pieces
2 onions, quartered
2 carrots, quartered
2 stalks celery, cut in 5cm (2in) pieces
large bouquet garni
10 peppercorns
2 cloves (optional)
head of garlic, unpeeled but divided into cloves
3-4 litres (6-8pts) water

Blanch the bones by bringing them to a boil in water to cover, simmering for 5 minutes, draining and rinsing in cold water. Add the vegetables, bouquet garni, peppercorns, cloves, garlic and enough water to cover generously, and bring slowly to the boil. Skim often at first; then simmer the stock for 4-5 hours, skimming occasionally.

Strain the stock, taste and if the flavour is not concentrated, boil it until well reduced. Chill quickly by placing the container of stock in cold running water and skim off any fat before using.

This stock can be kept for 2-3 days in the refrigerator. To keep it longer, boil it for 10 minutes and chill again. It can also be frozen.

FOND BRUN DE VEAU
(Brown veal stock)

Brown stock is used for making brown sauces and for adding to brown sautés and for stews of beef, game or lamb.

ingredients as for white veal stock
tablespoon tomato purée

Instead of blanching the bones, place them in a roasting tin and roast in a very hot oven, 230C (450F) gas 8, stirring them round occasionally, for 30-40 minutes, or until the bones are browned. Add the onions, carrots and celery and return to the oven until they are also browned. Transfer bones and vegetables to a stock pot with a metal spoon, leaving the fat behind.

Add the bouquet garni, peppercorns, cloves, if used, garlic, tomato purée and water and bring slowly to a boil. To enhance the colour of the stock even further, singe half an unpeeled onion, cut across the rings, over an electric plate or griddle or in a heated frying pan without oil and add to the stock. Continue as for white veal stock.

FOND DE BOEUF
(Beef stock)

Follow the recipe for brown veal stock, substituting beef bones for half of the veal bones.

Beef stock is used for rich brown sauces and for game dishes. The stock will be less syrupy than veal stock because it contains less gelatine.

FOND DE VOLAILLE
(Chicken stock)

Chicken stock is used for poultry dishes and sauces and can be used instead of white veal stock in most recipes.

Follow the recipe for brown veal stock, substituting 1.5kg (3lb) chicken backs and necks or a whole fowl for half the veal bones. Simmer the stock for 3-4 hours. If using a fowl, remove it after about 1½ hours, or when the thigh is tender when pierced with a skewer. The fowl can be served cold or used in some other dish.

FUMET DE POISSON

(Fish stock)

Fish stock is used in fish soups, for poaching fish and for making sauces served with fish and shell-fish. Makes 1 litre (1¾pts).

onion, sliced
15g (1 tablespoon) butter
700g (1½lb) fish bones, broken into pieces
1 litre (1¾pts) water
10 peppercorns
bouquet garni
225ml (8fl oz) dry white wine, or juice of ½ lemon (optional)
salt and freshly ground pepper

Cook the onion slowly in the butter in a heavy-based saucepan until soft but not brown. Add the fish bones, water, peppercorns, bouquet garni and wine or lemon juice, if used. Bring slowly to the boil, skimming occasionally, and simmer for 20 minutes, uncovered. Strain and season to taste. NOTE: never boil fish stock or it will turn bitter. Do not add fish skin to the stock as this darkens it.

MEAT AND FISH GLAZE

Veal, beef or fish stock can be boiled down to $\frac{1}{10}$ or $\frac{1}{20}$ of its original volume to make meat or fish glaze. When hot, it is syrupy; when cold, it sets to a warm jelly that keeps for months in the refrigerator. The flavour is extremely concentrated. A teaspoon adds flavour to sauces and stews.

CREME OLGA

Potato and onion soup is common in France, but this version is unusual in that the flavour of raw mushrooms permeates the crème.

SERVES 4
45g (1½oz) butter
large onion, chopped
large potato, thinly sliced
1 litre (1¾pts) milk
salt and pepper
bay leaf
125g (¼lb) mushrooms
few leaves watercress (for serving)
2 egg yolks
150ml (¼pt) double cream

Heat the butter in a heavy-based saucepan, add the onion and sauté lightly until soft but not brown. Add the potato slices and press a piece of foil on top. Cover with the lid and cook over very low heat, stirring occasionally, for 20 minutes or until the potato is very soft. Do not let them brown.

Stir in the milk with seasoning and bay leaf, bring to a boil and simmer for 10 minutes. NOTE: if the soup boils hard, it may curdle.

Discard the bay leaf and work the soup through a sieve or purée it in a blender. Purée the mushrooms separately and keep them tightly covered in a bowl so they won't discolour. Blanch the watercress leaves in boiling water for 1 minute and refresh. You can prepare the soup 6-8 hours ahead up to this point.

To finish, reheat the soup. Mix the egg yolks with the cream, stir in a little of the hot soup and add this liaison to the remaining soup. Heat gently, stirring until the soup thickens slightly but do not boil or it will curdle. Strain through a fine sieve and then add the mushroom purée. Taste for seasoning, adjust if necessary, and ladle the soup into bowls. Garnish each bowl with watercress leaves.

POTAGE D'AUTOMNE

(Autumn soup)

This recipe was originally set down by the illustrious Carême in the nineteenth century.

SERVES 6
white part of 3 leeks, cut in julienne strips
leaves of 2 celery hearts, cut in julienne strips
½ head cos lettuce, cut in julienne strips
tablespoon flour
2 litres (3½pts) chicken or veal stock
150g (5oz) uncooked green peas
pinch of sugar
pinch of white pepper
salt (optional)
for croûtons
6 slices bread (crusts removed), diced
120g (4oz) butter

Wash and drain the leek, celery and lettuce strips. Mix the flour to a paste with some of the stock and bring the rest to a boil. Add the flour mixture to the boiling stock, stirring, and then simmer the soup for 1 hour. Add the leek, celery and lettuce strips with the peas, sugar and pepper and simmer, uncovered, for 15-20 minutes or until the vegetables are tender. Taste the soup for seasoning and add salt and more pepper if necessary.

Meanwhile heat the butter and fry the croûtons, stirring, until browned on all sides. Drain them thoroughly on paper towels, spoon the soup into bowls or a tureen and top with the croûtons.

28
VEGETABLES
Earthly joys

On a summer day at Paris's famous market in the rue Mouffetard, it's the vegetables that steal the show. The first really red and juicy tomatoes take the centre of the stage with huge, globe-shaped Breton artichokes while burgundy-coloured aubergines, feather-leaved fennel and green and red peppers play the chorus. There are small courgettes and spring carrots in the wings, and leeks, fresh garlic and four or five varieties of lettuce as understudies. Stretching from the Mediterranean to the Channel, France has a profusion of vegetables no other European country can match, and the French treat these riches with respect.

The choice of cooking method for vegetables often depends on the season – the younger and fresher the vegetables, the better they are when very simply cooked. I personally think that plain boiled vegetables, tossed French-style in butter just before serving, are extraordinarily hard to beat. Above-the-ground (green) vegetables should be quickly cooked in quantities of boiling salted water until they just lose their toughness but are still firm and even crisp. They are then drained and refreshed with cold water to stop their cooking and set their colour. Under-the-ground (root) vegetables are cooked beginning with cold water in a covered pan so that they simmer and are not broken up.

Even for this simple treatment, boiling vegetables, then tossing them in butter is just the beginning of the story. The butter can be browned to a noisette to give more flavour, and the vegetables themselves can also be browned. In this case they are better blanched than completely cooked. A little garlic or finely chopped shallot can be added. Vegetables maître d'hôtel are dressed with melted butter flavoured with lemon juice and herbs.

After boiling, both green and root vegetables can be puréed in a blender or electric food processor or, more traditionally, by working through a food mill. The texture is usually very smooth – almost all vegetables puréed in a food processor or blender must also be pushed through a sieve to remove fibres (as in celery) or tough skins (as for peas). However, finely chopping rather than puréeing vegetables gives a pleasant texture. Either way, the purée is reheated in butter, often enriched with cream and seasoned with spices such as nutmeg. Enough butter and cream should be added so that the consistency is soft and fluffy, never sticky. Milk can also be used to thin the purée. When very diluted, the vegetable purée becomes a soup. Purées of fresh green peas, split peas, beans, lentils, tomatoes,

carrots, chestnuts and spinach date back for centuries, and some of these purées such as lentil and mushroom were also used for thickening sauces – cooks were apparently undeterred by the work involved in pushing vegetables through an old-fashioned drum sieve.

In classic cuisine, purées of vegetables with a low starch content, such as root celery or green beans, are bound with béchamel sauce or combined with a small amount of a high carbohydrate vegetable such as potato. Favourite combinations are green beans with dried flageolets, onions with potato, artichokes with flageolets and mushrooms with potato. Nouvelle cuisine purées often exclude these additions which smoothe and bind, and at the moment the simpler purées are 'le grand chic'. However, I don't think they will last – as the mother of two growing children, I find them all too reminiscent of commercial baby food.

Besides boiling there is braising. Not all vegetables lend themselves to braising, but those that do are excellent cooked in that way. Whole peeled chestnuts, hearts of celery, cabbage, lettuce, all may be braised in the classic manner on a mirepoix of vegetables moistened with stock. When cooked, the vegetables are drained, and a sauce is made with the cooking liquid. Some vegetables can be sautéed directly in butter without previous cooking, notably tomatoes, courgettes and aubergines. A few, such as cauliflower, broccoli and carrots, can be blanched, then dipped in batter and deep-fried, and mushrooms and aubergines can be deep-fried without blanching.

Each region has its own vegetable specialities using these various methods to cook the local produce. Dried beans are as evocative of Brittany as are cabbage of Picardy and wild mushrooms of the Alps. In cooking parlance 'lyonnaise' means with onions, and 'à l'alsacienne' denotes sauerkraut. Provence is the luckiest region of all. Its bountiful and lengthy growing season has helped to create dishes such as ratatouille and pissaladière, which have travelled

CHARLOTTE D'AUBERGINES

An updated version of a traditional dish – aubergines and tomatoes are flavoured with onion and garlic and set in a mould lined with aubergine slices. Yoghurt – a very popular ingredient with those who follow nouvelle cuisine – is layered with the vegetables. Serve with a tomato sauce

throughout France along with the vegetables that Provence supplies to the rest of the country. Aubergines, tomatoes, onions, garlic, peppers – these vegetables take kindly to the slow, relatively long cooking that fosters the melting texture and full flavour of such regional dishes.

One good, old-fashioned dish you can give me any day is a vegetable gratin. I cannot resist a rich sauce with chunks of well-cooked vegetables, crisp or melting as the case may be, topped by a golden crust of cheese or breadcrumbs. The sauce may be béchamel, mornay or, for root vegetables, just thick cream. For gratins, one vegetable is often stuffed with another: fonds d'artichaut favourite is an artichoke bottom filled with asparagus tips, coated with mornay sauce and browned, and artichoke Florentine substitutes spinach for the asparagus. Even more substantial is the popular endive au jambon – braised chicory wrapped in ham, coated with béchamel sauce and topped with cheese.

Gratins are firmly ensconced in French country kitchens – the most famous of all is gratin Dauphinois (potatoes in cream topped with cheese), but there are many more. Gratin Savoyarde – also from the Alps – uses stock instead of cream with the potatoes; from the north comes a gratin of leeks, and the central Bourbonnais region is well-known for a gratin of pumpkin, in which the vegetable is puréed then mixed with cream and flavoured with sugar. Many Provençal gratins dispense with sauce or cream, a reminder that dairy ingredients are less used in that land of the sun. In one recipe, aubergine is sliced, layered with tomato, garlic and herbs and topped with Parmesan cheese. Another calls for tomatoes to be stuffed with meat and baked, topped with oil and a coating of breadcrumbs.

And now this traditional repertoire is widening further. New menus offer more and more vegetable dishes and salads as entrées, rather than confining them to their conventional rôle as accompaniments to the main course. Typical is a kind of hot salad of lightly cooked vegetable julienne, sometimes spiced with bacon, sometimes spooned over greens such as escarole. Another idea is based on the northern flamiche – a bread dough filled with cheese-flavoured custard: the nouvelle cuisine version substitutes vegetables for the cheese. Even more popular, replacing the fish terrines that have held the stage for so long, are terrines of vegetables, whose invention is credited to the brothers Troisgros (their restaurant near Lyon enjoys top rating from both the conservative Michelin guide and the trendy Gault et Millau). Their terrines are made with multi-coloured layers of lightly cooked vegetables held together with a mousse of ham. Green vegetables such as spinach, sorrel, peas, beans, broccoli or courgettes are mandatory in such terrines, as are carrots, for colour, with perhaps a little mushroom or turnip for flavour. The terrines may be served hot, with butter sauce, or cold with a purée of fresh tomatoes that are not cooked at all.

These fashionable terrines are really no more than *pains* or vegetable loaves which have existed for centuries, the difference being that in a terrine the vegetables are set in multi-coloured layers like Neapolitan ice-cream. For a *pain*, the vegetables are puréed or cut in pieces, then bound with white sauce, eggs, and often with breadcrumbs (hence the name *pains*). The mixture is seasoned, poured into large or individual moulds and then baked in a water bath until set. For serving, the loaves are turned out and set like little castles around meat, or passed separately with their own sauce.

It is apparent that a definable nouvelle cuisine style is developing in vegetable cookery, as in sauces. Innovative chefs are looking for lightness and colour and for ingredients that are quickly cooked, and vegetables meet these criteria admirably. In contrast to the traditional approach, the nouvelle cuisine way with vegetables stresses light cooking – textures should be crisp and even crunchy, though not to the extent of tasting raw or feeling tough. Prime candidates for the new-style treatment are spinach, carrots, green beans, any vegetable that unites bright colour with good flavour.

Not everyone likes the new vegetable cookery. Certainly it will never oust old favourites like ratatouille and gratin of leek. The very existence of two schools of thought is further evidence of the seriousness with which the French take their vegetables, which are probably the finest in the world. A French meal without them would be strange indeed.

THE WAY TO SUCCESS

Entrées

1 Choose vegetables that need cooking for similar lengths of time, or vegetables such as tomatoes that can be cooked without spoiling for varying lengths of time. Alternatively, some vegetables can be partially cooked before they are added to the dish.
2 If substituting one vegetable for another, be sure they have similar textures and cooking times.
3 For attractive presentation, mix vegetables of contrasting colours.

Getting ahead

1 Most mixed vegetable dishes can be made up to 35 hours ahead and kept covered in the refrigerator; their flavour will mellow. If serving them cold, allow to come back to room temperature; if serving hot, cover and reheat in a moderate oven 180C (350F) gas 4.
2 Vegetable dishes that include bread or pastry should not be prepared more than 6-8 hours ahead and are at their best eaten immediately.
3 Due to their delicate texture, vegetable dishes do not freeze well.

TERRINE DE LEGUMES A LA MOUSSELINE DE VEAU

(Vegetable terrine with veal mousseline)

The vegetables used in this terrine can be varied according to season. Add or subtract as you like, but be sure to use vegetables of contrasting colours and textures.

SERVES 10-12

900g (2lb) fresh spinach
45g (1½oz) butter
salt and pepper
pinch of grated nutmeg
700g (1½lb) carrots
700g (1½lb) green beans
500g (1lb) turnips, quartered if large
for the veal mousseline
1kg (2lb) lean veal
1 egg yolk
45g (1½oz) butter, softened
1 egg white
300ml (½pt) double cream
salt and white pepper
pinch of grated nutmeg
3 litre (5pt) capacity rectangular terrine mould

For the spinach: remove the stems, wash the spinach thoroughly and blanch in boiling salted water for 1 minute. Drain thoroughly, refresh carefully under cold running water and drain as thoroughly as possible. Try to keep as many leaves whole as possible and pat them dry with a towel. Butter the inside of the terrine generously and line the bottom and sides with the most attractive spinach leaves. NOTE: there should be no holes in this layer.

Chop the remaining leaves. Melt 1 tablespoon of the butter, add the chopped leaves, salt, pepper and nutmeg and cook, stirring constantly, for 2-3 minutes or until nearly all the remaining moisture has evaporated.

For the carrots: shape each carrot into a rectangle and slice it lengthwise, if possible using a mandoline grater. Place the carrot slices in cold salted water, bring to boil and simmer for 7-10 minutes, or until tender. NOTE: if the carrots are undercooked, they will prevent the slices of terrine from holding together later. Drain thoroughly.

For the green bean purée: cook the green beans in a large pan of boiling salted water for 7-10 minutes or until just tender. Drain thoroughly and work them through a drum sieve. Alternatively, purée them in an electric blender or food mill and push through a sieve to remove any strings. Melt one tablespoon of butter, add the green bean purée, salt and pepper and cook, stirring, for 3-5 minutes or until nearly all the remaining moisture has evaporated.

For the turnip purée: place turnips in cold, salted water, bring to the boil and simmer for 5-7 minutes or until tender. Drain thoroughly and work them through a drum sieve or purée them in an electric blender or food mill. Melt one tablespoon of butter, add the purée, salt and pepper and cook, stirring, for 3-5 minutes or until nearly all remaining moisture has evaporated.

The vegetables can be prepared up to 24 hours ahead and kept in the refrigerator.

For the veal mousseline: work the veal twice through a fine blade of a mincer, then work it in an electric food mill or through a drum sieve until it becomes a smooth paste. Beat in the egg yolk and the softened butter. Beat in the egg white and place the mixture in a metal bowl of ice. Beat well over the ice until the mixture is thoroughly chilled. Gradually beat in the cream with a wooden spoon, beating vigorously after each addition. Season the mixture with salt, pepper and nutmeg to taste. Keep the mousseline in the refrigerator until ready for use; it should be cooked as soon as possible.

To assemble: heat the oven to moderate, 180C (350F) gas 4. Spread a layer of veal mousseline over the spinach leaves lining the sides and bottom of the mould, reserving some. Spoon a layer of green bean purée over the veal mousseline. Arrange three layers of carrot slices in the mould, all lengthwise. Spoon the turnip purée over the carrots and, lastly, the chopped spinach. If there is any room left, repeat the layers to make an attractive pattern. Seal the whole terrine by spreading another layer of veal mousseline over the top and cover with buttered paper or foil.

Place the terrine in a water bath, bring to a boil and place in the oven. Bake for 50-60 minutes or until the veal mousseline is set and a skewer inserted into the terrine comes out hot. NOTE: be sure the water keeps simmering in the water bath and add more as it evaporates. Drain off the excess fat and turn the terrine out onto a serving dish. Let it stand in a warm place for 10 minutes, slice and serve hot. If you like, serve Sauce beurre blanc separately.

ENDIVES AU JAMBON A LA CREME

(Chicory with ham à la crème)

Serves 8 as a starter;
4 as a main course

8-10 heads chicory weighing about 1kg (2lb)
50g (1⅔oz) butter
teaspoon sugar
salt and pepper
8-10 slices cooked ham weighing about 500g (1lb)
béchamel sauce (page 192) made with 900ml (1½pts) milk, slice of onion, bay leaf, 8 peppercorns, 70g (2½oz) butter, 40g (1¼oz) flour and a pinch of grated nutmeg
60g (2oz) grated Gruyère or Parmesan cheese (for sprinkling)

Set the oven at moderate, 180C (350F) gas 4. Wipe the chicory, discard any wilted leaves and trim the stems. With the point of a knife, hollow the stem so the chicory cooks more evenly. Butter an ovenproof casserole dish, arrange the chicory in it and sprinkle with the sugar, salt and pepper. Cover and bake in the heated oven for 1 hour or until the chicory is very tender. Let the chicory cool slightly.

Make the béchamel sauce.

Roll each cooked chicory in a slice of ham and arrange the rolls diagonally in a shallow, buttered ovenproof baking dish. Spoon the sauce over the vegetables and sprinkle with the cheese. The dish can be prepared 24 hours ahead and kept covered in the refrigerator.

To finish: bake in a hot oven, 200C (400F) gas 6, for 20-25 minutes until hot and browned.

CHARLOTTE D'AUBERGINES
(Aubergine charlotte)

A galette is often thought to be a cake, but in fact the term refers to any round flat dish, sweet or savoury. Depending on the shape of the mould in which it is formed, this dish is called a charlotte (deep) or a galette. (flat).

SERVES 4

3-4 small aubergines weighing about 800g (1¾lb)

salt and freshly ground pepper

150ml (¼pt) olive oil

1 medium onion, finely chopped

1 clove garlic, crushed

10 tomatoes, peeled, chopped and seeded, or 1kg (2lb) Italian-style plum tomatoes

300ml (½pt) plain yoghurt

150ml (¼pt) stock

1·5 litre (2pt) capacity charlotte mould or a 20cm (8in) diameter round cake tin

Wipe the aubergines, trim the stems, and cut in 1cm (¾in) slices. Sprinkle them with salt and leave for 30 minutes to rid the vegetables of excess juices. Rinse with cold water and dry on paper towels. Heat 2 tablespoons of the oil in a saucepan, add the onion and fry until lightly browned. Add the garlic, tomatoes, salt and pepper and cook, stirring occasionally, for 20-25 minutes until the mixture is thick and pulpy. Heat the remaining oil in a large frying pan and brown the aubergine slices on both sides.

Arrange a layer of overlapping aubergine slices in the bottom and up the sides of the charlotte mould or cake tin. Reserve a third of the tomato mixture. Spread the aubergine with a little of the tomato mixture, then with yoghurt and continue the layers, ending with a layer of aubergine. Mix the reserved tomato mixture with the stock to make a sauce. The mould and sauce can be prepared up to 24 hours ahead and kept, covered, in the refrigerator.

To finish: cover the mould with foil and bake in a moderate oven, 180C (350F) gas 4 for 40-50 minutes or until the aubergine is very tender. Cool a little, then unmould onto a serving dish. Bring the tomato sauce to a boil, taste for seasoning and spoon it over the mould.

POIVRONS FARCIS A LA NIÇOISE
(Stuffed peppers Niçoise)

Stuffed peppers can be served, hot or at room temperature, as starter or as an accompaniment to roast lamb or baked fish.

SERVES 4

4 medium red or green peppers, or a mixture of both

2 tablespoons olive oil

for the stuffing

medium onion, chopped

4½ tablespoons olive oil

250g (8oz) cooked rice (100g (3½oz) uncooked)

65g (2oz) stoned black olives, coarsely chopped

2 tablespoons capers, drained

45g or 1¾oz can anchovies, soaked in a little milk, drained and chopped

2 teaspoons dried thyme

teaspoon dried rosemary

juice of 1 lemon, or to taste

freshly ground black pepper

Cut the peppers in half lengthwise and discard cores and seeds. Coat a shallow baking dish with the 2 tablespoons of olive oil and then put in the peppers.

For the stuffing: fry the onion in 1 tablespoon of the olive oil until soft but not brown. Mix it with the cooked rice, olives, capers, anchovies, herbs, remaining oil, lemon juice and pepper, adding more lemon juice and pepper to taste; the anchovies will add enough salt. Pile the mixture into the peppers and cover loosely with foil. The peppers can be prepared up to 8 hours ahead.

To finish: bake the peppers in a moderate oven, 180C (350F) gas 4, for ¾-1 hour or until the peppers are very tender. Baste them from time to time, adding more oil if the dish gets dirty. Serve them hot or at room temperature – not chilled.

TARTE A LA TOMATE
(Tomato tart)

An unusual tart made with a tomato and quiche filling. Pâte brisée could be substituted for the puff pastry, but whatever pastry you use, be sure to drain the tomatoes very well to avoid a soggy crust.

SERVES 6-8

puff pastry (page 163) made with 160-200g (4-7oz) unsalted butter, 200g (7oz) flour, 4g (¾ teaspoon) salt, ¾ teaspoon lemon juice and 100-120ml (4-5oz) cold water or an equal quantity of puff pastry trimmings

1½kg (3lb) tomatoes, peeled, seeded and roughly chopped

3 eggs

250ml (⅜pt) double cream

100g (3½oz) Gruyère cheese

salt and pepper

23cm (9in) diameter cake tin

Make the puff pastry, roll it out to 5mm (¼in) thickness and line the cake tin with it. Chill for 30 minutes or longer.

Meanwhile, drain the tomatoes in a colander. Set the oven at hot, 220C (425F) gas 7. Whisk together the eggs, cream, cheese and salt and pepper until well blended. Stir in the tomatoes.

Pour the filling into the lined tin and set it on a baking sheet. Put it in the hot oven and in 15 minutes or when the pastry begins to brown, turn the heat down to moderately hot, 190C (375F) gas 5. Continue baking for a further hour, then allow to cool for 30 minutes before serving.

TARTE AUX LEGUMES DE PROVENCE
(Provençal vegetable tart)

A cross between a pizza and Pissaladière (page 242), this recipe makes an excellent light lunch dish served with a salad.

SERVES 8-10

for the yeast dough

400g (13oz) flour

15g (½oz or 1 cake) compressed yeast

150ml (¼pt) lukewarm milk

3 eggs

8g (1½ level teaspoons) salt

125g (4oz) unsalted butter, softened

for the filling

3 tablespoons oil

1 small onion finely chopped

1 clove garlic, finely chopped

6 tomatoes, peeled, chopped and seeded

bouquet garni

salt and freshly ground black pepper

1 small or ½ medium aubergine

2 courgettes

30g (1oz) butter

110g (3½oz) Gruyère cheese, thinly sliced

for the custard

2 eggs

50ml (¼pt) double cream

two 20-23cm (8-9in) diameter pie tins or sandwich tins

Sift the flour into a bowl, make a well in the centre and crumble in the yeast. Pour 4 tablespoons of the milk over the yeast and let it stand for 5 minutes, or until dissolved. Add the rest of the milk, the eggs and the salt. Beat with the hand, gradually drawing in the flour to make a dough that is soft and slightly sticky. Knead the dough by slapping it against the sides of the bowl or on a marble slab for 5 minutes, or until very elastic (see page 242). Beat in the very soft butter. Transfer to an oiled bowl and cover the bowl with a damp for 1-1½ hours or until doubled in bulk.

For the filling: heat one tablespoon of the oil, add the chopped onion and cook slowly, stirring often, for 5 minutes or until soft but not brown. Add the garlic, tomatoes, bouquet garni, salt and pepper and cook over medium heat, stirring frequently, for 25-30 minutes or until nearly all the moisture has evaporated. Peel the aubergine and scrub the courgettes; cut both into matchstick-thin julienne strips and season them. Heat another tablespoon of oil in a sauté pan, with one tablespoon of butter and gently cook the aubergine julienne for about 5 minutes or until slightly softened. In another pan heat one tablespoon of oil and one tablespoon of butter and cook the courgettes for about 3 minutes or until slightly softened.

For the custard: beat the eggs with the cream and season with salt and pepper.

Set the oven at hot, 200C (400F) gas 6. Knead the dough lightly to knock out the air. Butter the pie tins. Divide the dough in half and set it in the tins. With the oiled back of a spoon or your knuckles, flatten out the dough to line the tins. Place a layer of sliced cheese over the dough. Spoon on a layer of tomatoes, then the aubergines, the remaining tomatoes and the courgettes.

Pour the custard over the vegetables, pushing them slightly apart so the custard will run through each layer. Leave the tart in a warm place to rise for 15 minutes, then bake in the hot oven for 40-45 minutes or until the pastry is brown.

TOURTE DE LEGUMES VERTS
(Green vegetable mould)

SERVES 4

head of green cabbage

salt and pepper

5 leeks weighing about 500g (1lb)

250g (½lb) green beans

2 tablespoons butter

125g (8oz) mushrooms, sliced

for the custard mixture

2 eggs

2 egg yolks

150ml (¼pt) milk

450ml (¾pt) double cream

salt and pepper

pinch of grated nutmeg

23cm (9in) diameter cake tin or moule à manqué

Remove the large ribs from the cabbage leaves and wash the leaves well. Place them in a large pan of boiling salted water, bring back to a boil and boil for 7-8 minutes or until tender. Drain, refresh under cold running water and drain again thoroughly. Dry well.

Clean the leeks thoroughly, sprinkle with salt and steam over boiling water for 15-20 minutes or until barely tender but still slightly crunchy. Refresh under cold running water, drain thoroughly and gently squeeze out excess moisture. Cut in 2cm (1in) lengths.

Cook the green beans in a large pan of boiling salted water for 7-10 minutes or until just tender. Drain, refresh under cold running water, drain again and cut into three.

Heat the butter in a frying pan, add the mushrooms, salt and pepper and sauté over high heat, tossing often, for 3-4 minutes or until tender and lightly browned.

The vegetables can be cooked up to 24 hours ahead and kept in the refrigerator.

For the custard mixture: beat the eggs and yolks with the milk and double cream until smooth. Season well with salt, pepper and nutmeg. Heat the oven to moderate, 180C (350F) gas 4.

To assemble: butter the mould generously and line the bottom and sides with cabbage leaves, leaving them hanging over the sides of the mould. Chop the remaining leaves. Arrange a layer of sautéed mushrooms in the lined pan. Add a layer of leeks, then a layer of green beans and lastly, a layer of chopped cabbage. Season each layer with salt and pepper. Continue in this way until the mould is full. Pour in enough of the custard mixture to come to the top of the vegetables. Fold the overhanging leaves back to cover the custard. Bake for about 45-55 minutes or until the filling is set. Allow to stand for a few minutes before turning out.

CONCOMBRES FARCIS A LA DUXELLES
(Cucumbers with duxelles stuffing)

Serve these stuffed cucumbers as a starter, alone, or with other stuffed vegetables. They would be particularly good with stuffed tomatoes or aubergines.

SERVES 4

3 cucumbers together weighing about 900g (2lb)
15g (½oz) grated Gruyère or Parmesan cheese (for sprinkling)
15g (½oz) melted butter (for sprinkling)
for the duxelles stuffing
30g (1oz) butter
1 shallot, finely chopped
150g (5oz) mushrooms, finely chopped
salt and pepper
tablespoon chopped parsley
1 egg, beaten
mornay sauce (page 192) made with 300ml (½pt) milk, slice of onion, bay leaf, 6 peppercorns, 15g (level tablespoon) butter, 10g (level tablespoon) flour, salt, pepper, nutmeg, 1 egg yolk and 30g (1oz) grated Gruyère or Parmesan cheese
4 tablespoons milk (optional)

Peel the cucumbers lengthwise in strips leaving about half the peel on, cut them in 10cm (4in) pieces, halve them lengthwise and hollow out the centres with a spoon or small knife to make boat-shapes to contain the filling.

Alternatively, cut the whole cucumber into 5cm (2in) thick slices. Use the handle of a teaspoon or a melon ball cutter to scoop out most of the seeds from the slices, leaving small round cases ready for stuffing. NOTE: do not pierce the base of each case. Bring a large pan of salted water to the boil, add the cucumber cases, bring back to the boil and blanch them for 4 minutes. Drain, refresh under cold running water and drain the cases again thoroughly.

For the duxelles stuffing: heat the butter in a frying pan, add the shallot and cook until soft but not brown. Add the mushrooms with salt and pepper and cook over high heat, stirring, for 5-7 minutes or until all the moisture has evaporated. Stir in the chopped parsley, taste for seasoning and allow to cool. Stir in the beaten egg.

Heat the oven to moderately hot, 190C (375F) gas 5. Arrange the cucumber boats in a buttered, shallow baking dish and season them with salt and pepper. Spoon in the stuffing. Bake in the heated oven for 10-15 minutes or until the stuffing sets.

Make the mornay sauce and taste for seasoning. The sauce should just coat the back of a spoon – if it is too thick, stir in up to 4 tablespoons more milk.

Coat the baked stuffed cucumbers with the sauce, sprinkle with 15g (½oz) grated cheese and sprinkle on the melted butter. The cucumbers can be prepared up to 24 hours ahead but, if so, they should be undercooked to allow for reheating. Keep, covered, in the refrigerator.

To finish: if the cucumbers are still warm, brown them under the grill. If cold, reheat them in a moderate oven, 180C (350F) gas 4, for 20-25 minutes until browned. The finished dish can be kept hot in a low oven, 150C (300F) gas 2, for up to 15 minutes; do not keep it hot for longer or the cucumbers may overcook.

TARTE AUX COURGETTES
(Courgette tart)

SERVES 4

for the pie pastry
200g (7oz) flour
¾ teaspoon salt
1 egg yolk
50ml (1⅔oz) oil
3-5 tablespoons cold water
for the filling
2 medium courgettes weighing about 300g (⅔lb)
50g (1⅔oz) rice
tablespoon oil
½ onion, finely chopped
½ clove garlic, finely chopped
60g (2oz) grated Gruyère cheese
1 egg
salt and freshly ground black pepper
to finish
30g (1oz) grated Gruyère cheese
tablespoon oil
20cm (8in) diameter tart tin

For the pastry: sift the flour onto a working surface and make a large well in the centre. Put the salt, egg yolk, oil and 3 tablespoons water in the centre and mix together with the fingertips until the salt has dissolved. Gradually work in the flour, pulling dough into large crumbs with the fingertips. If the crumbs are dry, sprinkle over 1-2 tablespoons more water. Press the dough together firmly – it should be soft but not sticky. Work it by pushing the dough away with the heel of the hand and gathering it up with a

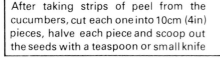

After taking strips of peel from the cucumbers, cut each one into 10cm (4in) pieces, halve each piece and scoop out the seeds with a teaspoon or small knife

For the smallest possible mushroom pieces, use a large knife, hold the point firmly and move the handle up and down in the classic chopping motion

dough scraper until smooth and pliable. Press the dough into a ball, wrap and chill 30 minutes.

Set the oven at hot, 200C (400F) gas 6. Brush the tins with oil, line them with the dough and prick with a fork. Line the shell with greaseproof paper, fill with beans and bake for about 15 minutes. Remove the paper and beans and return to the oven for 2-3 more minutes or until the base is lightly browned.

For the filling: slice the courgettes in 1cm (½in) slices but don't peel. Cook in boiling salted water for 10 minutes or until very tender. Drain thoroughly. Cook the rice in a large pan of boiling salted water for about 15 minutes or until just tender and drain. Heat the oil in a small saucepan, add the onion and cook slowly, stirring for about 5 minutes or until soft but not brown. Add the garlic and continue to cook for a further minute. Mash the courgettes with a fork; add the rice, onion, garlic, grated cheese, egg and salt and pepper to taste. Spread in the baked pie crust.

Sprinkle with the grated cheese and a tablespoon of oil. Bake for 25-30 minutes or until the filling is set and the topping is lightly browned.

THE WAY TO SUCCESS

Accompaniments

1 Use plenty of water for cooking green vegetables; a small quantity of water takes longer to come back to the boil after the vegetables are added, so that they cook more slowly.

2 Cooking time for vegetables can depend on how they are to be served. Vegetables to be served alone, or for a gratin, should be firmer than those destined to be puréed.

3 When reheating boiled vegetables in butter, be sure that they are well drained. Root vegetables can be dried in a pan directly over low heat before adding the butter; leafy green vegetables such as spinach should be squeezed with your hands or pressed between two plates before adding to a pan in which butter has been melted.

4 For a fresher flavour, vegetables can be gently heated directly in the pan, then the butter added off the heat so that it melts without cooking.

5 Be sure that vegetables are thoroughly drained before adding to a mixture for a gratin or vegetable mould. Even when drained, vegetables will produce liquid on further cooking.

6 Be sure to taste the mixture for vegetable moulds or gratins before browning.

7 Make gratins in a shallow baking dish so that each portion has plenty of browned topping. A shallow mixture also cooks more quickly, so that the vegetables give off less liquid.

8 Taste purées just before serving as the flavour can change on standing.

Getting ahead

1 Green vegetables can be cooked an hour or two in advance. Do not keep them hot, but just before serving reheat them in butter without cooking them further.

2 Root vegetables can be kept hot, covered, in a warm place for up to 30 minutes. They can also be prepared ahead and reheated as for green vegetables.

3 Vegetable purée can be kept hot for up to an hour in a water bath, though they lose some of their aroma. Unless they contain potato, they can be made 1-2 days ahead and kept covered in the refrigerator.

4 Vegetable gratins can be assembled ahead and kept overnight in the refrigerator.

5 Vegetable moulds and terrines can be cooked up to 24 hours ahead and kept in the refrigerator. They should be reheated in their moulds in a water bath. Vegetable moulds can also be served cold.

6 Before freezing, green vegetables must be thoroughly blanched or partially cooked.

7 Some leftover green vegetables, such as spinach and cabbage, reheat fairly well in butter the following day. Others, such as cauliflower, green beans and broccoli, can be tossed with vinaigrette dressing for a salad. Most cooked root vegetables are excellent if reheated by sautéing in butter or oil. Cooked potatoes, however, tend to blacken in the refrigerator and acquire a stale taste.

8 Leftover cooked vegetables, mixed or all of one kind, are excellent made into gratins or vegetable moulds.

Squeeze most of the cooked spinach by the handful to remove all the excess moisture before chopping it

Carefully line the buttered moulds with the blanched whole spinach leaves, overlapping to cover the filling well

PAIN D'EPINARDS

(Spinach mould)

This mould can also be made with frozen spinach. Substitute 1 large packet chopped spinach, cooked briefly and drained, for the fresh spinach, and do not line the mould with spinach leaves.

SERVES 4

750g (1½ lb) fresh spinach
salt and pepper
45g (1½ oz) butter
40g (1¼ oz) fresh white breadcrumbs
375ml (⅝ pt) hot milk
2 eggs, beaten to mix
1 egg yolk
pinch of grated nutmeg
mornay sauce (page 192) or tomato sauce (page 230)

plain mould or charlotte mould (750ml – 1 litre or 1½-1¾pt capacity) or 4 individual custard pots

Wash the spinach well, remove the stems and blanch 12-14 large leaves in boiling water for 1 minute. Drain on paper towels. Cook the remaining spinach in boiling salted water for 5 minutes or until tender. Drain thoroughly, refresh with cold water, squeeze thoroughly to remove all the water and chop. Do not chop the larger leaves that were blanched.

Butter the mould or custard pots and line with the blanched spinach leaves. Melt the butter, add the chopped spinach and cook for 3-4 minutes, stirring, until all the moisture has evaporated. Remove from the heat. Soak the breadcrumbs in the hot milk for 5 minutes and add to the spinach with the beaten eggs, egg yolk, nutmeg and seasoning. Spoon the spinach mixture into the lined mould or individual pots and cover with buttered foil. The dish can be prepared 6-8 hours ahead up to this point; keep covered in the refrigerator.

Three-quarters to one hour before serving, preheat the oven to moderate, 180C (350F) gas 4. Stand the mould or pots in a water bath (Chapter 29) and bring the water just to the boil on top of the stove. Bake in the heated oven for 45-55 minutes for a mould or 20-25 minutes for custard pots, or until the mixture is firm. Lift carefully from the water bath and allow to cool slightly before turning out onto a serving dish. Spoon some of the sauce around the spinach and serve the rest separately.

PAINS D'EPINARDS

Spinach leaves enclose chopped spinach cooked in a savoury custard mixture

COURGETTES AU GRATIN

Unpeeled slices of courgette are mixed with a cream and egg custard, topped with cheese and cooked to a golden brown

PUREES DE LEGUMES

(front)

A tri-colour dish of purées – carrot, cauliflower and Brussels sprout

SAUCE TOMATE
(Tomato sauce)

Unless fresh tomatoes are ripe and glowing red, tomato sauce made with canned Italian-style tomatoes has more flavour.

Makes about 600ml (1pt)

30g (1oz) butter
onion, chopped
20g ($\frac{2}{3}$oz) flour
375ml ($\frac{5}{8}$pt) veal stock, or veal stock mixed with juice from canned tomatoes
1kg (2lb) fresh tomatoes, quartered, or 750g (1$\frac{1}{2}$lb) canned tomatoes, drained and chopped
clove garlic, crushed
bouquet garni
$\frac{1}{2}$ level teaspoon sugar
salt and freshly ground black pepper
2 tablespoons tomato purée (optional)

Melt the butter in a saucepan and cook the onion until soft but not brown. Off the heat, stir in the flour. Pour in the stock or stock and tomato juice, and bring to the boil, stirring all the time. Add the tomatoes, garlic, bouquet garni, sugar and salt and pepper to taste and simmer, uncovered, for 30-40 minutes for canned (45-60 for fresh) tomatoes, or until the tomatoes are very soft and the sauce is slightly thick.

Work the sauce through a strainer and return it to the pan. Reheat and if necessary reduce it. It should be the consistency of thin cream. If the sauce has been made from fresh tomatoes and a deeper colour is desired, add the tomato purée. Taste the sauce for seasoning.

GRATIN DE POIREAUX
(Gratin of leeks)

This is a basic gratin recipe, which can be used for many different vegetables such as cauliflower, courgettes or spinach. They should all be cooked until just tender, then thoroughly drained before coating with sauce.

SERVES 4

6-8 medium leeks together weighing about 500g (1lb)
salt and pepper
60g (2oz) grated Gruyère or Parmesan cheese (for sprinkling)

tablespoon melted butter
béchamel sauce (page 192) made with 600ml (1pt) milk, slice onion, bay leaf, 6 peppercorns, 50g (1$\frac{2}{3}$oz) butter, 40g (1$\frac{1}{4}$oz) flour, salt and pepper and a pinch of grated nutmeg

Trim the leeks, discarding the green tops, split them twice lengthwise halfway to the root and wash the leeks very thoroughly. Cook them in boiling salted water 8-12 minutes or until tender, drain, refresh with cold water and drain again.

Make the béchamel sauce.

If not used at once, rub the surface of the sauce with butter to prevent a skin from forming. The sauce can be kept for 2-3 days covered in the refrigerator.

Spoon a little béchamel sauce into a buttered, shallow baking dish. Cut the leeks in 6cm (about 2$\frac{1}{2}$in) lengths, arrange them on top and coat with the remaining sauce. Sprinkle with the cheese and then the melted butter. The gratin can be prepared up to 24 hours ahead to this point and kept covered in the refrigerator, or it can be frozen.

To finish: bake the gratin in a very hot oven, 220C (425F) gas 7, for 10-15 minutes or until browned and bubbling.

VARIATION

For a more unusual gratin dish, substitute 500g (1lb) cucumber, cut in thick slices and sautéed in 15g ($\frac{1}{2}$oz) butter, in either of the two preceding recipes.

COURGETTES AU GRATIN
(Gratin of courgettes)

This is a simple form of the usual gratin made with béchamel sauce. To prevent excess liquid from the courgettes from diluting the custard mixture, be sure to drain them thoroughly after blanching.

SERVES 4

500g (1lb) courgettes, cut in 1cm (about $\frac{1}{2}$in) diagonal slices
2 eggs
300ml ($\frac{1}{2}$pt) double cream
salt and freshly ground black pepper
30g (1oz) grated Gruyère cheese

Blanch the courgettes in boiling salted water for 3-4 minutes and drain. Spread them in a shallow ovenproof baking dish. Beat the eggs until well mixed and stir in the cream and seasoning. Pour this custard over the courgettes and sprinkle with cheese. The courgettes can be prepared up to 6 hours ahead.

To finish: bake in a hot oven, 200C (400F) gas 6, for 10-15 minutes until the custard is just set and the top is browned.

ALIGOT

This recipe is a traditional dish of the Auvergne and is often served with sausages. If Cantal cheese is not available, use Cheddar or a strong-flavoured Gruyère instead.

SERVES 4-6

5-6 medium potatoes (1kg or 2lb), peeled
salt
60g (2oz) butter
300ml ($\frac{1}{2}$pt) double cream
350g (12oz) grated Cantal cheese

Cut each potato in 2-3 pieces of the same size, cover with cold water, add salt and bring to the boil. Simmer for 20-25 minutes or until tender when pierced with a knife or skewer – the potatoes should be quite soft.

Drain the potatoes and push them through a sieve. Put them in a heavy-based saucepan, add the butter and beat the potatoes with a wooden spoon over low heat until they are light and fluffy – the heat causes the grains of starch in the potatoes to expand. Gradually add the cream, still beating the potatoes over low heat. Lastly, stir in the grated cheese, beating hard over low heat until the mixture forms strings. NOTE: in contrast to other cheese dishes, Aligot is supposed to be stringy.

Aligot, because it contains so much cheese, is an exception to the rule that potato dishes can't be made in advance. It can be made up to 24 hours ahead and kept covered in the refrigerator. Pile in a serving dish and serve very hot.

PUREE DE CHOUX DE BRUXELLES

(Brussels sprout purée)

For a festive meal, serve a roast joint of beef or lamb with three vegetable purées: carrot, Brussels sprout and potato. Blanching the sprouts before cooking gives them a more delicate flavour.

SERVES 4

1kg (2lbs) Brussels sprouts
salt and pepper
90g (3oz) butter
pinch of grated nutmeg
tablespoon double cream
juice of $\frac{1}{2}$ lemon

Remove any discoloured outer leaves from the sprouts, trim the stems and wash well in cold water. Bring a large quantity of water to the boil, add the sprouts and blanch for about 2 minutes. Refresh under cold running water. Bring another large pan of water to the boil, add salt and the blanched sprouts. Boil them for about 15 minutes or until quite tender.

Drain the Brussels sprouts thoroughly and work them through a vegetable mill or purée them in a blender or electric food processor. The purée can be prepared a day ahead and kept covered at room temperature.

To finish: melt the butter, add the purée with nutmeg, salt and pepper and cook, stirring, until very hot. Stir in the cream and lemon juice. Taste the purée for seasoning and adjust if necessary. The purée should be just soft enough to fall from the spoon. Pile in a bowl and mark the top in waves with the blade of a knife.

PUREE DE CHOUFLEUR

(Cauliflower purée)

Cauliflower makes a surprisingly delicate-tasting purée.

SERVES 4

medium cauliflower
salt and pepper
30g (1oz) butter
pinch of grated nutmeg
1-2 tablespoons double cream

Divide the cauliflower into florets. Cook them in boiling salted water for 10-12 minutes or until just tender. Drain very thoroughly. Work the cauliflower through a vegetable mill or purée it in a blender or electric food processor. The purée can be prepared a day ahead and kept covered in the refrigerator.

To finish: melt the butter, add the purée with the nutmeg, salt and pepper and cook, stirring, until very hot. Stir in the cream; the purée should be just soft enough to fall from the spoon. Taste for seasoning, mark the top in waves with the blade of a knife, if you like, and serve immediately.

PUREE DE CAROTTES

(Carrot purée)

SERVES 4

750g (1½ lb) carrots
salt and pepper
15g ($\frac{1}{2}$ oz) butter
$\frac{1}{2}$-1 level teaspoon sugar (optional)
50ml (2oz) double cream

Peel and slice the carrots. Bring to a boil in salted water. Cook for 8-10 minutes or until the carrots are very tender. Drain and purée them in a blender or electric food processor, or work them through a food mill.

Melt the butter in a pan, add the carrot purée and heat. Add sugar, salt and pepper and beat in the cream a little at a time. Taste for seasoning. The purée can be made 2-3 days ahead and kept covered in the refrigerator.

To serve: reheat the purée if it has been cooked in advance. Pile in a bowl and mark the top in waves with the blade of a knife to decorate.

29
WATER BATH (BAIN MARIE)
From ancient Rome to Mrs Beeton

There are several ingenious, if apocryphal, stories to explain that curious name for a water bath – bain marie. One tale traces the bain marie back to the 14th century, when interest in this gentle cooking method coincided with a period of special devotion to the Virgin Mary. Another links it to Miriam (Hebrew for Marie), Moses' sister. Italians attribute their *bagno maria* to Maria de Cleofa, a lady alchemist. More plausible, if more prosaic, is the suggestion that marie is a corruption of mer, sea.

The origin of its name may be guesswork, but no cook is in doubt about the utility of a water bath. The principle of surrounding a cooking pot with water as protection from the fierce heat of an open fire must date back to primitive times. In his Renaissance cookbook 'Opera', Bartolomeo Scappi includes vivid woodcuts of pots with compartments for water at the bottom – the first chafing dishes. Today's water bath consists of a large shallow pan, often a roasting pan, with plenty of room for pots containing food to be set in the water. Many restaurants have a temperature-controlled water bath, like a miniature swimming pool with a grid in the bottom to keep the special tall saucepans off the hot base. Often a hot-water tap is installed over the bain marie so it can be filled easily. At home, almost any pan will do for a water bath, provided it is wide enough to hold the cooking pot and deep enough for a minimum 5cm (2in) of water.

A water bath is used in professional kitchens for two basic purposes: steady cooking at a low temperature, and keeping food hot. Water cannot get hotter than its boiling point of 100C (212F) so the temperature of any food set in it is automatically moderated. Nor, since the water produces steam, will the food get dry. A simmering water bath surrounds its contents with a constant, low, moist heat.

A water bath is essential for cooking a variety of dishes: custards, which curdle easily; light soufflé puddings; and pâtés and terrines, for which the heat must penetrate to the centre without melting the fat or forming a crust on the exterior of the loaf. A water bath is vital for fish and chicken mousselines – those tricky mixtures of pounded meat, egg white and cream – and for 'pains', moulds of meat, chicken, fish or vegetables that are set with eggs and thickened with béchamel sauce or breadcrumbs.

The correct temperature for baking in a water bath can vary, depending on the nature of the food. For custards, particularly when set in small moulds, the water should be scarcely bubbling; a rolling boil indicates that the oven heat, to which the top of the custard is exposed, is too high – and the dish may curdle. Mousselines and *pains* need a medium heat. On the other hand, pâtés and terrines can withstand comparatively strong heat, particularly when the terrine mould is thick; if the water simmers rather than bubbles, they will take a prodigiously long time to cook. Cooking time is estimated from the moment the water starts to simmer, so the water in the bath, with the pan inside it, should be brought to the boil before putting it in the oven to cook. Then it is simply a matter of making sure the water continues to simmer and keeping it topped up with hot water.

Cooks use stove-top water baths for a variety of purposes. In a water bath, it is easy to melt chocolate without scorching, to dissolve gelatine without cooking it, or to soften fondant icing without destroying its brilliance. The egg and sugar combination that is the base of génoise sponge cakes and some mousses can be whisked to the ribbon stage over a water bath. Cooked meringue (meringue cuite) must be beaten endlessly over hot water, but since the process requires the muscle power of a punter in good form, this meringue is generally passed over by modern cooks in favour of other types.

Sublime scrambled eggs (and they are one of the most difficult dishes of all) depend on patient stirring in a water bath for half an hour. However, few chefs can find the time, so scrambled eggs rarely appear on restaurant menus. Equally, a chef cannot lose precious minutes making a butter sauce or a hollandaise the safe way – in a water bath. He puts the copper pan over direct heat, and to hell with it. . . . (Perhaps that is one reason why the English double boiler, with its ceramic inner pan, does not exist in France.) In a restaurant a water bath on top of the stove is used mainly for

CREME CARAMEL
(back)
Cooked to perfection in a water bath (bain marie), a smooth-textured, classic combination of eggs and milk covered with a thin coating of liquid caramel

PETITS POTS DE CREME
(front)
Another rich custard mixture – also baked in a bain marie – flavoured first with vanilla, then with coffee and finally with chocolate

keeping things warm. Soups, vegetables, stews and sauces are all prepared, then placed in the hot water to wait until needed. The food dries much less than in the oven and need not be covered.

With a little care even delicate butter sauces keep for a few minutes without separating, and hollandaise holds for an hour or more. (For these sauces, the water bath should be warm, nowhere near the boiling point.) At La Varenne, the chefs put dishes that are ready to serve on racks set over the steaming pots – a variant of the bain marie method. Of course, keeping food hot for any length of time cannot improve it and often does harm – witness the food from cafeteria steam tables, which are no more than giant water baths.

Used in moderation, a water bath is a boon, a point appreciated by that master of kitchen management, Mrs Beeton, who wrote: 'So long ago as the times when emperors ruled in Rome, and the yellow Tiber passed through a populous and wealthy city, this utensil was extensively employed; and it is frequently mentioned by that profound culinary chemist of the ancients, Apicius. . . . If the hour of dinner is uncertain in any establishment, by reason of the nature of the master's business, nothing is so certain a means of preserving the flavour of all dishes as the employment of the bain marie.'

THE WAY TO SUCCESS

1 Food to be cooked in a water bath must be generously surrounded by water, otherwise it will cook at the *oven* temperature rather than at one moderated by the temperature of the *water*.

2 When cooking in a water bath, the cooking time is counted from the moment the water first comes to a simmer on top of the stove.

3 If a kitchen towel or piece of greaseproof paper is put in the water bath under the container of food, this insulates it from the base of the bath, thus protecting it from direct heat.

4 A water bath must be topped up with hot water during cooking. Cold water will slow the cooking.

Getting ahead

A water bath is one of the chief aids to getting ahead in the kitchen because prepared food can be kept hot at a steady gentle temperature. Advance preparation of dishes that are actually cooked in a water bath varies enormously: from terrines that can, and should, be made up to a week ahead, to butter sauces that are served at once. In general, water bath dishes contain eggs. Therefore, they are best served within a day or two of cooking and do not reheat well.

TURBAN DE SOLE

Turban of sole, with its delicate flavour and rich butter sauce, amply rewards the work involved; it can be kept warm for a short time and reheats well.

SERVES 6

8 sole fillets, together weighing about 750g (1½lb)
for the fish mixture
500g (1lb) whiting or haddock fillets
100g (3½oz) butter, softened
2 egg yolks
salt and pepper
pinch of grated nutmeg
1 egg white
150ml (¼pt) double cream
white butter sauce (page 194) made with 3 tablespoons white wine vinegar, 3 tablespoons dry white wine, 2 shallots, very finely chopped, 250g (8oz) butter, very cold, and salt and white pepper
for the garnish
6-8 cooked prawns
1 canned truffle, drained and thinly sliced (optional)
1 litre (1¾pt) capacity ring mould

For the fish mixture: discard any skin and bone from the whiting or haddock fillets. Work the fish twice through the fine blade of a mincer. Transfer the fish to a blender and purée it with the butter and egg yolks until smooth. Work the mixture through a fine sieve into a bowl and set the bowl in a pan of iced water. Add salt, pepper and nutmeg. With a wooden spoon, beat in the egg white, then gradually beat in the cream and taste for seasoning.

Butter the inside of the mould. With the flat part of a heavy knife, pound the sole fillets between two pieces of greaseproof paper. Halve each fillet crosswise, cutting diagonally. Line the mould with fillets, white side downwards, broad end to the outside, tail end hanging into the centre. There will be gaps between the fillets. Spoon the fish mixture into the mould and fold the fillets over the top. The mould can be assembled 3-4 hours ahead and cooked just before serving; keep it covered in the refrigerator.

Set the oven at moderate, 180C (350F) gas 4. Cover the mould with buttered foil, set in a water bath and bring it to a boil on top of the stove.

Transfer it to the heated oven and cook for 35-45 minutes or until the mixture is firm to the touch. Tip the mould sideways to drain off any excess liquid. The mould can be kept covered in a warm place for up to half an hour.

Make the white butter sauce and serve as soon as possible. If it must be kept warm for a few minutes, keep it over warm, but not boiling, water with a piece of buttered greaseproof paper over the top.

To finish: heat the prawns by putting them in boiling salted water; bring them just back to the boil and drain. Put a heated serving dish on top of the mould and invert both to turn out. Wipe away any liquid with paper towels, coat the moulded fish with sauce, top it with sliced truffle, if included, and arrange the prawns around the edge. Serve the remaining sauce separately.

TIMBALE DE QUATRE LEGUMES

(Four-vegetable timbales)

Any variety of vegetables in season can be used, but be sure to choose a good combination of colours. If fresh spinach is unavailable, frozen spinach can be substituted. Morels are a particularly delicious species of edible mushroom. Dried ceps may be substituted; otherwise cultivated button mushrooms will have to be used. They do not, alas, have anything approaching the same flavour. If they are fresh, they will not need to be soaked before cooking.

SERVES 8

small white cabbage or small cauliflower
1kg (2lb) fresh spinach
500g (1lb) carrots
500g (1lb) mushrooms
juice of $\frac{1}{2}$ lemon
4 eggs
salt and pepper
pinch of nutmeg
for the sauce
30g (1oz) dried morels
stick of celery, sliced
30g (1oz) butter
cooking liquid from the mushrooms and carrots
2 egg yolks
100ml ($\frac{1}{6}$pt) double cream

8 dariole moulds or individual ramekins each 150ml ($\frac{1}{4}$pt) capacity

Place the morels in a bowl, cover with lukewarm water and leave to soak for 1 hour. Thoroughly butter the ramekins. If using cabbage, cut it in thin strips and cook in a large pan of boiling salted water for 12-15 minutes, or until very tender. If using cauliflower, separate it into florets and cook in boiling salted water for 10-15 minutes or until it is very tender. Drain thoroughly.

Remove the stems from the spinach and wash the leaves in several changes of water. Cook in a large pan of boiling salted water for 2-3 minutes, or until just tender and drain well. Alternatively, steam the spinach above a large pan of boiling water for 2-3 minutes.

Peel and slice the carrots, put them in a pan with enough salted water to cover, bring to the boil and cook for 8-10 minutes or until very tender. Drain, reserving the cooking liquid.

Put the mushrooms in a saucepan with the juice of the $\frac{1}{2}$ lemon and 2.5cm (1in) water. Add salt and pepper, cover the pan and bring to the boil. Cook over high heat for 8-10 minutes or until very tender. Drain, reserving the cooking liquid.

After each vegetable is cooked, purée it in a blender or electric food processor and push the purée through a drum sieve. Dry each purée in a separate small saucepan over low heat, stirring constantly, until nearly all the liquid has evaporated. Add an egg to each purée and season to taste, adding nutmeg to the spinach purée.

Set the oven at moderate, 180C (350F) gas 4. Layer the purées in the buttered moulds: first, the cabbage or cauliflower; second, the carrot; third, the spinach and lastly the mushroom. Place in a water bath, bring to the boil on top of the stove and then transfer to the heated oven. Simmer for 10-12 minutes or until just set. Turn out on to a serving dish and keep warm.

For the sauce: drain the morels and slice them. Melt the butter in a saucepan, add the sliced morels and celery and cook slowly, stirring occasionally, for 5 minutes or until soft but not brown. Add the cooking liquid from the carrots and mushrooms, bring to the boil and simmer for 5 minutes, or until slightly reduced. The timbales and sauce can be made up to 1 day ahead and kept in the refrigerator.

Just before serving, beat the egg yolks and cream in a small bowl, whisk in a little of the hot sauce and return the mixture to the remaining sauce. Cook over low heat until slightly thickened, stirring constantly, but do not boil. NOTE: after the yolks have been added, the sauce cannot be reheated. Taste for seasoning and spoon the sauce around the timbales.

OEUFS MOULES VIROFLAY

(Eggs Viroflay)

Viroflay near Paris used to be famed for its fine spinach.

SERVES 8

sauce suprême (page 191) made with 600ml (1pt) chicken stock, 40g (1$\frac{1}{2}$oz) butter, 30g (3 level tablespoons) flour, 60g (2oz) chopped mushroom stalks, 125ml ($\frac{1}{4}$pt) double cream, salt and pepper
250g ($\frac{1}{2}$lb) fresh spinach
8 eggs
salt and freshly ground pepper
for the croûtons
8 slices white bread, cut slightly larger than the moulds
3 tablespoons oil and 3 tablespoons butter (for frying)

8 small moulds

Make the sauce suprême. It can be kept, refrigerated, up to 24 hours. *For the croûtons:* fry the slices of bread in the oil and butter until golden brown on both sides, drain on paper towels and keep warm.

Remove the stems from the spinach, wash the leaves well and blanch them in boiling water for 2-3 minutes. Refresh them with cold water, drain thoroughly and dry on paper towels, spreading out each leaf individually.

Butter the moulds as thickly as possible and line the bottom and sides of each mould with a layer of spinach leaves. There should be no gaps showing. Bring the sauce to a simmer. Heat the oven to hot, 200C (400F) gas 6.

Have ready a water bath large enough to hold all the moulds. Break an egg into each mould, season it lightly and fold the spinach leaves over the egg. Place the moulds in the water bath, cover it tightly with a piece of foil and put it in the oven. Adjust the heat so that the water simmers gently. Alternatively, place the moulds in a simmering water bath on top of the stove. Cook for 6-8 minutes or until the eggs just become firm. Remove the moulds from the water bath, leave to rest for 1 minute and turn out one onto each croûton. Coat each egg with sauce and serve.

PAINS DE FOIE DE VOLAILLE AU COULIS DE TOMATES

(Chicken liver ramekins with light tomato sauce)

This rich yet light starter is a good example of the finesse of nouvelle cuisine at its best.

SERVES 6

300ml (½pt) double cream
300g (10oz) chicken livers
3 eggs and 2 egg yolks
½ clove garlic, very finely chopped
salt and pepper
pinch of grated nutmeg
for the light tomato sauce
tablespoon butter
2 shallots, chopped
clove of garlic, crushed
1kg (2lb) tomatoes
6 ramekins, each 150ml (¼pt) capacity

Set the oven at moderate, 180C (350F) gas 4. Thoroughly butter the ramekins. Line a roasting tin with a teatowel, pour in water and heat it up. Bring the cream to the boil. Purée the chicken livers in a blender or food processor with the eggs and egg yolks. Transfer the mixture to a bowl and add the cream slowly, whisking all the time. Add garlic, season to taste and add the nutmeg. Spoon into the ramekins, filling them not more than ¾ full.

Set the ramekins in the water bath and bring almost to a simmer on top of the stove. Transfer to the heated oven and bake for 30-40 minutes, or until a skewer inserted in the centre comes out clean. Remove from the oven, keeping the ramekins in the water bath.

For the tomato sauce: melt the butter, add the shallots and cook until soft but not brown. Add the rest of the ingredients, season and simmer, uncovered, for 30-40 minutes or until the tomatoes are very soft. Purée the sauce and then strain it; return it to the pan to reheat and reduce, if necessary, to a light coating consistency. Taste for seasoning.

To finish: turn out each *pain* onto a serving dish and coat with sauce. Serve the rest of the sauce separately.

RAMEQUINS AU FROMAGE

(Cheese ramekins)

The croûton base provides just the right contrast in texture for these smooth, creamy ramekins.

SERVES 4-6

60g (2oz) cooked ham, cut in thin strips
2 eggs
350ml (12oz) double cream
100g (3½oz) Gruyère cheese, grated
salt and freshly ground pepper
for the croûtons
4-6 slices stale bread, cut to the same size as the ramekins
75g (2½oz) butter
2 tablespoons oil
4-6 ramekins or individual soufflé dishes

Fry the bread slices in the butter and oil until golden brown, turning them so that they brown on both sides. Drain well on paper towels. Butter the ramekins and arrange a few strips of ham in the bottom of each one. Beat the eggs until smooth, stir in the cream and cheese and season to taste. You can prepare the ramekins 6-8 hours ahead to this point; keep the cheese mixture in the refrigerator.

To finish: set the oven at moderately hot, 190C (375F) gas 5. Stir the cheese mixture and pour it into the ramekins. Set them in a hot water bath and bake in the heated oven for 15-20 minutes or until the tops are golden and firm to the touch. Remove the ramekins from the water bath and allow to stand for 1 minute. Run a knife around the edge of each, turn each out onto a croûton and serve.

FOR CREME CARAMEL

Pour the hot caramel into the dish and quickly turn the dish round so that the base and sides are evenly coated. Then leave the caramel to cool and set

CREME CARAMEL

The whole eggs in caramel cream bind the mixture, so that it turns out neatly.

SERVES 4

600ml (1pt) milk
vanilla pod, split lengthwise
80g (2½oz) sugar
2 eggs
2 egg yolks
for the caramel topping
75ml (⅛pt) water
100g (3½oz) sugar
soufflé dish or heatproof mould
1.25 litre (2pt) capacity
or 8 small ramekins or custard pots,
150ml (¼pt) capacity each

For the caramel topping: heat the water and sugar until dissolved, then boil steadily to a golden brown caramel. Remove from the heat. When the bubbles have subsided, pour the hot caramel into the mould and immediately turn the mould round to coat the base and sides evenly with caramel. Leave to cool and set. Set the oven at moderate, 180C (350F) gas 4.

Scald the milk by bringing it to the boil with the vanilla pod, cover and leave to infuse for 10-15 minutes. Add the sugar and stir until dissolved. Beat the eggs and egg yolks until mixed and stir in the hot milk mixture. Allow to cool slightly and strain into the prepared mould.

Set the mould in a water bath and bring to the boil on top of the stove. Cook in the heated oven for 40-50 minutes for a large mould, 20-25 minutes for individual ones, or until the custard has just set and a knife inserted near the centre comes out clean. Take from the water bath and leave to cool. Crème caramel can be made up to 48 hours ahead and kept covered in the refrigerator.

Not more than an hour before serving, run a knife around the edge of the cream and turn it out onto a serving dish.

COOKING IN A WATER BATH (BAIN MARIE)

To cook the Petits pots de crème, place the individual custard pots in a bain marie – the water should come halfway up the sides of the pots. Cover each one and cook in a moderate oven. Bains marie are for dishes which need gentle cooking; it is important that the temperature at which the food cooks is moderated by the surrounding water

PETITS POTS DE CREME

These Petits pots de crème are rich and smooth because of the number of egg yolks in the mixture; unlike Crème caramel which contains egg whites as well as yolks, the consistency is too soft for the crème to be turned out of the little pots successfully.

SERVES 9

| scant litre (1½ pts) milk |
| vanilla pod, split lengthwise |
| 100g (3oz) dark dessert chocolate, chopped |
| 12 egg yolks |
| 200g (7oz) sugar |
| 2 level teaspoons instant coffee dissolved in 1 teaspoon hot water |

9 individual mousse pots with lids, or 9 small ramekins

Scald the milk by bringing just to boiling point with the vanilla pod: cover and leave to infuse for 10-15 minutes. Melt the chocolate in a water bath, stirring from time to time. Remove from the heat when just melted and allow to cool. Beat the egg yolks with the sugar until light and slightly thickened. Stir in the hot milk and strain this custard mixture, reserving the vanilla pod for future use. Set the oven at 170C (325F) gas 3. Transfer the custard to a jug and pour about a third of it into three of the mousse pots or ramekins. Stir the dissolved coffee into the remaining custard in the jug and pour about half of it into three more mousse pots. Stir the cool but still melted chocolate into the remaining custard and pour into the three remaining mousse pots. NOTE: although this last custard combines vanilla, coffee and chocolate, the chocolate flavour will be predominant. Skim off the bubbles.

Set the mousse pots in a water bath and cover with lids or foil. Bring almost to a simmer on top of the stove. Transfer them to the heated oven and cook for 35-40 minutes or until almost set and a knife inserted in the centre comes out clean. NOTE: do not let the water boil and do not overcook, or the crèmes will curdle. Take them from the water bath and allow to cool.

They can be made up to 24 hours ahead and kept covered in the refrigerator. Serve at room temperature.

It is traditional in France for these petits pots de crème to be made in the flavours given here; we make all three at once at La Varenne, but an entire recipe for all 9 pots might be made with just one flavour – vanilla, coffee or chocolate – if preferred.

To melt chocolate in a water bath:
1 Chop or break the chocolate into pieces so that it will melt evenly.
2 It is especially important that the pan containing the water has lower sides than the one in which the chocolate is melted so that no water splashes into the melting chocolate. Drops of water can make the chocolate stiffen.
3 The water should only simmer, never boil.
4 Remove the pan of chocolate from the simmering water as soon as the chocolate is melted.

30
YEAST DOUGHS
Kneading a touch of luxury

No food has so captured our imagination as bread. The staff of life, the symbolic link between God and man – the imagery surrounding the humble household loaf is unending. Perhaps this fascination reflects our dependence on bread as a staple, or perhaps it arises from the seeming magic of yeast, which transforms an apparently inert lump of dough into a puffy, aromatic loaf.

The French tend to be conservative about their bread. With the exception of a few country breads made with wholemeal or rye flour, they stick to their famous baguettes, flutes and ficelles plus the plumper family loaves, all made from a basic dough of water and white flour, raised with yeast and baked to a crisp brown. Each is made (like butter-layered croissants) to a standard recipe and depends for its quality on the *tour de main* – the technique – of its maker. These are baker's breads: no restaurant chef or household cook would dream of competing with the boulanger, who has been at his trade from the age of 14.

It is the luxury breads that are made at home – brioche, golden with butter; savarin and babas soaked with syrup and rum; pizza and pissaladière that have spilled over the border from Italy; and the sweet Kugelhopf that is the traditional breakfast in Alsace. Brioche is the most versatile of these breads. There is a plain brioche for wrapping sausages, foie gras, or fillet of beef, and a richer brioche that can be flavoured with dried fruits or fried to make sublime doughnuts.

The richest dough of all is used for loaves, large and small, baked in a fluted mould and crowned with the characteristic ball of dough. Some bakers, pushing luxuriance to the limit and ignoring the usual rule of 'a half kilo of butter per kilo of flour', match every kilo of flour in their brioche with a kilo of butter. No wonder the Abbé Perrin, director of the first Paris opera in the 1600's, imposed on delinquent musicians fines which were used each month to buy a giant brioche for the whole orchestra. The culprits had to sew brioche-shaped emblems on their coats and soon 'brioche' entered the language as slang for mistake.

All these luxury breads are great fun to make and to shape – puffed and fluted Kugelhopf, bucket-shaped baba, ringed savarin or ball-crowned brioche, each dough has its traditional form. However, flavourings and fillings can be varied at whim – cinnamon, nutmeg, grated lemon peel and dried and candied fruits are some of the favourites in Alsace. The southern pissaladière, traditionally topped with onion, olives and anchovies, can also be flavoured with tomatoes or sausage.

Bread-making can never be an exact science as it depends so much on the idiosyncracies of yeast, its vital ingredient. Yeast is a living plant that can produce tiny bubbles of carbon dioxide and thus expand the volume of a flour and water dough. Like any plant, yeast is particular about its environment. It thrives at around 27C (85F); at lower temperatures it works more slowly or simply goes to sleep, and at 54C (130F), it expires. Yeast comes in a fresh cake or in dried granules and to dissolve it, the liquid into which it is sprinkled (usually water) must be at blood heat, ie no warmer than your hands. After about 5 minutes, and a couple of stirs, it should have been completely absorbed.

The average quantity of yeast needed is 15g per 500g ($\frac{1}{2}$oz per 1lb) of flour, but babas and savarins need more so that the dough will be riddled with holes and absorb plenty of sugar syrup. Remember that yeast is relatively more active in a large quantity of dough, particularly if the dough is soft.

The salt used in breadmaking is another essential, but it must be mixed with the flour, and never added directly to the yeast, as salt kills yeast. Salt not only gives flavour to bread, but also slows the rising, giving the dough a more even texture and a mellower flavour. The usual proportion of salt to flour is 20-25g per kilo (about $\frac{2}{3}$oz per 2lb). Saltless bread is a disaster; if you have forgotten the salt, better to add it late than never.

Sugar, on the other hand, activates yeast. It, too, is usually added to the flour along with the salt, since sugar tends to overstimulate the yeast if mixed directly into it. Eggs and butter (for richness) are common in many French yeast doughs, but milk is rarely used.

These ingredients are combined and mixed, according to the recipe instruction, to doughs of varying consistencies: soft but not sticky (for pissaladière and sweet breads), very soft (for brioche) and almost pourable (for savarins and babas). If you like, the flour

LUXURIES FOR HOME-BAKING

Pissaladière (back left) topped with tomatoes, onions, olives and anchovies; Saucisson en brioche (back right) – a French garlic sausage cooked in savoury brioche dough, and a classic savarin (front) – a ring of sweet yeast dough, baked then soaked in syrup and decorated with angelica and glacé cherries

and the mixing bowl can be warmed beforehand to boost the action of the yeast. Next comes kneading, the all-important exercise that develops the gluten in the flour and distributes the yeast throughout the dough so that the bread rises with a close, even texture. Ideally, kneading is done by hand – yeast loves warmth – but if you are making large quantities of dough, a heavy-duty electric mixer will ease the task.

For firm doughs, kneading is done on a floured board, pushing the dough away with one hand, folding it, turning and pushing again – this procedure is often called the English or American method. The French lift brioche in the air and throw it down on the board with gay abandon, while savarin and baba dough is kneaded in a bowl with the hand cupped like a spoon. Whatever the method, kneading should last several minutes, and the finished dough should look smooth and slightly shiny, with a characteristically elastic texture. The feel of well-kneaded dough is unmistakable, and when you have made bread once or twice, you will recognize it instantly.

Then the dough is put in a bowl, sprinkled with flour (for firm doughs) or brushed with butter (for soft doughs) and covered with a damp cloth to keep the dough from drying. It should be left in a humid, draught-free place at a temperature of about 25-30C (78-85F) to rise for an hour, or for longer, depending on the mixture. In the old days the dough went into the airing cupboard, but this refuge of warmth is fast disappearing, the modern alternative being the top of a radiator or the protected pilot light of a gas stove. Do not rush, but allow the yeast to leaven the dough at its own steady pace.

Most recipes say that the dough should double in bulk during the first rising. Actually it may rise less than that – La Varenne's pâtissier Chef Jorant says one and a half times the original bulk is ideal. Again, experience will tell you when dough is sufficiently risen. A savarin should look bubbly, and the test of a firmer dough is that it does not spring back when pressed with a fingertip.

Now comes 'knocking down' – cooking jargon for kneading lightly to deflate air bubbles. Left to its own devices, dough will go on rising and rising – as I discovered one summer morning when I went into the kitchen to find an amorphous sprawling mass had taken charge of the table – the bread dough I had started the night before.

To knock down brioche and other firmer doughs, turn them onto the board again and fold several times while patting with floured hands – this gives the yeast more strength during the final rising. For very soft doughs that were beaten in a bowl, additional ingredients such as butter, raisins or nuts are beaten in at this point. The beating knocks down the dough at the same time.

Next the dough is shaped or moulded: it is either rolled, twisted or flattened into shape on a floured board and set in a buttered mould or on a baking sheet; if very soft, it may be spooned into the mould. Then it is left to 'prove' (rise again), this time in a slightly warmer place so the yeast works more quickly.

Before baking bread it is vital to preheat the oven so that the yeast is killed almost at once by high heat – around 220C (425F) gas 7 for small breads like brioche and 190C (375F) gas 5 for large loaves. If the oven is not hot enough, the yeast will continue working and the bread will lose its shape. When the bread has browned and set, however, the heat should be lowered so that a loaf cooks completely without burning. The test of a well-cooked loaf is time-honoured – a tap on the bottom that brings a hollow sound.

Mixing, kneading, allowing to rise, knocking down, shaping, proving, baking. The effort yields the common yet magical breads and yeast cakes celebrated in custom and legend. It was customary for an Alsatian bride, as part of her trousseau, to bring a mould for baking raisin-studded Kugelhopf, and in Lorraine a braided brioche is still served to celebrate a baptism.

Rum babas are said to have been created by King Stanislas of Lorraine, who soaked his Kugelhopf in rum and found the result so delicious that he named it after the hero of his favourite romance, the 'Thousand And One Nights'. Such lore testifies to our fascination with this staff of life made from flour, water, the simplest of flavourings – and yeast.

Flour in bread-making

The gluten content is an all-important consideration in choosing flour for yeast doughs because it is the gluten, a type of protein, which gives elasticity to the dough and an even texture to the finished loaf.

1 Flours made from grains other than wheat have a lower, or non-existent, gluten content, and most must be mixed with wheat flour for bread-making. Rye flour can be used alone, but in France it is usually mixed with wheat flour for a finer loaf.

2 Plain flour makes perfectly good bread, especially when used for rich breads like brioche in which the gluten content is not as important as it is in less rich doughs.

3 'Strong' flour, intended for bread-making, is especially recommended. Hard wheat, which has a high gluten content, is included in the blend of cereals from which this flour is milled.

THE WAY TO SUCCESS

1 Have all the ingredients at room temperature or, in winter, slightly warm. Take eggs from the refrigerator in good time and soften butter.

2 To hurry rising, or on cold days, add a little more yeast. However, the flavour of dough may be harmed if more than 30g (1oz) yeast is added per 500g (1lb) of flour.

3 Yeast is relatively more active in a large quantity of dough, so when doubling a recipe, use a little less than double the yeast.

4 If dough rises too fast, the texture of the finished bread will be uneven and the flavour poor. If the dough gets much too hot, the yeast will be killed and the dough may start cooking on the bottom of the bowl or mould.

5 If dough rises too slowly, it may turn sour.

6 Dough that puffs too much during the second rising is crumbly when cooked; over-risen Kugelhopf and savarin doughs may become liquid and run out of the moulds during baking. Dough that hasn't risen enough is heavy.

7 So steam can escape, transfer bread to a rack *immediately* after baking.

8 If using dried yeast, check the instructions on the packet when adjusting the proportions.

Handling brioche dough

1 Brioche dough must rise at a relatively low temperature, around 18C (65F), so that the butter does not melt and run out of the dough.

2 After the second rising and before shaping, thoroughly chill the dough to ensure that it stays firm.

3 Keep brioche cool while working with it. If your hands are particularly warm, try lowering their temperature by plunging them into cold water.

Getting ahead

1 To slow rising, transfer dough to refrigerator.

2 After rising once, yeast doughs can be knocked down, left in the refrigerator and shaped the next day. On warm days, let the yeast dough rise not more than $1\frac{1}{2}$ times its volume before punching down and refrigerating. The dough will continue to rise very slowly in the refrigerator.

3 Dough can be shaped, then kept covered overnight in the refrigerator. It will rise during that time, and can finish rising just before baking.

4 If you want to keep the dough for more than 1 day, wrap it tightly after the first rising and freeze it for up to 1 week. Defrost in the refrigerator overnight.

5 Unbaked yeast dough that is shaped and ready for baking can also be frozen for 1-2 weeks. Let it thaw slowly in the refrigerator, then bake as soon as it shows signs of rising. Do not bake the dough while it is still frozen or the middle will not cook properly.

6 Baked yeast pastries freeze well. To thaw, let them come to room temperature, or defrost them more quickly by warming in a low oven. Savarins and babas keep especially well, because they can be reheated and moistened with syrup just before being served.

PISSALADIERE

Serves 6-8 as a starter

for the dough

about 400-450g (13-14oz) flour

150ml ($\frac{1}{4}$pt) warm water

15g ($\frac{1}{2}$oz or 1 cake) compressed yeast

2 eggs, beaten to mix

8g ($1\frac{1}{2}$ level teaspoons) salt

for the topping

4 tablespoons olive oil

4 large Spanish or other mild-flavoured onions, sliced

2 teaspoons mixed herbs (basil, thyme, rosemary)

salt and freshly ground black pepper

1 small can anchovy fillets, soaked in a little milk for 20-30 minutes, then drained

4 tomatoes, peeled, sliced and seeded (optional)

60g (2oz) Nice or Greek-style black olives, stoned

30-35cm (12-14in) diameter flan ring or pie tin

For the dough: sift the flour into a warm bowl and make a well in the centre. Pour the warm water into the well, sprinkle or crumble the yeast over and let it stand for 5 minutes or until dissolved. Add the eggs and salt and mix with the hand, gradually drawing in the flour to form a soft dough. Turn it out on a floured board and knead for 5 minutes or until smooth and elastic, working in more flour if necessary. Transfer the dough to an oiled bowl, turn it over so the top is oiled, cover with a damp cloth and leave to rise in a warm place for 45 minutes, or until about doubled in bulk.

For the topping: heat the oil in a saucepan, add the onions, herbs, salt and pepper and press a piece of foil on top. Cover the pan and cook, stirring occasionally, over very low heat for 15-20 minutes or until the onions are very soft, almost a purée. NOTE: do not let them brown. Cut

the drained anchovy fillets in half lengthwise. Grease the flan ring or pie tin and a baking sheet.

When the dough has risen, knead it lightly to knock out the air. Pat the dough out in the flan ring or pie tin, pushing it up the sides, and spread the onion mixture on top. If using tomatoes, arrange them on top and sprinkle with freshly ground black pepper (no extra salt is needed). Cover the pissaladière with a lattice of anchovy fillets and place an olive in each of the diamonds. Allow to rise in a warm place for 10-15 minutes or until the dough has once again almost doubled in bulk. Set the oven at moderately hot, 190C (375F) gas 5.

Bake the pissaladière in the heated oven for 40-50 minutes or until browned. Serve it hot or at room temperature.

BRIOCHE

More than any other bread, brioche puts butter in the limelight: excellent butter makes an outstanding brioche, while use of butter that is not so fresh will be instantly apparent in the finished bread.

500g (about 1lb) flour
12g (2½ level teaspoons) salt
30g (1oz) sugar
15g (½oz or 1 cake) compressed yeast
2 tablespoons lukewarm water
6 eggs
250g (½lb) unsalted butter
15 small brioche moulds; or two 21cm (6in) diameter brioche moulds

Sift the flour onto a marble slab or board and make a very large well in the centre. Place the salt and the sugar in little piles on one side of the well and the crumbled yeast or yeast granules on another side of the well as far from the salt and sugar as possible. Using your fingers, dilute the yeast with the lukewarm water without mixing in the salt or sugar. Mix about ⅛ of the flour into the yeast, still keeping the mixture on one side of the flour well. Leave to rise for 5-10 minutes.

Break in 5 of the eggs. With your fingertips, mix the eggs with the salt, sugar and yeast mixture; still using your fingertips, flick some of the flour over the centre mixture so the centre is no longer visible. Quickly draw in the rest of the flour with both hands – being careful not to let the liquid escape outside the well. Pull the dough into large crumbs using the fingertips of both hands. If it is dry, beat the last egg and add it. Press the dough firmly together – it should be soft and sticky.

Mix the dough by pinching off 2 small portions between the thumb and forefinger of each hand and placing the portions removed on the other end of the mass of dough. Repeat this pinching motion 5-7 times. Now knead the dough by lifting it up and slapping it down on a floured board or marble slab for 5-10 minutes or until it is very smooth and elastic.

Pound the butter to soften it thoroughly. Place the block of softened butter on the dough and mix it in with the same pinching motion used above. After 5-7 times, knead the dough by slapping it on the

KNEADING BRIOCHE DOUGH

Pick up the soft dough in your fingers, then quickly slap it down on a flat surface, withdrawing your hands at the same time. Repeat this lifting and slapping process for 5-10 minutes, until the dough is smooth and elastic

Mix in the softened butter by pinching off large portions of dough from the end nearest to you, then replacing them on the opposite end. Do this 5 or 6 more times, then knead until the butter is well blended into the dough

board as lightly as possible until the butter is completely mixed in.

Transfer the dough to a lightly oiled bowl, turn it over, cover the bowl with a damp cloth and let it 'prove' or rise again at room temperature for about 2 hours or until nearly doubled in bulk. Remove to a floured board or marble slab and fold it into three, patting it to knock out the air. Cover with a damp cloth and leave to rise again at room temperature until doubled in bulk, or leave overnight in the refrigerator. Brioche dough is much easier to handle if chilled. NOTE: up to 30g (1oz) yeast can be used if you want the dough to rise as quickly as possible.

Butter the brioche tins. Knead the dough lightly to knock out the air and divide it into 15 pieces (for individual brioches) or in half (for large loaves). Pinch off a third of each piece of dough and shape both large and small pieces into balls. Set a large ball in the base of each brioche pan, cut a deep cross in the top and nestle the smaller ball into it. The shaped brioches can be kept up to 36 hours in the refrigerator, or they can be frozen for up to 3 weeks.

Allow the brioches to rise in a warm place allowing about 15 minutes for small ones or 20-25 minutes for large loaves or until the pans are almost full. (Chilled brioches may already have risen sufficiently in the refrigerator.) Set the oven at hot, 220C (425F) gas 7. Brush the brioches with glaze and bake in the heated oven for 15-20 minutes for the small brioches or until they are well browned. For

large loaves, after 15 minutes turn the oven down to moderately hot, 190C (375F) gas 5, and continue baking 30-40 minutes or until the brioches pull away from the sides of the pan and sound hollow when tapped on the bottom. Cool them on a wire rack.

SAUCISSON EN BRIOCHE
(Sausage in brioche)

A little less egg is needed for this recipe than for brioche, since dough for wrapping should be relatively stiff so it can be rolled out easily. Serves 6 as a first course.

brioche dough made with 300g (10oz) flour, 8g (1½ level teaspoons) salt, 20g (⅔oz) sugar, 12g (⅔oz) compressed yeast, 2 tablespoons water, 3½-4 eggs and 165g (5½oz) unsalted butter
700g (1½lb) French garlic sausage
1 egg, beaten with ½ teaspoon salt (for glaze)
flour (for rolling)
large loaf tin 23×12·5×7·5cm (9×5×3in)

Make the brioche dough and leave to rise in a warm place. Remove the skin from the garlic sausage. Grease the loaf tin. If the dough is very soft, chill it in the refrigerator before rolling it out.

Roll out the dough on a lightly floured board to a 30×15cm (12×6in) rectangle and brush it with egg glaze. Brush the sausage with egg glaze also, and roll it lightly in flour. NOTE: this prevents he sausage and brioche from separating while baking.

Set the sausage lengthwise in the centre of the dough and roll the dough around it. Pinch the edges to seal well, turn it over so that the seam is underneath and place in the prepared tin. Cover with a damp cloth and leave to rise again in a warm place for 25-30 minutes, or until the tin is almost full. Be careful not to leave it in too warm a place or the butter will seep out. If the butter starts to do this, move the dough to a cooler place. Set the oven at hot, 200C (400F) gas 6.

Brush the loaf with egg glaze and make 3 holes in the top to let the steam escape. If you like, score the top with a small knife to make a decorative pattern, or decorate with trimmings of dough. Bake in the heated oven for 30-35 minutes or until the brioche is well browned and starts to pull away from the sides of the pan. Turn out onto a rack to cool.

Serve the brioche the same day or store it in the freezer. The loaf can also be shaped in the tin and frozen. It should be thawed and left to rise again just before baking.

To serve: cut the loaf in 2cm (1½in) slices, discarding the ends so each person has some sausage.

OEUFS POCHES EN BRIOCHE
(Poached eggs in brioches)

This recipe is a good example of how the French use various standard elements in their cuisine as building blocks to create an endless number of dishes. Brioche, poached eggs, duxelles and hollandaise sauce are all used repeatedly in the repertoire of French cooking. Here the four parts are put together to make an excellent first course. Eggs in brioches could also be served as a luncheon or supper dish.

Serves 8 as a starter or 4 as a main course.

8 small brioches
8 fresh eggs
hollandaise sauce (page 193) made with 180g (6oz) butter, 3 tablespoons water, 3 egg yolks, salt, white pepper and juice of ½ lemon
for the duxelles
30g (1oz) butter
½ onion, finely chopped
250g (8oz) mushrooms, finely chopped

Kugelhopf is baked traditionally in a high round, fluted metal or earthenware ring mould. The central hole permits the oven heat to reach the interior of the dough more quickly. Earthenware moulds are best because their thickness helps maintain a regular temperature. Alsatians also say that they gradually absorb butter and make each Kugelhopf better than the last.
Savarin moulds are plain metal rings that come in large and small sizes. Savarin is such a rich dough that it may stick if made in more elaborate moulds.
Babas are baked in plain dariole or individual bucket-shaped moulds. These moulds should be wiped clean after use but should not be washed or the babas will stick.

salt and pepper
tablespoon chopped parsley

Cut the tops from the brioches and hollow out the bases, leaving a shell 1cm (⅜in) thick.
For the duxelles: heat the butter in a frying pan, put in the onion and cook until soft but not brown. Add the mushrooms with salt and pepper and cook over high heat, stirring, until all the moisture has evaporated. Stir in the chopped parsley, taste for seasoning and adjust if necessary.

Poach the eggs for about three minutes, cooking them lightly so that they are still soft. Trim and transfer them to a bowl of cold water.

Make the hollandaise sauce and keep it warm in a water bath.

To finish: heat the brioches in a low oven, 170C (325F) gas 3, for 8-10 minutes. Reheat the duxelles and spoon some into each brioche. Transfer the eggs to a bowl of warm water to heat them, drain carefully on paper towels and place one in each brioche. Spoon a little warm hollandaise sauce over each egg, replace the brioche 'hats' and serve immediately. Serve the rest of the sauce separately.

KUGELHOPF

Recipes for Kugelhopf vary from bread dough to a rich pastry. Some pâtissiers make Kugelhopf by adding raisins to brioche dough.
SERVES 8

50g (1¾oz) whole blanched almonds, sliced
15g (½oz or 1 cake) compressed yeast
150ml (¼pt) lukewarm milk
400g (13oz) flour
30g (2oz) sugar
10g (2 level teaspoons) salt
3 eggs
125g (4oz) unsalted butter, softened
50g (1¾oz) currants
50g (1¾oz) raisins
icing sugar (for sprinkling)
18-20cm (7-8in) diameter earthenware Kugelhopf mould

Butter the mould generously and press the almonds around the sides and base.

Crumble or sprinkle the yeast over 4 tablespoons of the milk and let it stand for about 5 minutes until dissolved. Stir in about 100g (3½oz) flour, or enough to make a sticky dough. Cover and leave it in a warm place to rise for ½ hour, or until doubled in bulk. Sift the remaining flour into a warm bowl, make a well in the centre and add the yeast mixture, the remaining milk, sugar, salt and eggs.

Work the ingredients with the hand to a smooth dough, then knead the dough by slapping it vigorously on a marble slab, or in the bowl, for about 5 minutes or until the dough is very elastic. Work in the butter gently; work in the dried fruits. Transfer the dough to the mould – the bread should half fill the mould. Cover with a damp cloth and allow to rise in a warm place for 30-40 minutes, or until the dough is about 1cm (¾in) from the top. Set the oven at hot, 200C (400F) gas 6.

When the dough has risen, place the mould on a baking sheet and bake in the heated oven for 40-50 minutes or until the Kugelhopf is well browned, comes away from the sides of the pan and a toothpick inserted in the centre comes out clean. If the top begins to get very brown during baking, cover the Kugelhopf with a sheet of foil, turn down the oven to moderate, 180C (350F) gas 4, and continue baking.

Let the Kugelhopf stand for a few moments before turning out onto a wire rack to cool. Sprinkle it with icing sugar before serving.

Kugelhopf is best eaten the day it is baked, or it can be frozen, baked or unbaked, for up to 3 months.

TRANCHES DE BRIOCHE AUX AMANDES

(Almond brioche slices)

Brioche mousseline dough is richer than the normal brioche dough and, because of the large quantity of butter, it is too soft to be shaped. It is usually baked in cans.

SERVES 8

brioche mousseline made with 500g (1lb) flour, 12g ($2\frac{1}{2}$ level teaspoons) salt, 30g (1oz) sugar, 15g ($\frac{1}{2}$oz) yeast, 2 tablespoons lukewarm water, 6 eggs and 350g (13oz) butter

100g ($3\frac{1}{2}$oz) flaked almonds (for sprinkling)

icing sugar (for sprinkling)

for the almond cream

60g (2oz) butter, softened

60g (2oz) sugar

1 egg, beaten to mix

60g (2oz) ground blanched almonds

10g ($\frac{1}{3}$oz) flour

tablespoon rum

for the syrup

10ml (4oz) water

100g ($3\frac{1}{2}$oz) sugar

25ml (1fl oz) rum

two 680g (1lb 8oz) capacity empty cans

Make the brioche mousseline and allow it to rise overnight in the refrigerator. Bake the cans in a hot oven, 230C (450F) gas 8, for 45 minutes to sterilise them and allow them to cool.

Butter the moulds thoroughly. Add enough of the dough to fill them by a third to a half and leave in a cool place for 6-8 hours or until the dough rises to the top. Set the oven at very hot, 220C (425F) gas 7.

Bake the brioche mousselines in the hot oven for about 10 minutes or until they begin to brown. Turn the oven down to moderate, 180C (350F) gas 4, and bake for about a further 35 minutes or until they are firm. Turn them out onto a rack to cool.

For the almond cream: cream the butter, gradually beat in the sugar and continue beating until the mixture is soft and light. Gradually add the beaten egg, beating well after each addition. Fold in the ground almonds and flour. Add the rum.

For the syrup: bring the water and sugar to the boil in a small saucepan. Remove from the heat, allow it to cool slightly and add the rum.

To finish: set the oven at very hot, 230C (450F) gas 8, or heat the grill. Cut the cooled brioche into 1cm ($\frac{3}{8}$in) slices. Brush each slice generously with syrup. On one side of each slice of brioche, spread a thin layer of almond cream. Sprinkle the cream with the flaked almonds and then with icing sugar. Put the slices on a buttered baking sheet and bake in the very hot oven or grill until golden brown. Serve warm or cooled.

BEIGNETS BRIOCHES

(Brioche doughnuts)

These are most delicious when eaten hot, straight out of the pan.

MAKES 24

brioche dough made with 500g (1lb) flour, 12g ($2\frac{1}{2}$ level teaspoons) salt, 30g (1oz) sugar, 15g ($\frac{1}{2}$oz) compressed yeast, 2 tablespoons lukewarm water, 6 eggs and 250g ($\frac{1}{2}$lb) unsalted butter

125-200ml (4-7oz) strawberry or other whole fruit conserve

deep fat (for frying)

icing or caster sugar (for coating)

6-8cm ($2\frac{1}{2}$-3in) biscuit cutter

Prepare the brioche dough and let it rise, then knead the dough lightly and work in the softened butter. Chill it. Roll out the dough on a floured surface to about 1cm ($\frac{1}{2}$in) thickness and cut out rounds with the biscuit cutter. Put a teaspoon of conserve in the centre of each round. Brush the edges with water, pinch them together and roll the dough into balls so that the fruit is enclosed. Set them on a serving dish or baking sheet and leave in a warm place for 5-10 minutes or until just beginning to rise. NOTE: if preparing ahead, cover the doughnuts at this point and put them in the refrigerator to check the rising. They can be kept overnight in the refrigerator.

To finish: heat the deep fat to moderate, 180C (350F) on a frying thermometer. Fry a few doughnuts at a time for 5-8 minutes or until puffed and dark golden brown. Turn the doughnuts if necessary so that they brown evenly. Lift them out with a draining spoon, dry on paper towels and fry the remaining doughnuts in the same way. Shake the doughnuts one by one in a bag of icing or caster sugar until coated.

Butter the brioche tins. Knead the dough lightly to knock out the air and divide it into 15 pieces (for individual brioches) or in half (for large loaves). Pinch off a third of each piece of dough and shape both large and small pieces into balls. Set a large ball in the base of each brioche pan, cut a deep cross in the top and nestle the smaller ball into it. The shaped brioches can be kept up to 36 hours in the refrigerator, or they can be frozen for up to 3 weeks.

Allow the brioches to rise in a warm place allowing about 15 minutes for small ones or 20-25 minutes for large loaves or until the pans are almost full. (Chilled brioches may already have risen sufficiently in the refrigerator.) Set the oven at hot, 220C (425F) gas 7. Brush the brioches with glaze and bake in the heated oven for 15-20 minutes for the small brioches or until they are well browned. For large loaves, after 15 minutes turn the oven down to moderately hot 190C (375F) gas 5, and continue baking 30-40 minutes or until the brioches pull away from the sides of the pan and sound hollow when tapped on the bottom. Cool them on a wire rack.

SAVARIN

Savarin holds many possibilities: the dough can be varied by the addition of chopped candied fruit. The syrup for savarin can also be flavoured with cinnamon, coriander, mace, Kirsch, orange rind or puréed strawberries. When served cold, ice-cream, fruit salad or Chantilly cream mixed with fresh or poached fruit can be spooned into the centre. Savarin can also be served hot, with a fruit sauce flavoured with liqueur.

SERVES 8-10

300g (10oz) flour

4 tablespoons warm water

15g ($\frac{1}{2}$oz or 1 cake) compressed yeast

4 eggs

5g (1 level teaspoon) salt

25g ($\frac{5}{6}$oz) sugar

150g (5oz) unsalted butter, softened

3 tablespoons rum (for sprinkling)

for the syrup

250g (8oz) sugar

600ml (1pt) water

rind and juice of $\frac{1}{2}$ lemon

1·25 litre or 1¼pt capacity ring or savarin mould, or 2 small ring moulds (300-375ml (½-⅝pt) capacity)

Sift the flour into a bowl. Make a well in the centre and pour in the warm water. Sprinkle the yeast over the water and let it stand for 5 minutes, or until the yeast is dissolved. Add the eggs, salt and sugar and stir with the hand, gradually drawing in the flour to form a smooth dough. Beat with the hand, raising the dough and letting it fall back into the bowl with a slap, for 5 minutes – or until the dough is very elastic. Cover the bowl and allow to stand in a warm place for ¾-1 hour or until it has doubled in bulk. Set the oven at hot, 200C (400F) gas 6.

Beat the softened butter into the risen dough until the dough is smooth. Thoroughly butter the savarin mould, spoon in the dough to fill the mould(s) by one third, cover with a cloth and leave to rise in a warm place for 30-35 minutes, or until risen to the top. Bake in the heated oven for 20-25 minutes, or until the savarin is brown and shrinks from the sides of the pan. The savarin can be baked ahead and stored for up to 3 days in an airtight container or frozen for up to 3 months. A few hours before serving, warm it to tepid in the oven and soak with syrup.

For the syrup: heat the sugar in the water until dissolved, bring to a boil, add the lemon rind and simmer for 5 minutes. Remove from the heat, add the lemon juice and, if possible, place the savarin in the very hot syrup in the saucepan, spooning the syrup over the savarin until it absorbs as much as possible. If the savarin cannot be placed directly into the hot syrup, put it on a rack over a tray and keep spooning hot syrup over, reheating any that falls into the tray, until all the syrup is absorbed – the savarin will swell and become very shiny.

Just before serving, sprinkle the rum over the savarin. Melt the red currant jelly in a small pan, stirring gently, and brush over the savarin to glaze. Slice the cherries in half and cut diamond shapes from the angelica. Arrange the four cherry halves on top of the savarin and flank each with angelica.

To knead the dough: tilt the bowl slightly and, using your hand like a spoon – palm upwards – lift the dough and throw it back into the bowl with a slap. Continue until the dough is elastic

Carefully spoon enough of the dough into a well-buttered savarin, or ring mould, to fill it by about a third, then leave it in a warm place for 30-35 minutes for the dough to rise

Put the mould in a warm place and allow the dough to rise until it completely fills the mould before baking. Rising should take about half an hour, but judge by the dough not the clock

Spoon the warm syrup over the savarin until as much as possible has been absorbed – it may be necessary to warm the syrup again while you do so. The savarin will swell and glisten

SAVARIN CHANTILLY

Fill the centre of the savarin with Chantilly cream made with 300ml (½pt) double cream, stiffly whipped and flavoured with 1 tablespoon caster sugar and ½ teaspoon vanilla essence.

AN ANTHOLOGY OF FRENCH COOKING AND KITCHEN TERMS

Compiled by Jane Grigson

A

Acorns   Originally believed to be the first food of mankind:

> *'Those first unpolished matrons*
> *   big and bold,*
> *Gave suck to infants of gigantic*
> *   mould,*
> *Rough as their savage lords who*
> *   ranged the wood,*
> *And fat with acorns belched their*
> *   windy food.'*

Acorns certainly were popular throughout Europe in antiquity. People turn to them still in times of extreme hardship—coffee in France in the last war was often made from acorns.

Mainly, they have been a secondary food ever since people were prepared – and able – to give up some of their own provisions to feed animals. One of the most moving of the illuminations in the medieval illustrated manuscript 'Très Riches Heures' shows the swineherd in November striding to the forest with his pigs, where they will gorge and fatten on acorns. That was in central France in the 15th century, but even now, in such places as our New Forest, you may occasionally see pigs turned loose in autumn in the same way, to fatten for Christmas hams and charcuterie.

Aillade and **Ailloli** (Aioli)   These are Provençal forms of mayonnaise, heavily flavoured with garlic (ail). Aillade, which also contains walnuts, sometimes hazelnuts as well, is more usually served with fish, like the different nut sauces of the Mediterranean, and with snails and potatoes. **Ailloli** – especially in the form of *ailloli garni* or *le grand ailloli* – goes with an assemblage of vegetables, fish and meat, chosen according to the season. The bowl of sauce is placed in the centre of a huge dish and the other items are arranged around, in a still-life profusion of colour and shape.

Air   An important aim in any good cooking is to combine flavour with lightness, by incorporating air into a solid mass of ingredients – and retaining it. Yeast, eggs, much beating – for as long as four hours in some old cake recipes – were ways of achieving this, but the invention of reliable and controllable ovens made things easier. This was the great time in France for meringues, soufflés, choux pastry confections, brioches, sponge biscuits and cakes. The development in the 19th century of compact yeast, baking powder, regulated gas stoves, and in the 20th century of rotary and electric beaters and thermostatically controlled cookers, has brought these dishes into every home. But the professional chef still puts his egg whites into a copper bowl, and his cream over ice, and whisks them with a hand beater, for the greatest volume and lightness.

Alcohol   Two nations with the highest reputations for cooking, the French and the Chinese, habitually make use of alcohol. And of the two, the French have the advantage – with a huge range of table wines, fortified wines, cider and spirits to choose from. These fine flavourings are inimitable. They admit no substitute, and with meat, wine used in a marinade has a tenderizing effect as well.

Teetotallers and family cooks need not feel nervous – in most recipes the actual alcohol is burnt or cooked away completely. Only in sweet dishes is alcohol used straight from the bottle – pineapple with Kirsch, peaches in wine, pear sorbets and certain chocolate cakes.

There is indeed no substitute. If you have not got the one listed in the ingredients, it is better to use a different one rather than to leave alcohol out altogether.

Instead of Calvados, use whisky (preferably single malt).
Instead of Kirsch, use gin (perhaps with a drop of bitter almond essence added).
Instead of red wine, use white.
Instead of wine, use cider, or a smaller amount of dry vermouth or dry sherry.
Instead of Madeira, use Marsala, port, brown sherry, or a sweet muscatel wine.

Beer is used in northern French cookery, as you might expect, but is kept for robust dishes such as the various carbonnades, ox liver with prunes, ox tail, stewed beef and beetroot.

If you have no alcohol at all, and are making a beef or venison stew, use a tablespoon of wine or sherry vinegar with 2 lumps of sugar.

Remember that you rarely get more from a dish than you put into it. *Grands crus* apart, use the best wine you can afford that is appropriate to the dish. Rules are sometimes the refuge of the unthinking cook – sole and chicken and certain fish can be cooked with red wine; wine can be drunk with cheese. The delight of a sweet wine at the end of a meal, Monbazillac, Beaumes de Venise, Frontignan, Bonnezeaux and so on, is often overlooked.

Almonds   It cannot strictly be said that almond trees originated in the Mediterranean. Western Asia was their first home, and our name for almonds – like the French *amandes* – goes back beyond the Greek, or so it is said, to Hebrew words meaning 'divine fruit'. All the same, almond trees came westward thousands of years ago; cultivated, or as wilding escapes, they certainly grow all round the Mediterranean. It is from south European orchards that we still get most of our supplies, including Jordan almonds – which do not in fact come from the Holy Land, but from the 'garden', or 'jardin' variety

247

of the countryside around Malaga.

In Christian Europe of the Middle Ages, it was almonds with everything. A noble household would easily get through 5kg (11lb) a week – not so much when you consider that almonds with raisins, often from Malaga too, figs and dates were a normal dessert for the wealthy, and that on the many fast days almond 'milk' had to be substituted for cows' milk.

This prohibition was gradually relaxed, and by the 17th century the 'cuisine maigre' of France avoided only meat, game, poultry and the stocks made from them. Almost the sole relic of the great age of almond cookery is a soup sometimes called 'soupe à la reine', which was too good to be forgotten.

To French pâtissiers, almonds are indeed the divine fruit, one of their main ingredients. If you could, by magic, suddenly extract all the almonds from Parisian cake shops, the splendid displays would collapse into a meagre choice in a waste of crumbs. Operators without conscience, and this applies mainly to Britain, will cheat in the matter of almonds. If you want good tarts, cakes, biscuits in which they should be a major ingredient, you will have to be your own pâtissier. Hard work, and a good way to learn the high cost of skill.

Although that invaluable flavouring, praline powder, can be made in advance and stored in air-tight jars, blanched almonds, split and slivered almonds, chopped and ground almonds are best prepared just before they are used. It is cheering to discover that some cakes taste better when made with unblanched almonds ground to a coarse powder – but wash and dry them first.

One pleasure of a spring holiday in France is a basketful of green almonds. The shells are still soft and velvety to touch, the colour is exquisite. You split them in half with a knife, and extract the white young nut, which has little flavour but a crisp and agreeable juiciness.

Angel hair and **Angels on horseback** Angelic gastronomy has not been much of a stimulus to French chefs and cooks. Of the two examples I have found, **angel hair** is the name of a brilliant jam made with shredded carrots: its main use is to flavour the creamy interior of an angel hair charlotte. **Angels on horseback** are savouries made by grilling oysters which have been rolled up in bacon: they are then served on toast or fried bread. We have ignored angel hair, or so it seems, but around 1880 we took enthusiastically to angels on horseback, though with the rising price of oysters their popularity has declined. When the oyster millennium that we are promised every two or three years at last arrives, angels on horseback will canter rapidly back into favour.

Angelica Although angelica is easy to grow in this country, candying the hollow stalks is a laborious process and we have prudently left this to the French. The disadvantage is that after a lifetime of buying it in tiny packets, one can hardly think of it as a plant at all. I was startled when a pastrycook in Niort, a main centre of the angelica trade in France, waved a fresh, juicy stalk of it under my nose; but the smell was instantly recognisable.

Niort is more or less on the route to Spain and is well worth a visit. Close by is the Marais, a sunken bog which is drained by a network of canals. Bridges are few, so everything and everyone gets about by punt, including cows, goats, vegetables for market – and the angelica harvest. Such scenes modelled in angelica and almond paste can be bought from the pastrycook, as well as angelica frogs in angelica reeds, sugared violets on angelica stems with angelica leaves and – presumably as a gesture to La Rochelle and the seaside about 20 miles away – angelica lobsters and crabs in angelica seaweed. You can also buy angelica sweets, and an angelica liqueur – I will leave you to guess the colour – sometimes called 'Sève de Niort', the sap of Niort.

Apart from its general use with nuts and candied fruits in cakemaking, angelica does not have much of a rôle in classical French cookery, but in Poitou and the Charentes region, it flavours cream cheese tarts, cakes and galettes. The great collector of regional recipes, Austin de Croze, suggested a sybaritical dessert – put on the table a dish full of candied angelica stalks, a bottle of angelica liqueur, a carafe of iced water, a box of Egyptian cigarettes and a dozen burning hot brioches made with butter. Light a cigarette, drink a mouthful of iced water, crunch some angelica with the hot brioche and drink a few drops of angelica liqueur. Then you start again.

Anise In the form of anise-flavoured liquors such as pastis and anisette, it appears more in southern French cookery than in the regular repertoire, although there is always the delicious sauce for lobster, flavoured with anisette, given by Dumas in his 'Grand Dictionnaire de Cuisine'. The firm of Pernod and Ricard have produced cookery books of recipes using pastis which goes best of all with fish – in soups, to flavour cream pan sauces – and is not to be despised with snails. It is a flavour to be used with discretion.

Apples The French do not go in much for using sour apples in cooking. No Bramleys. One of the 'reinette' varieties is the usual thing or, if a purée or sauce is needed, an aromatic Calville. The Golden Delicious, originally from America, is a useful summer standby when the reinettes have given out; it has the extra advantage of resolutely holding its shape, which makes it quite a good choice for open apple tarts – indeed, I would say that the Golden Delicious is best kept for cooking as the heat seems to bring out what flavour it has.

However, in winter time, the best English substitute for the reinette apples is our Cox's Orange Pippin. If you can get them, Ellison's Orange, James Grieve and Allington Pippin are also sufficiently acid to cook well. Their natural sweetness and firm consistency make them especially good for use with poultry and pork. When baked they have a wonderful aroma, a richness that makes them irresistible.

Apricots These are used in French cookery with simplicity and directness. Their season is not a long one, and in northern France at least you have to look out for signs saying 'Buy your apricots now', to be sure of catching them at their height, when they are best and cheapest. Then, for a brief time, you see open apricot tarts, each halved fruit stuck with an almond, in the pastrycook's window, and find apricot ices on the restaurant menus. For home cooks it is the time for apricots en croûte (halved, placed on buttered brioche or fine white bread, and baked in the oven) and for making apricot jam. Later in the year, when the soft fruits are over, this jam with its huge pieces of apricot will be served with **coeur à la crème** (see **fromage frais**) and tuiles amandes biscuits.

The most assiduous lover of apricots, though, seems to have been an Englishman, Lord Alvanley, whose dinners were considered to be the best in England. 'He never invited more than eight people, and insisted upon having the somewhat expensive luxury of an apricot tart on the sideboard the whole year round.' Assiduous, yes; discriminating, no. Surely part of the joy of apricots is in their evanescence?

Arrowroot   The powdered rhizome of *Maranta arundinacea* comes mainly from the Caribbean island of Saint Vincent. Here it is cheap and easy to find at every chemist's shop. In France, it is expensive enough to be something of a luxury. Chefs prefer it to the cheaper potato flour (fécule) or cornflour (fécule de maïs), because it needs no cooking to speak of, it does not taste floury, and gives a more vivid gloss to a sauce than the other two. It follows that when you are using French recipes that list fécule, you can substitute arrowroot which is easier to get here than potato flour – and more delicate than cornflour.

Artichokes   These are a prime source of confusion as there are two distinct kinds. The original one – the one most eaten in France – is 'the noble thistle' improved into edibility by the Arab, Italian and French gardeners of the Renaissance. Its globe of spiky green leaves makes it easy to spot at the greengrocer's.

The other one, the one that we call the Jerusalem artichoke, is no relation at all. When Champlain, the explorer and founder of Quebec, first came across it in Indian gardens in 1603, he remarked that it tasted of artichoke. However, it was known in France at first as the Canadian apple, or Canadian truffle. Ten years later it was nicknamed 'topinambour', from the

Tupinamba Indians of Southern America, some of whom had been brought to France to be put on show as if they were exotic animals. And the nickname stuck.

Nonetheless, the artichoke idea caught on with crafty shopkeepers. At the beginning of this century jars of artichoke bottoms, 'qualité supérieure', on sale in Paris were often no more than carefully turned Jerusalem artichokes, which are much easier to grow than globe artichokes. However, as the true artichoke bottoms lose all flavour in bottling and canning, I do not think the deceit mattered very much.

Globe artichokes come to this country now from the fields around Roscoff in Brittany, and they are still something of a rarity. The characteristic French way of eating them, cold with a vinaigrette, or hot with a hollandaise sauce, is beginning to catch on, but I think it will be some years before they are a common feature of special dishes as they are in France.

The base alone is used as a garnish, or combined with shellfish mixtures as an hors d'oeuvre. Sometimes the central leaves and choke are removed, so that vegetable purées and light stuffings can be put into the 'cup'.

In southern France, as in Italy, tiny or 'poivrade' artichokes are eaten raw, perhaps as part of an 'ailloli garni' (at this early stage the choke is not formed enough to be a deterrent), or as an appetiser with coarse salt.

Asparagus   The difference between the asparagus in France and in England lies in variety and price. We prefer the green kind – a preference in which Escoffier (and other French chefs) concurred, to the extent that he persuaded the asparagus growers of Lauris in Provence to change to green asparagus for his wealthy clientèle at the Savoy. The French, however, go mainly for the huge yellowish and purple asparagus of Argenteuil. Whenever you see this name on a French menu, it indicates the use of asparagus, and it was at Argenteuil, beloved of the Impressionists, that Manet painted his asparagus still-life, the bundle tied round with a withy in the traditional and unchanged manner.

In prose, the great celebrator of asparagus was Proust. In 'Swann's

Way', he sees the beauty of asparagus in its basket, waiting to be prepared for the family lunch, each azure crowned head outlined 'star by star', like the flowers in a Giotto fresco at Padua.

No-one with a garden in France leaves asparagus to market gardeners. No doubt this is why the price is so low in comparison with ours. The opening of the six-week season is celebrated as much in cottages as in châteaux. There is much asparagus talk, and someone invariably quotes the tag that asparagus finishes at St Jean, ie. St John's or Midsummer day, 24 June, when the first red currants are ripe enough to pick.

Aubergines   came into southern France centuries ago, from Arab Spain as their name implies, being a form of *al-badinjan* softened on the French tongue. In spite of the fact that La Quintinie was growing them for Louis XIV in the gardens at Versailles, they have always kept a regional and exotic overtone, never being quite at home in the classical tradition – unlike **artichokes** (qv) which came in about the same time, or potatoes which were not taken up in any great way until the start of the 19th century. The names of the most celebrated dishes show this – 'aubergines à l'égyptienne', 'à la turque', 'à la provençale'.

The growing interest of the last 50 years in regional cookery has made ratatouille and *boumiano* (aubergines and tomatoes stewed, and flavoured finally with anchovy) canned clichés of the supermarket. In this form they are to be avoided. Processing destroys the vividness of such southern dishes.

Although the aubergine is thought of as a partner to lamb or tomato, it combines well with mushrooms and, more unexpectedly, with a stuffing of curd cheese. And for fritters, or simply dipped in flour and fried in olive oil, aubergines are high favourites in France.

Do not be put off if aubergines are not the colour or shape you expect – they can be a beautiful ivory white, and very round indeed. The only thing to worry about is their freshness. They should be firm and glossy, not wrinkled (as with humans, wrinkles are a sign of age and experience).

249

Aulx This is the plural of 'ail', meaning garlic. More of a puzzle or trick word than a practicality. Do not be too eager to display your knowledge in the marketplace: many French people are as unfamiliar with 'aulx' as we are. 'Trousses d'ail' (trusses of garlic), 'gousses d'ail' (cloves) and 'têtes d'ail' (heads, ie. the massed cloves on a single stem) are all different ways of avoiding this slightly uncomfortable word.

Avocados Not yet as popular in France, I would say, as they are in this country. Outside the largest towns, you cannot count on finding them and they are expensive. In Paris, it is another matter. The largest avocados I have ever seen – equal to about 5 or 6 of the usual kind – were on sale at Fauchon, the famous food store in the Place Madeleine. They came from Brazil. 'Worth trying?' I asked. The assistant drew in his breath, paused, looked me in the eye and said, 'No! They are tasteless.' The small Hass avocados with the purple-black skin have much more flavour.

At the other extreme are the tiny avocats-cocktail (cocktail is a favourite French adjective for miniature sizes of familiar things, as we say cocktail sausages). They are freaks, rather than a special variety, and unexpectedly have just as much – if not more – flavour than the normal kind. Pull out the quill, which is all they have by way of a stone, peel them and dip them in lemon juice to prevent discoloration. They can indeed be served on cocktail sticks at a party, but are better appreciated when turned into a salad with a little chopped chives or onion and an olive oil vinaigrette.

Avocados in France are normally served halved, with a vinaigrette or with shellfish. Sometimes they come sliced with smoked poultry, or mixed with grapefruit as an hors d'oeuvre. Sometimes they stimulate a chef to a *jeu d'esprit*, which will then be described by food commentators as 'original' (not always a compliment in matters of eating).

B

Bacon Bacon is a danger point for the unwary. Even if it is labelled 'smoked', it has not necessarily been through the smokehouse, but may have been given a smoky flavour in other ways. These other ways save time and shrinkage from loss of moisture, but they do not produce such good quality bacon.

If you cannot find a decent cure, such as Harris's Wiltshire, go to a delicatessen and look for bacon from countries which still demand a high standard in their pork products – Germany, for instance, or Austria (there is at least one Austrian smokehouse in London). *Geraücher Bauchspeck* is much closer to the French *lard* than most bacon on sale here, which loses all flavour if it is simmered in water before it goes into soup or stew. You do come across 'bacon' in France, but it is very lean, smoked meat from the loin; it is not the *lard* or bacon required by most recipes. Incidentally, *saindoux* is the French for lard. Confusing.

Another point – do not be trapped by certain English recipes into using large quantities of bacon when making pâté. It coarsens the flavour. Pork back fat can be added to the mixture if the pork used was on the lean side. Strips of thinly cut back fat, or a piece of pig's caul, can be used as a wrapping, to baste the meat as it cooks. But the use of bacon should be restricted to a few rashers.

Charcutiers in France will often cure the pork very lightly before making a pâté, or roasting a pork loin. This is to add flavour and improve the colour to a muted pink (the action of the saltpetre in the brine). Such curing has little to do with the business of producing bacon; it is another matter of seasoning.

Bain marie A bath of hot rather than boiling water, in which pans and pots of food can wait without their contents being spoilt by overheating or dryness (see Chapter 29).

The bath itself can be anything from a roasting tin to a fine closed copper cauldron, such as you may see in Avranches in Normandy at the Croix d'Or Hôtel. The outer rim is pierced with holes into which tall saucepans fit exactly, their bases in the water.

The name, from the Latin *balneum Mariae,* the bath of (the Virgin) Mary, presumably refers to the mildness of the heat. It goes back at least to 14th-century France. And when Denis Papin who was a Huguenot from Blois fled to London from Roman Catholic persecution in the late 17th century, he took the bain marie principle as the start of his 'Digester', the first pressure cooker. He described it as a 'screwed balneum Mariae' because the pot of food stood in water inside the tough container of cast brass. The lid was screwed down, and heat applied to raise the pressure. By 1687 Papin had thought of lining the brass with pewter, which meant he could put food in directly and do away with the inner pot.

If you go to Blois, you can see the statue of Denis Papin on the great flight of steps in the middle of the town, with his Digester at his feet.

Ballotine (*see* **Dodine**)

Barding is the excellent practice – too much neglected by our butchers – of giving prime lean meat a jacket of pork fat to make a permanent basting. Sometimes it is used in conjuction with **Larding**.

Skilful French butchers delight in cutting hard back fat into thin sheets, and then contriving strips of the correct size and shape to fit the breast of a bird or a piece of meat for roasting before it is strung into shape. It must be said, however, that some butchers these days buy vast sheets of fat, ready cut, from their wholesaler. Nonetheless, they shape and finish it off in great style, in contrast to the lump of bacon flung cheerfully by English butchers on to an expensive pheasant.

Barding can be applied to fish. One of the great setpieces of haute cuisine, carp Chambord, is characterised by a square of pork fat on the side of the fish, 'nailed' into place with truffles.

A simpler but equally effective form of barding is provided by caul fat. This web of fat has to be softened in warm water before it is supple enough to be stretched out and cut into squares. Very lean meat – a venison chop for instance – is sometimes wrapped in caul fat before grilling, but its principal use in French cookery is to baste and hold together small packages of chopped pork, seasoned with herbs and spices, and in winter seasoned perhaps with chestnuts or truffle. These *crépinettes,* like our faggots, can be cooked without coming to pieces. The thicker veins of fat turn an appetising brown in the heat.

Caul fat can also be wrapped round pâté, which is then gently pressed and eased into a terrine, loose ends underneath. Again, the fat will brown in the heat and give a homely finish that often appeals to people more than conventional barding strips.

Beans   Broad beans are eaten fresh in the spring in France as they are here, but with two differences. First, they are often cooked with the slightly bitter herb, savory. Second, the beans themselves will be skinned either before or after cooking. The latter is easier. At the turn of the century when wages were minimal, tiny skinned beans were the pride of every good restaurant. Now you will rarely find them on the menu – hand work of this kind costs money these days.

Green string beans, sometimes patched with purple streaks that disappear in the cooking, never cheap, properly small and stringlike, are another delicacy of the French table – the summer accompaniment to lamb. They are also eaten separately, with a little cream and butter to make a light sauce. Long yellow beans, haricots beurre, are larger, but they are cooked in the same way. As the heat of summer rises, the pods dry a little and only the beans inside are eaten. *See also* **Dried beans**.

Bercy   Butter and sauce for fish or white meats. Not 'Bercy' after some gastronomic banker or actress of the Belle Epoque, but after the great wine dépôts on the eastern side of Paris on the Seine. The two Entrepôts de Bercy, the Grand and the Petit are separated by a main road. You may walk along the perimeter fences and look down to the cobbled streets – rue de Mâcon, rue de Bourgogne, all the great wine names – with their old plane trees, and row after row of little offices. Unseen are the great cellars below.

Alas the transport of wine is

arranged differently these days, and the two Bercys are much neglected. A few merchants remain – La Varenne buys its wine from one of them – but there is no animation by comparison with, say, the 1870s. In the Siege of Paris meat may have been on the short side – official lists priced dog, cat and rat along with the beef – but there was plenty of wine. One merchant reckoned that there was a hundred litres for each man, woman and child – 'no likelihood of our having to drink water for some time'.

Naturally, wine is the keynote of the sauce – wine with a favourite partner, shallot. Boil 150ml ($\frac{1}{4}$pt) dry white wine with a heaped tablespoon of chopped shallot – gently at first, then fast – until you have a soft juicy purée. Either whisk in 150g (5oz) softened butter to make a cream, or 150ml ($\frac{1}{4}$pt) well-reduced fish or meat stock and double cream to make a sauce. Season with salt, pepper, parsley and lemon juice.

If you substitute red wine for white, and serve the result with grilled beef or lamb, you have Marchand de vins butter or sauce, reminding one of the portly merchants who once animated the little barge-boarded offices, as they saw to the barrels that came by Seine barge to the quays.

Bercy is in the news again. Officialdom wants to sweep away the ghosts and put a huge new sports complex on the site of Grand Bercy. The last of the wine trade will be clustered in Petit Bercy. Very rational, very sad.

Bigarade   The bitter orange has given its name to one of the most famous of the sauces served with duck. Until the second half of the 17th century, the oranges known to most Europeans were the bitter kind like our familiar Sevilles. Then the sweet China orange that the Portuguese succeeded in growing was imported into Northern Europe, and gradually ousted the bigarade. The triumph was more complete in France than in this country, where we look every January for Sevilles to make marmalade. At this time of year, it is worth making several pots of the old-fashioned bigarade sauce for the deep freeze: its flavour is much enhanced by the aromatic peel, too: cook 60g (2oz) butter to the noisette

stage, stir in a heaped tablespoon of flour, then $\frac{1}{2}$ litre ($\frac{3}{4}$pt) duck giblet stock. Flavour to taste with Seville orange juice, season with salt, pepper, sugar and a final lump of butter. Stir in fine shreds of the peel, which have been blanched in boiling water for 5 minutes. Out of season, you will have to follow the modern French style and use a mixture of sweet orange and lemon juices.

The sweet orange did not prevail quickly, which results in a certain ambiguity in cookery books of the latter half of the 17th century and the first half of the 18th. Modern adapters do not always remember this, so reflect whether you might not get a better result by using Sevilles with a little sugar, rather than sweet oranges with a little lemon juice.

Bladders   Pig's bladders have three uses post mortem, as far as Europe is concerned. The first is obsolete, few children now having to rely on them for footballs and balloons!

The second has unfortunately declined, and this is the bladder as a container for lard. Some pork butchers keep up this practical use, and the lard inside the bladder is usually of a higher quality and fuller flavour than the wrapped lard found in the supermarket.

The third use is for 'poulet' or 'poularde en vessie', chicken cooked in a bladder. It survives vigorously in the Lyonnais or the Ardèche. The idea is that you fill a chicken with good things – liver, truffles, foie gras – and slide it into a bladder that has been softened in warm water. You then pour in brandy, wine, superior juices of one kind and another and press out the air carefully, so as not to spill the liquor. Sew up the bladder and suspend it in water or stock to simmer for about 1$\frac{1}{2}$ hours. Check from time to time by wiggling the leg but do not pierce the bladder itself. Remove the whole thing to a dish, cut away the stitches and serve.

The bladder shrouds the chicken in semi-transparency and looks far more appetising than its modern equivalent, the 'roastabag'. Slit the bladder up and over the breast bone, then lay it to each side for easy carving. An English recipe I have, from 'The Epicure's Almanac' of

1841, by Benson E. Hill puts butter mashed with nutmeg and mace, plus 12 oysters and their liquor in with the chicken, which should be $1\frac{1}{4}$-$1\frac{1}{2}$kg ($2\frac{1}{2}$-3lb) in weight. It is delicious.

Blanquette A delicate stew, creamy white in colour as the name suggests, usually made of veal, sometimes of lamb, occasionally of lobster. The meat is not browned but 'seized' in hot butter, floured lightly and stewed in a pale stock. Whole small onions and button mushrooms cooked with lemon or milk are added towards the end of cooking. The sauce is thickened with cream and egg yolks.

'What a hole they had made in the blanquette. No one talked very much, but they all chewed stolidly. The bowl was emptying, the spoon stuck upright in the thick sauce, a good yellowish sauce which shook like a jelly. Everyone fished about for bits of veal – there were still some left – the bowl went from hand to hand and faces hung over it looking for the mushrooms.' Zola, 'L'Assommoir' (1876).

Blood Pig's blood, in France as in this country, goes mainly into black puddings. Indeed our North Country butchers sometimes win medals at the annual 'Foire aux boudins' which draws people from all over Europe to Mortagne in Normandy, every spring. But even our best puddings are hefty with groats and pearl barley. French 'boudins noirs' are lighter. The blood is mixed with onion, little cubes of pork fat, sometimes spices, and cream. Variations in different regions may include greenery or chestnuts but never cereals. These crumbly puddings make a cheap, delicious lunch when served with fried apple and mashed potato. Pieces left over can be used in an omelette. Incidentally, when a pig is killed on the farm in France, a very little of the blood will be gently cooked with fat and cream in a frying pan until set, to make a treat for the children.

Cooks in the South of England may be sceptical of the charm of black pudding, and with reason. Often, it consists of 'dehydrated black pudding products', reconstituted with water. You need to know the provenance of your black puddings.

The thickening capacity of blood is also put to good use in hare stew. The butcher should hand you a tiny bucket into which the blood has drained. Stir a spoonful of wine vinegar into it the moment you get home, to prevent coagulation. At the end of cooking time, use it to finish the sauce as if it were an egg yolk liaison – ie. make sure that the sauce is well below boiling point or the blood will curdle.

Cockerel's blood used in the same way provides a variation on the classic coq au vin. This poulet en barbouille, or poulet au sang, with its black sauce, is claimed by the cooks of Berry; elsewhere their title is disputed.

Bouquet garni Everyone, everywhere, has improved stock, soups and stews, with aromatic herbs, but it seems that only the French have turned the habit into a system. Jules Gouffé, one of the great chefs of mid-19th century Paris, and a pupil of Carême, defined the bouquet as parsley, thyme and a bay leaf. And this was the choice of Escoffier, the great reformer in the next generation of professional cookery. Now the elements of this bouquet garni are as familiar in Piddletrenthide as in Paris.

The bouquet was not always so exactly defined. Today there is a move back to earlier, more varied mixtures. Chefs will pack a curved layer of leek with extra herbs and aromatics such as dried orange peel. Then they string it firmly round, leaving ends to tie the package to the pot handle (for easy removal at the end of cooking). A roll of leek, or in summer a fat spring onion, makes a good substitute for the Welsh onion of the following bouquets. The earliest I found comes from the original La Varenne, founder of modern French cookery:

1651 La Varenne: parsley, Welsh onion, thyme
1656 Pierre de Lune: parsley, Welsh onion, chervil, 2 cloves, strip of streaky bacon or salt belly pork
1746 Menon: parsley, Welsh onion, thyme, bay, basil, 1 clove, 1 clove garlic
1883 Favre (for ragoûts, game, brown sauces): handful of mixed parsley and chervil; one sprig each of thyme, tarragon,

sage, basil, mint; small red chilli; $\frac{1}{4}$ nutmeg; 2 cloves; 2 cloves garlic

How, you may wonder, do you tie a clove into a bouquet? The answer is that you don't. You stick the cloves into the clove of garlic or the bacon, put it on top of the greenery, fold over both ends of the stalks to enclose it and tie the whole thing firmly together.

The use of a bouquet garni does not preclude the addition of other aromatics and herbs. It is a useful convention, not a straitjacket.

Bread In the French countryside, you will often see the ruins of an old oven built into a farmhouse wall, sometimes even built into the rock beside a cave dwelling. People outside towns and large villages had to make their own bread, and dreadful it often was (see Eugen Weber's 'Peasants into Frenchmen').

Then, about a hundred years ago, every village had by law to be provided with either a bakery or bread dépôt. The fine bread of the towns – what we regard as typical French bread – became standard. Nobody attempts to make white bread at home. It's the baker's job and he has to supply it twice a day as it rapidly goes stale, being made very light and from soft flour.

Do not be fooled by the 'French' bread in bakeries here. It is nothing like the real thing, apart from a similarity of shape to the baguette. Why bakers from France have not invaded this country since we joined the EEC, I do not know. They would have a huge success, especially in the South where decent bread is a rarity. So far, there seem to be only a handful of bold boulangers, installed in Bedford, Brighton, Bromley and Milton Keynes.

Nowadays, the French make bread from other flours. You find wholemeal bread with walnuts, rye bread, bran bread, five-cereal bread etc. If you are looking for an appropriate kind to serve with a French meal, you will do better to make or buy this kind of loaf, rather than hope to achieve those inimitable sticks of white bread, the ficelle, the baguette and the pain de livre.

The French religion of bread, as it seems to us, is well displayed at the Musée français du pain, 25bis rue Victor Hugo, Charenton, on the eastern outskirts of Paris beyond Bercy, open Tuesday and Thursday afternoons. There, in part of his mill, Monsieur Lorche and his brother show a collection of different-shaped loaves from all over France, utensils, signs, wafer-irons, posters, postcards, cartoons, paintings, even parts of old baker's shops and the mummified remains of bread from Egyptian tombs.

Butter   The flavour of different styles of French cookery depends on the correct fat being used: olive oil for Provençal vegetable and fish dishes, goose fat and lard for the rich meat and charcuterie of western and north-eastern France, butter for Breton and Normandy food and above all for dishes of the high classic style.

In France, as in many other European countries, butter is churned from ripened cream, ie. cream that has been lightly soured with a lactic starter (see **crème fraîche**). This gives it a different feel and flavour from sweet cream butter of the English kind. Another difference is that French butter is usually unsalted, or 'doux'. Demi-sel or lightly salted butter, especially from Brittany, may be popular for spreading on bread; but for cooking, in recipes and cookery books, butter means the unsalted kind, preferably from Normandy.

Such butter is widely sold in this country, at a far lower price than the French have to pay. If you cannot find it, use Danish butter; it will give a better result for French cookery than English butters, *unless* you want it for clarifying – in which case any type of butter can be used.

C

Cabbage (chou)   From Provence to the Belgian and German borders and across to the Atlantic, the French are good at cabbage. They even like it, having realised that it must either be cooked briefly, or for a very long time indeed. And that it needs richness – pork trotters, ears, tails, salt belly, good sausagemeat for instance, or goose and duck fat, butter or cream in generous measure.

Such confidence have they in

their ability to manipulate this difficult vegetable, that it appears in the highest reaches of fine cookery in happy alliance with partridge, as well as in the hundred and one homely variations of chou farci in the bourgeois style. The farmhouse cabbage soup of Gascony, garbure, is now much made in other parts of France. And sauerkraut – choucroute – can be bought every week in charcuteries that are hundreds of miles from Alsace and Lorraine. A special pleasure are the tiny cabbage rolls, enclosing fragments of chestnut and pork or bacon, or some ingenious stuffing. They may be cooked and served on their own, or used to embellish a soup.

In some parts of France, especially in rainy Auvergne and Limousin, where the winter can be as long and trying as ours, I would guess that as much cabbage is eaten as in the most cabbage-conscious parts of Ireland and Scotland – but with a great deal more pleasure.

Candied peel and **fruits**   These, with fruit pastes and so on, are a speciality of Clermond-Ferrand in the Auvergne, and of Apt in Provence. Both towns are close to fruit-growing districts of quality. Candied chestnuts, the marrons glacés of Christmas, come principally from Privas in the Ardèche, where chestnut forests cover the slopes of the hilly landscape.

This is the kind of confectionery that can be attempted at home, but once tried is usually left to the professionals (though there are families who enjoy making simple versions of marrons glacés in the Christmas holidays). What may have started as a way of storing fruit in the winter, a preserve, a few sugar plums for family enjoyment, has been developed especially in the last hundred years into a great luxury which is exported all over the world.

Cheaper items of the candying trade, cherries and lemon and orange peel, may be common enough in cake-making, and the target of secret raids on the larder, but the apricots, figs, greengages, strawberries, ranged in little papers in special wooden boxes, are for savouring one by one, slowly and with respect, in good company.

Capers   The buds of the caper plant, native to the Mediterranean region, are picked and pickled before they burst into one of the most exquisite of flowers. The finest, the little nonpareilles, come from the mouth of the Rhône and the Var, and appear in many Provençal dishes. Locally they are called tapeno, hence tapénade, the piquant mash of capers, olives and anchovies that is eaten as a snack with bread or hard boiled eggs. Capers also appear in salads, and in sauces such as raito which are served with salt cod.

Having been popular for hundreds of years in France, capers are comfortably established in standard cookery; their flavour is essential to a number of sauces, rémoulade, tartare, gribiche, and a few are always scattered over the favourite dish of skate, raie au beurre noir. The caper sauce we serve with lamb, the French eat with fish. And although salade niçoise and Montpellier butter come from the south, they have been Parisian favourites for a long time.

Sadly the caper trade of France is on the decline. Capers now come mainly from Spain and North Africa, where poverty makes the fiddly job of picking them worthwhile.

In 1787, Thomas Jefferson talked to caper pickers near Toulon, and hopefully despatched a few plants to the United States. He feared the accuracy of his information, as the people spoke 'no written language, but a medley, which I could understand but very imperfectly.' Because of the need for selection, 'every plant must be picked every other day from the last of June till the middle of October. But this is the work of women and children. This plant does well in any kind of soil which is dry, or even in walls where there is no soil,' – a nostalgic phrase for anyone who has come across flowering caper plants in the Mediterranean – 'and it lasts for the life of man.'

Caramel and **Praline**   In France, these are 17th century words. Caramel, which goes back, according to some, to medieval Latin *cannamella*, sugar cane, probably came in from Spain. It means toffee, and therefore toffee-flavoured puddings such as crème caramel.

French crème brûlée, burnt cream, is not our 17th century pudding with its mirror sheet of browned sugar, but a custard flavoured right through with sugar cooked to the rich brown stage. Caramelised root vegetables are cooked in various ways with sugar and butter, to enhance their natural sweetness and give them an appetising syrupy glaze.

Pralines are a sweetmeat made of sugar cooked to a deep brown, with almonds – what we might call almond brittle. They were invented by the cook of the Maréchal du Plessis-Prasline, who named them after his employer. In the 1650's, La Varenne gave a recipe for amandes à la Prasline, that is unchanged today – except that hazelnuts may sometimes be substituted for almonds.

Later chefs and pastrycooks had the idea of crushing these sweets to a powder, to make a flavouring for ices, creams, cake fillings, meringues, and cold soufflés. Those elaborate little cakes in the pâtisserie window will sometimes be decorated with discs and squares of praline, along with sugared violets and all the other delightful nonsense of the trade.

Caul   This is a veil of fat which surrounds the stomach of a pig. The butcher usually sells it in a stiff piece and it needs to be softened in hot water before use. It is placed over lean meat for roasting or grilling to make a permanent basting layer. It is also similarly used for **barding** (qv).

Cayenne, Chilli and **Curry**
Cayenne is not a true pepper, but ground red chillis that originally came, so it is thought, from Cayenne in French Guiana. Much used – though delicately, as highly seasoned food is not popular in France – to give a lift rather than heat to bland creamy sauces and certain fish and white meat dishes.

Whole chillis form part of preserving spices, and dominate *harissa,* the red spice paste of Algerian cookery. Over the last 15 years, refugee 'pieds noirs' and Arabs have begun to open couscous restaurants. I suspect they bear as much relationship to the real thing as most Cantonese and Taj Mahal restaurants in this country do to the

best native Chinese and Indian cookery.

Unfamiliarity with the many different members of the pepper family, both fresh and dried, can lead to confusion and the word 'piment' often occurs in French cookery writing without the qualifying adjective 'fort' or 'doux' (strong or mild). 'Fort' can be taken to mean chilli, 'doux' to mean sweet red peppers. If you have no experience of the dish you are attempting, look for clues at the quantity given (500g (1lb) must mean sweet red peppers), and the method.

Recipes for rouille, the red sauce stirred into fish soup in Provence, can be confusing in this respect; usually you need only chillis, but some recipes include sweet red peppers as well (and the method is often accompanied by a warning about the 'fiery' nature of the sauce). Nowadays, rouille may be no more than a mayonnaise coloured and mildly flavoured with harissa.

Curry, as in 'poulet au kari', does not mean meat or vegetables awash in a strong, yellow-brown sauce, Cheltenham style, but a thoroughly French sauce, often creamy, seasoned discreetly with a curry spice blend. The result has no connection whatsoever, even a bad one, with Indian cookery.

Charcuterie   The skilful art of preparing and cooking pork, sometimes with game and poultry but usually on its own, as practised in France. It is something which our trade has no experience of and no great interest in discovering, apart from a few ham curers and sausage-makers who stand out by their eccentric desire for quality. It would certainly take time and study to emulate this branch of French cookery, which has a long start on the rest of Northern Europe. After all, the Gauls were exporting hams to ancient Rome. The business has been expanding ever since, and is flexible enough to add new dishes as they come along, producing a range of cooked food that means you can camp or picnic – and eat like a king.

Nonetheless, I would suggest you avoid the cooked food on the outskirts of charcuterie. The scalloped fish and seafood patties are rarely as delicious as they look.

Stick to the excellent dishes for reheating – sauerkraut, tripe, roast chicken which will be put in a special bag that can go straight into the oven, pork knuckles, trotters, tail, ears – and the sturdy repertoire that has changed little for centuries. Hams, sausages for frying, sausages for reheating with lentils or beans such as the Morteau, 'saucissons secs', pâtés, above all the local specialities such as 'rillettes' in the West where they are chunky, the brown cubes of 'rillons' best bought hot to eat with fried apples, mashed potato and mustard, the various black puddings and white puddings, the 'crépinettes' and 'andouillettes', which are well-peppered chitterling sausages. Try the salted cooked pork known as 'petit salé', the fine lightly salted roast loin of pork, the brawns, the various salads from ox muzzle to mushrooms 'à la grecque', the little quiches and sausage rolls and 'petits pâtés' – though here we get back into the range of the variable, when you need to know your charcutier well . . .

Charlotte   This is the name of a pudding with two rather different versions. The earlier, hot pudding, which was certainly known in England as well as France in the 18th century, is still a favourite. A well-buttered mould is lined with buttered bread and filled with sliced apples of a firm, eating variety. It is covered with a lid of bread and baked until the whole thing turns crisp and brown. Other fruits can be used instead of apple and – in some versions – breadcrumbs are substituted for bread slices.

The cold charlotte was invented by the great chef Carême, early in the 19th century. At one stage in his career, he was supplying food for the tables of diplomats and foreign ministers as a caterer. He would send along his charlotte parisienne, which consisted of a palisade of sponge finger biscuits, filled with Bavarian cream. The word 'parisienne' was an assertion of French gastronomic superiority. Later, he changed the name to charlotte russe. . .

Cheese   Everyone knows the smug complaint – was it de Gaulle's? – that a country producing over 300 cheeses is impossible to govern. You may well prefer Zola's cheese symphony in 'Le Ventre de

Paris' – 'from Cantal and Cheshire and goat's milk cheeses came a dull and muffled booming like a melody on the bass, against which the sudden little waves of the Neufchâtels, the Troyes and the Mont-d'ors raised their shrill cries. Then the smells began to run wild, mixing violently with one another, thickening with gusts of Port-Salut, Limbourg, Géromé, Maroilles, Livarot, Pont l'Evêque, little by little merging and mingling, broadening out into a single explosion of smells'. Zola saw the attraction and repulsiveness, the variety, as a reflection of the prosperous and rotten society he was writing about.

These days, with pasteurisation and cold storage, cheeses are bland and often less interesting in consequence. You have to stretch over the piles of Babybel and imitation Camemberts to find the little local cheeses that Colette loved. She deplored the passion for slimming which was putting women off cheese. 'Time was, when a woman was better at choosing a cheese than a man. Feeling the rind, gauging the elasticity of the inside, *divining* a cheese, is to some extent a question of possessing a special X-ray sense. Studying the way in which a Camembert, a Reblochon, or a Maroilles had developed fissures in its ring, the way the centre of a Pont l'Evêque has become either a little cushion or a little saucer ... all such fine attention to details is now being lost.'

If she had a son of marriageable age, she would tell him, 'Beware of young women who love neither wine nor truffles nor cheese nor music'. If her daughter were to ask advice on what to take to a picnic, she would say, 'If you bring the desserts, the guests will be satisfied. If you choose the cheeses, they will repay you with gratitude.' But her daughter did not ask for advice. She brought both. Colette blushed with pride, then lectured her daughter on her thoughtless extravagance. 'Yes, Mummy' (she wasn't really listening). 'And we both felt, with equal satisfaction, that we had each discharged our respective duties.' From 'Paysages et Portraits'.

Cherries

'Un, deux, trois,
Dans les bois,
Quatre, cinq, six,
Cueillant des cerises'

– a rhyme you often hear children chanting, or muttering as they count stones, in the early summer in France. The 'cherries of the wood' are the small red and blackish *guignes*, sweet enough to eat, but a little sharp, the kind that go into brandy, or a country **clafoutis** (qv).

The classic cooking cherry came, and occasionally still does, from Montmorency, north of Paris, and the dish may take the name – canard Montmorency – duck with cherries. The term Montmorency now covers several varieties, but they all produce sour or acid fruit; as a substitute, use Morello or Kentish Red.

When the first large cherries of the summer arrive in the French shops, they will most likely be labelled 'bigarreaux' rather than 'cerises'. The word may be accurate and indicate a bigarreau variety, but it may well mean no more than 'excellent large cherries for eating'. Do not enquire too closely. Buy and be thankful, remembering the poignant brevity of the cherry season which has haunted many European poets.

Chestnuts

In the past a staple food of the poor. Going into Brittany from rich Normandy in early summer, you will be drenched with the cloying smell of chestnut trees in flower. Chestnut trees everywhere that once provided people with bread, soup, meat substitute, and puddings. Down in the Ardèche, where the huge chestnuts for marrons glacés are grown, they even have special chestnut drying houses.

In the museums you will see special boots with sharp nails underneath, for cracking away the shells once the chestnuts were dried. Nowadays we buy dried chestnuts from Italy, and add them as a treat to stews, or use them in making soup: very good they are, as long as you soak them for 24 hours, starting with boiling water.

In the prosperous wine districts, the more sparsely planted chestnut trees provide a whole day's pleasure in the autumn. In the morning, you go out and pick them up – leather gloves required, as the prickles are sharper than the sharpest pins. People with strong boots crack away the outer shells. The women set some aside for adding to crépinettes or black puddings, the rest are for the evening's sport.

After supper everyone draws his chair round the fire. Someone gets out the old shovel pierced with holes and starts roasting chestnuts over the red fire as quickly as they are 'nicked'. As they begin to blacken and burst, they are tossed round the circle. You catch and peel them quickly, clumsily, licking your burnt fingers as you go if you aren't good at manipulating them in your napkin. Then you drop them into a glass of new, cloudy wine (bernache) adding a little sugar if you like. Stir well and wait a moment before eating your chestnuts with a spoon.

Of course, you can quite well substitute white wine for the murky, pinkish bernache.

Chicken

'is to the cook what canvas is to the painter,' wrote Brillat-Savarin. Perhaps, but there is no need to exaggerate its nullity. By the time we have bought the items required to paint a frozen chicken into a masterpiece, we would have done better and cheaper to buy a proper bird, if we could ever find one.

That is the snag. Our chicken farmers are not in business to produce good food, but what seems to be cheap food to the ignorant consumer. Neurotic birds, sometimes stuffed with antibiotics, are killed at about 8 weeks, before they can acquire taste and experience. They are frozen and injected with water and sold without being hung. Alternatives are fresh and chilled chickens which, though better and water-free, do not have the right amount of flavour. I suspect that their free-ranging is confined to a crowded shed, and their food is what the French describe with disgust as 'powder'.

French chicken farmers have not been able to get away so easily. Large cabinets of frozen chickens do not dominate every supermarket. Fresh birds, a choice of them very often, will be proudly labelled, tied up with red ribbon and so on. You are given such information as '75 per cent cereal fed', 'finished with maize', 'at least 81 days old'. Such animals are started in intensive conditions, but spend the latter part of their life in a certain freedom and are given a decent diet of maize. This gives them the authentic flavour that only people over fifty, or the very lucky, will remember (though I notice that Harrods and Selfridges now sell maize-fed birds from France).

The aristocrat of French birds is the chicken of Bresse, reared in Brillat-Savarin country, and by methods similar to those of his time – an early version of factory farming. The aim, though, has always been to produce better rather than cheaper birds. Since 1957 they have borne an appellation contrôlée like a good bottle of wine. Numbers are limited to a million per year in a limited zone; 500 is the maximum number in each group. They run around outside, in 10 square metres each. They are fed on maize and dairy products. At 14 weeks, they go into confinement for fattening. Two weeks later they are killed and plucked by hand, all except for a little ruff of feathers which is their mark. Before going to market, they are vetted to make sure they weigh 1·4kg (3lb), and are unblemished.

Labelled 8 weeks, 11 weeks, 16 weeks – all these birds weigh much the same. This says everything about their comparative quality, the way in which they have been fed, and what they will taste like – which is, after all, the point.

Chinois   is the name given to a conical sieve that resembles a Chinaman's hat (see page 190); its advantage is that a sauce poured into it will emerge at the base in a single stream, falling tidily into basin or pan. Sieves of the drum or rounded kind allow liquid to splosh through in a manner that can be inconvenient, if not downright messy. These are best kept for purées and for straining stocks and soup.

Chocolate and **Cocoa**   The Spanish wife of Louis XIV is sometimes said to have introduced chocolate to France. She married Louis in 1660 and chocolate certainly became the rage at court during the next 10 years.

In 1671, Madame de Sévigné reported a bit of gossip. 'Madame de Coëtlogon drank so much chocolate last year when she was pregnant,

that she gave birth to a little boy as black as the devil, who died.'

Maria Theresa or her Spanish mother-in-law and aunt, Anne of Austria, may have popularised it, but the introduction had been made earlier on – as in England – in the early 1650s.

Chocolate began to be used in cookery, but gradually to flavour creams for instance; it was not until the second half of the 19th century that the great chocolate age began. There were several reasons for this – the lowering of duty made chocolate much cheaper, and the manufacture of eating chocolate began, first plain, then about thirty years later in 1876 the first milk chocolate from Peters, in Switzerland. Cocoa came from Holland, where in 1828 van Houten discovered how to extract enough fat – the cocoa butter – from chocolate to powder it successfully.

Chocolate is tricky to manage. Cocoa butter melts at a low temperature: it is all too easy to overheat chocolate, so that it turns into mud. No doubt this is why on the whole we have preferred to make cakes and puddings with cocoa.

The French have got round the problem by leaving chocolate confections to the trade. At home they content themselves with chocolate mousse, petits pots de crème au chocolat, and one or two rich, fragile cakes made with chocolate, ground almonds, eggs and hardly any flour – such cakes are frankly and openly 'sad', no one minds if they sink in the middle, and they are eaten as dessert with cream. The têtes de nègre, reines de Saba, chocolate marquises and opéra slices are treats to be eaten at a restaurant, or bought on Sunday from the pâtissier.

For home cooking, the French make no fetish about using chocolat Menier. Plain chocolat à croquer of any brand is the usual thing, though lately Poulain has put a chocolat à pâtissier on the market which is excellent, and worth bringing back. Here, I would recommend Terry's bitter chocolate, Suchard Velma, or a Côte d'Or. Some delicatessens, which deal with C. Costa and Co., stock unsweetened Baker's chocolate; but as most recipes are geared to using plain eating chocolate, you have to remember to use it in half quantities as it is so

strong, and perhaps add more sugar.

Making chocolate curls (caraque), discs and cigarettes is for the devotee. It needs time, care and practice. For ordinary purposes, you can produce chocolate curls quite satisfactorily by shaving block chocolate with a potato peeler, a sharp knife, or the long blade of a grater as they do at La Varenne.

Christmas   meals in France, family occasions as they are in this country, revolve round Midnight Mass. In Provence, the supper beforehand has become a traditional feast, the 'gros soupa'. Neither rituals nor food have changed much since the poet Frédéric Mistral was a child in the 1830s and 40s. He described the presents, cheese, figs, wine, the coming and going of relations, people without anywhere else to go, the ritual of bringing in a huge yule log cut from a fruit tree.

And then the evening meal, the table set with three cloths and three candles, a plate of sprouting wheat at each end, the dishes of snails, fried salt cod, mullet with olives, cardoons and celery. The long evening was slowly finished over the 'Treize Desserts', symbol of Christ surrounded by the twelve Apostles, with everyone telling stories, 'on parlait des ancêtres et on louait leurs actions'.

Here is a list of the desserts, a rather generously counted thirteen, from a modern Provençal cookery book: dried figs, almonds and raisins, glacé melon (melon confit), mandarins, sultanas (raisin pendu), dates, prunes, walnuts stuffed with coloured and flavoured almond paste (fruits déguisés), calissons d'Aix (oval almond biscuits with white icing), dark nougat, white nougat, oreillettes (fritters, see **ears**) and papillotes (wrapped sweets, with mottoes).

After Midnight Mass, the reveillon supper is a simple affair. In other parts of France, reveillon will be the large meal, a triumph of charcuterie – before the Mass one must stick to fish and vegetables – with black and white puddings, truffled crépinettes, truffles on their own if you can afford them – the finest meal you can manage.

Christmas ends on 6th January, Epiphany, the feast of the Three Kings. A special cake is eaten – brioche in a crown shape, or a puff pastry disc filled with almond cream – and in it a 'fève' is hidden. This is no longer a dried bean, but a small porcelain favour, a baby, horseshoe, duck, motorcycle etc. Whoever bites on the fève in the gâteau des rois is king of the evening (and very likely has to stand the wine and another cake).

Clafoutis   A cake of black cherries, ideally wild ones, sunk in a sweetened batter, which may also be flavoured with rum or cognac. One of the most over-rated dishes of French country cooking, unless you have a passion for flabby Yorkshire pudding, which in texture it often resembles.

Other districts of France make their versions with other fruits, but the people of the Limousin – the wet but beautiful country around Limoges – whose dish it is, would dispute that these cakes have any right to the name of 'clafoutis'.

Coeur à la crème *see* **Fromage frais**

Coffee   England may have been the first country in Europe to have a coffee house in 1650, but it's the French name, café, which has prevailed. Certainly the French drink more coffee than we do and have a better range of coffee puddings, creams and cakes.

Instant coffee, drunk in Europe since the First World War when the habit was introduced by American soldiers, is reasonable for flavouring cakes and biscuits. Lightly crushed beans or ground coffee produce the most subtle mocha creams and ices (Moka in the Yemen is the port from which Ethiopian coffee was brought to Europe in the 17th century). For cookery of this kind, go for a light or medium rather than a dark continental roast.

Dark coffee is for after dinner, the right end to a good meal, whether or not it is accompanied by brandy or some other 'digestif'. Some people pour it into tall cone-shaped beakers called Mazagrans (apparently after a fortress in Algeria, where iced coffee first became popular with French soldiers), and add marc. To me this is a desperate drink, tolerable only as a pick-me-up after a bad day, but certainly no end to dinner, when fine coffee in small cups is much to be preferred, with alcohol – if any – in a separate glass.

In 'Coffee', published by Faber in 1977, and much to be recommended, Claudia Roden remarks that a dark roast of the kind preferred by the French is less likely to keep you awake than the lighter kinds, as 'some of the caffeine has been sublimed off by the roasting'. True. But I note that it is easier and cheaper to buy decaffeinated coffee in France, beans, ground or powder, than it is here.

Decaffeinated coffee, sometimes referred to as Déca or café Hag after the best brand of instant, would not have done for France's greatest coffee drinker, the novelist Balzac. After four hours' sleep, he woke at midnight, put on his white monk's robe, and wrote. 'He wrote hour after hour and when he flagged and his head seemed to burst, he went to the coffee-pot and brewed the strongest black coffee he could find, made from the beans of Bourbon, Martinique and Mocha. He was resorting to a slow course of coffee poisoning, and it has been estimated that in his life he drank 50,000 cups of it.' He died at 51, but other excesses – including excessive work – contributed.

If you want to imitate Balzac's brew, Martinique is no longer available and you should use coffee from Haiti or Cuba instead.

Confits   generally meaning a preserve, as in fruits confits or confiture (jam), also covers that rich and glorious group of salted meats, cooked and potted in their own fat that everyone associates with the province of Aquitaine. Any meat can be treated in this way, but the prime choices are goose, duck and pork – all fat creatures – especially goose and duck that are stuffed with food to enlarge their livers. Confits were a consolation prize for farmers when foie gras went off the market. Nowadays they are almost as much of a luxury as foie gras.

You can make them at home, but unless you breed and fatten the animals yourself, the results will be disappointing. Meat sold over the counter is so lean that extra lard must be bought to augment the meagre fat. And the preserved meat itself – this is more serious – will be far less succulent, as it comes from animals too strictly dieted to have those invisible threads of fat running through the meat that

made the goose, duck and pork of the past such a splendid feast.

Cooking and **Eating**
'An operation which is performed two to three times a day, and the purpose of which is to sustain life, surely merits all our care.'

This one sentence, from 'The Memoirs of Hadrian' by Marguerite Yourcenar, sums up the attitude behind French cookery that distinguishes it above all others: to be in a right relationship with the earth and its produce, to treat the produce with respect, intelligence and love, so that things taste of what they are in simplicity and directness. As the world goes now, simplicity and quality are the two most difficult things to achieve. They need a high degree of care and skill.

Cotignac   To the Romans, the quince, the fruit of Venus, was the apple of Cydonia – now called Chania – on the north coast of Crete. And so cydonea, or cotonea, passed via the Provençal into French, particularly in the form of cotignac, which is a fruit paste made from coings ie. quinces.

The Orléanais claim cotignac as a local speciality, when it is really more of a survival (rather like haggis in Scotland). Peel, core, cook and sieve quinces. Add an equal weight of sugar to the purée. Stir over a steady heat until the mixture dries into a paste, leaving the sides of the pan. Spread out on a greasproof-lined tray, and complete drying in a warm place, eg. an airing cupboard. Cut into pieces, roll in sugar and store in layers in a box, with two or three bay leaves between each layer.

Couscous   is a preparation of semolina, that in France at least has given its name to the whole dish of grain and sauce. To make it from scratch, you need two kinds of semolina, medium coarse and fine. Soak the larger grains, stirring them about with your fingers for five minutes until the water is absorbed, then mix in a good handful of fine semolina to coat the grains. Roll them between your hands, or on a cloth-covered table. This process is repeated up to four times depending on the size of couscous you require (by the fourth time, it should be peppercorn-size). Then sift it in an appropriately sized sieve to get rid of the small bits, and any surplus fine semolina.

Put the couscous into a colander lined with muslin (unless you have a special couscousière), and set it to steam over the meat or poultry and vegetable stew that will accompany it as sauce. If the couscous seems to be sticking, run your fingers through it, and dab with large knobs of butter.

Happily, you can buy packets of couscous, ready prepared for steaming, in delicatessens and health food shops. Algerian and other North African cookery books are less easy to find here, though there is a good section in Claudia Roden's 'Middle Eastern Food' (1968). Visiting France, you will come across them in the Maisons de la Presse, even in quite small towns, such is the new enthusiasm for Algerian food.

Crème Chantilly means whipped cream, Chantilly to the north of Paris being a centre for dairy produce. I remember going to the market there many years ago, on a first visit to France, and being startled by the huge stoneware bowls of thick cream and the vast slabs of butter.

Cream intended for whipping should have spent several hours in the refrigerator. It then goes into a bowl, placed over another bowl of ice. This chill increases the volume and lightness of the cream as you beat it. Remember to add a spoonful or two of milk if you are using **crème fraîche** (qv) and a spoonful or two of single cream to our double cream (or more, up to ⅔). If you have whipping cream, it is ready for use as it is.

At home, French housewives will mix whipped cream with **fromage frais,** and then fold in a stiffly beaten egg white or two. An economy measure perhaps, but it tastes good and is excellent with tarts – and fruit. The proportion of cream to fromage frais is a matter of taste and pocket: the mixture will often be slightly sweetened as well, though this depends on what it is served with. **Fromage frais,** under the names of 'Jockey' or 'Quark', is now on sale in a number of supermarkets and delicatessens. It also makes a good cream-extender for fools, ices and cold soufflés.

Crème fraîche or fresh cream in France differs from ours in colour, consistency, taste and behaviour. It is yellower and thicker – but in a light sort of way – with a tiny amount of watery liquid that should be stirred back into it. The taste is slightly acid, which makes it agreeable in meat and fish sauces and with fresh fruit. When you whip it, a little milk must be added, and you have to catch it before it goes grainy. When you use it for a pan sauce, it does not reduce as quickly or as consistently as our double cream. It's no good adding it to coffee, as it curdles and tastes sharp.

You might infer from some of this that it is the same as our soured cream. Certainly it is produced in a similar way, being ripened after pasteurisation with a starter culture, but soured cream is made from single cream with 18% butter fat, whereas crème fraîche has a minimum fat content of 35% – not unlike our whipping cream (35-38%), less rich than our double cream (48%), and way below clotted cream (60%).

Nonetheless you can make a reasonable imitation of crème fraîche with soured cream. Mix it with twice the quantity of whipping or double cream in a pan. Raise the temperature slowly to 90°C, then pour into a pot, cover, and leave overnight in a warm place at a temperature of 75°C. Stir again and store in the refrigerator, where it will keep for about 10 days. To make another batch, use the last of this one, mix it with twice the quantity of whipping or double cream, and start again.

Incidentally, many French – and American – friends envy our choice of creams here, particularly our double and clotted creams. In the Paris Marks and Spencer's store, English cream sells fast, and at least one French restaurateur I know prefers the rich Jersey cream he gets from the Channel Islands to crème fraîche. It would be ideal if British dairies were to add crème fraîche to their repertoire and make our choice even wider.

Custard (crème anglaise) On a first visit to Fauchon's, the famous Paris food store, as we stood breathing in the air of passion fruit at no cost at all, a fine lady swept by in a mink coat. Behind her came an assistant burdened to the chin with big tins of Bird's custard powder. They went out to a Rolls. The chauffeur helped stow the tins of custard away in the boot as the lady supervised. Was she starting a charitable custard kitchen? Or were they going to join a great store of tomato ketchup, so that she and her friends would not be deprived of their little luxuries if the difficult times turned really bad?

How can the nation of Carême and Escoffier prefer to eat such things?

In fact crème anglaise, nicely made, has a more honoured place in high-class French cookery than it does here. And I mean as a pudding sauce, not only as an essential part of ices and so on. But our pleasure in custard has inevitably been corrupted by the torrent of reconstituted powder that has flowed through institutional kitchens and canteens in this country for over 130 years.

Dandelion leaves are a popular salad in France. You may grow a garden variety yourself, or blanch the dandelions growing wild by putting a plant pot over them with a stone over the hole, to exclude light. This blanching reduces the bitterness. Another way is to raise the large roots, trim off the green, and replant them in pots, like chicory, to sprout and blanch in a dark place such as an airing cupboard.

Dandelion leaves are sometimes added to other greenery in a salad, though the most popular way of eating them on their own, as a Salade de pissenlits, is given in Chapter 22.

Dariole This is the name given, since at least the 14th century both in France and England, to small bucket-shaped pasties, then to the moulds themselves and anything that might be cooked or shaped in them. Dariole was first, it seems, doriole, something gilded, referring to the colour of the pastry when it was cooked. Another name, *puits d'amour*, well of love, pictures the filling which was made from all matter of delicious bits and pieces, including dates or strawberries on occasion, as well as the more usual marrow from a beef bone and spices submerged in a custard. Later, the custard prevailed, but it still contained small delights such as almonds and a flavouring of orange flower water.

Darne   The name given to a steak cut from the thickest part of a large fish, such as salmon, tunny, or cod.

Dartois   A puff pastry sandwich, either large or small, savoury or sweet. According to the filling, it will be called dartois au fromage, dartois aux poissons, dartois aux pommes and so on.

But why dartois? Did it come from the province of Artois, centring on Arras? Or was it named in honour of the brother of Louis XVI, the Comte d'Artois? His youth was 'passed in scandalous dissipation', and Parisians loathed him. At 67, he became King Charles X, and provoked revolution by his reactionary behaviour. In 1830, his discreet departure for a life of repentance at Holyrood House was regretted by no-one. There, as one authority tartly remarks, he wasted his time expiating 'not his failure to grasp a great opportunity' – ie. as king – 'but the comparatively venial excesses of his youth'. Including, perhaps, too many dartois?

Daube   A dish of slowly braised meat, usually beef, often associated with Provence – which is not surprising as the word 'daube' comes from Italy next door, from *addobbo* meaning a garnish in culinary terms. One of the garnishings of the dish is pork skin, either in little rolls, or as lining to the pot: it makes an extra smoothness in the sauce. Plenty of herbs and aromatic vegetables give the daube a more rustic character than the elegant braises of high-class cookery.

By the beginning of the last century, a special heavy iron pot, a 'daubière', had been invented. The distinguishing feature was a rimmed lid, forming a top cavity to hold burning ashes from the fire – as the old cookery books say, 'Fire above and below'. Some firms still make these pots, and if you are given to cooking over a fire in the wintertime, you could use it on the hearth. Most of us will have to be content with putting hot water in

the top and transferring the whole thing to an oven. The point of this overhead heat is to speed up the condensation of steam rising from the contents, so that the meat is continually basted by moisture falling back on to it. To be successful, the lid needs to be stuck firmly on, either with a **luting** paste of flour and water, or with a dampened cloth, so that nothing can evaporate during the hours and hours of slow cooking.

Deglazing   is a simple but effective technique which is not much practised here (perhaps because it depends on careful frying in fat of good quality). The food, which may be anything from fish, game, poultry to apples, is cooked in butter, lard, goose fat or olive oil, until the stage required by the recipe, over a heat that is high enough to 'seize' it or brown it, without burning the fat. The food is then removed and any surplus fat poured from the pan.

The heat is raised and an appropriate liquid – water, or stock or wine, or a mixture – is poured in and the pan is scraped industriously so that all the delicious sediments are absorbed into the liquid. This is why the frying must be carefully conducted in the first place: burnt butter is not a good basis for anything.

During this process the liquid bubbles hard and reduces so that the flavour becomes richly concentrated. Cream, more liquid or butter can then be poured in to make a pan sauce, which will be seasoned and strained over the food. This deglazing technique may also be used at the start of a stew or a braise, or at the end of grilling or roasting to make a little rich gravy, by adding wine – table or fortified – and a small amount of stock. Not to be recommended is the English style of gravy in which flour or gravy browning is mixed into the residual juices, and turned into a copious sauce by the addition of unfortunate liquids.

Diable
1   An unglazed earthenware pot with handles, made in two identical halves, for cooking potatoes or chestnuts without water, over a low heat. About halfway through the cooking time, the pot is turned upside down to ensure that the

contents are evenly done. A utensil from the time when ovens were few and food was prepared on the fire, it is as popular today because the French are still reluctant to turn on their ovens without very good reason. Far more is cooked – most successfully – on top of the stove than we would ever attempt.
2   Meat or poultry cut in half, buttered, sometimes spread with mustard, then breadcrumbs, and grilled. The result is not as hot or highly spiced as our devilled dishes.
3   The piquant wine and vinegar sauce which accompanies such grills, or, on occasion, fried fish. The seasonings of this sauce diable include **cayenne pepper** (qv).
4   A gratin of boiled meat, pigs' ears, for instance, or left-over beef, spread with mustard, sprinkled with Cayenne and breadcrumbs, then with melted butter, before being baked in the usual way – a gratin de boeuf au diable.

Dieppoise   Dieppe has given its name to one of the most famous ways of cooking fish. Sole, bream, monkfish, scallops etc. are poached in white wine, decorated with mussels and shrimps and served with a cream sauce that includes the cooking liquor and mussel juice.

Dodine and **Ballotine**   Two similar preparations, often of duck, but also of poultry, game and some meats. The bird or joint is boned and re-formed round a pâté mixture, the more luxurious the better. Then the dodine is braised with wine and served hot with the juices (properly de-greased) as sauce.

The ballotine is poached in stock and wine on top of the stove, then left to cool under a light weight. The cooking liquor is used to make an aspic for glazing the dish; left-over jelly is chopped when cold and put round the ballotine.

Doyenné du Comice   Most famous of French pears, from the fruit-growing centre of Angers. When properly ripe, it is one of the best eating pears. When just ripe but a little on the firm side, it is ideal for cooking: peel the pears, leaving the stalks in place, poach them in a white wine syrup and serve well chilled. The juice can be given a lift with one of the pear eaux de vie, or the pears can be served with a raspberry purée.

The huge castle and the tapestries it contains make Angers one of the greatest sites of Europe. When you visit it, take a walk up the boulevard du Roi René. On the left by the university canteen – piles of students and bicyles intertwined – is a plaque set into the wall commemorating the pear and the garden that has disappeared:

In this garden
was raised in 1849-1850
the celebrated pear
Doyenné du Comice
by the gardener
Dhomme and by Millet de la
Turtaudière
President of the Comice Horticole

Doyenné might loosely be translated as 'star' – star of the Comice.

Dried beans   The dried beans of France have an honoured place in the culinary repertoire – cassoulet, lamb in the Breton style with dried white haricots, purée Musard with flageolets, purée Soissonnaise again with white haricots. Soissons is the famous bean centre of France, although Arpajon runs it close. Every year, in September, there is a bean fair at Arpajon, which is to the south of Paris on the eastern side of the Beauce. As well as the beans we all know, you will see the pale green flageolets which are the autumn and winter partner of lamb and mutton. When these beans are harvested, they are raised in mounds on four-legged wooden platforms that stride across the curves of the huge Beauceron fields. Underneath each, a small scatter of pale green indicates what is drying in the mass of tight, twisted pods.

There is no magic about soaking dried beans. It is merely a way of shortening the cooking time (and saving fuel). If the beans you buy are semi-dried, they need no soaking at all, but as the year draws on, their hardness increases. Overnight is the traditional time, but things can be speeded up by bringing the beans to the boil in water to cover, leaving them to cool, then starting again with boiling water. Two hours' soaking will then be enough. Beans will double their weight, more or less, in soaking. You can judge from this whether they are ready for the pot.

Drying   For herbs, orange peel, sliced onions, mushroom caps:

spread out on cheesecloth or muslin-covered wire cake trays, and put into the oven set at 50°C (120°F), gas low, until all moisture has gone. This can be done in stages, when the oven is cooling down after roasting for instance, or by putting them in the plate-warmer. Herbs and onions will be crumbly, mushrooms and orange peel rather leathery. Store in screw-top jars. No point in drying parsley: better to cram it into small plastic pots and freeze; then you can grate off what you require while still frozen. Another way is to fill an ice cube tray with chopped parsley and as little water as possible and freeze. When the cubes are solid, pack them into plastic bags and store in the freezer; add them to stews, soups and so on as they are, or put them into a sieve to thaw out if you need to get rid of the water.

Duxelles   A mushroom flavouring invented by La Varenne, écuyer de cuisine to Louis Chalon de Bled, Marquis d'Uxelles. His book, 'Le Cuisinier françois', was dedicated to the Marquis and so eventually was this mixture.

Soften a small onion and shallot, chopped, in butter. When golden, add 250g (8oz) or more chopped mushrooms. When the juices run, raise the heat to evaporate them, and cook steadily until the mixture dries out. It must not brown or burn. Flavour towards the end of cooking time with salt, pepper, nutmeg, and chopped parsley Store in the refrigerator, or deep freeze, in tightly closed containers. Add to sauces, stuffings, stews, soups; use as a base for baking fish, or intersperse with potatoes in a gratin.

E

Ears   Pigs' ears are, rightly, a favourite French dish. You buy them at the charcuterie, ready cooked, in their own jelly. You reheat them in the oven or under the grill with mustard, crumbs and butter (see **Diable**) and serve with a piquant white wine sauce, or a vinaigrette full of chopped parsley, shallot, capers, gherkins, and hard boiled egg (sauce gribiche).

In this country you may well get pigs' ears for nothing, or a copper or two, if you order them from the

butcher. They are easily cooked in water or light stock with the usual aromatic herbs and vegetables, taking about 40 minutes. Let them cool in the liquid, before draining and finishing as above, if you do not intend to eat them the same day. To eat, either scrape off the jellied meat, or eat the whole thing and enjoy the contrasting textures.

Little ears, oreillettes, are quite different. They are fritters much eaten in Provence. Any festival is an excuse for making them. Make a dough with 500g (1lb) flour, 4 egg yolks (or 2 eggs and a heaped tablespoon of unsalted butter), the grated peel of an orange and lemon, a tablespoon of orange flower water, and enough water, or milk, or rum and milk, to bind. Rest an hour in the fridge. Roll out thinly and cut into rectangles about 10×5cm (4×2in) with a serrated pastry wheel. Deep fry – they puff up into little cushions – and serve on a napkin in a basket, sprinkled with icing sugar.

In some places oreillettes will be made dinner-plate size, ending up as thin, bumpy discs larger than a poppadum but not unlike it in appearance.

Easter   brings every pâtissier out in a rash of chocolate symbolism: eggs, of course, enclosing sugar eggs; eggs in nests, with or without chickens on top; tiny eggs inside broody chocolate hens, tied up in a pink and white bow. The fish, the Christian *icthus,* is moulded in chocolate too, with little fish in its belly, and there will be bells, because from Maundy Thursday to the evening of Holy Saturday, the bells of the church go to Rome to see the Pope and bring back eggs for good children. 'In some villages, children actually watch for the return of the bells. Their parents take them into the field, or on to a hillock, and they then face towards Rome, waiting for the bells to descend' – presumably with a crash of sound from the village steeple. After lunch, the children look for the eggs brought back by the bells, in the house, in the garden, in the fields and stone walls.

Pâtissiers also make different cakes and pies according to the region – Easter is their busiest and most profitable time of the year. In our Bas-Vendômois, we have puff pastry fish filled with almond cream, and because we are not too far from the Berry, we share the Berrichon Easter pies of sausagemeat and hard-boiled eggs. In the south of France and Corsica, they make rings of enriched dough – enriched with eggs of course – and set hard-boiled eggs in them, like jewels in the crown, especially if the eggs have been dyed. To keep them in place, strips of dough are fixed across, so that they do not fall out as the ring is baked. The whole thing looks like a ring of bells; the Corsicans call them *Campanili.*

In Touraine, and no doubt elsewhere, eggs were dyed by putting nettles (green), violets (purple), coffee grounds (brown) or onion skins (yellow) in the water – an old habit. But when Ronsard, the poet of the Vendômois and Touraine, gave eggs as a present, he left them white, white and round like the sky 'which holds everything in its arms' – and so, he wrote, 'Je vous donne, en donnant un oeuf, tout l'univers.'

Incidentally, the main course at Easter lunch is provided by lamb – 'the pascal lamb indeed' – rather than turkey or chicken.

Eel Two kinds – the conger eel of the sea goes into Breton fish soups, the cotriades, to give a strong background flavour, but it is too coarse to appear much in classic or bourgeois cookery.

The other kind, the silver eel from the Sargasso sea that comes to many of the rivers of Europe, is caught at the mouth of the Loire in its tiny elver stage, as it is in the Severn estuary. These civelles are washed in plenty of water, acidulated with vinegar, then they go into a pan with aromatics and are covered with cold water. This is brought to the boil and left to simmer for a minute or two, until the elvers turn opaque, then they are quickly drained. They may be eaten cold with a vinaigrette flavoured with parsley, chervil, chives and gherkins, enriched just before serving with thick cream. Or reheated in butter with chopped garlic and parsley.

The fully grown eel is a special treat, whether cut in chunks and grilled over vine prunings at the wine cave, or turned into one of the splendid red wine **matelotes** (qv) of the rivers Loir and Loire.

A strange-sounding partnership

which works well is the combination of eel and chicken, in a sauté from Digoin that was a favourite dish of the great chef, Alexandre Dumaine, and in a 'pochouse' or freshwater fish soup from the country around Seurre, also in Burgundy.

Eggs Now that we follow the EEC sizing system for eggs, you might think that French recipes would be easier to follow accurately. Not a bit of it! I do not recall ever seeing an adjective attached to the word *oeufs,* let alone numbered sizes. Commonsense and experience are thought to be enough: if you feel short on these commodities, use a standard egg, size 3 or 4, weighing 55-60g (2oz).

For people who keep poultry, eggs are rarely standard. The chart below will help them to work out the total weight of eggs that they require, whether from bantams, ducks, geese or ostriches. Weigh them in their shells.

Old (ounces) New (grammes)

Old (ounces)	New (grammes)
Large	SIZE 1 — 70g
2 3/16 oz	SIZE 2 — 65g
Standard	SIZE 3 — 60g
1 7/8 oz	SIZE 4 — 55g
Medium	SIZE 5 — 50g
1 5/8 oz	SIZE 6 — 45g
Small	
1 1/2 oz	
Extra Small	SIZE 7

My useful egg ratios using eggs sized 3 or 4
For a firm custard to be turned out; 3 eggs + 3 yolks to each 600ml (1pt) liquid.
For a pouring custard; 2 eggs or 4 yolks to each 600ml (1pt) milk or milk and cream mixed.
For little pots de crème; 1 egg + 5 yolks to each 600ml (1pt) liquid.
For quiches and open tart custards; 2 eggs + 6 yolks to each 600ml (1pt) cream or cream and milk mixed.
For mayonnaise; 3 yolks to each 300ml (½pt) oil.
For soup liaison; 3 yolks + 100ml (3½oz) cream to each litre measured generously (2pts).

Elderflowers As neglected now in France, except for a few country districts, as they are here. A sad result of the move to towns, as elderflower syrup is a good standby

for cooking fruit (apples, gooseberries) or soaking it (strawberries, fruit salad), whenever a muscatel flavour is needed.

Dissolve 2½ kilos (5lb) sugar in 1 litre (1¾pts) water, and simmer for one minute. If you like, add a good pound of gooseberries at this stage. Simmer for 5 minutes. Prepare a muslin bag containing 8 or 10 heads of elderflowers and put it into the boiling syrup. Turn off the heat and leave to cool down. Taste from time to time, and remove the elderflowers when the muscatel flavour is strong enough. When cold, strain and freeze, or store in the fridge in screwtop bottles.

Use elderflowers for fritters – beignets de sureau. Shake them gently to dislodge any insects. Dip by the stem into batter and fry. Serve with a sprinkling of orange flower water (or orange juice) and sugar.

Essences A trap – and a temptation. Your eye catches the word 'Vanilla' or 'Almond' on the label. You buy the bottle without another look and discover, too late, that you are landed with vanilla or almond 'flavouring', which is not the same thing, but a poor-tasting imitation (compare 'rum flavouring' with rum). Read the small print with a cynical eye.

And the temptation? To use essence as substitute. For instance, ground rice plus almond essence for macaroons, rather than ground almonds.

Langdale's natural essences are to be found at health food stores. Some delicatessens stock superb German bitter almond essences in tiny phials, worth every penny, considering that they are used by the drop.

If you run out of vanilla essence, reduce a piece of vanilla pod to powder with some sugar in a blender, then add a teaspoon or so when you weigh out the ordinary sugar for the recipe.

F

Farce In its sense of 'stuffing', this French word was taken into our kitchen vocabulary centuries ago. And just as medieval cooks stuffed bits and pieces into capons and geese, so medieval players would stuff a comic interlude into their mystery plays, something to lighten them – a bit of fun for contrast – and that, too, became known as a farce. It's a name that has stuck, even when the farce became a play on its own. By that time it had come to mean a buffoonery, a comedy. In the kitchen, a farce has always been taken more seriously, with elegance rather than clowning.

Fasting   In France, as in neighbouring Belgium, 'fasting' does not mean going without food. It means going without meat, game and poultry on certain days. It also means the development of a wonderful 'cuisine maigre' to help one through these trying times, a development which seems to owe something to the Church itself and to parish priests (see Brillat-Savarin's description of the curé's dinner of crayfish soup, salmon trout and the famous carp roe and tunny omelette).

In 'Small Talk at Wreyland' (1918), Cecil Torr noted the pleasures of fasting and the cuisine maigre: 'The queerest table d'hôte I ever saw was at the "Singe d'Or" at Tournai, 26 March 1875. That was Good Friday; and it was a first-rate fish dinner, lasting close upon three hours. There were 80 people there, mostly from the town, as there were few travellers about, and we were the only English. The citizens went steadily through the 15 courses, and drank dozens of champagne, and then went home with a good conscience, feeling they had carried out the precepts of the Church in having a meatless day.' Do you think if Henry VIII had been a virtuous husband, we might have discovered how to cook and enjoy fish?

Fats and **Oils**   These divide French cookery into three main styles and two subsidiaries. Butter underpins the classic tradition, the Gauls having been the great butter-makers of the ancient world; olive oil is the base of the southern, Mediterranean style; and lard, which is the fat of the countryside and provincial cooking north of the olive line, triumphs in the elaborations of **charcuterie** (qv). Goose fat flavours many dishes in the south-west of France, and the foie gras districts of Alsace and Lorraine. Walnut oil, less now than in the past, has a rôle in Burgundian

and western French food; its strong flavour precludes much elaboration.

The characteristic nature of the different fats is something French cooks understand. I never remember seeing the word 'fat' used in a French cookery book as one sometimes does in English recipes – as if it did not much matter whether you used whale blubber, margarine or car oil. They realise that by changing the fat in, for example, a sauté, you alter the whole style of the dish and must change other ingredients to preserve the harmony.

Although cold storage of various kinds has made a big difference in France as elsewhere, fat is still used as a preservative. Pickled goose and pickled pork keep perfectly below a thick layer of goose fat or lard (see **confits**). Small soft cheeses last for months and improve in flavour when stored in olive oil flavoured with herbs. As with smoking, fat storage adds something, turns the main item into a new food. Often, food preserved in this way out of necessity in the past has become today's luxury.

Of course, the French are as nervous of fat these days as everyone else. Tasteless oils occupy much space in supermarkets. In the north, people prefer to use them for mayonnaise. Such bland, deodorised oils may have a rôle in deep-frying, on account of their high burning point. You might occasionally use a little of one – palm, soya or groundnut – to dilute a strong-tasting olive oil when making mayonnaise. But on the whole, stick to the classic fats, if your aim is good eating.

Fennel   The use of fennel as a herb – its stalks, leaves, seeds – belongs to the southern tradition of French cookery. Why it should be so confined I do not know, as the plant itself grows enthusiastically in the north. Once planted in your garden, you have it for ever, and it spreads all over the place. I suppose, though, that only in the heat of the south does the smell of fennel on sea cliffs make it irresistible, all-pervading. Primarily, fennel is a herb for fish and the dried stalks often make a bed for grilled mullet.

Fennel as a vegetable comes from Italy. We recall this in naming it Florentine fennel. To the French it has been familiar for so long that it

is just 'fenouil'. They have adopted Italian styles of fennel salad, fennel gratins in which the quartered, blanched bulbs are baked with butter and Parmesan, but they have also developed a range of fish dishes in which the fennel is emphasised by the use of pastis in the sauce.

One thing that has not survived is the old habit of eating fennel as dessert, along with fruit, nuts and sweetmeats, sometimes in candied form like angelica stalks, sometimes fresh.

Both 'fennel' and 'fenouil' come from the Latin name *faeniculum*, meaning 'little hay', on account of the fine, feathery leaves.

Filberts see **Hazels**

Fish-knives   In silver, with a pointed blade to make boning and filleting easier, these seem to have been a French idea of the mid-19th century. Sir William Hardman, wealthy barrister and friend of George Meredith, was an open-minded man who loved food. He gave a dinner in September 1863, when he returned from Paris: 'Meredith and Hinchcliffe dined with us, and our continental tour having enlarged our culinary ideas, we determined to air our novelties at home. Dinner commenced with prawns and bread and butter, and, after the soup, a slice of melon. The vegetable separate, and the Cabinet pudding iced. Fish knives for the first time . . .'

The usual steel knives were no good with fish, as they gave it an unpleasant flavour. People managed with silver forks and a piece of bread. Fish-knives made things much easier, but superior persons sniffed and thought them vulgar. I have heard of grandfathers in the 1950s still attending to fish in the old way. They must have been the only ones able to appreciate fully the horror of the first lines of 'How to Get On In Society', by Sir John Betjeman (1954):

'Phone for the fish-knives, Norman
As cook is a little unnerved
You kiddies have crumpled the serviettes
And I must have things daintily served.'

Nowadays, with stainless steel taking over, the need for fish-knives lessens – except for their elegance and that useful pointed end.

Flamiche means Flemish, a word that hints at the origin of this dish, popular from Burgundy – whose duke once ruled Flanders – right to the Belgian border. A flamiche is a dish with many variations, based mainly on the theme of leeks, cheese, egg and cream, enclosed in pastry. One old form of flamiche was made by putting the filling on a circle of dough, and then drawing the dough up in gathers, like a soft purse. Nowadays, puff pastry is used to make a simple round pasty, baked flat. Other versions come closer to our Cornish and Welsh leek double-crust pies.

Flan This, in its widest meaning, is an open tart, used for the kind of thing we loosely and incorrectly refer to these days as a quiche. The filling may or may not include some form of sweet or savoury custard. In the bakery or pâtisserie, a flan always means custard tart. Usually to be avoided – it is every bit as yellow and stodgy as anything our own manufacturers can produce.

Florentine This has two current meanings in French cookery. First, there is the delicious biscuit of chopped almonds, hazelnuts and candied fruit set in toffee and finished with a layer of chocolate. Second, the gratin in which a main ingredient – eggs, fish, ham – is placed on a bed of buttered spinach, and covered with a Parmesan-flavoured cheese sauce. Oeufs, sole ou jambon à la florentine all indicate the use of spinach, this being a favourite vegetable of Tuscan cookery.

Foie gras The one quotation from Sydney Smith we all know, is that heaven is eating foie gras to the sound of trumpets. Discreet trumpets, I would say, so as not to get in the way of Sydney Smith's elegant and witty conversation.

Complain about foie gras as we may, about the nasty business of stuffing the geese or ducks with a mash of maize, it is delightful to eat. Here you will not find it easy to buy in its best, fresh state; it comes mainly in pots and tins. A winter luxury from Alsace or Aquitaine, often prepared with truffles, a combination that was first thought of in Strasbourg towards the end of the 18th century.

If you happen to be in the Dordogne in winter, visit Sarlat, a great place for foie gras. In the market there a friend of ours went off and bought the largest foie gras he could find, as a surprise for his hostess. She was not used to cooking foie gras, but knew that it should be baked. She set the oven at moderate.

Both of them made a mistake. *He* should not have bought the largest foie gras, but a medium-sized one weighing about 6-700g (1¼lb). *She* should have baked it in the lowest of low ovens.

Result: a tough golf ball of skin and gristle in a sea of the most expensive fat in France.

Well, they did have the best fried potatoes in France for a week afterwards.

This is how they cook foie gras at one hotel in the Forez: remove all the skin and stringy bits and the gall bladder. Marinate the liver for two days in brandy and port. Pack into a metal mould, cover and stand in a **bain marie** (qv) with hot water. Bake at 30 minutes per 500g (1lb), at no more than 68C (155F) gas as low as possible.

Fouaces or **Fougasses**
Hearth-cakes that were baked on the foyer in the ashes, caused a battle between the bakers of Lerné and the shepherds of Gargantua's country. Early one morning in the autumn, just before the vintage, the cake-makers of Lerné set out with several loads of fouaces, intending to sell them at Parilly, near Chinon. As they passed the vineyards of Seuilly and Cinais, they were spotted by shepherds among the vines, who were scaring the birds away from the ripe grapes. Now 'it is a celestial food to eat for breakfast – hot fresh cakes with grapes, especially the frail clusters, the great red grapes, the muscadine, the verjuice grape, and the laskard ...' So the shepherds tried to buy some of the fouaces. The bakers refused to sell and called the shepherds rude names – and there was a fight. The shepherds got their cakes, but it ended in war and trouble.

Fouaces are more read about than eaten these days, I would say, though you do come across them in different parts of France. Recipes vary from the Rabelaisian requirements of 'fine butter, fine yolks of eggs, fine saffron and fine spices', but the result is usually a flat, plainish cake of the kind that is best eaten hot with butter. And nowadays they are baked in ovens. In the South of France, fouaces are made from a bread dough into a figure-of-eight shape and eaten with cream cheese.

Frangipane was the name given first – in 16th-century France – to a perfume for gloves made by the Italian Marchese Muzio Frangipani from the red jasmine of Mexico; second – in the 18th century – to fillings flavoured with almond and orange flowers and used in pâtisserie; and third – in the 19th century – to the flower from which the scent was derived.

Gâteaux and galettes des rois and gâteaux **Pithiviers** (qv) are filled with a version of frangipane cream that Margaret Paterson defines in 'The Craft of Cookery' (1978) as 'a sandwich cake mixture using ground almonds instead of flour'. As she remarks, a level dessertspoon of flour in addition to the ground almonds helps to stiffen the mixture slightly, and a few drops of almond essence accentuate the almond flavour, but this is the mixture I find most delicious for general use: 125g (4oz) each ground almonds and sugar, mixed with 60g (2oz) melted butter, 2 egg yolks and 2 tablespoons whipping or double cream.

Fricandeau A favourite of French cookery since the time of Rabelais, it is a piece of veal cut from one of the leg muscles of the calf, so that it looks like an oval cushion. It is well larded (see **larding**), then braised with wine and stock. Eventually the liquor is reduced to a concentrated richness, with which the fricandeau is glazed and sauced. Sometimes a large piece of tunny, salmon and so on, is called a fricandeau, because it has something of the same shape.

De Beaumarchais, author of 'The Barber of Seville' and 'The Marriage of Figaro', complained that the new restaurants of his day were always serving fricandeaux. They had become a bore. But one English traveller at least did not agree. 'Meat thoroughly subdued by human skill is more agreeable to me than the barbarian Stonehenge masses of meat with which we feed ourselves,' wrote Sydney Smith almost 50 years later, when fricandeau was still a standard item of the French menu.

Recently it has declined in popularity, but may well be due for a revival, being ideal for slow-cooking electric pots.

Fricassée from *frire* meaning to fry, is difficult to characterise separately and accurately from **ragoût** (qv). Both are elegant stews made with food that does not require long cooking. The principle is to cut up the main ingredient – chicken, veal, lobster, cucumber, mushrooms etc – and fry it in butter. Then a little stock, cream or ready-prepared sauce is added – just enough to complete the cooking and bind the pieces lightly together. The result is more of a sauté with a pan sauce than a stew.

These small dishes of French cookery, that demand a certain skill and taste, were once much despised by true-blue Englishmen who liked their meals massive:

'Muse! sing the man, that did to
*   Paris go,*
That he might taste their soups
*   and mushrooms know!*
Oh! how would Homer praise their
*   dancing dogs,*
Their stinking cheese and fricassée
*   of frogs!'*

from Dr King, 'The Art of Cookery', 1708.

Frogs' legs   or rather thighs, 'cuisses de grenouilles', are only avoided by the foolish. They look and taste like miniature chicken drumsticks. No horrors there. In France you will very often see them for sale at the fishmonger's strung by the dozen on wooden skewers. At the grocer's they are sold frozen. They are fried in butter, and served provençale-style with a chopping of garlic and parsley, or in a more classic manner with **poulette sauce** (qv). Sometimes cream will be stirred into the buttery juices with a little parsley and lemon juice – and that is all. Quick and simple.

With the rising standard of living in France, frogs' legs have become so popular that some familiar grounds, such as the Marais between Niort and La Rochelle, are fished out (if that is the right expression). Frogs' legs have to be imported from Russia, Eastern Europe, Turkey, Egypt and even the Far East.

Fromage frais (fresh cheese)
This unfortunately has no equivalent here. Low-fat cottage cheese is too granular, the moister medium-fat curd cheese is still too dry, and full-fat soft cheese has a texture too much like cloying white mud. Fromage frais has the light consistency of thick, drained yoghurt, which can be used as a substitute in some recipes. Its fat content can vary from nil to a medium 43 per cent or even higher, but the consistency remains the same. Any slight wateriness should either be poured off or beaten back into the cheese. In France, supermarkets stock several brands: you will also find local fromages frais made from cows' or goats' milk – or a mixture of the two – on sale at grocers' shops, market stalls and farms. They are sold in pierced plastic tubs, a modern version of the traditional stoneware 'faisselle' on little legs. (In this country supermarkets have begun to stock Gervais Jockey fromage frais, and Quark which is the German equivalent.)

Fromage frais is the basis of many family and regional dishes. It can be drained, then mixed with herbs and garlic. It can be beaten with cream for extra richness, and folded into beaten egg whites for extra lightness, and then served with soft fruit, fruit tarts, **Pithiviers** cake (qv), or home-made jam and biscuits. The most attractive form of this popular dessert is **coeur à la crème**: fromage frais drained and mixed with cream, and sometimes with sugar and beaten egg white. This is filled into little heart-shaped moulds of pierced white china and left to drain and set – if the mixture is on the moist side, the moulds are lined with muslin first so that the mixture is held together and only the whey falls through the holes. These hearts are turned out and served with cream and sugar, on special occasions with fraises des bois, otherwise with strawberries and raspberries.

In the past, the moulds were made of fine basket work, and I suppose that it was in this enchanting manner that Ronsard took his curd cheese on a picnic with Cassandra or Hélène, when they went to pick flowers in the spring, in the fields of the Vendômois.

Fromage frais is nowadays much used as a substitute for cream by chefs concerned with cuisine minceur. It can be used in making mousse and ice-cream mixtures, or to finish a sauce. Beaten with eggs and nutmeg, salt and pepper, it makes a lighter gratin sauce than the more usual béchamel.

In Poitou and the Vendée, great areas for goat cheese, they make tarts and cakes with fromage frais. It will be set with eggs and egg yolks, flavoured either with sugar and perhaps angelica, or with spring onions, according to whether you want a sweet or savoury tart. Of the many tartes, tourtes, tourteaux, the fromagés and fromagets, the gâteaux au fromage frais (which include flour), the most conspicuous is the black-crusted 'tourteau fromagé': although by definition it is a tart, being baked in a pastry crust, the consistency is cake-like, and the shape owes more to a pudding basin style of mould than to a flat tart tin. I suppose you might call it, and its numerous relations, a cheesecake, although the consistency is lighter and far more agreeable to many people than the tooth-sticking sweetness of the American cheesecake.

Drained and richer forms of fromage frais are sold in small squares and cylinders, under such brand names as Gervais and petit Suisse. Naturally they are more expensive, and kept for the cheese and dessert courses when they will be served on their own, or with sugar and cream, to be eaten with strawberries and raspberries etc, in the same way as coeurs à la crème.

Frontignac or **Frontignan**   is a sweet muscat wine produced at Frontignan, not far from Sète, in southern France. The English have loved it as much as – perhaps more than – the French, for drinking with dessert and for flavouring ices and creams. We even tried imitating it for ourselves, giving elderflower wine the flattering title of English Frontignac (see **elderflowers**).

Apart from the English, Frontignan has had two notable admirers. Thomas Jefferson declared it would be far more appreciated, more seen at the best tables, if only it were not so cheap. And Colette remembered Frontignan as the start of her education: 'I was no more than three years old when my father

oured out my first full liqueur
glass of an amber-coloured wine
which was sent up to him from the
Midi, where he was born: the
muscat of Frontignan. . . . This
initiation ceremony rendered me
worthy of wine for ever.'

Fumet meaning scent or bouquet,
is used of extra strong stock, the
kind that can be used to flavour a
sauce. The strength is achieved
either by boiling down stock to
reduce it well, or by simmering fish,
game, chicken, vegetables, in a
prepared stock, with or without
wine, to fortify the taste. In the case
of fish, 'fumet' can mean no more
than fish stock.

G

Galantine According to some,
this is a word of obscure derivation.
Does it come from snowdrops,
rushes with aromatic roots, the
Chinese spice of galingale which is
related to ginger, from gelatine,
from géline or galine meaning
chicken in Old French (from the
Latin *gallina*, a hen)? Larousse
plumps for the last explanation,
because galantine nearly always
means a boned, stuffed chicken in
jelly. If it is made with something
else, the galantine is qualified –
galantine de veau.

Clearly this is not right, because
long ago a galantine was a sauce
poured over meat, poultry or fish –
most often fish, judging by late
medieval cookery manuscripts. In
Chaucer's time the word may seem
to relate to gelatine:

*'Was never pyk walwed in
galauntyne
As I in love am walwed and
y-wounde.'*

But if you look up contemporary
recipes from court cookery, a
cookery much influenced by
France, you find that cold poached
pike is 'wallowed and wound' in a
sharp, oniony bread sauce, spiced
with galingale, cinnamon and
ginger, coloured red with saunders
very often, and poured hot over the
cold fish. More of a true chaudfroid
than what we think of as galantine.

And galingale? A bitter rather
than a gingery spice, perhaps more
difficult to come by than ginger as
some recipes for galantine sauce
leave it out and rely solely on
cinnamon, ginger and pepper.

Perhaps this goes against the
galingale derivation.

But then think about plum
pudding, made originally with dried
prunes, then gradually with dried
raisins and currants only as they
were easier and cheaper to buy.

Anyway, a puzzle.

Game By our standards game in
France is inadequately hung. We
like our birds to have a good flavour
and our venison a certain liveliness.
The French seem happy with wild
boar that is bred in forest parks in
special 'maternity units' and tastes,
in consequence, rather tame.

Where the French score is in the
ritualising business of La Chasse,
the autumn passion of every class of
society. The most famous shoot of
all was, I suppose, at Alphonse
Daudet's Tarascon in Provence:
'. . . every Sunday morning,
Tarascon flies to arms, lets loose
the dogs of the hunt and rushes out
of its walls, with game-bag slung
and fowling-piece on the shoulder,
together with a hurly-burly of
hounds, cracking of whips, and
blowing of whistles and
hunting-horns. It's splendid to see!
Unfortunately, there's a lack of
game, an absolute dearth.

'Stupid as the brute creation is,
you can readily understand that, in
time, it learnt some distrust.

'For five leagues around
Tarascon, forms, lairs, and burrows
are empty, and nesting-places
abandoned. You'll not find a single
quail or blackbird, one little leveret,
or the tiniest tit . . . Tarascon is
down in the black books of the
world of fur and feather. The very
birds of passage have ticked it off in
their guide-books, and when the
wild ducks coming down towards
the Camargue in long triangles, spy
the town steeples from afar the
outermost flyers squawk out loudly.

"Look out! there's Tarascon! give
Tarascon a go-by, duckies."
And the flock takes a swerve.'

So what do the sportsmen do?
They go out into the country, and
'gather in knots of five or six,
recline tranquilly in the shade of
some well, old wall, or olive tree,
extract from their game bags a
good-sized piece of boiled beef, raw
onions, a sausage and anchovies,
and commence a next to endless
snack, washed down with one of
those nice Rhône wines.'

Then they whistle the dogs to

heel, chuck their caps in the air and
shoot away. The one whose cap is
most tattered is king of the hunt. It
is always Tartarin, Tartarin of
Tarascon, the great hunter.

Vive la chasse!

Garlic 'I find as I suspected that
garlic is power; not in its despotic
shape, but exercised with the
greatest discretion,' said Sydney
Smith, reflecting on a visit to
France and Beauvillier's book
'L'Art du Cuisinier' which he had
bought there.

It's an opinion that most French
chefs would have echoed until the
last few years. Nowadays with the
new cookery so influenced by the
south of France, garlic is used by
the head rather than the clove, to
flavour and thicken sauces. Like
much else in the nouvelle cuisine,
this is not an original idea. Lamb
and chicken with 50 cloves of garlic
are old favourites from Périgord
round to Provence. In fact, the
garlic melts with the juices from the
meat to make a most savoury purée:
few people not in the know would
ever guess the main ingredient.

An even more naked assertion of
garlic's delight is the introduction
of a whole head of garlic baked in
its skin in a **diable** pot or in the
oven, as a first course. A head for
each person. The cloves are scraped
out of the hot golden skin and
spread on well-buttered bread. A
common dish of the past in Poitou,
where garlic is sometimes known as
'la thériaque des pauvres', the
antidote or cure-all of the poor.

For this kind of treatment, you
need the fat garlic of France, the
kind that begins to come into the
shops in July, looking fresh, the
white skin streaked with pink and
green and purple. There is
argument as to the best kind. Some
people swear by the rose-skinned
garlic of Albi for sweetness. Others
maintain that nothing can touch the
garlic of the Gers. I have a passion
for the garlic of Bourgeuil – and for
its wine – and buy at least two kinds
from the same grower every year: fat
purple-skinned heads for using first,
and a more compact white garlic for
keeping until the next St Anne's
day, 26 July, comes around when
the great garlic and basil fair is held
at Tours.

Garnishes In so many of our
eating houses, these have sunk to

such a decadence of parsley, frozen peas and fancy-cut tomatoes, that we tend to despise the whole idea.

A pity. Garnishes were not intended to disguise poor cookery or distract the eye, though at some periods splendour does seem to have been paramount. The great pâtissier Carême suspected that in some houses garnishing concealed the fact that the grand centre was served up day after day. People were not brave enough to dig a spoon into so lavish a sight. They said, 'Magnifique!' and ate from the smaller surrounding dishes. The practice is, I feel, not quite dead.

The true purpose of the garnishes that are such a large part of classic cookery is to add variety, to discover new compatibilities, to honour distinguished clients or events of the day, to wake people up. The names are a convenient shorthand and remind us of the past. Only when reading a menu do people remember Prince Demidoff or Count Orloff, or that peas were once grown in Clamart.

Nowadays nouvelle cuisine chefs are uninspiring in this respect, and simply give the main ingredients as the name of the dish. When trout is floured and fried in butter, it is much more entertaining that it should be called truite meunière, because of the miller's wife taking a trout from the mill pond in her floury hands. Such names make dishes memorable.

Escoffier went for pêches Melba, pêches Empresse Eugénie, poires Belle Hélène after the popular operetta by Offenbach (someone else invented consommé Réjane after the actress who appeared in it), pudding Malakoff because its palisade of boudoir biscuits reminded people of the redoubt at Sevastopol taken by MacMahon in the Crimean War.

The French have their special town and district names and use these to describe regional dishes. It's easy to work out pommes parisienne, short for pommes de terre à la parisienne, or sole normande. Can you place martégale, poniote, madrilène, mancelle, bittéroise? If not, read on.

Such titles as caneton à la montmorency, or consommé a la Jockey Club may look odd; so does moules marinière or boeuf bourguignonne, but these apparently mixed genders are, in fact, correct, since 'à la' or 'à la mode de' both meaning 'in the style of' have been omitted for convenience.

People complain about this litany of past fame but it is interesting to learn the history they conceal, or to make expeditions to see if the best cherries still grow at Montmorency, the best peaches at Montreuil, the best carrots at Crécy, the best asparagus at Argenteuil.

The great guide to classic garnishes and dishes is Saulnier's 'Répertoire de la Cuisine', translated into English and easily come by; it's the Bible of French classic cookery.

And martégale, poniote . . .? They designate Martigues, le Puy, Madrid, Le Mans and Beziers.

Genoese   Pâte à génoise is a fatless sponge to which melted butter is added at the end of the mixing. Whether baked as one large cake, or in a sheet to be cut into small discs and squares, it is the pastry cook's basis for drama and decoration.

Do not confuse pâte à génoise with pain de Gênes, Genoa cake. In France this is an almond cake, in England a fruit cake, often containing plenty of cherries.

Gigot   A leg of mutton or lamb has not always been the prized delight of the best French tables. Grimod de la Reynière would have wondered what all the present fuss is about. In his 'Almanach des Gourmands' of 1803, he observed that only from a few areas is the mutton worth eating. And it was only the rich who could afford it. He was less enthusiastic about the standard roast gigot of the bourgeois table. Grimod classed himself as an aristocrat through his mother's family: his paternal grandfather was a successful charcutier which tickled his bitter and ironical humour.

However, this rather common meat could be both nutritive and succulent, as long as it was 'anticipated as eagerly as a big prize in the national lottery, as mortified as a liar caught in the act, and as bloody as a cannibal'. 'Mortified' is a pun, because it also has the meaning of meat tenderised by marinating.

Grimod de la Reynière then goes on to discuss the art of roasting.

Disaster can lie in one turn of the spit, more or less. 'You can find a thousand good cooks to each perfect rôtisseur,' he declared, a remark later echoed by Brillat-Savarin, who concluded that rôtisseurs were born and not made. 'A hundred towns in Europe are famous for their excellent ragoûts, but superior roast meat is only to be found at Valognes.' The standard of meat cookery there is still high especially in the spectacular old kitchen of the Hôtel du Louvre. Local pré-salé lamb or veal preceded by a dozen oysters from St Vaas nearby, makes a good last meal before returning home from Cherbourg.

Gooseberries   are not much respected by the French. Even though you may see a basket of fine pinkish dessert gooseberries in Fauchon's food shop in the Place Madeleine in the summer, you will rarely come across a gooseberry bush in a French kitchen garden. I know of one or two round us that have escaped into the hedges of an old cottage, their fruit neglected, but that is all. They are called mackerel currants – groseilles à maquereau – which suggests a certain popularity in the past, the sharp fruit made into purée or stuffing to cut the richness of the oily fish.

This agreeable partnership has recently been revived again in England, but not yet I think in France, although one might expect it to appeal to the new chefs who make a greater use of fruit in savoury dishes than the classic tradition would allow.

Guineafowl   Pintade, or pintadeau for a young one, is far more common in France than here. In restaurants of the middling kind, it is already a cliché – and for the client a safer choice than chicken.

Guineafowl with their humpy, black and white chequered shape, are often seen in French farmyards. They are also reared in a semi-intensive way – in the early stages at least – for sale in the town butchers' shops and supermarkets. The dressed weight goes from $\frac{1}{2}$-1kg (1-2lb), and they are easy to pick out, being distinguished from chickens by their darker, yellower-skinned appearance and leaner shape. Happily, they taste more like under-hung pheasant han intensively-reared chickens, but they have the pheasant's disadvantage of being on the dry side.

Therefore it is prudent to lard a guineafowl (see **larding**), to stuff it with something moist – from a lump of butter to petits Suisses mashed with fresh or pickled fruit, and then to braise or pot-roast it in a moderate oven. Cooking time varies from 45 minutes to 1½ hours, according to size and oven temperature; start checking after 45 minutes.

All pheasant recipes are suitable for guineafowl. Favourite ways include braising it in wine and stock with raisins (sometimes with fresh grapes), or cooking it gently in a cocotte with cream, Cognac and mushrooms, or in the Normandy style with Reinette apples – substitute Cox's – fried in butter, and cinnamon, cream and Calvados. As well as the usual spirits and red or white wine, fortified wines work well with guineafowl – pineau des Charentes, port, Madeira, vermouths B & B (brandy and Bénédictine) – especially when the sauce consists mainly of the clear, reduced cooking liquor.

H

Ham   To the French, it is even more than it is to us as they have a range of hams that are eaten thinly sliced and uncooked, the aristocrat being the Bayonne ham, dark red, marbled with fat, up in the Parma class. Why we produce nothing equal to it I do not know. We import hams of this type at great expense, apparently with no thought of providing it for ourselves.

The Gauls were, it seems, the first producers of quality ham, the kind one buys by name for special occasions. In the first century AD, Strabo wrote that the Gauls had plenty of food, including milk (they were the original butter-makers, and butter is often served in curls on the same plate as ham in France and Italy). Their herds of swine were so enormous that they could supply 'salt meat, not only to Rome but to most parts of Italy as well'.

Part of the secret was the sea salt of Brittany, from the salt marshes behind what is now La Baule, a grey salt, full of flavour, still the best. Centuries later, in 1680, Madame

de Sévigné was gently chiding the extravagance of the Governor of Brittany, and of her daughter: 'I was wont to say that the Bishop of Rennes marked the pages of his breviary with slices of ham: it would seem your Valence would not despise the possession of a similar book-marker.'

The Sévigné ham, the ham required in most French recipes, usually means uncooked ham which is on sale in every charcuterie by the slice or in the piece. (Our uncooked English hams are only sold whole, as a rule, but gammon makes a good substitute.) The charcuterie will also have cooked ham on the bone of the highest quality, cut carefully in huge pink slices with a proper edging of fat. Ham on the bone is the only possible substitute here, even though it does not always match the French in quality.

This is not to say that the French do not suffer from very ordinary cooked jambon de Paris, or jambon de York, too. They also endure squared-off, water-injected, plasticated, pink 'ham', pork meat that has been divided into pieces, tumbled and massaged with a curing solution, so that it absorbs as much water as possible (some contain 31% water; some 38% and 42% when you come to canned hams). Then it is re-formed in various shapes.

Cheap food? Yes, perhaps, but expensive water.

Haricots   These cause confusion. Haricot beans, which to the English mean dried white beans and to the French green string beans, as well as many other varieties (see **dried beans**), all came to Europe in the 16th century, after the discovery of America.

But Taillevent, the royal chef who took three cooking pots and six roses for his coat of arms, was making 'haricots' in the 14th century. Haricot in this sense meant pieces, from the Old French *harigoter*, to cut in pieces and a fair enough name for a mutton stew, haricot de mouton.

The French soon discovered the affinity between lamb and mutton – and the new beans.

Is that how the name was transferred?

Probably not. It is more likely that haricot is a garbling of *ayacotli*,

the name for beans in the Nahuatl language of the Aztecs. A happy slide of language, from the exotic to the familiar.

Hay   An odd item, you may think, to come across in a cookery anthology. Hay was used in the past both in France and in England in the cooking of ham (and still is, by some people).

Elizabeth David has been discussing its precise purpose recently, in the first two numbers of 'Petits Propos Culinaires', Alan Davidson's new cookery magazine. She feels that the main purpose may well have been for some kind of cleansing, perhaps even for de-salting, and calls in evidence early recipes for cooking lampreys. Evidently hay was used to get rid of muddiness and slime. However, Mary Norwak writes that she has always added hay to the water when cooking bacon and ham, as her mother and farming ancestors had done, for the sweetness it gives to the taste (and the wonderful aroma in the kitchen). And I remember that when I was trying out jambon au foin for my book on charcuterie, using new dried grass from the orchard, there was an extra deliciousness to the meat. Though I do not recall that anyone eating it leapt to their feet, with a triumphant shout of 'Hay!'

When the season comes round, go out into the country and bring back a very generous handful of hay, and try it with a piece of gammon, putting it into the water like any other aromatic. A cheap way to fill the house with the smell of early summer at least, and perhaps to improve the gammon as well.

See what you think.

Hazels and **Filberts**   *Corylus avellana* and *Corylus maxima* provide much pleasure for pastrycooks, with hazelnut meringues, Florentines and other biscuits and hazelnut praline to flavour cakes and sweet butters. The best hazelnuts come from Avellino behind Naples, hence the botanical name. Filberts belong to St Phillibert, a 7th-century Norman saint, abbot of Jumièges on the Seine. They are the noix de filbert because they ripen round about his feast day, 20 August. Which is about right in a good summer, better still when you allow for the fact that by the old calendar his day falls at the beginning of September.

Once shelled, both hazels and filberts need grilling to get rid of the thin brown inside skin. Quite rapidly this skin darkens – turn the nuts regularly – and you can rub it off easily with a clean cloth. Both nuts can be substituted for almonds in some recipes; of course they alter the taste, but the result can be equally delightful. A good way of bringing out their best qualities is to range the nuts on a baking sheet and leave them in a low oven, 120-150C (250-300F) gas ½-2, until they are a very pale gold all through. Scatter them with sea salt crystals and serve with an apéritif.

Herrings in France are cooked resourcefully. They are stuffed, baked, grilled, fried, devilled, marinated in white wine and accompanied by various simple items such as onions and potatoes. The only thing the French do not know is the best way: herrings encrusted in oatmeal and fried in bacon fat. The Auld Alliance that the Scottish are so fond of evoking in matters of food from haggis to gigot, does not seem to have worked much in the other direction.

Of the pickled herrings, which include 'les kippers' (undyed and good), my favourite is the hareng saur or smoked herring, produced mainly at Boulogne. It is salted and smoked whole, like our bloater, which it somewhat resembles in richness of flavour. You can buy three kinds of hareng saur – the strong kind that have been salted for a week (they need soaking), the demi-sel or doux which are often sold ready-filleted in plastic packs and do not need more than an hour in some milk, and the light golden bouffis or craquelots which are the mildest of all, cured for a few hours only.

They are all served in the same ways after filleting. Simplest of all with a little olive oil poured over them and a squeeze of lemon, plus bread or a potato salad with an olive oil dressing. An alternative is to cut the fillets into pieces and chill them under a blanket of half soured cream and half double cream, scattered with chives. The Boulogne style is to make them the centrepiece of a salad, ringed with beetroot, dressed with a mixture of onion, oil and cream, and topped with chopped hard-boiled egg and onion rings.

Bloaters make a good substitute for harengs saurs, and can be served in all the above ways.

Horsemeat This is a well-established part of the French diet. Every town has its horsemeat shop, often with a gilded rocking-horse head over the door. Many markets have a stall. Children and invalids are given horsemeat hamburgers to build up their strength. Manual workers recover with a horsemeat steak. It's good meat with a rich flavour, appreciated by true carnivores.

Odd to think that horsemeat was introduced as a cheap food for the poor, and as a way of preventing cruelty to horses. If owners got a good price for them at the end of their useful life, they would keep them in better condition. In France the idea was promoted by the naturalist Isidore Saint-Hilaire in the 1850s and 60s. The high-spot of his campaign was the horsemeat banquet.

On such an occasion the great, the grand, the public-spirited of Paris – and a few from London, too – might start with consommé de cheval and end with sorbets 'anti-préjudice'. When a similar banquet was given at the Langham Hotel in London in 1868, the menu included purée of chargers, terrine of horse liver, roast fillet of Pegasus, sirloin with Centaur stuffing, marrow patties Bucephalus, veterinary's cake, lobster with mayonnaise Rosinante. So horsemeat triumphed as a quality meat. Look at the price list of any boucherie chevaline.

Horsemeat resembles beef, should be treated as respectfully and costs nearly as much and a good bit more than pork. And no wonder. The demand is such that the Japanese now breed horses specially for the French table.

I

Ice-creams and **Water-ices** came late to France as they did to England (soon after the Restoration in 1660). But the idea of chilling food and drinks with ice is much older, and one may speculate endlessly about the point at which a chilled fruit drink first became a granita (a slush which has to be eaten with a spoon) and then a sorbet (a firm ice which can be moulded).

By the time rich Romans of the 1st century AD enjoyed cold drinks in summer, the Chinese were well away with refrigeration and cold storage. A milk ice (surely the first ice-cream to be recorded?) of cow's milk, rice and camphor was served to a young T'ang emperor in 825 AD – a frozen rice pudding. Louis XIV was the first French king to try something of the kind, when Monsieur Audiger, who later wrote a book on the organisation of great houses, 'La Maison Reglée', returned from Italy in January 1660 and introduced his sovereign to ice-creams (and **petits pois**). Two years later Charles II, who had returned from exile in May 1660, was having an ice-house built in St James's Park. A decade later ice-creams – in rather meagre quantities – began to appear at the top table of court and official banquets.

These ices consisted of fruit and cream fools frozen. Custard-based ices did not come in until the 18th century, and then in France. Odd that this should be so, as England is always given credit for custard by the French, to whom it is crème anglaise (see **custard**). Frozen fruit juices, in other words water-ices, often elaborately moulded and coloured to look like the fruit itself, peaches or apricots or pears and so on, were a parallel preoccupation.

A pity that somehow, in this country, we seem to have forgotten that ices are a treat, that we have no pastrycooks – as the French still have – who glory in iced elaborations of cream, eggs, milk and fruit.

J

Japonais When Europe began to discover the beauty of Japanese prints and objects, in the wake of Monet and Whistler, the new craze was bound to be taken up by enterprising cooks in France.

The first salade japonaise seems to have been made by Dumas père, author of 'The Three Musketeers', who served it at a dinner round about 1860. Perhaps this was the mixture later described by Dumas fils in his play 'Francillon', a

268

mixture of potatoes, truffles and mussels. Another Japanese salad was invented by Escoffier to compliment a visiting Japanese delegation in the early 1900s (pineapple, tomato and orange in layers on a bed of lettuce, dressed with cream and lemon juice). Escoffier also gives a bombe japonais in his 'Guide Culinaire', consisting of peach ice filled with tea mousse – presumably green tea.

Pastrycooks were not left behind. Small japonais cakes began to appear, little discs of almond meringue sandwiched with butter cream, rolled in crushed nuts or meringue trimmings and topped with a small dark circle of icing that symbolises – or so I imagine – the rising sun.

Cooks in France have never worried about authenticity. They take an exotic item or idea that appeals to them, and come up with dishes that are firmly their own rather than an imitation of the real thing. Compare Sauté de poulet à l'indienne (Chapter 25) with curried Monday chicken, English-style. In the same confident way, they use the word japonais to cover Chinese ingredients – a meat dish à la japonaise will include elegant little tubers that first came to Paris from China in 1882. We call them Chinese artichokes; to the French they are 'crosnes du Japon'. In the spring, loquats, originally from China, will be sold as néfles du Japon, Japanese medlars.

Jardinière   means literally the gardener's wife, and is often the name given to the hot equivalent of a vegetable **macédoine** (qv). Young vegetables, cut up where appropriate, are cooked separately in water and finished all together in butter. Then they are put round a roast joint or bird.
Chefs sometimes cut the vegetables into even shapes, then boil and finish them separately, some in butter, some glazed. They will be spooned on to the serving dish in little piles. Certainly this makes a striking presentation, but it is tricky to manage in a family kitchen. And it seems a little far from the capabilities of the jardinière herself.

Jésus   may seem an unlikely candidate for a food anthology, but to people in the Lyonnais district, it means an extra good, small, fat pinkish-red sausage of the salami type – a saucisson sec – wrapped in a netting of string. One maker explains how his sausage, labelled Le Vrai BB Jésus de Lyon, got its name: 'Towards the end of the year, peasants who were killing a pig would prepare a sausage with the spare-rib and blade bone meat; it was swaddled like the Child Jesus and was eaten in December.'

To the people of Morteau, further north in the Jura, the jésus is a smoked boiling sausage. It is usually served hot, in slices, with grey-green lentils or a hot potato salad.

Julienne   means a piece of meat or a vegetable or truffle that has been cut into long shreds like matchsticks. By extension it gives its name to a clear soup, a consommé, garnished with a julienne of vegetables – see Chapter 5 for the recipe.

But why 'julienne'? No one seems to know. The word has been traced back to an early 18th-century edition of Massialot's 'Cuisinier roial et bourgeois', but where he found it remains a mystery.

Jus   in everyday French means juice – jus d'orange, jus de citron. But in cookery it has several specialised meanings. It may be the liquid from a piece of meat squeezed in a special press. More often it means the juices left in a roasting pan that can be used to make the basis of a small sauce, or to finish an accompanying vegetable.
Yet a third meaning equates 'jus' with sauce, when it consists of a stock well-flavoured enough to stand on its own with or without a thickening. Thus you get a dish of escargots au jus, snails in a sauce of wine and chopped greenery, thickened with egg yolk, walnut oil and chopped walnuts. But however the word is used, the point of jus is to make food juicy rather than wet. It should bathe the food lightly, coating rather than swamping, suffusing with its flavour rather than overwhelming it with liquid.

K

Kirsch   This is made from cherries and, with other clear fruit eaux-de-vie, is distilled in the eastern part of France, as well as in Germany's Black Forest area and northern Switzerland. Kirsch is the best known because of its popularity with French chefs and pastrycooks. So essential is its flavour for classic fruit dishes and certain cakes that it is paid the dubious compliment of an imitation known as 'kirsch fantaisie', which is cheaper by far. You can pay as much for a good fruit brandy as for a good Cognac, but if you can resist drinking the occasional glass, you will find that a bottle lasts a very long time.

With the growing emphasis on fruit sorbets in the nouvelle cuisine, similar distillations of pear (poire William), raspberry (framboise), wild strawberry (fraise des bois), bilberry (myrtille) and so on, are becoming more popular. These spirits seem to have the soul of the fruit in their bouquet. Poire William poured over a pear sorbet is a very special treat. And if you are cooking pork chops with tiny yellow mirabelle plums as they do in the Vosges, a dash of mirabelle eau-de-vie at the end will add delight to the sauce.

Kitchen   The ideal French kitchen, one every traveller hopes to find, is Victor Hugo's inn kitchen of the Hotel de Metz, at **Ste Ménéhould** (qv), where he stayed in July 1839, at the start of his journey to the Rhine.

It was a true kitchen, immense, one long wall covered with copper pans, another with china. Between them, opposite the windows, was the huge hearth with a splendid fire. From the ceiling's smoke-blackened beams hung baskets, lamps, a meat-safe and joints of bacon. In the fireplace was the usual spit, pot-hook, iron pot and an array of implements that shone and sparkled in the flames. The fire threw shadows on to the ceiling and light into the corners. It gave a rosy glow to the blue and white dishes. That kitchen was a world, the great fire its sun. And in all the bustle, in a cage hanging from the ceiling, a small bird slept . . . 'The most admirable emblem of confidence. That cave, that forge of indigestion, that terrifying kitchen is full of uproar day and night, the bird sleeps. Everything rages round it, men swear, women quarrel, children cry, dogs bark, cats mew, the grandfather clock strikes, the chopper thumps on the block, the dripping pan sizzles under the joint, the spit creaks, the tap drips, window panes shake as carriages pass under the archway like thunder; the little ball of feathers never moves – God is charming. He gives faith to small birds.'

Like other successful inns, the Hotel de Metz depended on the hostess. Inn-keepers are only good for drinking in a corner with the coach drivers; it's the woman who is the soul of such places, who veils with delicate attentions the ugliness of bought hospitality. And at Ste Ménéhould she was a girl of 15 or 16, who kept that great world of a kitchen turning, who was everywhere at once, yet managed to play a few notes on the piano as she went by.

Knives   Good knives are a cook's first need. I used to think that the universal cry of 'Sabatier' might be no more than a trendy myth, and tried other makes, both French and English. They were not so good. And I notice that at La Varenne, where the knives are used hard, they are all Sabatier's.

The superior kitchen knife is made of forged carbon steel and the complete blade is ground (in cheaper knives, the blade is stamped out of sheet steel; only the edge is ground). The blade is 'flat through tang', meaning it goes right through to the end of the handle (cheaper knife blades only go part way into the handle, which weakens them). Although it is not necessary with light, flexible filleting knives, the stronger cook's and boning knives have riveted handles for extra strength.

Carbon steel may stain, but can be cleaned – as rapidly as possible – with lemon juice, scouring powder or dampened soft emery paper; never put such knives into the washing-up machine. If they are not in constant use, grease them lightly to prevent rusting in this damp climate.

Never store them in a general kitchen drawer; even if you protect the tips with corks, the rest of the blade can be damaged (and you can cut yourself while rummaging about for something else). Keep them on the wall, either on a

magnetic knife holder, or in a slotted knife rack.

Acquire a range of about four good carbon steel knives, choosing wide or narrow blades, long or short, strong or whippy according to your needs. Boning and filleting knives will not be much use to vegetarians, but meat-eaters will find the larger kitchen knives useful for carving game, poultry and small pieces of meat. A small stainless steel knife is handy for preparing fruit, and a stainless steel palette knife that bends flexibly is essential for turning and lifting food as it fries, and for icing cakes smoothly. A heavy stainless steel cleaver is far more useful than you might at first suppose; not only is it essential for chining meat and jointing meat and poultry, but it flattens garlic efficiently – and escalopes and steaks (moisten the blade first); it also makes a useful chopper and slicer of vegetables and herbs. See also **Fish-knives**

Kouign (cake) **amann** (butter), or **Kuign amann**   is a drawing-room version of our west country lardy cake, as made in the Cornouaille district of Brittany.

The Breton yeast dough is spread with white sugar and butter, instead of brown sugar, lard and dried fruit. It is folded and rolled, then it is spread, folded and rolled again – and again, puff pastry-style. It emerges from the oven with a crunchy top and a yellow richness right through it, rather than the sticky dark lardy of lardy cake.

The idea seems simple enough, but there is some hidden tour de main, some 'truc', that makes it almost impossible for amateurs to rival the best kouign amann sold by the pastrycooks of Douarnenez.

Kugelhopf, Kougelhof, or **Kouglof**   is easily recognised by its tall shape of swirling segments and central hole. The sweet brioche dough it is made from includes raisins and currants (Chapter 30), sometimes soaked in Kirsch. The outside is embellished with slivered almonds scattered over the buttery mould before the dough goes in, and by a final sprinkling of icing sugar when the cake is turned out.

This cake of Austrian origin has collected several stories about its arrival and popularisation in Paris. Some say Marie Antoinette liked it;

others that Carême had the recipe from the Austrian ambassador's chef and made it popular. Others say that it came to Paris via Alsace, that it was brought from Strasbourg by a pastrycook called Georges, who set up in the rue de Coq with 25 workers, and was soon selling Kugelhopf by the hundred.

Perhaps all three stories are true, representing the usual stages of a new introduction – first court circles, then the households of rich and professional men, then the shops which are open to everyone. The same progression has occurred with sugar, ice-cream, petits pois, globe artichokes and so on. As far as the Kugelhopf is concerned, it is now so popular that you can buy the earthenware moulds for baking it in the markets and shops of western France, at the opposite side of the country from Alsace. These pottery moulds are better than the metal kind, as they conduct the heat more slowly and this suits the rich dough better.

L

Lard   or 'saindoux' to the French is lard made by rendering down the fatty parts of the pig to a white cream. Worth doing, if you can, as home-made lard has a superb flavour. You can see why, in the past, French country children loved to eat it spread thickly on bread.

To make lard, cut up the pieces into a roughly even size, put them into a heavy-based pan with 200ml (6-7oz) water to each kilo, and stir over a low heat until the fat runs. Leave to cook, stirring occasionally, until the pieces are reduced to crisp little nuggets of skin swimming in a clear liquid. Strain through a muslin-lined sieve into sterilised jars, filling them right to the top. When cold, press cling film on to the surface, then cover with foil.

The delicious bits and pieces left in the sieve should not be wasted: mix them into bread or brioche dough at the end of the first rising to make a pompe aux grattons – the bits are known as 'grattons' or 'grillons'.

Having made the lard, use it for making pastry, English lardy cake, and for frying potatoes. It comes in handy as a preserving medium – bits of salted goose, duck, pork and veal can be cooked in plenty of the lard, then be stored in it. Make sure that the lard is free of meat juices (cool, scrape the base free of jelly etc, then melt), and that it runs underneath the pieces of meat as well as round it, with a good thick layer on top.

The way to make sure of the bottom layer is to put two thoroughly cleaned wooden skewers into the jar before packing in the cooled meat. Cover as for lard and store in a cool dry larder. When you want the meat, melt the fat by standing the jar in a bowl of very hot water. Remove the piece you want with tongs, then allow the whole thing to set again, so that any pieces of meat remaining in the jar are once again enclosed in lard.

In Normandy, lard is sometimes replaced by graisse normande. This is made by melting together twice as much beef kidney fat as pork back fat. Once it begins to turn into liquid, aromatics are added – and it is simmered for 7 hours or so, and is then strained into pots as above.

Larding   Years ago in the art gallery at Nantes, we came across a strange sight: a still life painting of the 17th century, with a turkey hiding inside a hedgehog bristle of white bits, evenly and elegantly arranged. Some chef's pride and joy, that larded turkey. Turkeys are bred reasonably fat these days, but topside and rump of beef, veal, venison, pheasant and woodpigeon for braising and roasting can often be improved by this introduction of internal fat which keeps the lean meat moist and tender.

Slabs and pieces of pork fat, cut from the skin, cost little. Chill them before cutting them into strips of an appropriate size. Season them if you like, with salt, pepper and herbs. These strips are called lardons, a name also given to the small strips of salt belly pork or bacon which are added to stews and salads.

Fine larding needles in two or three sizes are easy to find in kitchen shops, but they will only do for birds and small pieces of meat if used too vigorously, they bend out of shape). The strips of fat slide into the open end, which has sections that can be bent out, then pressed back to hold the strips firmly in place. You then take a neat stitch in the meat, leaving the fat behind as you draw the needle through.

When you have finished larding,

with the stitches arranged as tidily as possible, the ends should all be trimmed to the same length. As the meat cooks, the fat will catch the heat and brown appetisingly.

The larding needle for beef and veal looks quite different and is extremely sturdy. You will only be able to buy one at a professional caterer's supply shop. The 'needle' is a strong pointed metal tube, about a foot long, set into a wooden handle. For most of its length, the top part of the tube is cut away, to make a curved trough into which really long strips of fat can be pressed. The whole thing is then pushed through the meat, and you catch hold of the fat as it emerges at the far end, before drawing the needle gently back.

Obviously you have to press the lardon well down into the needle, so that it does not catch in the meat as the needle is pushed through. If the piece of meat is not very long, you will find it easier to push the empty needle right through, then press the lardon into place before drawing the needle back. It sounds complicated when described, but in fact these large needles are much easier to use successfully than the small flexible kind. A piece of topside larded in this way will not only be more tender, but will also look handsome when cut into slices.

Lentils   have been much eaten in Europe, especially by the poor, for thousands of years. Like the other pulses, they are a useful source of protein. Pliny recalls that when the Emperor Gaius brought the obelisk from Egypt to set up in the Vatican, the ship was filled with lentils as ballast to keep it steady. Were they the red lentils that we still call Egyptian lentils? Or were they the dark brown and dark greenish kinds that are more commonly eaten in mainland Europe?

It is no use cooking our red and orange lentils if you want to make a French salade aux lentilles, dressed with olive oil, onion and herbs. They cook too rapidly into a purée. No good either if you want to serve them with various kinds of cured pork and sausages. Such dishes as these require the coherence and earthy taste of the dark lentils, which are grown at their finest – according to the French – around Puy de Dôme in the Auvergne.

Lentils of this kind you will have

to buy from a delicatessen or high-class grocery. Always pick them over for tiny stones.

Incidentally, the lens took its name from lentil, *Lens culinaris,* because the glass was ground to the same shape, not the other way round.

Liaison   is the culinary term in French for a thickening (and it is sometimes used in this sense in English, too). A good deal of the fun and success of cookery depends on understanding how the various liaisons work – and choosing the appropriate kind. A liaison may add a fine touch to a sauce, but it can also be a sort of first aid.

Liaison à la meunière– flour mixed to a cream with water – may be what the miller's wife does to her stews, but to me it comes close to boarding-house cookery. It can be useful if the stew is slightly fatty. Mix it in gradually to avoid lumps.

Liaison au roux– usually called a roux – is made from butter or some other fat which is melted in a pan, and flour which is stirred into the butter and cooked for a couple of minutes before the hot liquid for sauce or stew is added. By cooking the butter to an appetising brown, noisette brown, before adding the flour, you get a fawn or golden-brown roux. And if you cook the flour and butter over a more vigorous heat, you get a darker brown roux (be careful to avoid scorching). A roux is most often the start of a sauce, stew, soup or soufflé but it can be made separately and added to liquids towards the end of cooking.

Beurre manié– kneaded butter – is butter mashed to a paste with up to an equal quantity of flour. Add it in little knobs, one by one, to the liquid, which should be kept just below the boil. In a few minutes the sauce will be smooth and glossy. A paradox: a roux needs cooking for 15 minutes to eliminate the taste of flour, yet the brief cooking of beurre manié does not leave a floury taste behind. The traditional way of thickening matelotes and other fish stews, sometimes used for boeuf bourguignonne.

Potato starch, cornflour, arrowroot– these are mixed to a cream with an appropriate liquid and added to the sauce at the end of cooking time. They make a lighter, glossier thickening than flour, which is avoided by many chefs these days.

Cream – the simplest liaison of all. Much used for pan sauces, or to give a mellow richness to soups. A good corrective for slight oversalting.

Egg yolk/blood – the 'liaisons dangereuses' to the unskilful cook. Both need the same care. Egg yolks plus a little cream, or blood plus a little vinegar (to prevent coagulation), are mixed with some of the liquid from the main pan, and then the whole thing is stirred back and kept well below boiling point, at a temperature which should not be above 75C (175F). If egg yolk/blood overheats, it will curdle. A very slight curdling can be rectified by rapid transfer to a blender, which should be switched on to top speed, but you have to spot the danger fast and act quickly.

To prevent further cooking if you suspect you are getting near danger point, dip the base of the pan in a bowl of cold water. This is in any case a good idea with certain custards, which might go on cooking in the heat of a heavy pan after it has been removed from the stove.

Butter – today's most popular thickening. A stock will be much reduced to a good strong flavour and turned into a sauce by whisking in little bits of butter just before serving, off the heat of the stove. This process is called 'monter au beurre', and it has long been part of the classic tradition as a finishing process, to give a fresh buttery taste to, say, a Madeira sauce. Nowadays substantial quantities of butter will be worked in, so that it acts as a thickening rather than a finish.

These sauces certainly taste much lighter than the flour-based sauces of tradition. They have a clear strength of flavour too, and lack stodginess. For the cook at home who does not have time to make stocks and stand over a classic velouté, skimming and cherishing it, this method – which has become a mark of the nouvelle cuisine – has much to commend it.

Limes (citrons verts) have become steadily more popular in France over the last twenty-five years. First came the great success of the lime sorbet, which was also taken up over here, and more recently the nouvelle cuisine chefs have begun to use lime rather than lemon juice where a more delicate sharpness is required. Limes are used with other fruit, obviously, but also as a marinade for raw fish. For instance, slices of very fresh scallops will be marinated for about half an hour with lime juice and a little oil; then they are arranged neatly on a plate with a few lambs' lettuce leaves and a little heap of beetroot purée. Beautiful to look at, and good to eat – but the scallops must be fresh.

Does this idea come from Japanese *sashimi*, in which exquisitely cut fish is served with a soy sauce? Or from Peruvian *seviche*, in which the fish is 'cooked' by marinating it with lime, lemon or Seville orange juice and various aromatics? Or is it just an extension of eating oysters raw, something we have been doing in Europe since the earliest times?

Limeflowers The flowers of the lime tree (*tilleul*, in French), are mainly used to make a tisane. The winged pale green flowers are picked at their sweetest in late spring and are spread out on paper to dry in a cool place. When they come to the rustling papery stage, they are stored in paper bags for the winter. Like Proust, you may find limeflower tea and a madeleine comforting when you reach home on a wet, dark evening.

Another, more unusual way of using limeflowers is as an aromatic when cooking ham or gammon. Put two generous handfuls or more into the water, above and below the meat, and simmer in the usual way. There is some argument as to whether it really adds flavour – see **hay** – or just persuades everyone that it does, as the sweet smelling air wafts through the house from the kitchen.

Lotte (baudroie) often appears on French menus in the fish section and baffles many a traveller. I remember wrestling with the meaning 20 years ago at Briquebec in Normandy, quite unsuccessfully. The proprietor brought over his 'American' menu, then fetched his dictionary and phrase book. The mystery remained. And no wonder, for at that time lotte, otherwise baudroie, otherwise monkfish, never appeared in Britain at all.

These days we appreciate monkfish, though not as much as the French who buy much of our catch I believe, and price it with sole. They bake it on a bed of vegetables, the whole tailpiece, as if it were meat, and give it a name such as gigot de lotte, or lotte en gigot. The sweet firmness, the single easy bone, make monkfish ideal for cooking and serving with vegetable sauces (à l'américaine), wine sauces (matelote, à la tourangelle), cream sauces (charentaise, with mussels), butter sauces (béarnaise or hollandaise), for using in soups (bourride) and as a grill on skewers (en brochette). Here at least, it is still quite a lot cheaper than sole, which makes it the ideal fish for experiment as well as pleasure.

Lute comes from the French *luter*, and – if you go back far enough – from the Latin *lutum*, meaning clay or mud. It means to stop up a hole or close a join with cement or clay or, in the case of cookery, to fix the lid of a pot firmly in place with a luting paste of flour and water. The paste rapidly hardens in the heat to seal the join, so that no steam can escape. Ideal for daubes which are made with a small amount of liquid, and for pâtés (Chapter 18).

Luting paste is no more than a kindergarten dough of flour and water. You roll it into a long rope and press it round the rim of the pot. With the other hand you jam the lid in place and press the dough down to make a firm seal. If you are confident of your daube, you chip the lid away at table, so that the company can enjoy the wonderful smell that bursts from the pot. Less confident cooks – like myself – prefer to do this in the kitchen, in case the sauce needs degreasing or reducing, or just some extra pepper and salt.

Nowadays people use crumpled foil instead of luting paste, but it is not as efficient.

Lyonnaise 'in the style of Lyons' and its surrounding district, the Lyonnais – usually though not invariably means onions (bugnes lyonnaise, for instance, are sweet pastry fritters). The onions are sliced and cooked gently in clarified butter or lard, so that they melt rather than brown; they are sometimes finished over a higher heat with white wine and wine vinegar to make a sort of purée. If you want a sauce, add some basic brown sauce (Chapter 23) and sieve or liquidise. Alternatively, stir a tablespoon of flour into the purée, then add brown stock.

Two famous and favourite dishes are pommes de terre à la lyonnaise, and tripe à la lyonnaise. For the first, parboil and fry potatoes in clarified butter or lard until they are golden brown and crisp, then mix in onions, cooked more gently in the same fat, and serve immediately. A dish of wicked delight.

For the second dish, a superior form of tripe and onions, there are alternative methods: either cut the cooked tripe into strips, fry in clarified butter or lard until lightly golden brown, then mix in the cooked onions: or cut the cooked tripe into squares, coat them with egg and breadcrumbs and fry until crisp, then put them on top of the fried onions. In both cases, **deglaze** (qv) the pan with wine vinegar and pour it over the whole thing.

Lyophilisation You will often see the word 'lyophilisé' on cans of mushrooms, peppercorns in France. It is the term in modern chemistry for the process of freeze-drying. This is drying from a frozen state, the foodstuffs retaining their physical structure, ie. this method prevents the protein molecules concentrating and aggregating. The foodstuff is frozen, then dried in a vacuum so that the ice 'sublimes', passes from solid to vapour.

In plain terms, this means that freeze-dried foods taste a little more like their original selves than if they were dried at heat in the ordinary way. It also means that they cost more – quality has to be paid for.

M

Macaroni The Marco Polo pasta legend (Chapter 16) was a pre-war publicity invention of an enterprising Canadian firm. Surprising how the tale caught on, to the extent that it has to be denied by every cookery writer who mentions pasta.

More interesting than Marco Polo is the way that cooks far to the north of Italy began to make pasta several centuries ago, earlier than

one might have expected. Richard II's chief cook, who compiled a cookery manuscript about 1390 called 'The Forme of Cury', gives a recipe for macrows, ie. macaroni. His method would be the same today. Cut a thin 'foil' of dough into pieces and boil them; serve them interlayered like losyns, ie. lasagne, with butter and grated cheese.

If you ever buy pasta in France, go for an Italian brand with the durum wheat guarantee. Some French brands are made of soft wheat and lack the vigorous bite of proper pasta in consequence.

Macaroons have a long history in France, and a number of local variations. At Corméry in Touraine, so the legend goes, the pastrycook monk of the abbey made such superb macaroons that people came from miles around to buy them. The town bakers profited from the demand and sold inferior imitations. Soon the prior realized that the abbey macaroons needed a special trade mark. But what should it be? He prayed to St Paul, the patron saint of the abbbey, and vowed that the first thing he saw next morning would be the inspiration for the seal of guarantee. When he woke, he hurried to the kitchen where Brother Jean was preparing the oven for the first batch of the day. As he scooped out the embers, one of the coals jumped out and burned away part of his habit, exposing his navel. The abbot had the answer to his prayer.

Other macaroons, including those of Nancy and Melun, originated in convents and have attracted a less ebullient style of legend. Today the Nancy macaroon sets the standard, which is reasonably safeguarded in France.

Our own commercial macaroons are best avoided. Go for the packaged ones imported from France, especially if you want to make a special treat such as Biscuit Tortoni, a famous ice-cream from a famous ice-cream establishment of 19th-century Paris: whip 600ml (1pt) cream with 60g (2oz) icing sugar until stiff. Freeze until almost firm, then beat well and fold in a teacup of hard macaroon crumbs and a glass of sweet sherry. Freeze in a loaf tin. Turn out and coat with crushed macaroons.

Note that in France macaroons

are about 5cm (2in) across, and come 20 or 25 to 100g (3½oz). Useful to know if you have a recipe in which they are listed by number rather than weight, as for instance in a St Emilion au chocolat (macaroons are another speciality of this famous wine town).

Macédoine means a mixture of vegetables or fruit and refers to the Macedonian Empire that Alexander the Great put together from a jumble of small states. The word first appeared as a literary metaphor in 1771 – macédoine littéraire – but caught on more permanently in the kitchen. In 1814, Carême put a new dish in front of Czar Alexander I who was in Paris after Napoleon's defeat. It consisted of a jellied mould of chicken breasts filled with a macédoine of vegetables in mayonnaise. Presumably the first salade russe.

A vegetable macédoine, whether cold in jelly or mayonnaise, or hot in a velouté, should only be made in spring and early summer, when young vegetables are at their best. The end of its season coincides with the last asparagus of mid-June. Each vegetable should be carefully cut to size, and cooked separately. There should be just enough sauce to bind them.

The term macédoine was being used for fruit as well by the 1830s, with the advantage that this was a year-round dish. Fresh fruit, cooked fruit, even dried and glacé fruit softened gradually in water over a low heat, was set in a liqueur-flavoured syrup. The height of its glory came in mid-19th century at a time when the development of new fruit varieties, and the import of exotic fruits, were of passionate concern to the French.

The English version, given by Mrs Beeton in 1861 in her 'Book of Household Management', is a poor, tame affair more concerned with a trivial prettiness than with the dazzling chill and exquisite flavours of the macédoines of the great French chefs.

Macerate and **Marinate** mean very much the same thing, ie. soaking a food in flavoured liquid to improve the flavour and soften the texture. By convention 'macerate' is kept for fruit, and 'marinate' for meat and fish.

The liquor used is often, though not always, incorporated in the final dish. Often, though again not always, it includes some kind of alcohol. Its effect can be cosmetic and brief, as in fruit salad, or pork and lamb marinated into a semblance of wild boar and venison; or preservative and longer-term, as for peaches in brandy or mackerel in white wine.

Maize   Travellers driving these days across the ancient corn lands of France may be struck by the way maize has supplanted wheat. Stopping for a first sight of Chartres over the fertile land that paid for it, they will have to peer over walls of maize and listen to the dry crepitation of its leaves. This maize is not for eating, but for plastics, forage and oil.

But in Gascony, where maize crept quietly into the country first of all, in the 16th century, you will not only find dishes of cornmeal, but plenty of them. Peasants liked it better than the millet they had been used to (until a hundred years ago wheat flour was as much a luxury to Basques and Gascons as it was to the peasants of the English Lake District). They just put it into their dishes instead of millet, without bothering to change the names, even though colour, texture and taste were all different.

Liquid porridges and solid polenta-like dishes were still called milhas and millassou. The dough boiled in a pudding cloth continued to be known as mique. These firm yellow breads are at their best when sliced, fried and served with game or beef stews. Cornmeal does not rise easily, but mixed with half its quantity of wheat flour and given time (under an eiderdown, very often) for the yeast to work, it makes good grainy bread. When added to pumpkin, gold to gold, and sweetened, it can be turned into cakes and tarts. Sometimes prunes are added, for their dark softness of colour and their taste.

If you ever wonder why the chicken you are eating is so deliciously old-fashioned in flavour, or the foie gras so rich, you will find an answer in the maize field and the heads of grain it produces. Along the road, by the farmhouse, long *séchoirs* of wire netting, raised from the ground on poles in two parallel rows, are filled every autumn with maize. Their eccentric lines are as much part of the French landscape as the wild-angled telephone poles.

Marchand de vins sauce *see* **Bercy**

Margarine   On 17 July 1869, margarine was registered at the Société Impériale des Inventions et Recherches by Monsieur Hippolyte Mège-Mouriès, an engineer attached to the Ministry of Agriculture. Its importance was recognised. Napoleon III was rapidly persuaded to hold a competition to find a cheap edible fat which could be stored on board ship, in the navy, without going rancid like butter. Monsieur Mège-Mouriès was the sole competitor. He won.

Naturally the dairymen did not care for the new beurre économique. Over the years they made a fuss. The authorities came down on their side: margarine was to be sold in cubic packets. It was not to be used in public kitchens and canteens (except for certain stews). There were to be no mixtures with butter, and no verbal association with it.

This made France and French cookery safe for butter. Elsewhere margarine may have triumphed, but not in the land of its origin.

According to some French food writers, Monsieur Mège-Mouriès deserves to be remembered more charitably for his work on diseases of the vine and methods of preserving fruit and vegetables.

His last words were said to be: 'No, nothing can take the place of butter.'

Marmelade   A sweetened purée of fruit which has a certain consistency from being sieved, and if necessary cooked down to evaporate any wateriness. It is not as firm as our fruit cheeses. A marmelade de pommes, for instance, is often spread over pastry as the basis of an apple tart; it will then be covered with a beautifully arranged layer of apple slices. But often, the term is used loosely, and you may see pots of jam in the grocery labelled 'marmelade' with contents that have obviously not been sieved.

Marmelade – and our marmalade – go right back to the language of ancient Assyria and Babylon, to the Accadian *marmahu*, a quince. Was the quince the origin of all our fruit preserves? Perhaps. For however ripe it may be, however aromatic the smell, it cannot be eaten raw – 'It has the perfume of a loved woman, and the same hardness of heart.' One may conjecture that after it had lain in a bowl for a while, and sweetened Assyrian rooms 'like a censer', it was handed to the cooks to make something of. See **cotignac**.

Matelote   – from matelot, meaning sailor or mariner – is very much a dish of the Loire and of Burgundy, Touraine and Anjou through which it passes on its way to the sea.

Until the railways were built the Loire was a great highway. Barges and boats crowded the navigable channels of the treacherous river, taking goods and passengers to and from the heart of France.

Madame de Sévigné was once grounded on a sandbank, and spent the night in a hovel on a bale of straw. John Evelyn and his friends were luckier. They hired a boat at Roanne, then as now a fine gastronomic centre, and came singing down the Loire – 'the great poet Mr Waller' was one of the company – shooting at wild fowl, playing cards, alternately walking through fields and rowing, until they got to Orléans. I wonder if they picnicked on the banks and shared the boatman's matelote?

In its simplest form, matelote consists of a mixed bag of freshwater fish stewed in red or white wine. The method has been refined, and is nowadays applied to sea fish too. Nonetheless, there is nothing better than matelote of eel, served in a small river restaurant and made from eel trapped at a nearby sluice on one of the mill leats.

The trick of a matelote is to mature the sauce without overcooking the fish. Either make a velouté with wine, fish stock and aromatics, and stew it down slowly before adding the fish for 10-15 minutes. Or cook the fish, fast and briefly, in wine and stock with aromatics, then strain off the liquid, reduce it, and add a thickening of beurre manié: the fish then goes into the sauce to reheat, plus the separately cooked garnish, Burgundy-style, of glazed onions and fried mushrooms. Bread cut in hearts or triangles and fried in butter is tucked into the pot as it goes to table. One strange addition is prunes, for centuries a speciality of Tours, but they work well.

Matelote being such a favourite dish has many versions and local names – bouilleture, meurette and pochouse are three of them. It is mainly an angler's dish, since the mariners have gone from the Loire. You make it with what you have caught rather than what is listed in the cookery books.

Mayonnaise This basic sauce of everyone's repertoire we owe to the French. But when it was first made, or first noticed, remains a mystery. The name itself is odd. Some claim that it commemorates the capture of Port-Mahon in Minorca from the English in 1756, by the Duc de Richelieu (mahonnaise). Others say that over-indulgence in chicken chaudfroid made with his chef's new sauce caused the Duc de Mayenne to be beaten at Arques in 1589 (mayennaise). Grimod de la Reynière was all for Richelieu, but said it referred to his taking of Bayonne (bayonnaise). At this point the man of action stepped in, the great chef Carême: 'Nonsense! Every chef of my acquaintance calls it magnonaise because he knows it comes from manier meaning to stir. And this is a sauce one stirs.' You might expect every cook since to be with Carême, but not Prosper Montagné, author of 'Larousse Gastronomique'. He felt it should be moyeunaise, moyeu being Old French for an egg yolk. Etymologists of the great dictionaries just give up, as they so often do with culinary vocabulary.

Luckily, there is no mystery about making mayonnaise. Quantities and method are the same as given by Carême in the 'Cuisinier Parisien' in 1828, writing after more than 30 years' experience: 2 yolks, beaten with a little wine vinegar, and 250ml (8oz) olive oil added drop by drop, at first, with final seasoning and more vinegar to taste. Carême also added 4 or 5 tablespoons of firm jelly, as his sauce was mainly for binding moulded salads, and had to keep its firm consistency for long periods in hot rooms.

In today's circumstances, we emphasise the need for ingredients and utensils to be at warm-room temperature. But we echo Carême's

exhortation to go slowly at first. When his mayonnaise curdled, he would start again with a spoonful of thick béchamel, always to hand in professional kitchens. We take another egg yolk, or a spoonful of French mustard, adding the curdled mixture with slow care until the sauce comes back to its proper consistency, when we can go a little faster.

Méchoui To the Arabs a *meshwi* is any meat grilled or roasted over a fire; it might be doner kebab or shish kebab or kofta meshweya. To the French, who have taken to méchouis since the influx of people from Algeria, it means a whole lamb barbecued over a large fire.

At its best, a méchoui can be a lamb from your host's flock, skilfully cooked to brown crispness of skin and pink tenderness of meat, eaten out of doors on a sunny day with many salads and relishes, much wine and conversation. At its worse, a méchoui is a village beano centring on gobbets of underdone meat hacked from badly cooked carcases. And with any luck, the timing will have gone wrong, so that most people are a little sloshed, shouting to their friends across the wobbly tables of an overheated marquee, as they chew at the unlovely hunks.

Melons The French king Charles VIII was entranced by the gardens of Italy – 'all they lack is Adam and Eve to make them an earthly paradise' – and is said to have brought back melons to France. Amboise was his centre. The climate of Touraine and neighbouring Anjou must have suited the new fruit, because they rapidly became popular. In the Charentes to the south, the variety that we now see in every summer market in France was first developed.

The ancestors of our melons were taken on picnics by Ronsard. Catherine de Medici ate them so enthusiastically that she suffered appalling indigestion. And one was so good, so perfect, that the 17th-century poet, Saint-Amant, wrote a long ode in its honour. With exuberant joy he describes its thin green skin, its reddish yellow flesh which is firm and unwatery, its few golden seeds. He pictures its growth like a green snake with a rearing

head. It tastes better than coconuts, than apricots, than strawberries and cream, than the sacred pear of Tours, the sweet green fig or the muscat grape:
> '*O fleur de tous les fruits!*
> *O ravissant melon.*'

Menu, in the sense of a written list of dishes, is a fairly modern French idea, associated with the rise of restaurants in Paris at the end of the 18th, and beginning of the 19th centuries. Eating houses, inns, cooked food shops had often displayed boards, but menu cards belong to the superior tone of the restaurant. They give the style of the establishment, imply a regular repertoire of dishes and tell people politely and quietly how much they are likely to pay. Ledoyen, still flourishing elegantly under the trees of the Champs Elysées, was apparently the first restaurant to list the enormous choice it provided at the beginning of the 19th century, but it was not until about 1825 that printed menus became at all common.

In the prosperous Paris of the Second Empire (1852-1870), the menu was sometimes taken over by painters. They filled the borders with amusing drawings that might allude to the glorious deeds of the guest of honour, or to the season or event that had prompted a special dinner. This habit continued until modern printing costs made it too expensive.

The great change in dining brought about most notably by Escoffier in the last part of the 19th century, a change towards a simple – or simple-seeming – perfection, was reflected in refined menus. Escoffier would agonise over the choice of dishes for hours, but the result did not betray his concern. His carefully arranged sequence, in the Russian style, of one dish after another could be shown to far greater advantage on a menu card than the crowded offerings of the old French service with its three enormous courses. It required a wealthy and confident clientèle to turn from show towards simplicity, knowing that quality and skill are more valuable than opulence.

Although food styles have changed again, this still holds good to-day. It is the deep-freeze restaurant that has the vast menu. The three-star restaurant may stake its reputation on little more than a dozen dishes.

Meringue was being made at least half a century – and probably much longer – before it settled down with its present name. Two queens are sometimes credited with its popularity – Marie Leszczinska, wife of Louis XV, daughter of Stanislas Leszczinski of rum baba fame, and Marie Antoinette who apparently whisked up vacherins (Chapter 14) in her dairy at Versailles. Perhaps they made meringue fashionable, but it was nothing new.

In fact there is a meringue recipe in 'Le Pastissier François' of 1653, said to have been written by La Varenne, although Anne Willan doubts his authorship. His *biscuits de sucre en neige*, made from Italian meringue, are exactly like the little pink and white meringue biscuits at children's parties before the Second World War, as Elizabeth David has pointed out.

After La Varenne's death, enlarged editions of his 'Cuisinier François' came out. They included a recipe for *pets de putain*, consisting of Italian meringue, flavoured with orange-flower water, and baked in walnut-sized blobs. Another name of the time, less easy to understand, is mellandes, but in 1698 at last the word meringue appears – in Massialot's 'Cuisinier Roial et Bourgeois', 3rd edition. And meringue stuck, perhaps because the book went into many editions and was extremely popular.

Mesclun Provençal for mixture, is exactly that. The seeds of at least seven different kinds of salading are mixed together and sown in specially prepared ground. They are watered frequently, covered at night with plastic and scattered with powdered peat. Quite rapidly the closely sown rows of seeds turn to a thick green carpet of shoots that are longer and leggier than our mustard and cress, but still young and delicate. The mesclun is cut 1cm (½in) from the ground to give the slower seeds a chance to push up for a second crop, then it is washed and dressed with a vinaigrette. Bought from a greengrocer it is delicious, but what must it be like direct from the garden?

The plant mixture varies from region to region. Here is the Lyonnais choice – cress, non-hearting lettuce of the salad bowl type, lamb's lettuce, scarole chicory, curly endive, Verona chicory and cos lettuce. Fennel, chervil and rocket are sometimes included as well.

Metric weights and measures were devised by the French Academy of Sciences, initially for France but with the idea that in the end they should be 'for all times and for all peoples'. The system became law in 1795. What may seem at first a muddling confusion of names becomes simple if you remember that units have Greek prefixes when they are multiplied, and Roman prefixes when divided:

decalitre = 10 litres/
decilitre = 1/10 litre
hectolitre = 100 litres/
centilitre = 1/100 litre
kilometre = 1000 metres/
millimetre = 1/1000 metre

People take to such changes slowly. Even the French have not embraced the metric system as thoroughly as the reformers would have wished. In shops and markets you will hear 'livre' and 'quart' as often as demi-kilo or 500 grams – and 125 grams. Pound and quarter pound are convenient family measures, and as words they are more satisfactory both to the mind and tongue.

We had worked out improved standards for our old measurements by 1760, although they did not become law – as Imperial standard – until 1824. Americans kept to the English measurements, but confusingly preferred to adopt the 16oz pint (the Imperial pint is 20oz). Both countries are having to bow to world preference. It is to their advantage, but they make the change reluctantly.

As far as cookery is concerned, the change is easy once you grasp that a kilo is 2lb plus, and a litre under 2 pints. Easier still if you buy a marked measuring jug and balance scales – mine cost £3 from a local antique shop – with two sets of weights; with this basic equipment you need never attempt a conversion from one system to the other. If you prefer visual aids, get the children to make you graphs that you can stick up on the wall. A self-catering holiday abroad is one of the quickest, if more expensive, ways of learning how to cope with the metric system. The only way with oven temperatures is to pin up a chart by the oven itself:

Comparative oven temperatures
This table compares oven thermostats marked in C with those marked in F and with gas marks. These are specimen dial markings and not conversions.

260C	(500F)	
240C	(475F)	gas 9
230C	(450F)	gas 8
220C	(425F)	gas 7
200C	(400F)	gas 6
190C	(375F)	gas 5
180C	(350F)	gas 4
160C	(325F)	gas 3
150C	(300F)	gas 2
140C	(275F)	gas 1
120C	(250F)	gas ½
110C	(225F)	gas ¼
100C	(200F)	gas low
80C	(175F)	

Remember that individual ovens vary a great deal and that sometimes it is better to adopt 170C (325F) gas 3, and 130C (250F) gas ½. (This table is based on information given by the Electricity Council and by British Gas.)

Meunière on the menu – sometimes belle meunière, the miller's beautiful wife – means fish rolled in flour and fried in clarified butter. At first the fish was trout, from the mill pond, but the method is often used for sole and other fine white fish. The butter must be clarified to prevent it from burning. Then when the fish is dished up, with its lemon quarter and one or two tiny potatoes beside it, some sizzling golden brown beurre noisette is poured over it, and it is rushed to the table. Unfortunately practice does not always follow theory, and sole meunière may be no more than lemon sole carelessly fried in some anonymous restaurant fat.

The original truite à la meunière is said to have been served to Napoleon, in a mill at Royat near Clermont Ferrand, where the fresh streams were full of trout. A plain foursquare building has succeeded Napoleon's mill, but the same stream rushes beside and underneath. Tall capitals BELLE MEUNIERE top the façade, and that of the restaurant now jutting from the side, but alas you can no longer count on eating trout for your meal.

Minced meat Take a tip from the French who rarely buy minced beef or lamb ready prepared. They choose the cut they prefer, then ask the butcher to put it through his machine. Or they take it home, sharpen their heavy knives and chop it to the texture they require. Either way they are spared the unpleasant experience of seeing their money dissolve into a pan full of fat.

Sausagemeat is another matter. The charcutier has to use all meat for a start. And he tends to use proper meat rather than such dodges as emulsified pork skin. To give extra flavour and a good colour, he may first pickle the meat for a few hours, before he puts it through the mincer and adds a spice blend such as **quatre épices** (qv).

For such reasons as these, you may often see the word sausagemeat as an ingredient, used by reputable French cookery writers. Your best plan is to follow the advice of the first paragraph: buy a piece of neck or shoulder pork, with the rough proportion of $\frac{1}{3}$ fat to $\frac{2}{3}$ lean, and either leave it for 5 or 6 hours in brine, or add a small amount of bacon to mince or chop with it.

For stuffings and pâtés, this 100% sausagemeat is the best solution. For crépinettes and sausages, you may prefer the gentler style of our traditional sausage, the kind that disappeared after the Second World War when rusk superseded bread as the cereal filler (rusk has a long shelf-life – great advantage to commerce, disaster to gastronomy). Breadcrumbs from a homemade loaf, a drying stale loaf for preference, are the things to add: begin with 1 part to 5 or 6 parts of pork.

Mint (menthe) The French miss out badly on mint in cookery by comparison with the Eastern Mediterranean, or even with ourselves. I find they can be ecstatic at tiny new potatoes or English garden peas cooked with mint, but will shudder at the idea of mint sauce with lamb (reasonably enough, if it is made with much malt vinegar it also ruins the accompanying wine). At this point I say: 'But what about your sauce paloise?'

Sauce paloise (Chapter 23), called after Pau in the Pyrénées, is béarnaise flavoured predominantly with mint rather than tarragon. It is eaten with roast lamb, grilled lamb or poached duck.

Mirepoix Named after the Duc de Mirepoix, soldier and diplomat, who died in 1757, it is the vegetable equivalent of a bouquet garni. The three basic items are chopped carrots, onions and celery, in the proportion of 3:2:1, plus 2 parts of uncooked ham, gammon or salt pork when appropriate to the main ingredient of the dish.

Usually, a mirepoix goes into the base of a buttered pan, with a bouquet garni. It makes a bed for the meat, poultry, game or fish to be braised, or it can be the start of a stock or classic sauce. As it will later be strained out with all the flavour of the various ingredients absorbed into the liquid, the chopping can be fairly rough. On the rarer occasions when the mirepoix is to be a vegetable garnish, and separately cooked, the items need to be carefully diced. Just before it is put on to the serving dish, mix in chopped parsley.

Miroton sounds like the refrain of an old song. In reality it is a dish that the French have been making on Mondays for at least three centuries. It has its charm, when the cook takes trouble.

Briefly, a miroton is a gratin of leftover boiled beef – roast can be used too – which relies on piquancy to see it through. The modern version is often made by putting a layer of **lyonnaise** sauce (qv) on the base of a shallow dish, and then layering in thin slices of beef and fried onions. Over the top goes more sauce and breadcrumbs. The whole thing is browned in the oven or under the grill, and served bubbling hot. If the beef is on the short side, you put a ring of mashed potato round the edge and call it miroton **Parmentier** (qv).

I prefer the 18th-century bourgeois version. A piquant sauce of the lyonnaise type can be used, but the layers of beef are then alternated with finely chopped parsley, spring onion or Welsh onion (ciboule), capers, anchovies and a little garlic. A miroton of vigour.

Mouclade A version of moules marinière made in the Aunis, the district around La Rochelle. At Esnandes, up the coast on the huge Anse d'Aiguillon, you look past pink tamarisk to a shallow bay stuck with mile after mile of posts until the sea shades up into the sky. Men in flat-bottomed punts – called accons – manoeuvre along, cutting away the mussels which cling in bundles to the posts. These tiny moules de bouchots are sent far into France, to markets and fishmongers, to tempt everyone with their sweetness.

The trade is an old one. Legend traces it back to the 13th century, to 1253, when an Irishman by the name of Walton was wrecked off the coast. To keep alive, he netted sea birds. After a time he observed that mussels were growing on the posts he had put up to support his nets.

Like many food legends, this one was first recorded in the 19th century. It may not be true. But there is no greater pleasure, in that region of good eating, than to sit down in the small Hôtel de Port at Esnandes to a pot of bubbling mouclade. The sauce is yellow with saffron, flecked with herbs. It tastes sweet and piquant from the marriage of mussels and white wine. Cream and Charentais butter make it thick and rich. And that at least is true.

Mushrooms The French have been ahead in mushroom cultivation since the 17th century, though it was not properly understood and economically viable until the Pasteur Institute in Paris produced sterilised mushroom spawn in the 1890s. Now mushroom-growing is big business in the west of France, with Saumur as the centre. Worked-out quarry caves in the river cliffs of Loire and Loir country provide the perfect ambience of darkness and even temperature. There the familiar cultivated mushroom, *Agaricus bisporus*, is grown in oak trays and plastic sacks, with sometimes a smaller area devoted to the greyish oyster mushroom, *Pleurotus ostreatus*. Button mushrooms are easier to find in France than they are here. And you will see that they are sold complete with sandy base, rather than being cut across. In the early 19th century, Carême noted that the mushrooms on sale in England were well prepared and ready for cooking.

The French do not stop at

cultivated mushrooms. They use field mushrooms, and have a special appreciation of the morel of springtime, the yellow chanterelle or girolle, and the fleshy cèpe. The classic recipe of 'cèpes à la bordelaise' provides a special autumn treat: fry the cleaned and cut-up cèpes in olive oil, evaporating or pouring off any large amount of liquid (varies with the season), add a handful of chopped parsley and a couple of chopped shallots, and turn everything carefully for a few more minutes. With chanterelles, the recipe is altered to butter and garlic, rather than olive oil and shallots. Morels are cooked with butter and cream, and add their flavour to chicken sautés.

So popular are these mushrooms, so high their price, that it is worth flying them into Paris from Scotland where they are unappreciated and left to waste.

In the provinces mushroom-hunting is a favourite family sport. Beyond the classic favourites, the black 'horns of plenty', *russulas*, wood-blewits, parasols, rubber-brush (*Hydnum repandum*), and southern species such as the orange (*Amanita caesarea*) are all keenly sought. The puff ball is another one: every year giant specimens are recorded from the fields around Cholet (Maine-et-Loire) in our local paper – in 1979 the largest was 7.2kg or 15½lb. See also **truffles**.

Mustard is made differently in France. The basic ingredients are the same – black and white mustard seeds – but the French use more aromatic black mustard, while we have always gone for the fierce white kind. The difference can be compared to the differing heats of black and white peppercorns. Add to this the fact that the French soak and mix the seed with wine vinegar and wine, and you will understand why it is no good using English mustard for French cookery. Nor is it any good using imitations. Read the small print and make sure you buy mustard imported from Dijon, then read the small print again and make sure you are not buying one of the fancy mustards. What you require is the plain kind, or the kind described as 'moutarde forte au vin blanc'.

Dijon is the great mustard centre,

no doubt for the good reason that it is also the centre of Burgundy, the great wine country. Should a summer journey take you there, visit the mustard shop in Dijon's main street. There you can get advice, choose from a selection and admire the bright faience jars of an earlier time. As you drive away through the vineyards, reflect that mustard derives from Latin, *mustum ardens*, fiery must – 'must' being the unfermented juice that runs from the wine press.

Like pepper, mustard loses its fire if it is cooked for any length of time. For this reason it is usually a final addition to a sauce, whether the sauce is separately made or worked up from the pan juices of a sauté. However in the favourite lapin à la moutarde, the rabbit pieces are smeared with mustard at an early stage of the cooking so that its flavour penetrates the meat thoroughly: you can always add a touch of mustard to the sauce at the end, if it seems to need it.

French mustard can also be used to rescue a curdled mayonnaise: put a heaped teaspoon in a warm bowl, then add the mayonnaise drop by drop, beating all the time, going carefully. Mustard can also be used as part of a basting sauce, eg. for ham, and to liven veal escalopes, pig's ears, tails and trotters, cooked ox tail, before they are dipped in egg and breadcrumbs for grilling or frying.

N

Nantua on the menu means crayfish, usually in the form of a sauce or purée with fish and poultry. Nantua is a small town in the Alps where the streams run clear down to a lake. Crayfish like clear streams. If the water is muddy, they have a taste of mud – a 'goût de vase': if the water is really polluted, they die. Many country districts lost their crayfish when women started using detergents to wash clothes at the *lavoirs*. About the same time, their husbands were vigorously scattering nearby fields with artificial fertilisers, which leached into the streams and joined the detergents. Neither did the crayfish any good.

Now things are changing. Nearly everyone has a washing machine, and the wooden *lavoirs* rot into the

streams. Farmers use fertilisers more sparingly and a few crayfish are found again. But what really makes the difference is the establishment of the new fish farms. In disused water mills, people breed crayfish as well as trout for markets and restaurants. Sauce Nantua is found all over the place again, though often the menu will read, for instance, poulet aux écrevisses. The significance of Nantua was, I suppose, forgotten by many during the lean years.

Poulet aux écrevisses consists of sautéed chicken, with white wine and tomato providing the liquor. Crayfish are sautéed in another pan until they turn bright red. They are flambéed, floured, moistened with white wine and chicken stock, and spiced with onion, shallot and saffron. After a minute or two, the crayfish and the cooked chicken are put on to a serving dish. The liquids are amalgamated and reduced, flavoured with Madeira and cream, and the whole thing is poured over the dish. You need finger bowls and napkins.

Navarin is a ragoût of mutton or lamb, to be sampled at its best in spring when young turnips, the first peas and other vegetables are ready for the pot. The dish itself is an old one in French cookery – see **haricots** – that was renamed after the famous victory of Navarino in 1827. As a haricot usually contains turnips, 'navets' in French, some bright restaurateur or chef must have seen the chance of cashing in on a culinary pun.

Nivernaise Beef, pigs, and root vegetables all flourish in the Nivernais district of Burgundy on its western side, bordering the Loire. Nivernaise garnish consists of glazed onions, carrots and turnips, with braised lettuce and boiled potatoes, which are usually put round a large piece of beef or ham.

The simplest way to glaze root vegetables is to cut them to size if necessary (leave onions whole), put them in a pan with water to cover, a rounded tablespoon of sugar and a level tablespoon of butter – about 15g (½oz), plus a pinch of salt. Simmer steadily – no lid – until the liquid has reduced to a buttery caramel and the vegetables are tender. Turn the vegetables carefully to coat them in the glaze. Do not let the pan burn. Add plenty of pepper.

To braise lettuce, blanch whole in boiling water for 5 minutes. Drain, cool and cut in half. Fold top over cut side to base, and tie with thread or fine string. Put into pan on a bed of thin bacon, chopped onion and carrot, a bouquet garni. Cover and sweat them for 5 minutes over low heat. Add stock to cover. Simmer until tender – the liquor may be reduced if you need a little sauce, or kept for another dish.

Nougat   means literally 'made of nuts'. Sugar, syrup and honey are turned thick and opaque by the addition of beaten egg whites. Then nuts are stirred in, and the mixture is poured into moulds lined with rice paper to set. Tricky to make well, delicious to eat if the nougat is soft and chewy rather than hard.

The best nougat comes from Montélimar in Provence. Once upon a time the way south went through Montélimar. Every other shop on the main street seemed to be selling nougat. Boards overhead, at eye-level, in windows, over doors, on the pavement. Perhaps it's still the same, but now the motorway takes you to the east of the town and you have to buy nougat at one of the service stations, unless you like it enough to make a detour to the source.

Black nougat, another Southern speciality, is a dark nut confection with a more brittle consistency as egg whites are not used.

Nouvelle cuisine   has appeared at least once every hundred years, since the confidence of the new French cookery burst upon Europe in the middle of the 17th century. The initiators are always conscious of their aims – edging out old elaboration and fuss, bringing in new quality and simplicity. They tend to be noisy, unabashed that it has all been done before, and heedless of the thought that in their turn they will be shoved aside.
de Bonnefons, 1651 'Let cabbage soup taste of cabbage; leek soup of leeks; turnip soup of turnips and so on . . . and what I say about soup should apply to everything else that one eats.'
le Sieur R, 1674 'Today it's no longer the enormous glut of dishes, the abundant ragoûts and

gallimaufries, the vast pile-up of meat that make for good eating . . . but the exquisite choice of meats, the refinement of their seasoning, the style and neatness of their serving, their just proportion to the number of people present.'
Menon 1742 in 'La Nouvelle Cuisine' describes how the new taste, by reforming ancient ragoûts, is promoting delicacy at the aristocratic table: 'The new cookery based on the old style means less fuss, less paraphernalia and as much variety: it consists in extracting the quintessence of meats, by drawing out the light and nourishing juices, and by mixing and blending them together so that nothing dominates, yet everything makes itself felt.'
Menon, 1746 in 'La Cuisinière Bourgeois' introduced the new refinement to middle-class cooks: 'Cooking has become so diversified and elaborate that it can overwhelm someone who only wants to feed his family well. I have chosen dishes that are simple, good and new.' He did not wish to criticise the ancienne cuisine because it is the base of the nouvelle. He wanted to simplify method, and make the professional expertise of grand kitchens available to middle-class cooks.
Escoffier, 1902 'The number of dishes set before the diners being considerably reduced, and the dishes themselves having been deprived of all the advantages which their sumptuous decorations formerly lent them, they must recover, by means of perfection and delicacy, sufficient in the way of quality to make up for their smaller bulk and reduced spendour. They must be faultless in regard to quality; they must be savoury and light. Surtout faites simple.'
Curnonsky, 1872-1956 brought up in Anjou, loved the fine and delicate cookery of his native province, in which things 'have the taste of what they are'. He describes the qualities of his parents' cook, Marie Chevalier, as being 'moderation (mésure), taste, honesty, patience and simplicity'. He turned chefs and amateurs towards the regions of France.
Gault et Millau the most influential cookery writers of today; the 10 commandments of the nouvelle cuisine –
1 Avoid unnecessary complication.

2 Shorten cooking times.
3 Shop regularly at the market.
4 A shorter menu.
5 Abandon the hanging and lengthy marinating of game.
6 Avoid too-rich sauces.
7 Return to regional cooking.
8 Investigate the latest techniques.
9 Remember diet and health.
10 Constant invention.
The founding fathers were Alexandre Dumaine of the Côte d'Or, Saulieu, and Fernand Point of La Pyramide, Vienne. The disciples include Paul Bocuse at Collonges-au-Mont-d'Or; Jean and Pierre Troisgros at Roanne; Roger Vergé at Mougins; Michel Guérard at Eugénie-les-Bains; Alain Chapel at Mionnay.

Because they have all published books here, or have books in preparation, they tend to be the ones we know best. There are others, such as Jacques Pic at Valence or Jean-Pierre Billoux at Digoin, whose quieter style seems more attractive, more enjoyable. The best short discussion of the aims and realities of to-day's nouvelle cuisine is published by La Varenne: 'Nouvelle Cuisine: the ten commandments', by Anne Willan, 1979.

Noyau or **Noyeau**   often mentioned in early cookery books, is a liqueur of bitter almond flavour made from fruit kernels. Today we use almond essence instead, which is not altogether an improvement. If you have ever made your own cherry brandy, the hint of almond in the taste gives you an idea of what noyau is like.

Poissy, nowadays on the outskirts of Paris, has long provided confectioners of the capital with noyau for their cakes, ices and creams. And a crème de noyaux is still part of the wide repertoire of Dutch liqueurs, to be seen on the shelves in the bars of Amsterdam.

Nutmeg and **Mace**   The yellow fruit of the tree *Myristica fragrans* conceals two spices. Cut into it, and you will come first to a red aril, a netted skin, through which you can see the brown seed. Aril and seed are dried, and sold as mace and nutmeg.

Mace with its tone of nutmeg and cinnamon should be bought whole in 'blades' for stocks, sauces and stews. It is difficult to pound,

279

though an electric mill reduces it fairly well, so it is a good idea to have a little ground mace, although it is not much needed in French cookery: we have used it far more in this country, especially in potted fish and meat.

Nutmeg is another matter; it is the classic spice for cheese or onion sauces, for spinach and in charcuterie (see **quatre-épices**). Always buy it whole – it's easily grated. Have one of those small semi-circular graters, with a hiding place in the back for 3 nutmegs, hanging up near the stove.

Oils see Fats

Olive   like the fig, the vine and wheat, provides a staple food of Mediterranean civilisation, and so of southern France. It is 'assuredly the richest gift of heaven,' wrote Thomas Jefferson. 'I can scarcely except bread. I see this tree in among the Alps where there is not soil enough to make bread for a single family.' Jefferson was in Provence where the olive line – beyond which olive trees may grow, but will not fruit – swoops up the Rhône valley, defining the northernmost limit of the Mediterranean world in France. There, one may find a fine olive oil at Beaumes-de-Venise, to match the local muscat wine in elegant strength.

It seems wrong, however, to pick out one place. Different varieties, different terrains, all make for different oils. My ideal kitchen would have at least three: a refined, delicate oil for mayonnaise; one or two that *really* taste of the olive for salads; and a cheaper olive oil for frying – with fish, potatoes and many kinds of fritters, nothing can beat it. No wonder frying is so developed an art in the South.

If you happen to be in those parts in autumn, visit an oil mill or co-operative. Everything shines and smells of oil. You may be allowed to hold pieces of bread under the stream of new oil, one of the best of all snacks. Variations of this simple idea – toasted bread rubbed with garlic and sprinkled with oil; a baguette or other long loaf split open, soaked with vinaigrette and stuffed with salad, tomatoes, eggs,

anchovies, capers and olives (Provençal 'pan bagna', the best of sandwiches); bread dough covered with onions softened in olive oil, criss-crossed with anchovies, the lattice filled with black olives, all baked together (pissaladière, from Nice).

Nice, or the area round it, produces tiny black olives and uses them in many other dishes, salade niçoise, sauté of chicken niçoise, with wine, tomatoes and saffron, a garnish of small onions, basil – and olives, and so on.

Elsewhere, eels are baked on leeks with olives, salt cod is covered with a wine and tomato sauce with walnuts, capers and olives, beef is stewed in a **daube** (qv) and finished with olives, and braised duck is served with an olive sauce. These direct and sunny dishes have conquered us all. We return from Antibes or Narbonne and try to recapture their flavour at home – without success. When the Goncourt brothers wanted to take an envious dig at successful Daudet, successful Zola, they snarled that everyone from Provence was a cook at heart. Nowadays we would regard that as a compliment. I think the Goncourts would be startled to see how the South has encroached on our lives, both in northern France and in this country.

Olives can now be bought everywhere, if not in the profusion that exists in our French market in Touraine, where we have at best a choice of eleven different kinds, at worst eight. Olive-growing families long ago devised a series of different 'cures' to catch the virtues of the olive at every stage, from the first greenness, to a full plump tone, then to violet-brown, smooth black, and last of all to wrinkled black mildness. The olives will be crushed slightly, or slashed, or stuffed, or left alone. They will be pickled in wood ash solutions, then in brines. They will be suffused with chillis or herbs.

Expertise in wine is a great thing, slowly acquired, much respected: I have the feeling that expertise in matters concerning the olive may be a greater, if less recognised achievement, and one even more worthy of respect. But to our shame there is no great magnificent book on olives, their history, botany, products, manufacture, vintages,

cures, uses. One must gather the knowledge piecemeal, as one may. A private pleasure.

Olives (beef olives)   in English, alouettes or oiseaux sans têtes in French, are thin slices of meat rolled round a stuffing into plump oval cushions. They are tied into shape, browned in butter and braised. The usual meat is beef topside, but veal can be used instead.

When the string is cut away, and the packages are arranged in a neat row with their sauce for serving, they do look quite like small game birds without their heads – or giant olives.

Whatever name you choose, they make a good dish.

Omelette   A dish of beaten eggs cooked in a thin layer – the word comes from 'lamella', a blade – with or without flavourings. To foreigners the omelette is one of the bogies of French cookery, which is ridiculous. The only thing to avoid is overcooking: an omelette should remain foamy and liquid in the centre, 'baveuse' – a word that is also used for dribbling babies.
Late 14th-century merchant's omelette: pound smallage, rue, mint, sage, marjoram, fennel, parsley, chard, violet leaves, spinach, lettuce and some root ginger. Add to 16 beaten eggs. Cook in butter, oil or lard. Scatter with grated cheese.
17th century: a well-known unbeliever was eating a bacon omelette on a Friday, at Saint-Cloud. A thunderbolt fell nearby. 'What a fuss for a bacon omelette!' he said reprovingly, and continued his meal.
Early 19th-century curé's omelette: a pair of carp roes stiffened in simmering water, chopped with an egg-sized lump of marinated tunny and shallot. Add to 10 or 12 eggs, cook in butter, turn on to a dish spread with maître d'hôtel butter. Good – the pity is that it's more quoted than eaten.
Late 19th-century tourist's omelette: before the causeway was built over to Mont St Michel, arrivals were unpredictable. Anxious visitors arrived ravenous at all hours. How to feed them quickly and well? An inn-keeper's wife, Annette Poulard, found the answer – omelettes. They became so famous that everyone

was after the 'secret'. No secret, said Mère Poulard, plenty of Normandy butter, well beaten eggs, that's all. At her inn to-day, the eggs are so well beaten that the omelette is much puffier than those of the classic style.

Orange flavourings in French cookery, beyond orange juice, are provided in three main ways. First, by the addition of orange liqueurs – Cointreau, Grand Marnier etc. – to cakes, chocolate mousses, certain charlottes and soufflés; second, by adding a curl of dried orange peel to the aromatics of a fish or meat stew (take off the zest of an orange in a long curl, hang it up to dry and, when leathery, store it in a jar or plastic bag); third, by flavouring custards, creams and cakes discreetly with orange flower water, a Provençal habit that gives a strangely magical note of the South, of that southern rim of France where orange trees grow and do not have to be wheeled away into sheds before the onset of winter.

Orange flower water can be bought at the chemist's, but I have an idea that the quality is better if you can find the French *eau de fleurs d'oranger naturelle* from a delicatessen. It comes in Bristol blue bottles, with a gold and orange label. Store it in the dark, so that the flavour is kept for as long as possible. In time it will fade and light hurries this along. Use it in meagre quantities at first. It has a flavour all its own, not orangey at all, but a recollection of the strange fragrance of the tree that bears flowers and fruit together.

Ox If you have ever wondered how long and how deeply France has influenced our eating, consider this observation from André L.Simon's 'Concise Encyclopaedia of Gastronomy': 'All the main joints and the best pieces of beef are known by their Norman-French name – Beef, but all tidbits which were presumably left by the Norman lords to their Anglo-Saxon menials have retained their original Anglo-Saxon Ox prefix' – ox tail, ox kidney, ox cheek and so on.

It seems as if this class distinction, this idea of upper and lower parts, has remained with us. To the French it is all 'boeuf', each part with its own virtues, its appropriate dishes, with 'tripe à la

mode de Caen' as much appreciated as an 'entrecôte bordelaise'.

Oysters Cheap oysters are one of the best things about France. You can buy them most of the year round too, though they are finest in autumn and winter. From September onwards oyster stalls appear at street corners, outside restaurants and bars. A sturdy well-wrapped figure in a blue apron will open your oysters rapidly, arrange them on a bed of ice and seaweed, with wedges of lemon. With bread, butter and white wine, you have the cheapest, best possible lunch.

In Paris, Savoyards used to be in charge. They had to leave their high villages in winter to save food and find work. Being accustomed to cold, they took to shellfish. Now that tourists go skiing, the Savoyards can stay at home. Arabs are taking their place, Kabyles from the mountains of North Africa who are as accustomed to cold as the Savoyards.

For most visitors, oysters have to be a summer treat. From Normandy and Brittany down the coast, 'the sign says BAR – CREPERIE – DEGUSTATION D'HUITRES, and the word "dégustation" means what it says: not "consumption of" but "tasting", "savouring". It does not mean having a snack, with no suggestion beyond feeding your face. You are in the country of good food, and this dégustation is very like what you do in an art gallery, unless your soul is lost.'

That was Eleanor Clark in her book – the devotee's bible – 'The Oysters of Locmariaquer'. She and her husband, the novelist Robert Penn Warren, spent a sabbatical in the Morbihan, near Carnac, and this picture of the district, centred on the oyster trade, was the result. In those parts round flat oysters, the 'plates', are the thing. Further south towards the Gironde, you get the long, craggier 'portuguaises', tinged with green, and recently enlarged by the introduction of the big Japanese oyster. From Marennes you should take the causeway road between canal and oyster 'parcs', to the tiny port at Cayenne. Stop on the way at the oyster museum, then sit down to your oysters, the best ones of the neighbourhood, the 'spéciales' and the 'fines de claire'.

'You are eating the sea, that's it,

only the sensation of a gulp of sea water has been wafted out of it by some sorcery.'

P

Pain d'épices As you drive into **Pithiviers** (qv) by a back road from the Beauce, you are suddenly enveloped in the sweet cloying smell of warm honey and spice. Then you come to a small factory, where they make 'pain d'épices', which has been – according to legend – a speciality of Pithiviers since the 10th century. In 992, an Armenian bishop, Gregory, took refuge in the town, living as a hermit in a cave on the outskirts. It made a pleasant walk for the spiritually-minded.

After refreshing the souls of his visitors with canticles and psalms, Gregory would refresh their bodies with his own spiced Armenian honey cake. 'As they tasted it, his guests thought they were enjoying the delights of Paradise.'

Given this uplifting start, pain d'épices soon became popular. Different versions were made elsewhere, notably at Dijon. Hucksters sold it at fairs, baked in all sorts of shapes, some of them too explicit for the prudes of the 19th century. Nowadays one buys pain d'épices in decorous slabs, hygienically plastic-wrapped for long life.

In English books, you will sometimes see pain d'épices translated as gingerbread. Although the ancestors of both cakes may have been similar, they are quite different from each other now. Pain d'épices is not gingery, and its texture has an over-spiced rubberiness that seems disagreeable to me in comparison with our good dark, sticky gingerbread.

Pancakes known as crêpes, galettes and pannequets are a Breton speciality. Cookery writers try to maintain a division between them. Crêpes, made of wheat flour and used for sweet fillings, belong to Basse-Bretagne, and the town of Quimper in particular. Galettes, made of buckwheat flour and used for savoury fillings, are from Haute-Bretagne. Pannequets – the word is less common than the other two – are wheat-flour pancakes used for savoury fillings. However, as any traveller knows, the wheat flour crêpe of the crêperie is filled with sweet or savoury mixtures indiscriminately.

Confusion is compounded by the way in which both words – galette and crêpe – are used for biscuits, for instance a 'crêpe dentelle' which is normally used for a lacy delicate pancake but it can also be a crisp rolled biscuit of the wafer type.

When you are faced with this variety, and see Brittany so shiny bright, a tourist trap with swinging signs and clashing tills, it is difficult to believe how recent its prosperity is. And as you run your eyes down the crêperie menu, desperately trying to choose one filling out of thirty or forty on offer, it is even more difficult to believe that pancakes were once the daily bread of a poor and scattered countryside. The boulangerie might be a long muddy walk away, firing too scarce to heat the huge bake-oven. Pancakes were quickly made on the hearth, along with a pot of cabbage soup or porridge (bouillie). On prosperous farms, pancakes were wrapped round grilled sausages, served with tripe and bowls of cider, sliced into meat soup. Sometimes when the pancake was turned, an egg would be broken on top, and a little cheese added as well for extra flavour.

Poverty drove Bretons out to seek work elsewhere. Year after year they took the same roads, often to the grape harvests of the Loire valley. Their passage is still marked in far-away towns by streets called La Bretonnerie. And they are still on the march. A Breton pancake and waffle stall, or a seller of Breton specialities, ham, gâteau breton, rye bread, is a familiar sight at most markets and fêtes in western France.

Parmentier on a menu is synonymous with potatoes – potage Parmentier, potato soup, hachis Parmentier, shepherd's pie. Antoine Augustin Parmentier (1737-1813) was not the first or the only savant in France to push the cause of potatoes primarily as a bread substitute or as an addition to flour in bread-making, but he was the most persistent. His efforts, backed by the National Convention, at last established potatoes and potato flour (fécule) in French cookery at the beginning of the 19th century.

Parmentier first came across potatoes as a prisoner in Germany during the Seven Years War. There was nothing else to eat. A less intelligent man might have decided never to touch a potato again, but Parmentier saw its possibilities. He did not forget about potatoes as a cheap food, easily grown, when he got back to France; famines in the late 1760s brought him many supporters. Voltaire praised his 'pure' glory, saying that popular heroes were usually brigands, whereas Parmentier deserved the approbation of all who loved humanity. Louis XVI backed him, accepted buttonholes of potato flowers. Marie Antoinette wore potato flowers in her hair. Parmentier followed the French publicity idea – see **horsemeat** – of a dinner in which every dish was based on potatoes: it included the first Savoy Cake to be made with potato flour, a practice which is still followed.

Parmentier's real backing came with the Revolution. Marat planted a potato patch in the Tuileries (apparently Robespierre had it grubbed up). And in the year III, a small cookery book came out, 'La Cuisinière Républicaine', devoted entirely to potatoes – potato custard, potato cake (though not Parmentier's Savoy cake), potato croquettes, baked potatoes with onions, potatoes with parsley butter, and so on. There was a good potato salad with suggested variations, a matelote (velouté sauce made with stock and wine, herbs to flavour, add sliced cooked potatoes to heat through), potatoes in mushroom sauce (put cooked potatoes in a pan with butter, mushrooms, shallot, Welsh or spring onion: turn well: add a pinch of flour, stock to cover: when everything is cooked, boil the sauce down slightly and thicken with 2 yolks beaten with a little vinegar) – and recipes which were to become standard favourites such as baked potatoes in their jackets, and potatoes cooked under the joint.

Petits pois Tender green peas were first developed by Italian gardeners of the Renaissance. The French who were introduced to them in the middle of the 17th century called them petits pois, to distinguish them from the large, ancient pea that had for centuries been dried for winter stores. One of

the first Frenchmen to taste them – in January 1660 – was Louis XIV. He liked them and pea mania began.

At first the price was ridiculous, but that did not put people off. Thirty years later the court was still going mad about peas every May. In a letter of 1696 Madame de Maintenon, Louis XIV's second wife, wrote that for the last four days, the princes had talked of nothing else but peas: their impatience to eat them, their delight in having done so, and the joyful thought that they would soon be eating them again.

Ladies of the court who had taken supper with the king and eaten well, risked indigestion by having peas again at home before they went to bed. From a fashion, peas had become a frenzy.

Something of the same excitement about the first peas of the year was possible until deep-freezing took over our lives. Even canning – peas were among the earliest and most popular foods to be canned – did not spoil the pleasure. The best French and Belgian brands cannot compete with the real thing, though they are worth eating sometimes in winter for a change.

No wonder the French thought of the summer combinations of duck and green peas, lamb and green peas. It surprises me that they never thought of adding a little mint to emphasize the freshness. Their style is different, the peas are laid on a bed of lettuce with a few tiny onions, some butter and very little water. The lid is put on tightly, so that they cook in very little liquid and benefit from the soft juice of the lettuce. As the season continues and the peas get larger, a few bacon dice may be put in as well.

Pigeon, pigeonneau
*'Il y avait un jeune homme de Dijon,
Qui n'avait que peu de religion.*
   Il dit: 'Quant à moi,
   Je déteste tous les trois,
Le Père, et le Fils, et le Pigeon.'
This limerick, reputed to be by Norman Douglas, will help to remind you that the French pigeon is more likely to be a young squab from the dovecot (pigeon de volière) than a woodpigeon (ramier) from the wild. Being tender, it is rapidly cooked. Therefore in using French recipes with our English birds, you

will need to increase cooking time and cooking liquid which can be boiled down afterwards to a concentrated sauce.

Pigeons are cooked in the same style as small game birds, eg wrapped in vine leaves, or like chicken in the crapaudine manner (Chapter 12). They are particularly good with young peas, or later in the year with grapes and wine in the sauce, and have far more flavour than the quail that are now so popular.

Pithiviers   A town on the eastern side of the Beauce, the great corn plain to the south-west of Paris. In the matter of pies and pâtés, but its fame has long rivalled Chartres, but its fame is a cake, the gâteau de Pithiviers feuilleté, known to pastrycooks simply as Pithiviers. The recipe is unchanged since at least the beginning of the 19th century, and it keeps its characteristic shape of a formal rose (Chapter 20).

There is very little difference between a Pithiviers and an Epiphany galette or gâteau des rois (see **Easter**). It's a matter of shape and putting in a dried bean or porcelain 'favour'. Whoever finds either becomes King of the Feast. You leave the cake in a plain round – some have the lower edge curled up over the top pastry, others have the edges trimmed flush like the pages of a book. Then you score the top with a diamond pattern or a large star, and brush it with egg. No sugar glaze, as a rule.

Poulette   French for pullet – it describes a velouté sauce thickened with egg yolks and cream (or butter), and seasoned finally with a little lemon juice and parsley. The velouté is made with an appropriate stock, eg. chicken or veal, or mussel liquor, or other fish stocks. The result is a yellowish creamy sauce, with a rich yet refreshing flavour. It goes well with light meats, chicken, veal, brains, and with fish and shellfish.

Blanquette of veal is essentially veal in a poulette sauce. The same applies to some versions of moules marinière and **mouclade** (qv).

If you have no stock, tackle sauce poulette another way. Lightly fry mushrooms in butter, add shallots and a good glass of white wine. Boil down to a moist purée. Add cream and stir into a béchamel sauce. Beat

two eggs with 4-8 tablespoons of cream and stir into the sauce, which from then on should not boil. Finish with lemon juice and parsley.

Prunes   Plums were once dried in every European household with access to an orchard, as part of the winter stores. In this country as in Touraine, the Ste Cathérine was a favourite variety for the purpose. The prunes of Tours were much in demand in Paris, especially in Lent.

Tours is still the place to find prune tarts, prune sweets stuffed with marzipan and apricot paste, a **matelote** (qv) of eel or river fish with prunes, and the famous porc aux pruneaux de Tours (a sauté of pork loin noisettes, with Vouvray wine to make a little sauce and for soaking and cooking the prunes; cream and redcurrant jelly are used to finish the sauce and the prunes are put in to heat through last of all).

Sad to know that the prunes themselves are more likely to come from Agen than the old villages near Tours, and more likely still to come from Santa Clara in California. The industry there was started by a Frenchman in 1856, and at least he planted the Agen variety. Every summer I lay in a good store of Agen prunes from our local market at Agen, but this is more a matter of sentiment than true preference. No one could tell the difference between the two, when the prunes are cooked in a dish.

The habit of adding them to meat dishes has spread all over western and northern France. Down in Aquitaine, in the Agenais you will get stews and pies of chicken with Armagnac and prunes. In the north of France, prunes are added to hare, rabbit and beef. Prunes in brandy is a popular home preserve. Prunes are often stuffed into a bottle of coarse country *marc*, in a desperate attempt to soften its rasping fire.

One prune that you may read about in letters and journals of the past is the brignole. It was a golden plum, the perdrigon, dried, stoned and carefully flattened, the most delicious of all. When Jefferson returned to America, he took a supply with him – more than you could do these days. Last summer I tried to find them around Brignole in the Var, but nobody knew what I was talking about.

Q

Quail   in the shops here are all bred on farms; wild quail are protected. This is not the case in France, where you may sometimes find them on the menu. The flavour is richer, the price is higher – as you would expect. Incidentally, in England wild quail say 'wet my lips'; in France 'Payes-tes-dettes'.

These plump little birds are a useful size – one per person – and make good eating. They cook quickly by the sauté method, taking 20-30 minutes. Quail with grapes, 'caille aux raisins', is a popular way of cooking them. Tie a vine leaf (optional) and a thin sheet of fat round each bird. Brown in plenty of clarified butter, lower the heat, cover and leave for 15 minutes. Turn occasionally. Meanwhile, skin and pip some grapes, preferably muscat. Add them to the pan 5 minutes before the quail are done, and flame with 4-5 tablespoons brandy. Cover and leave to finish cooking. Serve on slices – or in little 'boxes' – of fried bread with the grapes round them. Deglaze the pan with stock or white wine to make a little sauce, and pour over the quail.

Other ways of cooking them, with cherries, olives or mushrooms, are equally simple. You can use port or Madeira. Juniper berries, lightly crushed, are often put inside the birds: you could complete the sauté with gin, stock and cream. Quail can also be roasted or grilled on a spit and served with rice in the Italian style.

Quatre-épices   is the essential spice blend in charcuterie, giving the characteristic flavour to rillettes, rillons, confits, pâtés, sausages etc. You can buy it in any grocery in France, but I have never seen it on sale here. To make your own – which is easy with an electric coffee mill – whizz to a powder 7 parts black peppercorns, 1 part cloves and 1 part cinnamon. Grate separately (it is too hard for the mill) 1 part nutmeg. Mix together and store in a tightly covered jar.

'Larousse Gastronomique' gives a different version: 125g (4oz) white pepper, 10g ($\frac{1}{3}$ oz) cloves, 30g (1oz) ginger, 35g (generous oz) nutmeg.

Be prepared to find allspice

referred to in some French books as 'quatre-épices' or 'toute-épice' or 'herbe aux épices', on account of its rich flavour that seems to be a blend of different spices. Usually, though, it is called 'poivre de Jamaique', Jamaican pepper, which is less confusing. You must judge from the context.

Quatre mendiants   An old winter dessert that has been ousted by imports of fresh fruit or our own fruit that has been kept in cold store as André L. Simon pointed out in his 'Concise Encyclopedia of Gastronomy': 'The Quatre Mendiants are dried figs, raisins, filberts and peeled almonds. The name is a reminder of the four chief orders of mendicant friars, the black friars (Dominicans – raisins); the white friars (Carmelites – peeled almonds); the grey friars (Franciscans – figs); and the Austin friars (Augustines – filberts).'

Quatre-quarts   Four-quarters cake – ie. four equal weights of eggs, butter, flour and sugar – what we used to call a pound cake in the days when families were large and we used a pound of everything. Now a $\frac{1}{4}$lb (125g) is the usual choice. In France where they do not use self-raising flour, people add baking powder ('levure alsacienne', as opposed to 'levure de boulanger', yeast).

The traditional method for a quatre-quarts is to beat the yolks and sugar until thick and creamy, add the cool, melted butter, then the flour and baking powder. Finally the whipped whites are folded in, and the mixture is baked in a moderate oven, 180C (350F) gas 4, for 40-60 minutes – according to the depth of the cake tin.

If you use softened butter, self-raising flour *plus* a level teaspoon of baking powder, the ingredients can rapidly be mixed together with an electric beater. This is the ideal cake for the non-cake-makers – who by and large include most French housewives.

Improvements can be added, and flavourings: 2 tablespoons liqueur, brandy or other appropriate liquid are a good idea. Substituting a heaped tablespoon of ground almonds for a heaped tablespoon of flour gives a better, moister texture. Candied peel, glacé cherries, chopped preserved ginger, dates and

walnuts, caraway seeds, brown sugar instead of white, are ways of turning one useful recipe into a whole repertoire of cakes.

Quenelles   from the Alsatian *knödel* meaning dumpling, were often part of the decoration of grand dishes, one item among many in the magnificent displays of *haute cuisine*. Then they disappeared as the kitchen boys and scullery maids found better things to do, to make a comeback with the arrival of electric blenders, choppers and processors.

The base of the quenelle is a purée of meat, game, poultry or fish, extended with a panada of breadcrumbs, or with egg whites and cream which make a lighter mixture.
Panada version: moisten 150g (5oz) white breadcrumbs with a little milk; squeeze out surplus to leave a thick paste. In the processor or blender, reduce 250g (8oz) skinned and boned meat, game, poultry or fish to a purée. Add the bread paste, then 125g (4oz) softened butter and 2 egg yolks. Whisk the 2 whites until stiff and fold in the panada. Season to taste. Roll or pipe into croquette shapes. Turn in flour and poach in barely simmering water, a few at a time, for 5-8 minutes. Try out an experimental quenelle first.
Mousseline version: purée meat, game etc. as above. Add 2 large egg whites, then 300ml ($\frac{1}{2}$pt) double cream. Season and chill. Shape the mixture with 2 warm tablespoons and slide into simmering water. Cook as above.

Quetsche   is a variety of dark, bloomy plum much grown – for drying and distilling as well as cooking – in Eastern Europe, Germany, Alsace and Lorraine. Baked or stewed with sugar, it may accompany roast pork and game.

In one dish, tiny ortolans are perched on top of baked quetsches for the last 5 minutes of their cooking time. I would have thought this too strong a partnership, but I cannot say so from experience. Crtolans are birds of fantasy for most of us. The nearest acquaintance we may have with them is through Colette's 'Gigi', who was taught how to eat them, crunching up bones and all, as an essential part of every courtesan's education.

The most popular way of using quetsches is in a 'tarte'. Pastry is covered with a layer of pastry cream (Chapter 4) and half baked. Then the stoned plums are set on top, cut side up, with a good sprinkling of sugar. When it comes out of the oven, the tart can be glazed in the French manner with a heavy syrup.

Quiche   (from the Alsatian *kuche*, a cake) is by strict definition an open tart made in Lorraine and parts of Alsace. The essential filling is a 'migain' or custard of eggs and cream, seasoned with salt and pepper. Extra ingredients are added to give variety. The classic quiche lorraine, for instance, is flavoured with a scatter of smoked bacon dice. Occasionally fruit and sugar appear as a quiche, but such dishes are usually called 'tarte' (see **quetsche**).

Today the word is used interchangeably with flan or 'tarte' in France – and in this country too. Often it is a disaster, flabby and heavy when the 'migain' has had béchamel sauce or milk added – a meanness you will find in both countries. (An English authority said recently that we were suffering as a nation from quiche-poisoning.) I wonder the people of Nancy have not started a Society for the Protection of Quiches.

The simplest quiche requires a tart tin lined with shortcrust pastry – in times past, bread dough was often used but most people now prefer pastry. Beat together 3 large yolks, 1 large egg and $\frac{1}{2}$ litre ($\frac{3}{4}$pt) double cream. Flavour with salt, pepper and nutmeg and pour into pastry crust. Dot with butter – 30g (1oz) or a little more. Preheat oven to 200C (400F) gas 6, and slide a baking sheet on to the centre shelf. When hot, put in the quiche on the sheet, and leave for 15 minutes. Turn the heat down to 160-180C (325-350F) gas 3-4, and leave for 15-20 minutes until the filling is puffed and lightly browned. Serve warm, rather than very hot or cold.

For the quiche lorraine, scatter the pastry with strips of smoked streaky bacon, lightly fried to get rid of some of the fat, then pour on the filling. To the bacon, some people add an equal quantity of sliced onion cooked slowly in butter and a scatter of fines herbes. Sometimes **fromage frais** is substituted for half the cream.

I like making a quiche

tourangelle when we're in Trôo. The pastry is covered with **rillettes** and a couple of coarsely chopped **rillons** (qv). Plenty of parsley. Then half quantity of the migain, well seasoned, is poured on top.

Quinces (coings)   An important thing about the quince is its smell, first the tiny fragrance of the flowers in spring, then in the autumn, when the fruit is brought into the house, so rich and powerful a sweetness that it fills the house from hall or kitchen.

The point is to keep quinces until they are golden and ripe. Then the last of the grey down should be washed and rubbed away to expose the full beauty of colour and shape. I do not think the French have our former habit of putting one quince into an apple pie or tart (which it will flavour far better than any clove), but they make it into fruit paste (see **cotignac**) – and use it for liqueur-making at home.

To do this, grate two fine quinces, including peel and core. Put into a litre (1¾pt) bottling jar, and add sugar to come a third of the way up. Fill up the jar with brandy, rum or vodka. Add spices if you like, cinnamon, ginger or mace. Make sure the liquid covers the fruit, then cover tightly and keep in a dark place for as long as possible. Taste from time to time, after two or three months, to see how it is coming along. Depending on the ripeness of the quince, the liqueur may only come to full virtue after a year, or even longer.

See also **marmelade**.

R

Radishes   are a favourite summer dish in France, nicely scraped pink and white radishes, slightly peppery, crisp and sweet, with 6mm (¼in) tuft of green stalk and a little leaf to show how fresh they are. Visiting a peasant neighbour, dining in a two-star restaurant, in the season you will be given radishes. Spread them with a dab of unsalted butter, dip them in salt and eat them with a mouthful of bread to follow.

Radishes in France are sold in huge bundles. Sitting in the sun, preparing them for lunch or a picnic, is one of summer's best pleasures.

Ragoût   used to be a word in our chauvinist armoury against the French – like celery, mushrooms, champagne, frogs and snails. The poet Rochester lampooned the English food bore in the 17th century, who took a guest out to dinner saying:

> 'Our own plain fare, and the best
> terse the Bull
> Affords, I'll give you and your
> bellies full.
> As for French kickshaws, celery
> and champagne,
> Ragoûts and fricassées, in troth
> w'have none.'

What was served up was beef, carrots, pork, goose and so on, with 83 sauces. Our faults it seems were already set (can we ever escape them?) – thoughtless cooking (plain fare), gross eating (bellies full) and overloaded plates.

In fact a ragoût is nothing more than a stew, but a stew carefully made and seasoned to arouse the palate (which is what the word means). In white ragoûts, meat, fish or vegetables are just seized in butter, then simmered in light stock; in brown ragoûts, they are coloured in butter and simmered in brown stock, both with appropriate seasonings. The ragoût technique was the base for civets, blanquettes, stews à la bourguignonne, and the delicious mixtures that go into **vol-au-vent(s)** (qv), or accompany roast and grilled meat. As the emphasis lies in subtle flavouring to set off the main ingredient, and in producing a small amount of sauce, ragoûts give any cook a chance to show skill and taste, something which our idea of a stew – at least in the past, and still in institutions – with its wash of liquid and gobbets of tough meat, did not.

Ragoûts also meant that much more of an animal's carcase was available to the good French cook and to the good French table; plain fare John Bull was restricted to the prime cuts suitable for roasting and grills. No doubt this was a reflection of the comparative wealth of the two countries. Three centuries later things are different. We need the skill of making a ragoût of secondary cuts, offal and so on, and of presenting vegetables with their sauce, rather than merely as watery adjuncts to a joint.

Raisin   can be a confusing word in French – a point to watch if you

ever use an English version of a French cookery book.

Raisin on its own means grape.

Raisin sec means what *we* mean by raisin.

Raisin de Corinthe means currant.

Raisin de Smyrne means sultana.

And you may come across raisiné. This can be grapes boiled down, sieved and boiled down again, to make a grape cheese. In Burgundy it may be made from other fruit – principally apples and pears, but sometimes quinces and melon – cooked to a jam in grape juice. Sugar is not usually necessary, but should be added if the grapes are not sweet.

The ideal grape for the classic dish of sole Véronique is a tiny seedless white grape of quality. This is difficult to find these days – the seedless grapes on sale now often lack flavour – so go for the muscatel grape of the autumn season, skinned, halved and de-pipped. The dish was invented by Monsieur Malley of the Ritz hotels in Paris and London (and chronicled by Louis Diat). He told a young chef working for him to add grapes to the white wine sauce that was to be served at an evening party with sole. Then he went out for the afternoon. On his return he found the chef in a high state of excitement. His wife had just given birth to a girl, who was to be called Véronique. 'We'll call the new dish sole Véronique,' said Monsieur Malley.

To make it, poach rolled sole fillets in white wine and water. The liquid is then reduced to an essence, and added to a creamy béchamel sauce with an egg yolk and cream liaison. Peeled grapes, heated through in simmering water, are placed round the sole. The sauce is finished with a good knob of butter and two tablespoons of cream that have been lightly whipped. Pour it over the fish and grapes, and glaze under the grill.

Chicken can be cooked in the same way. Or you can prepare a chicken sauté (Chapter 25), just seizing the chicken in butter rather than browning it, and completing the cooking in white wine and chicken stock. The rest as above.

Ratafia   In France this name covers many home-made liqueurs which do not involve distillation. The general principle is to fill a large bottling jar with soft fruit or orange peel, pour in enough heavy sugar syrup to come just under halfway up, and then enough brandy or less glorious alcohol to cover the fruit generously. The jar is then closed and left to infuse for several months.

The most picturesque of these ratafias is made with a pear that has grown inside the bottle. Choose a fat bottle with a small neck and fasten it over a very young pear on the tree, supporting it from underneath with a forked stake. The pear will grow in this miniature greenhouse. When it is ripe, remove the whole thing from the tree, add syrup and brandy and leave it to mature.

Wild fruit ratafias, like our sloe gin, are still made in some country districts. In the autumn, people go to their favourite sorb or wild service trees, and pick the fruit. Back home, they spread it out on large dishes to soften to that dark bruised state of soft ripeness that medlars also have to reach before they are edible. Then it can go into bottles, to make the best liqueurs of all.

Wine-making districts make their own pineau – freshly pressed grape juice from the vintage mixed with a quarter or more of its volume of brandy. In the Charentes, pineau is now big business, with special labels and promotions to encourage its use as an apéritif or in cooking. To me these regulated productions have far less delight than the pineau of peasant households which tastes different every year, and is enjoyed as a little luxury of autumn evenings. A seasonal treat like the cloudy fermenting wine, the 'bernache', that is drunk with oysters, chestnuts, or with new bread and fresh walnuts.

Ratatouille   Best-known of Mediterranean vegetable stews, consists of equal parts – more or less – of onion, aubergine, sweet peppers, courgettes and tomatoes cooked in olive oil with garlic. Coriander seeds, and basil or parsley, provide a final seasoning.

The problem of making ratatouille with northern vegetables is wateriness, lack of the sun. Salting and draining before cooking, then brisk cooking in a wide uncovered pan, once the juices flow, is the best solution. A pinch of sugar, a splash of wine vinegar may be needed to raise the flavour.

Ratatouille – an odd name – seems to be a mixture of 'tatouiller' and 'ratouiller', forms of an old Provençal verb 'touiller', meaning to stir and crush.

Rate   French for spleen. The long, flat, dark red piece of meat is rolled up round its line of fat, stuck with a small wooden skewer and cooked in with the **rillons** and **rillettes** (qv). It is eaten cold with plenty of Dijon mustard, bread and butter. Cheap and well worth trying, when you are buying a picnic, as part of a mixed bag of charcuterie.

Ravigote and **Rémoulade**   cover five piquant sauces in which a similar collection of lively items is added to different basic sauces, according to the main food they are to accompany.
1 *Ravigote chaude:* reduce 2 chopped shallots, 4 tablespoons each wine vinegar and dry white wine, to a purée with chopped chervil, tarragon and parsley. Add to a velouté made with appropriate stock, or to basic brown sauce.
2 *Ravigote chaude:* use the shallot reduction above as the basis for an hollandaise. Add 3 egg yolks and incorporate 250g (8oz) butter. A dab of mustard can be added to either of these versions for extra flavour.
3 *Ravigote froide:* vinaigrette with chopped fines herbes, gherkins and capers. A little hard-boiled egg, shallot or onion, can be put in as well, but then you are coming close to:
4 and **5** *Rémoulade:* can be a vinaigrette with chopped hard-boiled egg yolks, fines herbes, gherkins, capers, anchovy fillet, onion. Or a mayonnaise flavoured with the same things, minus egg yolks and plus mustard.

Ravigote means an invigorating sauce, a sauce to which you add a ravigote – a 'livening' – of herbs etc. Rémoulade is trickier to understand. By way of explanation etymologists have called in large black radishes, wild horseradish (rémola, ramolas) and even an ointment rubbed into horses in Italy (*remolata*) . . .

Reine Claude   Originally 'prune de la reine Claude', ie. plum of Claude, the wife of François I, who became queen of France in 1515, with her husband's accession, and died in 1524, worn out by repeated childbirth. If introduced into France from Italy, in her time, the Reine Claude or Greengage would be an item of the French Renaissance along with the turreted pleasure-château of Chambord and the elongated nudes of the artist Primaticcio.

And greengage? That was called after Sir William Gage of Hengrave Hall, Bury St Edmunds, who brought back reine claude trees from France in 1724, and lost the labels.

Réligieuse   This is a cake made in the delightful form of a nun's head and shoulders in her veil, seen from behind.

The small version consists of a small choux puff placed on a larger one, the top iced with coffee or chocolate and piped elegantly with cream. Coffee or chocolate cream fills the inside. The large réligieuse is a cone-like construction of éclairs, placed on end on a round pastry base, inclining slightly; decreasing circles of choux paste complete the cone, with a tiny choux bun on top. The whole thing is filled with coffee and chocolate creams, covered and piped in swirls with coffee and chocolate icing and dotted discreetly with silver and gold balls. Altogether a charming cake, best left to the pâtissier. It was first made at Frascati's, one of the best pastrycooks in Paris, in 1856.

Rillettes and **Rillons**   These are great delicacies of the charcuteries of Anjou and Touraine. Both are made with large cubes cut from the belly of fat pigs, though other pieces and scraps may be added. A friend who lives near us in France notices that winter rillettes are of better quality and more succulent than the rillettes of summertime. Without visitors to buy the roasting and grilling cuts for quick cooking, the butcher has to use up pig carcasses in the staple items that permanent residents buy. Every household in western France always has a large pot of rillettes in the fridge for snacks, breakfast, the children's 'goûter' when they return from school, or for a first course at lunch when friends arrive from regions less privileged in charcuterie.

All the pork that is going, the

cubes, the scraps, the bits of fat, the odd chops, are put into a huge pot with a ladle of water to prevent sticking in the early stages. Herbs and **quatre-épices** (qv) are added. The whole thing is cooked for four or five hours, very slowly, either on top of the stove or in the oven. In the medieval kitchen of a château in the Sarthe, there is a special circular depression in the brick floor for the fire, with an inner rim to support the huge rillettes cauldron above it. A step down, cut out at one side, meant that someone could manoeuvre the whole thing more easily, or sit down to the steady stirring that a huge quantity of slowly cooking meat demands.

Towards the end of cooking time, the best, most sightly cubes are removed for browning off at a higher temperature. These are the **rillons,** which can be eaten hot with apple sauce and mashed potatoes, or cold with mustard, gherkins and so on. The rest of the contents of the pot will be smashed to a thready pulp – use the heavy beater of an electric mixer. The final result should be a light mass, to which you add more (Le Mans style) or less (Touraine style) of the cooking fat.

In Normandy one often sees pale, impacted **rillettes,** chopped, moulded and sliced as if they were a kind of pâté. Very disagreeable.

To pot rillettes (or rillons), reheat them and check the seasoning. Put into sterilised stoneware jars (the traditional kind are like very thick mugs – and jugs without a pouring lip) or glass bottling jars. With rillons, pour fat all round; when cool, cover with a centimetre's depth (to about $\frac{1}{2}$in) of more fat, or use some melted-down bought lard. Keep in the refrigerator or – for longer storage – in the freezer.

Rissoles   In France, these are not the unpleasant objects of Monday cookery that we remember from schooldays, but little pasties filled with something delicious and then deep-fried. The name goes back to the 12th century – 'rousole' figures in one of the chansons de geste – and means something reddish, something nicely coloured by the process of frying. I would say that these small delights are the French equivalent to Middle Eastern *bourekia* or Indian *samosas*.

The right English translation for the true rissole is kickshaw, a corruption of quelquechose, something or other, said – of course – with a sniff by 17th-century patriots who preferred quantity in food to delicacy. Nevertheless, some of our 18th-century writers give recipes for kickshaws filled with jam or candied fruit, then fried. Very good. An honourable way of using up pastry scraps.

Robert   Sauce Robert is a piquant onion sauce, often served with pork. It has a long history. Rabelais mentions it; so does Perrault in his version of the Sleeping Beauty: 'It is my wish,' said the Queen, 'to have my grand-daughter served up with sauce Robert.'

This is the way it was made in Perrault's time, according to La Varenne. Spit-roast a boned loin of pork, basting it with a bunch of sage dipped in **verjuice** (qv) and vinegar. Take some of the fat which falls into the dripping pan and fry sliced onions in it. Then mix the onion with the basting sauce (which by this time will include meat juices from the pork), and simmer together. I can see it would go nicely with a tender grand-daughter. . . .

The modern version is not too different. Cook 2-3 large chopped onions until golden brown in butter. Stir in a little flour, then enough stock to make a sauce. Sharpen to taste with vinegar and lemon juice. Simmer a little longer to reduce the sauce and mature the flavour. Season finally with Dijon mustard to taste, a pinch of sugar, some salt, pepper, chopped tarragon and parsley.

With the move to banish flour from sauces, the most progressive cooks of to-day would prefer the La Varenne version, which ends up as a lively confiture d'oignons, rather in the style of Michel Guérard.

Roes   France is not without its own caviar, from such sturgeon as can survive the pollution of the Gironde, but it is not easy to come by even – I believe – in Bordeaux.

'Caviare blanc', alias boutargue, alias poutargue, is a less expensive rarity, a speciality of Martigues on the Mediterranean coast. Ideally, it is made from the roes of grey mullet, but other mullet, bass and tunny roes are also used. They are salted, pressed and dried in the sun, then encased in wax for long keeping. You may see boutargue in the best Parisian food shops – it is easy to spot from its flat shape and pearly-grey covering (and from the astounding price). However, each roe weighs little more than 100g ($3\frac{1}{2}$oz), and you eat it in tiny slivers – removing the wax first – either with an apéritif, or shaved over haricot bean and chick pea salads to liven their blandness. Considering the careful use of boutargue the price is not too bad, certainly far below that of caviar from Bordeaux or the Caspian Sea.

Try it at least once, to learn the taste of ancient pleasure. These roes were being cured in the same way over 4,000 years ago in Egypt: their flattened oval shapes are carved on tomb walls at Giza and Saqqarah. They were a luxury export, so expensive that in later centuries the Greeks of Cyprus and Crete had the idea of adding olive oil to make them go farther – hence taramasalata.

Without knowing it, we still acknowledge our debt to Egypt: European names, boutargue, Italian *bottarga*, English botargo, derive from the historic Egyptian word *batarekh*, which in turn comes from the Coptic *pi-tarikh*. I have made taramasalata with boutargue and it is good, slightly different in taste, and a pinkish-yellow in colour.

Soft roes of herring and other fish have had more of a place in classic French cookery. Simmered with hardly any water and a little lemon, then mixed with cream, Cayenne and parsley, they make a filling for omelettes or puff pastry cases. Ali-Bab recommends fritters in his 'Gastronomie Pratique' – dip the roes in a beer batter lightened with whipped egg whites, and fry them golden brown. Serve with a mustard-flavoured velouté, finished with egg yolks and cream (see **liaison**).

Rognons blancs   'white kidneys', is the polite French name for testicles, usually veal. They do have a kidney flavour, but are finer and more delicate. The butcher sells them skinned, and split almost in half. They should be floured, fried in butter and finished either with a chopping of garlic and parsley, or with cream.

They lose a good deal of juice during cooking, so raise the heat the moment their liquid starts to swill about the pan. Be prepared also to remove the cooked rognons blancs from the pan and reduce the liquid, which can then form the base of a pan sauce with cream and some alcohol. The point to watch is overcooking.

Romaine or 'laitue romaine' is French for Cos lettuce. Some people claim it was introduced by Rabelais, who certainly sent packets of seed for salad greens home to France from Rome in the 1530s. It seems more likely, however, that it came via the gardens of the Papal court at Avignon and that the name came with it – to the Italians it is *lattuga romana*.

Rye and Buckwheat Rye flour has long been used in Brittany for breadmaking – the pain de seigle – and with the spreading craze for such things as 'pain biologique', wholemeal bread, it becomes more and more popular all over France. Even supermarkets sell rye bread, sliced, in plastic bags.

Part of its popularity comes from the fact that it goes well with fish, especially shellfish. If you only know the dark, close, sweet rye bread of more northern countries, this may startle you. French rye bread is light coloured, a little tough, with just a hint of sweetness that brings out the sweetness of oysters and similarly fine fish. Rye flour contributes something, too, to the chewy texture of **pain d'épices** (qv) as made in Pithiviers and Dijon.

If you buy flour in Brittany to bring home, do not confuse farine de blé noir with rye flour (easily done – we think of rye bread as black bread). Blé noir, or blé sarrasin, Saracen corn, means buckwheat flour, much used – though less now than in the past – for **pancakes** (qv) and galettes.

To poor Breton farmers buckwheat had advantages: it was sown after the corn harvest, it ripened before winter, 'it cost little to cultivate, its flowers drew bees (at a time when honey made up for lack of sugar), and surpluses could be sold as poultry feed or to distilleries.'

S

Sabayon This is the French for Italian *zabaglione*, which is a fluffy mixture of egg yolks beaten over hot water with Marsala. It can be eaten on its own, or served as a sauce with some other dessert. The French see sabayon more as a sauce, or as a manner of finishing a sauce – for instance Michel Guérard's blancs de volaille au sabayon de poireau, a complex dish of stuffed chicken breasts served with a leek, cream and port sauce, thickened finally with egg yolks beaten first with a little water.

In another dish, made with John Dory, the cooking juices are well reduced, seasoned with white peppercorns, and finished in the same way – Saint Pierre en sabayon de poivre.

Saffron The use of saffron has diminished in France as it has in England. Once it was grown near Orléans, but people have now found easier ways to make a living from the land. It takes up to 250,000 – yes, a quarter of a million – blue and purple saffron crocuses to make a $\frac{1}{2}$ kilo (1lb). Think of the picking of the flowers, the careful removing by hand of the central stigmas, the drying, the shrinking and the packaging. No wonder there is such a temptation to adulterate saffron (buy the hairy red filaments, never the powder), to substitute turmeric, or to make saffron 'optional'. Unfortunately it is not; because of its unmistakable flavour, nothing else will do.

French dishes that demand saffron nowadays come mainly from the south of France. It is characteristic of fish soups, for instance. Elizabeth David has recorded a mussel dish from Avignon with a saffron sauce: 3-4 kilos (roughly 7-9lb) mussels are opened by boiling with $\frac{1}{4}$ litre (8fl oz) water, a bouquet garni, a chopped onion and 8 fennel seeds. Saffron is infused in the hot liquor, which is then added to 300 ml ($\frac{1}{2}$pt) very thick béchamel sauce; if necessary, reduce the sauce to the right consistency by rapid boiling. Stir in 2 heaped tablespoons chopped cooked spinach and the mussels. Turn into a gratin dish, sprinkle with crumbs and melted butter and brown under the grill or in the oven.

Saffron also flavours and colours the mourtayrol of Languedoc. First a fat boiling fowl, a piece of boiling beef of 1½ kilos (3lb) and half its weight in gammon are simmered in water with pot herbs. These meats form the main course of the meal. A good hour before lunchtime, an ovenproof pot is filled with slices of pain de campagne, country bread, which is sometimes toasted first. A little of the stock from the meat is used to infuse a generous pinch of saffron, then tipped on to the bread, plus a $\frac{1}{2}$ litre ($\frac{3}{4}$pt) more stock. Bake at 150C (300F) gas 2 for an hour, adding more stock when necessary. This is the mourtayrol, which should turn to a creamy yellow panada, to be served as a first course.

St Honoré whose feast day is 16 May – was Bishop of Amiens, about 600 AD. One day when he was celebrating mass, 'A divine hand sent down a loaf of bread. Thereupon the bakers adopted him as their patron saint.' Later on, the street of bakers and pastrycooks in Paris was called after him, the rue St Honoré running parallel to the rue de Rivoli. And later still, in 1879, one of them – the pastrycook Chiboust – at last made a cake in his honour, the gâteau St Honoré, filled with a special light cream, crème Chiboust.

St Honoré appears on the façade of the church halfway along his street, holding a sheaf of corn and a baker's peel. In a niche on the opposite side is **St Roch** (qv) to whom the church is dedicated. He also has food connections.

St Jacques – feast day 25 July. The great pilgrimage centre of Western Europe, particularly in the late Middle Ages, was Santiago di Compostela, where the martyred body of the Apostle St James the Greater was said to lie. Just as the routes into Spain are marked by his churches (our own village has a frescoed church of St Jacques-des-Guerets, St James of the Ploughlands, by a ford across the Loir), so his pilgrims are marked in statues and paintings as they were on the journey by a scallop shell in their hats. These are the coquilles Saint Jacques. I hope that the pilgrims had a dish or two of them on their way towards Galicia and the shrine.

Why the scallop shell? No one knows. Legends were made up after it became a symbol, to account for it. The most puzzling thing is that

Compostela is not on the coast, but about 16 miles inland. One group of tales related with variations how a knight on his horse rode across an inlet of the sea, and emerged covered with scallops.

I believe that today many of the coquilles St Jacques consumed in France come from around the Isle of Man, and from elsewhere in our waters.

St Laurent – St Lawrence to us – is the patron saint of cooks. He carries a gridiron as his symbol, of a kind you can still buy at any ironmonger's shop in France. Why? The poor fellow was martyred on a grill. His feast day is 10 August, appropriately at the hottest time of the year. *He* would have understood the saying, 'If you can't stand the heat, keep out of the kitchen.'

Ste Ménéhould – this time not the saint, a holy virgin who lived in Champagne in the 5th century, but the place, the town of Ste Ménéhould, near Verdun, where charcutiers have a special way of preparing pigs' trotters. By cooking them slowly for hours, the bones are reduced to an edible crumbliness. Long cooking was held to be the 'secret' by Urbain Dubois who investigated the matter in the last century. I spoke to a local charcutier's wife who hinted at a 'secret' herb, but I have sometimes wondered whether the secret wasn't in fact an old-fashioned pressure cooker operating at much higher pressures than is normal these days. When John Evelyn tasted the food cooked in Denis Papin's original pressure cooker, in 1682, he described the bones of the meat as a sort of crumbly cheese that could be scattered on bread (the meat seems to have turned into a thick purée). Papin's pressure was from 35 to 50lb to the inch, whereas to-day's pressure is only 15lb, which is why our meat is not transformed in the same manner.

But however they are cooked, the trotters are rolled in breadcrumbs and left to cool. They are grilled or fried to reheat them for the meal, and served – sometimes – with a sauce Ste Ménéhould. You get a triple contrast of soft, gelatinous meat, crisp breadcrumbs and hard-soft biscuity bones. The sauce can, of course, be served with trotters prepared by boiling in the ordinary way. It goes too with pigs' ears, pigs' tails and boiled salt pork.

Soften 2 tablespoons chopped onion and a tablespoon of chopped shallot in butter. Add 2 tablespoons white wine vinegar and 8 of white wine. Boil down until hardly any liquid remains. Pour in ¼ litre (8fl oz) beef stock and simmer with a bouquet garni for at least half an hour, with the pan covered. Thicken with beurre manié (see **liaison**), after removing the bouquet, and flavour finally with mustard, chopped gherkins, fines herbes, pepper and salt.

St Pierre is the name the French give to that sad-looking, firm-fleshed fish, the John Dory. And this is why: one day on the Sea of Galilee, Christ and the Apostles were being harried by some tax collectors. To get rid of them, Christ told St Peter to catch a fish – which he did – and take the coin out of its mouth to pay them off. To this day you can see St Peter's dark fingerprints on either side of the John Dory's head, where he picked it up.

Do not let this legend confuse you, however. Saint Pierre or John Dory in either language is a salt-water fish. In Israel you can eat a scaly fish, 'St Peter's fish', that really comes from the Sea of Galilee, but it tastes dull by comparison with John Dory or Saint Pierre. And the ones I ate in Tel Aviv were so well grilled that I couldn't see whether St Peter had left his fingerprints on them or not.

St Roch – feast day 16 August – was a rich young man of Montpellier at the beginning of the 14th century. He sold off all his goods and went to Rome as a pilgrim. In Italy he was caught up in epidemics of the plague. Whether he had learnt something about medicine in the famous school of Montpellier, or whether he was just a saint, I do not know, but he nursed the sick until – at Piacenza – he himself fell ill of the plague.

No one intended to look after St Roch. Instead, they drove him out of the town into the forest. There he would have died of starvation rather than the plague, had not a dog brought him a loaf every day. St Roch is usually shown with his pilgrim's robe raised to expose a plague sore on his thigh. At his feet there is a little dog with a large bun in its mouth.

Salad is essential to a French meal. A simple green salad dressed, if you are lucky, with olive oil, appears after the main course at lunch or dinner. Most people eat it from the plate used for their main course, so that the last juices from the meat or sauce are not wasted, but blend with the lettuce and dressing to make a last delicious mouthful or two. Other people prefer their salad on a side plate to eat on its own, or with cheese and bread.

As you read about the food of the past, you have sadly to conclude that today's green salads, whether in France or in this country, are poor by comparison with our ancestors' expectations. John Evelyn worked out a 'growing and picking' scheme for a mixed salad every day of the year, to help his gardener at Sayes Court, and his small book 'Acetaria' devotes pages to salad-making, salad seasoning. It amplifies and explains Milton's lines in 'Paradise Lost', describing Eve's salad:

> *'What order, so contrived as*
> *   not to mix*
> *Tastes, not well joined,*
> *   inelegant, but bring*
> *Taste after taste upheld with*
> *   kindliest change.'*

That this expectation of a good salad was not confined to the wealthy, is joyfully explained in a poem by 16th-century Joachim du Bellay, friend of Ronsard. It is a translation, or rather a re-writing and re-setting of a poem by Virgil. The poor peasant – in this case an Anjou peasant living near du Bellay's village of Liré – gets up, quickly mixes a dough for bread and puts it into the oven. As it bakes, he goes out to the garden to pick a salad for breakfast – he chooses from mallow, sorrel, chives, spring onion, onion, lettuces, Orléans cress, endive, rocket, garlic, coriander, parsley, rue, shallot and chard. (The best vegetables he does not touch – they are for taking to market, to sell to the comfortable bourgeoisie.) He mixes his salad with oil and vinegar, gobbles it up with the hot bread, and thus fortified for the day takes his hat, puts on his gaiters and goes off with his oxen to plough.

In less civilised parts, people would make a choice of wild herbs for their salad – the origin of **mesclun** (qv) in the south of France. Or the two kinds might be mixed, garden greenery with watercress from the brook, for instance.

Salambos or Salammbôs are, I conclude, the voluptuous namesakes of Flaubert's Carthaginian heroine. 'Salammbô' was published in 1862 during the great inventive period of French pâtisserie.

Salmi A dish of ancient cookery – recipes for it occur in late medieval collections – that is still made in the same way. Game, poultry, meat or fish are half-cooked by roasting, then finished in a wine sauce. A good dish when well made, especially good for game which turns out to be tougher than you at first suspected. The snag of the dish is obvious – salmi can be a grand-titled way of using up restaurant leftovers, a 'dustbin' dish with little freshness or vigour.

Salt Crystals of gros sel, coarse salt, whether from rock or sea are an essential part of the French kitchen. Apart from their general use in all cooking, they are put on the table with boiled beef – boeuf au gros sel – and sprinkled over sauté potatoes, the point being crunch as well as saltiness. Salt sprinkled over the top of bread before baking gives the same kind of pleasure. Gros sel is also the salt used for curing meat, fish and vegetables as it has no additives. And it is sometimes used in enormous quantities to enclose fish or chicken – in the Chinese manner – which will then be baked in the oven. The salt forms a crust that keeps in all the juices. After the meal is over, the best of the salt can be broken up and used again.

Since Elizabeth David started writing, after the last war, we have all followed her counsel and become addicts of sea salt. We can buy it from our own as well as French sources. Nevertheless, much of the salt you see in high-class groceries comes from the shining moon landscape of Mediterranean salt pans, via the Salins du Midi company. These distributors may be French, but the salt comes from all over the Mediterranean area.

My own preference is for the grey sea salt of Brittany, claimed by

many to be the best in Europe for its savour and health-giving elements. One 18th-century expert claimed that it was so mild yet so full of flavour that it was thought to have aphrodisiac properties. Today the active salt pans, the 'oeillets' as they are called, near the town of Guérande to the north of La Baule, are reduced from twenty-thousand to just over nine-thousand, less than half of what they used to be. Every summer almost every local paper in western France carries a valedictory article about them. Yet the salt still appears in groceries there, thank goodness; and it is cheap, too cheap perhaps for its survival.

If you take a holiday in those parts, stow as many bags as you can in the car to bring home. The salt workings of Guérande, threatened by the conscienceless resort interests of La Baule, are worth saving – and not just as a museum for tourists in search of what is known as 'folklo', but as a living industry.

Snail eating This tradition goes back to the melting of the glaciers, to the rainy world of the mesolithic period. You can stuff yourself full of good snails with garlic butter at Mas d'Azil in the foothills of the Pyrénées, where beds of fossilised snail shells have been found in prehistoric caves outside the village.

The snail of high French cookery, classic and regional cookery, is the escargot gros bourguignon, *Helix pomatia*; found at its best – if rarely these days – in the vineyards of Burgundy. But, as in Britain, these large buff and white-shelled snails are local. They have to be bred in snail farms to try and meet the demand. The snail sought by amateurs on wet summer nights, the family snail, is the garden snail *Helix aspersa*, with a mottled brown shell, that you find behind bushes and stones, smaller than the big Burgundy snail, only 2cm – an inch or so across.

Basic preparation for both kinds is the same. They need to fast for at least a week to get rid of any poisonous leafage they may have eaten (poisonous to us, not to them). Keep the bucket or basket in a cool place, with a lid across the top, well weighted down. If a bucket is used, pierce it with plenty of air-holes, and if you do not like the idea of the

snails fasting, put in lettuce, rosemary and thyme for them to nibble. Some people think flour is a good idea, too.

The next stage of de-sliming is not so pleasant. Put on rubber gloves, dissolve a handful of coarse salt in half a bucket of water, swish the snails round in it, leave them for a moment or two, then swish again until they start to exude a transparent slime. When this begins to dominate and change the consistency of the water, throw it away and start again. Four rinsings are usually enough.

Simmer the snails in a prepared 'court bouillon' until tender – from 40 minutes to well over an hour, depending on the snails. Try one from time to time – removing them with a draining spoon – and you are in business. Do not be in a hurry to throw out the bouillon; some soups and sauces will benefit from it. Hoick out the snails from their shells with a pin stuck into a cork, remove the tiny round opercula. Put some garlic butter into the shell, replace the snail, and add a final plug of garlic butter. Arrange on shell dishes, or on a huge slice of bread, pierced with holes (use an apple-corer), and quickly heat through in the oven. For fuller instructions and more recipes, turn to my book 'Good Things', published by Penguin.

In some parts of France, such as the Charentes and the country bordering the Gironde, snails are popular in soups and ragoûts. This saves the business of stuffing the shells and in some recipes the initial cooking liquor, an embellished court bouillon, is the sauce without more ado. Most people, though, prefer the classic stuffed snail with its sizzling aromatic butter. At the Escargot-Montorgueil, the old and famous Paris restaurant with the large gold snail as its sign, they serve snails with five different stuffings – Burgundy garlic butter of course, and four more dominated by Roquefort, fennel, mint and a mixture of curry spices. You can order a tasting plate – le colimaçon, which is another word for snail – with two or three of each kind. And ragoûts of snail are also served in cassolettes.

Sorrel Everyone should cultivate a patch of sorrel. It grows anywhere without trouble; being perennial it survives from year to year and it lasts from February or March through to the first severe frosts of the following winter. Its dark sharpness has won it a cherished place in French family cooking, and the great chefs have not despised it in a purée or sauce to go with veal, fish and eggs.

Young sorrel leaves can be used as they are (after a good rinse). Medium and larger leaves – avoid the largest and toughest – benefit from having the stalks and main rib cut away. Fold the leaf in half, upper-sides together, and snip out stalk and rib with a pair of scissors. Roll up the leaves together and cut across the bundle, again with scissors. This leaves you with a pile of neat shreds – a chiffonade – which can be reduced to a purée in a minute or two, if cooked in a little butter. You now have the basis for a sauce (add concentrated stock and cream), and a means of flavouring omelettes and potato soups. With a liquidiser or food processor, you begin to discover the freshness of raw sorrel when making quick versions of emulsified sauces (hollandaise, mayonnaise) or very smooth soups. Until you are used to its sharpness, be extra careful not to overdo the quantity. The flavour of sorrel is strong.

And do not forget that a few leaves of young sorrel in a green salad make a lively seasoning.

Soubise may be a grand name in French history, but in cooking it means onion sauce. An elegant, mid-18th century onion sauce, it must be admitted, and one made in the first instance to go with duck – the work of Constant, chef to Charles de Rohan, Prince de Soubise.

Blanch ¾kg (1½lb) sliced onions for 4-5 minutes in boiling, salted water. Drain. Melt a good tablespoon of butter, add the onions, 150g (5oz) long grain rice, and ⅔ litre (1¼pts) appropriate light stock. Simmer uncovered until very tender, then sieve. Reheat, adding butter and cream to taste. This is more of a purée than a sauce, so use less rice and more stock if you require a pouring consistency.

Soufflé We still suffer from a hangover of nervousness about the making of soufflés, dating from the time before modern ovens, the temperatures of which can be quickly set and exactly controlled.

Soufflés – the word mean 'puffed up' – became important in French cookery in the time of Carême, when chefs were concerned with miracles of lightness – see also **vol-au-vent** – as well as grand presentation.

To get the mixture to rise, to time it exactly right, needed professional skill and coolness when the oven heat was tested by the time it took a piece of paper to brown, or just by an experienced hand. So the soufflé acquired its mystique. In fact it is a good-natured affair (Chapter 26). Anton Mosimann, head chef at the Dorchester, insists that a dish containing the soufflé mixture can be set in a bain marie for up to an hour to keep warm, and then finished off in the oven to suit your convenience. In his special oven in the Dorchester kitchens, which has revolving shelves, he can bake soufflés for 800 people at a time. His expertise is unquestionable, yet I have never quite had the nerve to put his bain marie theory to the test. The mystique again . . .

T

Tarragon An essential herb in French cookery, whether as a leafy branch, chopped leaves, or as part of the mixture of fines herbes for Montpellier butter and so on. It is the star of béarnaise sauce (Chapter 23) and of poulet à l'estragon, which in a number of versions is a favourite of summer meals all over France. Mashed into butter with lemon juice, tarragon leaves convey their flavour well to grilled chicken and fish. Elizabeth David has a good recipe for firm tomatoes cooked whole, and gently mixed with tarragon butter before they collapse to a sauce.

Tarragon is not easy to grow in our climate. It needs warmth. In the sun the leaves have a dry anise smell, on the tongue a peppery anise sharpness. I find it irritating to see large careless bushes of tarragon in our neighbours' gardens in France – barely 300 miles south of London – growing so abundantly that at least half must go to waste.

If you want to try it here, make sure first of all that you get the seeds of true French tarragon, *Artemisia dracunculus.* There is a false tarragon around, Russian tarragon, *Artemisia dracunculoides,* which looks similar, grows here easily and has nothing to give by way of flavour except disappointment.

When tarragon reached England early in the 16th century, people translated the name into Garden Dragon from *Dracunculus hortensis.* All the European names go back to the Arabic *tarkhun,* dragon plant. But why dragon in the first place?

Tetragon may puzzle summer visitors to France. The diamond-shaped leaves, bright dark green and vigorous, are obviously not spinach, yet if they ask for spinach, this is what they will most likely be given. Of all the leafage that optimists group under the 'like spinach' heading, tetragon is closest to the real thing.

It was brought to Europe in 1771 by an Englishman, Sir Joseph Banks, when he returned from Captain Cook's voyage round the world. He had found it growing wild, as it still does, in New Zealand (we call it New Zealand spinach, and a few nurserymen sell the seeds). Soon he was growing it successfully at Kew. It was bound to become more popular in France – where it started to catch on in the 1820s – for its advantage is that it can be grown in a summer heat that more tender spinach plants dislike. You cook it in exactly the same way, but the flavour is coarser.

Timbale is a general and confusing term. It started off as a drinking cup – in Arabic. Then it became a bowl large enough to serve two people when filled with food, in the medieval mess-mate style. In grand cookery, 'timbale' came to mean round and oval metal forms, with straight or sloping sides, used for deep pastry cases to be baked blind. The case was then filled with a separately cooked mixture.

In less splendid circumstances, the timbale served to shape the mixture without the pastry crust: the mixture was made firmly enough, or coherently enough to be turned out. So you get timbale de pêches à la Condé (peaches and rice pudding), timbale de caneton (duck).

Timbale de Brillat-Savarin, as given in 'Larousse Gastronomique',

291

demonstrates an easy way out of the pastry dilemma. You bake a brioche dough in a charlotte mould, then you cut off the top, scoop out most of the inside and replace it with layers of lightly cooked pear and pastry cream mixed with macaroon crumbs. On top, pieces of pear should be nicely arranged and scattered with candied fruit. The whole thing is then warmed through in the oven and served with an apricot purée flavoured with Kirsch. The knack is to put everything together while warm, and to take care when hollowing out the brioche, so that there is no danger of the whole thing collapsing.

I reflect that the original Bakewell pudding was baked in an oval timbale, of a kind rarely seen these days.

Tourin   From reading some books and articles, one might conclude that France has only invented one onion soup – the clear soup with onions and slices of bread and cheese that was part of the life of Les Halles in Paris. Now that the markets have been cleared out to Rungis, onion soups from elsewhere in France may get more of a look-in.

Tourin, for instance, is quite different from the Halles soup. It comes from the large south-west area that regional revivalists like to call Occitanie. Several versions are to be found in 'La cuisine occitane', by Huguette Castignac (Solar, 1973), including the practical soupe à l'édredon: the tourin was made in double quantity and after lunch the pot was slipped into the bed, under the eiderdown, to keep what was left of the contents warm for the evening meal.

Basic tourin consists of sliced onions, plus a sliced clove of garlic per onion, slowly softened in goose fat in a covered pan. When they are tender, but still cream-coloured, flour, seasoning and a pinch of sugar are sprinkled on. Water or light stock is added and the whole thing is simmered for an hour. To thicken the soup, 2 eggs are beaten with a little vinegar and stirred in last of all (the soup must not boil after this addition). It is then poured into the soup tureen over toasted slices of bread. It's the touch of vinegar that lifts the soup out of the ordinary.

This habit of pouring soup on to bread, 'tremper la soupe' – soaking the soup, has become synonymous with 'supper's ready', or 'time for supper'. When our neighbour comes for a chat and an evening drink, and the seven o'clock angelus rings down from the church tower, she soon gets up to go, saying, 'Il faut tremper la soupe'.

Tripe   The first thing you notice about tripe in France is that it's a different colour, a pale brownish tone that relates it to meat. Ours is blanched to a whiteness that looks – and what is worse, tastes – pallid by comparison. I suspect that this is why we do not eat much tripe in the south, and why it is almost never seen on restaurant menus.

For this reason, tripe is something to be enjoyed once you cross the Channel into Normandy, mainly at Caen – the capital of tripe cookery – it is true, but in other towns as well. We sometimes stop at St Hilaire du Harcouet, on the edge of Normandy almost into Brittany, where the proprietor of the Lion d'Or has won prizes for his tripe. The first time we ate there, we sat a long way from the kitchen door, but we could hear the sizzle, smell the unique, appetising smell as the bubbling pot was carried into the dining room.

The secret of the Normandy style is calf's foot (and very often Calvados as well). It smoothes and jellies the sauce, so that you need to keep licking your lips. The great pots for cooking tripe, the tripières, are among the most beautiful of kitchenware. The colour is usually golden yellow and the shape a squashed roundness with lugs at each side, and in the centre of the top part is a small hole with a lid. The lid is sealed into place with a luting paste, so that there is no evaporation through the long slow cooking.

Charcutiers and groceries in many parts of France sell tripe cooked with carrots in a sub-Normandy style; you can buy it by the slice, cut from a huge jellied block studded with carrots, or in jars; worth buying for picnics. Cook down some wine with a tomato or two, then add the tripe to reheat. Finish with a generous grinding of pepper – a cheap and delicious meal, especially in poor weather.

Tripe is cooked in many other

ways. Bretons may grill it, heat it richly in butter and cream, or stew it with prunes. Some people turn it into fritters. Lyonnais cooks fry it and mix it with separately fried onions and a dash of vinegar. In any region where beef cattle are raised, tripe is an honoured dish, a speciality.

Truffles   are treated at some length – and with just a little scepticism – by Brillat-Savarin in his 'Physiologie du Goût'. He says the best come from the Périgord and Haute Provence, dismisses the white truffles of Piedmont as inferior, enquires into the indigestibility of truffles and quotes against it the experience of a doctor who used to eat truffles enough to upset an elephant, yet lived till he was 86.

He states that in 1780, when he was a young man, truffles were hardly known in Paris. But by 1825 – when he wrote his book – the truffle had reached 'the height of its glory' (in fact it was only the beginning – by 1868, according to one authority, the total truffle production of France was one and a half million kilos; by 1890, two million kilos).

After calling the truffle 'the diamond of the kitchen', he concludes that truffles were popular because everyone believed that they were 'good for bed'. He and some knowledgeable friends went into committee and concluded that truffles were not positively aphrodisiac, but that on certain occasions they could make women more willing and men more attractive. Not a word about truffles as delicious eating or delicious flavouring.

After trying those expensive little tins and jars of truffles and truffle peelings, I conclude that Colette was right when she said, 'If I can't have too many truffles, I'll do without truffles.' She thought they should be eaten like potatoes, and if there was enough money in the bank, she would ordain a truffle day once a year. She cleaned them herself, trusting no one else with so delicate a task. Then some bits of bacon were lightly fried and put into a little black stew-pan with seasoning and half a bottle of dry champagne. When it all came to the boil, the truffles went in. 'A divine and slightly suspect odour, like everything that smells really good, floats through the house,' wrote her husband Maurice Goudeket. Then the pan itself was put on the table, and the liquor was poured into port glasses for drinking with the truffles.

The only time I have eaten truffles on anything approaching that scale, was in a lavish plateful of scrambled eggs aux truffes, down in the Var. It made me understand Colette's point of view.

V

Vanilla was first used for perfuming chocolate by the Aztecs, who discovered how to process the long yellow seed capsules of the trailing orchid *Vanilla planifolia* by a sweating process that turns them into the dark pods that we know. So startlingly sweet and delightful a flavouring was bound to be taken up by the Spanish invaders, and so vanilla came to Europe. Early on after the French acquired Bourbon, ie. Réunion, in the West Indies 1649, the island's vanilla was imported via Bordeaux, and the best French vanilla bears the label Bourbon. Nowadays the main source is Madagascar, which the French captured in 1895.

Vanilla pods are common in French shops, far more so than here. One can also buy the tiny packets of concentrated vanilla sugar for adding to larger quantities of sugar when baking etc. I find it a nasty substance (if not as nasty as synthetic vanilla essence). Much better is the old habit of keeping vanilla pods in a large jar of sugar. I suppose that it was this mode of storing that Sydney Smith had in mind when he complimented Lady Holland, 'Ah, you flavour everything; you are the vanilla of society.' Not only do the pods flavour the sugar, they can themselves be used several times so long as they are washed and dried after each use. For a specially dominant vanilla flavour, split the pods and scrape out the soft black part inside. If you combine it with sugar from the vanilla jar, you have the very best way of flavouring vanilla ice-cream and biscuits.

Verjuice Green – ie. sharp or sour – juice was pressed from unripe grapes, and was much used before lemons and bitter oranges were accessible. It gave a fruitier sharpness than vinegar. In places where grapes were not grown, the juice of sour apples, crab apples, gooseberries or sorrel might be used instead. Verjuice survived longer in medicine than in cookery, and longer still in popular sayings about the sour nature of men and women.

Vine leaves in French cookery are used mainly to wrap round the breasts of small game birds, or such fish as red mullet. They have a light lemony sharpness that has an excellent effect of seasoning.

There is another purpose that I have never seen recorded in any book on regional cookery. A neighbour at Trôo told me about it over the garden fence one day. Long ago, her parents would wrap up the hard ends of cheese – usually goat cheese, but it works for almost any kind – in vine leaves, making little packets which were then put into a shallow dish, seam end down. The dish went into the oven when the bread came out. After about 10 minutes the leaves began to brown and the cheese to soften, all ready for eating with the bread.

This works beautifully with a moderately hot oven. You can add refinements such as brushing the packages over with olive oil, but this is not necessary. Fresh leaves can be used, or fresh leaves that have been blanched for a minute in boiling water to wilt them, or pickled leaves first soaked to remove excessive saltiness.

Vinegar (vinaigre) means exactly that – sharp wine. And in French cookery the word vinegar always means wine vinegar, except when the contrary is specified. It is much more used there than here, especially as a basic ingredient of the many piquant sauces, which often start with a reduction of wine, wine vinegar and shallots or onion.

It is used in a simple vinaigrette of course, and in a fine complex cream sauce such as the saupiquet des Amognes (see 'French Provincial Cooking' by Elizabeth David). So buy at least one good wine vinegar. Go for an Orléans brand labelled 'vieille réserve', or 'à l'ancienne', or with some English phrase indicating that the vinegar has been matured in casks. The word 'vieux' is apparently not enough – it sometimes appears on vinegars that have been whizzed through the process in a matter of hours, in vast turbines.

Orléans was the port where people and goods, including wine, left the Loire to go to Paris. Perfectly sound wine from vineyards up and down the river would go sour on this unpredictable highway with its delays, sandbanks and storms. It was held back at Orléans and turned into vinegar. The old process may still be seen at Martin Pouret in Orléans. In the great halls, row upon row of casks mature the wine into vinegar at a steady temperature of 27-28°C (and in a powerful smell of vinegar, that has soaked into every beam of the place). These days the wine comes from abroad, though sometimes an old peasant will bring in a barrel or two – as he has done all his life, and his father did before him. The wine is mixed with a proportion of vinegar, and the process begins.

Flavoured vinegars are much sold in France. It is cheaper to make your own. Pick tarragon, mint or rosemary, just before they flower. Put the lightly bruised leaves into a measuring jug and mix in with an equal volume of wine vinegar (white is best). Store in closed jars for at least 3 weeks. In the early days of using these vinegars, top them up from time to time while the flavourings still have some strength. Garlic vinegar requires a head of garlic cloves, peeled, crushed slightly, to a litre (1¾pts) vinegar. Sweet raspberry vinegar has become fashionable lately with the chefs of some smart restaurants. Put crushed fruit and its juice into a measuring jug. Infuse for a week with an equal volume of white wine vinegar. Stir daily and keep it covered. Strain into a measuring jug, then pour into a saucepan. Add ½ kilo (1lb) sugar to each 600ml (1pt) juice. Boil for 15 minutes, skim, cool and bottle. Or just soak raspberries in wine vinegar for a month, then strain and bottle.

One friend tells me that in her Yorkshire childhood, when they started a meal with Yorkshire pudding, raspberry vinegar was poured over it rather than the more traditional gravy. She is amused by the idea of going, say, to Digoin to eat a dish of calf's liver with a raspberry vinegar sauce at a starred restaurant.

Vol-au-vent The story is that Carême one day made a turret of puff pastry so light that he exclaimed 'Elle vole au vent', which could be translated, 'It's light enough to fly'. Certainly this puff pastry case with any one of a hundred lively fillings was a Parisian invention of the 1820s, and certainly in 1835 the French Académie accepted 'vol-au-vent', shortened from 'vole-au-vent', as a permissible French word. Very useful and delicious, too, the vol-au-vent, as long as it isn't filled, bad-restaurant-wise, with chunks of battery chicken and a few mushrooms (tinned), awash with a slime of poorly contrived velouté sauce.

One of Carême's fillings – for a vol-au-vent d'huitres à la Maintenon – consisted of oysters which you cook gently in melted butter with chopped truffles and mushrooms, seasoned with lemon juice and nutmeg just long enough for the flavours to mingle. Transfer to a bain-marie to keep warm. Prepare a sauce normande (page 206). Drain the liquor from the oysters, and sauté them a little faster this time, in more butter. Stir in some of the sauce, and fill the hot puff pastry case. Replace the lid, and use the rest of the sauce to mask part of the vol-au-vent. A delightful combination of richness and lightness, even if you have to leave out the fresh truffles – which in this country are beyond our reach.

W

Walewska A garnish of sliced lobster and truffle with a Mornay sauce, served with poached fish, especially sole.

Marie Walewska was thrown into Napoleon's arms in Poland, for political reasons, and ended up by falling in love with him. She also bore him a son.

The Walewska garnish, however, has nothing Polish about it. It was, it seems, invented much later on when the son, Count Walewski, became a minister of the French government in 1862. He liked his food and the dish named after his mother, but in his honour, became part of the repertoire of grand cookery. In these less grand days, it is a dish to be avoided except in the best restaurants. You are only too

likely elsewhere to end up with lemon sole covered with a poor cheese sauce, a couple of chunks of canned lobster and three or four black specks that look like smuts but which are the dregs of canned truffle peelings.

Walnut To the French the walnut is 'the nut', le noix. To us, further north, it is 'the foreign nut', wal- like Welsh meaning foreigner, cf. Welsh onion.

Walnut country began with the Loire and Burgundy until the dreadful winters of the late 19th century as well as determined buyers of wood for furniture-making decimated the trees. Now you need to go further south, to the Corrèze, to Vaucluse, before walnut orchards begin in earnest. In the past the walnut harvest led to much sociability. Everyone in a hamlet would gather at one house, to hold a veillée. Elderly people would tell stories, someone would play the violin, while the younger people shelled the walnuts and gossiped as fast as they could go. Nowadays the nuts are taken straight to the factories, some for oil, but most for shelling and packaging, or for sending in bulk to pâtissiers and grocers abroad, as well as in France.

We import a certain quantity of fresh walnuts every November. These are the ones to use for walnut soup (reduce with garlic and stock in a liquidiser, reheat with seasonings and cream), for walnut and onion bread, or just for eating as they are with plain new bread, unsalted butter, coarse salt and a glass of wine. It is a good idea to remove the fine yellow skins which taste bitter – pour boiling water over them, leave for 2 minutes, and they come away easily. A good tip for later in the year (the walnut year that is, rather than the calendar year): pour boiling milk over the dry walnuts and leave them to soak for a while.

Walnut oil was once produced for painters as well as cooks (to mix with their pigments). Now there is little of it, and the price – in the olive oil range – puts people off. It's a good oil for salads, especially hot salads, both for the dressing, and for cooking bits of bacon or cubes of bread rubbed with garlic (chapons). Walnut oil goes extra well with salads of lambs' lettuce.

Water-ices *see* **Ice-creams**

X

Xérès A word that puzzled me for a long time. It did not occur often enough for me to bother to look it up, but one day I did and discovered it meant 'sherry'. Obvious, once you know. The French do not use much sherry in their cooking, but lately sherry vinegar has become popular. In the onion chutney, confiture d'oignons, that is sometimes served with pâté, sherry vinegar is required for its stronger taste. It needs to be used with discretion, but can be useful when making certain stocks.

Z

Zest is the thin outer peel of citrus fruit, removed with a grater, a potato peeler, a lump of sugar, or a useful little gadget called a lemon zester which scrapes away the oily zest without including too much of the pith.

Zewelwai The Alsatian name for onion tart (see **quiche**). Onions are gently stewed in lard without colouring, and placed on the pastry with blanched lardons of bacon. You then cover them with a béchamel or an egg and milk or an egg and cream custard, according to the strength of the stomachs you are cooking for (they are listed in ascending order of deliciousness and, alas, indigestibility). It is the slow cooking of the onions that brings out their sweetness.

USEFUL CONVERSIONS
From imperial to metric measures

PINTS TO LITRES

imperial	metric
1 fl oz	25 ml
2 fl oz	50 ml
4 fl oz	100 ml
¼ pt (5 fl oz)	150 ml
6 fl oz	175 ml
⅓ pt (7 fl oz)	200 ml
8 fl oz	225 ml
½ pt (10 fl oz)	300 ml
¾ pt (15 fl oz)	400 ml
1 pt (20 fl oz)	500–600 ml
	(568 ml = 1 pt)
1¼ pts	700 ml
1½ pts	900 ml
1¾ pts	1 litre
2 pts	1.1 litres
2¼ pts	1.3 litres
2½ pts	1.4 litres
2¾ pts	1.6 litres
3 pts	1.7 litres
3¼ pts	1.8 litres
3½ pts	2.0 litres
3¾ pts	2.1 litres
4 pts	2.3 litres
4¼ pts	2.4 litres
4½ pts	2.6 litres
4¾ pts	2.7 litres
5 pts	2.8 litres
5¼ pts	3.0 litres
5½ pts	3.1 litres
5¾ pts	3.3 litres
6 pts	3.4 litres
6¼ pts	3.5 litres
6½ pts	3.7 litres
6¾ pts	3.8 litres
7 pts	4.0 litres
7¼ pts	4.1 litres
7½ pts	4.3 litres
7¾ pts	4.4 litres
8 pts (1 gallon)	4.5 litres

OUNCES TO GRAMS

ounces	grams
½	15
1	30
1½	45
2	60
2½	75
3	90
3½	105
¼ lb	120
4½	135
5	150
5½	165
6	180
6½	195
7	210
7½	225
½ lb	250
8½	255
9	270
9½	285
10	300
¾ lb	360
14	420
1 lb	500
18	540
20	600
1½ lb	750
1¾ lb	875
2 lb	1 kilo

INCHES TO CENTIMETRES

inches	centimetres
⅛	0·3
¼	0·5
⅜	0·75
½	1
¾	2
1	2·5
1¼	3
1½	4
1¾	4·5
2	5
2½	6·5
3	7·5
3½	9
4	10
4½	11·5
5	12·5
6	15
7	18
8	20·5
9	23
10	25·5
11	28
12	30·5
13	33
14	35·5
15	38
16	40·5
17	43
18	45·5
19	48
20	51

NOTE: Comparative oven temperatures are given in The Kitchen Anthology under 'Metric weights and measures' on page 276.

BIBLIOGRAPHY

Huge numbers of books have been written in French about the cooking of France. The following are those we used most often when researching this book. The date on the original edition is indicated as well as the date of reprints when available.

Ali-Bab, *Gastronomie Pratique,* Paris, 1928. Reprinted 1955. Abridged translation by Elizabeth Benson under title *Encyclopedia of Practical Gastronomy,* New York, 1977.

L'Art Culinaire Français, Paris, 1948. Several reprints with translation into English as *The Art of French Cooking.*

Delplanque, A. & S. Cloteaux, *Les Bases de la Charcuterie,* Paris, Editions J. Lanore, no date (c. 1977).

Dictionnaire de l'Académie des Gastronomes, 2 volumes, Paris, Editions Prisma, 1962.

Escoffier, Auguste, *Le Guide Culinaire,* Paris, 1902. Several reprints with translations into English under the title *A Guide to Modern Cookery.*

Escoffier, Auguste, *Ma Cuisine,* Paris, 1934. Several reprints with translation into English under same title.

Gringoire, Th. & L Saulnier, *Le Répertoire de la Cuisine,* London, 1914. Several reprints and translations under same title.

Montagné, Prosper, *Larousse Gastronomique,* Paris, 1938. Several reprints (reissued under title *Nouveau Larousse Gastronomique* with translations under title *New Larousse Gastronomique*).

Pellaprat, Henri-Paul, *L'Art Culinaire Moderne,* Paris, 1935. Several reprints, with translations into English under title *Modern French Culinary Art.*

Saint-Ange, Madame, *Le Livre de Cuisine de Madame Saint-Ange,* Paris, 1927. Reprint by Editions Chaix, Grenoble, 1977.

Sylvestre, J & J Planche, *Les Bases de la Cuisine,* Paris, Jacques Lanore, 1969. Several reprints with translation into English available from same publisher under title *Fundamentals of French Cookery.*